The Context of Ancient Drama

The Context
of Ancient Drama

Eric Csapo
and
William J. Slater

Ann Arbor

THE UNIVERSITY OF MICHIGAN PRESS

2005   2004   6   5   4

A CIP catalogue record for this book is available from the British Library.

Library of Congress Cataloging-in-Publication Data

Csapo, Eric.
    The context of ancient drama / Eric Csapo and William J. Slater.
       p.   cm.
    Includes bibliographical references (p.   -   ) and index.
    ISBN 0-472-10545-0 (hardcover : acid-free). — ISBN 0-472-08275-2
(acid-free)
       1. Classical drama—History and criticism—Theory, etc.
    2. Theater—Greece—History—Sources. 3. Theater—Rome—History—
Sources. 4. Civilization, Ancient—Sources. I. Slater, William J.
    II. Title.
    PA3024.C75   1994
    792′.0938—dc20   94-24681
                                                              CIP

For Heather and Bob Jordan

Preface

This book has some of the qualities of an adjustable wrench, a standard all-purpose implement for the general handy(wo)man, but one that is useful to the specialist only when the right tool is out of reach. It is a series of selections from the evidence about ancient drama, translated and grouped under what we trust are suitable subtitles, and introduced by essays designed to make the the ancient sources accessible and intelligible. It grew (alas slowly) out of an urgent need. Both authors, working at neighboring institutions, found themselves teaching undergraduate courses on the "History of the Greek and Roman Theater," titles that implied a heavy concentration on the mechanisms that created drama, the festivals, audience, actors, theaters, political, religious, and social contexts. No adequate text or texts existed for these topics. Unlike many classicists who find themselves in a similar predicament, we did not resort to the common subterfuge of substituting a course in dramatic literature; but our refusal to capitulate may have been due less to idealism than to the fear that students in large translation classes do not have the same tolerance for the tedium of textual commentary that we demand of language specialists. The results have been more than satisfactory. Our students have taught us that there are few topics as rich and fascinating as the social and institutional history of ancient drama. Our primary reason for writing this book was to facilitate the creation of a new approach to teaching the ancient theater for colleagues who may be no less aware of the topic's enormous appeal but are less reckless with their time and energy.

But since this book is the first of its kind, we have not attempted to imagine a single individual reader. We found it equally undesirable to prescribe its use with precise parameters. For the Greekless and Latinless undergraduate with little or no background in classical antiquity, it is designed to be accessible and challenging, but it is not entirely self-contained and presupposes an instructor with independence, interest, and imagination. It is less well suited to courses that require virtual redundancy between lecture and text. For more advanced students of classics, drama, or theater history, undergraduate or graduate, this book serves a still more pressing need. Most classical graduates, even those specializing in ancient drama, are woefully ignorant of the background to their texts, largely because of the inadequacy of traditional training methods; and the same is true of graduates in theater and drama because of the inaccessibility of the primary evidence. We have also tried to envision the needs of our colleagues in literature and drama departments who are disadvantaged because of language and discipline barriers. We even hope that this book will be useful to most general professional classicists, or specialists in ancient drama, who do not have easy access to large libraries, or who are in need of a quick reference. No doubt many will find that the book lacks focus and tries to serve too many needs at once, but we hope that nearly everyone with an interest in the ancient theater will find in it much that is useful, and will be enabled to pass over easily that which is not specifically relevant to their task.

Others will say unkindly that this book has the qualities of an overstuffed sofa—the lumpiness of too much here, not enough there. We should plead that the evidence itself has come to us in extraordinary lumps and holes, and smoothing it out for the use of others has not always been easy, or successful, or desirable. Nevertheless, while we cannot promise total comfort, we do try at least to provide solid support. We have therefore refrained from burdening readers with the many interesting details of Euripides' domestic problems that may derive from the comedy industry, while on the other hand we have made demands on their patience with long festival inscriptions. There are, and will be, large holes, or, more often, disconnected scraps, in what was once a coherent fabric. Thus some matters of stage design proved too insubstantially woven from modern or ancient speculation. Discussions of dramatic genres or purely literary topics were both too vast and easily accessible elsewhere. For mime and pantomime, however, we made an exception, since the principal evidence for these genres is documentary. Costume received no continuous treatment, but is touched on at various places in the text. This is because the artifacts provide the only really reliable evidence, and this made comprehhensive treatment impracticable. The criterion for the selection of passages on any given topic has also not always been consistent. The inclusion of a particular source does not necessarily mean that we assign it some kind of "truth-value." Some of the documents listed contain obvious lies or highly questionable statements, but they appear simply because they were often cited in the literature, or often misused, or because they are characteristic of the ancient testimony on a topic or they pose interesting and typical problems. Exhaustiveness was not possible: we would rather invite those who are more conscious of their pocketbooks to admire our economy in treating a topic of such scope.

Thanks are due to Dr. Ellen Bauerle, who, throughout the production of this book, has given us encouragement, understanding, and wise advice.

Contents

Explanatory Note

Brackets Used in Translating Sources

[...]	A lacuna exists in the text that is being translated.
...	A passage is omitted from the text translated.
(*factio*)	The original word that is being translated is italicized and attached to the translation.
(this is not true)	The words in parentheses represent an editorial comment or explanation inserted by the translator.
<word>	The translators have supplied a word not in the original to make the sense clearer, e.g., <Augustus> for "him."

Dates

All dates are A.D. if not otherwise specified.

Greek Names

All Greek names sufficiently well known to merit separate entries in the *Oxford Classical Dictionary* are spelled as they appear in that work (normally Latinized). Other names and all Greek words appear in standard transliteration.

Referencing

The text is not necessarily designed for the linear reader. There is a minimal amount of redundancy to allow easy flipping back and forth. One could, for example, read the sources first and then the chapter introduction, or read both at once, constantly referring from one to the other. For this reason we have given essential data (name of author, date of composition) with each numbered source, even when the same author and date appear earlier or even immediately before. To keep catalog numbers to a minimum, we have numbered consecutively throughout entire sections, not through individual chapters. Section numbers (I, II, III, IV, V) are added only when the cross-reference is to a passage in a different section. When a cross-reference is to a chapter, rather than to a specific source in the chapter, then section subdivisions (A, B, C, or i, ii, iii) are included in the reference.

Abbreviations

BGU	Aegyptische Urkunden aus den staatlichen Museen zu Berlin, Griechische Urkunden
BCH	Bulletin de Correspondance Hellénique
CIL	Corpus Inscriptionum Latinarum
CMG	Corpus Medicorum Graecorum
C.Ord.Ptol.	Corpus des Ordonnances des Ptolémées
CR	Classical Review
FD	Fouilles de Delphes
FGrH	Fragmente der griechischen Historiker
FIRA	Fontes Iuris Romani Anteiustiniani
GVI	Griechische Versinschriften
ID	Inscriptions de Délos
IG	Inscriptiones Graecae
IGRR	Inscriptiones Graecae ad Res Romanas pertinentes
IGUR	Inscriptiones Graecae Urbis Romae
ILS	Inscriptiones Latinae Selectae
JRS	Journal of Roman Studies
MAMA	Monumenta Asiae Minoris Antiquae
OGIS	Orientis Graecae Inscriptiones Selectae
OMS	L. Robert, *Opera Minora Selecta* I–VII
ORF	Oratorum Romanorum Fragmenta
PCG	Poetae Comici Graeci
PHibeh	Hibeh Papyri
POxy	Oxyrhynchus Papyri
SEG	Supplementum Epigraphicum Graecum
SIG	Sylloge Inscriptionum Graecarum
TAM	Tituli Asiae Minoris
TrGF	Tragicorum Graecorum Fragmenta
ZPE	Zeitschrift für Papyrologie und Epigraphik

I. Kinds of Evidence: Their Nature and Reliability

IA: The Texts

IAi. The Dissemination of Athenian Drama and the Survival of the Texts to Hellenistic Times

The earliest manuscripts of the classical dramatists date from the 10th or 11th c. In many places they have obvious omissions; in some places obvious gibberish. The age of a manuscript is a factor of limited importance: better readings can very often be found in much later manuscripts stemming from an independent tradition; papyrus finds may bring us 800–1200 years closer to the original text of a play but rarely contain readings not found in the manuscript tradition of preserved plays. This allows us to feel reasonably confident that our modern critical editions are close to the texts that were in circulation in the 3rd c. B.C. But how close are we to the original texts of the 5th c. B.C.? It is generally supposed that the texts sustained more damage in the first century of their existence than in the following twenty-three altogether. The transmitted text of Aeschylus inspires so little confidence that at least 10 percent has been condemned by one editor or another, while the number of proposed emendations far exceeds the number of words.

How did the texts suffer so much damage so soon after their conception and at a time when the fame of the tragedians and interest in their works was highest? Paradoxically, the popularity of the tragedians in the 5th and 4th c. B.C. both ensured the survival of their works at this critical period and led to the massive corruption of their texts. The Greek book trade did not exist when Aeschylus produced his plays (499–458 B.C.), was in its infancy during most of Euripides' dramatic career (from 455 B.C.), and seems not to have become a profitable business until just a few years before his death (407/6 B.C.). Though we find the dead Euripides of Aristophanes' *Frogs* (943) claiming to have nursed the ailing art form he inherited from Aeschylus with an "infusion drawn from the blather of books," it is not till the last decade of the 5th c. B.C. that we hear of books being widely circulated (10, 11). By the end of the century, books travel far and wide: in 400 B.C. Xenophon saw the Thracian Black Sea coast littered with debris from wrecked cargo ships including "couches, boxes, written books" (*Anabasis* 7.5.14); Plato mentions Anaxagoras' treatise selling for, at most, a drachma at the book stalls in the Athenian marketplace (*Apology* 26d–e). From this it appears that, by the turn of the century, books were relatively expensive but easily acquired, and they soon came to be collected by cultured Athenians (cf. 10–12).

The earliest drama whose survival is attributable to a purely literary transmission is in fact a comedy (2). There is conclusive evidence to show that our text of Aristophanes' *Clouds* is not the text of the play performed at the Dionysia of 423 B.C. but a revised version. The sources claim that the revision was undertaken for the purpose of a second production (cf. 1, 3), which never materialized. Two other comedies of the late 5th and early 4th c. B.C. seem to owe their survival entirely to book circulation (4). From the mid-4th c. B.C. the revision of dramas for circulation appears to have been taken for granted (5). Nevertheless book circulation cannot fully account for the survival of 5th-c. drama, particularly drama produced before the last two decades of the 5th c. B.C. Despite general literacy, books had a relatively low appeal to most ancients. Reading was a costly and difficult art. Ancient papyrus books were cumbersome continuous rolls, up to seven meters long, without word separation or punctuation, with the lines of verse all strung together like prose, with speakers often unidentified, with changes of speaker sometimes unmarked, and without stage directions. Such technical difficulties conspired to make the average ancient considerably less bookish than Euripides. Most ancients, even scholars, preferred to cite from memory rather than hunt a passage down in a text. No compulsion was felt for verbatim accuracy: Aristotle owned the largest library in Athens (15A) but made errors in 80 percent of his citations from Homer.

Most Greeks of the 5th and 4th c. B.C. became acquainted with drama through oral tradition and performance. Choral lyrics and monodies often became popular songs (9) and common entertainments at drinking parties (6). The custom of singing songs and reciting iambic speeches from tragedy at drinking parties, well known from the later period, seems already to have come into fashion by the late 5th c. B.C. (7, 8). Memorable phrases, mostly in succinct, proverbial form (*gnomai*) embellished conversation, and schoolboys learned to cite tragic speeches from memory. Of the performance tradition there is little direct evidence. It is often said that Greek plays were written and produced for a single performance, but the statement is misleading. The City Dionysia and the Lenaea were the most important dramatic competitions. Originally, archaic cult probably required new compositions for presentation to the god; even the Hellenistic hymn of the *phallophoroi* insists on an offering of "virgin song" (II 9). But in addition to the reentry of "revised" plays at the Dionysia and Lenaea (1–3), we hear, by the early 5th c. B.C., of the reperformance of plays at the smaller festivals of the Rural Dionysia (16; IIIAib), and by the end of the century there is evidence for the reperformance of comedy at the main festivals (18, 19). Sometime after the death of Aeschylus, the Athenians voted to allow his plays to be reproduced at the major festivals (17). From 386 B.C. onward, "old tragedies" were regularly reproduced at the City Dionysia, and by 339 B.C. the same was true of "old comedies" (22).

We have less information about performances outside of Attica during the 5th c. B.C. The earliest were those of Aeschylus in Sicily in 471–469 and 458–456 B.C. (23). Euripides' *Andromache* is said to have been first produced outside of Athens (24). Later he went to Magnesia and then, along with Agathon, took up residence at the court of the Macedonian king Archelaus at Pella (25–27). By the last decade of the 5th c. B.C. the sources imply that Athenian tragedy was having an impact on common people outside of Attica (27, 28, see also on 2). About the same time, we begin to hear anecdotes about tragic and comic actors touring the Greek world (29–31).

The anecdotes about the survivors of the Battle of Syracuse are likely to be greatly exaggerated even if true, but they provide a nice illustration of how dramatic culture might be disseminated even without a performance tradition (9). Even if one takes these tales at face value it is not easy to determine whether they indicate a prevalence or dearth of tragic performance in Sicily: the former is suggested by the popularity of Euripides, the latter by the lengths to which the Sicilians went to hear his verses. Possibly an active performance tradition was interrupted by the war with Athens; this in turn would suggest the absence of native tragic actors in Sicily or Italy at the time. Satyrus' version of the tale does suggest that no books were available to satisfy the longing for Euripides' verse (9). Plutarch, however, speaks specifically of Euripides' songs, and, although about eleven dramatic papyri with musical notation have been found, it is doubtful whether books were ever an adequate medium for music (IVC). In any case, archaeological finds confirm the main point of these anecdotes: South Italian and Sicilian imports and local imitations of Attic terra-cotta figurines and vase paintings do attest a keen interest in Attic drama from about 420 B.C., and particularly for Euripides (128, 129). Greeks from Italy and Sicily soon became major exponents of Attic theater: among them we may note the tragic actor Aristodemos of Metapontum, whose first Lenaean victories can be dated ca. 370 B.C.; Dionysius the tyrant of Syracuse and part-time tragic poet (8A), who had a Lenaean victory in 367 B.C.; and Alexis of Thurii, one of the most important poets of Middle Comedy, whose first Lenaean victories came in the 350s B.C. Many of the most prominent dramatists in the first half of the 4th c. B.C. came to Athens from the periphery of the Greek world.

The oral tradition made a significant contribution to the survival of our playtexts. In most cases, indeed, the oral and book tradition are inextricably mixed. Actors appear to have played a major role in both. Though poets apparently revised their plays in the 5th c. B.C., we are explicitly told that the rewriting was aimed at reperformance, not circulation in book form (1–3). Not until the 4th c. B.C. do we have evidence for a regular practice of book publication following production (5), or, exceptionally, without production (4). Even then a popular play was not likely to avoid contamination. In an age that knew no copyright, the poet had little control over the text of his play. Booksellers felt no obligation to use authorized versions of plays, when any one of the people involved in the production could have sold them working copies or memorized texts. Even if an author released his text immediately, actors traveled faster than books. There is no reason to think that a bookseller in Syracuse would copy only the best Athenian edition. The book tradition may never have been independent of the oral tradition, and it was subject to the same hazards. The scholia allege a great many actors' interpolations in our surviving texts (13), and their assertions are sometimes confirmed by the appearance of transposed lines or alternate versions of whole sections of plays. When important speeches seem to ramble on or drift clumsily, suspicion normally, perhaps reasonably, falls upon the actors' hamming up the poet's text to magnify their roles and expand the crowd-pleasers.

Around 330 B.C. the Athenian politician Lycurgus attempted to curb the degeneration of the texts of Aeschylus, Sophocles, and Euripides by passing a law requiring the preparation of an official text to which actors would be forced to adhere when performing "old tragedy" at Attic festivals (14). In composing the official text, there is no reason to believe that the Athenian public secretaries had anything more reliable to work

with than the mixed oral and written tradition that was circulating at
the time. The official Athenian texts are said to be ancestors of our
manuscripts: Galen describes how Ptolemy stole them for the Museum
in Alexandria (15B), where Hellenistic scholars busied themselves with
the task of producing authoritative versions that became the standard
editions of the plays in later antiquity (see IAii).

Sources

Written and Oral Texts

1. Hypothesis to Euripides, *Hippolytus*. The second *Hippolytus* was
performed in 428 B.C.
> This is the second *Hippolytus,* also called *Garlanded Hippolytus*.
> It is manifestly the one written later. That which was distasteful
> and deserved condemnation is corrected in this drama.

2A. Aristophanes, *Clouds* 522–25. *Clouds* was performed at the Dionysia in 423 B.C., but the text was later revised by the author sometime
between 420–417 B.C. as the following passages show, and it is this revised
version that survives today. The date of the revision is established by the
references to Eupolis' *Marikas,* performed at the Lenaea in 421 B.C. (cf.
Clouds 553), and the ostracism of Hyperbolus in 416 B.C. (cf. *Clouds*
550–58); Aristophanes implies that the work could have been presented
elsewhere, had he not decided to favor the "clever" Athenian audience.
We should not assume that first performance of a play was necessarily
the privilege of the Athenian audience.
> I considered this to be most clever of all my comedies and so thought
> it proper that you should be the first to experience this work upon
> which I labored harder than on any other. But then I lost out to
> tedious clowns, though I did not deserve such treatment.

2B. Second Hypothesis to Aristophanes, *Clouds*.
> The first *Clouds* was produced at the City Dionysia during the archon-
> ship of Isarchos (424/3 B.C.), when Cratinus won with *Wineflask,*
> Ameipsias <came second> with *Konnos.* So, Aristophanes, tossed
> out unreasonably, thought it necessary to produce the second *Clouds*
> and chastise the audience. But his luck was even worse with this
> and he did not thereafter produce the revised version. The second
> *Clouds* dates to the archonship of Ameinias (i.e., 423/2 B.C., which
> is wrong; the revision was probably never produced).

2C. Scholion to Aristophanes, *Clouds* 553.

"Eupolis was the first to haul in Marikas": Clearly the *Marikas* was performed before the second *Clouds*. Eratosthenes (ca. 275–194 B.C.) says that Callimachus (ca. 305–240 B.C.) found fault with the *Didaskaliai* because they show *Marikas* being produced two years later than *Clouds,* though here it is clearly stated that it (*Marikas*) was produced first. Eratosthenes says that Callimachus was ignorant of the fact that no such thing was said in the version that was produced, and there is nothing strange about it being said in the later revision. Obviously the *Didaskaliai* list the plays that were produced. How can he be ignorant that in the *Marikas* Cleon is already dead, whereas in the *Clouds* it is said: "Then the leather tanner (Cleon), hated by the gods..."?

3. Galen, *Commentary on Hippocrates' Regimen in Acute Diseases,* *CMG* V.9.1. p. 120.5. Written second half of 2nd c. Cf. *diaskeue* in 38.

A book written after the model of an earlier work is said to have been "revised" ("made into a *diaskeue*"), whenever it has the same argument and most of the phraseology is the same, but some things are omitted, some added, and some changed. If you wish an example for the sake of clarity, you may take the second *Autolycus* of Eupolis (ca. 418 B.C.), which is a revision of the first (ca. 420 B.C.).

4. Athenaeus 270a. Written ca. 200. Athenaeus cites from two comedies that he claims were never produced, the *Thouriopersai* of Metagenes, who was active after 410 B.C., and the *Sirens* of Nicophon, who was active in the last decade of the 5th c. B.C. and the first two decades of the 4th c. B.C.

I know that the *Thouriopersai* and the drama of Nicophon were not produced, which is why I mentioned them last.

5. Chamaeleon, *On Comedy,* book 6 in Athenaeus 374b. Chamaeleon lived from ca. 350 to after 281 B.C. Anaxandrides, a poet of Middle Comedy, was active from 376–349 B.C.

<Anaxandrides>, being of a sour temperament, did the following to his comedies. Whenever he did not win, he took them and gave them to the incense seller to be cut up as wrapping and did not revise them like most poets. He destroyed many elegant plays out of spite for the audience in his old age.

6. Aristophanes, *Knights* 526–30. Produced Lenaea, 424 B.C. The passage comes from the *parabasis* in which the chorus speaks of Aristophanes' rival comic poet, Cratinus (active ca. 450–420 B.C.), as if he were

senile. It shows that Cratinus' lyrics were popular songs for the drinking parties (*symposia*) in their day.

> And then he (Aristophanes) thought of Cratinus, who once surged forth with mighty applause. . . . It was impossible to sing anything at drinking parties but "Figwood-sandled Doro" and "Crafters of clever hymns."

7. Aristophanes, *Clouds* 1353–72. Written ca. 423–416 B.C. From the second agon, in which Strepsiades recounts the cause of a quarrel between himself and his son Pheidippides. Simonides is the lyric poet (ca. 556–468 B.C.). It was customary at drinking parties to pass around a myrtle branch and take turns singing popular songs. It appears from this passage that reciting tragic speeches had also become symposium entertainment by the late 5th c. B.C.

> STREPSIADES: I'll tell you how our quarrel first began! When we had dined, as you know, I first asked him to take the lyre and sing a song by Simonides, the one about how Krios was shorn. He immediately started saying that playing the *kithara* and singing while you drink, like a woman grinding barley, is old-fashioned. . . . and he said Simonides was a bad poet. And I could hardly hold my temper at first, but I did. Then I asked him to take the myrtle branch and to recite something from Aeschylus for me. Then he says right off, "I really think Aeschylus is the first of poets <for being> full of rumbling, incoherent, bombastic, and pompous." You can imagine then how my gall was piqued. Nevertheless I bit my lip and said, "So recite whatever is clever in your modern poets." Immediately he launched into a speech of Euripides in which a brother—O Heracles!—screws his own half-sister (the *Aeolus*). I couldn't stand it any longer . . . (the quarrel begins and turns from abuse to physical violence).

8A. Ephippus, *Twins, PCG* F 16. Produced probably before 367 B.C. Theodoros was a famous tragic actor in the early 4th c. B.C. (see III 92; IV 20, 21, 32).

> (The speaker perverts the formula of an oath, which normally requires that the oathtaker call various calamities upon himself if he is guilty of perjury): May I have to learn the dramas of Dionysius by heart, and Demophon's lampoon against Kotys, and may Theodoros recite <tragic> speeches to me over dinner, and may I live next door to Laches, and may I pass cups to Euripides while feasting him.

8B. Diodorus 16.92. See IV 30H.

8C. Nikoboule in Athenaeus 537d. Nikoboule was a Hellenistic author of unknown date. She describes an event in 323 B.C.

> Nikoboule says that at dinner all of the contestants did their best to please the king (Alexander) and that at his last banquet he competed by reciting from memory an episode from Euripides' *Andromeda* and then he eagerly drank down toasts of even unmixed wine and forced others to do so.

9A. Satyrus, *Life of Euripides* (*POxy* 1176, fr. 39, col. 19). Written in the form of a dialogue ca. 200 B.C. See 81. The events purportedly took place in the years following the defeat of the Athenian forces in the Battle of Syracuse, 413 B.C. This tale should be read with particular caution; Athenians loved to tell tales about how their city was saved, despite military defeat, by its superior culture (e.g., Plutarch, *Lysander* 15). Plutarch's fuller version of the same tale seems to indicate that he and Satyrus both draw from a common, earlier source.

> You did not state it badly, for the appreciation of the Athenians was worthless, since they perceived the greatness of the poet after the Macedonians and the Sicilians. At any rate it is said that when Nicias led his expedition against Sicily and many Athenians were made prisoner, a great number of them were saved by the poems of Euripides. All those, namely, who retained some of his verses, taught the sons of their captors. To such a degree did Sicily marvel at Euripides. And indeed by Archelaus [...

9B. Plutarch, *Nicias* 29. Written ca. 115, describing events from 413 B.C. onward.

> Most of the Athenians perished in the stone quarries from disease and malnutrition, since they received a daily ration of a pint of barley groats and a half pint of water. Some, however, were sold into slavery or managed to pass themselves off as slaves. When they sold them as slaves they tatooed them with the figure of a horse on their foreheads—indeed there were some who suffered even this in addition to slavery. Respectful and orderly behavior aided these men too: either they were soon freed or they stayed with their masters in privileged conditions. Some were even saved by Euripides. It seems that the Sicilians, most of all the overseas Greeks, had conceived a passion for his music. Whenever they were able to get snatches and morsels of his music from people coming from overseas, they learned it by heart and passed it on to each other. At that time, in any case, they say that many of the survivors

who managed to get home greeted Euripides warmly and some would tell that they were released from slavery after teaching all they could remember of Euripides' poetry; others said that they wandered about after the battle and got food and water in exchange for singing his songs. Nor should one be surprised that they say when a Caunian ship had been chased by pirates and tried to put in at Syracuse harbour, the Syracusans would not at first receive them, but kept them outside. Yet when they were asked if they knew any songs of Euripides and they said yes, they allowed them in and brought the ship to shore.

10. Aristophanes, *Frogs* 52–54. Produced Lenaea, 405 B.C.
DIONYSUS: And then, while I was on board ship reading the *Andromeda*, suddenly an unimaginably powerful longing struck my heart.

11. Aristophanes, *Frogs* 1105–18. Produced Lenaea, 405 B.C. The chorus encourages Aeschylus and Euripides to pull no punches in the contest of poetic prowess. The bookishness of the Athenian audience is no doubt greatly exaggerated to make the comic rhetorical point.

Whatever you may have to argue about, speak, go straight to it, dredge up the old and new, dare to say what is subtle and clever! Don't be afraid that the audience's ignorance will prevent it from understanding subtleties! Things are not like that any more. They are veterans and every one of them clutching a book learns ingenuities. Their minds—normally first-rate—are especially well honed today. Fear nothing as far as the audience is concerned. Broach any subject. They're enlightened.

12. Athenaeus 164b. Written ca. 200. Athenaeus describes a scene in Alexis' *Linus* (*PCG* F 140) probably produced ca. 350–340 B.C.

He has Heracles receive his education at the house of Linus. Linus asks him to choose a book from a number lying beside him and read it. Heracles picks up a cookbook and holds it very eagerly in his hands. This is what Linus says: "Go over and take any book you like from there. Examining the titles carefully, you will read quietly and at your leisure. Orpheus is there, Hesiod, tragedies, Choerilus, Homer, Epicharmus, all kinds of works. You will reveal the bent of your nature." HERACLES: I'll take this one. LINUS: First show me what it is. HERACLES: A cookbook according to the title. LINUS: Clearly you are a philosopher, since you chose the work of Simos out of so many writings. HERACLES: Who's Simos? LINUS: A very talented man. He has now taken an interest in tragedy and of all the actors is the best of cooks, so his patrons say, though his audience thinks him the worst actor among cooks. (Either Athenaeus omits some lines, or some stage action intervenes: perhaps Heracles starts eating the book.) LINUS: This guy has a fierce appetite. HERACLES: Say what you like. I'm hungry, you know.

13. Scholion to Euripides, *Orestes* 1366–68. The scholia are filled with charges of interpolation and alteration of the text by actors (e.g., 38, 45, 56, 75, 84). As we have it, the text of the *Orestes* (first produced 408 B.C.) at lines 1366–74 has the Phrygian slave escape from the palace where Orestes and Pylades are supposedly murdering Helen, as follows: "CHORUS: But there is a noise at the bolts of the palace doors. Be quiet. A Phrygian is coming out. From him we will find out how matters stand in the palace. PHRYGIAN: I have fled from death, the Argive sword, in my barbarian slippers, over (or beyond the confines of) the cedar beams of the gallery and the Doric trigyphs, away, away, earth, earth, with barbarian runnings." This scholion sees a contradiction in the descriptions of the mode of exit given by the chorus and by the Phrygian, and blames the actors, probably unfairly.

> One would not readily concede that these three lines <of the chorus> (cited above) are by Euripides, but rather <one would say they are> by the actors, who, so as not to injure themselves by jumping off the palace roof, open the door a little and come out wearing the Phrygian's costume and mask. They added these verses, then, so that they would seem justified in exiting through the door.

14. Pseudo-Plutarch, *Ten Orators* 841.The author lists various pieces of legislation initiated by Lycurgus, a very influential Athenian politician, ca. 338–326 B.C.

> ...and <Lycurgus> introduced another law requiring bronze statues of the poets Aeschylus, Sophocles, and Euripides to be set up and their tragedies to be written down and kept in the public treasury and the state secretary to give a public reading to the actors, as they were not permitted to act except in accordance with the texts.

15A. Athenaeus 3a–b. Written ca. 200. The first two books of Athenaeus survive only in excerpts by an epitomator: this passage is one of them.

> <Athenaeus> says that <Pindar> (518–438 B.C.) possessed so many ancient Greek books that he surpassed all others renowned for their collections, Polycrates of Samos (died 522 B.C.), Pisistratus the tyrant of Athens (died 527 B.C.), Eukleides also of Athens, Nikokrates of

Cyprus, the kings of Pergamum, Euripides the <tragic> poet (ca. 485–406 B.C.), Aristotle the philosopher (384–322 B.C.), and Theophrastus (ca. 370 to ca. 285 B.C.), and Neleus, who preserved the books of the two last mentioned. <Athenaeus> says that our (Egyptian) king Ptolemy (II), surnamed Philadelphus (308–246 B.C.), purchased <Neleus'> entire library and transported it, along with the books he acquired in Athens and Rhodes, to beautiful Alexandria.

15B. Galen, *Commentary on the Epidemics of Hippocrates* 2.4. Written second half of 2nd c. Galen describes the theft of the official Athenian copy of the tragedies of the three tragedians by Ptolemy III (Euergetes), who used them to build up his library, the Museum, in Alexandria ca. 247–222 B.C.

> <Ptolemy> gave <the Athenians> a security of 15 talents (90,000 drachmas) of silver and took the books of Sophocles, Euripides, and Aeschylus on the pretext that he only wished to copy them and would immediately give them back safe. After preparing a costly copy on the very finest quality of papyrus, he kept the books that he received from Athens and sent back the copies he himself had prepared, inviting them to keep the 15 talents and take new books for the old ones they gave him.

Reperformance in Athens and Attica

16. Herodotus 6.21. Written ca. 430 B.C. Miletus was retaken by the Persians in 494 B.C., after a short period of independence during the Ionian Revolt.

> The Athenians made quite clear the extent of their grief at the capture of Miletus, particularly when Phrynichus produced his drama *The Capture of Miletus* and the audience was reduced to tears (ca. 492 B.C.). They fined him one thousand drachmas for reminding them of their own misfortunes and passed a regulation that no one was ever to make use of this drama in the future.

17A. Aristophanes, *Acharnians* 9–12. Produced Lenaea, 425 B.C. Theognis is a minor tragedian much ridiculed by Aristophanes for the frigidity of his compositions. The speaker, Dikaiopolis, is recalling events that took place just before the presentation of the tragedies at one of the dramatic festivals, possibly even referring to events that happened earlier at the very festival in which *Acharnians* was being produced.

> I suffered a tragic pang when I was waiting open-mouthed for

Aeschylus and then the herald announced, "Bring in your chorus, Theognis." Imagine the shudder that ran through my heart.

17B. Scholion to Aristophanes, *Acharnians* 10.

Aeschylus received the highest honor from the Athenians and by popular decree his plays continued to be produced even after his death, an honor granted to his dramas alone.

17C. Philostratus, *Life of Apollonius* 6.11. Written after 217.

The Athenians considered <Aeschylus> the father of tragedy, and called him up to the Dionysia even when he was dead, since by decree the works of Aeschylus were presented anew and won fresh victories.

18. Third Hypothesis to Aristophanes' *Frogs*. *Frogs* was first produced at the Lenaea, 405 B.C.; Dicaearchus was active from ca. 326–296 B.C.

The drama is well and painstakingly composed. It was produced in the archonship of the Kallias who followed Antigenes. It was so admired because of its *parabasis,* in which he reconciles those who have retained their civic rights with those who have lost them and the citizens with the exiles, that it was produced a second time, as Dicaearchus says.

19. *IG* XIV 1098a (= *IGUR* 215). From the Roman *Fasti* (103). The inscription gives a list of the placement attained by comic poets at the main Athenian festivals, poet by poet, in the order of their first production. The plays are listed in order of their placement, with Dionysian prizes preceding Lenaean. The first part of the fragment is thought to deal with the career of Teleclides because we know that he wrote plays named *Sterroi* and *Hesiods*. Moreover the Athenian Victor Lists for the Lenaea put Xenophilos just before Teleclides. The reversal of the order here is probably due to Teleclides winning a victory at the Dionysia before Xenophilos. "Still extant" appears to be a reference to the holdings of the library in Alexandria contained in the document from which this list was copied.

- - - In the archonship of] Eu<thy>d[emos (431/0 B.C.)
- - -]ai Lenaea [- - -
- Ste]rroi a second time [produced -
- - -] fourth [- - - -
- with He]siods still extan[t
- with ?Sold]iers. [poet X was second, Dionysia?, with X,
never attained a victor]y or th[ird or fourth, was fifth,
Lenaea?, with X,
in the archonship of X]

Xenophilos [won, Lenaea? in the archonship of X,
never attained th]ird or fourth [...

20. Plato, *Laches* 182d–83b. Written ca. 400–390 B.C., but set in the
late 5th c. B.C.

LACHES:...if there was such a science <as military science>, the
Spartans would know about it, since they have no other interest
in life than to seek out and occupy themselves with that learning
and practice that would make them superior to all others in matters
of war. But if they don't know it, then the teachers of military
science certainly haven't failed to notice that they more than any
other Greeks are preoccupied with this sort of thing, and that in
Sparta a teacher of military science could gain honor and more
money than anywhere else, just as we honor tragic poets. Surely
anyone who thought himself a good tragedian would not travel the
circuit outside, going around Attica and performing in the other
cities, but would in all likelihood be brought straight here (Athens)
and perform for this audience.

21. Plato, *Republic* 475d. Probably written 380–370 B.C., but dramatically set ca. 410 B.C.

(Socrates speaks) "The man who compulsively wishes to sample
every kind of study and eagerly embraces learning and never knows
surfeit, this is the man whom we would justly call a philosopher.
Not so?" And Glaukon said: "A strange and motley group this
would be. Indeed, theater-lovers all seem to be of this group insofar
as they love to learn something. And those who like to hear new
things would be a very strange group to number among philosophers. These people have no time for argument and serious debate,
but, as if they had rented out their ears, they run around to all of
the Dionysia and don't leave out a single one whether in the cities
or towns. Are we to call all these and all enthusiasts of similar and
minor arts 'philosophers'?"

22A. *IG* II² 2318, col. viii. *Fasti,* inscribed ca. 315–310 B.C.; the
inscription refers to the City Dionysia.

In the archonship of Theodotos (387/6 B.C.)
    the tragedians first added a production of an
    old drama to the festival
    Antiochis won the boys' dithyramb
    Euegetes of Pallene was *choregos*
    Aigeis won the men's dithyramb

Iasos of Kollytos was *choregos*

22B. *IG* II² 2318, col. xii.

In the archonship of Theophrastos (340/39 B.C.)
the comedians first added a production
of an old drama

Performances Outside of Attica

23A. *Life of Aeschylus* 8–11. Aeschylus' first visit to the court of Hieron, tyrant of Syracuse, was in 471–469 B.C.; his second visit lasted from 458 till the time of his death in 456 B.C.

He went off to the court of Hieron, some say because he was vexed by the Athenians and had been defeated by the young Sophocles, others say because he had been beaten by Simonides in the competition to write a grave epigram for those who fell at Marathon. . . . Still others say that in the production of the *Eumenides* while the chorus came on in separate groups spaced at intervals, it created such an impression on the audience that young children fainted and women miscarried. He therefore went to Sicily at the time when Hieron was founding the city of Aetna and produced *Women of Aetna*, which augured a good life for those inhabiting the city. He received very high honors from the tyrant Hieron and the people of Gela and stayed on there till he died as an old man after two years. . . . The people of Gela gave him a costly burial in the public cemetery and paid him grand honors. They gave him the following epitaph:

This monument covers Aeschylus the Athenian, son of Eu-
phorion, who perished in wheat-bearing Gela;
the famous grove of Marathon could speak of his courage
and the long-maned Medes knew it.

All those who gained their livelihood from tragedy used to visit the monument, both to make offerings to his spirit and to perform his dramas.

23B. *Life of Aeschylus* 18.

They say that Hieron conferred upon <Aeschylus> the honor of producing the *Persae* again in Sicily and that he was immensely popular.

24. Scholion to Euripides, *Andromache* 445 (produced in the 420s B.C.).

It is not possible to determine the date of the drama with exactitude, because it was not produced in Athens. Callimachus says he found the name of Demokrates inscribed as author of the tragedy (but perhaps we should read "Timokrates," an Argive claimed by an unnamed source in the anonymous *Life of Euripides* to have authored Euripides' songs).

25. *Life of Euripides* 21–25. Cf. 9A.

<Euripides> moved to Magnesia, where he was honored by an ambassadorship and an exemption from taxes. From there he went to Macedonia, where he spent his time in Archelaus' circle and wrote a drama named *Archelaus* to please him and was active alongside Archelaus even when <the latter> occupied himself with government.

26A. Scholion to Aristophanes, *Frogs* 83. *Frogs* was first produced at the Lenaea, 405 B.C. The scholiast comments on the statement that Agathon has gone off "to the banquet of the blessed."

Either he speaks of him as dead, as if he had said "the isles of the blessed," or he says this because <Agathon> was in Macedonia along with many others at the court of King Archelaus until his death, and he says that life in the palace is a "banquet of the blessed."

26B. Plato, *Symposium* 172c. Written ca. 384–379 B.C. The dialogue's frame story is set sometime in the last decade of the 5th c. B.C.

Don't you know that Agathon hasn't lived in Athens for several years now?

26C. Aelian, *Varia Historia* 13.4. Written early 3rd c.

Archelaus, the king, prepared a lavish dinner party for his friends. As the drinking progressed, Euripides drank a little harder than usual and somehow gradually became drunk. He then embraced and started kissing Agathon, the tragic poet, then roughly forty, who was lying beside him on the couch. When Archelaus asked him if he thought Agathon still worthy of such attentions, he answered: "Yes, by Zeus. Not only is the spring most beautiful of all, but the autumn as well."

27. Plato, *Republic* 568a–b. Written in the 380s B.C., but dramatically set ca. 410 B.C.

"It is no wonder," I (i.e., Socrates) said, "that tragedy appears to be an altogether wise thing and that Euripides is outstanding in it." "Why so?" "Because among other things he uttered this profoundly intelligent phrase, that 'tyrants are wise because they keep company

with the wise.' He clearly meant by wise the companions we have
described." He (i.e., Glaucon) said, "He also sings the praises of
tyranny as something godlike and says many other such things—
both Euripides and the other poets do this." "No doubt," I said,
"the tragic poets in their wisdom will forgive us and others who
have a constitution like ours, if we do not receive them in our state,
since they sing hymns of praise to tyranny." "I think," he said,
"that those of them who are smart will forgive us." "I think they
will go around to the other cities, gathering crowds, hiring those
who have good, loud, and persuasive voices, and dragging states
into tyranny and democracy." "Very likely." "In addition, then,
they will be paid and honored by them, especially, in all likelihood,
by the tyrants, but secondly by the democracies...."

28. Aristophanes, *Thesmophoriazusae* 390f. Produced 411 B.C. The
women of Athens hold a secret council at the Festival of the Thesmophoria and discuss plans for dealing with Euripides' misogynistic slander;
the passage is from the opening speech at this meeting.

Where has <Euripides> not slandered us? In brief <he has slandered
us> wherever there are audiences and tragedies and choruses.

29. *Life of Sophocles* 14. The earliest notices of actors on tour outside
of Attica are set at the very end of the 5th c. B.C. Though these circumstan-
tial details are often credible enough, they often serve as background for
silly anecdotes.

Istros and Neanthes (3rd c. B.C.) say that Sophocles died in the
following manner (405 B.C.). Kallippides the actor was returning
from an engagement at Opous (in Locris) at the time of the Festival
of the Cups and sent some grapes to Sophocles. As the grapes were
still unripe Sophocles got a pip stuck in his throat, and because of
his extreme old age he choked on it and died.

30. Polyaenus 6.10. Written ca. 162 and referring to 399 B.C. Nikostratos' career as a tragic actor lasted from ca. 425 to 392 B.C.

Alexander the garrison commander of Aeolis hired some of the
best performers from Ionia, the pipers Thersander and Philoxenus
and the actors Kallippides and Nikostratos, and announced a spectacle. Everyone, lured by the fame of the competitors, gathered from
the neighboring cities. When the theater was full, Alexander sur-
rounded it with the soldiers and barbarians he used to guard the
country and seized all the spectators, including women and children.

He released them after receiving a large ransom, then gave the country over to Thibron and left.

31. Demosthenes (?), *Against Euboulides* 18. Delivered ca. 345 B.C. The speaker, whose Athenian citizenship has been impugned, responds to evidence brought by his opponent that his father spoke with a foreign accent. Presumably Kleandros, an Athenian, was in Leucas for professional reasons, perhaps traveling through with immunity, since Leucas was a stopping place en route to Italy. The meeting must have taken place in the late 5th/early 4th c. B.C.

They have denounced my father as speaking with an accent, but they omitted to say that he had been caught by the enemy during the Decelean war (413 B.C.) and sold off to be a slave in Leucas, where after many a year he chanced to meet the actor Kleandros and was brought home safe to his relatives.

IAii. Legacy of Ancient Scholarship

In classical Greece and Rome, dramas were usually written on rolls of papyrus, in capital letters, without stage directions or assignation of speaker. There was no copyright, and people could copy or alter or annotate any text in their possession; as one would expect, readers, especially actors, were always doing so. For in order to use a text, even a reader needed to divide words, and assign roles, and, especially with comedy, add stage directions, as we see most clearly in Donatus' commentary on Terence (59, 60). This activity, if uncontrolled, would lead very soon to the corruption of a text beyond repair, and this was realized throughout antiquity. Quality control was exercised by grammarians and booksellers, seeking good texts, but notably by the larger institutions such as the library at Alexandria in Egypt, which was in turn part of the Museum. This had been set up by the Ptolemies, the Greek successors to the Egyptian kings, as part of their palace, and from ca. 300 B.C. they employed scholars in philological and scientific work, including the collection and preservation of manuscripts. They produced catalogs of surviving texts and made determinations of authorship and authenticity. Just what their role was in the production of texts is unclear, but we can observe from 150 B.C. a standardization in the texts of Homer and disappearance of some obviously wilder texts. The same is probably true of other classical Greek texts. The Greek methods of philological scholarship were eventually applied also to the Latin dramatists, notably by Varro.

Since papyrus paper is derived from the stalk of a tall Egyptian bullrush, it is highly perishable in use outside the extremely dry conditions of Egypt. It must be recopied within about thirty years; even so, the beginning and end of the roll are likely to be lost. Later on, in Roman times, a form of papyrus, more like our book, called a codex, came to be popular because it was easier to consult. In the 2nd c. B.C. a more durable writing material called parchment (or vellum) was developed from animal skins, but it was very expensive. After the Arab conquest of Alexandria in the 7th c., the papyrus supply was cut off, with the result that writing materials became more difficult to obtain. It is between this period and the introduction of paper in the 11th c. that most classical texts, already neglected by a Christian education system in economic hardship, tended to disappear. Only a handful of manuscripts of the dramatists survived, and even if these were recopied in early medieval times, the mistakes in these few manuscripts will have remained. Most

Latin manuscripts perished in the barbarian invasions from the 5th c. onward. Yet Terence, unusually, is preserved in a manuscript, the *Codex Bembinus,* of the 4/5th c. But for most authors we are dependent on much later sources, written as much as seventeen hundred years after the first performance. The sack of Byzantium by the Crusaders in 1204 destroyed the last remaining manuscripts of many ancient works. In the early Renaissance, Western interests in importing and collecting Greek manuscripts preserved many others before the general destruction of the Turkish conquest of Byzantium in 1453. The manuscript texts can sometimes be supplemented by quotations from ancient sources and fragments of Egyptian papyri. The surviving texts are very unevenly distributed. For example, while only a small fraction of the work of the three main Greek tragedians survive, we have almost all of Terence and Plautus, but practically nothing of Hellenistic or Roman tragedy. It is impossible under these circumstances to construct complete literary histories of the theatrical genres.

It is important to realize how the texts of the dramatists could have been altered and corrected, since many questions of detailed interpretation depend on how the text is punctuated or divided or altered. Some texts, especially Aeschylus, are very corrupt, and in places incomprehensible. Translations usually conceal this. The primary source of error was mechanical corruption in copying and accidental destruction of passages. To these can be added deliberate omission of, e.g., choral passages that were found irrelevant. But more complex are the changes caused by actors' interpolations in antiquity and the scholars' efforts to locate and correct these and other errors. We cannot now estimate accurately how far these have affected our texts. On grounds of internal consistency it is arguable but not provable that in extreme cases large sections are not what was originally written, e.g., the end of the *Seven against Thebes* of Aeschylus or the end of the *Oedipus Tyrannus* of Sophocles. There was also the insertion of lines by both actors and scholars. The correction of texts has been the aim of philologists since the time of Aristotle; most remaining problems will never be solved, but we illustrate here the kinds of problems faced by the ancient scholars and their attempts at solutions.

Scholarship on the ancient drama may have started with the dramatists themselves, since Sophocles is said to have written a book on the chorus. But the sophist Hippias, a contemporary of Sophocles, was already using data from the Olympic festivals for dating purposes, and someone must have been recording the details of the Dionysiac festivals for bureaucratic purposes. Aristotle (33) and his school collected information about the dramatists, in a work called *Victories in the City Dionysia and the Lenaea* by one scholar and *Dionysiac Victories: Volume One* by another. At the same time, information from the Athenian archives was being assembled. This is found in the later inscription known as the *Fasti* (see 100). There is no real evidence for a pragmatic interest in editing a text for the stage. In fact the absence of music or even metrical arrangement in early texts suggests rather that texts were made available primarily for the benefit of the reading public, and the scholarly notes that we possess are largely meant to explain details for this public or for students. Nor is there any proof that any of the surviving stage directions are anything but additions by later scholars. Indeed there is a general dearth of interest in the realities of production, especially in stage machinery.

The highest point of ancient scholarship was reached in the Alexandrian Museum between 300 and 140 B.C. under a series of great librarians and scholars, especially Callimachus, Eratosthenes, Aristophanes of Byzantium, and Aristarchus. All of these scholars concerned themselves with drama, organizing and commenting on texts that were assembled and cataloged in the library. They seem to have concentrated on determining authenticity, which entailed dating the performances. For this purpose, comedy was particularly useful, because of its contemporary references. But we are ill informed of scholarly activities pertaining to the publication of dramatic texts.

Texts of the dramatists were subject to two kinds of interference. *Diaskeue* (38) is the alteration made by a dramatist (including the writer) or actor for the purpose of updating, adapting, and improving a drama for the stage. The published version of a play could differ from the acted; several acted versions could exist. *Diorthosis*–"correction"–is the attempt by grammarians to establish the original text; this could result in another text. The confusion was only augmented by the fact that there were many comedies—and tragedies—that were composed by different authors but carried the same title; e.g., at least three comic poets wrote a drama called "Lookalikes." A text, therefore, may contain actors' interpolations or false corrections, as well as mistakes and omissions of all kinds.

We have evidence of the difficulties of scholars faced with these defective texts and their explanations. They attempted to make lists, and discovered that there were different poets with the same name (33), the same drama with different names (35), titles with no text (34), the same play ascribed to two poets (36), and variants of the same drama (38). Attempts at dating were made difficult by reworked dramas (37). Reworkings could not be easily separated from forgeries (38). Most of our information is contained in mixtures of notes, called *scholia,* written in the margins of our medieval texts by different hands (40) and of very different quality. A major source of information for drama are the notices attached to the texts of dramas in medieval manuscripts; these are called *hypotheses* (43–45), and give not only a summary of the plot but details of the original performance obviously derived from excellent sources, though now much abbreviated.

Most ancient scholarship is intended to help readers (47, etc.) by providing much-needed explanatory material. The texts had no stage directions (49), or even indications of speaker, or even word division (68); in fact, inserted stage directions could eventually corrupt the text (48–50). There was interest in actors' performance (51, 52), and breaches of convention (54), though very rarely do we even suspect that the scholar has knowledge of the details of an early production (57, 58). The scholars were aware the stage directions were sometimes built into the text (55), and our scholia in general try to supply commonsense guidance for the reader (59, 60), while popular scholarship (61) often sought sensational biography.

The later scholars also used theories of meter to restore the text (62–64), since the original music and dancing was lost or preserved only among actors. Their central interest was making sense of the text, deleting lines (69), and spotting omissions (78), suspicious passages or words (70–73, 79), wrong ascriptions (67), and false readings (74)—often with a great deal of disputatiousness (76). They developed signs to indicate to the learned reader what difficulties existed (78, 92).

The school system encouraged treating these texts as a series of problems (*zetemata*) to which solutions had to be found. A favorite solution was the irresponsible guess, sometimes based on alleged historical details (81–83), and these guesses eventually affected the scholarly biographies of the poets. Likewise, the search for solutions (84) led to irrelevant associations and unjustified assertion (87, 88) or accusation (85), while the need to find problems could lead to hypercriticism (86). The general training in rhetoric also tended to encourage treating the text from the point of view of rhetorical categories (91–94), which could lead to psychological insight, as well as banality.

The grammarians and the educational system have preserved for us our texts, despite the alterations of actors. In fact, the texts are in remarkably good condition, when one considers the difficulties they faced. This is undoubtedly because of the schools' respect for the text itself in direct opposition to the adaption in which acting troupes were obligated to indulge.

Especially in late antiquity, the written text of drama increased in importance: the writing of dramas for recitation and reading became more common, and acquaintance with classical drama in its orginal form was largely through texts; private performance was matched by private discussion and reading.

Sources

Production Records

32. Johannes Tzetzes, *Prolegomena de Comoedia* I X1A p. 22 Koster. Tzetzes wrote in the 12th c., and we do not know where he got this very suspect information. Alexander and Lycophron were themselves dramatists.

> Alexander of Aetolia and Lycophron of Chalcis, incited by large payments from the king, edited the dramatic books for Ptolemy Philadelphus (288–247 B.C.), i.e., those of comedy, tragedy, and satyrs, Eratosthenes, the chief librarian of such a large library, being present to help them. Callimachus wrote up the catalogs of these books. Alexander edited the tragic works, Lycophron the comic...

33. Scholion to Aristophanes, *Birds* 1379. Aristotle was the first person we know to reduce the records of the Athenian festivals to some order. This was the first step in any study of drama. He wrote a book of "Production Records," a book "On Tragedies," and "Dionysiac Victories," which were the basis for much later work. But such remarks as this could come from other works.

> Aristotle says in his *Didaskaliai* ("Production Records") that there were two people called Cinesias.

34. Callimachus, fr. 439 Pf. from Athenaeus 336d. Athenaeus wrote ca. 200; Callimachus lived from ca. 305–240 B.C. The scholars of the Alexandrian age, especially Callimachus, listed all the works known to them, but many had not survived.

> Alexis in his *Asotodidaskalos,* says Sotion of Alexandria in his book *On the Satires of Timon*—I haven't myself run into the play...nor am I aware that it has been deemed fit to be cataloged by anyone, for neither Callimachus nor Aristophanes (of Byzantium) listed it, nor those who composed the lists in Pergamum.

35. Callimachus, fr. 440 Pf. from Athenaeus 496e. Athenaeus wrote ca. 200; Callimachus lived from ca. 305–240 B.C. A major problem in cataloging was that the same play went under different names.

> Diphilus in his play *The Walltaker*—but Callimachus calls this play *The Eunuch* ...

36. Athenaeus 127b. Written ca. 200.

> I will begin by citing these lines from the *Anteia* of Antiphanes.... But the same play is also ascribed to Alexis, with very divergent readings in a few places...

37. Callimachus fr. 454 Pf. from a scholion to Aristophanes, *Clouds* 553. See 2C. The line from Aristophanes is first quoted, and then the comment on it, which is preserved in the margin of the medieval manuscript. The dating of plays was hampered by the fact that two editions were sometimes produced, or the fact that a drama could be reworked after production. Here we see a major disagreement between the top scholars of Alexandria in the 3rd c. B.C. about dating comedies.

38A. Athenaeus 663c. Written ca. 200. It was not easy for ancient scholars to distinguish genuine remakes or reworkings by the author himself or later actors from the originals, or to discover if these were forgeries. The Greek word *diaskeue* is used for all these, sometimes pejoratively, and always for comedy, which suggests that the constant reperformance of "new" comedies meant in fact usually reworking "New" comedy. We are ill informed about the basis for many of these scholarly conclusions.

> The complete quotation, which comes from the reworked drama with the title *Demetrios* (of the poet Alexis).

38B. Athenaeus 496f.

> Diphilus in the *Eunuch* or *Soldier*—the play is a reworking of the *Walltaker* ...

38C. Athenaeus 429e.

> Alexis in the reworking of the *Phrygian* says...

38D. Hesychius, s.v. Lydizon. Probably written 5th c. We are told that there were nine plays circulating under the name of Magnes, one of the earliest poets of Old Comedy (victorious at Dionysia in 472 B.C.): all were deemed to be forgeries.

> The *Lydians* of Magnes is not preserved; it (i.e., what we have) is a reworking.

39A. Aulus Gellius 3.3.12. Written ca. 180, from Varro (116–27 B.C.). It was equally difficult to determine which plays of Plautus were genuine. The stories are rather improbable.

There are transmitted under the name of Plautus about 130 comedies, but that most learned man L. Aelius Stilo (teacher of Varro,
ca. 100 B.C.) thought that there were only 25 <genuine> comedies
of Plautus. However there is no doubt that those that do not appear
to have been written by Plautus but are attached to his name were
the work of poets of old but were revised and polished up by him,
and therefore smack of Plautine style. Now Varro and several others
have recorded that the *Saturio,* the *Addictus,* and a third comedy,
the name of which I do not now recall, were written by Plautus in
a bakery, when, after losing in trade all the money that he had
earned in jobs connected with the stage, he had returned penniless
to Rome.... So too we are told of Naevius that he wrote two plays
in prison, the *Soothsayer* and the *Leon,* when by reason of the
constant abuse and insults he aimed at the leading men of the city
after the manner of Greek poets, he had been imprisoned by the
triumvirs at Rome.

39B. L. Aelius Stilo, fr. 4 Fun. (= Suetonius, *On Grammarians* 2).
Suetonius wrote ca. 110.

L. Aelius Stilo (early 1st c. B.C.) considered that there were only 25
comedies of Plautus.

39C. Aulus Gellius 3.3.1.

I am convinced by the truth of the statement that I have heard
made by men well trained in literature, who have read a great
many plays of Plautus with care and attention, viz., that with regard
to the so-called doubtful plays, they would trust not the lists of
Aelius or Sedigitius or Claudius or Aurelius or Accius or Manlius,
but Plautus himself and the characteristic features of his manner
and diction. Indeed this is the criterion that we find Varro using.
For in addition to those twenty-one known as "Varronian," which
he set aside from the rest because they were unquestioned, and by
common consent attributed to Plautus, he accepted some others
also, influenced by the style and humor of their language, which
was characteristic of Plautus; and though these had already been
listed under the names of other poets, he claimed them for Plautus.

39D. Servius, *Commentary on Vergil, Aeneid* 4.14. Written ca. 400.

There is no question here about the number of books, though that
is a question found with other authors; for some say that Plautus
wrote 21 plays, others 120.

40. Scholion to Euripides, *Orestes* at end. It is clear that ancient commentaries could be drawn from sources with different texts. The writer is probably at the end of antiquity.

The notes have been made against several copies, from the commentary of Dionysius entirely and the mixed ones (i.e., those by several hands).

41. Donatus, *Commentary on Terence, Adelphoe,* Preface 3.8. Written 4th c. The commentator identifies the Greek originals of a Latin play; blending of this kind was called *contaminatio.*

This has been composed out of two comedies, the *Brothers* of Menander and the *Dying Together* of Diphilus.

42. Dio Chrysostom 32.94. Written 69–79. The orator is criticizing the inhabitants of Alexandria.

Just as in comedies and remakes (*diaskeuai*) when the poets bring on a drunken Karion or Daos, they do not get a real laugh, but it seems funny when Heracles is seen in that condition, paralytic, and as usual dressed in yellow.

43. Hypothesis to Aeschylus, *Persians.* Much ancient information is preserved in the brief and often abbreviated introductions, called *hypotheses,* to plays in the medieval manuscripts. In the fuller versions, details have been preserved about a play's time and place of production, whether it won, and who the competing dramatists were, as well as a brief summary of the plot.

Glaucus in his work *On the Myths of Aeschylus* claims that the *Persians* were adapted from the *Phoenician Women* of Phrynichus— he even quotes the beginning of that play thus.... But there there is a eunuch who announces at the beginning <of the play> the defeat of Xerxes, and sets out some seats for the companions of the king; here a chorus of old men speaks the prologue.... The scene of the drama is beside the tomb of Darius. The plot (*hypothesis*): Xerxes has invaded Greece; defeated with his infantry at Plateaea, with his fleet at Salamis, he flees through Thessaly to Asia. Aeschylus won under Menon (473/2 B.C.) in tragedy with <the plays> *Phineus, Persians, Glaucus Potnieus, Prometheus* (a satyr play).

44. Hypothesis to Euripides, *Hippolytus.* Care is taken to distinguish this play from the other earlier and notorious play about Hippolytus and Phaedra, which no longer survives.

The scene of the drama is in Thebes (false: actually Troizen). It was produced in the archonship of Epimeinon in the 87th Olympiad, year 4 (429/8 B.C.). Euripides was first, Iophon second, Ion third.

This is the second *Hippolytus,* called also *Stephanites.* It was clearly written later <than the first *Hippolytus*>. For what was improper and worthy of criticism is revised in this play. The drama is among the first.

45. Hypothesis to Euripides, *Rhesus.* Perhaps an even greater problem was the number of forgeries in circulation. The principal task of a grammarian was considered to be the separation of the genuine from the false texts. It was often impossible.

> Some people have suspected this drama is not genuine, and not by Euripides; that it displays rather a Sophoclean touch. However in the *Didaskaliai* it is listed as genuine, and the wordiness about the heavens in it smacks of Euripides. There are two prologues transmitted. Dicaearchus (a pupil of Aristotle: 4th c. B.C.), setting out the plot of the *Rhesus,* writes exactly as follows:... In some of the copies there is another prologue transmitted, pedestrian and not suiting Euripides; perhaps some of the actors could have written it in. It goes like this.

Interest in Stage Production

46. *POxy* 2257 (= *TrGF* 3, p. 126 R.). This papyrus fragment was almost certainly a discussion of the lost play of Aeschylus called the *Women of Aetna.* It was produced in Sicily (cf. 23). No extant tragedy has so many changes of scene; it looks as if at least five acts are described.

> In the first part of the drama the scene is set in Aetna, in the second Xouthia, in the third Aetna again; then it changes from there to Leontini and becomes Leon[tini?], after that Syracuse, and the rest is brought to a close in the [?Temeni]tes, which is a place [. . .

47A. Scholia to Aristophanes, *Acharnians* 770 and 860. All scholiasts will provide simple help to the reader such as these remarks about entrances and exits, and gestures. They need not indicate any knowledge of a production but merely explain the text.

> He addresses the spectators. . . . He comes on with his shoulder sore from supporting the pack.

47B. Scholion to Aristophanes, *Frogs* 40.

> He nods toward Xanthias.

48. Scholion to Aristophanes, *Thesmophoriazusae* 99. Some commentators apparently recommended inserting stage directions for the benefit of readers.

Between the two lines some scholars think it right to insert <the word> "trilling," for there are many stage directions like that.

49. Scholion to Aeschylus, *Eumenides* 117. Here the word "muttering" is an obvious insertion in the text. This is one of the very few remarks, perhaps four, that could be an original stage direction from an actor's copy; but it could equally be a guess by a reader.

> <Muttering>: *Parepigraphe* (i.e., stage direction). This is what the poet says, "They muttered." That <the Furies> all wake up from their slumber together is not credible; so they will simulate their awakening gradually as they come up.

50. Scholion to Euripides, *Orestes* 1384. But we see that the ancient scholars suspected too readily that some words in the text were originally inserted stage directions.

> "A charioteer's charioteer's melody": Some people say this is a *parepigraphe,* like in comedies. Apollonios of Cyrene says that this is a stage direction (i.e., which has got into the text)....But if it really were, it would have been written only once.

51. Scholion to Euripides, *Orestes* 269. Cf. 13 and scholion to *Orestes* 1287. This is one of a number of notes comparing the contemporary with the assumed ancient acting of the play. The *Orestes* was the most popular of all classical plays and was accordingly most frequently reenacted, and altered.

> He follows Stesichorus in saying that he got his bow from Apollo. So the actor had to get a bow and shoot arrows. Those who act the hero (Orestes) nowadays ask for the bow and, without getting it, make a show of shooting arrows.

52. Scholion to Euripides, *Orestes* 643. The ancient commentator in rhetorical terms unreasonably criticizes contemporary acting.

> "ORESTES: You need only repay your debt, Menelaus, what you got from my father. I don't mean money...": When Orestes says this, the actors (i.e., those playing Menelaus) raise one hand, as if Menelaus were distressed that <Orestes> is saying that he (Menelaus) had had a sum of money entrusted to him by his father (Agamemnon). But Menelaus is silly to harbor such a suspicion. For if he didn't know the speaker or what he wanted, perhaps the action would have some plausibility; but since he does know, the gesture is unnecessary and useless.

53. Scholion to Euripides, *Orestes* 57. Obviously the introductory scene was, in the times of the commentator, grandiosely staged with booty and captives with no regard to the original text.

Some actors are not correct nowadays when they make Helen and
the booty <from Troy> come on the stage at dawn. For literally
(i.e., according to the text here) he says that she departed during
the night, and the action of the play takes place in daytime.

54A. Scholion to Euripides, *Hecuba* 484. The commentators were
aware of the conventions of the early stage, and they noted exceptions.
They believed that the suicide of Ajax took place before the audience in
Sophocles.

Polyxena has been dispatched without it being mentioned. For it is
the custom with the tragedians not to kill in front of the spectators:
they would be upset by such a sight.

54B. Scholion to Sophocles, *Ajax* 815 Christod. Cf. IV 64.

The scene has changed to some remote region, where Ajax has got
his sword ready and utters a speech before he dies, for it would
be silly for him to come in and fall on his sword without saying
anything. Situations like this are rare in ancient writers. They usually
announce what has happened in messages. What is the reason <here
for the exception>? Aeschylus is the first to announce Ajax' death
in his *Thracian Women* by means of a messenger. Perhaps then
Sophocles, wanting to be original and not follow the ideas of
someone else, has put the action before our eyes; or perhaps he
wished to dazzle (*ekplexai*) <the audience>. It is pointless and
impious to condemn one of the ancients.

55. Scholion to Euripides, *Orestes* 168. The general principle enunci-
ated here of "implicit stage directions" is very important.

Some people say that the chorus employed a mourning tone that
cannot be indicated in writing, a wail or something rougher, which
women are accustomed to utter in overwhelming misery. For what
cannot be indicated in writing is expressed by other characters, e.g.,
in Aristophanes, when a slave laments, another actor says: "Do you
hear how he laments?"

56. Scholion to Euripides, *Medea* 85. This looks like a guess at the
reason for a text variant.

"Who of men does not? Do you now realize this?": The actor who
did not realize that there was a stop <in the middle of the line>
altered it into: "Who of men does not clearly realize this?"

57. Scholion to Aristophanes, *Clouds* 889b–c. This is a peculiar re-
mark, and it is debated whether it is merely a guess or based on
experience. See 132.

The Greater and the Lesser Arguments are speaking. The Arguments are shown on stage in little wicker cages, fighting it out like cocks.

58. Scholion to Aeschylus, *Prometheus Bound* 287. The scholia, on the other hand, are almost excessively interested in the stage movements, since they are writing for readers, not for actors.

Ocean, coming in, gives the chorus a chance to get down from the *mechane*.

59A. Donatus, *Commentary on Terence, Adelphoe* 210. Written 4th c. The Latin commentaries of Donatus on Terence's comedies are particularly rich in explanations of the more complex action of comedy, adding stage directions to help the reader understand the text, including "asides." Here the incoming speaker enters the stage from the house door and in the middle of his speech catches sight of someone on stage.

The first part <of the speech> is spoken at the back of (lit. "behind") the stage, this part on the proscaenium.

59B. Donatus, *Commentary on Terence, Eunuchus* 391. From the beginning of a scene where two characters enter in the midst of a conversation.

This conversation is produced in such a way that it is understood to have begun behind the stage.

59C. Donatus, *Commentary on Terence, Andria* 456. Here an aside to the audience must be understood.

He (the slave) said, "That stung him" (*commovi*), to himself, so that the spectator hears, not the old man.

59D. *Ibid.* 495.

He says this in such a way that the spectator hears but not Simo.

59E. Donatus, *Commentary on Terence, Eunuchus* 394.

The third character comes on the stage, but speaks apart and to himself.

59F. *Ibid.* 987.

The old man says this aside, his eyes fixed on Parmeno.

60A. Donatus, *Commentary on Terence, Adelphoe* 127. Written 4th c. Donatus is also very interested in gesture, as it might accompany the words and demonstrate character by action. This is probably due to the influence of rhetoric, and intended for schoolchildren declaiming.

This is pronounced with the gesture of one leaving or going to leave.

60B. Donatus, *Commentary on Terence, Eunuchus* 549.

In this scene the words indicate the gesture and expression of a person leaving whom a character runs into.

60C. Donatus, *Commentary on Terence, Phormio* 52.

"There, take it!": This is said with the gesture of offering.

60D. Donatus, *Commentary on Terence, Andria* 110.

Because he has said, "I was thinking like this," he expresses a gesture of thinking. So it's mimicry.

60E. Donatus, *Commentary on Terence, Eunuchus* 771.

Here again the vainglory of the silly soldier is made clear in that he proceeds to his girlfriend as to a fearsome army, with anger aroused, hasty step, cloak waving, tossing and shaking his head.

61. Athenaeus 21e. See IV 304. It is alarming to find that comedians are considered good sources for tragic stage production. Much of this information must be considered suspect.

Interest in Meter

62A. Dionysius of Halicarnassus, *On the Composition of Words* 22, p. 102, 2 R. Written last quarter 1st c. B.C. It was not known even in antiquity who had devised the systems of meters that were in early Roman times found applied in the manuscripts, but the grammarian Aristophanes (ca. 200 B.C.) was a popular choice.

Assume that I mean by cola (metrical units) not those into which Aristophanes or some other metrician arranged the odes.

62B. *Ibid.* 26, p. 140, 19 R.

The lines are written not according to those divisions that Aristophanes or some other metrician devised.

63A. Scholion to Aristophanes, *Clouds* at end. The medieval manuscripts of the comedian Aristophanes do contain information about the metrical forms, which they attribute to the metrician Heliodorus, active ca. 50.

The colometry <has been taken> from Heliodorus.

63B. Scholion to Aristophanes, *Peace* at end.

The colometry <has been checked> against Heliodorus.

64A. Donatus, *Commentary on Terence, Andria* 536. Written 4th c. Our information about what ancient scholars thought is often confused. Here we have three separate pieces of information, which show that the commentator Donatus knew of two readings in the text of Terence but preferred one, apparently for metrical reasons.

Both *pauca* and *paucis* are read.

64B. Priscian, *Grammatici Latini* 3.320.10. Written early 6th c.

Pauca: this is what the ancient manuscripts had according to Donatus, the commentator on Terence.

64C. Priscian, *Grammatici Latini* 3.281.12.

Pauca: a quaternarius iambus does not scan any other way; the commentary of Donatus also recommends it (sc., as the correct reading).

Interest in Text

65. Scholion to Euripides, *Medea* 759. None of the attributions of parts in our texts is secure; even in antiquity there was uncertainty about roles.

Some scholars attribute these words to the chorus, others to Medea.

66. Scholion to Sophocles, *Ajax* 354. A scholiast offers a rule of thumb for assigning roles in reading a text.

For in places where the roles are unclear, one should guess at the character, and make a distinction accordingly.

67. Donatus, *Commentary on Terence, Adelphoe* 287. Written 4th c. There are many such notes in both Greek and Latin dramatic texts.

Some people want this verse to be added to the role of Syrus, but it is clear that the words are those of Ctesiphon from what follows.

68. Aristotle, *Rhetoric* 1407b. Written ca. 330 B.C. Likewise, the earliest texts were written in capitals without word division or punctuation. It required skill to make sense of the lines so written. Various signs were used by the readers.

To punctuate Heraclitus is no easy task, because we often cannot tell whether a particular word belongs to what precedes or what follows it.

69. Scholion to Euripides, *Orestes* 640.

Some athetize (i.e., decree to be false) this and the next line, for they lack the Euripidean touch.

70. Scholion to Euripides, *Orestes* 1227–30.

In the copy, these four iambic lines are not recorded, and in another also.

71. Scholion to Euripides, *Orestes* 1394.

In many copies the line is not written.

72. Scholion to Euripides, *Medea* 87.

The line is added and redundant, containing elaboration.

73. Scholion to Sophocles, *Antigone* 46.

Didymus (ca. 50 B.C.) says that <the line> was considered spurious by the commentators.

74. Scholion to Euripides, *Andromache* 89.

According to some <scholars?> the line is written without "not," so that the opposite is meant, in sarcasm.

75. Scholion to Euripides, *Andromache* 330ff. These lines are else-where cited from Menander, so that there is a suspicion that they have been inserted in one or the other author. Sometimes playwrights of New Comedy did take lines from other works, and actors almost certainly did make such insertions.

Didymus (ca. 50 B.C.) criticizes these lines as unsuitable to the action; the language is too grand for a barbarian woman in misery.

76. Scholion to Aristophanes, *Thesmophoriazusae* 162. Ancient schol-ars not only emended texts but assumed that others had already emended them too. Here there is a disagreement whether the text of Aristophanes had the word "Achaios" or "Alkaios." All our manuscripts now have only "Alkaios," which is obviously correct.

In some <writers? manuscripts?> the <word> "Achaios" is written, and the older copies had this. Aristophanes (the grammarian ca. 200 B.C.) is the one who made the change to "Alkaios," for the argument is about men of old, and Achaios is too recent. As for what is said by Didymus (ca. 50 B.C.) against Aristophanes, that he can't be referring to Alkaios—for the works of Alkaios were not popular, he says, because of their dialect—that is utter rubbish. Even in the drama before this one, the *Birds,* there is a parody <of Alkaios>—"here are some birds of Ocean from the ends of the earth"—and in the *Wasps*—"this man here seeking great power." Elsewhere Didymus says the reading can stay, but he (i.e., Aristoph-anes the poet) would not be referring to the lyric poet—saying exactly the same again, viz., that the works of Alkaios were not popular—but to the lyre player, whom Eupolis mentions in his play *The Golden Age,* "O Alkaios Sicilian and Peloponnesian." But why <should he refer> to a lyre player here when the whole point is about a poet?

77. Scholion to Aristophanes, *Frogs* 152. The ancient scholars set signs in the text to indicate text problems. Here the two signs indicate that two lines in the text are alternatives, and that one should not be read. Note that other scholars recommended removing one of the two lines altogether. The two lines are still in our texts, and they are indeed

alternatives, but the signs are only once more mentioned in the whole of antiquity.

> Some <scholars?> do not write the line that begins...(i.e., line 152), but they remove it and write the next line thus....Therefore Aristophanes the grammarian sets a sigma and antisigma beside the lines.

78. Scholion to Aristophanes, *Clouds* 889a, 889d. Here it was noticed that a choral ode was missing. In the texts of Menander it is normal that the odes, being irrelevant to the drama, are not written out, and that only the indication "of the chorus" is given (see IVD). The signs *diple* and *koronis* are indications by a grammarian that a choral ode is expected after the departure of the actors.

> The part with the chorus is missing but there is a marginal note "of the chorus." A *diple* and a *koronis,* because the actors have gone off. There is not a choral ode, only "of the chorus" is written in the middle.

79. Pliny, *Natural History* 18.107. Written ca. 77.

> Plautus already calls it *artopas* ("baker") in a play, which he entitled *Aulularia* (400), though there is a great argument among the learned whether the verse is actually his.

80. Varro, *On the Latin Language* 9.106. Written ca. 43 B.C. Cf. Cicero, *Letters to Friends* 9.16.4.

> Whether the error belongs to Plautus or his copyist, it is not (sc., the theory of) analogy but the writer that is to be blamed.

Interest in Biography

81. *POxy* 1176 (= *Vita di Euripide* 39 X Arrighetti). This is one column from a papyrus, which comes from book 6 of a work by Satyrus of Alexandria (ca. 200 B.C.) called *Register of the Lives of Aeschylus, Sophocles, and Euripides,* and which surprisingly is written as a popular dialogue. Many of the legends in the *Lives,* which were already old by this date, recur here, along with the citations from the dramas that were supposed to prove them. The story of the women attacking him is clearly adapted from Aristophanes' *Thesmophoriazusae* (cf. 135).

> Euripides was hated by all the men because he was a misanthrope, and by the women because of the criticisms of them in his poetry. He got into considerable danger with both groups. For he was acquitted on the earlier-mentioned charge of impiety brought by

Cleon the demagogue; and the women plotted against him at the
Thesmophoria festival and came in a mob to the place[. . .

82A. Athenaeus 229e (= *Aristophanes, PCG* T 12). Written ca. 200.
The invention of often absurd biographic details to explain questions in
the text is an embarrassing feature of ancient scholarship. Here a question
on the text of the *Clouds,* "Why does Aristophanes mention the Nile?"
has been answered by the scholar Heliodorus with "Because he was an
Egyptian." This comment has become part of the biographic tradition.
Similarly the story of his being an Aeginetan derives probably from a
misinterpretation of *Acharnians* 652–54. Much of what we are told about
the lives of the poets may derive from such remarks.

> Aristophanes the comic poet whom Heliodorus the Athenian says
> in his work *On the Akropolis* (ca. 150 B.C.) was from Naucratis (in
> Egypt).

82B. Scholion to Aristophanes, *Clouds* 272. Here the text mentions
the Nile.

> The poet, wanting secretly to make a show of his own circum-
> stances—for he was an Egyptian by birth—finding an opportunity,
> makes mention of the Nile.

83. Arethas on Plato, *Apology* 19c (= Aristophanes, *PCG* T 3). Written
after 895. But in principle useful biographical information could be
derived from the works of ancient authors if used carefully; this warns
us not to dismiss all biographic details. Here a learned Byzantine bishop
is writing a note in the margin of his Plato manuscript.

> Aristophanes the comic poet was bald, as he himself says in the
> *Peace* (771). He was mocked for joking at Euripides but imitating
> him. Cratinus (*PCG* F 342):
>
> > Who are you? a smart spectator would ask. Superfinewordy,
> > neatexpressionhunting, euripidaristophanizing.
>
> And he himself (!: this is most unlikely) confesses it in the *Women
> Pitching Tents* (*PCG* F 488):
>
> > For I employ the elegance of his language, but I make my
> > minds less vulgar than his.
>
> Aristonymus (*PCG* F 3) in the *Freezing Sun* and Sannyrion in
> *Laughter* (*PCG* F 5) say that he was born "on the fourth" (a
> proverb meaning "to hard labor"), because he wasted his life work-
> ing for other people. Because those who are born on the fourth by
> working for others provide them with the profits, as Philochorus
> says in the first book of *Concerning Days* (328 *FGrH* 85). On this
> day they say that Heracles was born. <Aristophanes> had three

sons: Philippos, who competed with the plays of Eubulus; Araros, who competed with his own and his father's plays; and a third, whom Apollodorus (244 *FGrH* 75) calls Nikostratos, but Dicaearchus and his followers (fr. 83 W.) Philetairos. <Aristophanes> was allotted land in Aegina, as Theogenes says in his book on Aegina (300 *FGrH* 2). He is also mocked in comedy because he took out the colossal statue of Peace: Eupolis in the *Autolycus* (*PCG* F 62), Plato in *Victories* (*PCG* F 86).

Zetemata and False Cross-References

84. Scholion to Euripides, *Medea* 169. Nothing excited the ancient scholars so much as an apparent contradiction in the text: this gave rise to a "question" (*zetema*); scholars wrote books of solutions to them.

This is one of the most hotly debated questions, how Medea can call on Themis and Artemis (60), whereas the old woman says (169) that Medea called on Zeus and not on Artemis. Apollodorus of Tarsus says that the actors are responsible for the ambiguity by confusing the parts for the chorus with those of Medea (sc., in line 147)....Didymus (ca. 50 B.C.) says that by saying "May fire from heaven go through my brain" (144) she is calling on Zeus. For who else would be able to send lightning upon her if not Zeus? But if the old woman hasn't remembered everything that Medea said in her prayer, we shouldn't be surprised; she was content with the very solemn names. Others claim that "I swear by Zeus and Themis" is missing from the text (i.e., should be inserted).

85. Scholion to Euripides, *Orestes* 1366–68. See 13.

86. Donatus, *Commentary on Terence, Phormio* 1005. Written 4th c. The grammarian Probus (late 1st c.) was apparently prepared to query the text on moral grounds, a common procedure in antiquity.

Probus asks whether a married woman could rightly speak so familiarly to a stranger; but the question is pointless. For the language of women, even if not <intended as> flattery, is flattering.

87. Scholion to Aristophanes, *Frogs* 1206. Ancient scholars felt obliged to detect references and cross-references, but often they made mistakes.

Some people say that this <line> is the beginning of <Euripides'> *Archelaus;* wrongly. For there is no such line of Euripides recorded now. For it can't be, says Aristarchus, unless <Euripides> himself changed it later, and Aristophanes mentioned the original.

88. Diogenes Laertius 2.44. This scribbler of the 3rd c. is copying out authors who used much earlier sources. The passage illustrates well how popularizing scholars—even of the 4th c. B.C.—made wild deductions from the texts, especially by equating characters and poet, and finding illegitimate references to historical events. In the *Palamedes,* performed in 416 B.C., seventeen years before the death of Socrates, the chorus is mourning the unjust death of the hero Palamedes.

> Euripides also criticizes the Athenians in the *Palamedes* (fr. 588 N.), saying: "You killed, you killed the most wise one, O Greeks, the nightingale of the Muses who did no harm," and so on. But Philochorus (328 *FGrH* 221) says that Euripides died before Socrates.

Rhetorical Comment

89. Scholion to Sophocles, *Electra* 1171. This is a type of rhetorical criticism that is very common in ancient commentary. The word "necessary" is paralleled by the comments "probable, persuasive, effective, economical, useful, and timely," which are rhetorical categories. When all else fails, the word "wonderful" will do.

> It's necessary for Orestes to be revealed, for the connection of the plot would have been destroyed if he were silent.

90. Scholion to Sophocles, *Ajax* 66.

> The entrance of Ajax is persuasive; for thereby the emotional effect of the tragedy is greater when the spectators see him now raving, and a little later sane.

91. Scholion to Sophocles, *Oedipus Tyrannus* 946. Ancient comments are often moral and suited for schoolrooms.

> There is a didactic element in the drama, viz., that one should not despise the gods. Those who have said such things will show their nature clearly after a while.

92. Scholion to Sophocles, *Antigone* 735. The greek letter *chi* (i.e., X)—like some other marks—was set in the margin of the text by ancient commentators to indicate some point of interest. But it needed to be explained, as here. The point was of interest either for moral-didactic purposes or to stress the stage psychology.

> The *chi* because Haemon addresses his father in a severe tone.

93. Donatus, *Commentary on Terence, Andria* 485. Written 4th c. There is interest in the general nature of typical characters and in

psychology generally, partly under the influence of rhetorical theory of character types.

Observe that he is imitating the authoritative and vain manner of doctors when he says, "As I ordered."

94. Donatus, *Commentary on Terence, Andria* 288. Written 4th c.

"I beg you, my nurse, what is now to be done?": This is the imploring of someone in fear rather than the question of someone who does not know.

Nonperformed Drama

95. Pliny, *Epistles* 6.21.2–4. Written ca. 100. Since the time of Aristotle (*Rhetoric* 3.12.3) there had existed drama that was meant to be read. Genuine dramas were often in whole or part simply read rhetorically or dramatically before an audience, often at dinner (see 6–8), and eventually dramas were written to be so read like poetry. It is often assumed that Seneca's tragedies were of this type. The fashion for reciting tragedy in lecture halls may have been invented by Asinius Pollio in the second half of the 1st c. B.C.

And I have just been listening to Vergilius Romanus reading to a small group a comedy he wrote so well in the manner of Old Comedy, that one day it too could be a model (i.e., of Old Comedy, which here means Aristophanes)....he has written comedies in imitation of Menander and others of that era (New Comedy); you could put them among those of Plautus or Terence. At the moment for the first time, he is showing his ability in Old Comedy, but not as though he was a beginner.

96. *CIL* 9.1164 (= *Carmina Epigraphica* 97). Date: after 117. A grave epigram records a similar attention to Hellenistic comedy.

In order not to pass my leisure time like an animal, I translated a few clever comedies of Menander, and even invented a few new ones myself. That, whatever it was worth, is long since committed to paper...

97. Tacitus, *Dialogus* 2.1. Written ca. 85. But even a nonperformed drama could be published and have considerable effect. Maternus had already published a *Medea* and was working on a *Thyestes*. Previously Mamercus Scaurus had written an *Atreus* that Tiberius took as a personal attack, and Mamercus was forced to commit suicide (IV 222). Tragedy continued to be politically sensitive, especially when written by the aristocracy.

... Curiatus Maternus had given a reading of his *Cato,* when powerful spirits are said to have taken offense at the way he forgot himself
and thought only of Cato in the plot of a tragedy, and there was
a lot of talk in town about it.

98. Aulus Gellius 2.23.1. Written ca. 180. The standard of literary
appreciation of drama could still be very high in later imperial times.
The author is thinking about classical Roman and Greek drama, now
more than three or four hundred years old.

I often read comedies that our poets have adapted and translated
from the Greek,... and while I am reading them, they do not seem
at all bad; on the contrary, they appear to have been written with
wit and charm that you would say absolutely could not be surpassed. But if you compare and place beside them the Greek originals from which they came... the Latin versions at once begin to
appear exceedingly commonplace and mean, so dimmed are they
by the wit and brilliance of the Greek comedies.

99. Aulus Gellius 2.23.4–12. Written ca. 180. Cultivated people in
the 2nd c. were very familiar with classical texts.

I was reading the *Plocium,* or "Necklace," of Caecilius, much to
the delight of myself and those who were present. We had the idea
of reading also the *Plokion* of Menander, from which Caecilius had
translated the comedy. But after we took Menander in hand, my
goodness, how dull and lifeless and how different from Menander
did Caecilius appear. ... he (the slave) gives expression to his fear,
anger, suspicion, pity, and grief. In the Greek comedy all these
feelings are wonderfully vivid and clear, but in Caecilius they are
dull and without any grace and dignity of expression.

IB. Inscriptions

We give a few examples here from the hundreds of inscriptions that provide us with evidence for aspects of drama in the ancient world, which we should not otherwise know. The best-known examples are those listing the competitions of the major festivals of Athens; after that we offer some other illustrations of the kinds of information that we can derive from records on stone. The so-called epigraphic habit of the Greeks and then the Romans led them to carve on stone many items of their bureaucracy that would otherwise be lost to us, including decrees honoring actors, winners of festivals, building inscriptions, and other details central to the history of drama. However these inscriptions very seldom form a coherent series and are often fragmentary; they also reveal *what* was done, but do not explain normally *why* or *how*. It will be seen that the information is often dependent on local habits of recording.

For Athens we are fortunate in having four different types of inscriptional information about the two major festivals, the Dionysia (IIIAia) and the Lenaea (IIIAib), and their actors in classical and Hellenistic times. All are badly damaged. Nonetheless we can document from these some crucial changes in the history of the theater. Originally we can assume that poet, director, and chief actor would have been the same person; but already Aeschylus employed a chief actor, and Aristophanes used a director, whose principal chore was to train the chorus in music and dancing throughout the year. While in the beginning the reason for recording the details of drama were financial—and therefore the producer (*choregos*) and his chief associate, the director (*didaskalos*), are those named in the *Fasti*—neither poet nor chief actor are named. Competition for leading chorus directors was great. Yet already in ca. 447 B.C. there was a prize for actors at the Great Dionysia and, shortly afterward, for comic actors at the Lenaea. The importance of the actor continues to rise at the expense of poet and director. The reperformance of classic plays in the next century meant that the actor-director, especially of tragedy, now became the most important personality in drama. The power of the actor brought with it certain difficulties, since the reputation that the actor had with the population would tend to sway the judges to award the prize to the play he acted in, irrespective of the quality of the play. We find that various regulations were introduced to try to circumvent this problem.

Reperformance not only removes the poet from prize consideration and elevates the acting profession. The actors are made independent of poets; they can develop a repertoire, play at short notice, and move with greater freedom. The audiences, on the other hand, will tend in turn to become connoisseurs of these "classic" dramas, and raise again the importance of the actor. "Old tragedy" in festival programs usually means Euripides or the tragedians of his time; "old comedy," however, usually means what we call "New Comedy" or comedians like Menander. We have no record in inscriptions that Aristophanes was reperformed.

Sources

Athenian Inscriptions Relating to the Dionysia
and Lenaea

100. *Fasti.* This is a modern title for an inscription found near the Agora at Athens, representing parts of thirteen columns of text, the beginning of which is lost. The remnants are fragmentary records of the Great Dionysia festival from 473 to 328 B.C.; originally it went from an unknown date just before 500 B.C. to about 316 B.C., but additions had been made after 346 B.C. The *didaskalos* ("teacher" or "director," as we translate it) was at first the poet himself, who would orginally have been chief actor also. But already in the 5th c. B.C. professional directors appear, who train the chorus in particular. The following items are listed under the entry for each year:

    1. The name of the presiding archon

    2. The name of the victorious tribe in the boys' dithyrambic contest and its *choregos*

    3. The name of the victorious tribe in the men's dithyrambic contest and its *choregos*

    4. The name of the victorious *choregos* and director (*didaskalos*) in comedy who would not always be the poet

5. The name of the victorious *choregos* and director in tragedy
For the year 449 or 447 B.C. the name of the victorious actor in tragedy
is added to no. 5. Over the first four columns was written a now damaged
heading: [... FIR]ST KOMOI WERE T[O DIONYSUS] TRAGIC D[... ;
and it is not known what the word *komoi* ("revels") refers to, since it
is not elsewhere used for drama; perhaps the dithyrambic choruses could
be so called. Where the compiler got all this detailed information is
unknown; the assumption that he could have gotten it from lists made
by Aristotle and his school cannot be proved, since nothing survives of
these lists except the title. The information would be more likely to
interest officials, since the people mentioned are those financially involved.
Reconstruction is rendered even more difficult by the inconsistencies that
developed over the course of the years, e.g., a joint-*choregia* at the end
of the fifth century. See III 29; IV 11.

   101. *Didaskaliai.* This series of inscriptions (*IG* II² 2319–23), now
in many fragments, comes from one building set up on the south slope
of the Akropolis, probably in the 3rd c. B.C., and was added to by various
hands for another century. There were undoubtedly considerable changes
in the festival program, some unknown to us, which took place in the
350 years covered by this inscription, e.g., tragic trilogies were at some
point replaced by single dramas; and in some years no festival could be
held at all. The list records, though not certainly in the following order,

   1. (Comedy at the Dionysian festival): archon; winning actor/director
of "old" comedy with the name of the play and its original composer;
first victorious poet with name of play and chief actor; second poet,
play, actor; third, etc., ... up to the fifth; prize for best actor

   2. (Comedy at the Lenaean festival): archon, etc., as at the Dionysia

   3. (Tragedy at the Lenaean festival): archon; first poet, play(s),
actor; second poet, play(s), actor; winning actor

   4. (Tragedy at the Dionysian festival, where only Hellenistic dates
survive): archon; victorious poet of satyrplay with name of play;
winning actor/director of "old" tragedy with name of play and its
original composer; winning poet of original tragedy with two plays,
followed by the actor in each; second poet with two plays and actor
in each; third poet with two plays and the actor in each; winning actor.
The name *Didaskaliai* has been given to this list on the assumption that
its origin has something to do with the lists made by Aristotle. Notably
missing are *choregoi* and dithyrambic victors. This list is more concerned
with the history of drama, and with poets and actors; it is a reasonable
guess that the Artists of Dionysus would be interested in such information

(see IVAii). Unfortunately, little information from the classical period survives on the stones.

In 341/2 B.C. each of three playwrights still offers three tragedies, but no longer a satyrplay. The "old tragedy" is simply called "the old" in the inscription, because only tragedies at that point are recorded; in the list of comedies, "the old" means of course a reperformance of usually New Comedy; these reperformances are irregular in the 4th c. B.C. but become established at the Dionysia before 386 B.C. for tragedy and 311 B.C. for comedy. It is not known what the status of "old" drama was at the Lenaea, but it is not mentioned on the fragments we have. Most interesting here is the fact that in 341 B.C. there are only three actors for the nine plays (IV 16). Each actor gets to play the lead in the first play in one trilogy, the second in another, and the third in another. This complex and demanding arrangement can only be a response to demands for fairness in tragic competition; no such demand appears in comedy. But in the next year only two principal actors perform six plays by three poets; one concludes that in the absence of one actor, the system of fairness was maintained by allowing only two plays per poet.

In 155/4 B.C. the actor/director Damon wins with a reperformance of an old standby from New Comedy, but he also acts in two other new comedies. We note that no other "old" comedies are ever recorded except the winning one. The actor Kallikrates also appears in two comedies, as does Asklepiodoros in 311 B.C. (IV 14). There were clearly star comic actors as well as tragic.

A small fragment (Mette, *Urkunden* 149ff.) from a totally different set of similar lists has also been found recently in Athens, and it surprisingly gives a list of victories in the restaging of older plays. The previously known *Didaskaliai* give only one "old" comedy or tragedy, which might suggest that only one was performed. Here, however, we learn that, at least in 255/4 B.C., there was a complete competition for "old" comedy, "old" tragedy, and even "old" satyrplay, with three plays entered in each category. We cannot tell what this otherwise unknown competition has to do with the Dionysiac or Lenaean festivals, if anything. It was clearly a competition for the actor-directors rather than the poets, but the fact that the main competition in Athens has to be described in the 3rd c. B.C. as "the competition for new tragedians (i.e., for original tragedy) at the Great Dionysia" instead of as before as "the competition for tragedians at the Great Dionysia" seems to prove that there was indeed a competition for "old" tragedy there. See III 74, 75, 77; IV 14, 16.

102. Victor Lists. In the same building that contained the *Didaskaliai,* there was also a different kind of inscription, now broken in many pieces, which listed victorious poets and actors, from the beginning down to the mid-2nd c. B.C., as follows:

1. Victorious poets of tragedy at the Dionysia
2. Victorious actors of tragedy at the Dionysia
3. Victorious poets of comedy at the Dionysia
4. Victorious actors of comedy at the Dionysia
5. Victorious poets of comedy at the Lenaea
6. Victorious actors of comedy at the Lenaea
7. Victorious poets of tragedy at the Lenaea
8. Victorious actors of tragedy at the Lenaea

The order at the Lenaean festival is explained by the greater importance of comedy there. The order within each section is chronological; that is, each individual is ordered according to the date of his first victory, though neither date nor anything else is indicated, and a numeral is added to indicate the total number of victories won by that individual at that festival. Obviously such a list could be compiled by going through the *Didaskaliai* from the beginning. It is notable that it is the poets and not the directors they may have used that are listed. See III 68; IV 12, 13.

103. Roman *Fasti.* Small fragments of a huge inscription (*IGUR* 215–31: Mette, *Urkunden* 190ff.) with another type of list come from a now unidentified building in central Rome. This contained at least lists of

1. comic poets and all their placings in the two great Athenian competitions and elsewhere down to fifth place, along with the dates of these. This information could not normally be derived by reorganizing the details from the *Didaskaliai.* The order was
   a. name of poet
   b. his first-placed plays in chronological order, listed by archon
   c. his second-placed plays listed in the same way
   d. his third-placed plays listed in the same way, and so forth
2. actors in tragedy
3. actors in comedies and tragedies
4. victories of individual actors in tragedies and comedies

But other lists are now missing; additional information was given, e.g., whether the play mentioned was preserved, or even if its name was no longer known. It is noted, e.g., that the *Bacchae* of Lysippus was the only surviving play by that poet. See III 41.

Other Attic Festivals

104. *IG* II² 3091; *TrGF* 1, p. 39. Choregic monument. Date: early 4th c. B.C. It is often by chance that we learn that there were dramatic or similar competitions at the many other festivals at Athens and in the surrounding territory, where several theaters have been discovered (see III 48–52, 54–60). This puzzling inscription is said to come from the theater of Aixone in Attica, but it may represent a list of victorious local *choregoi* at the main Athenian or local festivals.

E[... won as *choregos*] in comedians (= comedy).
Ecphantides was *didaskalos* of *Attempts*.
Thrasyboulos as *choregos* won in comedians.
Cratinus was *didaskalos* of *Cowherd*.
Thrasyboulos as *choregos* won in tragedians.
Timotheos was *didaskalos* of *Alkmaeon, Alphesib[oea* ...
Epichares as *choregos* won in tragedians.
Sophocles was *didaskalos* of *Telepheia* (plays about Telephus)

105. *IG* II² 3157 (= *TrGF* 1, p. 42). This fragment is on the base of a statue from the 1st c., and rare evidence for the inclusion of tragedy at the great athletic and thymelic festival of the Panathenaea. New tragedy even at this time must have had a chorus. Drama was also included in the Pythia of Delphi about this time also, as part of the general expansion in early imperial times.

...] he competed with cyclic choruses of men for the Kekropidan tribe, acting himself as *choregos* and director, and he produced a new tragedy at the Great Panathenaea and[

106. *IG* II² 3103. This is a baffling inscription from the deme Xypete in Attica, which may take us back to the original country rituals. Two *komos* (revel) leaders are also *komasts.*

The people of Xypete won. Aristophon was archon (330/29 B.C.).
Komos-leaders: Philton, son of Aischytos; Pamphilos, son of Aischytos; Peisidamas, son of Peisidos; Lykinos, son of Lykon.
Komasts: Pamphilos, son of Aischytos; Philton, son of Aischytos; Kephisios, son of Kephisios; Philaios, son of Philon; Pytheas, [son of ...

Greek Inscriptions Outside Attica

107. *IG* XI 106. Cf. Mette, *Urkunden* 63ff. One of a series of lists of *choregoi* and performers at the Dionysia and Apollonia in Delos.

Date: 282 B.C. There are regularly six *choregoi* each for tragedy and comedy, of whom two in each category are foreign residents. It looks as if two teams of two citizens plus a resident alien looked after each genre (cf. Sifakis, *Studies* 31). "A presentation for the god" we find at other sanctuaries: these should mean freely donated performances by visitors.

> Under the archon Kleostratos these were *choregoi* at the Apollonia (sc., for the boys' dithyramb). Pleistainetos, son of Teleson; Didymos, son of Antigonos; Stesileos, son of Skymnos; Apemantos, son of Herodikos.

At the Dionysia:

> for the boys': Kallidikos, son of Diodotos; Ortygenes, son of Tychandros; Ergoteles, son of Theophanes
>
> for comedians: Androlas, son of Sattos; Pyrraithos, son of Nesiotes; Theorylos, son of Diaktorides; Aristeides, son of Charilas; from the resident aliens Antigenes, Heraiskos
>
> for tragedians: Ampithales, son of Philonymous; Neokrontides, son of Blephyros; Kraton, son of Mnesides; Agloneas, son of Ostakos; from the resident aliens Delikos, son of Drimakos, Dorion

Artemis slave of Euthymos was freed

These made a presentation for the god:
Piper: Xenophantes of Thebes
Comedians: Phaidros of Athens, Hephisios of Histiaia
Kitharist: Heris of Kalchedon
Tragedians: Theodoros of Megara, Themistonax of Parion, Nikostratos of Kassandra

108. *SIG*³ 648B. Here a famous piper and singer to the *kithara* gives a performance in Delphi in 194 B.C. Note that he performs in the stadium.

> Satyros, son of Eumenes, of Samos: he has been the first and only performer to appear in the pipe contest without any competition, and to have been deemed worthy to offer a performance to the god Apollo and the Greeks after the athletic contest at the sacrifice in the Pythian stadium of a song "Dionysos" with chorus and a lyre solo from the *Bacchae* of Euripides.

109. *SIG*³ 659 (= *FD* 3.1.48). Honorary decree. Date: 165 B.C. This inscription, along with the next two, is important for showing how performances could take place outside of regular festival competition. In this case we know from another inscription that Nikon as *tragoidos* was honored and we also learn the names of the two Argive synagonists, who were honored with him, but as usual they are not even mentioned here. The Hellenistic inscriptions of Delphi record many well-paid individual performers like these, including water-organ players and female harpists, who were hired to amuse the crowds who came to the shrine.

> The city of Delphi in full session resolved with the appropriate votes: whereas Nikon, son of Nikias, of Megalopolis, tragedian, was even aforetime well disposed to the city, and now while sojourning here donated on request a day to the god and performed with success: to praise Nikon, son of Nikias, of Megalopolis, and to grant him and his descendants rights of hospitality from the city, right to prior consultation, freedom from arrest, a front seat in all the contests that the city holds, and all other honors that it gives to the other guest-friends and benefactors, and the archons are to invite him and those with him (i.e., the synagonists) also to the town hall (*prytaneum*).

110. *IG* XII 7, 226; Ghiron-Bistagne, *Recherches* 187. Honorary decree. Date: end of 3rd c. B.C. The Samians of Minoa on Amorgos promise a crown to the visiting actor Nikophon of Miletus, who has with his troupe perhaps stopped on the way home.

> Decision of the *prytaneis:* whereas Nikophon, son of Ainios, of Miletus, a comedian, has stopped in our harbor and announced that he will contest three dramas in three days, it is decided by the people to crown Nikophon, son of Ainios, of Miletus, with a golden crown to a value of a hundred drachmas, and he is to be a guest-friend and benefactor of the people of the Samians who dwell in Minoa like their other benefactors, and this decree is to be written up in the temple of Delian Apollo; and the temple officials under Ainesileos are to supervise the writing up.

111. *TrGF* 1, p. 41, no. 12. This honorary decree from Koronea in Boeotia records a visiting artist from Asia in the mid-2nd c. B.C. It is important for illustrating how tragedies were now being broken up for practical purposes of performance by touring virtuosos.

> Zotion, son of Zotion, of Ephesus, poet of tragedy and satyrs, has firstly while staying with us conducted himself with honor and in a manner worthy of himself, and in the present time, having composed entertainments (*akroamata*) from his repertoire by virtue of his poetic skill, distinguished himself greatly in a manner worthy of our city and of Athena, who guards it along with the other Olympians from the beginning.

112A. Boeotian Inscriptions. *IG* VII 423. Dedication from the theater in the sanctuary of Amphiaraus. Date: ?2nd c. B.C.

> ...] appointed priest (dedicated) the stage building (*skene*) and doorways (*thyromata*) to Amphiaraus.

112B. *IG* VII 1830 (cf. 2873). Dedication from Thespiae. Date: 2nd c. For a temple with *thyromata,* presumably openings between the pillars. Was it used as a backdrop?

> Phileinos, son of Titus Flavius Mondon and Flavia Archela, as *agonothetes* set up the Eros and the *thyromata* in the fore-temple at his own expense and refurbished the temple.

112C. *IG* VII, p. 745. Dedication from the theater of Oropus. Date: ?2nd c. B.C.

> As *agonothetes* Nikon, son of Nikon, priest, dedicated the *proskenion* and the *pinakes* to Amphiaraus.

113A. Inscriptions from Teos in Ionia. LeBas-Waddingon, *Voyage* 92; Mette, *Urkunden,* p. 48. Dedication. Date: 2nd c. B.C.? The Teian inscriptions preserve types of information not recorded elsewhere. This inscription and the next are a rare record of an actor of satyrplay, but the first may be a private dedication of a winning family troupe.

> ...] dedicated the masks and the garlands... in the Dionysia. Actor of satyrs, Hermotimos, son of Archikleios, son of Diotimos, from Magnesia on the Meander. Of tragedies Metrodoros [...] Hermodotos. Actor Diotimos, son of Diotimos, from Magnesia on the Meander.

113B. LeBas-Waddington, *Voyage* 91; Mette, *Urkunden* p. 48. Date: 2nd c. B.C.?

> ...] <Prize> of satyrs: Anaxion, son of Thrasykleides, of Mytilene, with a drama, *Persians.* Asklepiades, son of Herakleides, of Chalcis was actor. [...

114. *CIG* 3059. Here prizewinners at Teos are listed for the younger class in the gymnasium. Date: 2nd c. B.C. Declamation of drama rather than just reading is implied by these sometimes unique terms. This sheds some light on the appearance of competitions for "boy comedians" in some festivals (e.g., *Hesperia* 1970, 80, at the Kaisareia of the Isthmus). "Rhythmography" is unknown, but suggests metrical notation. We know from other sources that dramas could be performed in school with masks. Psalmody is "singing to the harp."

> Of the younger age group: for answering, Herakleos; for reading [...], for calligraphy [...], for torch (race) [...], for psalmody [...], for kithara playing [...], for singing to the kithara [...],

for rhythmography [. . .], for comedy [. . .], for tragedy [. . .], for musical notation (melography) [. . .]

115A. Delian Inscriptions. *IG* XI, 2 105. Date: 284 B.C. A number of inscriptions of Delos, nos. 105–34, running from 284–170 B.C., conform to a pattern, whereby *choregoi* are listed for the Apollonia and Dionysia festivals, then voluntary performances by artists, sometimes accompanied by a list of articles donated or transmitted by the archon. It is clear that there were at least two comedies and two tragedies and probably two dithyrambs presented at the Dionysia. The performers who donate their services include marionette artists, harp players, a type of mime artist called a *romaistes* (169 B.C.), and female entertainers, as well as the usual *technitai* (for the term, see IVAii).

In the archonship of Aristokritos, there was health and prosperity. These were *choregoi* for the Apollonia: (four names)

For the Dionysia:

for the boys' <dithyramb>: (four names)

for comedians: (two sets of three names, each of two citizens plus a foreigner)

for tragedians: (two sets of three names, each of two citizens plus a foreigner)

The following donated their services for the god when Aristokritos was archon:

Tragedians: Theodoros of Megara; Philokleides of Chalcis

Comedians: Telestes of Athens; Sannion, son of Sannion; Dexilaos; Diodoros of Athens; Diodoros of Sinope

Piper: Kaphisias of Thebes

Singers to the lyre: Memnon of Athens, Xenokrates of Ambrakia, Philodamos

Harpist: Diomedes of Methymna

Kitharist: Epikrates of Argos, Tellenokrates

Rhapsodes: Archelaos of Thessaly, Glaukos of Athens

115B. *IG* XI, 2 113.21ff. Date: 263 B.C. The "entertainer" (*thaumatopoios*) Kleopatra appears on another list also.

The following donated their services to the god:

Piper: Antigeneidas

Singers to the lyre: Megistokles, Andreas of Tegea

Kitharist: Antiphanes

Comedians: Ergophilos, Phanylos, Parion, Eritimos, Philonides, Nikolochos of Arcadia

Comic poet: Nikomachos of Athens
Tragedian: Theodoros
Entertainer: Kleopatra

Roman Inscriptions

116A. Theater of Pompey. *Res Gestae Divi Augusti* 4.9. The emperor Augustus recounts his munificence in a posthumous inscription. Date: 14. The theater of Pompey, built in 55–53 B.C., was the most famous in the Roman Empire. This is a reminder that many of the great surviving theaters were only constructed and maintained with imperial help.

> ...and the theater of Pompey, works involving great expense, I rebuilt without any inscription in my own name.

116B. Tertullian, *On Spectacles* 10. Written ca. 200. We add an illuminating excerpt about its founding. A Christian polemicist reminds us that the ancient Greek or Roman theater was always connected with the worship of gods, and was preceded by sacrifice; this was the primary reason for the antipathy of the church fathers. We do not need to believe that Pompey deliberately intended to deceive in the way alleged. Temple theaters, where the temple steps formed the seating, had been built for a hundred years earlier in southern Italy, though not at all in the same proportions. But all the African and Gallic theaters with smaller temples on the *summa cavea* (see ID) are later than Pompey's, and therefore imitate it.

> Also the general preparations are in this respect in agreement (i.e., between circus and dramatic spectacles) that the road to the dramatic performances takes its start from temples and altars and that wretched business with incense and blood (i.e., sacrifice) in the middle of pipes and trumpets, and with the two most polluted managers of burials and sacrifices, the director (*dissignator*) and the entrail consultant. The theater is really a shrine of Venus. In this way in fact this kind of construction has arisen over time. For often (surely an exaggeration!) the censors tore down theaters that were in the process of being built out of concern for public morals, which they saw greatly endangered by its lasciviousness.... And so when Pompey the Great, who was only less great than his own theater, constructed that fortress of all vices, he feared that sometime there would be a censorial stain on his memory, and put a temple of Venus on top; when he called the people by edict to the dedication, he called it formally not "the theater" but "the temple of Venus,"

below which he said we have laid down rows of seating for spectacles. In this way he used the term "temple" as a pretext for the damned and damnable work.

117. *CIL* 8, *Suppl.* 4.26606. Dedication from the theater of Dugga (Thugga) in Africa. Date: 166–68. At Pompeii the original gymnasium in the colonnades behind the theater was turned into a gladiatorial school.

P. Marcius Quadratus, priest of the god Augustus... constructed from the ground up with his own money the theater with its foyers (*basilicae*) and portico and arcades (*xystica*) and the stage building with its curtains (*siparia*) and all its ornamentation, and dedicated it by giving scenic games and donating free food baskets both in a public feast and in the gymnasium.

118. *CIL* 13.1642. The inscription is set up by a priest of the god Augustus in the time of the emperor Claudius, ca. 60, in Segusiavum near Lyon. It records what must have happened in most theaters.

Sacred to the god Augustus. For the safety of Tiberius Claudius Caesar Augustus Germanicus (= Claudius), Titus Claudius Capito, son of Arucas, priest of Augustus, restored with his own money in stone the theater which Lupus, son of Antus, had established in wood.

119. Romanelli, *Notizie degli Scavi* 1931, 342. This fragmentary inscription records the protocol of the Secular Games of Septimius Severus in 204. After the recording of the circus games and beast hunts (*venationes*) are mentioned the dramatic presentations, which seem to consist entirely of pantomime. Three theaters are mentioned: the Theater of Pompey, the Odeum, which must be the Theater of Domitian, and the wooden theater that served also as the religious center in the sacred area near the Piazza Navona known as the Tarentum.

... (lines 43 ff.) order of the honorary games. On the day before the Nones of June, the first day, in the wooden theater a new presentation (*commissio*) in which the pantomime Pylades <performs>. Likewise on the first day in the Odeum a new presentation, in which the pantomime Apolaustus <performs>. Likewise on the first day in the theater of Pompey in which the pantomime Marcus <performs>. On the Nones [of June], the second day, in the wooden theater the pantomime Marcus, likewise on the second day in the Odeum the pantomime Pylades, likewise in the theater of Pompey the pantomime Apolaustus. On the eighth day before the Ides of June, day three, the pantomime Apolaustus in the wooden theater, likewise on the third day in the Odeum the pantomime Marcus, likewise on the third day in the theater of Pompey the pantomime Pylades.

120. *OGIS* 510 (= *Teatri Asia Min.* no. 16 = *Inschriften von Ephesos* 2039). This inscription from the large theater in Ephesus comes from the mid-2nd c., and is a unique testimony that even the very large theaters could have a roof over the stage; a *petasos* (cf. *IGRR* 4.1632) is actually a broad-brimmed hat.

> The first and greatest metropolis of Asia, twice temple guardian of the Augusti, repaired or constructed from its own resources the *petasos* of the theater, the *proskenion,* and the *podoma* (? front wall of the seating) and the *seipharoi* (= *siparia,* curtains) and the rest of the wooden apparatus for the theatrical <shows> and the missing doors and the marble pavement in the theater. Publius Vedius Antoninus, Asiarch, was secretary, Publius Aelius Menodotus and Gaius Attalos, son of Attalos, of Berenike, were in charge of the work.

121. *Inschriften von Ephesos* 2042. Date: ca. 240. There seems to have been a temple of Nemesis, often associated with the amphitheater, in the theater.

> Good luck! the people repaired the front hall of the temple of Nemesis from the income of Iulia Potentilla, when Marcus Arunceius Mithridates was secretary.

122. *TAM* 2.408 (= *Teatri Asia Min.* no. 11). The Latin word *vela* is written in Greek. Date 147.

> [For Antoninus Pius] ... and her most happy fatherland, the city of Patara, mother city of the Lycian race, Velia Prokla of Patara, daughter of Quintus Velius Titianus dedicated and sanctified the *proskenion,* which her father Q.V.T. had constructed from the foundations up, and its decoration and surroundings and the erection of statues and ornaments and the construction of the *logeion* and the pavement that she constructed. And the eleventh step of the second bank of seats (*diazoma*) and the awnings (*vela*) of the theater constructed by her father and herself were dedicated beforehand and handed over according to the vote of the Supreme Council.

123. *IGRR* 3.803 (= *CIG* 4243d = *Teatri Asia Min.* 4 no. 26). This inscription in Latin and in Greek is written over the entrances to the orchestra in the well-preserved "Roman" theater of Aspendos in Asia Minor, the legacy of a very wealthy benefactor. Date: ca. 165.

For the gods of our country and the imperial house from the will of A. Curtius Crispinus, A. Curtius Crispinus Arruntianus and A. Curtius Auspicatus Titinnianus constructed <it>.

IC. Artifacts

A series of twenty Attic vase paintings dating from ca. 560 to ca. 480 B.C. show choruses of dancers in exotic costumes accompanied by pipers (II 6). As the dancers are depicted as moving in lines, not in formation, and there is nothing to hint at a broader narrative context, the vases may represent festive processions (*komoi*) rather than actual comic or protocomic performances. It is true, however, that our earliest certain depictions of drama are of choruses. From ca. 500 to ca. 470 B.C. three or four vases depict tragic choruses in a manner very like the *komos* vases, but all give clear indications of a narrative context, and one shows the chorus in rectangular formation (124). From ca. 470 B.C. a number of "genre scenes" also show choreuts dressing before or after performance (136, 137). The focus on choral subjects may indicate that the vase painters took their subjects from paintings commemorating performances by victorious *choregoi* and dedicated in the temple of Dionysus Eleuthereus (137; III 99, 100). The scenes are not common on Attic pottery, but they are remarkable for their relatively "literal" reproduction of performance and theater life.

The theater's chief influence on Attic vase painting took a different form. Attic artists generally ignored drama's signifiers in direct contemplation of what it signified: it is the impact of the dramatic illusion, not the performance, that one can detect on many hundreds of mythological scenes in Attic art. This is most true of tragic subjects, somewhat less of satyrplay. Satyrplay is the first dramatic genre to influence the treatment of myth, perhaps not surprising, given the choral bias among earlier painters. From ca. 520 to 510 B.C., satyrs grow increasingly human in appearance, and their range of occupations begins to include the kind of cultural symbols and pastimes with which the Greek dramatists liked to confront their *Urmensch* (fire, sports, musical instruments, tools, machines) in order to rediscover, through the satyrs, the thrill of that originary impulse that first separated culture from nature. The influence of satyrplay extends also to theatrical trappings: many 5th-c. B.C. vases show satyrs dressed in dramatic costume, without any express intention thereby of departing from a mythological conception of their paintings. It is not until much later, about 460 B.C., that Attic pottery begins to show the impact of tragic narrative on a large scale. Here the illusion is much more carefully preserved, but the influence of tragedy is palpable from the choice and treatment of the mythological subjects, from the dress and expansive gestures of the figures, and from architectural details in the background. A more subtle dramatic influence may be seen in changes in the whole technique of narrative exposition beginning already in the early 5th c. B.C., when vase painters begin to center their compositions on a pathetic scene, very often one of domestic violence, to which numerous marginal figures register emotional reactions, frequently women staring at the central action and running frantically to the side. The whole creates a "splash" effect of emotional reaction radiating from a central action and analogous to that of actors and chorus (already visible on 126). Many of these Attic vases are preserved because they were exported to Italy, where it was customary to use them as grave gifts. By ca. 440 B.C. the Italiot Greeks begin to produce their own imitations of Attic pottery, soon developing a distinctive local style with an even greater interest in Attic theater and a stronger taste for dramatic effects (128, 129). Attic drama continues to exert its influence on South Italian vase painting for nearly a century after Attic vase painters lose interest in it (ca. 390 B.C.).

The influence of comedy on Attic vase painting is very slight and, except for genre scenes, limited to a very few vases produced from ca. 420 to ca. 390 B.C. (131, 132). In contrast to the mythological character of the other genres, the comic vases show a high degree of theater realism and depict actors and performance rather than choruses or myth. Exceptional in date is a single Attic vase of ca. 360 B.C. showing a comic chorus. Some Attic vases were exported to southern Italy, where they gained great popularity. Comic scenes were imitated from at least 400 B.C. till about 350 B.C. Afterward single figures and masks became more popular subjects, in red-figure until about 320 B.C. (133–35) and in Gnathia-ware until 273 B.C. The vases are erroneously called "phlyakes," after a form of local farce produced in South Italy in Hellenistic times (II 8A), but since the discovery of 135, there can no longer be any doubt that some, if not most, of these vases take their direct inspiration from Attic comedy, just as other South Italian vases show the influence of

Attic tragedy and Attic satyrplay. The South Italian vases of tragic inspiration generally tend to grow more theatrical by the mid-4th c. B.C., but only two vases by a Sicilian painter of the third quarter of the century can properly be said to show tragic performance, rather than myth, in the theater-realistic style characteristic of the "phlyax" vases (130). It is not clear whether the images were derived from performance, from "high-art" models (such as votive paintings), or from the painters' own imagination tempered with a knowledge of the theater and theater practice. It is probably wrong to posit a single source for this highly variable output. Visual memory seems best to account for a series such as the Attic and South Italian vases inspired by Euripides' *Andromeda*, where the paintings have little in common beyond the basic *schema* of Andromeda's posture. In the case of the two South Italian scenes from the same Attic comedy (133, 134), however, the details of the resemblance are so great as to suggest a hard-copy transmission, and this may also be indicated by the citation of dialogue.

By the beginning of the 4th c. B.C. Athens also produced and exported terra-cotta figurines of costumed actors, especially comic, in a highly realistic style (138). In this case the production continued until very late antiquity and was also copied by local centers of production, not only in Italy but throughout the Greek world (139–42). The dramatic figurines number among the thousands and are evenly distributed in time, so that they are our best index of changes in costume. The production of terra-cotta imitations of theatrical masks was equally diverse and still more prolific, especially with the rise of New Comedy from 320 B.C. onward. The artifacts were produced for a relatively undiscerning mass market, and it is unlikely that much effort or originality went into their production. In several cases we can demonstrate that they were copied from other artifacts (140–41).

From the Hellenistic and Roman period, well over a hundred paintings, mosaics, and reliefs show a clear intent to represent scenes from dramatic performance in a highly realistic style (143–46); several of the later artifacts have labels with author's name, play title, and even scene number (145, 146). All certainly identifiable comic scenes are from plays of Menander; all identifiable tragic scenes from plays of Sophocles and Euripides. There is good evidence to show that some, if not most, of these scenes are copies of famous easel paintings of the early 3rd c. B.C. and hence contemporary evidence for the staging of New Comedy and early Hellenistic tragic performance. A large number of the artifacts come from the wall and floor decorations of upper-class villas and town houses in the cities buried by Vesuvius in 79, particularly from mural decoration of the Third and Fourth Style (ca. 20 B.C. to 79), in which it was common practice to include copies or adaptations of famous Greek Hellenistic easel paintings as if they were themselves easel paintings hanging on the wall.

The clearest evidence comes from multiple copies of scenes from two plays by Menander, *Theophoroumene,* act 2, and *Synaristosai,* act 1. The earliest versions of both scenes are from Pompeian mosaics of the late 2nd c. B.C. (143, 144). A 1st-c. copy of the same scene as 143 was also found in a wall painting at nearby Stabiae. The existence of 2nd-c. B.C. terra-cottas copying each of the two young men (140, 141) in these scenes shows that the Campanian artifacts are copies of a much earlier archetype, which can be dated stylistically to the early 3rd c. B.C. Stylistic considerations urge the same date for the archetype for the *Synaristosai* scene (144), which has a 3rd-c. copy in Mytilene (146). That a linkage between these scenes and the early Hellenistic era is not isolated to these two examples, but is likely to be a more general phenomenon, seems assured by the recent demonstration that a 1st-c. comic scene on a relief from Naples (MN 6687) derives from the same original as a late Hellenistic cameo and a Boeotian terra-cotta dated ca. 300 B.C.

The evidence suggests two possible sources for these scenes. The appearance of many of these pieces on Campanian frescoes in the form of *trompe l'oeil* easel paintings and the demonstrable derivation of some scenes from early Hellenistic archetypes suggest the possibility that the archetypes may be votive paintings dedicated in commemoration of a victorious first performance at the Athenian Dionysia (or elsewhere). Another possibility is that the archetypes of these scenes were painted as part of a set, perhaps a decorative program for a famous public building. The consistency in the treatment of most of the comic and tragic scenes seems to go beyond the generic features common to early Hellenistic art. The scenes tend to concentrate on key moments in the dramas; they focus generally on lively interactions between two or three central figures, sometimes with smaller, framing figures present (143–46); most seem to have minimalistic background details, though a great deal of attention is given to·movable stage furniture, such as the table in 144/146. Some argue, on the analogy of the Terence manuscripts (147), that these Hellenistic theater scenes were first produced as book illustrations, but the argument is largely based on a retrojection of medieval attitudes and modes of production: papyrus books were too impermanent to serve as a medium for high art and the comparatively low status of book illustrations makes them an unlikely model for mosaicists or fresco painters. There is very slim evidence for illustrated editions of Menander and Euripides in antiquity and none at all for the luxury editions hypothesized.

Sources

Choral Scenes

124. Basel, Antikenmuseum BS 415. Attic red-figure column krater in the Mannerist Style, ca. 500–490 B.C. See Plate 1A.

> This is one of three early 5th-c. B.C. vases that give fairly realistic renderings of tragic choruses in performance. Three pairs of young men (or a hemichorus?) move with identical gestures toward an altar decorated with boughs and ribbons. Illegible letters (not visible on the photograph) issue from their mouths to show that they are singing. Their faces are all alike, and the gaping mouths, jutting chins, and extended chin lines show that the artist attempted to render masks, or at least something between masks and faces. The costumes are not identical but give the general impression of uniformity. They suggest that the young men are meant to be warriors, but the painter demonstrates his desire to depict performance rather than a dramatic narrative by covering their heads with diadems, not helmets. A figure appears to stand or rise from behind the altar. This is generally taken to be an actor playing the rising ghost of a dead hero, like Darius in Aeschylus' *Persians*. Alternatively, one could take the truncated figure as a depiction of the icon of Dionysus dressed with mask and a garment (as in II 7) and placed upon the altar to witness the performance in his honor. The original publication took the scene for dithyramb, but the use of masks (cf. 125) and the chorus' rectangular formation argue for tragedy (IV 313; app. A).

125. Copenhagen 13817. Attic red-figure bell krater by Kleophon Painter, ca. 425 B.C. See Plate 1B.

> The bell krater seems to depict an abbreviated dithyrambic chorus. On either side of what appears to be a portable ivy-covered maypole of unknown function stand a piper and five elaborately dressed, garlanded, and unmasked figures. The figure immediately to the left of the pole faces the viewer and, unlike the pair of figures bordering either side, appears not to be singing; possibly he is the *choregos*

or poet. Contrary to what we might expect of the dithyramb, none
of the choreuts shows any sign of dancing. Inscriptions (not visible
on the photograph) identify each of the figures by name. All are
ordinary Athenian names. The frontal figure, named "Phrynichus,"
is thought by some to be the comic poet (who may also have written
dithyrambs), but the name was fairly common.

Tragic/Mythological Pots

126–27. Boston MFA 63.1246. Attic red-figure calyx krater by
Dokimasia Painter, 475–450 B.C. See Plate 2. Side A: Death of Agamemnon. Side B: Death of Aegisthus.

The initial publication of this vase argued that "the Boston Oresteia
krater is one of the best candidates among early fifth-century vases
to be considered a direct, deliberate illustration of literature." It
noted three major links between Aeschylus' drama and the vase
painting: (1) the "organic" connection between the death of Agamemnon and the death of Aegisthus, which imitates the movements
of the trilogy; (2) the combination of weapons in the death of
Agamemnon scene, that is the axe carried by Clytemnestra and the
sword carried by Aegisthus; (3) the net/robe thrown over Agamemnon in the same scene. Others have noted Agamemnon's nakedness
on the vase, which suggests that he has just stepped out of the
bathtub. All of these links are problematic. The organic link between
the murders of Agamemnon and Aegisthus is in fact too strong to
reflect the influence of Aeschylus' *Oresteia*. The dramatic trilogy
emphasizes the dominant role of Clytemnestra in the first episode
and the murder of Clytemnestra in the revenge sequence; in either
case Aegisthus is only a secondary figure. The combination of axe
and sword is also a very weak link, since both weapons are used
by Clytemnestra in Aeschylus; Aeschylus leaves it very unclear just
how he imagined the murder. Cassandra and the Chorus seem to
refer to Clytemnestra's use of an axe with their vague kennings
"black-horned device," "projectile cutting at both ends (or sides)"
(*Ag.* 1127, 1496, 1520), but, although one might wish to dismiss
the mention of the sword at line 1262 (Cassandra's vision) and at
line 1528 (Clytemnestra stressing the link between Agamemnon's
and Iphigenia's death) as metaphorical, the *Libation Bearers* (1011)
insists upon the use of Aegisthus' sword, apparently on loan to
Clytemnestra, as the murder weapon. There is no evidence that

either weapon ever appeared on stage, so Aeschylus was free to
remain vague and inconsistent and to choose the weapon whose
connotations best suited the verbal imagery of any particular context. It is most likely the iconographic tradition that evoked the
ambiguity in Aeschylus' conception of the event: earlier pots show
sword alone in the murder of Agamemnon, but Clytemnestra regularly appears with an axe (as here on side B) in the traditional
iconography of the death of Aegisthus. If so, we have a case of
drama "illustrating" art and not the reverse. There is, however, no
clear instance of the "net/robe" in earlier art, but, given our ignorance of tragedy and lyric poetry before Aeschylus, it is very unsafe
to assume that he invented it. Agamemnon's nakedness does seem
to require explanation, although male nudity, particularly "heroic
nudity," is commonplace on Greek vase paintings. One could argue
that the artist chose to paint Agamemnon this way in order to avoid
the visual confusion that could arise between the net/robe and lines
of clothing revealed underneath, or to arouse pathos by stressing
Agamemnon's utter helplessness. Given that the normal criteria for
the stylistic dating of Attic red-figure would favor a date around
470 B.C., well before the performance of Aeschylus' *Oresteia* in 458
B.C., it seems best, for want of closer links, to assume that the vase
is evidence for an earlier tradition than to assume that it was painted
in the 450s in an antiquated style. Yet even if it was later, it would
be an exaggeration to speak of the vase as an "illustration of
tragedy": neither murder was staged in Aeschylus, but simply described, and so both scenes at most illustrate the dramatic "story,"
and not a scene from the drama; Aegisthus, the principal agent in
the Dokimasia Painter's version of the murder of Agamemnon,
does not participate directly in the murder of either Cassandra or
Agamemnon in Aeschylus' play; the vase painter's portrayal of
Aegisthus' death conforms to the traditional iconography of this
scene in a number of important details that are also inconsistent
with Aeschylus' *Libation Bearers*: Aegisthus is not surprised while
sitting in repose in the palace; Clytemnestra does not manage to
get hold of an axe and, in any case, asks for it to save her own
skin, not to defend Aegisthus, for whom she is in any case too late;
Orestes does not wear hoplite armour, but is disguised as a mer-
chant; there is no mention, or place, for any of the peripheral
running women on either side of the vase, except perhaps the second
female to the right of Agamemnon, tentatively identified by her

cropped hair as the slave princess Cassandra. The use of the term "illustration" in this case, however much qualified, is an instance of scholarly hyperbole.

128. Berlin F 3296. Early Sicilian calyx krater by the Dirce Painter, ca. 380–370 B.C. See Plate 3A.

This calyx krater does not depict a tragic performance. The figures represent the gods and heroes of myth, not actors. The setting is not a stage but a landscape. It exhibits events and combinations of events that could not appear in the Greek theater. Yet full appreciation of the painting is impossible without an exact knowledge of the specific tragedy from which the myth is derived. The scene renders the climactic moment of the myth of the Theban heroes, Amphion and Zethos, as narrated in Euripides' *Antiope*. Zeus fell in love with Antiope, daughter of Nykteus, and raped her. Her father discovered she was pregnant, refused to believe her a victim of Zeus, and threatened her. She ran off. Nykteus killed himself, but first charged his brother Lykos, king of Thebes, to punish her. Lykos took her captive and brought her back to Thebes, but en route she gave birth to twins. The twins, Amphion and Zethos, were exposed, but were discovered by a cowherd who reared them. Antiope was thrown into prison and maltreated by Lykos and his wife, Dirke, for some eighteen years, until one day, suddenly, her chains dissolved and she escaped, making her way, unknowingly, to the cowherd's cave dwelling. Dirke happened to appear leading a group of maenads in worship of Dionysus. She found Antiope and commanded the cowherds to tie her to the horns of a bull, but Antiope was recognized by her sons, who, instead, treated Dirke in the prescribed fashion. In the final episode of Euripides' play, which survives on papyrus, Lykos appears in search of the runaway Antiope. The cowherd then tricks Lykos into entering his cave without his bodyguard by telling him that Antiope's confederates plan to ambush him in some other nearby building. But Amphion and Zethus prepare the real ambush inside the cave.

> COWHERD: I'm glad I got you well away from danger. LYKOS: Did you not say, sir, that the hut would be safe? COWHERD: Something must be done. But I know that they are dead. LYKOS: If you are certain, let's make the proper arrangements. COWHERD: What other course is there than to go inside this cave that has long been my home? LYKOS: [I would be a fool] if I allowed the strangers [to catch] me.

COWHERD: [But you must] leave your bodyguard outside the door. LYKOS: [Good idea!] So all fear may be removed. COWHERD: [Inside] you and I will set things right. LYKOS: [How many] are the strangers? COWHERD: [...] but they do not have [weapons?] in their hands. LYKOS (to body-guard): [...] guard the area around this cave [look]ing [in all directions]. If somebody comes out of the building (perhaps the royal palace? or a shrine?), [grab them. I want to kill] the daughter of Nykteus with my own hands. She will soon learn how vainly she boasted [about her divine lovers, when she sees what] useless allies they are. CHORUS: [May he be struck down unaware of the plot,] god willing, inside this hut soon.... LYKOS: Ay, me, me! CHORUS: Hark, hark. The youths' hands are indeed [at work!] LYKOS: Servants, won't you come [running] to save me? CHORUS: The hut resounds with cries. He shouts [...] LYKOS: O land of Cadmus, city of Asopos! CHORUS: Do you hear? Do you see? He calls the city to his aid in his terror. Retribution for bloodshed, indeed retribution, though long in coming, yet seizes impious mortals whenever it sees them. LYKOS: Alas, I will die without a helper at the hands of two. AMPHION: Aren't you going to grieve for your dead wife? LYKOS: Is she dead? You tell me of a new calamity. AMPHION: Yes, torn apart by being dragged by a bull. LYKOS: Who is responsible? You? I want to know. AMPHION: I would like it to be very clear to you that she died at our hands. LYKOS: Do you have parents with whom I'm unacquainted? AMPHION: Why do you ask? You'll learn this from the ghosts when you are dead. HERMES: I command you to stop this murderous assault! (there follow about fifty lines of a very typical *deus ex machina* solution, in which Hermes commands Lykos to hand over his kingdom to Amphion and Zethos and everyone is reconciled).

Euripides' tragedy explains not only the details of the scene, but even its visual configuration. In *Antiope* the action inside the cave was made visible to the audience by means of the *ekkyklema* (see IV 78), a trolley on which interior tableaux were wheeled out from the central door of the *skene* onto the stage. Hermes almost certainly appears suspended from the *mechane* (IV 77). 128 reproduces the illusion as the dramatist wished to create it: upon a rocky platform as if seen through the mouth of the cave. Lykos kneels, held fast

by Amphion and Zethos, who stand ready to cut his throat. They
appear momentarily distracted. Hermes appears in the air above the
left side of the cave opening. Further left, the painter depicts the
death of Dirke, an event merely narrated in the drama: its appearance here and its lack of synchrony with the main scene, though
irreconcilable with performance, nevertheless shows close adherence
to the tragic narrative in which the heroes torment their prisoner
by boasting of Dirke's murder. The painter is responsible for other
details, which could not have appeared in performance but nevertheless serve to create an impression of theatricality. A woman, right,
runs from the scene in terror (perhaps we are to think of her as
Antiope). Though she had no part in the performance of the play's
final scene, she nevertheless provides a fine example of the painter's
theatrical "rhetoric," a kind of choruslike emotional response to
the central action adding pathos and terror. Note also how an
arched-over tree impressionistically renders the cave mouth: instead
of drawing a real cave mouth, the painter depicts a piece of artifice.
Frequently, red-figure pottery will show its theatrical inspiration
by granting staginess to minor peripheral details, even while preserv-
ing the illusion in rendering the main points of the narrative.

129. Würzburg H4696 and H4701. Fragments of a South Italian
(Apulian) Gnathia-ware vase, Konnakis Group, ca. 350 B.C. See Plate 3B.

This vase is an early example of Gnathia-ware, a technique of
polychrome painting on black glaze. In the mid-4th c. B.C. its subjects
and style are closely parallel to the red-figure tradition, though it
develops its own idiosyncracies and outlasts red-figure (to ca. 273
B.C.). The fragment shows a young woman, left, eavesdropping
through a doorway. To the right stands a young man wearing a
pilos, generally worn by travelers, and looking dejected. Farther
right is a much-worn figure of an older man who holds a *phiale*
(a ritual vessel) and appears to be pouring an offering over an altar
(lost). At the far right another woman stands in front of another
doorway. It has been argued that the scene illustrates Jason's arrival
in Iolcus in Euripides' *Peliades* or Bellerophon's return to Proetus
in Euripides' *Stheneboia,* but neither of these suggestions adequately
accounts for the details. The older man is performing a ceremony
of purification for the young man. In myth and tragedy this is
required after someone has spilt the blood of a relative and left his
home in exile. The scene better suits Euripides' *Peleus,* in which the
hero accidentally killed his father-in-law and went to Acastus in

Iolcus, who purified him and acted as his host. Acastus' wife, Astydameia (one of the eavesdropping women?), fell in love with Peleus, but he resisted her advances. In revenge she wrote to Peleus' wife that Peleus was about to marry Acastus' daughter, Sterope (the other eavesdropping woman?). The vase is of particular interest for the architectural details that seem to reproduce a stage set. Some argue that it represents a theatrical scene-painting with a perspective drawing on a flat board that the pot painter has reproduced literally. Others take it as rendering a stage with a (three-dimensional) projecting wing (*paraskenion*). In any case the background details are highly theatrical (as in 128) even though the mythological illusion dominates the painter's interpretation of the characters.

130. Syracuse, Museo Archeologico Regionale "P. Orsi" 66557. Sicilian calyx krater by Capodarso Painter, ca. 350–325 B.C. See Plate 4A.

In earlier South Italian vases that depict scenes influenced by tragedy, myth rather than theater emerges as the dominant frame of reference. This vase is one of only two vases, both decorated by the Capodarso Painter in Sicily in the third quarter of the 4th c. B.C., where "theater" may safely be designated the primary frame. The transformation needed only very small shifts in the art's visual rhetoric: the depiction of the stage platform; slightly larger heads with more fixed facial expressions; the theatrical dynamics of the scene in which the old man to the left makes a speaking gesture with his left hand in the direction of the central male figure and the woman on the right, but rather than turning toward them, he speaks frontally as if to an audience. Along with this, we may note the austerity of the background, decorated only by columns to give the effect of the stage (as 129), and without the layered or floating references to other characters or further events in the narrative that we find on many earlier South Italian and Attic vases (see 128). The scene almost certainly depicts the messenger scene in Sophocles' *Oedipus* 924ff., where the messenger, depicted left, brings news of the death of Oedipus' presumed father, Polybus, in Corinth, but reveals, upon questioning, that Polybus and Merope were not Oedipus' true parents and that the messenger himself was given the child by a slave of Laios and took him to the childless couple in Corinth. By the end of the scene, Jocasta has guessed the true secret of Oedipus' parentage and leaves the stage in anguish to hang herself. The vase shows the moment of Jocasta's recognition: the female

figure on the left raises her right hand to her chin and her left hand
to her cheek in standard gestures of grief and anxiety in Greek art
(and doubtless also in the theater). In contrast, Oedipus, center,
seems to stroke his beard in puzzlement. There is no evidence in
Sophocles' text that the children, probably Antigone and Ismene,
appeared in this scene, though they do appear in the final scene of
the play. Their presence in the vase painting is a caution against
taking the scene as a "literal" reproduction of an actual performance. No doubt the children are here to add pathos. The same
must be said of a female figure (not visible on the photograph) who
stands behind Jocasta and echoes her gesture with her back turned
to the others.

Comic Pots

131. Vlastos Collection, Athens. Attic red-figure chous, ca. 420 B.C.
See Plate 4B.

This is the earliest of nine known Attic vases depicting scenes of
comic performance and the most directly comparable to the South
Italian "phlyax" vases (133–35). It is the only Attic vase to show
a stage and the only ancient Greek painting to depict a theater
audience. The low stage is identical to that found on the "phlyax"
vases and is approached by a ladder with three rungs to give the
actor easy access to the orchestra (cf. 133). Upon the stage, an actor
plays the part of Perseus, indicated by the scythe (*harpe*) in his left
hand and the magical bag (*kibisis*) over his left forearm, in which
he carries the head of Medusa. There is nothing masklike about the
face, except perhaps the gaping mouth, but the lines on his right
wrist mark the ends of his tights, showing that he is "stage-naked"
(i.e., wearing only the sleeved tights and padding that conventionally
signify comic flesh). He raises his left arm as if to shade his eyes
as he looks in the distance (perhaps the dance figure called *skops*,
IV 319, 321, 322). At a guess the actor mimes Perseus flying over
Ethiopia and descrying Andromeda in the distance. We know that
Phrynichus, the comic poet, produced (ca. 430–415 B.C.) a parody
of Andromeda in which a drunken old woman dancing the *kordax*
(IV 317, 318) was about to be devoured by a sea monster (*PCG* F
77). The object cutting across the back of the stage may be a
curtain. To the left the *theatron* immediately abuts the stage:
the painter has excised the orchestra. Two wreathed figures, one

bearded, the other beardless (possibly female), form a synecdoche for the audience. They sit in elegant chairs called *klismoi:* it is interesting to note that the marble *prohedria* of the later Lycurgan theater imitates wooden *klismoi,* and it is likely that the two figures are conceived as sitting in the front rows. Possibly one is the priest of Dionysus, the other another priest or priestess; possibly they represent Dionysus and Ariadne, or the *choregos* and poet. Many of the details of our drawing are reconstructed since the pot itself is much damaged and most of its finer details unclear.

132. Malibu 82.AE.83. Attic red-figure calyx krater, ca. 420–410 B.C. See Plate 5.

The interpretation of this scene is divided into two main camps, each placing the image in a different subgenre. One view compares 132 with the series of *komos* vases (II 6), which regularly show a piper and men dancing in identical or nearly identical costumes, and concluded that 132 was a contemporary illustration of Aristophanes' *Birds* (414 B.C.). One objection to this view is chronological: the *komos* vase series dies out ca. 480 B.C. (although similar choral scenes with pipers appear on a vase of 360 B.C. and on two mid-4th c. B.C. Athenian reliefs). Another objection is philological: in the *parodos* of Aristophanes' *Birds* (297ff.) the actors point to each of the twenty-four choreuts and identify them as different birds, some as female, but the birds on 132 are unambiguously both chickens and both male. Others are therefore inclined to compare 132 with contemporary Attic counterparts (131) of the Italian "phlyax" series. Pipers accompanied not only the chorus but also the actors in lyric and recitative (IV 259–61, 264), and they appear on "phlyax" vases accompanying actors on stage. It has been argued that 132 depicts the *agon* between the Greater and Lesser Arguments in the *Clouds* (423 B.C.); the scholiast there (57) tells us that "the Arguments are shown on stage in wicker cages fighting like cocks." This interpretation better suits both the costume and the movements of the figures, which are not the uniform dance movements of a chorus but individuated and mutually aggressive. There is, however, no sign of a wicker cage, but it is very likely that the scholion has condensed two thoughts, since cocks do not fight in cages, though they may be caged when brought into the ring. It has been argued in favor of the choral interpretation that the ithyphallic shorts worn by the cocks are nearly identical to those used by satyr choruses (137), but this detail can also be used to argue that the figures are not generic birds, but specifically fighting cocks, which to the ancients emblematized virile sexual and martial aggression.

133–34. New York MMA 24.97.104. South Italian (Apulian) red-figure calyx krater by Tarporley Painter, ca. 400 B.C. Boston MFA 69.951. South Italian (Apulian) red-figure bell krater by McDaniel Painter, ca. 370 B.C. See Plate 6.

This pair of "phlyax" vases is unique in showing two scenes from the same comedy and a remarkable testimony to the iconographic tradition's ability to preserve accurate details of costume, mask, and staging for over a quarter century. The two principal figures in 133 can easily be recognized in 134, and all doubts must be dispelled by the recurrence of the unique detail of a basket holding two goats juxtaposed to a goose. Many "phlyax" vases attest to the free movement of the actors between the low stage in front of the *skene* and the orchestra; 133 is a particularly good example. The actors wear costumes and masks typical of Athenian Old and Middle Comedy (as known from other sources, mainly figurines). 133 is particularly valuable in that it quotes comic dialogue. Although the pots were produced in Doric Tarentum, the dialect of the inscriptions is Athenian. On 133, an actor, wearing the costume and mask of an old man and "stage-naked," stands on tiptoe in the orchestra with his hands raised. Behind him, also "naked," a young man approaches with a stick. To the right, on a roughly four-foot-high stage, an actor costumed as an old woman stands in front of the *skene* door making a speaking gesture toward the pair in the orchestra. By her feet is a basket with two goats (the ears of the second are just visible on the right side of the basket) atop a piece of cloth or garment and beside a dead goose. The inscriptions help make some sense of the scene. The central figure says, "He (or she) has tied up my hands." The woman declares, "I shall hand over (or provide) <?>." The young man, however, speaks gibberish: "Noraretteblo." The nonsense is usually interpreted to mean that the young man is a foreigner, perhaps a Scythian, since Scythians were employed in Athens as police. The interpretation of the woman's words depend on what we take as the implied object: suggestions are "witnesses," "blows," "trouble," "the goose and basket," "myself." Because the verb does not express its object, it is easiest to take it as a legal formula: the verb "provide" (*parexo*) can be used alone to mean "I will stand surety." We prefer to take the old woman's words as a legal formula for handing over her slave (the implied object) for punishment or to give evidence under torture. It appears, then, that the old man is about to get a beating, and this in part accounts for his posture, since it was normal practice to tie slaves by the hands and suspend them in the air to be whipped (or, as here, caned). As there is no rope around the old man's wrists and because the words for "tie up" can also mean "cast a spell on," some scholars suggest that the old woman has cast a binding-spell upon him. It may be, however, that the actor merely mimed being tied up, and the lack of rope is to be explained by the artist's realistic depiction of his non-illusionistic performance: it would be very difficult to find a spot from which to suspend someone in the middle of the orchestra. The "phlyax" vases often show masks or implements floating above their comic scenes or depict characters in an upper register who are somehow related to the scene but not actually a part of it. Just to the left of the old man there floats a slave (?) mask. The figure to the upper left is labeled, curiously, "tragedian." If the life cycle of a goose can serve as an index of time, 134 would be an earlier scene from the drama. The old man, apparently in possession of the goats and goose, puts oil on his hand from an oil flask as if he is about to wrestle with the "Scythian." To the left of the "Scythian" stands a herm, a phallic icon of Hermes commonly placed by house doors, in the market, or in gymnasia. On top of the herm's head is a garment, presumably the "Scythian's" *chiton* and another oil flask.

135. Würzburg H5697. South Italian (Apulian) red-figure bell krater by Schiller Painter, ca. 370 B.C. See Plate 7A.

This scene is clear evidence of a close connection between Attic comedy and the South Italian "phlyax" vases. In Aristophanes' *Thesmophoriazusae,* Euripides' (father?)-in-law is dressed up as a woman in order to infiltrate the Thesmophoria (an exclusively women's festival characterized by days of communal fasting and abstinence), where the women of Athens (chorus) plan to consider collective action against Euripides for his supposedly misogynistic tragedies. At the women's "assembly," word comes that the meeting has been infiltrated and suspicion falls upon the disguised in-law, who has just spoken in favor of Euripides and who is not known to any of the other women. In desperation the in-law jumps upon the altar for asylum, but for added security grabs as hostage what appears to be the baby of one of the women and threatens it with a knife (in an elaborate parody of the climax of Euripides' *Telephus*). Several women run in search of kindling to light a fire around the altar and drive the in-law from his sanctuary (730ff.):

> IN-LAW: Go ahead, kindle! Burn! (To the baby) But you, off with this wrap right now! For your death, child, you have only your mother to blame. Hey, what's this? The girl has turned into a skin full of wine and wearing booties at that! O most flagrant women! O most bibulous of creatures, stopping at nothing to contrive an opportunity for drink!...WOMAN: What have you done? You've stripped my child naked, tiny as she is, you pervert! IN-LAW: Tiny! (Ironically) I'll say she's tiny.... WOMAN: But give her back! IN-LAW: No, by Apollo who stands here (probably a reference to the statue of Apollo by the central door of the stage)! WOMAN: We'll set you on fire, then. IN-LAW: Go ahead! Burn! But this baby's going to get her throat cut, this instant! WOMAN: No! I beg you! Do whatever you like to me, but spare her! IN-LAW: I see you have a very maternal nature. But her throat will be cut nonetheless. WOMAN: Oh, my child! (To a slave) Mania, give me the *sphageion* (a sacrifical bowl in which a victim's blood was collected) so that I can at least save the blood of my child. (A temporary truce is finally called between the women and the in-law; the wineskin is saved).

The *Thesmophoriazusae* agrees with 135 on the following points: the refuge on the altar; the wineskin threatened by a knife; the booties on the wineskin; and the woman rushing in with a large vessel to catch the "blood" of the wineskin. The figure on the altar also reveals details of costume that are consistent with those mentioned in the elaborate dressing scene in which the in-law is shaved, dressed in women's clothing, and lent a feminine headband by Agathon. The first two details are all the more striking since male characters on the "phlyax" vases normally wear beards and *phalloi*. Above the in-law's knife stands a mirror: it is unclear whether we are to imagine this mirror as fixed to the *skene* wall, or whether we are to take it as the kind of filler, frequently found on "phlyax" vases, of objects related to the scene depicted but not an integral part of it. In the first case, we can note the use of a mirror in the

in-law's dressing scene immediately before this one. In the second,
we can perhaps read it as alluding to the feminine ambience of the
Thesmophoria.

Theater Life

136. Boston MFA 98.883-II. Attic red-figure pelike by Phiale Painter,
ca. 450 B.C. See Plate 7B.
    From ca. 470 B.C. several Athenian red-figure vases show scenes of
    actors or choreuts dressing before or after a production. These
    "genre scenes" are realistic in style and give unambiguous informa-
    tion about tragic costume. Here two choreuts are shown at different
    stages of dressing up as young women. Note the high, flat-soled
    boots and the realistic features of the mask and costume.
137. Naples M.N. 3240. Attic red-figure volute krater by Pronomos
Painter, ca. 400 B.C. See Plate 8.
    The "Pronomos Krater" is the most famous of the theatrical "genre
    scenes." The choregic monuments, columns with tripods, located
    beneath the handles on either side, show that the scene is set in the
    sanctuary of Dionysus (III 88, 102). In the center of the upper
    register Dionysus himself (labeled) is present on a couch that he
    shares with his wife, Ariadne. Another female figure sits at the end
    of the couch holding a female tragic mask. She is probably a
    personification of satyrplay. Between them flies a winged boy labeled
    Himeros (Desire). To the right of the couch stands an actor labeled
    Heracles, who wears tragic costume and carries a mask of Heracles,
    a breastplate, quiver, and club. Next, to the right, is the actor who
    plays Papposilenos, the father of the satyrs, wearing woolly tights,
    leopard skin, staff, and masks. The third actor stands to the left
    of the couch with the costume of a tragic hero, possibly an Oriental
    king. The vase shows that the heroes of satyrplay wore costumes
    identical to those of tragic heroes. The costumes and the winged
    Desire, which fastens upon the female figure holding the female
    mask, may hint that the play dealt with the story of Heracles and
    Omphale; some argue for the story of Heracles and Hesione (which
    suits the implied love interest less well). In the center of the lower
    register sits the piper Pronomos (labeled), known from literary
    sources as one of the most famous musicians of the late 5th c. B.C.
    Next but one left, sits a young man labeled Demetrios, evidently
    the poet of the satyrplay, since he holds a scroll. The eleven

remaining figures are members of the satyr chorus. Nine of the choreuts are labeled, but unlike the actor, they are given their own names, not those of their fictitious characters. They are depicted in conversation, as if before or after the drama, and hold their masks in their hands. The exception is the figure between Demetrios and Pronomos, who has put on his mask and dances the *sikinnis* (IV 317, 318). All but two wear a hairy loincloth (*perizoma*) to which a tail and an erect *phallos* are attached. One has a *perizoma* of cloth, while the figure to the right of the right choregic monument is much more elaborately dressed and is probably distinguished as the *koryphaios* (chief choreut). The fact that there are only eleven choreuts has raised questions about the status of Papposilenos. Some maintain that he is the *koryphaios* and that the total satyr chorus numbered twelve as in early tragedy. The difficulty is that Papposilenos, though closely identified with the satyrs, acts independently and often converses with the chorus in iambic dialogue (where the *koryphaios* is normally its spokesman). One scholar would solve the problem by elevating the *koryphaios* for the preceding tragedies to the function of "quasi actor" as Papposilenos, though he would still technically have him numbered a member of the chorus, while a "sub-*koryphaios*" would speak for the satyrs. The problem with this is that the pot would then show only two actors, whereas we know three were used in the late 5th c. B.C. (IVAi). It is perhaps not safe to assume that the pot's scene is complete. Its composition and setting suggest that the pot is copied from a votive painting set up in the temple of Dionysus Eleuthereus (cf. III 99, 100). The fact that two choreuts' names are missing shows that the painter was not punctilious in reproducing his model and through lack of space may have excised some of the choreuts who appeared on the margins of his model. The missing complement of choreuts may be hinted at by four mythologized satyrs who appear on the reverse of the pot, which is not demarcated in any other way from the scene on the front except by its mythological mode. The vase is not clear evidence that the satyr chorus was any less than the tragic, i.e., fifteen, members.

Terra-cotta Figurines

138. New York MMA 13.225.13, 14, 16, 18, 19, 21–23, 25–28. Attic terra-cotta figurines, 400–375 B.C. See Plate 9.

Twelve of these (Old or?) Middle Comic comic figurines are said
to have come from a single tomb in Athens and are therefore
contemporary. The figure of an old woman at the bottom right
was bought from the same dealer. Up to five others may be associated with this group for stylistic reasons, and the entire group is
thought by some to derive from archetypes made by a single artisan.
By the second quarter of the 4th c. B.C. we know that about eighty
different types of comic figurines were produced in Athens and
exported and copied throughout the Greek world and as far away
as Spain, North Africa, and South Russia. The old woman not from
the tomb group is the earliest datable type. Of nine known examples,
one from a worn mold was found by systematic excavation in the
Athenian marketplace in a context datable to 410–390 B.C. In any
case, examples of six of the tomb group were found at Olynthus
in Chalcidice and must therefore predate its destruction in 348 B.C.
(IV 30F). Scholars traditionally divide the tomb group into a "red"
and "yellow" group based on the shades of the clay, as if the two
groups were fired in separate kilns or at separate times, but the
distinction is suspect and the collection may be random. From top
to bottom and left to right the figures are: slave carrying a water
jar (missing); old man (or slave) clutching or opening money bag
and seated on square altar; old man wearing a traveler's hat (*pilos*)
and drying his eye with his *himation*) old man wearing *pilos* in
thinker pose seated on round altar; slave carrying basket; old woman
with *himation* over head; young woman or prostitute hiding face;
seated slave on "stump"; Heracles wearing lion skin and club on
left shoulder; slave seated on "stump" in thinker pose; younger
man; young woman or prostitute with *himation* over head; old
woman. Note the universal use of stomach, buttock, and breast
padding for male characters and the *phallos* that is generally exposed
beneath the abnormally short *chiton*. The *phallos* and short *chiton*
disappear by the New Comic period (from ca. 320 B.C.), when the
padding is used only for slaves (139–41, 143, 145, 147).

139. Athens NM 5027 (Misthos 544). Terra-cotta figurine from Myrina, 2nd c. B.C. See Plate 10A.

New Comedy opposes the world of its heroes, the urban bourgeois
family and its slaves, to an antisocial demimonde of urban poor—
pimps, whores, professional charlatans, and sycophants, normally
motivated by jealousy, greed, and self-interest—that lurks, awaiting
any opportunity to avail itself of the bourgeois family fortunes. The

toady and parasite are typical of this demimonde (app. A, New Comic masks 17 and 18). They have dark skin from spending most of their time in gymnasia and stalking the streets. Their names often reveal their predatory nature: e.g., "Jawbone," "Sponge," "Breadgnawer." They usually wear black or gray and carry a strigil and a bottle of oil so that they can scrape down their patrons in the gymnasia (app. A, Costume and Props). 139 holds his oil bottle suspended from his left wrist, but the strigil he once held in his right has been lost. The ancient physiognomic writers give frequent insight into the significance of the features that appear on New Comic masks. The toady's and parasite's hooked nose indicates shamelessness. Their shoulders are hunched, signifying their unfree state (i.e., they are not economically self-sufficient). The short neck is a sign of a treacherous nature. The ears have a battered look from being frequently boxed by his patron. According to Pollux, the parasite is distinguishable from the toady in that the parasite has a more cheerful look while the toady has his eyebrows raised more malevolently and ears in slightly better shape. The raised eyebrows are said to show mischievousness and vehemence. 139 is often said to be a parasite, but comparative material, particularly the terra-cotta masks found at Lipari, show clearly that this is the more malevolent toady.

140–41. Athens NM 5060 (Misthos 543) and Berlin 7969. Terra-cotta figurines from Myrina, 2nd c. B.C. See Plate 10B–C.

The figurines reproduce the young men playing cymbals and *tympanon* from the archetype of 143, 145, but are much earlier than either and help corroborate the stylistic dating of the archetype to the early 3rd c. B.C. Two other Myrina terra-cottas reproduce the character and pose of 141: none of them preserves the hands and *tympanon*. 140 and 141 give firm evidence to show that the terra-cotta figurines sometimes copy figures from models depicting specific scenes: possibly the figurines were sold in sets to be arranged in imitation of the scene.

142. Paris, Musée du Petit Palais, DUT 192. Ivory statuette, 1st–3rd c. See Plate 10D.

This statuette of an imperial tragic actor accords well with Lucian's description of the actors of his day (IV 103). The top-swelling (*onkos*), the gaping mouth, and the elevator boots begin to appear in the illustrations ca. 300 B.C. The top-swelling and elevator boots are evidently designed to give extra height and majesty to tragic heroes and it is tempting to connect this with the development of the Hellenistic theater that placed actors at a greater distance from the audience through the introduction of the high stage and the building of larger theaters with greater seating capacity (148, 149). Contrast the naturalistic masks and flat soles of the 5th and 4th c. B.C. on Würzburg H 4600 (cover), 130 and 124.

Wall Paintings, Mosaics, Manuscript Illustrations

143–44. Dioskourides Mosaics: Naples MN 9985 and Naples MN 9987. Produced 125–100 B.C. See Plate 11.

Comparison with 145 and 146 shows that 143 illustrates act 2 of Menander's *Theophoroumene* (The Possèssed Girl) and 144 act 1 of Menander's *Synaristosai* (Women Breakfasting Together). Lyric verses of the *Theophoroumene* survive on papyrus, probably from act 2, since music and song are rare in the New Comedy of Menander's day (see IVC–D). Another fragment of text seems to come from the part of the play immediately preceding the scene illustrated on 143 and 145:

> LYSIAS? (reporting a conversation): . . . "My gifts,"—you hear?—the girl says, "they took away my gifts." He says, "Why did you take them, slut? How do you know this guy who gave them to you? What [did?] the young man [do]? And why are you walking around outside wearing a garland? Are you crazy? Then why can't you be crazy locked up inside?" KLEINIAS?: That's nonsense! She's not just putting it on, Lysias. LYSIAS: It can be put to the test. If she really is divinely possessed, she'll come leaping out here in front. Pipe [a tune] of the Mother of the Gods, or rather of the *Korybantes* (her priests)! And you, stand here by the door of the inn! KLEINIAS?: Yes, by Zeus, excellent! Truly excellent! I like this! A beautiful sight!

The cult of Cybele, the Mother of the Gods, involved orgiastic dancing and divine possession. The lyric fragment is a hymn to Cybele. It is clear that a girl, probably the love interest of one of the young men, is possessed by the goddess, but the other characters consider her behavior a pretense, until she emerges from the inn in response to the music like a charmed snake. The *tympanon,* played by the young man to the left, the cymbals, played by the young man on the right, and the pipes are all associated with cult of

Cybele. The piper wears a female mask; possibly this is the real official piper incorporated into the stage action. The boy to the left has no mask and seems to be an extra, the piper's assistant, or another musician, since he holds a pipe in his hand. Note that the doorway, probably the inn door mentioned in the fragment, is a prominent feature in the background, signifying its importance to the scene. The young men's masks are normally differentiated by the tilt of their eyebrows, but this seems largely an effect of the artist capturing the difference in the angle of their gaze (in fact the *tympanon* player's crucial stage-left eyebrow forks both up and down). If the reproduction is accurate they appear to me both to wear the mask of the tender youth (perhaps twin brothers) said to be "whiteskinned, unsunned with signs of delicacy" (app. A, no. 13). A soldier complaining about a rival to his beloved prostitute in Plautus' *Truculentus* 610f. describes the mask: "Do you love that curly, soft adulterer, brought up in the shade, a *tympanon* banger, good-for-nothing?"

The opening scene of *Synaristosai* is known from Plautus' adaptation of the play in *Cistellaria*. Three women converse, having just finished breakfast: an old bawd, her daughter, and their hostess and mutual friend. 146 shows that in Menander's play they were named Philainis, Pythias, and Plangon, respectively. Plangon is the concubine of the young man who owns or rents the house in which the party takes place. He has promised Plangon's adoptive mother (who brought her up as a foundling) that he will marry Plangon, but his father recently announced his intention to force him to marry the daughter of a prosperous relative. Plangon is broken-hearted and Plangon's mother wishes her to return home. The problem will of course be happily resolved when it is discovered that Plangon is in fact a lost daughter of the prosperous relative and hence a perfectly acceptable bride for the young man. The bawd Philainis, generally supposed to be wearing Pollux' "fat old woman" mask (app. A, no. 29) sits at the right, holding a silver wine goblet. To her left stands the figure of an unmasked female house slave referred to by Philainis in a surviving fragment of Menander's play (385 K.-Th.): "By Artemis, I've breakfasted well. [Everything would be to my liking,] if only someone would give some more to drink. But the slave girl took the wine away from us along with the table." Facing us at center is Plangon, wearing the mask of the "second false maiden" (app. A, no. 35). "False maiden" implies a girl living as a prostitute or concubine, but virtuous at heart, and normally recognized to be of citizen birth and married by the end of the play (precisely Plangon's position). Plangon is less adorned than the prostitute Pythias to her right, who wears a *mitra* bound in her hair (thus identifying her as Pollux' mask no. 41, app. A). In *Cistellaria* 113f. Pythias draws attention to the contrast implicit in Plangon's plain adornment: Plangon replies that it suits her bleak fortunes. The bands of color framing the scene appear to be an attempt to give an impression of architectural depth, probably to show that the scene is an interior scene set within the *thyroma* (149, 150) of a Hellenistic theater.

145–46. Maison de Ménandre, Mytilene. Mosaics, late 3rd c. See Plate 12.

A wealthy provincial town house excavated in 1961 contained mosaic copies of scenes from eleven plays of Menander. Of these, seven scenes, labeled with the title of the play, act number, and character names (145, 146), were found in the *triclinium* (formal dining room) along with a mosaic portrait of Menander, one of Thalia, the Muse of Comedy, and a scene from Plato's *Phaedo*. In a portico just off the *triclinium,* four others were found with play and act labels only. The subjects were well suited to the context: the custom of performing scenes from drama, especially Menander, at private dinner parties is widely attested in imperial times: Plutarch devotes one of his *Convivial Questions* to the topic: "What are the entertainments at dinner?" (711a–13f.), and the discussion gives particular praise to the presentation of Platonic dialogues (hence the *Phaedo* scene), mime, and comedies of Menander.

The Mytilene *Synaristosai* (146) unquestionably reproduces the same scene as 144, although differences in the arrangement and in costume led some scholars to suppose that the two mosaics depict different productions. This misapprehends the nature of the relationship between art and drama in this period. Rather, the difference in details are due to the qualitative difference in the craftsmanship, and to a translation or updating of the stylistic idiom, such as one finds in the tradition of the manuscript illustrations of Terence (147). The independent stylistic evolution of the scene is most easily explained through a copybook tradition, such as that which medieval mosaicists employed, though there is no direct evidence for antiquity. In such a tradition, artists copy their patterns from other artists over a long period of time, without referring back to the archetype, and they introduce gradual changes to the image as they perceive and reinterpret it within a changing conceptual framework: so here the masks have become more grotesque and the costume more elaborate in consonance with changes in the theater and changing notions of theatricality. A close comparison of the *Synaristosai* mosaics gives further confirmation of the copybook hypothesis: 146 is a mirror-image reversal of 144, including even the small figure on the right of 144, whose head has been squeezed in above the seat and behind the head of the old bawd in 146 (hardly explicable as a reference to a different production!). The patterns in the Mytilene mosaicist's copybook evidently took the form of stencils that could be laid on the floor and brushed over for a quick reproduction of the basic outline: the Mytilene mosaicist was apparently indifferent as to which side of the pattern sheet faced upward.

Most scholars take the Mytilene *Theophoroumene* (145) to represent a later moment in the same scene or a later scene in the same play as 143. A garlanded young man, labeled "Lysias," plays cymbals left. An actor dressed in slave costume, labeled "Parmenon," stands center with a curious pose. To the right a young man, "Kleinias," also garlanded, holds a round object in his right hand (barely visible in the photograph): it is a good deal smaller than the *tympanon* one would expect from a comparison with 143. The reproduction of two scenes close together in the same play has been used to support the idea that they derive from illustrated book editions of the plays. However, it is worth considering whether the changes are not analogous to those between 144 and 146 but greater, due to a corruption of the scene in the copying tradition. Note that the young man playing cymbals appears in both scenes in a roughly similar pose, and that the little figure to the left holding a single pipe in 143 appears on the right in 146 and is also holding a single pipe. He is apparently the piper's assistant and holds his pipe case with an extra pipe. Note also that the cymbal player has been dressed in a costume normally worn by slaves (though his name clearly shows that he is a free youth), while the pose of the slave, center, looks as if it may be a misinterpretation of the reversed stance of the *tympanon* player. Note in particular the scarflike object hanging over the slave's left arm, which looks like an attempt to interpret an indistinct copy of the end of the *tympanon* player's *himation* folded around his waist and appearing to hang from his left elbow.

147. Miniature illustration of Terence's *Phormio,* act 2, scene 3, in Vaticanus Latinus 3868, 9th c. See Plate 13.

Thirteen medieval manuscripts of the comedies of Terence preserve miniature illustrations drawn from an archetype that can be dated on textual and iconographic criteria back to the "Calliopian edition" of Terence, no earlier than ca. 400. Several scholars of the late 19th and early 20th c. optimistically believed the illustrations to be drawn directly from performance, but examination of the miniatures shows that they are heavily dependent upon the text. As Roman playwrights wrote texts for continuous performance, there existed no "organic" criteria for dividing plays into scenes, and the divisions in our manuscripts are arbitrary, yet the illustrations follow these late editorial divisions faithfully. Moreover, the illustrations are linked to these scene divisions by function. In the illustrated manuscripts they serve to separate the scenes: the manuscripts without illustrations also do this by providing a list of the characters appearing in the scenes, like that above the figures' heads in 147. The intention of the illustrator was evidently to provide a pictorial supplement to the list of names, since it is his general policy to depict everyone who appears in any given scene, but he also wished to present the characters in such a way as to summarize the action in the scene. The two aims were frequently at odds, however, particularly in scenes like 147, where no single moment unites all characters in a coherent action. In this section of the play (348–440), the slave, Geta, and the parasite, Phormio, pretend to be in a heated conversation that they wish the old man, Demipho, to overhear as he enters the stage accompanied by three legal advisers: Hegio, Cratinus, and Crito. Demipho then interrupts and argues with Phormio directly. Phormio leaves and the scene ends. In the following scene Demipho sends Geta off, and then turns to address his advisers directly. In 147, the illustrator attempts to capture all of this action at once. The characters are shown from left to right in the order in which they speak in the text. Geta and Phormio are shown in heated conversation. Demipho stands to the left of Geta because he is the first to speak in this scene. The artist also tries to show by Demipho's posture and position that he later also has a conversation with Phormio, but the artist's desire to condense these actions and reconcile them with the order of speakers results in the irrational placement of Demipho on the opposite side of the pair from that of the advisers with whom he entered. The scene is further divorced from performance by the fact that the artist anticipates the next scene by showing Cratinus pontificating rather than watching in silence. Indeed the next illustration (*Phormio,* 2.4) is nearly identical except for the excision of Phormio and the transposition of Geta to the far left departing from the scene. Though the function and inspiration of the miniatures is purely textual, the costumes show that the original illustrator had some familiarity with the iconographic tradition of theater illustration (not with the theater itself). As in the Mytilene mosaics, masklike features are reserved for old men, slaves, and lower-class professionals. As in the Mytilene mosaics, the cloak (*pallium*) is the chief means of distinguishing free men from slaves (whose masks are often identical to those of old men). In addition, slaves almost invariably carry scarves over their left shoulders, as does Geta here. This attribute has nothing to do with stage costume but is derived from a progressive misconstrual of the manner in which slaves wear their *pallia* in the iconographic tradition (the scarf can be seen over the left arm and right shoulder of "Parmenon" in 145). The stiff and conventional gestures also have their counterparts in earlier theater illustrations. On the whole, however, the correspondence with the early tradition is less impressive than the discrepancies. Nonetheless some scholars feel that the former can only be explained by supposing that the originals of the Terence manuscripts were modeled after a much earlier archetype closely connected to the performance tradition.

ID. Theater Buildings

Sources

148. Plan of Theater of Dionysus at Athens. See Plate 14.

There is no general agreement about the appearance of the earlier phases of the Theater of Dionysus. Most of the evidence has been destroyed: the theater was frequently rebuilt in antiquity, used as a marble quarry in the Middle Ages and subject to the experiments of early archaeology in the 19th c. The Archaic remains are scant and their interpretation disputed. According to Dörpfeld, who published the results of the 19th-c. excavations, the earliest attempt to increase the steepness of the embankment of the *theatron* took place ca. 500 B.C. since no later pottery could be found in the lowest layers of imported earth. By the same time, the Old Temple of Dionysus was built. A fragment of a wall (SM3) in Archaic polygonal masonry survives undisturbed by the later rebuilding and probably marks the line of the earliest wall separating the sanctuary from the west *parodos*. Two more lines of Archaic wall (J3 and SM1) are preserved under the later *skene* building. Dörpfeld took them to be fragments of the retaining wall marking the circumference of the Archaic orchestra. Many now doubt the curvature of these wall fragments. An important point in their favor is a growing body of evidence demonstrating that the classical orchestras in other theaters were rectilinear or trapezoidal. It is uncertain whether early drama was played against a backdrop. The *Oresteia* of Aeschylus (458 B.C., cf. 126–27) seems to presuppose the existence of a (wooden) stage building (*skene*) though the earlier extant plays do not.

A major rebuilding of the theater took place probably in the latter half of the 5th c. B.C., most likely in conjunction with the construction of the Odeon of Pericles (built ca. 440 B.C.). This large concert hall (and site of the *Proagon,* see III 4–8) obviously encroached upon the *theatron* from the east. The center of the orchestra and the whole *theatron* may have been shifted slightly to the north and west to minimize the encroachment. Probably at the same time, a colonnade (or stoa) was built across the northern edge of the sanctuary of Dionysus, which is three meters lower than the theater area. Abutting the back wall of the stoa and sharing its foundation (though not bonding with it) is a 73.1-meter-long wall (H-H) with ten slots cut into it at regular intervals (S1-S10), evidently to receive wooden beams, and a rectangular stone projection (T) jutting out 2.7 meters to the north of H and measuring 7.9 meters west to east. Some think that T supported the *skene* or stage machinery or both. The cuttings S1-S10 may have held the back wall of a long *skene* building or simply a screen behind a *skene* supported by T. At least by the 420s, literary and iconographic sources also attest the existence of a low wooden stage attached to the *skene* and probably connected by steps to the orchestra (131, 133; IV 76). The audience sat on wooden bleachers built onto the slope of the acropolis (IV 130, 153, 154, 169). A row of stone seats for dignitaries (*prohedria*) was also built at the foot of the *theatron* at the edge of the orchestra (IV 143–50).

From 330 B.C. to the late 4th c. B.C. the theater underwent extensive rebuilding initiated by Lycurgus, the leading financial official of the period ca. 338–326 B.C. (cf. 14; III 78). The *theatron* (auditorium) was rebuilt in stone; most of its present remains belonged to the Lycurgan theater. It was built around a round orchestra, twenty meters in diameter. There are twelve sets of stairs dividing the thirteen *kerkides* (wedges of seats) in the *theatron* below the *diazoma* and about twenty-one above. A street, called the *peripatos,* was rerouted across the top.

The visible front of the *skene* (V-V) was twenty meters long. At either side square buildings in stone, called *paraskenia,* projected forward five meters. Later rebuilding has unfortunately obscured the evidence for the appearance of the Lycurgan *skene.* Elsewhere in Greece (149, 150) theaters built after the theater of Lycurgus have high stages, formed by adding a second story to the *skene* building and then attaching another one-story platform to the front of the *skene,* called the *proskenion* (literally, "building before the *skene*"). The actors were moved up to the *proskenion*'s roof, called the *logeion* (literally, "talking place"), and the second story of the *skene* served as a backdrop, called *episkenion*. It is a reasonable guess that the late 4th-c. B.C. theater in Athens was the first to use a raised stage, possibly of wood, and thus served as the model for the other theaters. The raising of the acting area from the low wooden stage to the *logeion* made impossible the kind of easy communication between actors and chorus, stage and orchestra, that we find in earlier drama. Some confirmation for a high stage already in the late 4th-c. B.C. theater in Athens comes from the texts of New Comedy (performed in the "Lycurgan" theater) that show that the actors had ceased to interact with the chorus (IVD).

In a Hellenistic rebuilding, possibly of the 2nd c. B.C., the *paraskenia* were brought back two meters closer to the *skene*. In front of the *skene* a *proskenion* was built (P-P), creating an acting surface twenty meters long and only about three meters deep. In the time of Nero (54–68) the *skene* was drastically remodeled with a two-story pillared stone facade, but on much the same basis as the Hellenistic theater, and with *paraskenia*. The *parodoi* were never roofed over. A stage in the Roman style (*pulpitum*, cf. 151–53) was erected, with a curtain, which extended forward to the *theatron*, and went through a number of alterations. Further changes were made to accommodate gladiatorial fights in the 1st c., and the orchestra was later adapted as a swimming pool.

149. Elevation of a Hellenistic Theater (labeled). See Plate 15A.

The Hellenistic theater in its most advanced form has a narrow and high stage—up to nine feet—to allow performances at two levels, either on the stage (*logeion*) or at orchestra level. Both levels have a facade of pillars or pilasters, which can be filled with wooden flats, suitably painted. The openings to accommodate these are called *thyromata*. These flats are called *pinakes* (singular *pinax*) or, confusingly, *skenai* (the plural of *skene*) as at Delos, where several sets were said to be stored. This system could allow for not very quick changes of scene, and even for different arrangement of doors. Presumably it would be possible to play at the lower level dramas such as Old Tragedy, which would require use of the orchestra for dancing, and connection between orchestra and performing area, while the high *logeion* proper would suit New Comedy, where no connection with a chorus or orchestra was required (cf. 148). This arrangement however would have the obvious disadvantage that the *logeion* could not easily be reached from the orchestra. Yet we hear of a set of wooden steps being made for the Hellenistic stage at Delos, and perhaps some dramas required it.

Some, but by no means all, Hellenistic theaters, e.g., at Athens and in other Greek areas including South Italy, have *paraskenia,* square buildings at each side of the stage, projecting several feet forward, even beyond the front of the *proskenion,* so as to enclose it between wings, though we do not know the height of the stage when the first *paraskenia* were built. These could also be fitted if necessary with *pinakes,* as at Delos, or be more substantial constructions of stone, or only be pillared porches at the upper level. There is great variety in this respect; and later there is observable a tendency to move these projecting wings back toward the facade, so that they represent side doors. In the illustration, we indicate only where these *paraskenia* would be. The two levels could if necessary be connected by ramps at the ends of the *logeion* alongside the *parodoi,* thereby allowing entrance to the stage from the side. But obviously actors would usually come out from the side of the stage building in order to enter the *logeion* from the side. Though we use the word *paraskenion* in this technical sense, one must note that in antiquity it was used to mean both any annex at the side of the *skene* and also the *parodos* doors.

The orchestra is usually so shaped as to contain an open circle, thereby leaving a considerable distance, up to twenty yards, between the middle of the front row and the *proskenion.* The seating area is divided by stairways into up to twelve even, wedge-shaped sections (*kerkides*), to which were allocated the specific divisions of the citizen body, while the magistrates and priests sat at the front. The *kerkides* are divided horizontally by passageways called *diazomata.* The *skene* is always separated from the seating area (*theatron*) by the two entranceways (*parodoi*) on either side, which sometimes have a decorative gateway, but are not roofed over. There is no barrier or change of elevation between the front seats (*prohedria*) and the orchestra (cf. 131).

In a few theaters can be found an underground passage, called Charonian steps by Pollux (app. A), from the stage building to an exit in the middle of the orchestra. This is one of the many ways in which the Hellenistic theater achieved considerable stage effects, which we cannot reconstruct. There was clearly much wooden machinery to emphasize the epiphany of gods and special effects demanded by tragedy (IV 77–79). There seems, e.g., to have been methods of rotating painted flats beside the side doors to indicate a change of genre (IV 81–82).

150. Model of the Theater at Epidaurus (Royal Ontario Museum). See Plate 15B.

The Theater of Epidaurus was built in two stages. The first construction was a design by the architect Polykleitos ca. 330–300 B.C. and held ca. 6,200 spectators in 34 rows; in 170–160 B.C. it was enlarged by an additional 21 rows of seats to hold ca. 12,000 people, and it was not later remodeled. It is the largest surviving theater of Greece, though not the largest in antiquity. It is constructed on the basis of a measure called the "pheidonic cubit" = .4903 meters to an exact mathematical plan. It is the only theater based on a pentagon, drawn in the orchestra circle. The exact and unique harmonic form and the fact that it was a theater for pilgrims to the cult of the healing god, Asclepius, and not for the city of Epidaurus, whose theater lay elsewhere, suggests that the plan was meant to have a more profound significance, related to Pythagorean/Platonic ideas of perfect form, and it is therefore untypical. We know of no certain example of an earlier theater with circular orchestra, though the Theater of Lycurgus at Athens (148) is contemporary.

In the lower section there are twelve *kerkides* (wedges of seats) with thirteen staircases: in the later addition, there are twenty-two sections and twenty-three stairways. The semicircular *theatron* flares out almost imperceptibly at the outside *kerkides* toward an oval. The orchestra is marked out in limestone blocks as a perfect circle forty cubits across, i.e., 9.8 meters in radius; the diameter of the circle defined by the edge of the front row of seats (*prohedria*) is fifty cubits. From the center of the orchestra to the back of the original *theatron* is eighty cubits; to the back of the later *theatron* is an additional forty.

Unfortunately we know little of the original *skene* building, save that at ground level it had projecting *paraskenia*. The second *skene* had ramps built over these *paraskenia*, leading up to a high *logeion* less than four meters deep and ca. twenty meters long. The first stage may have been similar, but we cannot be certain. The *episkenion* had the usual *thyromata*, openings that could be left open or closed with paintings, while the front of the *proskenion* consisted of pillars, between which painted flats (*pinakes*) would be placed.

Even in antiquity the theater of Epidaurus was admired for the perfection of its form, and it was not, like so many other theaters, adapted for nontheatrical purposes in later times. It must therefore be borne in mind that it was not a typical city theater, but a cult building in the service of Asclepius, not Dionysus.

151. Elevation of a Roman Theater (labeled). See Plate 16A.

Vitruvius at the time of Augustus already recognizes that there is a basic difference in architecture between Greek and Roman theaters. In his day it is possible that the theaters he knew in Rome still had wooden stage buildings. But most surviving Roman theaters have had their stage facades rebuilt, sometimes several times, in imperial times, and their remains usually represent a state reached in the 2nd c., after which they were often further adapted for wild-beast shows or nondramatic purposes. Typical is a highly elaborate stone facade (*scaenae frons*) with many columns, usually three stories high. Some Roman theaters are well preserved; e.g., Bosra in Syria (152) or Aspendos (ca. 170) in southern Turkey provide good examples of a Roman theater, because they are built according to a consistent plan and show the Roman theater in its most developed and coherent form. Most theaters of Asia or South Italy, however, were to some degree adaptations of earlier Greek theaters to the Roman model, seldom consistently realized: these are classified as "Greco-Roman" theaters (153).

In the Roman theater the stage building is completely integrated with the auditorium (*cavea* = Greek *theatron*), so that the curve of the seating reaches right up to the *versurae*, which are the Roman equivalent of the Hellenistic *paraskenia,* and which thereby match the height of the *cavea*. The seating is usually much steeper. The side entranceway to the stage (Vitruvius' *iter versurae,* or "*versura*-path") is partially concealed by the projecting wall of the lower *cavea* seating. The entranceways to the orchestra (*aditus maximus*) below them are vaulted over and hidden behind the lowest wall of the seating (the Greek *analemma*). Over the *aditus* are the *tribunalia,* seats of honor for the presiding magistrates. The *cavea* is divided horizontally into the three levels by gangways (*praecinctiones*) and vertically into six or more wedges (*cunei* = Greek *kerkides*) by stairways. In the orchestra are low steps (*subsellia*) for the seats of distinguished spectators at dramatic events. But there is also a parapet around the orchestra acting as a barrier between them and the rest of the spectators. Later this barrier was useful when the orchestra in some theaters was used for more violent spectacles.

The *scaenae frons* can be flat or indented, as here, but is increasingly decorated with many columns. These facades were of wood but were replaced with stone during the first two centuries A.D. Most Roman theaters of the 2nd c., however, had three doors set back into curved or rectangular niches (*exedrae*), but facades with five doors are also found. The doors usually had steps down to the stage, which would itself have a wooden roof at the third story. The stage proper (*pulpitum* = Greek *logeion*) is made of wood set on pillars, with room below it (*hyposcaenium*) for machinery. The facade of the stage proper, the *proscaenium,* was normally about five feet high, made of elaborate stone, and sometimes incorporating a mechanism for the stage curtain to be raised.

Generally speaking, the Roman imperial stage is about eight by fifty meters, though the stages in Rome itself may have been much larger, and unadapted stages are smaller. The stage of the Theater of Pompey must have been an amazing ninety meters wide. But many variants exist; sometimes an originally narrow stage has been extended forward into the orchestra on rows of pillars, as at Miletus. Often steps are integrated into the *proscaenium* to enable actors to enter the orchestra, or possibly to allow for nontheatrical movement, since the theater was often the main place for the people to convene.

In Aspendos and some other theaters there is notably missing the large assembly rooms (*basilicae*) or foyers that are sometimes found on either side of the long but narrow stage building, and that could contain stairs to upper stories. Like the columned porticos along the top of the *cavea,* they were perhaps meant to be added afterward. In African theaters a temple is also found at the top of the *cavea.* Even when the Roman theater utilizes the slope of a hill it is essentially conceived as a freestanding unit.

152. Theater of Bosra. See Plate 16B.

The well-preserved theater of Bosra in Syria was built to a consistent plan in the 2nd c. The irregular stage facade is more elaborate than that of Aspendos, and it has two large peristyle courts instead of *basilicae* at each side of the stage building: these are connected by a large vaulted corridor running all the way behind the facade and giving on to the stage. These courts allow direct access to the side entrances to the stage and the entrances to the orchestra. The parapet of the seating is ca. 1.25 meters high and was surmounted by a metal railing, so that the first seats are almost 2 meters above the orchestra, while the stage is 1.75 meters high, and about 50 meters by 9 meters in area. Part of the colonnade at the top of the *cavea* survives. There are three sets of steps built into the *proscaenium* front, as in many imperial theaters, allowing easy access to the orchestra. Note that the bases of the pillars on stage form a solid front six feet high, showing that they are purely decorative; one cannot hide behind them. The three levels of the *cavea* are divided vertically into ten *cunei*. The orchestra is part of a perfect circle whose far side would touch the front of the central stage door (*valva regia*). Since the *cavea* is totally preserved, it is possible to observe clearly how small are objects on the stage seen from the back of the seating. There is no sign that the theater was adapted for beast hunting, and no amphitheater is known in the area.

153. Theater of Aphrodisias (Greco-Roman Theater). See Plate 17.

Almost all surviving theaters have been modified in some way, especially in regard to the stage building; but none more so than the Greek theaters, whose history encompasses nearly seven hundred years of development. The earliest theaters focused on the orchestra, while later drama focused on the stage and did not have much use for the orchestra. The tendency was therefore to magnify the size and importance of the stage building, until in later imperial times the orchestra resumed its importance for animal hunts and gladiatorial combat, at least in places where no amphitheater was available. The great theaters of Miletus and Ephesus and many others give evidence of several stages of these alterations, all of which differ in detail and in execution. Three developments in particular are evident: first, an increase of the depth of the stage at the expense of the orchestra; second, the conversion of the facade into a grandiose stone structure; and third, varying attempts to connect the *theatron* architecturally with the *skene*.

Aphrodisias in Asia Minor has one of the best-excavated theaters, and several inscriptions deal with alterations to it, showing that despite its lateness and relative simplicity, there were more than seven building phases. There is no complete publication, and what follows is very provisional. But it is not typical, perhaps because Aphrodisias was famous for its marble and sculptors. It was built in the time of Augustus, already with a stone facade in two stories, but it was never a typical Hellenistic theater nor was it ever converted fully into the Roman form, and the form of the stage is approximately that of the original Augustan building, which is Hellenistic Greek in inspiration. The *theatron,* which could hold about eight thousand spectators, was less steep than a Roman theater, and never connected to the *skene* building. The first stone theater was dedicated in 28 B.C.: an inscription records the gift of the *logeion* and the *proskenion* (i.e., stage front) and its decoration. Further major construction over several years took place around 60, especially in the auditorium. In the 2nd c. statues were placed on the *logeion,* suggesting that it had fallen out of use.

Archaeology reveals that, as originally designed in the 1st c. B.C., the stage, ca. 30 meters long, had a *proskenion* with fourteen Doric columns, supporting a *logeion* ca. 3 meters deep, much of the acting space being limited by the large column pedestals behind. At both ends the *proskenion* is angled slightly away from the orchestra to form one wall of the *parodos.* The *scaenae frons* with the usual pillars and three doors was at least two stories high and decorated with marble pillars and statues: this is a remarkably early example of this kind of stage, especially when allied with the old high *logeion.* The *proskenion* pillars were designed to accommodate wooden painted flats (*pinakes*), each 2.64 meters by 1.5 meters. The *logeion* is, as it now stands, 3.5 meters above the orchestra level. The stage building is separated from the *theatron* by the *parodoi,* which were not built over. It was in this form, if one ignores the grandiose *scaenae frons,* a typical late-Hellenistic theater with a high, long, and narrow stage, but it was antiquated by Roman standards even at the time it was built. The narrow stage would have been unsuitable for anything but older drama without a chorus, having a clear acting area little more than 2 meters deep, but 30 meters wide.

Possibly in the middle of the 2nd c. most of the orchestra was lowered 3 meters to make almost a pit for spectacles and well-attested gladiatorial events, and among other changes, the front seats were removed, and the resulting auditorium front wall was plated with marble. New doors were constructed in the new lower arena as access for hunters and animals. This left an acting space about 5 meters deep and 20 meters wide, floored with marble slabs, between the new pit and the front of the old *proskenion* at the earlier orchestra level; eventually the spaces between the *proskenion* pillars were mostly walled up to leave entrance doors. Inscriptions reveal that this area was used for pantomime and mime performances as late as the 5th c., the mimes having their quarters in the rooms behind the old *proskenion.* Perhaps the original *logeion* was abandoned as early as the 2nd c., so that mimes could be said to perform in the orchestra. Eventually the *theatron* became part of the Byzantine fortifications of Aphrodisias, as at Miletus, which helped to preserve it from stone robbing.

II. Origins of Greek Drama

Of the fragments of the inscription known as *Fasti* at Athens (I 100), one tantalizingly records the surprising information that the dramas were not called tragedies and comedies or even, as they are oddly but normally called, "the tragedians" and "the comedians," but *komoi.* A *komos* is usually a drunken procession of young men after a drinking party and is best known to students as the word that Aristotle in the *Poetics* takes to be the root of com-edy, a *"komos-*song." A *komast* is one who performs a *komos,* whatever it is (cf. I 106). The word can be applied to tragedy because of the procession of the chorus in honor of the god of wine. But archaeology tells us more about the origins of drama than literature or epigraphy, though its evidence is more difficult to interpret.

Usage decrees that we call komasts the dancers who appear on Greek vases from about 630 B.C. and continue in changing form until well into classical times. The importance of these komasts lies in what they can tell us about the origins of drama and ritual at a time when our literary sources are deficient. Our first existing dramas come from about 480 B.C., and we are largely dependent on vase painting for the previous 160 years.

Here is a rough list of the types of komasts and the characters connected with them who appear on early vases:

1. Komasts, i.e., simply normal dancing men in groups
2. Padded dancers: dancers with padded bellies and posteriors
3. Solo or group komasts with unpadded costumes of various types
4. Satyrs or silens wearing smooth or hairy loincloths
5. Satyrs wearing nothing
6. Hairy satyrs, usually phallic
7. Women, connected with some of the above, especially satyrs later, and possibly to be called nymphs or maenads in some circumstances. They wear usually either long dresses (*peplos*) or short tunics (*chitoniskos*)

These all appear in great numbers, in different combinations, and in a variety of contexts. There are a number of other rarer varieties. Those Attic vases that can be directly associated with satyrplay in general run from only about 500 B.C. onward (IC) and are therefore of interest only in shedding light on contemporary formal satyrplay. More important for the history of drama are the vases that seem to suggest drama long before its official existence. Apart from those vases that illustrate animal choruses, the komast vases are the most important for this purpose.

In particular the komasts who are dressed as padded dancers have attracted attention, since this costume has some similarity to that worn in later comedy. Especially in Corinthian, and consequently in the vase painting of Attica, Chios, and elsewhere, the earliest komasts have often protruding posteriors and stomachs, which makes one think of padding, though the deformation may be due to natural fat at times. More commonly these komasts simply wear a skintight tunic, sometimes later painted so sketchily that they appear naked. At first they appear particularly on Corinthian ware as individuals, but soon in groups, forming a *komos* proper; they are particularly fond of dancing around a large wine krater, often with a piper among them, and later in the 580s B.C. they are accompanied in their dancing by "females." Komasts proper are in general, but not always, distinguished by an energetic dancing, not the kind of dancing that we would think of as being suited for tragedy; some are shown with musical instruments and associated directly with myth. Despite their costumes, early komasts, unlike the comic actors, are almost never phallic; and they never have the tails, ears, and *phalloi* of true satyrs. In fact they are almost never to be found together with satyrs, despite the features they do have in common. The artists treat them as separate motifs, and we should consider them to be separate entities.

The komasts or padded dancers are certainly to be connected with wine drinking but not necessarily with Dionysus. This prevents us from associating them with the one literary reference that could, with any probability, be said to have any connection whatsoever with them, a fragment of the earliest iambic poet from the island of Paros in the 7th c. B.C., Archilochus (1), who speaks of leading off the dithyramb drunk. The dithyramb is traditionally Dionysus' dance, and iambics are the basic meter of all classical drama; therefore it could be argued we have on the vases representations of a drunken dance for Dionysus. But that in fact does not take us very far, because we do not know what a dithyramb looked like in 630 B.C., 150 years earlier than our literary fragments of dithyrambs, which are not in the least drunken dances and which have sometimes nothing obviously to do with Dionysus, but tend to relate in complex style some mythical story (cf. I 125). It remains therefore no more than a possibility that some of the komastic dances that we see were called dithyrambs by their performers. The dance "kordax," for example, which is often alleged to be the dance of the komasts, is connected with later comedy (IV 317, 318) but is not in itself Dionysiac.

The first komasts start appearing as individuals almost entirely without context on vases from 630 B.C. onward. There are more than 400 vases from Corinth showing them; they principally occur on *aryballoi* (scented-oil bottles) of the Early and Middle Corinthian period, where there are signs of mass production. But the padded dancers appear only down to about 540 B.C. in Corinth or anywhere else, and thereafter only satyrs or ordinary komasts, i.e., men in drunken procession, are found. Very few representations of komasts are overtly sexual, very unlike the satyrs. It has been alleged by many art historians that they represent, in fact, fertility demons or spirits of some sort. The principal evidence for this was that they often occurred together with mythological scenes, and since the mythological characters were clearly not real, then the komasts were not either. This view now finds less favor than the view that these komasts and the padded dancers are closely related and both represent ordinary people dressed up; it is also agreed that it is not unreasonable to think that they are in some way connected to drama. Second, there are a few vases that do give a context and suggest that the mythological connection can be otherwise explained as related possibly to the theme of the dance or the song. Third, the komasts known from Chiote and Ionic painting are dressed in a peculiar local style, which suggests that they represent some local reality. These dancers then could well be professional entertainers of some sort at a public festival or a cultic ceremony or private party. They cannot, however, as yet be equated with any god's or goddess' worship, unlike satyrs who are early associated with Dionysus. One of the peculiarities of Corinthian and Laconian komasts is that quite a number of them are pictured with a grotesquely deformed foot, which reminds one at least of the lame god Hephaestus (cf. 3), who is a comic figure in Homer. (Likewise one finds that early satyrs can be given one horse's foot by artists.) But the center of their interest is almost always a wine krater and never the god of wine, unless of course he is supposed to be represented in that form.

In only a very few examples before 540 B.C., notably on the so-called Dümmler krater (2), do these dancers seem to be involved in a dramatic story, but in view of its phallic figures this vase is not typical. The

Athenians took up the komast theme along with its subthemes of drinking and dancing on their pottery from at least 580 B.C. and after enjoying great popularity the padded and associated komasts disappear entirely around 540 B.C.

Satyrs, on the other hand, who are known to earlier epic and appear roughly at the same time as the komasts, are not nearly so popular in art as they become after 550 B.C. A hairy, phallic but tailless protosatyr appears uniquely on an *amphoriskos* from Corinth about 600 B.C. (3). There appear also about 570 B.C., in Attic painting, the first truly hairy satyrs, i.e., bearded with sidewhiskers and grotesquely furnished with *phallos* and horse's tail, which seems in fact to be already a costume for men dressing as Dionysiac satyrs. There need be no meaningful difference between the hairy and nonhairy satyrs, though the *Papposilenos* of satyrplay is regularly given a woolly outfit, to distinguish him from the other satyrs with their smooth stage-skin and smooth or hairy shorts, as on the Pronomos vase (I 137). But there is a clear distinction to be made between the komasts and the satyrs.

The humanizing of the padded komasts in art into ordinary komasts, which starts already in the 560s B.C., is paralled by the great increase in the popularity of satyrs, who, hairy or not, are to be found dancing often with Dionysus and "maenads"; again, because they are painted mostly as mythical beings and not actors, it is impossible to assert that they are to be connected with drama in the 6th c. B.C., unless there are signs of a costume or formal choral activity. The history of vase painting therefore shows that komasts, especially tunicated or padded, are replaced thematically by realistic komasts or mythical satyrs, who in turn are confused eventually with dramatic satyrs, inspired by satyrplay. It is much debated just how all of these are to be related to reality. There are of course a number of important vases (I 124, 125) that show choral dancing, often of a more serious kind. There is some 5th-c. B.C. evidence to suggest that men dressed as satyrs could perform in musical chorus, and many of these representations may have to do with early choral dancing rather than dramatic comedy; that is, there could well be genres and rituals that were nondramatic and that could be performed by people dressed as satyrs.

One has to reject the idea that, e.g., komasts turn iconographically into hairy satyrs, because the two occur independently for fifty years. Nor do they turn into ordinary satyrs, since these, too, start appearing after 580 B.C. and are clearly different, and indeed they continue to be distinguished from komasts. But there are good reasons of course for saying that komasts and satyrs were in some iconographical way linked, i.e., they suggested similar ideas; this seems to be proved by a unique black-figure cup in Florence showing a *phallagogia*, i.e., a ritual *phallos-*carrying procession (4A–B). The importance of the vase rests in the demonstration of the iconographic relationship, though not identification, of the fatman/komast and the satyr on each side of the vase, and the differentiation of the carriers. These phallic rituals, first described by Aristophanes (III 26), are referred to by later writers (13, 14) also, and they are for Aristotle the origins of comedy (11, 12).

Smooth satyrs are not exactly the same as hairy satyrs, who are relatively rare; but by 560 B.C. the artists already fail to distinguish the two. By the end of the 6th c. B.C. one finds human dancers together with satyrs, both with female companions and connected with Dionysus. At this time, too, the first vases affected by satyric drama begin to appear. In general the mythical, constantly and perhaps increasingly in the 6th c. B.C., intrudes between us and the representation of the dramatic.

The connection of satyrs with public amusement is confirmed by a number of Athenian vases that show a ship procession of Dionysus accompanied by satyrs, who are as we know citizens in costume (5). This is known to be part of a festival (*katagogia*) in many Greek cities that brought back Dionysus after the winter. It is likely that at such times the disguised satyrs sang rude songs and made the sort of jokes that resulted in the Greek word for "to conduct a procession" carrying also the meaning "to insult" (III 62C). These ritual insults (III 62) are attested for a number of Athenian festivals, including the Anthesteria festival of Dionysus, and are to be connected indirectly with the iambic meter of comedy. It seems certain that both satyrs and padded komasts performed dances in either a private or festival context from the late 6th c. B.C. Their costumes suggest that they were professionals.

About twenty vases from ca. 560 to 480 B.C. are our only certain evidence for the existence, from the mid-6th c. until the mid-5th c. B.C., of *komoi* of men dressed as animals or on dolphins or on stilts (cf. 8C); they are generally accompanied by a piper. These mimetic musical perfor-mances inevitably recall the titles of many old comedies, such as *Wasps* or *Birds,* and suggest choruses like these are the origin of early comic choruses, which had no fixed costume. But we cannot show that they were more than a pantomime dance by themselves, though the earliest dolphin-rider vase has "on a dolphin" written on it, which suggests the first words of a song. We illustrate one of these in Boston (6). Six of the vases (510–480 B.C.) show dolphin riders, making it the most popular theme; but though it is tempting to think of the story of Arion (cf. 15), more probably the theme recalls some actual chorus at Athens prior to the official establishment of comedy.

A large number of Attic vases in two series illustrates an unknown ritual in which women worship a mask or masks of Dionysus, on a pillar or in a basket. They are portrayed sometimes as maenads but are clearly Athenian matrons. These vases are called "Lenaean" vases, because it was thought at one time that they illustrated a ritual at the festival of the Lenaea, but there is no firm evidence to connect the vases with any known festival of Dionysus. They are valuable in demonstrating the continuing worship of Dionysus as a mask god throughout classical times, and for explaining why masking ritual was Dionysiac at Athens. We illustrate here (7) one of the last and best known from the series (480–420 B.C.), a stamnos now in Naples, to be dated ca. 430 B.C.

Apart from the evidence of art, we are very reliant on information from antiquarians of the Hellenistic age, and sources which depend on them. One group of witnesses (8) calls attention to masked dances of various sorts in Sparta, and it is likely that Artemis there represented for masked ritual and comic abuse what Dionysus represented in Athens. A Hellenistic writer (9) shows that there was a considerable variety of choral and masked rituals in the worship of Dionysus. More typical is a story (10) about realistically described semidramatic rituals in Syracuse in Sicily, which are alleged without much likelihood to be the origins of bucolic poetry. Though such stories preserve valuable details without context, they also involve much scholarly guesswork and contradictory assertion. It is alarming to see that even Aristotle (11, 12), who is the first to deal with the origins of drama, is largely guessing and extrapolating from the customs of his time and such early dramas as he could read.

We do not list here all the existing biographical data about the "inventors," such as Thespis, of different genres of drama, who are sometimes said to be Sicilian or Corinthian. Much of this information is suspect, and the result of learned speculation in antiquity. Some allegations (15) are credible, especially the connection of leading poets with the courts of early tyrants, and it is likely that in Sicily, Athens, and Corinth, the policies of tyrants in building temples and promoting festivals also effected an increase in public musical and protodramatic religious festivity. In particular, Pisistratus and his sons are likely to have promoted the Panathenaea and Dionysia festivals at Athens, and earlier Periander (15B) may well have encouraged choral performances at Corinth, since this agrees with the evidence of vases. But it is clear that the ancient scholars had less certain knowledge than would appear from our surviving information. It may well be, e.g., that Pratinas was the first person to have appeared on the official lists of satyrplay poets at the Athenian festivals (16); but he was not likely to have been the first to write such plays.

Sources

1. Archilochus, fr. 120 W. Written mid-7th c. B.C. These are two lines from a lost poem and without any context.

> For I know how to lead off (*exarxai*) the beautiful dithyramb song of the lord Dionysus, my mind blasted by wine.

2. Louvre E632. Corinthian krater, 600–575 B.C. See Plate 18A–B.

> The "Dümmler krater" uniquely seems to illustrate some dramatic action that does not belong to myth. On the top left there are two padded figures, one a piper and the other a bearded dancer who is singing and gesticulating; he touches his posterior in a manner typical of the komasts. Whether he is wearing a mask or not is disputed. On the right two men, who carry a vase, are being controlled by a grotesquely phallic person, with two curved sticks (these sticks are typical later of satyrs). Though none of these three is padded, the markings on the shoulder of the left-hand one indicate that the artist hints that he is costumed, and perhaps we should hold this true for all the figures. The three are labeled "Eunos" (beneficent), "Ophelandros" (man-helping), and "Omrikos," which is at present meaningless. Eunos looks at the singer, so tying the scenes together. Below there are six stacked kraters, a woman with a plate of cakes, and two men in stocks, one of whom is naked and fettered, the other clothed. The interpretation of the whole as a dramatic representation of wine thieves and their punishment must be discarded; wine was not stored in kraters. It is not at all certain that the two registers even belong together.

3. Athens NM 1092 (664). Corinthian amphoriskos, 600–575 B.C. See Plate 18C.

> This is normally taken to be a very early representation of the Return of Hephaestus, who appears on a donkey drinking wine from a horn, and who is identifiable by his misshapen foot. That he has been overcome by the power of wine is emphasized by the attendant figures on the left who carry an amphora and a vine stem with bunches of grapes. It follows that the grandly dressed figure

whom they follow must be Dionysus, though he is not usually so portrayed. More problematic still are the two figures who appear to greet Hephaestus. The ithyphallic figure clearly wears a costume reminiscent of Attic comedy, as does his companion. His wild hair allows us to think of him as a protosatyr, even if he has no tail. He appears to be "stonethrowing," a gesture we find on other Corinthian vases, but whose meaning is unknown. It is difficult to avoid the conclusion that a comic version of the Return is meant. In later versions of this theme on vases, a komast is occasionally found instead of the protosatyr here.

4A-B. Florence 3897. Attic black-figure cup, ca. 560 B.C. See Plate 19A–B.

On side A we see seven *phallos* bearers. An eighth man faces them from in front and leans hard toward them, but it is uncertain that he is helping to lift the *phallos* pole since his hand is clearly outlined in front of the pole, not underneath it. We are to think of him as "leading off" the procession, perhaps in the way suggested by Archilochus (1) and Aristotle (11). Those supporting the pole are shown as uncostumed, save for erect *phalloi* which are added in red paint; the man facing is further differentiated by the absence of a *phallos*. The men support a *phallos* pole from which another pole rises diagonally; on it sits an enormous satyr who is part of the float, since a small person sits on his back. Side B has six men without *phalloi* carrying a less elaborate pole but with a large fat figure, like a padded komast, riding the attached secondary pole. The same system of ropes is found in both pictures, which are obviously meant to complement each other.

5. Demosthenes, *On the False Embassy* 287. Delivered 343 B.C. The orator is implying that it was normal for citizens to wear a mask (sc., of a satyr) in the Dionysiac processions of his time.

… and the accursed Kurebion, who revels (*komazei*) in the processions without a mask.

6. Boston MFA 20.18. Attic black-figure cup, ca. 500–490 B.C. See Plate 20A.

A line of six helmeted and cloaked warriors on dolphins are shown facing a piper. On the other side of the same vase are six ostrich riders. It is worth observing that the artist could not make his mind up whether to show the feet of the dolphin riders, as he does with the first and third from the right, or to conceal them, as he does with the others. That is, he could not decide whether to show the reality—since the riders would have had to use their feet in the procession for dancing—or to sustain the fiction postulated by the presentation of dancing dolphins.

7. Naples MN 2419. Attic red-figure stamnos by Dinos Painter, ca. 430 B.C. See Plate 20B.

On this so-called Lenaean vase, a mask of Dionysus, with clothing attached, sits on a pillar; in front of it is a table for offerings on which stand a *kantharos*—the wine vessel most associated with Dionysus—and two *stamnoi*, i.e., vases of the same shape as the vase on which they are painted. The stamnos was obviously the sacred vessel of the ritual itself. On each side are two women dressed as maenads, one of whom ladles presumably wine from the vessel into a *skyphos*, a drinking cup, while the others dance in ecstatic fashion with tambourine and the Dionysiac staff called a *thyrsos*. On some of the vases, the artists introduce a satyr, so that there must always be a question about the amount of artistic license taken with the ritual itself.

8A. Masked ritual in early Sparta. Athenaeus 621d. Written ca. 200.

Among the Spartans there was an ancient variety of comic pastime, as Sosibius (a writer of ca. 300 B.C.) says, not taken very seriously, because in such matters also Sparta follows simplicity. In simple language one would imitate persons stealing fruit, or a foreign doctor talking.... Those who pursued this kind of pastime among the Spartans were called *deikelistai*, as one might say, *skeuopoioi* (mask-creators) or mimes. But there are many local terms for the type of *deikelistai*. The people of Sikyon call them *phallos*-carriers, others *autokabdaloi*, others *phlyakes*, like the Italian Greeks, but most people skillmongers (*sophistai*).

8B. Hesychius, s.v. *brydalicha*, s.v. *bryllachistai*, s.v. *lombai*. Written ca. 5th c. The first entry is corrupt, but masks of old women from classical times have been found in an Artemis temple in Sparta.

Brydalicha: female mask put on because ridiculous and ugly ... and female clothing is put on. Therefore also they call ... *brydaliches* in Laconia.

Bryllachistai: men who put on the masks of ugly women and sing hymns.

Lombai: women who begin the festival sacrifices for Artemis, from their outfit in the merriment. *Phalloi* were called thus.

8C. Pollux 4.104–5. Written ca. 180.

There were also some Laconian dances on Malea. There were silens and satyrs with them dancing in fear. And *ithymboi* in honor of Dionysus, and Caryatids in honor of Artemis. And *baryllicha*—invented by Baryllichos—and dances by women for Apollo and Artemis. The *hypogypones* imitated old men with sticks. The *gypones* mounted on wooden legs to dance, and were swathed in diaphanous Tarentine material.... And they called the dithyrambic dance *tyrbasia*. And they called mimetic(?) the dance in which they mimed those who were caught stealing stale meat. *Lombroteron* was what they (masc.) danced naked with ritual abuse.

9. Athenaeus 622a. Written ca. 200. Here too antiquarians collected evidence for early folk rituals, from which drama arose.

Semos of Delos (a Hellenistic writer) in his work *On Paeans* says: "the *autokabdaloi*, as they were called, recited their pieces standing, wearing wreaths of ivy. Later they were named *iamboi*, as also were their poems. The so-called *ithyphalloi*," he says, "have a mask representing drunken men and wear white stripes and are belted with a fancy apron that covers them down to the ankles. After entering the portal in silence, when they reach the center of the orchestra, they turn toward the audience and recite:

> Give way; give way; make room for the god; for the god
> wishes to march through your midst upright and bursting.

But the *phallophoroi*," he says, "do not wear a mask, but binding on their heads a bonnet of tufted thyme and holly, they place on top of this a thick wreath of violets and ivy; wrapped in thick mantles they come in, some by the side entrance, some by the middle doors, marching in step and reciting:

> To thee, Bacchus, we lift up this music
> Pouring forth a song with varied melody
> New and undefiled and in no way used in older
> Songs; no, untouched is the hymn we dedicate.

They would then run forward and jeer at anyone they picked out; they did this standing still. But the man who carried the *phallos* pole marched straight on, covered with soot."

10. Scholion to Theocritus, p. 2.21ff. Wendel. The scholiast gives several versions of the origins of bucolic poetry. This is a rare but convincing example of the folk rituals that must have been common in classical times, disguised by antiquarian lore.

In Syracuse (in Sicily) there was once a revolution and many citizens were killed, and when the mob finally settled down in peace, Artemis was seen to be the cause of the reconciliation. The farmers brought gifts and sang songs joyfully to the goddess. After that they made room as a custom for the songs of the farmers. (Variant) They say that they sang, bedecked with bread in the form of different kinds of animals, a wallet full of seeds of all kinds, and a goatskin of wine. They poured libations to those they met; they wore a garland and had deer horns on their heads and a stick for hitting hares in their hands. The victor took the bread from the vanquished, and while he stayed in town in Syracuse, the vanquished went into the surrounding villages collecting sustenance for themselves. They sang verses full of fun and laughter, and ended with the benison "Good luck be with you, good health too, which we bring from the goddess, which she's brought(?) <you>."

11. Aristotle, *Poetics* 1449a2–25. Written ca. 330 B.C. This is one of the most important passages about ancient drama, but it is very obviously a set of ill-written lecture notes not intended for publication. Perhaps more alarming is the thought that some of the sentences could be later additions by someone else, e.g., the sentence beginning "Sophocles <invented>."

When tragedy and comedy appeared, people were attracted to each <kind of> composition according to their personal disposition. Some became composers of comedies instead of iambics, while others directed tragedies instead of epics, because comedy and tragedy are greater and more noble in their forms than are iambics and epic. To consider whether tragedy is now developed in its elements or not, and to judge it in itself and in relation to its audience, is another matter. <Tragedy> arising from improvisation—both it and comedy, tragedy from those who "led off the dithyramb," comedy from those <who led off> the phallic songs, which still remain the custom in many of our cities even now—grew gradually as they developed each aspect that came to light; and after going through many changes, it stopped when it attained its proper nature. Aeschylus first raised the number of actors from one to two, and reduced the choral element and gave the leading role to the spoken part. Sophocles <invented> three <actors> and scene painting. Also as to <tragedy's> greatness, starting with insignificant plots and ludicrous diction because it was transformed from a satyr <performance?> it was late in becoming serious, and the meter changed from tetrameter to iambic. For in the beginning they used the tetrameter because the composition was for satyrs and more in the nature of a dance performance; but after speaking had come in, nature herself discovered the appropriate verse form. For of all the verses, the iambic is the most like ordinary speech.

12. Aristotle, *Poetics* 1449a37–b9. Written ca. 330 B.C.

The changes that tragedy went through and the persons responsible for them have not been forgotten. Comedy, on the other hand, was disregarded at first because it was not taken seriously; in fact it was at a late date that the archon granted a chorus of comedians; <before,> they were volunteers. Those called its poets were recorded only when it already possessed certain elements of form; but who gave it masks or prologues or its number of actors and all that sort of thing remains unknown. Composing story plots, however, came from Sicily originally and of those at Athens it was Crates who was first, giving up the iambic character and composing universalized stories and plots.

13. P. Veyne, *BCH* 109 (1985) 621. Date 3rd c. This inscription was found in Chalcis in Euboea; it seems to refer to roughly the same kind of ritual as is shown on 4 over seven hundred years earlier. "Carried" likely indicated a sacred function.

For Junior—For Marcus Ulpius Callinicus Junior, "carried" and first to have made fifty-five circles in the theater for Dionysus successfully, and who went on his own to the Capitolium, without the *thyone* (= *phallos*?)-bearer from the time he picked <it> up till he put it down, soaked (drunk?) during the whole performance and . . . [. . .]festival[. . .

14. Lucian, *On the Syrian Goddess* 16 (cf. 28). Written ca. 160.

The Greeks raise up *phalloi* for Dionysus, upon which they carry also something like this, small men made from wood, with large genitals; these are called marionettes (lit. "string-pulled").

15A. Arion. *Suda,* s.v. *Arion.* Written ca. 1000. These unreliable details of the life of the semilegendary poet Arion, principally known for being saved by a dolphin from pirates, are typical of the assertions about the origins of drama. But the date does suit the evidence of the vases, and the connection with the tyranny is likely enough.

Arion: of Methymna (in Lesbos), lyric poet, son of Kykleus, flourished in the 38th Olympiad (628/4 B.C.). . . . He is also said to have been the inventor of the tragic style, and to have been the first to organize a chorus, sing a dithyramb, and give a title to what the chorus sang, and the first to introduce satyrs speaking verses.

15B. Herodotus 1.23. Written ca. 420 B.C.

<Arion> had spent the greater part of his life, they say, at the court of Periander (tyrant of Corinth, 625–585 B.C.).

15C. John the Deacon, *Commentary on Hermogenes* (= Solon 30a W.). Written 10th c.

The first performance of drama was introduced by Arion of Methymna, as Solon (ca. 585 B.C.) stated in the poems entitled *Elegies.*

15D. Scholion to Aristophanes, *Birds* 1403.

Antipater and Euphronios (Alexandrian grammarians) say in their notes (*hypomnemata*) that Lasus of Hermione was the first to organize circular choruses, but the older authorities, Hellanicus (of Lesbos, 5th c. B.C.) and Dicaearchus (4th c. B.C.), say that it was Arion of Methymna, Dicaearchus in his work *On the Dionysiac Contests,* Hellanicus in his *List of Carnean Victors.*

16. *Suda,* s.v. *Pratinas.* Written ca. 1000. This is clearly the first name that ancient scholars found recorded on their victory lists at Athens. The numbers, if credible, obviously do not match the normal tetralogy.

Pratinas: son of Pyrronides or Enkomios, of Phlious, poet of tragedy; he competed against Aeschylus and Choerilus in the 70th Olympiad (i.e., 499/6) and he was the first to write satyrs. When he was giving the performance, the scaffolding on which the spectators were sitting fell down, and as a result a theater was built at Athens (cf. III 65). He gave fifty dramatic performances, of which thirty-two were satyric; he won once.

III. Organization

IIIA. Classical Athens

IIIAi. Festivals

IIIAia. The Great Dionysia

Greek drama was performed as part of a religious festival. The importance of the religious context must not be underestimated, but one must also beware of overestimating it. In contrast to the various paradramatic rites and pageants found in other traditional societies, Greek drama is distinguished by its secularity. Drama developed out of ritual at a time when most of Greek society underwent a transition from a dominant rural aristocratic society to a dominant urban democratic social formation, and traditional pieties began to be replaced with a civic ideology suited to the new social structure. The so-called Age of the Tyrants in Greece (7th–6th c. B.C.) was a period in which ambitious men took advantage of the new accumulation of wealth through trade and commerce to oppose the old land-based aristocracy and seize political power. In further developing their urban power-base, the "tyrants" found it convenient to eclipse many traditional rural festivals, which were largely under the control of local aristocrats (through priesthoods, maintenance or ownership of shrines, and funding of sacrifices), by relocating important cult objects to the urban centers and by introducing large urban festivals. Several tyrants took a particular interest in the worship of Dionysus. Not only did the Dionysiac cult, largely centered on wine and revelry, have an enormous popular appeal, but Dionysus, like death, was a great leveler: the forms of his worship overrode class distinctions, while his worshipers were ideally projected in myth as an undifferentiated harmonious collective. Though these festivals were still, strictly speaking, religious in nature, they gave a new secular form and slant to the traditional myths and rituals. The purpose of the new festivals was to foster and display the power of the unified state, centered politically upon the city and ultimately upon the tyrant himself, and to promote a common cultural identity and a system of values consistent with the new political reality. The new historical conditions that gave rise to the "tyrants" eventually led to their expulsion and replacement by more democratic constitutions in Athens (510–503 B.C.) and elsewhere.

The "Great Dionysia," also called "City Dionysia," was one of the new urban festivals created by Pisistratus, who was tyrant of Athens on and off from 561 and securely from 546–527 B.C. Pisistratus superimposed his festival upon an old local festival and for the purpose appears to have brought an important cult idol of Dionysus down from the town of Eleutherai on the border with Thebes (and added a suitable myth to give the newly transformed cult the sanctity of hoary antiquity, 9). The urban festival had two sacrificial processions for the god (the "Introduction" and the "Procession"), each slightly different in character, and the doubling is perhaps a vestige of the operation that grafted the new civic and secular festival upon the old religious cult.

The original pre-Pisistratid cult no doubt resembled the many local festivals to Dionysus that survived in Attica until late antiquity and came to be known collectively as the "Rural Dionysia" to distinguish them from the urban festival (IIIAib). It appears that these festivals originally consisted of a phallic procession to a cult center followed by sacrifice. The ancient sources attest to the use of the *phallos* pole and the singing of obscene songs in the rural Dionysiac procession (24, 26). A mid-6th c. Attic black-figure cup depicts a phallic procession (II 4A–B). Semos of Delos (II 9) describes a dramatized phallic parade from the third c. B.C. (?), which involved a ritual song, described as a "virgin dedication," a *phallos* pole, and also improvised abuse by the chorus of members of the audience. Semos mentions two different kinds of choruses of *phallos*-bearers, both costumed, one called *ithyphalloi* (i.e., "erect *phalloi*"), who are masked, and another called *phallophoroi* (i.e., "*phallos*-bearers"), who are not. It is interesting to note that the cup in Florence shows one group of *phallos*-pole bearers with ithyphallic costume. Comparative material shows a close connection between phallic processions, ritual abuse, and obscenity and the use of masks in Greek cult, particularly Dionysiac cult. Whatever the original practice of the rural Dionysia, which may well have differed in detail from one township to the next, the procession of the later festival does appear to have employed masked participants (24, 25).

The Rural Dionysia took place in December or early January, but the City Dionysia took place in the month of Elaphebolion, roughly late March, when good weather and the beginning of the sailing season permitted national and international participation. The competitors were selected well before the start of the festival by the archon eponymous (in the classical period) or by the Agonothete (in the Hellenistic), who was in charge of the festival (17); it is perhaps a sign of the Pisistratid reorganization that the new festival was not given to the "king archon," who assumed most of the religious functions of the earlier Athenian monarchy, while the archon eponymous was the principal political office in the Athenian state. The criteria for selection remain somewhat obscure. It appears that a poet could be excluded if he made a poor showing at the previous festival (42), but factors other than quality control clearly came into play (1), and in the Hellenistic period we hear of direct political censorship (3). On the 8th Elaphebolion at the latest (4) was an event called the *Proagon* ("Before the Contest"), which took place (after ca. 440 B.C.) in a building called the Odeon ("Music Hall") adjacent the theater. At the *Proagon* the poets who were to compete in the dramatic contests mounted a platform accompanied by their actors and chorus, all garlanded but without masks or costumes, and they spoke "about their compositions" (5–8).

On or before the 9th Elaphebolion, the religious ceremonies began with a procession called the "Introduction" (*Eisagoge*), which was said to commemorate the original introduction of the god Dionysus from Eleutherai in Boeotia to Attica (9). The icon of Dionysus Eleuthereus was a wooden shaft with a mask attached (II 7), one of the most common ways of representing Dionysus in Greece. During the Introduction the icon is dressed, garlanded with ivy, and carried in procession from his temple on the south slope of the acropolis to the Academy (10, 14), a grove outside the city, on the road to Eleutherai, where hymns were sung (12). The icon may have remained at the Academy for one or several days. On the 8th or 9th Elaphebolion, after sacrifices were made, they brought Dionysus back to his theater (in the urban sanctuary) with a torchlight parade (11).

This cultic activity appears not to have been considered part of the offical public celebration, which began only the next day. On Elaphebolion 10 the law forbade the holding of the Assembly and the commencement of any legal proceedings (15, cf. 4). Even the prisons were opened and prisoners released on bail to attend the festival (16). The first rite of the official festival was the "Procession" (*Pompe*). We do not know the precise route of the parade, but it is a reasonable guess that it began at the city's principal gate, the Dipylon, where the road from the Academy entered the city, in a building called the "Pompeion," in which the objects used in various sacred processions were housed (the building, or one near it, later became the Council Chamber of the "Artists of Dionysus," cf. IV 48). The procession included the various strata of Athenian society carrying provisions for the sacrifice and feast, each symbolically appropriate to their rank. It was led by a virgin of "good" (i.e., aristocratic) family, who carried a golden basket containing the "first fruits" of the sacrifice (19, 26). The particular order is unknown, but somewhere behind her followed male citizens carrying wineskins and huge loaves of bread on spits (20, 21). The resident aliens ("metics") carried basins probably filled with honeycombs and cakes, and their daughters carried water jugs (21); the carrying of utensils was evidently regarded as subservient since colloquial Attic used "basin bearers" as a derogatory term for metics. The *choregoi* (IIIAiia) appeared in lavish costume (22). Young men of military age (ephebes) escorted the bull "worthy of the god," which was to serve as the principal sacrifice (11). Hundreds of other sacrifices followed (18). At the end of the procession appeared groups of men singing hymns and carrying large *phalloi* (9, 23, 24, 26, II 9). It is not certain whether the icon of Dionysus was present: Athenian pots show the icon carried in a wheeled ship, but it is uncertain whether the the the rite belongs to the Great Dionysia or another Dionysiac festival. The procession stopped for hymns and dances at the shrines en route (27) and proceeded to the sanctuary of Dionysus Eleuthereus for the sacrificial feast.

Contests for choral songs called dithyrambs (I 125; IVC) were probably held on the same afternoon and would likely have continued well into the night. Each of the city's ten tribes produced a chorus of fifty boys and a chorus of fifty men for the competition (28, 29). The *choregos* of the winning chorus of each competition received a crown and a tripod (31, 32), and the poet probably received a bull to sacrifice to Dionysus. Both were then taken home in a victory procession, or *komos* (II).

Up to this point the Athenian Dionysia was more splendid but not qualitatively different in form from archaic Dionysiac festivals in rural Attica and elsewhere in Greece, with the exception perhaps of the tribal competition for dithyrambs. Though dithyrambs were a common element of Dionysus worship throughout Greece, 45 suggests that the dithyrambs were not organized into a competition until the earliest years of the Athenian democracy. If the contest came after Cleisthenes' democratic reforms (ca. 503 B.C.), then the tribal organization of the competition may have been introduced to help consolidate Cleisthenes' massive reorganization of the Athenian tribes from regional and economic to purely administrative units. It was the last three or four days of the festival (Elaphebolion 11–14), given over to dramatic competitions, which were originally unique to the Athenian festival. This innovation probably goes right back to Pisistratus, since the traditional date for the first tragic competition in Athens is ca. 534 B.C. (45). Comic competitions were not introduced to the Dionysia until 486 B.C. (46).

Considerable controversy surrounds the order of the dramatic competitions and the number of days devoted to them. The dominant view, until recently, was that before and after the Peloponnesian War (431–404 B.C.) five comedies were presented on Elaphebolion 11, followed by three days that were each given to the production (by a single poet and *choregos*) of three tragedies and a satyrplay. Another possibility is that five days were given to competitions in this order: day one—boys' dithyramb plus comedy; day two—men's dithyramb plus comedy; days three through five—tragic tetralogy plus comedy. Numbers 41, 43, and 44 name five comic competitors in 434 B.C., 388 B.C., 312 B.C., and 311 B.C. (cf. 82; I 19). Because the hypotheses to Aristophanes' *Clouds* (Dionysia 423 B.C.), *Peace* (Dionysia 421 B.C.), and *Birds* (Dionysia 414 B.C.) all name only the first-, second-, and third-prize winners, it appears that only three comedies were produced during the war, and it is assumed that this was because of economic cutbacks. It was therefore assumed on the basis of 39 that during the war, each group of three tragedies plus satyrplay were performed in the morning and one of the three comedies were performed on the afternoon of each day of Elaphebolion 11–13. The publication of 42 in 1968 occasioned a challenge to the notion that the number of comedies was reduced from five to three during the war. It may be, however, that the fourth comedy mentioned was produced in the years of the nominal peace between Athens and Sparta in 420–416 B.C., in which case the older view needs only a partial modification.

The competition opened with a number of ceremonies: a ritual purification of the theater (33), followed by a libation (wine offering to the gods) by the ten generals, the most important elected officials in the Athenian state (34). It is of some interest to see that the libations were poured not by the priest of Dionysus or any other sacred office but by civic heads of state. Four rituals followed that were purely civic in character. Along with other proclamations (36A), the public herald presented and announced the names of distinguished citizens and benefactors of the state, who had been awarded golden crowns by the Assembly for their services to Athens (36B; a ceremony, Demosthenes explains, designed not only to encourage benefaction but to display the magnanimity of the state to its benefactors, 37). As the sailing season began at the time of the Dionysia, the (subject) allies were required to send their tribute to Athens at the time of the festival, and this was brought down from the Treasury and displayed to the audience (35). This display of power was discontinued after Athens lost its empire in 404 B.C. (35). At the time of the empire, the orphaned sons of the war dead who had reached the age of majority were presented with suits of armor and invited to sit in the front-row seats (35, 36). Judges were selected (34, IIIAiib). The order of appearance of the contestants was decided by lot, probably before the festival (38). A herald announced each performance (40). On the last day, after the judges had turned in their verdicts, the winners were proclaimed and the prizes awarded: a crown of ivy leaves for the victorious tragic and comic poets (38). The victorious poets and *choregoi* were then led home in a victory procession (*komos*). Plato's *Symposium* gives a detailed portrait of the private celebration that followed Agathon's tragic victory in 416 B.C.

Sources

Archon's selection

1. Cratinus, *The Cowherd, PCG* F 17. Produced ca. 453–423 B.C.
   <The archon> did not give a chorus to Sophocles but gave one to the son of Kleomachos (Gnesippos), whom I would not think worthy of producing a chorus for me even at the Adonia.
2. Plato, *Laws* 817a–d. Written ca. 347 B.C.
   If some tragic poets were to come to us and ask something like "O strangers, shall we visit your city and countryside or not, and should we bring our poetry or what are your thoughts on the matter?" what answer would we give to the marvelous fellows? Here is what I think: "O best of strangers, we ourselves are poets, to the best of our ability, of the most beautiful and best tragedy possible. So all our government is an imitation of the most beautiful and best life—and this is what we call really the truest form of tragedy. So now you are poets and we are also poets of the same genre, your rivals and competitors in the most beautiful drama, which only true law can bring about, or so is our hope. Do not suppose that we will so easily allow you to set up your stage in the

marketplace and bring onto it actors with beautiful voices, who can speak louder than ourselves, and permit you to harangue the children and women and the whole mob, addressing the same concerns as we do, but for the most part saying just the opposite. We and our whole city would be completely mad if we allowed you to do what I've just said, without the authorities first judging whether what you wrote is fit to be said in public or not. So now, you children of dainty Muses, first demonstrate your songs to the archons alongside our own, and if they appear to say the same or better than ours, we will give you a chorus, and if not, my friends, we could never do so."

3. *POxy* 1253. Written 2nd c. The papyrus contains plot summaries and some production information of plays of Menander. The Athenian general Lachares had been a supporter of Cassander, the Macedonian regent who served as the main prop of the oligarchic faction in Athens. In 300 B.C. he employed his mercenary troops to make himself tyrant of Athens. He was not finally ousted until 295/4 B.C.

The *Imbrians,* of which the first line goes "God its been a long time since I [last saw?] you, Demeas, my friend." <Menander> wrote the play in the archonship of Nikokles (302/1 B.C.) [...] on the seventy-[first? third? sixth? ninth? day] and submitted it for production at the Dionysia. It was not produced because of Lachares the tyrant. Later Kallippos of Athens acted it.

Proagon

4. Aeschines, *Against Ktesiphon* 66–67. Delivered 330 B.C. Inscriptional evidence contradicts Aeschines and shows that the Assembly often met up to and on the 9th Elaphebolion. The fact that Aeschines was able to get away with this statement perhaps attests to the confusion created by the disjunction between the religious and the civic holidays.

<Demosthenes introduced> a decree that the executive officers (*prytaneis*) hold an Assembly on the 8th Elaphebolion, when we sacrifice to Asclepius and hold the *Proagon,* on a holiday, a thing that no one can remember ever having been done before.

5. Scholion to Aeschines, *Against Ktesiphon* 67.
A few days before the Great Dionysia in the so-called Odeon there took place a contest (*agon*) of the tragedians and an exhibition of the plays with which they intended to compete (*agonizesthai*) in the theater. Therefore it is called *proagon* in accord with the original

meaning of the word (i.e., "precontest"). The actors entered uncostumed, without masks.

6. Scholion to Aristophanes, *Wasps* 1109.

Those in the Odeon: a place in which they used to announce the compositions before the announcement in the theater.

7. Plato, *Symposium* 194. Written ca. 384 B.C. Fictional date: 416 B.C. Note that 70B places this event at the Lenaea, but there is some room for doubt: we have no knowledge of a *Proagon* at the Lenaea, moreover Plato (70A) refers to a large international audience that would sooner suit the Dionysia.

"I would be very forgetful, Agathon," said Socrates, "after I saw you mount the platform with your actors and face such a large audience with courage and poise to talk about your composition, revealing not the least sign of stagefright, if now I were to think you would be flustered before so small a group as we are."

8. *Life of Euripides.* Written 1st c. B.C. or later. The event dates to 406 B.C.

They say that when Sophocles heard that <Euripides> died, he appeared in a black *himation,* and introduced his chorus and actors without garlands in the *Proagon,* and that the people shed tears.

The "Introduction" (Eisagoge)

9. Scholion to Aristophanes, *Acharnians* 243. One would infer from the following legend that the sanctuary of Dionysus Eleuthereus was the oldest in Athens, but Thucydides (2.15.5; cf. Philostratus, *Life of Apollonius* 3.14) tells us that this is not so; the cult of Dionysus in the Marshes appears in Thucydides' account to have been an integral part of the Anthesteria as worshiped by the Ionians and therefore must predate the Ionian migration (before ca. 900 B.C.), while Pegasos is associated in legend with King Amphiktyon (dated ca. 800 B.C.). The story type is typical of those attached to Dionysus in the Archaic period and it is likely that the story in its present form was made up for the purpose of providing the Pisistratid festival with an ancient foundation myth. Comparison with other stories of this type indicate that the "disease" mentioned below is a permanent erection, hence the ithyphallic parades commemorating the event.

A *phallos* is a long piece of timber fitted with leather genitalia at the top. The *phallos* came to be part of the worship of Dionysus by some secret rite. About the *phallos* itself the following is said.

Pegasos took the image of Dionysus from Eleutherai—Eleutherai is a city of Boeotia—and brought it to Attica. The Athenians, however, did not receive the god with reverence, but they did not get away with this resolve unpunished, because, since the god was angry, a disease attacked the men's genitals and the calamity was incurable. When they found themselves succumbing to the disease, which was beyond all human magic and science, envoys were hastily dispatched to the divine oracles. When they returned they reported that the sole cure was for them to hold the god in all reverence. Therefore, in obedience to these pronouncements, the Athenians privately and publicly constructed *phalloi,* and with these they paid homage to the god, making them a memorial to their suffering.

10. Pausanias 1.29.2. Written ca. 150.

Outside of the city, in the townships and along the roads, are sanctuaries and the graves of heroes and men. Nearest is the Academy, an estate once owned by a private individual, but in my day a gymnasium. As you descend into the Academy you find a precinct of Artemis...Then there is a small temple to which they carry the icon of Dionysus Eleuthereus every year on fixed days.

11. *IG* II² 1006.12–13. Date: 121 B.C. An inscription honoring the ephebes (young men beginning military service) and describing their activities. The use of the word *eschara* shows that the altar of Dionysus is that in the Academy; note that the "Introduction" is distinguished from the "Dionysia," the latter term being used to designate the "Procession."

After sacrificing, they also brought (literally, "introduced"; the Greek uses a cognate of *eisagoge*) Dionysus from the altar (*eschara*) to the theater by torchlight; and at the Dionysia they led in procession a bull worthy of the god, which they also sacrificed in the precinct during the Procession.

12. Alciphron, *Letters* 4.18.16. A fictional letter by "Menander" written 2nd or 3rd c. The use of the word *eschara* again shows that the altar of Dionysus is that in the Academy.

May I always be able to garland my head with Attic ivy and sing hymns every year at the altar (*eschara*) of Dionysus.

13. Philostratus, *Lives of the Sophists* 549. Written in the second or third decade of the 3rd c. Herodes was an important Athenian politician and sophist who lived ca. 101–77.

Whenever the Dionysia came around and the icon of Dionysus went down to the Academy, <Herodes Atticus> would supply wine to citizens and foreigners alike while they lay on couches of ivy.

The Festival

14. Oracles of Delphi and Dodona in Demosthenes, *Against Meidias* 51–54. Written 348–346 B.C.; the date of the oracles is unknown. Bacchos and Bromios are cult titles of Dionysus.

> Of course you know that you do all these dances and hymns for the god not only according to the customs that govern the Dionysia, but also by oracular decree: in all the oracles, those of Delphi and Dodona alike, you will find that the city is commanded to perform dance with song according to ancestral custom and to fill the streets with the smoke of sacrifices and to wear garlands. Read me these oracles. (The court clerk reads the oracle of Apollo at Delphi:) "I say to the children of Erechtheus who inhabit the town of Pandion (i.e., Athens) and regulate festivals by ancestral custom, to be mindful of Bacchos, and to give thanks to Bromios all together in the wide streets, and to make smoke rise from the altars and to tie your head with garlands...." (Oracle of Zeus at Dodona:) "The prophet of Zeus in Dodona commands that you make public sacrifices and mix craters of wine and perform dance with song, that you sacrifice an ox to Apollo the Warder of Evil, and that free men and slaves put on garlands and keep holiday for one day. To Zeus the Protector of House and Property sacrifice a white ox."

15. Law of Euegoros in Demosthenes, *Against Meidias* 10. The speech was written 346 B.C.; the date of the law is unknown.

> Euegoros moved: whenever there is the procession for Dionysus in Piraeus and comedy and tragedy, whenever there is the procession at the Lenaion and tragedy and comedy, whenever there is at the City Dionysia the procession and the boys' <dithyramb> and the *komos* and comedy and tragedy, and whenever there is the procession and contest at the Thargelia, may it not be permitted to take security or to arrest another, not even those past due in their payments during these days. If anyone violates any of these regulations, let him be liable to prosecution by the injured party and let charges be brought against him in the Assembly held in the precinct of Dionysus as a wrongdoer, just as has been decreed in respect to other wrongdoers.

16A. Demosthenes, *Against Androtion* 68. Date: 355 B.C.

> He asks if the prison was built for nothing. I would say so, since your father escaped from it after dancing in the procession of the Dionysia wearing his chains.

16B. Scholion to Demosthenes, *Against Androtion* 68.

It was customary in Athens to release prisoners from jail for the duration of the Dionysia and the Panathenaea upon bail.

The Procession (Pompe)

17. Aristotle, *Constitution of the Athenians* 56.4. Written ca. 330 B.C.

<The Archon Eponymous> is in charge... of the procession of the Great Dionysia along with his Overseers, who, ten in number, used to be elected by the people and used to pay the cost of the procession from their own pockets, but now the people appoint them by lot, one from each tribe, and give them ten thousand drachmas for the expense.

18. *IG* II² 1496.80f. and 111f. These accounts of the Treasurers of Athena and the Overseers record money received from the sale of hides of animals sacrificed at public festivals. The first of our entries dates to 333 B.C., the second to 332 B.C. It has been calculated, based on an estimated 3–4.5 drachmas per hide, that 240 animals were sacrificed during the Dionysia of 333 B.C. Another estimate of 7.6 drachmas per hide gives only 106 animals. The hides sold may not reflect the actual numbers sacrificed.

<Received> from the City Dionysia from the Cattle-Purchasers: 808 drachmas, 4 obols

... <Received> from the City Dionysia from the generals: 306 drachmas.

19. Scholion to Aristophanes, *Acharnians* 241.

At the festival of the Dionysia at Athens, maidens of aristocratic families carried the basket. The baskets were made of gold. In them they placed the "first fruits."

20A. Pollux 6.75. Written ca. 170.

Obeliai are loaves of bread that the so-called *obeliaphoroi* carried to the sanctuary of Dionysus. They are of one, two, or three *medimnoi* (= 12, 24, or 36 imperial gallons) in bulk and held together by spits (*obeloi*), whence the name.

20B. Athenaeus 3.111b. Written ca. 200.

The bread is called *obelias* either because it is sold for an obol or cooked on spits... Those who carry them around on their shoulders at processions are called *obeliaphoroi*.

21A. *Suda*, s.v. *askophorein*. Written ca. 1000. Metics are foreign residents of Athens.

In the processions of Dionysus some things are done by the citizens; other things the metics were ordered to do. Metics wore purple gowns and carried basins, whence they were called "basin-bearers." Citizens wore whatever they liked and carried wineskins on their shoulders, whence they were called "wineskin-bearers."

21B. *Suda* s.v. *skaphephoroi.* Demetrius of Phaleron lived from ca. 350 until after 283 B.C.

Demetrius in the third book of *On Legislation* says that the law enjoined metics to carry basins in processions and their daughters to carry water jugs and parasols.

22. Demosthenes, *Against Meidias* 22. Date: 346 B.C.

Demosthenes, for whom I testify, paid me to prepare a golden crown and make a golden *himation* so that he could walk in them in the procession of Dionysus.

23. *IG* I³ 46.11–13. Date: 446/5 B.C. The inscription gives instructions to the Athenian colonists of Brea in Thrace.

To bring an ox and a suit of armor to the Great Panathenaea and a *phallos* to the Dionysia.

24. Plutarch, *On the Love of Wealth* 527d. Written ca. 110. Plutarch implies the absence of masks in the early Dionysia, though, if so, this is unlikely to be more than a guess motivated by his desire to draw a strong contrast between the extravagance of processions in his day and the simplicity of the past.

Our traditional festival of the Dionysia was in former times a homely and merry procession. First came a jug of wine and a vine branch, then one celebrant dragged a he-goat along, another followed with a basket of dried figs, and last came the *phallos*. But nowadays this is disregarded and gone, what with vessels of gold carried past, rich apparel, carriages riding by, and masks.

25. Demosthenes, *On the False Embassy* 287. See II 5.

26. Aristophanes, *Acharnians* 240–65. Produced Lenaea, 425 B.C. The hero of the play, Dikaiopolis, has arranged a separate peace with Sparta, and so can go back to the country and celebrate the rural Dionysia. The procession here described is the prototype for the civic festival.

DIKAIOPOLIS: Keep holy silence; holy silence! The basket bearer, go forward a little! Let Xanthias (the slave) stand the *phallos* upright! Put down the basket, daughter, so that we may begin the sacrifice! DAUGHTER: Mother, hand me the ladle, so that I can pour soup over the cake here. DIKAIOPOLIS: Well, that's fine. Oh Lord Dionysus, look graciously on me, as I make this procession and sacrifice; may I with my household celebrate in all good fortune the Dionysia in the country, free of campaigning, and may the thirty-year treaty (which he has privately concluded with the Spartans) bring me good luck. Come daughter, see that you carry the basket nicely with a savory-eating look in your eye . . . Forward, (to daughter) and in the mob take good care that no one unnoticed nibbles off your gold things! Xanthias, it's the job of you two to hold the *phallos* upright behind the basket carrier. I shall follow and sing the phallic song. You, wife, look at me from the roof! Advance! (He sings) Phales, comrade of Bacchos, companion-reveler, night wanderer, adulterer, boylover.

27. Xenophon, *Hipparchikos* 3.2. Written ca. 388–355 B.C.

I think that the processions would be most pleasing to the gods and spectators alike if, starting from the Herms (in the Athenian marketplace), one rode around to all the shrines and cult statues in a circle honoring the gods. Indeed the choruses at the Dionysia pay their respects to the other gods and the twelve with their dancing.

Dithyrambic Contest

28. Scholion to Aeschines, *Against Timarchus* 10. It was once argued on the basis of considerations of timing and the ambiguity of this scholion that each tribe provided only one dithyrambic chorus, men's or boys', but 29 and 30 are clear evidence against this.

By custom the Athenians put on choruses of fifty boys or fifty men for each tribe, so that there were ten choruses, since there were also ten tribes. The dithyrambs are called "circular choruses" and the "circular chorus." . . . in circular choruses the piper stood in the middle.

29. *IG* II² 2318.320–24. *Fasti* for the year 333/2 B.C. Cf. *IG* II² 3061, where the same tribe also wins both events.

In the archonship] of Ni[kokrates
<the tribe> Kekrop[is <won the dithyramb> for boys
Diophantos of Halai was *choregos*
<the tribe> Kekropis[<won the dithyramb> for men
Onetor [was *choregos*

30. *Hesperia* 37 (1968) no. 51, frr. a–b, col. 2, 1–24. An inscription listing dedications of silver vessels (*phialai*). Date: 331/0 B.C. The inscription seems to indicate the existence of a law requiring all liturgists to

dedicate a vessel on the termination of their liturgy (IIIAiia). Eight names are listed in traditional tribal order (as shown by the deme names) under the heading for boys' dithyramb. This leaves no doubt that there were normally ten men's and ten boys' dithyrambs. We must assume that the winner was exempt, since he dedicated a tripod, and that a *choregos* could not be found for one of the tribes for the Dionysia of 330 B.C. (cf. 84). Another fragment of the inscription contains dedications of silver vessels by tragic *choregoi*.

[These dedicated vessels for litur]gies in the archonship of A[ristophanes]

for b[oys'] dithyrambs
Sosistr[atos - - - -]
of the deme Euonym[on, weight: 50 drachmas]
Thymokles [- - - - -]
of the deme Prasia[i, weight: 50 drachmas]
Aischylos [son of Hippiskos]
of the deme Paionida[i, weight: 50 drachmas]
Polyarato[s son of Periander
of the deme Cholargos, w[eight: 50 drachmas]
Theophilos son of Tr[- - - -]
of the deme Athmonon, we[ight: 50 drachmas]
Philokrates son of Ph[- - - -]
[of the deme O]inoe, weig[ht: 50 drachmas]
[Ka]llikrates son of Ar[istokrates]
[of the deme Aph]idna, we[ight: 50 drachmas]
[Le]ptines son of Olym[p- - - -]
[of the deme Alo]peke, wei[ght: 50 drachmas]
[for men]s'
[. . . .]as son of Ariston[- -]
[of the deme ?], weigh[t: 50 drachmas]
[Lysik]les son of Lysiade[s]
[of the deme Leukon]oion, weig[ht: 50 drachmas]
[- - - - -]es [.]tin[- - -]

31. Demosthenes, *Against Meidias* 63. Date: 346 B.C.
    Although they say Iphikrates was a most hated enemy of Diokles of Pitthos, and in addition to this it happened that Teisias the brother of Iphikrates was a rival *choregos* of Diokles.... they had to endure seeing him win and being crowned.

32. Demosthenes, *Against Meidias* 5–6. Demosthenes was *choregos* of the tribe Pandionis for the dithyramb at the Great Dionysia of 346 B.C.

Since this man corrupted the judges and because of this the tribe was wrongfully deprived of its tripod, and I myself was subjected to blows and was outraged as no other *choregos* I know of.

Ceremonies Preceding the Dramatic Competitions

33. *Suda,* s.v. *katharsion.* Written ca. 1000.

The Athenians were accustomed to purify the Assembly and the theaters and practically all gatherings of the people by sacrificing very small piglets, which they called "purificatory." This the so called *peristiarchoi* do, whose name comes either from lustration (*peristichein*) or from the hearth (*hestia*).

34. Plutarch, *Cimon* 8.7. See 112.

35A. Isocrates, *On the Peace* 82. Written in 356 B.C. Isocrates speaks of the Athenians of 454–404 B.C.

They so precisely found the means by which men can best inspire enmity that they voted to divide the incoming public revenues into talents and bring them into the orchestra during the Dionysia when the theater was full. This they did and they brought the orphans of the men who died in the war, making a display at once both to the allies of the extent of their wealth that these mercenaries had carried off, and to the other Greeks of the great number of orphans and the suffering caused by this lust for wealth.

35B. Scholion to Aristophanes, *Acharnians* 504.

It was decreed that the <subject> cities should bring the tributes to Athens at the Dionysia, as Eupolis says in *Cities* (422 B.C.).

36A. Aeschines, *Against Ktesiphon* 41–43. Delivered 330 B.C. Aeschines explains why a law was passed regulating proclamations in the theater. He seems to indicate that the proclamation of crowns (to honor distinguished citizens and foreigners) was restricted to meetings of the legislative assembly, but, if so, there were certainly exceptions to this rule, which in any case, could only have been short-lived, since inscriptions dating throughout the 4th c. B.C. require the proclamation of crowns in the Theater of Dionysus.

At the time of the tragic performances in the city, people would make proclamations without the approval of the Assembly: that so-and-so was being crowned by his tribe and others by the townships; others called upon the Greeks to witness that they were freeing their slaves; most presumptuous were the proclamations engineered by people who acquired ambassador status (*proxenia*) in foreign cities, that the people of Rhodes or Chios or whatever other city was crowning them, if such was the case, on account of their virtue and rectitude.

36B. Aeschines, *Against Ktesiphon* 153–54.

Suppose for a little while that you are not in the court but in the theater. Imagine that you see the herald approaching and that the proclamation of <Ktesiphon's> decree <that Demosthenes should be crowned> is about to take place. Now consider whether you think the relatives of those who died (sc., at the battle of Chaeronea in 338 B.C.) would shed more tears for the tragedies and heroic sufferings that will come on after this, or for the insensitivity of the city. What Greek, what man who has had the benefit of a free man's education, would not be pained, if for nothing else, then at the thought that once on a day like today before the performance of the tragedies, at a time when the city was governed by better men, the public herald, bringing alongside the orphans, young sons dressed in armor of those men who died in the war, came forward and made the most noble and most inspiring proclamation, that the people brought up these young men whose fathers died as brave men in the war, and that now the people presented them with a suit of armor and left them with good wishes to follow their own fortunes and now also invited them to take front-row seats (*prohedria*)? In those days this is what the herald announced, but not now. Instead he brings alongside the man who made the children orphans and what will he say, what words will he utter? If he follows the instructions of this decree—but the shameful truth will not be silent! It will seem to contradict the herald's voice that the people crown this man, if this is a man, for his virtue, this coward for his bravery, this wimp and deserter. I beg you, Athenians, do not erect in the orchestra of Dionysus a victory monument built from your own spoils, do not convict the people of Athens of madness in front of all Greece.

37. Demosthenes, *On the Crown* 120. Delivered 330 B.C.

But by the gods are you so stupid and insensitive, Aeschines, that you are unable to perceive that the crown gives the same joy to the person crowned wherever it is proclaimed, but that the proclamation is made in the theater for the benefit of those who confer it? This is because all the audience is encouraged to do service to the city, and they applaud the gratitude of the giver more than the receiver. This is why the city made this law.

The Dramatic Contests

38. Aristides, *On Rhetoric* 2. Written 2nd c.

For tragedians and kithara players and other musicians being best and performing first is not the same thing, otherwise it would suffice just to take lots, but the best contestant is crowned and proclaimed as the first, even if he happened to perform last.

39. Aristophanes, *Birds* 786–89. Produced Dionysia, 414 B.C. The word here translated as "brunch" is misleading, since our terms "break-fast," "lunch," and "supper" imply mealtimes, whereas the Greek equivalents have more to do with levels of formality, the evening meal being the only formal shared meal, and the one or two earlier meals being more like snacks. The *ariston* was normally taken at a pause after the morning's work, and if one can speak of normal times, they differed greatly from country to city and from workday to holiday. The passage is taken from the *parabasis,* where the chorus addresses the audience in the double persona of birds and choreuts.

If any of you spectators had wings, then, when he was feeling hunger pangs during the tragic choruses, he could fly off home to have brunch and then return with a full stomach to us (the comic choruses).

40. Pollux 4.88. Written ca. 170 and referring to an event in the last quarter of the 5th c. B.C.

Hermon was a comic actor. As he was scheduled by lot to perform after several others, he was absent from the theater exercising his voice. Because all the other performers were booed out of the theater, the herald called upon Hermon, but the latter did not come forward and incurred a fine. From that time on they introduced the performers by trumpet.

41. *IGUR* 216 (= *IG* XIV 1097). A fragment of the Roman *Fasti.* The inscription shows that five comedies were produced at the City Dionysia before the Peloponnesian War, 431–404 B.C. The hypotheses to plays of Aristophanes produced during the war mention only three prizes. Yet 42 seems to indicate that, if the number of comedies was reduced, it did not remain so for the duration of the war.

]In the archonship of Antiochides (434 B.C.) with the *Cy[clops*
]s with a comedy fourth prize in the c[ity
. . .
with the *Frog]s* fifth prize in the archonship of Antiochides[

42. *POxy* 2737, fr. 1, col. ii, 1–17. See 71.

43. Fourth Hypothesis to Aristophanes, *Plutus*. It is not said whether the *Plutus* was produced at the Dionysia or the Lenaea, but it appears that five comedies were the norm in either festival after the Peloponnesian War (see 77).

It was performed in the archonship of Antipatros (388 B.C.) in competition with Nikochares with the *Lakonians*, Aristomenes with the *Admetos*, Nicophon with the *Adonis,* and Alcaeus with the *Pasiphae.*

44. *IG* II² 2323a. See IV 14.

45. The "Parian Marble," *FGrH* 239.54–55, 58, and 61. The Parian Marble is a chronology of major political and literary events compiled and inscribed in 264/3 B.C. The first event, probably fictitious, can be dated by its position on the stone to between 580–560 B.C., the second to ca. 534 B.C., the third to the archon year of 509/8 B.C. The "chorus of men" appears to be men's dithyramb. The date 508 B.C. would associate the introduction of the contest with the democratic reforms (508/7 B.C.) after the fall of the Pisistratids, though the Cleisthenic constitution was probably not instituted until ca. 503 B.C. Note that the *Fasti* begin about this time (I 100).

From the time when in Ath[en]s a com[ic cho]r[us was est]ablished, the people of Ikarion being the fi[rst to pro]duce it, Sousarion inventing it, and the first prize was established as a basket of dried figs and 40 liters of wine... [two hundred years and... years have elapsed and the archon was...]

From the time when Thespis the poet first [act]ed, who produced a [dr]a[ma in the c]it[y], and the goat was established as the [prize], 250 [plus ??] years have elapsed, the archon in Ath[ens be]ing...]naios, the Elder.

From the time when the choruses of men first competed, when Hypo[di]kos the Chalcidian won, 236 years have passed, the archon in Athens being Lysagoras.

46. *Suda,* s.v. *Chionides.* Written ca. 1000. The word translated as "the originator" (*protagonisten*) may conceivably mean "the principal actor," in which case the introduction of comedy to the Dionysia would have been before 486 B.C.

Chionides: Athenian, writer of Old Comedy, whom they also say was the originator of Old Comedy and produced eight years before the Persian Wars (i.e., eight years before 480 B.C. by the usual inclusive reckoning gives 486 B.C.).

IIIAib. The Lenaea, Rural Dionysia, and Anthesteria

In Attica and Athens, each of the four winter months included a Dionysian festival. Our sources give the impression that all the rural festivals of Dionysus took place in the month of Posideion, roughly our December (47, 48, 49G, 49H). They did not all take place on the same days in Posideion, however, since Plato's theater addicts go from one to another without "missing a single one" (I 21). Plato's claim may be exaggerated, but possibly some attempt was made to coordinate festival calendars (such as we find in Hellenistic times; see IIIB). The middle of the following month, Gamelion, our late January, was given to the celebration of the Lenaea at Athens. One month later the Anthesteria was celebrated from the 11th to the 13th Anthesterion, and precisely one month after that Athens was celebrating the Great Dionysia. By the late classical period all of these festivals included dramatic contests.

The ancients most readily associated phallic processions with the rural Dionysia (24, 26), though it is unlikely that they ever surpassed the phallic procession of the Great Dionysia in magnitude and splendor. The processions had a relatively greater importance to the rural festivals and there was, perhaps, a feeling, that in the country the procession was more in its rustic element. The phallic procession was probably the only common denominator; at a guess most demes had little more to offer. The later tradition has many murky references to contests involving dancing on greased wineskins; the reader will be grateful to have to seek these elsewhere. Direct evidence for drama comes from only thirteen demes (49–60); others doubtless existed. The thirteen include the largest demes, Piraeus (49), Akharnai (54), Eleusis (52), and Salamis (55), as well as the deme of Kollytos, located inside the walls of Athens itself (53). Ikarion (50) is prominent as an important cult center for Dionysus because of its legendary connections with the first introduction of wine in Attica. The central government in Athens took a direct interest in the management of the Dionysia at Piraeus (49A, B, D–F, H), which far surpassed that of other demes: it included both the parades familiar from the Athenian Dionysia, an "Introduction," and a "Procession" (49B–E), ending in sacrifices nearly half as voluminous as those of the Great Dionysia (compare 49D and 18), followed by both tragedy and comedy (49B), to which dithyrambs were added by the late 4th c. B.C. (49H), and, in the late 2nd c. B.C. at least, apparently lasting four days (49E). The full slate of dithyramb, tragedy, and comedy are otherwise known only from Eleusis (52A–C) and possibly Akharnai (54); both tragedy and comedy were performed at Thorikos (50bis C, D), Kollytos (53), and possibly Ikarion (50A–C, F, G); dithyramb and (much later) tragedy are attested at Salamis (55), tragedy only in Paiania (57), comedy only in Aixone (51A), Rhamnous (56), and Anagyros (59). There is little evidence for the actual number of performances within each genre: the evidence consistently shows that the performances were part of a competition, we can safely assume a minimum of two performances in each genre, and the Ikarian decree shows a total of only two tragedies (50A). Beyond this we hear only of three dithyrambs competing in Piraeus in the later 4th c. B.C.

The choregic monuments show that *synchoregia* was very common at the rural festivals (i.e., the sharing of production costs by two or more *choregoi,* see III 108). Of the twenty-two choregic offices attested (50–59), there are ten instances of *synchoregia,* two of which are shared by three *choregoi* (50C, E), with several demes showing great flexibility in the practice (esp. 50). Otherwise the rules for the *choregia* appear to have been the same as in Athens, except in perhaps one other respect. It is not entirely clear whether foreign residents (metics) were called upon to serve as *choregoi,* an office from which they were debarred at the Great Dionysia (72). The decree from Ikarion (50A) distinguishes demesmen and residents, though this may mean resident citizens of Attica who are not citizens of the deme. 52B is a certain instance of a metic *choregos,* but this case may well have been exceptional. Note that the demotic *choregia* outlived the abolition of the institution in Athens ca. 317 B.C. (29). Literary sources sometimes treat the deme festivals as third-rate entertainments (53A, B; I 20), but both literary and epigraphical sources show the presence of first-rate competitors (49G; 50bis C, E; 52A, 53C, 54A, 55A).

Of the Lenaean festival we know little. There was a parade, supervised by the archon, named "king archon," who took over many of the religious duties of the prehistoric monarchy (61); unlike the Great Dionysia, the Lenaean festival was a very old institution; it was common to the Ionians, who migrated from Attica around 1,000 B.C. Our comprehension of the character of the festival would be greatly enhanced if it could be proved that the so-called Lenaean vases actually referred to the Lenaea and not the Anthesteria (see II 7). What little information we do have points to the release from inhibition characteristic of Dionysiac festivals; at any rate the procession seems to have involved ritual abuse, unless the scholia and late lexicographers are confusing Lenaea and Anthesteria (62). Indeed, the confusion of Lenaea and Anthesteria is not limited to late antiquity. On the evidence of 67, many modern scholars have argued that the Lenaion, where the Lenaea was celebrated, and the sanctuary "in the marshes," where the Anthesteria was celebrated, were one and the same. Apart from the improbability of having two names for a single sanctuary, each invariably associated with a different festival, we are explicitly told in the speech *Against Neaira* that the temple in the "Dionysion in the marshes" was open only for a single day in the year, the evening of the Festival of the Cups, and it seems inconceivable that the Lenaea would be held at a sanctuary where the temple remained locked. All the surviving testimony, albeit late and perhaps unreliable, assigns the Lenaean contests to a location in the Athenian marketplace for the period before the construction of the Theater of Dionysus, and to the Theater of Dionysus afterward (63–66). At any rate, the Lenaean performances must have moved to the Theater of Dionysus by ca. 440 B.C., when the state established a formal contest for *choregoi* and poets (68). Plato writes of an audience of thirty thousand at the Lenaea of 416 B.C (70); the Theater of Dionysus was the only venue in Athens that could accommodate a crowd even a half or a quarter of that size. Unlike the Great Dionysia, the Lenaea is generally characterized as a purely Attic affair, as we would expect at a midwinter festival (69, 71), though Plato exceptionally, perhaps rhetorically, stresses the international character of the audience, calling it "Greek" not "Athenian" (70). The relatively less cosmopolitan character of the Lenaea seems to be reflected in the relaxation of restrictions on noncitizen *choregoi* and choreuts (72, 73—since the propaganda of pure Attic content seems directed at an international audience) and in its lower status as a competition (71). The *Didaskaliai* show that tragic poets competed with only two tragedies (74, 75). Less clear is the number of tragic competitors: the *Didaskaliai* show two tragic poets in 418 B.C. and three in 363 B.C. and it is impossible to know which represents the norm. The hypotheses to Aristophanes' Lenaean plays, like those for the Dionysian plays, name only three comedies (76, cf. 44). The only other evidence for the comic competition, the *Didaskaliai,* shows five comedies produced in 284 B.C. (77). There is no better evidence than this for the usual handbook dogma that five comedies were regularly produced at the Lenaea except during the Peloponnesian War (the years covered by the hypotheses in 76). The *Didaskaliai* (75) and the Law of Euegoros (49B) mention no satyrplay or dithyrambs and it is generally inferred that they were not included at least in the classical period: there is inscriptional evidence for dithyramb at the Lenaea in the 3rd c. B.C. For drama at the Anthesteria the evidence is slim (78–81). It is less likely that dramatic competitions took place there earlier than the late 4th c. B.C., died out, and then were revived by Lycurgus, as 78 implies; if the sources are at all reliable, the dramatic competitions were probably a Lycurgan (ca. 330 B.C.) or later innovation.

Sources

Rural Dionysia

47. Theophrastus, *Characters* 3.5, "The Chatterbox." Probably Written ca. 319 B.C. The chatterbox is characterized by his excessive fondness for relating trivia, truisms, and clichés. The scholiast to Plato's *Republic* 475d, the scholiast to Aeschines' *Against Timarchus* 43, and a grammarian in Bekker's *Anecdota Graeca* all flatly state that the Rural Dionysia are in Posideion.

> The chatterbox is the sort of man who (says)...That the mysteries are in Boedromion, the Apatouria in Pyanopsion, and the Rural Dionysia in Posideion.

48. *IG* II² 1183.36f. This inscription contains regulations governing the handling of public money in the deme of Myrrhinous. Date: after 340 B.C. As at Athens (49B), the special meeting of the Assembly probably follows immediately after the festival.

> ...on the nineteenth of the month of Posideion they are to conduct business concerning the Dionysia.

49A. **Dionysia in Piraeus.** Aristotle, *Constitution of the Athenians* 54.8. Written ca. 330 B.C.

> They also choose the archon for Salamis by lot and the mayor for Piraeus, who look after the Dionysia in either place and appoint the *choregoi*. In Salamis the name of the archon is also recorded (on public documents, cf. 55B).

49B. **Law of Euegoros. See 15.**

49C. *IG* II² 380. Decree of Piraeus. Date: 320/19 B.C.

Let the market inspectors (*agoranomoi*) see to it that the broad streets on which pass the processions for Zeus Soter and Dionysus be leveled and prepared as well as possible.

49D. *IG* II² 1496.70. This series of inscribed stelae gives the accounts of the treasurers of Athena at Athens for 334/3 to 331/0 B.C. The accounts list money received from the sale of the hides of sacrificed animals and follow the order of expenditures. Cf. 18.

(Posideion, 334/3 B.C.) From the Dionysia in Piraeus from the cattle purchasers: 311 drachmas.

49E. *SEG* 15.104.25f. One of a large number of decrees from the late 2nd c. B.C. onward honoring the ephebes in part for their service in the "introduction" and "procession" of Dionysus both in Athens and in Piraeus (cf. 11). Date: 127/6 B.C.

<the ephebes> also sacrificed to Dionysus for the people of Piraeus and they introduced the god (*eisagoge*) and had an orderly sojourn in Piraeus for four days.

49F. *IG* II² 456. A decree by the Assembly in Athens awarding a long list of honors to the people of Kolophon for remaining faithful to Athens, their "mother city." Date: 307/6 B.C. For the *architekton*, see IVBi.

... and that the theater manager (*architekton*) give the <ambassadors of Kolophon> a seat at the Dionysia in Piraeus.

49G. Aelian, *Varia Historia* 2.13. Written late 2nd or early 3rd c. The event is supposed to have taken place in the late 5th c. B.C.

Socrates frequently attended the theaters, especially when Euripides the tragic poet was competing with new tragedies. And when Euripides was competing at the Piraeus, he even went down there.

49H. Pseudo-Plutarch, *Ten Orators* 842a. The author lists various pieces of legislation introduced by Lycurgus, a prominent Athenian politician, ca. 338–326 B.C.

... and to hold a contest of no less than three dithyrambic choruses in the Piraeus in the month of Posideion and to give the winners one thousand drachmas, those judged second eight hundred, and those judged third six hundred.

50A. Dionysia in Ikarion. *IG* I³ 254. Decree of Ikarion. Date: 440 to ca. 415 B.C. Though the decree envisions a pair of *choregoi*, each competing with one (?) tragedy, the other inscriptions from Ikarion show great flexibility in dividing a single *choregia* between one, two, or three *choregoi*.

This stele [is sacred to Dionysus]. The people of Ikarion have decreed; Menest[ratos proposed. The people of Ikarion will choose two] from the demesmen and from the residents of Ikarion who have not yet served as *choregoi,* whichever two should [...], exchange of pr[operty (*antidosis*) should take place before] the mayor within twenty days [... if there is no] exchange the may[or ... the] two *choregoi* should reveal (or give an inventory?) thrice (or in front of three witnesses) [... and these two] are to enroll tr]agic chorusmen from the [...] and the *choregoi* are to swear that they have not [...] within ten days if there is no denial by oath [... they are to put their hands upon?] the (cult) statue [before] the mayor and the [mayor to administer to] them the oath [... to those] managing a chorus for the first time not to [...] fifteen [...] whenever the year [...] send away if not [...] or pay a fine of fi[ve...] to the tragic chorusmen the cho[... fif]teen men each... (there follow twenty-six very fragmentary lines).

50B. *IG* II^2 3094. Inscribed block found in Ikarion. Date: beginning of 4th c. B.C. Aristophanes had a son, also a comic poet, named Nikostratos, but there is also a dithyrambic poet of that name.

[A]rchippos son of Archede[ktos], victorious, set this up for Dionysus. Nikostratos was *didaskalos.*

50C. *IG* II^2 3095. Inscribed marble statue base found in Ikarion dedicated by a father and two sons. Date: before the middle of the 4th c. B.C.

Ergasos, son of Phanomachos; Phanomachos, son of Ergasos; Diognetos, son of Ergasos; victorious when they served as *choregoi* in tragedy, set this up.

50D. *IG* II^2 1178. Honorary decree. Date: before the middle of the 4th c. B.C.

Kallippos proposed. The people of Ikarion voted to honor Nikon the mayor and crown him with a crown of ivy and have the herald proclaim that the people of Ikarion are crowning Nikon and that the deme of Ikarion crowns its mayor, because he conducted the festival and the contest for Dionysus well and justly, and to honor the *choregoi* Epikrates and Praxias and crown them with a crown of ivy and make a proclamation as for the mayor.

50E. *IG* II^2 3098. Inscription on a small shrine found at Ikarion. Date: middle of the 4th c. B.C.

Hagnias, Xanthippos, Xanthides, victorious, set this up.

50F. *IG* II² 3099. Inscribed marble slab. Date: mid-4th c. B.C.
Mnesilochos, son of Mnesiphilos, won as *choregos* in tragedy.

50G. *SEG* 22.117. An honorary decree. Date: ca. 330 B.C.

> [The people of Ikarion decreed: since - - - aios, son of Sos]igenes
> of Ikarion sacrificed the victims to all the gods [as is the local custom
> and looked after everything else] well and zealously, etc.... [to
> praise - - -]aios and crown him with a golden crown worth 10
> drachmas for his virtue and justice toward the demesmen... and
> to proclaim the crown at the tragic performances at the Dionysia.

50^{bis}A. **Dionysia in Thorikos.** *Thorikos* VIII, no. 75. Decree of the
deme of Thorikos. Date: end of 5th c. to beginning of 4th c. B.C. The
reference to three *choregiai* is intriguing. Since there is no evidence for
dithyramb in Thorikos, it may indicate that there were three tragedies
or three comedies, and that only one genre is being discussed here.

> G]ods! Lysippides was ma[yor? and] put it to the vot[e. It was
> decreed by the people of Thori]kos. Teleas m[ade the motion to
> assign the?] three choregia[i to those who make the lar]gest offers
> - [- - - not] less than thr[

50^{bis}B. *Thorikos* IX, no. 85. Dedicatory verse inscription found at
Thorikos. Date: ca. 400–350 B.C.

> T]his Py[- - -
> he was *choregos* [- - -
> having pray[ed - - -
> You in return?[- - -
> a fine[- - -

50^{bis}C. *Thorikos* VIII, no. 76. Dedicatory inscription on a statue base
found in the theater at Thorikos. Date: 375–325 B.C. If the restoration
is correct, the inscription may refer to Theodoros, one of the most
celebrated actors of the 4th c. B.C. (92; I 8A; IV 20, 21, 32). Note that
in this inscription, and in the two that follow, comedy is listed before
tragedy, presumably following the order of events at the local Dionysia.

> D]emocharides for comedy, [Sp]eusiades was actor; [De]mochares
> for tragedy, [The?]odoros was actor; [...]ades for comedy, [...]
> was actor. [Having served as *choreg]oi,* they made this dedication.

50^{bis}D. *Thorikos* IX, no. 83. Decree of the deme of Thorikos. Date:
4th c. B.C.

> - - -]was *choregos*[- - -
> - - -]of the *choregia* Tho[rikos?- - -
> and the] time and for the com[edies- - -
> and for the tr]agedies and that the regis[trars

write up] an official record [- - -
- - -] Ameipsias Mnes[i- - -
these men were *cho]regoi*- - -
- - -]of Lidos Mnesi[- - -
- - -]os son of Dorokle[s- - -

50^bisE. *Thorikos* IX, no. 84. A marble stele found in the theater of Thorikos. Date: 4th c. B.C. The list would seem to record the winners of an actors' competition. The name Pindaros may be that of the actor criticized by Aristotle (IV 60). If so, then the list seems to give the victorious comic actor, followed by the victorious tragic actor.

When so-and-so was mayor]: Pindaros, son of Proteas. When Epeusthenes was mayor: Diphilos, son of Astyphilos; Diotimos, son of Hermod[. . .]. When Mikinos was mayor: Polykrates, son of Polykrates; Polystratos, son of Polykrates.

51A. Dionysia in Aixone. Mette, *Urkunden* 136. This decree by the Attic deme of Aixone is dated to the archonship of Theophrastos, but two archons of this name are known, in 340/39 B.C. and 313/2 B.C., and the date is disputed. Another honorary decree proposed by Glaukides and dated to Theophrastos' archonship is known: here also two demesmen receive crowns to be announced during the Dionysia at the time of the comedies (*IG* II² 1202). In demes where honorary decrees call for proclamations "at the comic contest," it seems a reasonable assumption that no tragedy was performed. See also I 104.

G]laukides, son of Sosi[pp]os, moved that, since the *choregoi* Aut[ea]s, son of Autokles, and Philoxenides, son of Philip, performed their task as *choregoi* well and zealously, the demesmen decide: to crown them each with a golden crown worth one hundred drachmas in the theater at the time of the comedies that take place after the archonship of Theophrastos, so that future *choregoi* will perform their tasks with zeal; that the mayor Hegesileon and the treasurers give them ten drachmas for a sacrifice; that the treasurers also have this decree written on a stone stele and set up in the theater so that the demesmen of Aixone always produce the best possible Dionysia.

51B. *IG* II² 1198. An honorary decree. Date 326/5 B.C. The wording is nearly identical to *IG* II² 1200, another decree honoring two choregoi in 317/6 B.C.

Phil]oktemon, son of Chremes, proposed: since the *choregoi* appointed under the archonship of Chremes, Demokrates, son of Euphiletos, and Hegesias, son of Lysistratos, performed their *cho-*

regia for the people of Aixone well and zealously, we should honor them and crown them . . . etc.

52A. Dionysia in Eleusis. *IG* II² 3090. A statue base found at Eleusis. Date: last decade of 5th c. B.C. The inscription generally used to be interpreted as referring to two victories by Eleusinians at the City Dionysia, but Capps studied the spacing on the fragments of the *Fasti* (I 100) and found room for only one *synchoregia* in 406/5 B.C. (108, 109). It is now generally interpreted as referring to the Eleusinian Dionysia. The use of the term *didaskalos* should indicate that Sophocles and Aristophanes directed their own works at Eleusis.

> G]nathis, son of Timokedes, Anaxandrides, son of Timagoros, were victorious as *choregoi* for comedy. Aristophanes was *didaskalos*. <They had> another victory in tragedy; Sophocles was *didaskalos*.

52B. *IG* II² 1186. An honorary decree of the Attic deme of Eleusis. Date: mid-4th c. B.C.

> K]al[li]machos, son of Kallikrates, spoke. Whereas Damasias of Thebes, son of Dionysios, has settled in Eleusis and always led an exemplary life, well disposed to all inhabitants of the deme, both he himself and his students, and since, during the Eleusinians' celebration of the Dionysia, he showed commitment and zeal, toward the gods, the people of Athens, and those of Eleusis, that the Dionysia be the best possible and, equipping two choruses at his own expense, one for boys and one for men, he voluntarily offered them to Demeter and Kore and Dionysus: may it please the people of Eleusis to praise Damasias the Theban, son of Dionysios, for his virtue and piety toward the goddesses and crown him with a golden crown worth ten drachmas. May the mayor who takes office after Gnathis announce at the tragedies during the Dionysia at Eleusis that the deme of Eleusis crowns Damasias.

52C. *IG* II² 3100. Inscribed base found in Eleusis. Date: mid-4th c. B.C.

> Athenodoros, son of Go[- - - was victorious] as *choregos* in comedy.

52D. *IG* II² 3107. Inscribed base found in Eleusis. Date: 4th c. B.C.

> As *chore[gos* in - - -] Hieron, son of - - -, v[ictorious, set this up.

53A. Dionysia in Kollytos. Demosthenes, *On the Crown* 180. Delivered in 330 B.C. Demosthenes ridicules Aeschines not only for being a tritagonist but also for playing the circuit of the Rural Dionysia—see also IV 165—but note that the deme of Kollytos where Aeschines is said to have fallen disgracefully and thus gained the appellation "clod-hopping Oenomaus" (242) is hardly rustic. Kollytos is located within the city walls of Athens, not more than five minutes' walk from the Athenian acropolis, and its Dionysia was very likely conducted in the Theater of Dionysus. The date of Aeschines' performance must be ca. 370–360 B.C.

> What role would you have me assign to you and what to myself on that day? Would you have me be "Battalos," as you call me when you abuse and ridicule me, and yourself, not any old hero, but one of those from the stage, Kresphontes or Kreon or Oenomaus whom you once made hash of in Kollytos.

53B. Demochares, *FGrH* 75 F 6a, in *Life of Aeschines* 7. Demochares (ca. 360–275 B.C.) is also cited by several other later sources. Hesychius adds that the *Oenomaus* in question was by Sophocles. For Sannion cf. 107.

> Demochares, the nephew of Demosthenes, if he is to be trusted when he speaks about Aeschines, says that Aeschines was the tritagonist of the tragedian Ischandros and that when he was acting the part of Oenomaus chasing Pelops he fell disgracefully and was helped to his feet by Sannion the chorus director—this is why Demosthenes calls him Oenomaus, mocking him before an audience well aware of the fact—and he wandered the countryside with Sokrates and Simylos the ham actors. From this he is called a "clod-hopper."

53C. Aeschines, *Against Timarchus* 157. Delivered 346 B.C. The speech is a prosecution, for political motives, against an associate of Demosthenes on the grounds that he had prostituted his body and was therefore to be deprived by law of his citizen rights. Aeschines contrasts Timarchus with citizens of good character so that the judges "can assign him his proper rank." The comic actor Parmenon was a Lenaean victor around midcentury.

> Again <choosing examples> from among the young men and those who are even now still boys, take first the nephew of Iphikrates and son of Teisias of Rhamnous, the namesake of the present defendant. Though he is good-looking, so far is he from disgraceful conduct that the other day during the comic performances at the Rural Dionysia at Kollytos, when Parmenon the actor delivered an anapaestic line to the chorus, in which it was said that there are some big Timarchian catamites, no one understood this to refer to the youth, but everyone thought of you.

54A. Dionysia in Akharnai. *IG* II² 3092. Dedicatory inscription. Date: beginning of 4th c. B.C. Several fragments of the tragedian Dikaiogenes are extant and he is said also to have written dithyrambs; nothing is known of Ariphron or Polychares.

Mnesistratos, son of Misgon; Diopeithes, son of Diodoros, were *choregoi*. [Di]kaiogenes was *didaskalos*. Mnesimachos, son of Mnesistratos; Theotimos, son of Diotimos, were *choregoi*. Ariphron was *didaskalos*. Polychares, son of Komon, was *didaskalos*.

54B. *IG* II² 3106. Dedicatory inscription. Date: 4th c. B.C. No comic poet of the name Speuseades is known.

- - - ?son of Dem]os[t]ratos victorious in the [round] chorus (i.e., dithyramb) and in comedy set this up. Chares of Thebes played the pipes. Speuseades was *didaskalos*.

55A. Dionysia in Salamis. *IG* II² 3093. Dedicatory inscription on base found on Salamis. Date: beginning of 4th c. B.C. Telephanes was one of the most famous pipers of his age (cf. 106).

Diodoros, son of Exekestides, victorious with a boys' chorus. Paideas was the *didaskalos*. Telephanes of Megara was the piper. Philomelos was archon.

55B. *IG* II² 1227. An honorary decree. Date: 131/0 B.C. A proclamation at the (new) tragic contest at the Dionysia in Salamis also appears in *IG* II² 1008 (118/7 B.C.), 1011 (106/5 B.C.), and *SEG* 15.104 (127/6 B.C.).

Theogenes . . . proposed . . . to honor the annual gymnasiarch who held office during the archonship of Ergokles, Theodotos, son of Eustrophos, of Piraeus, and, as is customary, to crown him with a golden crown for his zeal toward the deme of Salamis and to proclaim this crown at the tragedies of the Dionysia in Salamis, when it next occurs.

56A. Dionysia in Rhamnous. *IG* II² 3108. Dedicatory inscription on base of an *exedra* found in Rhamnous. Date: 4th c. B.C.?

- - -] of Rhamnous [set this up being victorious as *choregos*] in comedy.

56B. *IG* II² 3109. Dedicatory inscription on statue base inside the small temple of Nemesis at Rhamnous. Date: beginning of 3rd c. B.C.

Megakles, son of Megakles, of Rhamnous, set this up for Themis when he was crowned by his demesmen for his justice during the priestessship of Kallisto and when he was victorious serving as gymnasiarch for men and boys and when he was *choregos* in comedy.

57. Dionysia in Paiania. *IG* II² 3097. Dedicatory inscription found in Paiania. Date: mid-4th c. B.C. This Demosthenes may be a relative of the famous orator, who was also from Paiania.

De]mosthenes, son of D[emainet]os, of Paiania was victorious as ch[orego]s in [t]ragedy.

58. **Dionysia in Aigilia.** *IG* II² 3096. Dedicatory inscription found near ancient Aigilia. Date: before the mid-4th c. B.C.

> Timo]sthenes, son of Meixonides; Meixonides, son of Timosthenes; Kleostratos, son of Timosthenes; victorious as *choregoi* set up this statue and altar to Dionysus.

59. **Dionysia in Anagyros.** *IG* II² 3101. Dedicatory verse inscription found near ancient Anagyros. Date: second half of 4th c. B.C. Cf. IV 307.

> When with the sweetly laughing chorus I won the Dionysia, I set up this gift to the god both as a monument to my victory and an adornment to my deme, an honor to my ivy-crowned father, even before whom I won the ivy-bearing contest.

60. **Dionysia at Myrrhinous.** *IG* II² 1182. An honorary decree. Date: mid-4th c. B.C. On *prohedria* see IVBi.

> And they are to have *pr]ohedr[ia in]* all the [specta]cles that the people of Myrrhinous produce.

Lenaea

61. Aristotle, *Constitution of the Athenians* 57.1. Written ca. 330 B.C. The king archon looks after . . . the Lenaean Dionysia. This is [both the procession and the contest.] The king archon and the supervisors together organize the procession. The king archon arranges the contest.

62A. Scholion to Aristophanes, *Knights* 547. The expression "from the wagon" appears frequently in ancient literature meaning unbridled abuse.

> The Lenaea is a festival in Athens, in which to this day poets compete composing some songs to be laughed at. That is why Demosthenes says (*On the Crown* 122) "from the wagon," because the singers sitting on wagons recite and sing the verses.

62B. Photius, *Lex.* s.v. *ta ek ton hamaxon.* Written 9th c.

> "The things from the wagons"; because at Athens in the Festival of the Cups (i.e. day two of the Anthesteria) the revelers on the wagons mock and insult everyone they meet. Later they did the same thing at the Lenaea also.

62C. Harpocration, s.v. *pompeias kai pompeuein.* Written 2nd c.?

> "Processions and to have a procession": instead of "abuse" and "to abuse" . . . the metaphor is from people abusing each other on the wagons in the processions of Dionysus. Menander, in the *Perinthia*

(= fr. 4 K.): "there are some 'processions' on the wagons, highly abusive."

63. Hesychius, s.v. *epi Lenaio agon.* Probably written 5th c.
The Lenaion is in the city and has a large enclosure and inside it a temple of Dionysus Lenaios. In it the contests of the Athenians took place before the theater was built.

64A. Demosthenes, *On the Crown* 129. Delivered in 330 B.C.
I am not at a loss for things to say about you (Aeschines) and your family, but for choosing a place to begin . . . or I could mention the fact that your mother earned the means of nourishing you, her lovely manikin and super-tritagonist, by selling her body afternoons in the shed by the shrine of the hero of the probe (a nickname for the statue of the surgeon Aristomachus).

64B. Patmos scholiast to Demosthenes, *On the Crown* 129.
Shed: a building with big doors in the marketplace . . . The sanctuary of <the hero of the probe> is near the Lenaion.

65. Photius, *Lex.* s.v. *ikria* (bleachers). Written 9th c. Pollux 7.125 also connects the "bleachers" with the marketplace.
Those in the marketplace from which they used to watch the Dionysian contests before the theater in the sanctuary of Dionysus was built.

66. Photius, *Lex.* s.v. *orchestra.* Written 9th c. Cf. Plato's *Apology* 26d, which mentions books for sale in a place called the orchestra. Orchestra means "dancing circle," and the name of the spot in the marketplace is most easily explained as a carryover from the time when it was really used as such.
<A spot> was first called <"orchestra"> in the marketplace, then also the lower semicircle of the theater, where also the choruses sang and danced.

67. Hesychius, s.v. *Limnai* (Marshes). Probably written 5th c. "Laia" is obviously corrupt and is often corrected to "Lenaia." But even if the emendation is correct, and this is far from certain—"Limnaia" is a possibility—the statement is extremely doubtful.
A place dedicated to Dionysus in Athens, where the Laia is put on.

68. *IG* II² 2325. "Victor Lists" of comic poets at the Lenaea, col. i. Most of the beginning of the list of Lenaean comic victors survives and this enables us to arrive at an approximate date for the beginning of the comic contest at the Lenaea and also presumably for the beginning of the official regulation of drama at this festival. The list gives comic poets/directors in the order of their first victory at the Lenaea. Each

name is followed by the total number of victories won at the Lenaea over the individual's entire career. The key to dating the beginning of the Lenaean contest is the absence of the name of Aristophanes, whom we know (from the hypotheses and scholia) to have won a Lenaean victory with *Acharnians* in 425 B.C. Since neither the name of Aristophanes nor his director (*didaskalos*) Callistratus appears on the surviving part of the column, all of the poets on the column won their victories previous to 425 B.C. This makes the earliest conceivable date for Xenophilos' victory 434 B.C. Moreover, we hear from late sources that Eupolis began his career no earlier than 429 or 427 B.C. It is clear therefore that Aristophanes' victory of 425 B.C. must have appeared just below or very close to the break. Some considerations, however, urge a date before 434 B.C. for Xenophilos' first victory. The activity of Teleclides seems not to have extended beyond ca. 430 B.C. The inclusion of Teleclides' other four victories would push the earliest date back to 438 B.C. Similar considerations urge the inclusion of the second victories of Cratinus and Hermippus taking us to at least 440 B.C.

Lenae]a[n Victories of Comi]c [Poe]ts

X]enophilos 1
Teleclides 5
Aristomenes 2
Cratinus 3
Pherecrates 2
Hermippus 4
Phrynichus 2
Myrtilos 1
Eu]polis 3

69A. Aristophanes, *Acharnians* 501–8. Produced Lenaea, 425 B.C.
What I will say is terrible, but just. Cleon will not now slander me saying that I have maligned the city in the presence of foreigners: this contest is the Lenaea and we are alone. The foreigners are not yet present because neither the tribute nor the allies have come from the cities. But now we are winnowed clean—I call the metics the bran of the citizens.

69B. Scholiast to Aristophanes, *Acharnians* 504.
The <subject> cities were ordered to bring the tribute to Athens at

the time of the Dionysia, as Eupolis says in *Cities* (*Poleis,* produced at the Dionysia, 422 B.C.)

70A. Plato, *Symposium* 175e. Written ca. 384 B.C. The fictional setting is a private party celebrating Agathon's first victory for tragedy in 416 B.C. This passage is included here on the basis of the testimony in 70B, but the ascription to the Lenaea is problematic. See 7.

(Socrates to Agathon) Your wisdom is brilliant and will grow; indeed, though you are young, it shone forth brilliantly and became famous two days ago before more than thirty thousand Greeks.

70B. Athenaeus 217a–b. Written ca. 200.

But Plato's *Symposium* is complete nonsense, because when Agathon had his victory, Plato was fourteen years old. The former was crowned at the Lenaea in the archonship of Euphemos (417/6 B.C.), but Plato was born in the archonship of Apollodoros (430/29 B.C.)

71. POxy 2737, fr. 1, col ii, 1–17. The papyrus, written before the end of the 2nd c., contains a fragment of a commentary, probably on Aristophanes' *Anagyros*. The comic poet Plato's *Theater Police* is to be dated some time between 427–413 B.C. The commentator seems to be explaining the line "those granting choruses should have considered the contest at the Lenaea," probably from the epirrhema of the *parabasis*. The text is very fragmentary and uncertain up to "Eratosthenes."

I have sai]d the thea[trical productions] were [of two types]: the Lenae[an appear not to have been equ]ally reputable, perhaps also because of the fact that in s[pring the al]lies had already c[ome from abroa]d to see [the performances and do b]usin[ess. With "t]o the city" the Dionysia is indicated. Eratosthenes also says of Plato (the comic poet) that as long as he had his plays produced by others, he did well; but when he first produced a play on his own, *Theater Police* (*Rabdouchoi*), and placed fourth, he was pushed back again to the Lenaea.

72. Scholion to Aristophanes, *Plutus* 954.

It was not permitted for a foreigner to dance in the city choruses ... but it was in the Lenaea, since even resident foreigners (metics) acted as *choregoi*.

73. *Hesperia* 40 (1971) no. 4. An inscription on a herm base found in the step of the stoa of the king archon in the Athenian marketplace. Date: end of 5th or beginning of 4th c. B.C. Since Sosikrates' profession is given and not his father's name, we can infer that he is a metic.

Onesippos, son of Aitios, of the deme of Kephisia, the king archon, erected this monument. These *choregoi* were victorious during Onesippos' tenure of office as king archon. For comedy Sosikrates, the bronze-merchant, was *choregos;* Nikochares was *didaskalos.* For tragedy Stratonikos, son of Straton, was *choregos;* Megakleides was *didaskalos.*

74. *IG* II² 2319, col. ii. The *Didaskaliai,* a list of tragedies at the Lenaea for the years 420–417 B.C. See I 101.

Eir[... (= a tragedy)
The actor was [X
The actor [X won first prize
In the archonship of A[styphilos (420/19 B.C.) poet X with
Aga[memnon etc.
The actor was [X
Herak[leides was second with]
These[us etc.
The actor was [X
The actor [X won first prize
In the archonship of Arch[ias (419/8 B.C.) poet X (Sophocles?) with]
Tyro, T[roilus?
The actor was Lysikrat[es
Callistratus [was second with]
Amphilochus, Ixio[n
The actor was Kallippi[des
The actor Kallippid[es] won
In the archonship of A]ntiph[o]n (418/7 B.C.) S[...

75. *Hesperia* 40 (1971) 302f. A new fragment of the *Didaskaliai* listing Lenaean tragedies from the years 364/3 B.C.

The actor was] Hephai[stion
Ni]komachos [was third with
Amymone, T[...
The actor was [X
The actor Hephaistio[n won
In the archonship of Timokrate[s (364/3 B.C.) poet X with
Oinopion, Heka[...
The actor was Arexis
Theodorides was second with
Medea, Phaetho[n
The actor was Androsthe[nes
Kleainetos was t[hird with
Hypsipyle, Ph[...

The actor was Hippar[chos
The actor Arex[is won
In the archonship of Charik[leides (363/2 B.C.) poet X

76A. First Hypothesis to Aristophanes, *Acharnians.*

It was produced in the archonship of Euthynos (426/5 B.C.) at the Lenaea by Callistratus (he was *didaskalos*) and he was first. Cratinus was second with *Storm-Tossed.* It does not survive. Eupolis was third with *Firsts of the Months.*

76B. Second Hypothesis to Aristophanes, *Knights.*

The drama was produced in the archonship of Stratokles (425/4 B.C.) publicly at the Lenaea by Aristophanes himself. He won with first prize, Cratinus was second with *Satyrs,* Aristomenes third with *Wood-Carriers.*

76C. First Hypothesis to Aristophanes, *Wasps.*

The drama was produced by Philonides (i.e., he was *didaskalos*) in the archonship of Ameinias (423/2 B.C.) in the 89th Olympiad. It was second at the Lenaea. And Philonides won first prize with *Proagon,* Leucon was third with *Ambassadors.*

76D. First Hypothesis to Aristophanes, *Frogs.* Date: 405 B.C.

The drama was produced by Philonides (i.e., he was *didaskalos*) at the Lenaea in the archonship of the Kallias who comes after Antigenes (406/5 B.C.). It was first. Phrynichus was second with *Muses.* Plato was third with *Cleophon.*

77. *IG* II² 2319, col. i. *Didaskaliai* listing comedies at the Lenaea in 285/4 B.C.

...fourth with ...]*stis*
The actor was Aristoma]chos
...]es was fifth with *The Rescued Girl*
The actor was Ant]iphanes
The actor Her]onymos won
In the archonship of Di]otimos, Simylos with
Ephe]sian Woman; the actor was Aristomachos
Diodorus was second with *The Corpse*
The actor was Aristomachos
Diodorus was third with *The Lunatic*
The actor was Kephisios
Phoe]nik[id]es was fourth with *The Poet*
The actor was Antiphan?]es

Anthesteria

78. Pseudo-Plutarch, *Ten Orators* 841. The author's source appears
to be Philochorus' *Atthis* (79), which was written ca. 261 B.C. Like 71,
this passage suggests that success at other festivals could qualify a poet
for the Great Dionysia, presumably of the following year. The Anthesteria
was a three-day festival whose days are called "Opening of the Wine
Jars," "Festival of Cups," and "Festival of Pots."

<Lycurgus> also introduced legislation (ca. 338–326 B.C.), one on
comic performances establishing a competition in the theater at the
Festival of the Pots (i.e., day three of the Anthesteria), and had the
winner enrolled as a competitor for the City Dionysia, a thing not
formerly permitted, and thus restored a contest that had fallen into
neglect.

79. Scholion to Aristophanes, *Frogs* 218.

The Pots: a festival in Athens...The so-called contests of the Festival of the Pots are held there, as Philochorus says in the sixth book
of the *Atthis*.

80. Diogenes Laertius 3.56. Probably written first half of 3rd c. Thrasyllos was an astrologer and friend of Tiberius, active till 36. There is
inscriptional evidence for the performance of "new tragedy" at the
Panathenaea in the 1st c. and dramatic contests in the 2nd c. B.C.

Thrasyllos says that <Plato> even published his dialogues after the
manner of tragic tetralogies, just as <the tragedians> contested with
four dramas at the Dionysia, Lenaea, Panathenaea, and Festival of
the Pots.

81. Philostratus, *Life of Apollonius* 4.21. Written ca. 200 and referring
to the second half of the 1st c. Apollonius was a mystic philosopher.
The author appears to be describing pantomime. Cf. V 37.

<Apollonius> is said to have rebuked the Athenians with respect
to the Dionysia, which they perform in the month of Anthesterion.
He thought that they were attending the theater to hear monodies
and lyrics, *parabaseis* and measures, but when he heard that they
danced to the music of a pipe suggesting lithe twistings, and that
they acted like Hours, Nymphs, and Bacchants to the epics and
theology of Orpheus, he reproached them and said, "Stop dancing
away the memory of the brave men of Salamis."

IIIAii. Regulation

IIIAiia. The Choregic System

The main burden of organizing the dramatic festivals at Athens fell upon citizens—and in some cases probably metics (72)—whom the archon appointed to be *choregoi*. The *choregos'* principal responsibility was to foot the bill for equipping and training a tragic, comic, or dithyrambic chorus, but the office (called *choregia*) also involved a great deal of organization: the secondary selection from the archon's list of a poet and piper, the primary selection of members of the chorus (a very irksome duty to judge from 94), and the hiring of a chorus director (94, 106, 107), if the chorus was not taught by the poet himself (IVD). The financial burden far outweighed the organizational. The choregos was required to provide a training ground (94) for the chorus, to house and feed the chorus and actors (IV 19; 92, 95, 96 attest to high expectations in this regard), and to pay for the costumes and accessories used in the performance (91, 106), including extra actors (98). In the event that the *choregos* won first prize in the contest, there was the additional cost of a dedication to Dionysos (88, 102, and cf. 30).

The *choregia* formed one of a variety of public services, such as paying the upkeep of a warship for the period of a year (trierarchy), or paying for the training of a team of athletes for an athletic contest (gymnasiarchy), which were collectively called "liturgies" (*leitourgiai*). These may be described as special taxes imposed by the Athenian democracy upon the rich. Property qualification for the performance of the more expensive liturgies lay somewhere between three and four talents (18,000 and 24,000 drachmas). The lower limit is more than a skilled laborer could hope to earn in an entire lifetime (1 drachma is the daily wage of a common soldier or a master craftsman in the late 5th c. B.C.). Appointment to the most expensive liturgy, the trierarchy, was generally confined to an elite class of about 300 to 400 citizens, roughly one percent of the (adult male) citizen population (numbering from around 43,000 in 431 B.C. to about 21,000 in 313 B.C.). The attitude of the liturgical class to the *choregia* was generally ambivalent: as far as possible it was a thing to be avoided, but once assigned, the *choregia,* more than any other liturgy, could become something of a potlatch, a display of public zeal and conspicuous consumption pushed to the very brink of financial ruin (88, 91, 92).

Certain exemptions existed to protect wealthy citizens from overextending their resources by performing more than one liturgy at a time or by performing several liturgies in close succession (82). The evidence is clearest for the 4th c. B.C.: those who acted as trierarchs were not required to perform other liturgies (85); apart from the trierarchy (85), no one was required to perform (precisely) the same liturgy twice (i.e., not "*choregos* for the men's dithyramb at the Dionysia" twice—see 82); again, apart from the trierarchy (85), an exemption of one or two years (82, 85) intervened between the performance of liturgies; finally, certain benefactors of the city might be voted the honor of *ateleia,* or freedom from taxation, which meant an exemption from the requirement to perform liturgies other than the trierarchy (85). In addition, a law forbade those under forty years of age to act as *choregos* for the boys' dithyramb (82). It is questionable whether some of these exemptions existed in the 5th c. B.C.: the speaker of 88 and the Thrasyllus mentioned in 85B both performed the trierarchy and other liturgies simultaneously, and neither interrupted his service for the exemption period, possibly out of pure zeal, but more probably because the exemption did not yet exist despite Demosthenes' rhetorical appeal to "longstanding laws"; moreover, the speaker of 88 was in his early twenties and Alcibiades in his early thirties (105) when they acted as *choregoi* for boys' dithyrambs, and it seems that the minimum age law mentioned by Aristotle (82) and other 4th-c. authors was not yet in effect.

The state exercised a strict compulsion upon those selected to perform liturgies. As a last resort, an unwilling candidate could instigate a procedure called *antidosis* (literally, "exchange of property") by presenting the archon with the name of a candidate he thought better qualified to perform the liturgy. It was then open to the new candidate to take up the performance of the liturgy, or to exchange property with the original appointee, who would then perform the liturgy with the financial resources acquired in the exchange (82, 86, 87, cf. 50A). Although the procedure was fully regulated by law, the risks were considerable and probably served as a deterrent to any but the most desperate (87).

The evidence for the cost of the various liturgies gives us a sense of the enormous importance of the dramatic festivals to Athenian society. The speaker of 88 claimed to have served as *choregos* at the Dionysia three times and to have spent 3,000 drachmas for tragedy, 1,600 for a comedy, and 5,000 for the men's dithyramb. The only comparable figure is also from a speech of Lysias, referring to two tragic *choregiai* performed some fifteen to twenty years later, which are said together to have cost 5,000 drachmas (89); the slight difference between this sum and that of 88 may be due to less zeal or more careful management, but since the festivals at which the latter tragic *choregiai* were performed are not named, it is possible that one or both were at the Lenaea, which was less expensive since it involved only two tragedies as opposed to three plus a satyrplay at the Dionysia (cf. 74, 75). Similarly, comic *choregiai* were cheaper since they involved only one performance, despite the larger size of the chorus, but it is interesting to see that they were much more cost-intensive than individual tragedies. Demosthenes also attests to the greater cost of the dithyramb (90), due not only to the greater size of the chorus but also probably to the fiercer competition that seems to have attended its tribal rivalry. It is impressive to note that the cost of this dithyramb, at most one half-hour's public entertainment, was just slightly less than the cost of running a warship for an entire year (5,143 drachmas). If the rival competitors of the speaker of 88 spent as much as he did, then three days' entertainment cost Athens 113,800 drachmas in choregic contributions, to which may be added an estimated state expenditure of 36,000 drachmas. The resulting figures show that Athens, at war, and fighting for its very survival, spent on a single dramatic festival an amount equivalent to the total annual expenditure on one-tenth of its navy. Plutarch's claim (92, cf. 93)—that the Athenians spent "more on the production of *Bacchaes* and *Phoenician Women* and *Oedipuses* and the misfortunes of Medeas or Electras than they did on maintaining their empire and fighting for their liberty against the Persians"—though exaggerated, is not wildly so.

The victorious dithyrambic *choregos* won a tripod, which was normally dedicated in or near the precinct of Dionysus on expensive monuments that added no small sum to the cost of the *choregia* (88, 102; I 137). The successful tragic *choregos* is said to have won a goat to sacrifice to Dionysus, and the successful comic *choregos* is said to have been given a basket of figs and a skin full of wine. As opposed to dithyrambic *choregiai,* there are relatively few stone inscriptions relating to dramatic victories. This is probably due to the fact that dramatic *choregoi* rarely made dedications of this sort. The literary testimonia refer rather to the dedication of masks and costumes (88) or to the dedication of *pinakes* (= plaque, tablet, or painting—see 99, 100), which, as the evidence seems to show, were paintings of scenes relating to the drama or its production. Many of the pots, figurines, reliefs, mosaics, and wall paintings with theatrical or theatrically influenced mythological scenes probably derive from these dedications (IC). Theophrastus' illiberal man stands out because he merely dedicates a text recording his name on a slab of wood, not an artifact of intrinsic value relating to the context of the victory (101).

It is not the stinginess of the illiberal man per se that makes him ridiculous to his contemporaries but his failure to use his money for the "attainment of respect or distinction" (101). Although the institution of the *choregia* probably goes back to the time of the democratic reorganization of the Dionysia around 502/1 B.C. (see I 100), it is likely that it merely formalized a customary sponsorship of village sacrifice and festival worship undertaken by local potentates for the sake of prestige and good will. The shift from voluntary largesse to obligatory service did not eliminate the potential benefits of the system for the donors. They were, in Isocrates' words, "a burden, but one which conferred a certain honor on those who undertook them" (*Panathenaikos* 145), so that they were frequently assumed by volunteers (84), and even those who acted under compulsion were likely to spend more than the legal minimum (88, 103). *Choregiai* and other liturgies were used in canvasing popularity for political ends (102). The memory of public largesse was openly viewed as a form of litigation insurance if one fell foul of the law, as wealthy Athenians frequently did (103, and, conversely, 104). We owe a great deal of our evidence about the liturgical system to the common practice of winning over the sympathy of the popular juries by recounting past public services (e.g., 84, 88, 89, 90). In addition to these motives, the performance of conspicuous liturgies like the *choregia* provided an outlet for the fiercely competitive *ethos* of the Greek aristocracy, which frequently led to more than financial excess (105–7). For most, however, the cost of the *choregia* far outweighed such potential benefits, and the elite seem to have agitated continually for some alleviation of the burden. Their growing success can be seen, for example, in the apparent growth in the number of exemptions available in the 4th c. B.C. In 359 B.C. the burden of the trierarchy was considerably lightened by the assignment of trierarchies to corporations of sixty men (called *symmoriai;* 85B, 109), though the number of co-contributors was reduced in 340 B.C. The *choregia,* probably because it required much more personal initiative, seems to have been more resistant to this kind of cost distribution scheme. The contradictory evidence for the shared responsibility for the *choregia* (*synchoregia*) has made this a celebrated problem of contemporary scholarship. A scholion on Aristophanes quotes Aristotle to the effect that by decree, the drama at the Dionysia in 410 or 406 B.C. was jointly sponsored (108). This is the only secure evidence that exists for the *synchoregia* at the urban festivals in Athens (cf. IIIAib). A statement of Demosthenes seems to imply that he knew nothing of the practice (109). The *choregia* was abolished under the oligarchic constitution set up by Demetrius of Phaleron, a Peripatetic philosopher, installed as governor of Athens by Cassander (IV 131–33), and the *choregoi* were replaced by an annually elected official called the *agonothetes,* who organized dramatic and other festivals and seems to have contributed large sums from his own private purse (110). The Aristotelians, at least, were conscious of potential benefits that the coupling of an elected office with choregic functions had for the consolidation of an oligarchic constitution (111). In any case, the abolition of the *choregia* so soon after the restriction of the franchise attests to its unpopularity among the wealthier class, while any opportunity the *choregia* may have provided for winning prestige and popular favor survived in the *agonothesia* in augmented form. The *agonothesia* survived the various constitutional modifications that attended the social and political conflicts of the following centuries.

Sources

Selection of Choregoi

82. Aristotle, *Constitution of the Athenians 56.3.* Written ca. 330 B.C. The transfer of the responsibility for appointing comic *choregoi* from the archon to the tribal organizations must already have taken place by 348/7 B.C. since tribal appointments of *choregoi* are mentioned in that year in a speech by Demosthenes (*Against Boiotos Concerning the Name 7*).

> As soon as he takes up office the eponymous archon first proclaims that everyone shall hold and retain till the end of his term of office all the property he owned at the beginning of his term of office. Next he appoints for tragedy three *choregoi* who are the richest of all Athenians. In former times he also appointed five *choregoi* for comedy, but now the tribes appoint them. Then he receives the *choregoi* put forward by the tribes for the men's and boys' dithyramb and the comedies at the Dionysia and for the men's and boys' dithyramb at the Thargelia—at the Dionysia the *choregoi* are appointed one to each tribe, but at the Thargelia one to a pair of tribes; in other words each tribe of a pair takes its turn. The archon

looks after the exchanges of property (*antidosis*) and introduces the exemptions in cases where the candidate claims to have performed this liturgy in the past, to be exempt because the period of exemption following another liturgy he performed has not yet elapsed, or not to be of age, since the law requires *choregoi* for boys' choruses to be over forty years of age.

83. Second Hypothesis to Demosthenes' *Against Meidias*. The author of this hypothesis is very ignorant about some things and naive about others, but he alone preserves the following piece of information that may have been taken from a reliable source. In any case, 93 indicates that *choregoi* were chosen long in advance of the festival.

> In the first month after the end of the festival the names of the *choregoi* for the next festival were put forward.

84. Demosthenes, *Against Meidias* 13–14. Written 348–346 B.C. Demosthenes' *choregia* was at the Dionysia, 348 B.C.

> When two years ago no *choregos* had been appointed for the tribe Pandionis and the assembly was held at which the law requires the archon to allot pipers for the choruses, as there was a great row with the archon accusing the overseers of the tribe and the overseers the archon, I came forward and voluntarily offered myself as *choregos,* and when the lots were drawn and I got first pick of the pipers, you, men of Athens, all welcomed most favorably both my announcement and the outcome of the draw, and made such clatter and applause as to praise and congratulate me.

85A. Demosthenes, *Against Leptines* 8 and 18–19. Delivered in 355/4 B.C., this speech expresses Demosthenes' opposition to a proposed law that would rescind and permanently do away with grants of freedom from the responsibility of performing annual liturgies (*ateleia*), which till then had been awarded to notable public benefactors. Those supporting the legislation claimed that so many of these grants had been made that there were not enough rich men to be found to assume the liturgies and that they now devolved upon "poor men."

> (8) Still one has to keep in mind that according to the existing laws that have long been in force . . . each person performs liturgies at one-year intervals, so that half the time he is exempt from contributions. . . . (18–19) Of those taxes levied for the pursuit of the war and for the safety of the city and of the trierarchies, by longstanding laws, rightly and justly, no one is exempt . . . Let us consider whom <Leptines> (sponsor of the law against exemptions) will add as *choregoi* to those liturgies and, if we don't listen to

him, how many it will leave out. Now the richest citizens, as they are trierarchs, are always exempt from the *choregia*. Those who have insufficient property, enjoying the exemption imposed by necessity, also lie outside the purview of this tax. Therefore no one of either of these groups will be made *choregos* for us through this law.

85B. Isaeus, *Estate of Apollodoros* 38. Written ca. 354 B.C. The law of Periandros, 357/6 B.C., created the system of *symmoriai,* by which corporations of sixty contributors jointly defrayed the cost of a trierarchy. Thrasyllos, the father of Apollodoros, who is the subject of this passage, died serving in Sicily in 415–413 B.C.

> We beg you <jurors> to come to our assistance both for Apollodoros' sake and for the sake of his father, for you will find that they were not useless citizens, but as solicitous as possible about your affairs. His father both performed all the other liturgies and acted continuously as trierarch, not as a member of a *symmoria,* as they do at present, but at his own expense, not even as the second member of a pair of trierarchs (i.e., syntrierarchy), but all alone, and not even interrupting for two years after each year of service, but serving continuously, and not even acting perfunctorily, but providing the very best service possible.

86A. Bekker, *Anecdota Graeca* 1.197.3, s.v. *Antidosis.*

> *Antidosis:* someone giving his property to someone wealthier to make him pay the cost of an imposed liturgy, as they are expensive, or, if the latter does not wish to perform the liturgy, the latter giving his property in exchange, and the former receiving it and performing the liturgy.

86B. *Lexicon Rhetoricum Cantabrigiense,* in *Lexica Graeca Minora* p. 69, s.v. *antidosis.*

> *Antidosis:* whenever someone summoned to perform a liturgy claims that another is wealthier than he and summons the other to perform the liturgy or to discharge the responsibility by giving his own property and receiving that of the other person.

87. Demosthenes, *Against Phainippos* 1–4. Date uncertain: ca. 355–325 B.C. The speaker was appointed to a liturgy and challenged Phainippos to an exchange of property. Phainippos, however, did not carry out the exchange in the proper manner, so the question of which party was to perform the liturgy was submitted to a jury, a form of trial called *diadikasia.*

> Gentlemen of the jury, I wish first you all well, and then Solon, the man who established the law concerning exchanges of property

(*antidosis*). For if Solon had not clearly set out what parties agreeing to an exchange of property had to do first, second, and so on in order, I don't know what limit Phainippos' impudence might have reached, since even now when the law prescribes the entire procedure, he nevertheless treated its codified justice with contempt, and instead of giving me the inventory of his property in three days as he swore to do in accordance with the law, or since he didn't wish to do this, instead of giving me the list on the 25th of Boedromion, a date he himself set after requesting an extension and on which he agreed to give the inventory, he did neither of these things, but dismissing both us and the law, he gave me the list more than a month later, just two or three days before coming to trial, and made himself scarce in the entire interval. Instead of leaving the sealings with which I sealed the buildings, he went to his farm, opened the buildings, and carried off the barley and other things, as if the law had given him permission to do as he pleased and not as is just. I, gentlemen of the jury, would happily have seen myself prospering with my former wealth and remaining a member of the three hundred. Since, however, I shared the general misfortune with those who operate the silver mines, but also privately lost my wealth through the imposition of enormous fines, and, to cap it all, must now deposit three talents (18,000 drachmas) with the city, a talent per share—I unfortunately had shares in the confiscated mine—I am compelled to try to find someone to set in my position who is not only richer than I am at present but also richer than I was previously and also someone who has never performed a liturgy for you or paid the special tax on wealth to the state. I beg you all, gentlemen of the jury, if I show that this Phainippos has transgressed the justice of the laws and is richer than myself, to come to my assistance and have this fellow enrolled among the three hundred in my place. It is for this reason that the laws allow for exchanges of property (*antidosis*) once a year, since the joy of continuous prosperity is wont to remain with few citizens.

Costs and Responsibilities

88. Lysias, *Defense Against a Charge of Bribery* 1–5. Delivered 403/2 B.C. or soon after. This is the beginning of the defense of an unnamed defendant charged with accepting bribes. The defendant's liturgical career is unique in its intensity and expenditures, amounting to 63,300 drachmas over a ten-year period.

Men of the jury, enough has been said about my accusers; I think it right that you learn the rest so that you will know what sort of man you are judging. I was enrolled as a citizen (i.e., reached the age of majority, eighteen) in the archonship of Theopompos (411/10 B.C.) and was appointed *choregos* (at the City Dionysia) for tragedy. I spent 30 mnas (3,000 drachmas) and two months later I won first prize as *choregos* of a men's dithyramb at the Thargelia at a cost of 2,000 drachmas. In the archonship of Glaukippos (410/9 B.C.) I spent 800 drachmas on the *pyrrhiche* at the Panathenaea. Once again *choregos* for the men's dithyramb in the same year, I won first prize at the Dionysia and spent 5,000 drachmas, monument for the tripod included. Also in the archonship of Diokles (409/8 B.C.), I spent 300 drachmas on a circular chorus (i.e., dithyramb) at the lesser Panathenaea. Meanwhile I was a trierarch (i.e., responsible for the upkeep of a warship) for seven years and spent six talents (36,000 drachmas). Even though I incurred such expenses and risked my life daily on your behalf and endured absence from home, I nevertheless contributed to the special property tax, 30 mnas (3,000 drachmas) on one occasion and 4,000 drachmas on another. When I returned from service in the archonship of Alexias (405/4 B.C.) I immediately became gymnasiarch for the Prometheia and won first prize at a cost of 12 mnas (1,200 drachmas). Later I was made *choregos* for a boys' chorus and I spent more than 15 mnas (1,500 drachmas). In the archonship of Eucleides (403/2 B.C.) I won first prize in comedy as *choregos* for Cephisodorus (an Old Comic poet whose victory at the Dionysia of 402 B.C. is independently attested by the "Victor Lists") and spent 16 mnas (1,600 drachmas), including the dedication of the masks, and at the lesser Panathenaea I was *choregos* for the youths' *pyrrhiche* and spent 7 mnas (700 drachmas). I won first prize competing in the boat race at Sunium at a cost of 15 mnas (1,500 drachmas). This is not to mention leading the sacred embassy and the Arrephoria and other such things, on which I spent more than 20 mnas (3,000 drachmas). And of those things I've listed, if I had wished to perform these liturgies only to the standard required by the letter of the law, I would not have spent a quarter of what I did.

89. Lysias, *For the Property of Aristophanes* 42. Written in 388 or 387 B.C. The *choregiai* mentioned were performed sometime from 394

to 389 B.C. Earlier in the speech (29), we learn that "on his own behalf and on behalf of his father" refers to two separate *choregiai* for tragedy and that the trierarchy was for three consecutive years.

> Now Aristophanes had land and a house worth more than 5 talents (30,000 drachmas). He performed the *choregia* on his own behalf and on behalf of his father at a cost of 5,000 drachmas, as trierarch he spent 80 mnas (8,000 drachmas).

90. Demosthenes, *Against Meidias* 156. Written 348–346 B.C. Demosthenes' *choregia* was at the Dionysia, 348 B.C.

> This man (Aeschines) once served as *choregos* for tragedy, I for a men's dithyramb, and surely no one is ignorant of the fact that the latter expense is much greater than the former.

91. Antiphanes, *Soldier*, PCG F 201. A poet of Middle Comedy, Antiphanes was active from about 385 to about 335 B.C.

> Whoever thinks, being human born, that any possession is safe in life, couldn't be more wrong. Either some tax snatches away everything, or incurring a lawsuit he is wiped out, or he goes into debt after becoming a general, or he is chosen *choregos* and furnishing golden robes for the chorus he himself wears rags, or he hangs himself while trierarch.

92. Plutarch, *On the Glory of Athens* 348d–349b. Written ca. 115.

> Do you wish us to introduce the men themselves carrying the tokens and insignia of their occupation, giving their own entrance to each? From this side let the poets come forward chanting and singing to the music of flutes and lyres (= Aristophanes, *Frogs* 353ff.), "Keep holy silence and stand out of the way of our choruses whoever is untutored in this form of discourse or is impure in mind or never sang nor danced the mysteries of the noble Muses or was never initiated in the Bacchic rites of the bull-eating tongue of Cratinus," and carrying props and masks and altars and stage machines and *periaktoi* and victory tripods. And let the tragic actors enter with them, the Nikostratoses and Kallippideses and Mynniskoses and Theodoroses and Poloses, like the beauticians and stool bearers of the rich woman Tragedy, or rather following along like the painters, gilders, and dyers of statues. Now bring forth the unruly mob of props and masks and purple robes and stage machines and chorus directors and supernumeraries. Looking at all this, a Spartan once said, quite appositely, that the Athenians were making a big mistake in lavishing so much on their love for play, in effect pouring the expense of large fleets and the provisions of armies into the theater.

If the cost of the production of each drama were reckoned, the Athenian people would appear to have spent more on the production of *Bacchaes* and *Phoenician Women* and *Oedipuses* and the misfortunes of Medeas and Electras than they did on maintaining their empire and fighting for their liberty against the Persians. Generals frequently gave the order to bring uncooked grain and led the men off to battle. And, by Zeus, the trierarchs provided the men rowing the ships with barley flavored with onion and cheese and marched them aboard ship. But the *choregoi* set before the members of the chorus eels and lettuce and prime ribs and brain and continued feasting them for a long time while they lived in the lap of luxury and had their voices trained. In return, what was there left over but for the *choregoi* who lost to be abused and ridiculed, and for those who won, a tripod, not a monument to a victory, as Demetrius said, but a libation to a squandered livelihood and a cenotaph to a lost home. Such are the ends of poetry and from it comes nothing more glorious.

93. Demosthenes, *Philippic* 1.35–36. Delivered early 351 B.C.

Yet why then, men of Athens, do you suppose that the festivals of the Panathenaea or the Dionysia always take place at the regular time whether experts or ordinary citizens are chosen to oversee the preparations, though such great amounts of money are spent on these festivals as would never be spent on any military expedition, and though they involve so much trouble and preparation that I don't know if there is anything at all comparable; instead, all of our military expeditions arrive late, for example, the forces sent to Methone, Pegasai, and Potidaea? It is because the former are entirely regulated by law, and everyone of you knows long in advance who is to be *choregos* or gymnasiarch of his tribe, when, with what, and from what source one has what to do, and nothing has been left unforeseen or unprescribed?

94. Antiphon, *On the Choreut* 11–13. Delivered sometime between 422 and 411 B.C. The speech is a defense by a *choregos* for the boys' dithyramb on a charge of murder, since one of the boys in training at his house died taking a drug intended to improve his voice. The *choregos'* responsibility for two tribes is probably an arrangement specific to the Thargelia.

When I was appointed *choregos* for the Thargelia and was given by the lottery Pantakles as chorus director and the tribe Kekropis in addition to my own (i.e., Erechtheis), I performed my duties as well and as fairly as I could. I first built in the most convenient part of my house a schoolroom, which I also used for training when I was *choregos* for the Dionysia. Then I chose the best chorus I could, without penalizing anyone or levying distraint by force, or incurring anyone's hostility, but taking care to arrive at the most mutually agreeable and convenient terms: I set about making requests and solicitations, and they sent their sons voluntarily and gladly. When the boys arrived, I had at first no leisure to attend and oversee the instruction. I had a dispute with Aristion and Philinos, in which it was important to me to make a fair and accurate presentation to the Council and the rest of the Athenians, since I had initiated impeachment proceedings. While I applied myself to this affair, I charged Phanostratos to look to the chorus' needs. He is a demesman of my accusers here, but my relative by marriage, since I gave him my daughter, and I considered him fit to take the best possible care of the chorus. In addition, there were two others: Ameinias of the tribe Erechtheis, whom the tribesmen themselves voted to put in charge of assembling and overseeing the tribe on every occasion, thinking him the best man for the job, and another fellow of the tribe Kekropis, who always used to assemble that tribe. There was, moreover, a fourth, Philippos, whom I put in charge of purchasing and paying for whatever the chorus director or either of the other three needed to ensure that the boys receive the best service from their *choregos* and that no one want for anything because of my preoccupation.

95. Aristophanes, *Acharnians* 1150–55. Produced Lenaea, 425 B.C. The passage is from a quasi-parabatic choral ode; it appears that the first-person singular refers to the choreuts, though it could conceivably refer to the poet himself, or both. The scholiast here jumps to the conclusion that the chorus' hostility to Antimachos is due to some decree injurious to the chorus, though the actual words of the chorus make it clear that he merely cheated his chorus (or Aristophanes) of the expected banquet (at the cast party?) while *choregos*.

Antimachos, the son of Sputter, the lyric poet! In a word, may Zeus destroy him utterly, since he let me go, poor wretch, without a dinner, when he was *choregos* at the Lenaea.

96. Scholion to Aristophanes, *Clouds* 338f. In the play, Strepsiades has just quoted some fragments of a dithyramb and said, "then in return for these <bits of song> I wolfed down great big delicious fillets of *kestra*

(an unidentified delicatessen fish) and the meat of thrushes (also a delicacy)." The scholion comments:

> The whole passage alludes both to those being feasted at the houses of *choregoi* and those who always have their meals at the *prytaneion.*

97. Eupolis, *PCG* F 329. From an unnamed comedy produced 429–ca. 412 B.C.

> Did you ever see a stingier *choregos* than this?

98. Plutarch, *Phocion* 19.2–3. Written ca. 115. Phocion was active from 350 to 318 B.C.

> Once when the Athenians were watching a new tragedy (i.e., not a revival), the tragic actor who was supposed to come on stage as a queen had asked the *choregos* for a large number of richly adorned attendants, but as he did not provide them, he got angry and kept the audience waiting by refusing to come on stage. The *choregos,* Melanthios, pushed him out into the theater and shouted, "Do you not see Phocion's wife, who always goes about in public attended by a single servant? But you're putting on airs and corrupting women." The shouts were overheard and the audience received them with a great deal of boisterous applause.

Victory Dedications

99. Plutarch, *Themistocles* 5. Written ca. 115. Themistocles' victory was at the Dionysia of 476 B.C.

> In his ambition <Themistocles> surpassed everyone...He won a victory as *choregos* for tragedy, though at that time already the contest was pursued with serious rivalry, and he dedicated a tablet (*pinax*) in commemoration of his victory with the following inscription: "Themistocles of the deme Phrearrioi was *choregos;* Phrynichus was poet; Adeimantos was archon."

100. Aristotle, *Politics* 1341a34–36. Written ca. 330 B.C. Aristotle is arguing against the use of pipes in musical education, one reason being that it distracts from more important pursuits, "hence our ancestors were right to reject the practice of pipe playing for youths and free men," but he concedes that in earlier times, in the leisure society that emerged after the Persian Wars, the practice was encouraged. Ecphantides is an Old Comic poet, whose first victory is 457/4 B.C. It seems fairly clear that Aristotle is referring to something visible on the tablet, perhaps

Thrasippos himself playing the pipes, and that this *pinax* is a votive painting of a scene probably related in some way to the performance.

> And at Athens pipe playing took such hold that most free men took up the practice: this is clear from the tablet (*pinax*) that Thrasippos dedicated when he served as *choregos* for Ecphantides.

101. Theophrastus, *Characters* 22.1–2. Written ca. 319 B.C.

> Illiberality is a kind of absence of inclination toward the attainment of any respect or distinction that involves the expenditure of money. The illiberal man is the sort who, after winning a victory in tragedy at the Dionysia, will dedicate a slat of wood with his name inscribed upon it.

Public Recognition for Service

102. Plutarch, *Nicias* 3. Written ca. 115. Nicias lived ca. 470–413 B.C.

> Now Pericles governed the state by virtue of his genuine excellence of character and the power of his eloquence and did not need to cultivate his image or to curry favor with the mob. Nicias lacked these qualities but had an abundance of wealth, which he used to advance his political popularity. And since he doubted his ability to match the slick vulgarity with which Cleon catered to the Athenians, he won over the populace by taking on the expense of furnishing choruses (*choregiai*), training and maintaining teams for athletic competitions (*gymnasiarchiai*), and undertaking other costly enterprises of this sort while surpassing all predecessors and contemporaries in elegance and munificence. Among his dedications there survive even till the present day both the statue of Athena on the Acropolis, which has lost its gold, and the temple surmounted by choregic tripods in the sanctuary of Dionysus; he was often victorious as *choregos* and was never defeated.

103. Lysias, *Defense on a Charge of Subverting the Democracy* 12–13. Delivered ca. 399 B.C. The unnamed defendant is accused of having had oligarchical sympathies.

> I held the trierarchy five times and fought at sea four times and made many financial contributions during the war, and for the rest I took on liturgies with no less enthusiasm than any other citizen. And yet I spent more than was required by the state in order to be thought better of by you and so as to be better able to defend myself in case any misfortune befell me.

104. Isaeus, *On the Estate of Dikaiogenes* **36. Delivered ca. 389** B.C.
You have no reason, gentlemen, to pity Dikaiogenes because he is
poor and in financial difficulty, nor to benefit him as one who has
done some service to the city, for neither of these is the case, as I
will demonstrate, gentlemen. I will show that he is at once both
rich and the meanest of men to the city, to his relations, and to his
friends. Although this man received by your judgment an inheritance
that brought an annual income of 80 mnas (8,000 drachmas), and
although he has enjoyed it for ten years, he claims that he has no
money and yet is unable to say what he spent it on, gentlemen. It
is a matter worthy of your consideration. For this man, when he
acted as *choregos* for his tribe at the Dionysia, came fourth, and
came last in tragedy and in the *pyrrhiche*. Being forced to do only
these liturgies, this is how well he managed from such a large
income.

Competitiveness

105. Pseudo-Andocides, *Against Alcibiades* **20–21.** This speech, set
in 415 B.C., is generally considered to be a late forgery. The events in
this passage probably took place in 417/6 B.C. and are also mentioned
by Demosthenes, *Against Meidias* 147 and Plutarch, *Alcibiades* 16.5.
Alcibiades drove off one of Taureas' choreuts during a performance, but
the "him" driven off in the text seems to refer to Taureas, who was
metaphorically driven off insofar as his chorus' performance was aborted.
   Consider Taureas, who was Alcibiades' rival *choregos* in the boys'
   dithyramb. As the law permits anyone who wishes to remove any
   foreigner participating in a chorus and does not permit anyone to
   obstruct the removal, <Alcibiades> drove him off with blows in
   front of you and the rest of the Greeks in the audience, including
   all of the archons. As the spectators sided with Taureas and loathed
   Alcibiades, to the extent that they praised the former's chorus and
   did not wish to hear the latter's, Alcibiades took no further action.
   But the judges gave Alcibiades the victory, placing greater weight
   upon the man than on their oaths, since some were afraid of him
   and the others were anxious to please him.
106. Demosthenes, *Against Meidias* **14–18. Written 348–346** B.C. Demosthenes' *choregia* was at the Dionysia, 348 B.C. Demosthenes brings a
charge of impiety against Meidias, who assaulted him, beat him, and

ripped his garments in the orchestra of the Theater of Dionysus during the performance of the men's dithyramb.

> And <Meidias> stalked me throughout the entire term of my liturgy, obstructing me continually in matters both great and small. As to the hindrance he provided in opposing the exemption of my choreuts from military service or putting himself forward and urging that he be made overseer of the Dionysia, and all the other things of this sort, I will pass over them without mention. . . . But I will say that which will arouse the indignation of every one of you alike. . . . The sacred garments—I consider sacred everything that is prepared for the festival until it is used—and the golden crowns that I had commissioned as ornaments for the chorus he planned to destroy by breaking into the house of the goldsmith at night. And he did destroy them, though not all of them, because he was unable (Demosthenes says the goldsmith appeared and stopped him). And yet no one claims ever to have heard of anyone attempting or performing such a crime in this city. This, however, did not satisfy him. No, but he even tried to bribe my chorus director and had Telephanes, the finest of pipers, not been with me at the time and driven the man off when he noticed what was afoot, and, had he not felt it necessary to organize and direct the chorus himself, we would not have been part of the contest, Athenians, but the chorus would have entered the theater untrained and we would have suffered the ultimate disgrace. But Meidias' insolence did not even stop there. He had such an abundance of it that he bribed the invested archon, led the *choregoi* in a conspiracy against me, stood by shouting and threatening while the judges took their oath, fenced off the *paraskenia,* nailed them shut, public property, though he was a private citizen, and continued to make indescribable troubles and problems.

107. Demosthenes, *Against Meidias* 58–61. Written 348–346 B.C. Demosthenes' *choregia* was at the Dionysia, 348 B.C. Meidias' assault on Demosthenes is contrasted with the customary respect shown for the sacred and civic solemnity of the performance; the "misfortunes" suffered by the men who are the subjects of the following anecdotes are the loss of citizen rights because of their convictions for serious offenses.

> As you probably know, there is a certain Sannion who directs tragic choruses. This man was convicted of avoiding military service and suffered calamity. After his misfortune an ambitious tragic *choregos*

hired him, Theozotides, I think. So at first his rival *choregoi* were indignant and claimed they would stop him. Yet when the theater was full and they saw the crowd gathered for the contest they recoiled, allowed him to go on—no one touched him—but such pious reserve could be seen by any in each of them that he has been directing choruses ever since and not even his personal enemies try to stop him, let alone *choregoi*. There is another Aristeides of the tribe Oineis, who also suffered the same sort of misfortune. He is an old man now and perhaps less of a choreut, but he was once the leader of his tribal chorus. As you know, if anyone removes the chorus leader, the rest of the chorus falls apart. But though there have been many ambitious *choregoi,* none of them ever saw their way to this trick: no one dared to remove him or obstruct the performance. This is because of the requirement that one has to do this by laying hands on the man—it not being permitted simply to summon him to the archon—just as if you wanted to remove a foreigner, and everyone balks at the outrage of being seen laying hands on someone. Is it not then shocking, men of the jury, and mean spirited, when of the *choregoi,* who consider their victories to depend upon it, who have frequently spent their entire fortunes on the liturgies, no one ever dares to lay hands even on those whom the law permits, but they are so cautiously and so piously and so moderately disposed that they, who have spent money and are eager to win, nevertheless refrain and respect your wishes and the solemnity of the festival, while Meidias, working on his own behalf, who spent nothing, but because he has given offense to someone and become his enemy, abuses and beats him who is spending money, is acting as *choregos,* and is in possession of his full citizen rights, and does so without consideration for the sanctity of the festival, for the law, for public opinion, or for the god?

Synchoregia

108. Scholion to Aristophanes, *Frogs* 405. The scholiast quotes Aristotle, possibly from the lost *Dionysian Victories.* The Cinesias mentioned is the famous dithyrambic poet and exponent of the "New Music" (IVC) and this alone suffices to explain the epithet "chorus-killer." Since the fragment from Strattis comes without context, it is impossible to decide if the scholion is based on more than a possibly false inference from the fragment of Strattis; the scholia are full of such false inferences, cf. 95

and Scholion to *Frogs* 153: "Cinesias...took measures against the poets so that they would be without choruses."

He seems to indicate that the poets were already suffering from a reduction in choregic support. At any rate Aristotle says "in the archonship of this Kallias (410 or 406 B.C.) it was decreed that *choregoi* would jointly defray the costs of the tragedies and comedies at the Dionysia." So perhaps there was a similar arrangement governing the Lenaea (*Frogs* was produced at the Lenaea, 405 B.C.). Not much later Cinesias did away with the *choregia* altogether. This is why Strattis says in a comedy named after him (produced not long after the *Frogs*): "stage of the chorus-killer Cinesias."

109. Demosthenes, *Against Leptines* 23. Delivered 355/4 B.C. Demosthenes' statements strongly suggest that *synchoregiai* were far from normal practice.

But if indeed the numbers of those able to perform *choregiai* did fall short, by Zeus, would it be better to have the cost of the *choregiai* defrayed by joint contributions, as we do the trierarchies, or to take back what we have given to our benefactors? I would say the former.

The Agonothetes

110. *IG* II² 3073. "The Monument of Xenokles" is an inscribed monument found in the Theater of Dionysus at Athens and provides the first inscriptional record of the *agonothesia*. Date: 306 B.C. Since two choregic inscriptions survive from 319 B.C., the end of the choregic system must be dated to the period 318–307 B.C. The order of the listings, tragedy first, then comedy, indicates that the inscription refers to the Lenaea (contrast the order of the *Fasti,* I 100).

The people assumed the costs of production in the archonship of Anaxikrates.

The *agonothetes* was Xenokles, the son of Xeinis, of the deme Sphettos.

In the tragic competition the victorious poet was Phanostratos, son of Herakleides, of Halikarnassos.

In the tragic competition the victorious actor was Hieromnemon, son of Euanorides, of the deme Kydathenai.

In the comic competition the victorious poet was Philemon, son of Damon, of the deme Diomeia.

In the comic competition the victorious actor was Kallippos, son of Kallias, of the deme Sunium.

111. Aristotle, *Politics* 1321a31–42. Written ca. 330 B.C. Aristotle advises oligarchs on how to acquire and maintain a hold on power within the *polis*. Although Aristotle claims that the propertied class of his day (before the restriction of the franchise in 322 B.C.) did not employ it, the conversion of the *choregia* into a magistracy, sometime during the restricted democracy, is an excellent expression of this strategy.

> Moreover, to the chief magistracies, which are to be held by those enjoying full citizen rights, liturgies should be attached so that the common people will gladly have no part in them and show indulgence toward those in office, who pay a great deal for the privilege. It is appropriate, upon entering into office, to offer magnificent sacrifices and undertake some public works, so that the commoners will be glad to see the (oligarchic) constitution remain in place when they participate in the feasts and to see the city adorned with monuments and buildings. As a result the leading citizens will also have monuments to their expenditures. But at present, oligarchs do not do this—just the opposite. They pursue profit no less than honor.

IIIAiib. Judges

A close correspondence between a playwright's success and contemporary estimation of his merits is generally assumed; much, for example, is made of the report that Euripides produced ninety-two plays but won only four victories in Athens. But in order to assess the correlation between success and contemporary reception, one needs to consider the manner in which judging took place and the factors that might influence a judge's decision. Above all, one must keep in mind that the prize was not awarded to a play but to a production: though the poet and *choregos* each won separate prizes, a single decision determined the success of both together.

What most strikes the modern observer is the degree of public participation and public scrutiny that went into the process of judging the dramatic and dithyrambic contests at Athens, making them more akin to our national elections than to the secret deliberations of Nobel Prizes and Academy Awards. The state went to great lengths to prevent corruption, bribery, or influence peddling. Each of the ten Athenian tribes appears to have submitted a list of possible candidates to serve as judges (112, 113). The Council (*Boule*) then approved the candidates, and the names were put into jars, sealed by the *choregoi* and taken up to the state treasury on the Acropolis (113). At the beginning of the competition the jars were brought into the theater and the archon, before the assembled audience, appears to have selected one name from each (112). It is not clear whether the same judges sat for all of the contests or whether different judges sat for each (as perhaps implied by 112). The judges then came forward and publicly took an oath of impartiality (112, 114, 117, 118, 125) and were seated in a separate section of the theater, presumably close to the orchestra (116, 124). The Calendar Frieze, an Attic relief sculpture possibly of late Hellenistic date, shows the judges sitting at a table heaped with crowns and other prizes.

The choice of ten judges seems a reasonable inference from 112 and the reference to a plurality of jars (see on 113), but scholars have debated the number since late Hellenistic times (119–21). The tradition best represented names five judges, though four (119), seven, and "however many" (121) are also mentioned. The simplest way to reconcile the evidence is provided by 122: Lysias states clearly that not all the judges necessarily contributed to the final decision. He refers to a judge whose vote was not "selected by lot." Most scholars take this as evidence of a second lottery in which only five of the ten ballots cast by the judges were selected for the final decision. This second lottery might be explained as a further precaution against corruption: if there were only one group of judges for all the contests during the four or five days of the festival, it is not out of character for the Athenian democracy to have added this further obstacle to attempts to compromise the integrity of the judges over the interval. This is true even if each contest had its own judges, since the tragic and comic contests (at least during the Peloponnesian War) each seem each to have extended over three days (IIIAia). It may be added that the whole purpose of using voting tablets (122, 123) presupposes a second lottery, since 122 makes it clear that there is no question of using the tablets for a secret ballot; Lysias' speaker assumes that had the judgment in question been read, everyone would have known whose judgment it was.

The difficulty with the theory of a five-ballot selection is the low probability that five ballots would ever produce a clear ranking even of three sets of tragedies, let alone five comedies and ten dithyrambs. This is true even if each prize (first, second, third, etc.) were voted on independently. It has recently been suggested that the contradictions in the sources could best be reconciled by supposing that there were ten judges but that only as many votes were counted as assured placement. A given candidate would normally need five, and hence the proverb in 120. This would have the advantage of speeding up the process and avoiding the embarrassment of a tie in a case where five judges voted for Eupolis and five for Aristophanes (though admittedly adding an element of chance to the evaluation). But the five votes in favor of Eupolis might only be acquired on reading the ninth ballot (cf. 121), while any leftover ballots could be said to have missed being "selected by lot" (122). The main problem with this scheme is that it is scarcely economical since in the case of three, and especially in the case of five or ten contestants, one is not likely to leave many ballots uncounted in producing five votes for a single candidate. Indeed, chances are against any candidate getting as many as five votes.

It would make more sense to assume that a decision would be attempted on a draw of five ballots, with an option of choosing as many more as necessary to break a tie. The advantage of such a system would be less one of saving time (though this would in most cases be a welcome side effect) than to avoid indecision. We know of no procedure that would have forced a judge to alter his decision if the balloting ended in a dead heat, and one can scarcely imagine what such a procedure would be, or how the volatile Athenian audience would endure a mechanical remedy for tie breaking. A five-ballot selection would have the advantage of breaking a tie vote before the fact. Let us suppose a number of worst-case scenarios in a tragic contest where the judges' ballots are distributed as follows: 1-1-1-1-1-2-2-2-2-2. In this case, selecting five ballots will force a decision that would otherwise be impossible. But what of a case, surely the most common occurrence, where the vote distribution allowed no sure placement with five votes? Consider a contest with five comedies where the vote is distributed 1-1-1-2-2-2-3-3-3-4. Chances of breaking the tie are far greater with an initial selection of five, with two or more votes to the winner, or if two candidates receive two votes each, with a clear winner emerging by the time the eighth ballot is chosen. There are still several problems unresolved by this theory. A vote distribution such as 1-1-2-2-3-3-4-4-5-5 could only be resolved if one or no pairs emerged in the selection of five ballots. Moreover, this system is only economical from the point of view of determining the winner, not ordering all the contestants from first to third, fifth or tenth, prize as was the practice at these festivals. Total ranking adds a completely new dimension to the calculation. Two possibilities present themselves: either each rank was voted on individually, making for nine rounds of voting in the case of dithyramb, or a single vote was meant, ideally, to determine all of the places. The former procedure is implied by the wording of 122, which suggests the judge simply wrote "tribe X wins" on his tablet, and 123, which also implies a single choice. The latter procedure is envisioned by 124, but this anecdote may have no connection at all with Athenian practice.

It is most difficult to imagine how dithyrambic victors were chosen, given the fact that the dithyrambs were a tribal competition. If each tribe put forth a list of candidates, surely it did so with the expectation that its candidates would vote for the nominating tribe, and this indeed is the expectation clearly expressed by 122. The process described above would leave each competitor with only one vote; indecision could only be avoided by selecting a single vote by lot, which would make a mockery of the notion of a competition. An attempt to envision the practicalities of the business reveals how little we know. The tragic and comic competitions were no doubt less partisan. The sources seem to assume that the judges allowed themselves to be swayed by the will of the crowd; some suggest that this was the judges' obligation (123–26). The comic poets frequently include commands, admonitions, and entreaties to the judges (possibly a cue for partisans and claqueurs to shout their approval).

The extant sources leave us with a strong sense of paradox. Despite the enormous precautions taken by the state, charges of corruption, bribery, and manipulation meet us at every stage in the procedure (113–15, 118, 125, 127). On the other hand, there is no evidence at all for a failure to award a clear ranking of prizes, though the process of selecting winners hardly seems workable so far as we can reconstruct it.

Sources

112. Plutarch, *Cimon* 8.7–9. Written ca. 115 and referring to an event in 468 B.C. The passage implies that the generals were apt substitutes for the judges since they came (normally or unusually?) from each of the ten tribes. The anecdote goes on to explain that Aeschylus left for Sicily in a tiff at Sophocles' victory. The historicity of the event is extremely doubtful, but Plutarch seems to have envisioned a separate selection of judges for each genre.

When Sophocles, still a young man, entered his first production in the contest, Apsephion the archon did not choose the judges of the contest by lot, because he saw great rivalry and partisanship in the audience, but after Cimon entered the theater with the other generals and made the customary libations to the gods, he would not allow them to leave but forced them to take oaths and sit as judges, being ten, one from each tribe. Then the competition gained in ferocity because of the dignity of the judges.

113. Isocrates, *Trapeziticus* 33–34. Delivered ca. 393 B.C. The reference to a plurality of water jars seems to confirm the tribal basis of the selection: unless one candidate from each tribe was required, there is no reason to put names in separate jars.

Which of you does not know that Pythodoros, the fellow known as the "bum" who does and says anything for Pasion, opened the water jars last year and took out the names of the judges that the Council had deposited? So why would anyone be surprised if a man who for small gain would risk his life and open these jars, which were marked by the Executive Officers of the Council (*prytaneis*), sealed by the *choregoi,* guarded by the treasurers, and stored in the Acropolis...

114. Second Hypothesis to Demosthenes, *Against Meidias.* Cf. 106.

Meidias, a very rich and powerful citizen and an enemy of Demosthenes, for reasons Demosthenes will give shortly in his speech, frequently obstructed and hindered him, and especially, as Demosthenes says, when the judges were taking their oath to give the victory to the one who sang well, Meidias kept inciting them saying "except Demosthenes."

115. Pherecrates, *Krapataloi, PCG* F 102. Produced late 5th or early 4th c. B.C.

To the judges who are now judging I say do not perjure yourselves nor judge unjustly, or by Zeus, God of Friendship, Pherecrates will tell you another tale far more abusive than this.

116. Aristophanes, *Acharnians* 1224f. Produced Lenaea, 425 B.C. In the *exodos,* Dikaiopolis wins the drinking contest of the Anthesteria and is carried out in a victory procession (*komos*). The passage's primary reference is to the awarding of a wineskin as a prize in that contest. A humorous metatheatrical reference to the theatrical contest is obvious: the king archon presided over the Lenaea (61); a wineskin is said to be the prize of a comic *choregos* (IIIAiia).

Carry me to the judges. Where is the king archon? Give me the wineskin!

117. Aristophanes, *Birds* 445–47. Produced Dionysia, 414 B.C. After the *agon* the chorus is asked to swear to a peaceful settlement with Pisthetairos, but delivers a comic oath instead.

> CHORUS: I swear on the heads of all these people (gestures to audience), that I will win by all the judges and all the spectators. PISTHETAIROS: It will be so. CHORUS: If I transgress, may I win only by a single judge.

118. Aristophanes, *Ecclesiazusae* 1154–62. Produced 392/1 B.C.

> I wish to make a little suggestion to the judges: may the ones who are wise be mindful of this play's wisdom and vote for me; may the ones who like to laugh be mindful of this play's humor and vote for me; that is to say I encourage just about everyone to vote for me. Don't let the lottery and the fact that our play was produced first be to blame for anything, but remember all of this. Don't perjure yourselves, but always judge the choruses fairly! Don't behave like bad whores who can only ever remember their last customers!

119. *POxy* 1611, 30–37. This fragmentary papyrus, written sometime in the late 2nd or early 3rd c., is a copy of a literary commentary, probably of Hellenistic Alexandrian scholarship, possibly by Didymus (ca. 80–10 B.C.). It seems fairly certain that the reference is to the judges of the comic contest: in a surviving fragment of the *parabasis* of Cratinus' *Plutuses,* the chorus declare that they deserve to win but express some anxiety about the impatience of the judges.

> "[...] now [...] you see us, being two, and the judges four": He thus shows that there were four (the papyrus actually reads "and thus it is clear there were forty judges"; this is usually emended but may be correct), but Lysippus in the *Bacchae* shows there were five, and Cratinus says the same thing in the *Plutuses.*

120A. Zenobius 3.64. Date: 2nd c.

> "It lies on the knees of five judges": proverbial for such things as are in the power of others. The proverb was used insofar as five judges judged the comic choruses, as Epicharmus says.

120B. Hesychius, s.v. *pente kritai.* Written 5th c.

> "Five judges": So many judged the comic choruses, not only in Athens, but in Sicily.

120C. Scholion to Aristophanes, *Birds* 445.

Five judges judged the comic choruses. Those who received all five
votes were happy.

121. Lucian, *Harmonides* 2. Written ca. 170. The dialogue presents
a piper advising his student to play not to the crowd but to the few of
discerning taste, if he wishes to be famous.

In the contests the mass of the audience know how to clap and
hiss, but the judges are seven, five, or however many.

122. Lysias, *On the Wound by Premeditation* 3. Delivered late 5th
to early 4th c. B.C. This passage is valuable evidence for the selection of
judges' ballots. Of particular interest are the argument's presuppositions
that the candidate put forward by the tribe would vote for it; that the
audience would know who cast the ballot; that the audience would have
been able to infer that the speaker and the judge were friends. This last
presupposition may indicate that the judge did not belong to the speaker's
tribe, since this would otherwise seem sufficient. Great caution is needed
in pressing Athenian forensic arguments for logic.

I wish that his vote had been selected by lot when he was judge at
the Dionysia, so that it would be clear to you that we were
reconciled, since he judged that my tribe won. But as it is he wrote
this on his tablet, but it was not selected. Philinos and Diokles
know that I am telling the truth. They are not allowed to give
evidence, however, since they did not make a deposition in relation
to the charge against which I am now defending myself, and yet
you know well that we were the ones who put his name forward
in the selection and that he was sitting as judge on our behalf.

123. Aelian, *Varia Historia* 2.13. Written ca. late 2nd c. to 235. Aelian
claims to describe the audiences reaction to Aristophanes' *Clouds* at the
Dionysia, 423 B.C.

They applauded the poet as never before and shouted that he
should win and commanded the judges from above to write no
other name but Aristophanes.

124. Vitruvius, *On Architecture* 7, prooem. 4 ff. Written ca. 25 B.C.
The anecdote, which supposedly took place ca. 195 B.C., is absurd and
anachronistic, but at least it shows us how Vitruvius' source imagined
judging took place at the games consecrated by Ptolemy Philadelphus to
the Muses and Apollo. There is no reason to suppose that the judging
of this contest was modeled on the judging of Athenian contests, but
there may be some relation, and this is the only detailed description of
the process in ancient literature.

Once these arrangements were made and the games were at hand, learned judges had to be chosen to evaluate them. When the king had chosen six citizens and could not easily find a seventh suited to the task, he consulted the directors of the library and asked if they knew of anyone available for the task. They mentioned a certain Aristophanes (of Byzantium) who with great application and diligence was daily engaged in systematically reading all of the books. So when the crowds had gathered for the games and the judges had been assigned seats set apart from the rest, Aristophanes was summoned to take the place marked out for him along with the others. The first competition was for poets, and while they read their texts the entire populace by their shouts warned the judges what they should vote for. And so, when they were called upon one by one to express their judgments, the six were unanimous and gave first prize to the poet whom they noticed most pleased the multitude and gave second prize to the next most pleasing. But Aristophanes asked them to proclaim the man who least pleased the crowd. When the king and the entire audience grew indignant, he rose and obtained permission to speak. When there was silence he explained that his choice was the only poet among them—all the others had recited other poets' work—and that judges should reward what was written, not stolen. While the crowd was dumbfounded and the king was wavering, Aristophanes, relying on his memory, produced an enormous number of rolls from certain bookshelves and by comparing them with the recited poems forced the contestants to admit their plagiarism. And so the king ordered them to be arrested for theft and sent them off condemned in disgrace, but he heaped Aristophanes with honors and put him in charge of the library.

125. Pseudo-Andocides, *Against Alcibiades* 20–21. See 105.

126. Plato, *Laws* 659a–c. Written ca. 357–347 B.C. Cf. IV 172.

The true judge should not learn from the audience nor be impressed by the noise of the many or by his own ignorance . . . It was possible for him, according to the old Greek custom, just as the present custom in Sicily and Italy, to leave it to the majority of the audience and judge the winner by a show of hands.

127A. Aulus Gellius 17.4. Written ca. 180, the anecdote is set in the late 4th or early 3rd c. B.C.

Menander was repeatedly beaten by the inferior poet Philemon through his influence, friends, and supporters. When he once chanced to meet him in the street he said, "Pardon my asking, Philemon, but tell me, are you not ashamed when you win?"

127B. Quintilian 10.1.72. Written late 1st c.

Philemon, who was often preferred to Menander in the corrupt judgments of his day, deserved to be second in the opinion of all, I believe.

IIIAiic. Freedom of Expression

Most literary historians from the Hellenistic period onward explained Old Comedy's freedom to abuse individuals as a "law" or "right" acquired when it was discovered that public abuse embarrassed malefactors into giving up their evil ways, but the "right" was eventually repealed, either because poets began to attack "good people" or because the "malefactors" eventually ganged up on the poets (128, 129). This theory still has its modern supporters, though modern scholars generally prefer to find the cause of comic license in the festival context of Athenian drama, mixing sacred inviolability with psycho-sociological notions of "carnival." Neither theory is really adequate. No 5th- or 4th-c. B.C. texts support either view. Moreover, comic freedom rose and declined without any significant change in its festival and religious setting. In our view, comic outspokenness was a liberty not granted but assumed at a calculated risk when the political climate seemed to offer a chance of impunity, not a creation of conscious policy or sacred tradition but a by-product of the factional struggle between the democrats and oligarchs at Athens. This is in fact the explanation offered by our 5th- and 4th-c. B.C. writers (130, 131) and repeated by one of our later sources on comedy (132), whose views may go back to the school of Aristotle (cf. 133). There are three main reasons for preferring a purely political explanation. First, there was a close synchrony between the tide of poetic freedom and rise of the Athenian democracy, its ebb, and the supremacy of the oligarchs. Second is the fact that poets were never entirely secure in expressing their views: we have evidence of two legal prosecutions of poets in the 5th c. B.C. (136, 139–41) and some possible attempts at censorship legislation (137, 138, 142, 143), both inconsistent with any stable or generally recognized privilege. Third, and perhaps most important, the freedom exercised by the comic poets in the theater did not in fact differ markedly in kind or degree from that exercised by ordinary citizens in the democratic law courts (146–57).

Aristophanes and Eupolis are the most distinctive representatives of the political comedy that was the dominant style of Old Comedy during the period of the "radical democracy" in Athens (from about 430 to 415 B.C.). Two features typical of the style were the appearance of individual Athenians as characters in a comedy and the incidental ridicule of public personalities in the comic dialogue. Aristophanes may have been the first to devote an entire comedy to ridiculing a single individual (Cleon) with *Knights* (424 B.C.). Many other such comedies followed, but their numbers drop sharply ca. 415 B.C. and eventually give way to less direct treatments and in the 4th c. B.C. to apolitical paratragedies, myth-travesties, and social comedies. By the Middle Comic period the ad hominem plot is extremely rare and generally reserved for prominent and unpopular foreigners, who constituted safe targets. In addition to the real personalities who appear in the drama, the 430s and 420s also saw an increase in people verbally ridiculed. Aristophanes' comedies contain a great number of such victims of abuse (*komodoumenoi*): *Acharnians* (425 B.C.), 45; *Knights* (424 B.C.), 44; *Clouds* (423 B.C.), 45; *Wasps* (422 B.C.), 81; *Peace* (421 B.C.), 40; *Birds* (414 B.C.), 61; *Lysistrata* (411 B.C.), 14; *Thesmophoriazusae* (411 B.C.), 17; *Frogs* (405 B.C.), 55; *Ecclesiazusae* (ca. 392 B.C.), 41; *Plutus* (388 B.C.), 19. One notices a decline in the statistics for the last two plays, and a very significant drop in the two plays of 411 B.C. that coincide with the unsettled period just before and just after an oligarchic coup in Athens. Peisander, a leader of the conspiracy, is the only person in *Lysistrata* to come under political attack, but Aristophanes could not at that time have anticipated his importance. Democracy was restored the next year, and its recovery is adequately reflected in the statistic for *komodoumenoi* in *Frogs*. The fragments of Middle Comedy show that the practice of ridiculing by name declined only gradually during the 4th c. B.C. By the period of New Comedy, it is rare, and the productive years of this genre coincide with a period of oligarchy at Athens from 322 to 307 B.C. (almost continually) followed by a long period in which the government remained unstable and continually changed hands. It is probably significant that the latest two *komodoumenoi* that survive are from comedies written during democratic restorations, and one of these may have had an ad hominem plot in the old style (134, 135).

The best-attested attempt to muzzle a comic poet came after the production at the Dionysia of 426 B.C. of Aristophanes' *Babylonians,* a satire on Athenian imperialism. Aristophanes reports that Cleon dragged him (or his *didaskalos* Callistratus) to the Council Chamber, where he was "inundated with slander and abuse" (139A). The fact that Cleon brought Aristophanes before the Council of the Athenian Assembly indicates that he used a legal procedure called *eisangelia,* normally reserved for serious crimes threatening the safety and welfare of the whole community. Two passages in the *Acharnians* mention the actual charge laid against Aristophanes: that he spoke ill against the city in the presence of foreigners (139B) and that he ridiculed the city and committed an outrage (*hybris*) on the people (*demos*) (139C). The scholiasts claim that the case went to trial: not only does Aristophanes mention nothing of this, but his words in 141, whether they refer to this affair or a subsequent event, imply that an out-of-court settlement was reached. This is a good example of the manner in which scholia fabricate facts on the basis of inferences from the text and then frequently proliferate them: the mention of charges in *Acharnians* led to the fabrication of a trial, which led to the fabrication of a multiplicity of charges, which led to the fabrication of a multiplicity of trials to accommodate all the charges. A similar scenario is not unlikely for most, if not all, of the "laws" passed against comic ridicule (cf. 143, 144).

The other 5th-c. B.C. "censorship trial" was the much earlier prosecution not of a comic poet but of the tragedian Phrynichus for the production of a tragedy on the recapture of Miletus by the Persians in 494 B.C. (136). Athens had given, but later withdrew, aid to the revolt: clearly the city was sharply divided in its policy, not least of all because the Persians continued to support the remnants of the exiled Pisistratid tyranny against the young Athenian democracy. Phrynichus' play and its punishment (if historical) must be seen as moments in a bitter factional struggle. It is worth noting that historical tragedy flourished briefly in the first three decades of the 5th c. B.C. In addition to *The Capture of Miletus,* we know of two plays dealing with the Persian Wars (480–479 B.C.): Phrynichus' *Phoenician Women* (probably 476 B.C.) and Aeschylus' *Persians* (472 B.C.). Aeschylus' play is extant and includes partisan propaganda in aggrandizing the role of the democratic leader Themistocles. Tragedy on sensitive current events then disappears in the wake of conservative ascendancy under Cimon, never to return to the Athenian theater. The case of Phrynichus would suggest that contemporary subjects in tragedy, as in serious art generally, were simply too hot to handle directly.

The late tradition has several reports of censorship legislation. The first, 137, said to have lasted from 440/39 B.C. to 437/6 B.C., cannot be confirmed by independent sources, but it is generally accepted because of the precision of the scholiast's information and the fact that it is not an obvious inference from the text. The second, 138, is almost certainly a mistaken inference drawn by a later scholar from a passage in Aristophanes. The third, 142, legislation by Cleon, was probably fabricated in an attempt to sort out the profusion of charges and prosecutions of Aristophanes, generated by uncritical ancient scholars. The fourth, 143, the decree of Syrakosios, is a little harder to dismiss: though the existence of the law is reported only by scholia and clearly based on inference, the inference in this case is drawn from a passage of a lost comedy, which the scholiast cites, but the reconstruction and interpretation of the fragment is very controversial. In any case, if the "Law of Syrakosios" was a general ban on ridiculing people by name, then its existence as legislation appears to be contradicted by the fact that Aristophanes' *Birds* and Phrynichus' *Antisocial Man,* produced at the first Dionysia after this putative legislation, both ridicule, among others, Syrakosios himself. Some take it to be a ban on ridiculing those accused of the mutilation of the herms (415 B.C.). If so, it was evidently designed to avoid exciting partisan violence in the audience. The last reported piece of legislation, 144, appears to be another fabrication of ancient scholarship, probably arising from an attempt to reconcile the legislation theory with the myth of Eupolis' death, which seems to have become a centerpiece of the rival political theory of Old Comedy in the Hellenistic period (132, 142, 144, 145).

No discussion of dramatic freedom of expression could be of any value without a consideration of the limitations on free speech outside the theater, both as they existed in law, and as they existed in practice. An examination of the law will show that comic poets did occasionally violate some legal restrictions, though here "occasionally" and "some" may be more telling than the violations. But an examination of speeches delivered in Athenian courts and subsequently published show that ordinary Athenians lavished abuse on one another in flagrant violation of the law, and did so in the expectation of getting away with it.

The slander law attributed to Solon (148) was superseded at least in part by the *dike kakegorias* (149), probably some time in the 5th c. B.C., although we cannot be sure of its existence earlier than 384/3 B.C. (149). There is some evidence that "Solon's" provisions against abusing the dead were covered by this new law (149), but our best evidence makes it clear that it specified four insults that may not be brought against the living: "murderer," "mother beater," "father beater," and "shield thrower" (152). Perhaps separate from this law is a law that forbade ridiculing the profession of any citizen working in the marketplace (clearly a law directed at "classist" remarks, 154). The charge of *hybris* differed both in procedure and in the gravity of the charge from *kakegoria*. The latter was a *dike,* a purely private remedy, and could only be pursued by the injured party or their legal representative. The former was an indictment (*graphe*) and could be brought by any citizen (146, 147); since acts of *hybris* (mistreatment, outrage, or assault) were thought to pose a threat to the security and welfare of the community as a whole, its punishment was every citizen's business. Briefly stated, an act was considered *hybris* if it showed contempt for the rights of one's fellow citizens. There was, finally, a law against abusing civic magistrates; the penalty was loss of civic rights (147, 156, 157). Because most of our information about Athenian law comes from the 4th-c. B.C. orators, we cannot be sure that all these laws existed in the late 5th c. B.C. The exceptions are the indictment for *hybris,* which is amply attested in comedy, and presumably also the law of Solon, if it had not yet been superseded by the later slander law. Assuming, for the sake of argument, that they were all in existence during the heyday of political comedy, we find several violations in the fragments of Old Comedy, but on close inspection the violations show signs of restraint and do not show clear evidence that comic poets were exempt: rather they seem to honor them in the breach. The only apparent violations of the taboo on abusing the dead are in Aristophanes—two rather mild passages ridiculing Pericles for starting the war (150) and two more vigorous assaults on the recently dead Cleon (151), both of which, to make the issue even muddier, are rather indirect. The first attack was placed in the mouth of a fictitious foreigner in the audience; the second was couched in a figure of *praeteritio,* virtually, "now that he's dead, we musn't say anything bad about him...that he was a crook, a blabbermouth, an extortionist, etc." As for the *dike kakegorias,* a similar mixture of freedom and restraint is shown in the use of the taboo words: no *komodoumenos* is ever called a "murderer," "mother beater," or "father beater" in all of our extant fragments of comedy, although otherwise anonymous characters called "father beaters" do appear, and indeed fathers are even beaten on stage. But one Kleonymos is persistently ridiculed as a "shield thrower" in five Aristophanic comedies (153). Similarly, though there is frequent ridicule of "tradespeople" in the fragments of Old Comedy, the tradespeople who appear on the stage are generally either unnamed or probably fictitious; in cases where real people's names are used we can never prove that the person actually was a tradesperson, but we can sometimes prove the opposite (155). Finally, though the scholia at *Clouds* 31 appear to think that Aristophanes made slight alterations on the name of the archon so as to mock him with impunity (157), there is some evidence to suggest that the name, not deformed, refers to a *komodoumenos* known elsewhere and someone other than the archon, but more importantly, Lysias and Demosthenes show quite clearly that the law only prohibited the abuse of magistrates in public offices and performing their official duties (147, 156).

It is difficult to say, then, whether the two or three serious violations of Athenian slander laws show that dramatists were exempted, or whether they are merely the exceptions proving that they were not. The problem is in thinking that the violation of the laws of slander would necessarily lead to prosecution. Law is one thing, but actual legal practice is quite another. An examination of forensic and political speeches shows that Attic orators took the same liberties in abusing their opponents as we find in the comic theater. One need only consider the example of 152, where the speaker, while prosecuting Theomnestos, who had gratuitously called him a "father killer" at a previous trial, not only abuses Theomnestos' dead father as a "worthless good-for-nothing," but mocks Theomnestos throughout as a "shield thrower," a charge that he also generously extends to his father; yet the context shows the charge to be unambiguously slanderous, since Theomnestos had already been acquitted of the charge by a jury. Similarly, we owe our knowledge of the law about ridiculing the occupation of tradespeople in the agora to the fact that it is violated in the prosecution of the speaker of 154. Though Theomnestos' prosecution shows that slander trials did occur, it is the only private suit for slander that survives from antiquity. Such cases seem to have been quite rare. It is of great interest to note that Theomnestos feels it necessary to apologize for bringing the suit under the *dike kakegorias:* "I think it vulgar and excessively litigious to prosecute for slander" (152). There are in fact many good reasons why someone like Kleonymos would have willingly foregone his right to sue Aristophanes, quite apart from the expense and trouble of prosecution. Whatever the prospects for success, the risks were considerable. One had only to consider such precedents as Cleon's attempted prosecution of Aristophanes, which only inflamed the poet to intensify his abuse and added motive and an air of legitimacy to his charges. From what we know of ancient courtroom practice, a suit against a comic poet was less likely to lead to the restoration of one's good name than to provide an opportunity for more comic abuse at the trial itself (cf. 141A), let alone future comic productions. A normal trial involved a jury of five hundred random citizens, usually of the ardently democratic lower classes, and there was no reason to think that they would condemn in the courts what they approved in the theater.

Sources

Comic License

128. Cicero, *On the State* 4.11 A philosophical dialogue written 54–51 B.C. A "law" is also mentioned by Themistius, *Orations* 8.110.

> SCIPIO: Except when habit of life permits it, comedy could never have won from audiences the approval of its excesses. And indeed the older Greeks preserved a certain harmony in its vicious reports; among them it was even conceded by law that comedy could say whatever it wanted about whomever it wanted by name... AFRICANUS: Whom did it not affect, or rather whom did it not molest? Whom did it spare? Granted, it injured shameless populists (i.e., "radical" democrats), men who were undermining the state, like Cleon, Cleophon, and Hyperbolus.... but it was no more decent that Pericles, who had already been head of the state with supreme power for a great many years in peace and war, should be attacked in verse, and that these verses should have been paraded on stage, than if our Plautus.... or Naevius abused Publius or Gnaeus Scipio.

129. Horace, *The Art of Poetry* 281–84. Written ca. 19 B.C.

> Old Comedy followed these men (Thespis and Aeschylus) not without great praise, but license lapsed into excess and violence, which needed to be checked by law. The law was passed and the chorus fell shamefully silent, once it lost its right to abuse.

130. "Old Oligarch," *Constitution of the Athenians* 2.18. Written ca. 430–420 B.C. In this passage the word *demos* is left untranslated in order to preserve its ambiguous reference both to the "people," meaning lower classes as opposed to the elite, and the "people" as sovereign political authority within the democratic state.

> They do not permit anyone to ridicule the *demos* in comedy, or to abuse it, so as not to suffer ill repute themselves. If, however, anyone wishes to ridicule a private citizen, they bid him do so fully

aware of the fact that those ridiculed in a comedy are generally not of the *demos* nor of the mass, but the rich, noble, and powerful. A few poor people or democrats are ridiculed in comedy, but only because they are busybodies and anxious to rise above the *demos*. Consequently, they do not mind seeing such people ridiculed in comedy.

131. Isocrates, *On the Peace* 17. Delivered 355 B.C.

I know that it is arduous to oppose your intentions, and that as there is a democracy, there is no freedom of speech, except here for those who are most thoughtless and have no regard for you, and in the theater for the comic poets.

132. Platonius, *On the Differences of the Comedies.* Written in the late Hellenistic period or later. Platonius or his source is an eclectic and has clearly added to the basic framework of a political theory of comic evolution a "terror" arising from the supposed "murder" of Eupolis by Alcibiades, a general fear of prosecution among the poets, and a particularly confused statement about the effect this had on the availability of *choregoi.* The various causes are specifically aimed at explaining the three major distinctions perceived by later theorists between Old and Middle Comedy: the disappearance of personal abuse, the disappearance of direct political satire, and the disappearance of the chorus. This distinction seems to owe something to Aristotle's distinction between the abuse (*aischrologia*) of early comedy and the innuendo of modern (i.e., Middle) comedy in *Nicomachean Ethics* 1128a.

> It is good to indicate the reasons why Old Comedy has a certain form peculiar to itself, and Middle Comedy is different from it. In the times of Aristophanes, Cratinus, and Eupolis democracy ruled in Athens and the people held all the power, being itself the autocrat and master of its political affairs. Since everyone had freedom of speech, the writers of comedy had license to mock generals, judges who gave bad judgments, and also any of the citizens who were either greedy or behaved wantonly. For when the people heard the comedians vigorously insulting such persons, as I said, they exempted them from terror of reprisal. We know that the people by nature have been opposed to the rich since time immemorial and that it rejoices in their discomfiture. So in the time of the comedy of Aristophanes, Cratinus, and Eupolis some poets were pitiless against those who erred, but for the rest, when the democracy was driven back by those who wanted to set up a tyranny in Athens and an oligarchy was established and the power of the people had

gone over to a few men and the oligarchy was in charge, terror
seized the poets: it was not possible to mock anyone openly when
the offended parties could demand justice from the poets. And so
we know that Eupolis, upon producing the *Baptai,* was drowned
in the sea by the man against whom he launched the *Baptai*
(Alcibiades). Because of this they grew more wary of mockery and
the *choregoi* began to grow scarce, for the Athenians no longer had
the will to elect the *choregoi,* who defrayed the expenses of the
choreuts. At any rate Aristophanes produced the *Aiolosikon* (388
B.C.), which has no choral odes (doubtless a false inference from the
noninclusion of choral *embolima* in the textual tradition). Since the
choregoi were no longer being elected (!) and the choreuts had no
sustenance, the choral odes were taken out of comedy and the
character of the plots changed. The object of Old Comedy being
the people's mockery of the judges and generals, Aristophanes
omitted the usual mockery because of the great terror and jeered
at the drama *Aiolos* written by the tragedians (i.e., Euripides, before
423 B.C.) as badly made. The character of Middle Comedy is such
as the *Aiolosikon* of Aristophanes and the *Odysseuses* of Cratinus
and the majority of ancient comedies that are without choral odes
or *parabaseis....* The poets of Middle Comedy both changed the
plots and left out the choral songs since they did not have *choregoi*
to defray the costs of the choreuts. These are the plots of Old
Comedy: to censure some generals and judges who do not judge
rightly and make money through injustice and have taken up a
wicked way of life. Middle Comedy gave up that sort of plot, and
proceeded to mock the stories told by the poets, because such things
as mocking Homer for saying something or some tragic poet or
other are not liable to prosecution. Even in Old Comedy one can
find dramas of the same sort as those produced in the end when
the oligarchy had consolidated its power. At any rate the *Odysseuses*
of Cratinus censured no one but was a mockery of the *Odyssey* of
Homer. For such are the plots in Middle Comedy. Placing in their
comedies certain myths that were told by earlier authors, they
mocked them as badly told and they rejected *parabaseis,* as there
were no choruses because of the lack of *choregoi.* They did not
even bring on stage masks made the same way as in Old Comedy:
in Old Comedy the masks resembled the people ridiculed in the
comedy, so that, even before the actors said anything, the identity
of the ridiculed person was obvious from the likeness of the mask's

appearance; in Middle and New Comedy they deliberately constructed the masks with greater comic distortion since they were
afraid of the Macedonians and the terror that was attached to them,
and so that the appearance of the mask would not coincide by
some chance with the features of some Macedonian ruler and the
poet incur a penalty because he was thought to have acted deliberately. At any rate we see the shape of the brows on the masks of
Menander's comedy and how the mouth is distorted and not of
human proportion.

133. Aristotle, *Poetics* 1448a28–40. Written ca. 330 B.C. The assumption that comedy must have developed out of a democratic state is at
least as old as the Megarian claim to comedy on the basis of the fact
that Megara had a democracy long before Athens. Megarian tradition
placed the first democracy before 600 B.C. Aristotle himself recognizes a
Sicilian Dorian contribution to comedy (II 12). Analogous is Aristotle's
explanation that rhetoric developed in Sicily when tyranny gave way to
democracy (fr. 125 Gigon).

> Wherefore some also call these <forms of mimesis> "dramas," since
> they imitate people in action (*drontas*). For this reason the Dorians
> lay claim both to tragedy and to comedy; for the Megarians, both
> those on the mainland <claim to be the inventers of comedy>
> alleging that <it arose> at the time of their democracy and also
> <the Megarians> of Sicily, since the poet Epicharmus, who was
> much earlier than Chionides and Magnes came from there; and
> some of the Peloponnesians claim tragedy. They adduce the names
> as proof. For they call their townships *komai,* but the Athenians
> call them "demes." They suppose that "comedy" is derived not
> from the word "to revel" (*komazein*), but from the fact that they
> were despised and wandered out of the city about the townships
> (*komai*). And they say *dran* (whence "drama") for "to produce
> poetry" (*poiein*), whereas the Athenians say *prattein.*

134A. Plutarch, *Demetrius* 12 (= PCG F 25). Written ca. 115. Referring to events in 307–302 B.C. In 307 B.C. Demetrius the Besieger put an
end to the oligarchy under the regency of Demetrius of Phaleron (see IV
131–33) and restored the democratic constitution. Athenians lavished
divine honors upon Demetrius and his father Antigonus, among other
things renaming the Dionysia the "Demetria" and decreeing that the
figures of Demetrius and his father should be woven onto the robe in
which the statue of Athena was dressed at the Panathenaea (302 B.C.).
The comic poet Philippides ridicules Stratokles, the principal agent of

this sycophancy. All three fragments probably come from a single comedy produced in 301 B.C. before the defeat of Demetrius and Antigonus at the Battle of Ipsus. It provides one of the last survivals of a direct attack on an Athenian politician in comedy. The last line in the first passage is taken by some as an indication that Stratokles advocated some restriction of the comic poets' freedom of speech.

> The gods showed their disapproval of most of these things. When the robe <of Athena>, on which it had been decreed that the figures of Demetrius and Antigonus be woven between Zeus and Athena, was carried in procession through the Kerameikos, a sudden squall arose and ripped it in half... On the day of the celebration of the Dionysia they canceled the procession because of an unseasonable cold snap and, as a deep frost fell... the cold blighted all the vines... Because of this, Philippides, an enemy of Stratokles, wrote the following verses on him in a comedy: "because of whom the frost blighted the vines, because of whom the robe was torn in half, since he acted impiously in making human the honors due to the gods. This, not comedy, destroys the people."

134B. Plutarch, *Demetrius* 26 (= *PCG* F 25). Written ca. 115. The event took place in 302 B.C.

> Breaking camp <Demetrius> wrote to Athens that he wished to be initiated to the Eleusinian Mysteries as soon as he got to Athens and to undergo the whole rite from the Little Mysteries to the *Epoptika* (the highest grade of initiation)... Stratokles made a motion and they voted to declare the month of Mounichion the month of Anthesterion, and they performed for Demetrius the Lesser Mysteries at Agrai, and after that Mounichion became Boedromion back from Anthesterion and Demetrius completed his initiation, even participating in the *Epoptika*. Because of this Philippides abused Stratokles in writing as "the man who compacted the year into a single month," and, for allowing <Demetrius> to set up his quarters in the Parthenon, as "the man who supposed the Acropolis was a hotel, and introduced prostitutes to the Virgin (Athena)."

134C. Plutarch, *Amatorius* 750e (= *PCG* F 26). Written ca. 115. This passage suggests that an actor may have represented Stratokles on stage.

> Philippides the comic poet, ridiculing the politician Stratokles, wrote, "you can hardly kiss her when she turns her head away."

135. Demetrius, *The Areopagite, PCG* F 1. Performed after 294 B.C. when Demetrius the Besieger returned to Athens a second time and ousted the tyrant Lachares after a siege that caused severe famine. This is the latest datable example of ridicule of an Athenian by name in comedy.

> A BRAGGART COOK: What I have accomplished in this art of mine no actor has ever accomplished. This art is an empire of smoke! I was made *aburtake*-chef (a sauce of leeks, cress, and pomegranate) at the court of Seleucus. And at the court of Agathocles I first introduced Imperial Lentil Soup to the Sicilian. I did not tell you the most important thing. At the time of the famine, when Lachares was giving a dinner party to his friends, I provided refreshment by introducing capers.

Censorship Laws and Prosecution of Poets

136. Herodotus 6.21. See I 16.

137. Scholion to Aristophanes, *Acharnians* 67. The wording of the scholiast's summary of the law is *me komoidein*, which can mean either "not to write comedies" or "not to ridicule in comedy"; since we know from a fragment of the *Didaskaliai* that a comedy was produced in 437 B.C., either the former meaning is excluded or the testimony of the scholiast in its present form must be discredited. Perhaps we are meant to understand "not to ridicule by name."

> "In the archonship of Euthymenes (437/6 B.C.)": this is the archon in whose term was dissolved the law against ridiculing, which was passed in the archonship of Morychides (440/39 B.C.). It was in force during that year and the two years following in the archonships of Glaukinos (439/8 B.C.) and Theodoros (438/7 B.C.), after which it was dissolved in the archonship of Euthymenes.

138. Scholion to Aristophanes, *Acharnians* 1150. The chorus of *Acharnians* complain about having been deprived of a meal by Antimachos who was their (or Aristophanes') *choregos* at the Lenaea (95). The text of Aristophanes, perhaps corrupt, refers to Antimachos as a *syngrapheus,* which can mean "composer," "drafter of legislation," or "historian." The scholiast's own words ("Antimachos appears to have") show that in this case the legislation is a simple inference from the text. Elsewhere (scholion to *Clouds* 1022) a scholiast gives us a list of Athenians named Antimachos, which include a "historian," clearly another inference from our text by another scholiast. The inference does not easily follow from the text, which is a simple complaint about a stingy *choregos,* but falls neatly in line with the late tradition that links a putative piece of legislation with the putative simultaneous disappearance of political comedy and choruses. It does not often happen that scholiastic inferences are obstructed by such patent counterevidence as the fact that Antimachos is abused by name in the very passage on which the theory is spun.

> For they say that he drafted a law, with the result that the choruses got nothing from the *choregoi*. This Antimachos appears to have produced a law that one must not ridicule in comedy by name, and for this reason many of the poets did not come forward to get a chorus, and many of the choreuts were clearly starving. Antimachos was *choregos* at the time when he introduced the law.

139A. Aristophanes, *Acharnians* 370–82. Produced Lenaea, 425 B.C. The hero Dikaiopolis lapses into the persona of the poet while making his defense before the hostile chorus of farmers from Akharnai.

> And yet I am very much afraid because I know the ways of the farmers, who are overjoyed when some windbag praises them and the city whether justly or unjustly. And then they can't see that they're being sold out. And I know the hearts of the old men that look for nothing beyond stinging someone with a voting pebble (used for giving verdicts at jury trials). I myself know what I suffered at the hands of Cleon because of last year's comedy. He dragged me to the Council Chamber and slandered me and screamed lies into my face, and bellowed and inundated me, so that I nearly died from mucky persecution.

139B. Aristophanes, *Acharnians* 496–519. The hero of the play, Dikaiopolis, addresses the spectators directly and adopts Aristophanes' own persona. The word translated "comedy," *trygoidia,* is a coinage formed on the analogy of "tragedy" (*tragoidia*). The point seems to be that comedy has its truths just as does tragedy.

> Men of the audience, do not begrudge me if I, a mere beggar, intend to speak before the Athenian people on matters of state while producing a comedy. Comedy (*trygoidia*) also knows the truth. I will say things that are terrible but true. For now at least Cleon will not slander me by alleging that I spoke ill of the city in the presence of foreigners: we are alone and this contest is the Lenaea; the foreigners are not yet present; the tribute has not yet come nor the allies from the cities. . . . But since we are friends present at this discussion, why do we blame the Spartans for these things? I ask because men among us—and I do not say the city; remember this, that I do not say the city!—but rotten, bogus, worthless, ill-begotten, phony little men, kept denouncing the little cloaks of the Megarians.

139C. Aristophanes, *Acharnians* 628–32. The chorus addresses the audience in the *parabasis*.

From the time that our poet took charge of comic choruses, he has not yet come forward toward the audience to say that he is clever. But since among the quick-counseled Athenians he has been slandered by his enemies, who say that he ridiculed our city and committed an outrage (*hybris*) upon the people, it is necessary for him to give an answer now to the fickle-counseled Athenians.

140. Scholion to *Acharnians* 378. The *Life of Aristophanes* (19–26) also mentions the trial for wrongful acquisition of citizen rights and adds, "and he was acquitted after being falsely accused a second and a third time."

"I myself know what I suffered at the hands of Cleon because of last year's comedy": he means *Babylonians;* Aristophanes produced this play, in which he abuses many people, before the *Acharnians*. He ridiculed both the public offices assigned by lot and the elected offices and Cleon in the presence of foreigners. This is because he entered the drama *Babylonians* at the festival of the Dionysia, which is celebrated in spring at the time when the allies bring the tribute. For this reason Cleon indicted him on a charge of wronging the citizens, alleging that he had written these things to commit an act of *hybris* upon the people (*demos*) and the Council, and he indicted him for wrongful acquisition of citizen rights and he brought him to trial.

141A. Aristophanes, *Wasps* 1284–91. Produced Lenaea, 422 B.C.

There are some who said that I came to terms with Cleon when he attacked me, shook me, and battered me with abuse. Then while I was being flayed, the spectators outside ("outside the building"? or possibly "those not involved") kept laughing, caring nothing for me, but only interested in seeing whether, when pinched, I might emit a little joke. To show my contempt for all this, I've played a bit of a trick and so now the stake has fooled the vine.

141B. Scholion to *Wasps* 1284e.

It is unclear whether he still now refers to the bringing of charges against Callistratus (the *didaskalos* of *Babylonians*) to the Council, because Cleon brought charges against him, or to another bringing of charges against Aristophanes himself, or perhaps there was no bringing of charges but just a threat, which seems more likely.

142. Scholion to Aelius Aristides, *Orations* 3.8 L.-B.

After Cleon prosecuted Aristophanes on a charge of *hybris,* he made a law that it no longer be permitted to ridicule people by name in comedy. Others say that they used to ridicule people by name in comedy until the time of Eupolis, but Alcibiades the general and politician did away with this. For he was ridiculed in a comedy by Eupolis (*Dippers*), and while he threw him into the sea, when he was a soldier in the expedition in Sicily, <Alcibiades> said: "you dipped me in the theater, now in the waves of the sea / I will destroy you, dipping you in most bitter waters."

143. Scholion to Aristophanes, *Birds* 1297. In *Birds* the name "jay" is given to Syrakosios. *Birds* was produced at the Dionysia, 414 B.C., as was Phrynichus' *Antisocial Man (Monotropos)*, from which the scholiast cites. The apparent metrical complexity of the citation seems to indicate that it comes from a choral ode, perhaps the *parabasis,* but the text is obviously corrupt, and there is dispute about where it ends. The words "because he took," etc., may be the words of the scholiast and not the fragment, although in this case it is difficult to see how the citation supports the scholiast's claim that the passage is evidence for the law; similarly the words "therefore they assault him," etc., may belong to the citation and not the scholiast.

This man (Syrakosios) is one of the politicians. Eupolis also ridicules him in *Cities* (422 B.C. = *PCG* F 220) He appears to have made a law against ridiculing anyone in comedy by name, as Phrynichus says in *Antisocial Man* (Dionysia, 414 B.C.): "May the mange take Syrakosios, may it be conspicuous on him and grow luxuriant (?end of citation), because he took away the right to ridicule whomever I (or they) wished" (or possibly "because he took away those whom I wished to ridicule"). Therefore they assault him even more bitterly.

144. Iohannes Tzetzes, *Prooemium* 1.87–97. Written 12th c. The word translated as "ridicule" in this passage can also mean "comedy" or "to write comedy."

The first comedy had unveiled mockery; it was satisfied to ridicule thus in unveiled fashion until the time of Eupolis. When the latter tossed off a jest at the expense of Alcibiades the general and openly reviled his lisp—they happened to be on the warships at the time awaiting battle—he gave an order to the soldiers, and they either threw him out once into the sea and he perished, or they kept drawing him up and throwing him back into the sea tied to a rope and finally saved him when Alcibiades said to him: "You dipped me in the theater, I will immerse you in the most briny waters."

Whether it happened this way or he perished once and for all in the waves, he put a stop to open and symbolic ridicule, or, when he was saved from such a death, he no longer pursued unveiled ridicule, but Alcibiades made a law to ridicule figuratively in comedy and not openly, and Eupolis himself, Cratinus, Pherecrates, Plato (the comic poet), Aristophanes, and others practiced symbolic mockery, and the second comedy sprang into being in Attica. When the Athenians began to break the law and did not wish to be exposed through symbols (i.e., comic allegory), they passed a law that ridicule should not take place symbolically, except that directed against slaves and foreigners alone; whence also the third comedy appeared, to which Philemon and Menander belonged.

145. Cicero, *Letters to Atticus* 6.1.18. Written 20th February, 50 B.C.
Who does not say that Eupolis the poet of Old Comedy was thrown into the sea by Alcibiades while sailing to Sicily (415 B.C.)? Eratosthenes proved it false (later 3rd c. B.C.); for he adduces plays produced by him after that time. Duris of Samos (ca. 340–260 B.C.), an exceptional historian, is not laughed at because he made this mistake along with many others, is he?

Comedy and the Slander Laws

146. Isocrates, *Against Lochites* 20.2–3. Delivered ca. 400–396 B.C.
For all other charges the perpetrator is only liable to prosecution by the person who was wronged, but in the matter of *hybris,* it being considered a matter of common concern, it is permitted to any citizen who wishes, after bringing an indictment before the *thesmothetai* (a board of six of the nine archons) and to appear before you <judges>. They thought it so terrible a thing that one citizen strike another that they even established a law that requires any who say something forbidden <to another citizen> to pay a fine of five hundred drachmas. And so how great must the retribution be on behalf of those who have actively suffered ill, when you appear so angry on behalf of those who have only verbally heard ill.

147. Demosthenes, *Against Meidias* 31–33, 47. Written 348–346 B.C.
He did not only do violence to me, as Demosthenes, on that day, but also to your *choregos;* how important this distinction is you may learn from the following. You know of course that of these *thesmothetai* none is named "Thesmothetes," but each has whatever name. Now then, if anyone commits assaults (i.e., commits *hybris*)

or abuses one of them in his capacity as private individual, he will be prosecuted on a private indictment (*graphe*) for assault (*hybris*) or a private charge of slander (*dike kakegorias*), but if <anyone assaults or abuses one of them> in his capacity as thesmothete, he will at once be deprived of his citizen rights. Why? Because anyone who does this assaults (commits *hybris* against) the very laws and your common garland (badge of office) and the name of the city, for *thesmothetes* is no individual's name, but that of the city. And again if someone strikes or abuses the archon, the same situation: if <he strikes or abuses> while the archon is wearing his garland, he will be deprived of his citizen rights; if <he strikes him> in his private capacity, he will be liable to a private prosecution . . . (citing from the text of the law:) If anyone commits an act of *hybris* against anyone else, whether child, woman, or man, whether free or slave, or does anything illegal against any of these, let anyone who wishes, of those Athenians entitled, lay an indictment (*graphe*) before the *thesmothetes,* and let the *thesmothetes* bring him before the court of the Heliaia within thirty days of the indictment, if no public business prevents it, otherwise at the earliest opportunity.

148. Plutarch, *Solon* 21.1–2. Written ca. 115. Solon's laws date to the early 6th c. B.C.

Also praised is Solon's law that forbade speaking ill of the dead. Indeed piety demands that we regard the dead as sacred, justice that we abstain from assaulting those who no longer exist, and good policy that we avoid the perpetuation of feuds. It also forbade speaking ill of the living in sanctuaries, courts, the offices of magistrates, and whenever there were contests at a festival. It set a fine of three drachmas to be paid to the injured party and two more to be paid to the public treasury.

149. *Lexicon Rhetoricum Cantabrigiense,* in *Lex. Gr. Min.* 78.18f., s.v. *kakegorias dike* ("charge of slander").

Charge of slander: if anyone speaks badly of any deceased person, even if he should be spoken badly of by his children, being condemned, he owes fifty drachmas to the public treasury, and thirty to the private person <who brought the prosecution>. Hyperides in the speech *Against Dorotheos* says those speaking ill of the dead are fined one thousand drachmas and those speaking ill of the living five hundred.

150. Aristophanes, *Acharnians* 530–34. Produced Lenaea, 425 B.C. Pericles died in 429 B.C. Pericles is also ridiculed in *Peace* 606–14.

And then in anger Pericles, the Olympian, lightened, thundered, set Greece in commotion, and proposed laws written like drinking songs: "the Megarians ought not to reside on land, in the market, on the sea, or in the air."

151. Aristophanes, *Peace* 42–48 and 642–56. Produced Dionysia, 421 B.C. Aristophanes boasts in his revised *Clouds* (549f.) that, unlike his rivals, "I punched Cleon in the stomach when he was most powerful but was not so presumptuous as to jump on him when he was laid low." Nevertheless Cleon is here openly ridiculed, just months after he was killed in battle at Amphipolis.

HOUSE-SLAVE: So now some smart-aleck youth in the audience will ask, "What's going on? What's the dung-beetle for?" And an Ionian sitting beside him will say, "I suspect that it alludes to Cleon, since he eats excrement shamelessly" (or "in Hades" according to a plausible emendation).... HERMES (describing how corrupt politicians manipulated the events of the war): The city, pale and crouching in terror, would happily eat up whatever anyone slandered to it (a pun based on the similarity of the words "toss" and "slander"). When your allies saw the blows that were being administered to them, they stuffed with gold the mouths of the perpetrators of these acts and made them rich as a result. But meanwhile you did not notice that Greece was being turned into a desert. And the man who did this was the tanner (Cleon). TRYGAIOS: Stop, Lord Hermes, stop, don't speak, but let that man be where he is down below. That man is no longer ours but yours (Hermes is usher of the dead). Anything you might say about him—that he was a crook, when he lived, and a blabbermouth and an extortionist and a troublemaker and a peace disturber—all this you will now say of one of your own.

152. Lysias, *Against Theomnestos* 1–12. Delivered 384/3 B.C. The speaker prosecuted Theomnestos for libeling him as a "father killer."

I see that many of you judges were among those present when Lysitheos impeached Theomnestos for speaking in public after he had flung away his shield, this not being permitted. In that trial <Theomnestos> said that I had killed my father. Now I would have forgiven him for what he said if he had accused me of killing *his* father, because the latter was a worthless good-for-nothing. And I would not have prosecuted him if he had said any other of the forbidden things, since I think it vulgar and excessively litigious to prosecute for slander, but it seemed to me a shameful thing not to seek vengeance from the man who said this about my father, who was such a worthy man to you and the city. . . . Now perhaps, judges, he will offer no defense concerning this, but will say to you what he dared to say even before the arbitrator, namely, that if someone says "he killed his father," it is not one of the things that it is forbidden to say, since the law does not forbid this but rather does not permit one to say "murderer." I think, judges, that you have to argue not about words, but about their meanings, and that you all know that all who are killers also murdered somebody. It would be a lot of work for the legislator to write down all the words that have the same significance. Rather, speaking of one, he signified all. If, Theomnestos, someone called you a father beater or mother beater, you would certainly not think he should pay you a penalty and at the same time suppose that he should go unpunished if he said that you "beat your female parent" or "your male progenitor." I would be delighted to know, since you are an expert in the matter and have taken up both the practice and the theory, if someone were to say that you flung away your shield—the wording of the law is "if anyone says someone threw away <his shield>, let him be liable to prosecution"—would you not prosecute him, contenting yourself with having flung away your shield, and saying that the abuse is a matter of indifference to you, since "throwing" and "flinging" are not the same thing. . . . And you yourself brought a charge of slander against Lysitheos when he said you had flung away your shield. And yet nothing is said of "flinging" in the law, but rather it requires that anyone saying someone "threw away his shield" pay a penalty of five hundred drachmas.

153. Aristophanes, *Clouds* 353f. Kleonymos is the only *komodoumenos* ridiculed for shield throwing in extant Old Comedy. Aristophanes alludes to his alleged shield throwing ten times in the extant comedies, but always with some slight comic distortion (e.g., *Wasps* 592, "Toadyonymos the shield flinger"). This passage is the only direct reference. The penalty in Athens for throwing one's shield, i.e., running from the battlefield, is given by Andocides (1.74) as loss of citizenship rights, but Kleonymos was certainly never convicted of this crime, since he is likely to be the same Kleonymos who proposed decrees concerning the tribute in 426–5 B.C. (*IG* I² 57.34 and 65.5) and again authored a decree setting a reward for information about the mutilation of the herms in 415 B.C. (Andocides 1.27). In any case it is clear from Aristophanes that he is an active politician and not a disenfranchised nonentity (he is

said to be a perjurer at *Clouds* 400, a supporter of peace at *Peace* 673, and a sycophant at *Birds* 1479). Socrates has just explained that the clouds mimic people that they spot.

> STREPSIADES: So that's why when these clouds saw Kleonymos the shield thrower yesterday, they recognized that he was the biggest coward ever and for this reason turned into deer.

154. Demosthenes, *Against Eubulides* 30. Delivered ca. 345 B.C. The speaker appeals a decision to strike him from the citizen lists on the grounds that he was a foreigner. One of the arguments used for excluding him was that his mother was not a citizen, and that this was somehow indicated by the fact that she sold ribbons in the marketplace.

> I will speak concerning my mother since they slandered even her, and I will call witnesses for what I say. And yet, Athenians, not only did Eubulides slander us contrary to the legislation dealing with the marketplace, but also contrary to the laws that make anyone who disparages the occupation of any male or female citizen working in the marketplace liable to prosecution for slander.

155. Aristophanes, *Acharnians* 475–79. Produced Lenaea, 425 B.C. The comic poets frequently mocked Euripides' low birth, claiming that his mother was a greengrocer. In reality she was of high birth (Philochorus *FGrH* 328 F 218).

> DIKAIOPOLIS: Dearest, O sweetest little Euripides, may I perish horribly if I ever ask again for anything, except one thing alone, just this one, just this alone: fetch me a piece of chervil from your mother.

156. Lysias, *On Behalf of the Soldier* 6. Delivered ca. 395–387 B.C.

> All that I've just related was spoken at the table of Philios. When someone told them that I had abused them (the officials in charge of drawing up the muster rolls for conscripting citizens for a military expedition), they along with Ktesikles the archon decided to fine me contrary to the law, since the law forbids anyone to abuse a magistrate in the Council Chamber. . . . You have heard that the law clearly requires the punishment of those who speak abuse in the Council Chamber, but I provided witnesses to the effect that I did not go to the magistrate's office, but have been fined unjustly, and am not obligated to incur the fine or to pay the penalty.

157. Scholion to Aristophanes' *Clouds* 31. Ameinias was archon in 423/2 B.C. at the time of the production of the first *Clouds*. The scholion comments on a character named "Amynias" in the text, but refers the name to the archon "Ameinias." However, the Venetus, one of the two most important of the manuscripts of Aristophanes, has "Ameinias" at *Clouds* 31 and 686. Further confusion is added by the fact that a prominent politician by the name of Amynias is mentioned in the *Wasps,* and it may well be that Ameinias and Amynias are two distinct people who both happened to be politically active at the time. It is quite likely that the legislation mentioned by the scholiast was invented as a theory to explain why "Amynias" appeared where some ancient scholar wanted the passage to refer to "Ameinias."

> Amynias: ... he mentions him also in the *Wasps,* but in the present passage he mentions him not because he is attacking that man, but rather he uses that man's name because he wishes to mock the archon. At that time Ameinias, son of Pronapes, was archon. (At this point the manuscripts give two versions to the scholion.) (A.) Not wishing to mock that man he turned the "i" to "y" and changed the spelling in a humorous way, since there was a law in Athens that no one could openly ridicule the archon in comedy. For this reason he said also Amynias, not Aminias. (B.) Since the law formerly forbade the Athenians to ridicule the archon in comedy, he took away the "i" and added the "y," and changing it a little called him Amynias instead of Aminias.

IIIB. The Greek World from Hellenistic to Imperial Times

In this section we deal with mainly inscriptional evidence concerning the dramatic program of festivals in Hellenistic and Roman Greece. In the majority of cities, drama would only have been possible when there were festivals that would attract the actors; we do not know of any permanent companies attached to a theater, only of companies attached to a place or sanctuary, to a patron, and to individual chief actors. Drama attached itself increasingly from the late 4th c. B.C. onward to existing athletic and musical competitions (160). More commonly, festivals were upgraded by the inclusion of further contests or by greater prizes, in an attempt to achieve greater prestige. We therefore cannot know what the full program of a festival was at any given time unless we are certain that we have a complete list of victories.

The number of festivals also caused organizational problems as the actors, especially those who were in the guild of the Artists of Dionysus (IVAii), were required to travel from one festival to another. An early example of this enduring problem is illustrated by a damaged inscription (162) from the island of Euboea. The four main cities of the island clearly found it difficult to control the artists, who, by failing to show up for festivals, could cause embarrassment for the political organizers in the independent cities. The inscription records the cities' attempt to regulate the artists, while agreeing to a synchronism of their calendars. An artist could scarcely be blamed for canceling an engagement if the date of the festival suddenly moved by several days or even a month. The first requirement for an organized dramatic festival was placement in the overall festival calendar of the Greek world. Later, actors would move with ease from Asia Minor and Palestine to Rome and Greece, but only after an international synchronism had been established by Julius Caesar.

Some dramatic festivals, on the analogy of the athletic ones, were more prestigous than others. Those that were "sacred" and "crowned" were superior to those that merely offered money prizes, called among other names "thematic" or "talantiaios," meaning that the prizes were supposed to amount to a talent in value. Dramatic festivals proper were "scenic" or, if the major part was musical, "thymelic" or "musical." It is important to recognize that all Greek festivals were in theory contests (*agones*), with prizes, sometimes second and third prizes (168), to attract competitors. Sometimes even all competitors were allowed a subsidy for upkeep from some date in advance of the competition (168, 170). Sometimes we know that competition was only a pretense, since second prizes could not be awarded through absence of competitors in poorer cities or in times of poverty (161). Elsewhere we know that no one at all showed up in individual events, or they were disqualified if they did. We note how at Oinoanda (158) the mimes and other spectacles (*akroamata, theamata*) are specifically not to be given prizes; they are hired to entertain the people. Prestige attached to the concept of competition, even when it was only apparent.

The value of the prizes could vary greatly according to the nature of the event and the endowment and prestige of the festival. At Oinoanda (158) tragedy was more valuable than comedy, but less valuable than singing to the lyre. But the list of prizes from Aphrodisias (159) in Asia Minor shows that dramatic prizes were small by comparison with the athletic, whereas local athletic events were relegated to one day at the end of the Demostheneia (158). At Samos (166), as elsewhere, the local gymnasia contributed athletics to a dramatic festival of Hera. The actor of old drama usually was more highly rewarded than anyone else in dramatic events, but singers to the lyre were better rewarded than actors—who have to pay their companies—or playwrights at Oinoanda (158) and Tanagra (161).

Likewise there is visible a tendency to have a specific order of musical and dramatic competitions (e.g., 159A), beginning with trumpeter and herald, typical even in athletic competitions; presumably these two were required for the organization of announcements and prizegivings that followed perhaps at an interval of some days; they are the lowest paid. But this order was not followed precisely. One can observe from the detailed Oinoanda inscription (158) that even a minor festival could be spread over most of a month, with allowances made for traditional market days, religious rituals, and public feasting, while a major festival like the Great Dionysia at Athens occupied only a week (IIIAia). All such extensive festivals date from the period of Roman imperial rule, and we may suspect that economic considerations were paramount.

Perhaps the most detailed of the lists outside Athens comes from the Festival of the Soteria at Delphi (165), which in Hellenistic times could mount three groups in tragedy and four in comedy, but no mention is made of a tragic chorus, despite the piper. In drama a special problem attaches to the use of the words "old comedy," "new comedy," "old tragedy," and "archaic tragedy," especially in the inscriptions. There is no likelihood that there was a standardization of such terms throughout all the festivals, but we can say that "old comedy" normally (160) means what we should call "New Comedy," i.e., the comedy of Menander and his fellows. "New comedy"—which uses the word meaning "brand new" in Greek—usually implies that the comedy is newly composed, though of course it might mean rather "performed for the first time at this festival." "Archaic comedy," however, may mean a version of what we should call Old Comedy, though this is far from certain. Again, while satyrplay as an event is always referred to as "the satyrs," as in, e.g., "poet of satyrs," comedy and tragedy can be referred to as "comedians" and "tragedians" but also as "comedy" and "tragedy." "Comedian" means "comic actor" as opposed to "poet of comedy," and likewise with tragedy. On the other hand, we note that "tragic dancing" always means pantomime, specifically in the grandiose phrase "actor of tragic rhythmic dancing," while "dancer" probably often but not always means pantomime; possibly even "comedian" can mean pantomime in some late places. Official contests for mimes or pantomimes are not recorded until the end of the 2nd c., but probably existed in the early empire in Italy.

The Romans introduced Greek-style games into their territory, though these will have had forerunners in the Greek area of Italy, especially in Campania. We are, however, ill informed about their programs since no complete lists have survived of their contests. Best known were the Sebasta—the Italika Romaia Sebasta Isolympia—at Naples, which were started in 2 and acquired scenic games probably after the death of Augustus (14), and the prestigious Capitolia at Rome, established in 86 by Domitian in specific imitation of Greek models; though it contained dramatic contests, little is known about them (173). The Eusebeia at Puteoli were founded by Antoninus Pius in 138. The Neronia of 61 were a short-lived eccentricity, but there were quite a number of Greek competitions at Rome later. In general it seems true that in Italy drama was associated principally with religious festivals, games to honor the dead, and games given by magistrates and emperors for the entertainment of the people, rather than forming a part of the contests that were typical of the Greek world.

Sources

158. M. Wörrle, *Stadt und Fest im kaiserzeitlichen Kleinasien*, p. 8, ll. 38ff; *SEG* 38.1462B; S. Mitchell, *JRS* 80 (1990) 183ff. This inscription lists a number of documents recording the foundation of a festival called the Demostheneia by a wealthy benefactor called Julius Demosthenes in Lycia in 124, and it is our last detailed record of the institution of dramatic festivals. There are twelve days of competition, with nine contests, of which four have second prizes, and one—the "overall" competition—has a second and third prize. The prizes from highest to lowest are solo singer to the lyre, tragedy, comedy, overall winner, piper with chorus, poet and prose-encomiast—probably praising the emperor—trumpeter, and herald. Compare the greater variety even in a small festival like the Sarapieia (161). At least part of the intention of the long festival was to encourage trade in the local market, which had been built by Demosthenes himself.

...The order and the days of the contests are subscribed to this announcement. On the Augustus day of the month Artemisios, competition of trumpeters and heralds, to the winners of whom shall be given 50 denarii each. Then after the meetings of the Council and of the Assembly on the 5th, a competition of prose encomiographers, to the winner of whom shall be given 75 denarii. On the 6th an intermission because of the market held then. On the 7th a competition of poets, to the winner of which shall be given 75 denarii. On the 8th and 9th a competition of pipers with choir, to whom shall be given as first prize 125 denarii, as second prize 75 denarii. On the 10th and 11th a competition of comedians, to whom shall be given as first prize 200 denarii, as second prize 100 denarii. On the 12th sacrifice for Apollo of Ancestors. On the 13th and 14th competition of tragedians, to whom shall be given as first prize 250 denarii and as second prize 125 denarii. On the 15th the second sacrifice for Apollo of Ancestors. On the 16th and 17th competition of singers to the lyre, to whom shall be given as first prize 300 denarii, as second prize 150 denarii. On the 18th an open competition (*dia panton*), and as first prize shall be given 150, as second 100, and as third 50 denarii. There shall also be given 25 denarii to the person who provides the stage apparatus.

On the 19th, 20th, and 21st hired performances (*paramisthomata*), among which shall be mimes and performances for eye and ear (*akousmata* and *theamata*); for these there are no prizes, though other spectacles that please the people shall be included in these days, toward which shall be paid out 600 denarii. On the 22nd gymnic competition of citizens, for which 150 denarii shall be spent.

159A. *CIG* 2758; Liermann, *Analecta* 168ff. Date: ca. 100? These are fragmentary lists from Aphrodisias in Asia Minor. Note that the "cyclic" piper is the same as "piper with chorus" in the previous inscription. The Pythian pipes are solo pipes. As the contest becomes wealthier, it is noticeable that the number of second and third prizes increases. The basic order of the competition that can be derived from the lists, excluding the athletic contests and other additions, was as follows: trumpeter, herald, encomium writer, poet, pythian piper, comedian, tragedian, cyclic piper, singer to the lyre, overall winner.

(Stone A: columns 1+2)

Trumpeter	150 denarii
Herald	150
Encomium writer	200
Poet	200
Boy singer to the lyre	150
Pythian piper	200
Comedian	400
Tragedian	500
Cyclic piper	350
Adult lyre player	500
Overall	200

For the athletic competition of the citizen boys: [??]

Furlong race men	[...]
Wrestling men	[...]
Pankration men	[...]
Boxing men	[...]

[??]

(Stone E: column 1, from a later series of contestants at the same festival)

Trumpeter	500
Herald	500
Pythian piper	1,400
" second prize	400

cyclic piper	?
" second prize	100
Comedian	1,600
" second prize	500
" third prize	300
Tragedian	2,700
" second prize	800
" third prize	600
[. . . a section is missing]	
furlong race men	2,000
furlong adolescents	2,000
pentathlon "	3,800
wrestling "	3,800
[etc. . . .]	

159B. *MAMA* 8.420; *CIG* 2759; Liermann, *Analecta* 115ff.; Reynolds, *Aphrodisias and Rome,* p. 192. Date: late 2nd c. The term translated "joint comedies, joint tragedies" used here is *"koine* of comedians/of tragedians," a rare and unclear term, possibly meaning "open to all age groups in all categories of comedy, or tragedy" (Robert, *Bull. Ep.* 1968, 254); the low amounts among other reasons suggest that it was not the same as an "overall" prize, as might be suspected.

The prizes in the quinquennial contest, musical only, with money prizes, established by Flavius Lysimachus <are> written below:

trumpeter	500
herald	500
encomiast	750
poet	750
Pythian pipes	1,000
<"> 2nd	350
solo *kithara*	1,000
<"> 2nd	350
boys' *kithara*	750
<"> 2nd	250
choric pipes	1,500
<"> 2nd	500
tragic chorus	500
choric *kithara*	1,500
<"> 2nd	500
comic actor	1,500
<"> 2nd	500

<"> 3rd	300
tragic actor	2,500
<"> 2nd	800
<"> 3rd	400
joint comedies	200
joint tragedies	250
new comedy	500
archaic comedy	350
<"> 2nd	150
new tragedy	750
pyrrhiche	1,000
<"> 2nd	350

160. *SEG* 3.334; Jamot, *BCH* 19 (1895) 341ff., no. 16; Mette, *Urkunden* 60. Catalog of the victors at the Festival of the Muses at Thespiae in Boeotia. Date: ca. 160. New comedy and tragedy are still being written and acted.

Poet of processional: Eumaron, son of Alexandros, of Thespiae

Herald: Gnaios Pompeios Zosimos, Corinthian and Thespian

Trumpeter: Zosimos, son of Epiktetos, of Thebes

Encomium for the Emperor: Markos Antonios Maximos of NeoCaesarea

Encomium for the Muses: M. Antonios Maximos of NeoCaesarea

Poem for the Emperor: Threptos, called Nikanor [?? . . .

Poem for the Muses: Zosimos, son of Tryphon, of Argos [. . .

. . . .]mophanes, son of Bromios, of Thespiae

Rhapsode]: [. . . . .], son of [. . .]ios, of Hypata

Pythian pi]pe: [. . . . . .]

Kithara player: Kastrianos, son of Kastrianos, of Chios

Comedian (i.e., actor/director) of old comedy: Cl. Apollonios of Miletus

Tragedian (i.e., actor/director) of old tragedy: Metrobios, son of Metrobios, called Philemon, of Athens

Poet of new comedy: L. Marios Antiochos of Corinth

Actor of new comedy: Flavios Ennychos of Thespiae

Poet of new tragedy: Apollonios, son of Apollonios, of Aspendos

Actor of new tragedy: L. Marios Antiochos of Corinth

Singer to the *kithara*: Memmios Leon of Larissa

Choric piper: M. Antios Artemidoros of Alexandria

Writer of satyrplay: L. Marios Antiochos of Corinth

Overall competition: Klaudios Apollonios of Miletus

161. *SEG* 19.335; Mette, *Urkunden,* p. 53; M. Calvet, P. Roesch, *RA* (1966) 297–332. Competitions at the Sarapieia—a festival for the Egyptian god Sarapis—about 85 B.C. from Tanagra in Boeotia, with the most detailed accounting of any known festival; at least two of the victors are relatives of Glaukos. The normal unit of coinage is the Attic silver drachma, in which the accounting is done, but the gold crowns have their values given in their weight of gold, expressed in whole gold coins—gold <staters>—and fractions thereof. The extraordinary complexity of these crowns, which are not really very valuable, is due to the difficulty of obtaining 16 crowns of four different values in a precise ratio from 69 gold staters. The prizes are so organized that the difference between the four levels of first prizes is in a descending ratio of 1:2:3. We give a possible overall explanation at the end of the inscription.

<The work> of Glaukos, son of Boukattes: these won the contest of the Sarapieia:

<1.> trumpeter: Antandros, son of Eredamos, of Aigira

<2.> herald: Praxiteles, son of Theogenes, of Athens

<3.> rhapsode: Boukattes, son of Glaukos, of Tanagra

<4.> poet: Athanias, son of Phrynon, of Tanagra

<5.> piper: Artemon, son of Myrton, of Thebes

<6.> singer to the pipes: Parmenion, son of Parmenion, of Athens

<7.> lyre player: Philon, son of Philon, of Tarentum

<8.> singer to the lyre: Timokles, son of Herodotos, from Aeolian Kyme

<9.> poet of satyrs: Alexander, son of Glaukos, of Tanagra

<10.> poet of tragedies: Asklepiades, son of Hikesios, of Thebes (N.B.: a mistake for Athens)

<11.> [actor]: Diogenes, son of Antigon, of Thebes

<12.> poet of comedies: Poses, son of Ariston, of Athens

<13.> actor: Demetrios, son of Demetrios, of Athens

<14.> the old tragedy: Silanos, son of Demetrios, of Thebes

<15.> the <old> comedy: Hipparchos, son of Apollodoros, of Thebes

<16.> the epinician (i.e., overall winner): Asklepiades, son of Hikesios, of Athens

(a total of 16 crowns and first prizes)

Accounting of Glaukos, son of Boukattes, *agonothetes* of the Sarapieia. I received from the office of Kaphisios, son of Boukattes, Attic[. . .]silver, from which I purchased 69 gold <staters>, each being Attic gold. [<Total>...] Attic 2,070 <silver drachmas>. To Sotades for construction of crowns 4 <silver> obols per Attic gold <stater>: in total 46 Attic <silver drachmas>.

I gave to the victors:

<1, 2:> to Antandros the trumpeter and Praxiteles the herald each a crown, @ 3 gold 4 obols 6 bronze (i.e., 101 1/4 silver drachmas)

<3:> to Boukattes the rhapsode a crown @ [3] gold <4> obols 6 bronze; to Aristodikos, son of Demokrates, of Opous, a second prize of 40 Attic <silver drachmas>

<4:> to Athanias the poet a gold crown @ 4 1/2 gold; and to Diogenes, son of Leonidas, of Thebes, a second prize of 40 Attic <silver drachmas>

<5:> to Artemon the piper a crown @ 5 1/2 gold 1 1/2 obols; to K[l]eitophon, son of Athenodotos, of Athens, the second prize of [50] Attic <silver drachmas>

<6:> to Parmenion the singer to the pipes a crown @ 3 1/2 gold 3 obols

<7:> to Philon the lyre player a crown @ 4 1/2 gold; to Metrodoros, son of Dionysios, of Smyrna, second prize of 40 Attic <silver drachmas>

<8:> to Timokles, son of Herodotos, the singer to the lyre a crown @ 5 1/2 gold 1 1/2 obols

<9:> to Alexander poet of satyrs a crown @ 3 gold 4 1/2 obols; and to Athenion, son of Nikarchos, of Anthedon, second prize of 40 Attic <silver drachmas>

<10:> to Asklepiades poet of tragedies a crown @ 4 1/2 gold; and to Publius, son of Publius, of Rome, second prize of [50] Attic <silver drachmas>

<11:> to Diogenes the actor (of tragedy) a crown @ 3 gold 4 obols 6 bronze

<12:> to Poses poet of comedies a crown @ 4 1/2 gold.

<13:> to Demetrios the actor (of comedy) a crown @ 3 gold 4 1/2 obols

<14:> to the tragedian [space left blank, presumably Silanos] <who won> the old <tragedy> a crown @ 5 1/2 gold 1 1/2 obols; and to Praxiteles, son of Theogenos, of Athens, a second prize of 50 Attic <silver drachmas>

<15:> to Hipparchos the comedian (i.e., who put on and acted in "old" comedy) a crown @ 4 1/2 gold; and to Demetrios, son of

Demetrios, the Athenian, a second prize of 40 Attic <silver drach-mas>

<16:> to Asklepiades poet of tragedies for the epinician (= over-all?) crown for @ 5 1/2 gold 1 1/2 obols; to Philon, son of Philon, of Tarentum, (the lyre player) second prize of 50 Attic <silver drachmas>
(a total of 16 first prizes and 9 second prizes)

———

Costuming [. . .] Attic <silver drachmas>

———

For the tragic <chorusmen?> and satyrs 100 Attic <silver drachmas> and for the comic <chorusmen?> along with their chorus directors 50 Attic <silver drachmas>. For the chorus directors who produced the new tragedies and satyrs 50; for the pipers who [played for?] the tragedy 28; and for the comic <pipers> 12 Attic <silver drach-mas>.

———

Sacred sacrifices for Sarapis and Isis and the other gods and the feasting of those in the decree 300 Attic <silver drachmas>.

———

I gave back to Kaphisias for the second prizes that were uncontested, <viz.,> singing to the pipes 40 (no. 6), singing to the lyre 50 (no. 8), and the second prize for the poet of t[ragedy] 50 Attic <silver drachmas> (N.B.: a mistake for no. 12: the poet of comedy, since no. 10 and all others are accounted for; there are no second prizes for actors, trumpeter, or herald.)

———

Total: 3,276 <silver drachmas>

———

and other expenses for the daily oaths and the feasting of the daily participants, judges and [. . .] and choruses and victors, and for the incense and [. . .] I do [not] account since I paid the money from my own resources.
(There follows a detailed accounting of the endowment funds)

* * *

(The total could be arrived at as follows:

16 crowns	2,070
Construction of same	46
9 second prizes: (540 less 140 returned)	400
Costuming	[230]

tragedians and satyrs [?the chorus]	100
comedians with chorus directors	40
chorus directors of new tragedy and satyrplay	50
tragic pipers	28
comic pipers	12
sacrifice and banquet	300
Total	3,276

The prizes are allocated in four levels as follows:

1. piper, singer to lyre, old tragedy, epinician: 5 1/2 gold 1 1/2 obols = 168 3/4 drachmas

2. poet, lyre player, tragic poet, comic poet, comedian: 4 1/2 gold = 135 drachmas

3. singer to pipes: 3 1/2 gold 3 obols = 112 1/2 drachmas

4. trumpet, herald, rhapsode, satyric poet, 2 actors: 3 gold 4 1/2 obols = 101 1/4 drachmas)

162. *IG* XII 9, 207 and p. 176; *IG* XII Supplement p. 178; + *SEG* 34.896; Ghiron-Bistagne, *Recherches* 180–82; *Festivals*[2] 306–8; Stephanes, *EpThess* 1984, 499ff. Date: ca. 290 B.C. This important text is badly damaged, and in places uncertain; missing parts of the stone, usually about twenty-five letters at the start of every line, are indicated by [...]. The inscription describes the attempt by four cities of the island of Euboea—Chalcis, Karystos, Eretria, and Oreos—to organize their festivals. The performers for several months are to visit all the cities for the Dionysia and then in reverse order for the Demetrieia. Much remains unclear.

[It was decided] to choose men who would go to Chalcis to allocate the work among the *technitai,* [in the month of Apatourion in the Chalcidian] calendar, the month of Ares in the calendar of the Histiaians, the month of [...] in the calendar of Eretria. [...]

OATH: that those who have been chosen take oaths in their own city, [...] and when they arrive in Chalcis, that they [... administer?] the same oath [...] to the best of the professional *technitai* [..."I shall ...] without partiality or animosity; I shall not [accept] gifts [...] by no craft or excuse ?canceling [... by ...] and Apollo and Demeter and Dionysus. Good luck to me if I keep my oath, otherwise bad luck."

ON CONTRACTS: when they (the cities' representatives) [have made their oath, let them award the jobs] after having them proclaimed by herald and announcing them to the *technitai* from the twentieth [of Apatourion. Let them arrange for?] three pipers, three tragedians (i.e., leaders of troupes), but for Karystos two[... and comedians?] four as well as three choruses of children and three of men, except for the ch[oral? ... and a w]orker who will provide all the costumes for the tragedians and comedians they may need. Let them accept worthy guarantors except non-Euboeans from each of the *technitai*.

[ON OFFICIAL VISITORS:] The cities are to choose [and send] to the contests of the Dionysia and Demetrieia official visitors (*theoroi*) [bringing] the offering [according to] the decree, getting money from the individual cities in the amount of [...]; they are to join in procession and perform all the other acts according to the law of Euboea.

[ON PAY:] Each [city is to give] 600 drachmas of Demetrian coinage to a piper; to a tragedian [...] contest 100 drachmas, to comedians 400 drachmas, to a costumer 300 drachmas.

ON PROVISIONS: Each city is to give living allowances to the *technitai* for five days at 9 obols a day and for intercalated days [... and to the dire]ctors (*didaskaloi*) of tragedians and comedians for ten days, and for the [directors?] of cyclic choruses [...] 20 drachmas.

ON THE CONTESTS: The contests of the Dionysia are to take place in Karystos in the month [...] as the Karystians conduct them from the 12th, then in Eretria in the Lenaean month, as the Eretrians conduct them, from the [...], then in Chalcis in the Lenaean month as the Chalcidians conduct them from the 20th, then in [Oreos ... as the Histiaeans] conduct them from the 8th from the end of the month.

{ON INTERCALATED DAYS: If they should have need in advance of [...] intercalated days, they are allowed to intercalate up to three days. (This seems to be an afterthought.)} The pipers are to lead off [... and] bring in the chorus, and the tragedians who have contracted for work [...] are to [apportion?] for the pipers[... ?] and for the choruses of the men tragedians to the actors(?: this important line seems to be corrupt and cannot be restored) to [provide?] costumes (*himatia*) as new [for those that each?] brings in; and the *choregoi* who have been appointed in the various cities are to welcome the *technitai* [and entertain them?] according to the laws.

ON THE JUDGING: When the contest takes place, let the judges select [...] having inscribed [...] in the secretariat and put into public view [... and] let him announce the names of the *choregoi* for the *technitai,* and let the archon [...] those selected [... and let the ?] of the drama win.

ON THE DEMETRIEIA: For the Demetrieia the contracts are to take place in [Chalcis ...] from the cities, and let them hold the contest first in Oreos in the month of Demetrion, as the Histiaeans conduct it from [...] then in Chalcis in the month of Hippion as the Chalcidians conduct it from the twelfth [then in Eretria ... then in Karystos, etc.]. The judgings of the *technitai* in the Demetrieia in the cities [...] as has been written for the Dionysia. The Karystians are to use the *technitai* for the Aristonikeia.

[ON PENALTIES:] If any of the *technitai* abandon any of their jobs assigned to them, let them pay a penalty of double the value of the job they undertake, and let it be exacted from the *technites,* the contractor or the guarantor in each of the cities where they have abandoned the job. Let them be liable to arrest within Euboea in person and be deprived of all that they possess in their journeying through Euboea, until they pay the penalty that is set down. Money exacted from those failing their engagements is to be sacred to Dionysus in the city where the job is, but as regards all they possess in their journeying, let half belong to the one who takes it and half the city's from which the taker comes. If anyone in the city proposes or votes that one should acquit of the fine any of those who have abandoned their engagement, let the proposer and seconder be held responsible for illegal force, unless the king sends some other direction about them. Let them use the funds accruing from this in the cities for the temple of Dionysus, and nothing else.

{ON INTERCALATED MONTHS: concerning intercalation of months, the archons in the cities are to ensure, along with those chosen when appropriate, that they should happen simultaneously throughout Euboea. (This too is an addition)}

ON OATHS OF INNOCENCE: *technitai* who have abandoned some assigned job may take an oath of innocence by appearing in person at the city where they abandoned the task in the six months before winter—before that they may not claim exemption—while the contracting employers are present; if any of the *technitai* who contracted for the jobs in Euboea is competing in a contest in any city from which it is not possible for him to attend at the times at which the contests are held in Euboea, he may take an oath of innocence.

The accords are to be written up by the archons in each of the cities on a stone slab and set up in the entranceway to the theater. The cost for the slab each group is to reckon off for itself as a cost to the theater, when they make the hiring for the next Dionysia. (Here follows a long addition in two parts.) (A: dealing with the hiring.) In order for the <contracting> to take place, the cities are to choose men according to the decree (*diagraphe*) and send them to Chalcis before the twentieth of the month of Apatourion, as the Chalcidians conduct it, so that they may tender the jobs to the *technitai*. The Councilors (*probouloi*) and generals of the Chalcidians are to send someone to announce the contracts to the *technitai*, and in order that those who wish to get contracts may be present in the month of Apatourion, as the Chalcidians conduct it, before the twentieth by the religious calendar; if any of those *technitai* who have been previously fined in the cities wish to contract for the Euboean work before the coming into effect of the law, they may when they are present take' an oath of innocence and be acquitted of their previous fines. (B: clarifying the legal status of the performers.) There is to be immunity from civil prosecution for those *technitai* who have undertaken contracts in all the cities in Euboea during the time, if they are in town for the contests; the archons and generals in the city are to ensure their immunity. If any of the *technitai* abandon any of their jobs, the contracts for all their jobs are to be annulled, if they are not done, <and?> *technitai* are to be hired from elsewhere to replace the missing ones, if they can; those who have been hired are to be at the disposal of other cities, where work has been abandoned. If the *technitai* or any of the contractors who can undertake the work do not do so when the archons are prepared to give them the work, but [practice?] contrary to the laws of the Euboeans established about them, they are to be taxable on all their possessions while resident in Euboea, both imported and exported. Those who tendered out the work are to indict in the individual cities whomsoever of the *technitai* or contractors they adjudge to be guilty in this. Those who are selected to make the tenders are to take care, by whatever means they know, that those indicted pay the taxes according to the decrees of the Euboeans. If any of the *technitai* disregarding any of the rules of contest are fined by the *agonothetai,* the fines are to be deducted from their salaries the moment they receive them.

163. *SIG*[3] 1080. A memorial to the victories of an unknown actor of "old tragedy" from Tegea in Arkadia. Date: mid-3rd B.C. His boxing victory shows why he was particularly good in Heracles roles. The most prestigious contests are named first, where a crown was the prize; those where a money prize was allotted are not named.

The Great Dionysia at Athens with the *Orestes* of Euripides. The Soteria at Delphi with the *Heracles* of Euripides, the *Antaios* of Archestratos. The Ptolemaia at Alexandria, men's boxing. The Heraia (at Argos) with the *Heracles* of Euripides, the *Archelaos* of Euripides. The Naia (of Zeus) at Dodona with the *Archelaos* of Euripides, the *Achilles* of Chairemon, and scenic contests in individual cities, Dionysia, and other contests that cities conducted: 88.

164. *SIG*[3] 1079; Mette, *Urkunden,* p. 47. A list of the victors in festivals of the Romaia, honoring the goddess Rome, at Magnesia on the Meander. Date: second half of 2nd c. B.C. and first half of 1st c. B.C. Notable is the restriction to newly composed dramas, including satyrplay, called here a drama, though for that there was as often no actor's prize. We give only the first two lists.

While Apollodoros was crown bearer, and Euandrides, son of Euandrides, Mandrodoros, son of Kleainos, Apollodoros, son of Leonteus, were festival managers, the following won the contest of the Romaia as poets of new dramas:

Of tragedies (victor) Theodoros, son of Dionysios, with the drama
Hermione: actor was Apollonios, son of Apollonios
Of comedies: Metrodoros, son of Apollonios, with the drama
Lookalikes: actor was Agathokles, son of Agathokles, of Miletus
Of satyrs: Theodoros, son of Dionysios, with the drama *Thytes*

While Sokrates was crown bearer, and Diagoras, son of Demetrios, Dionysarchos, son of Lampon, Gerontides, son of Gerontides, were festival managers, the following won the contest of the Romaia as poets of new dramas:

Of tragedies (victor): Glaukon, son of Glaukon, of Ephesus; actor
was Herakleitos, son of Menodoros, of Mallos
Of comedies: Diomedes, son of Athenodoros, of Pergamon; actor
was Menodotos, son of Metrodoros, of Pergamon
Of satyrs: Polemon, son of Neon

165A. Two of a series of somewhat confused and untypical Hellenistic inscriptions recording the victors at the Amphictyonic Soteria of Delphi; these were biennial, and may have been a display for the *technitai* rather than a genuine contest. *SIG*[3] 424A; Mette, *Urkunden,* p. 67: G. Nachtergael, *Les Galates en Grèce* 305ff. Date: 256 B.C. Notable are the regular seven comic dancers, who were perhaps entre'acte entertainers. The actors are listed together and not separated into chief actor and *synagonistai.* In tragedy the piper must have accompanied the actors' arias and not a chorus, which is not recorded here, though a tragic chorus is mentioned later (161; IV 293). The list seems to be a complete list of the finalists rather than the actual victors, as the inscription declares. We do not write out all the names.

In the archonship of Aristagoras, while Philonides, son of Aristomachos, of Zakynthos, was priest, and the sacred commissioners were ... etc. These were the victors in the contest of the Soteria:
    <A: Musical and poetic contests: 2 finalists>
        Rhapsodes: (2 names)
        Lyre players: (2 names)
        Singers to lyre: (2 names)
    <B: Choral contests: 2 finalists, presumably with 5 per chorus>
        Boy choreuts: (5 names and space for 5 more)
        Men choreuts: (5 names and space for 5 more)
        Pipers: (2 names)
        Directors: (2 names)
    <C: Dramatic contests: 3 tragedies and 4 comedies, each with their own director (*didaskalos*) and piper>
        Tragedians:
            <1.> <Actors>: (3 names)
                Piper: (1 name)
                Director: (1 name)
            <2.> <Actors>: (3 names)
                Piper: (1 name)
                Director: (1 name)
            <3.> <Actors>: (3 names)
                Piper: (1 name)
                Director: (1 name)
        Comedians:
            <1.> (3 names)
                Piper: (1 name)
                [Director]

<2.> (3 names)
    Piper: (1 name)
    Director: (1 name)
<3.> (3 names)
    Piper: (1 name)
    Director: (1 name)
<4.> (3 names)
    Piper: (1 name)
    Director: (1 name)
    Comic choreuts: (7 names)
    Costumers: (3 names)

165B. *SIG*[3] 690; Nachtergael, p. 492. This is the only catalog of competitors in the relatively insignificant Winter Soteria from ca. 135 B.C.; the order is the same as above. Those without city are perhaps local members of the guild. Note that the kitharode is also leader of the men's chorus, which may have been supplemented from local non-guild resources.

Ambassadors having been sent by the city of the Delphians to the Commonweal of the *Technitai* from Isthmus and Nemea, *viz.*, (three names follow), on the subject of the contest of the Winter Soteria, so that they may perform (lit., "contend together") in the yearly competition to the god, the *technitai* have acceded to the request and sent the following to perform as a gift to the god:

Kitharist: Dionysios, son of Theodotos, of Thebes

Kitharode: Tyrannias, son of Automedos, of Thebes

Choreuts (boys): Xenon, son of Doros, of Thebes; Theogeiton, son of Kleimedos, of Thebes; boy leader: Ariston, son of Straton

Leader of the men: Tyrannias

Choreuts (men): Athenokles, son of Xenokles, of Thebes; Ismenon, son of Timokles, of Thebes

Comedian: Apollas of Pheneos

Synagonists: Soteles, Theokritos

Choreuts of the comedian: Xenolaos, son of Sosikrates, of Opus; Myrton, son of Menophilos, of Thebes; Aristokleidas of Thebes; Menekrates, son of Sopatros, of Thebes

166. G. Dunst, *ZPE* 1 (1967) 230; Mette, *Urkunden*, p. 49. This is a victory list from Samos in the games for Hera in the 2nd c. B.C. The musical and dramatic part is interrupted by two torch races, to be connected with the gymnasium; whether the "teachers" belonged there too, we do not know. Likewise the technical term "those from the first" is not explicable. It is interesting that the actor/director of the old tragedy is also awarded a prize as actor in the new tragedy as well. Those without a place of origin are presumably locals. Rarely is a satyrplay competition specified as "new," though competitions for "old" satyrplay occur at Athens, and the competitions of satyrs at the Romaia of Magnesia are under the heading "new" (164).

Under Antipatros, when Hermippos, son of Moschion, and Aristeides, son of Apollodotos, and Nikolaos, son of [. . .], were *agonothetai,* and Sosistratos, son of the younger Sosistratos, was head of the gymnasium, these were the victors:

<1.> Trumpeter: N[. . .], son of Menekles, of Tralles

<2.> Herald: Eubios, son of Sosistratos

<3.> Actor of old tragedy: Demetrios, son of Nikaios, of Miletus

In the torch race of Hephaistos, those from the first [*apo proton*]: Leonides, son of Theodoros, of the Chesean tribe

Torch race leader: Aristomenes, son of Aristippos, of the Chesean tribe.

Teachers of the lyre players: Kallikrates, son of Kallikrates

<4.> Piper: Neileus, son of Ammonios, of Corinth

<5.> Lyre player: Nikon, son of Antigonus, but naturally of Simakon

<6.> Singer to the lyre: Lykon, son of Lykon, of Tarentum

In the torch race of Aphrodite, those from the first: Soton, son of Kallikrates, of the Chesean tribe

Torch race leader: Poseidippos, son of [ ], of the Chesean tribe

<7.> The poets of the new satyrs: Archenomos, son of Hermias, of Rhodes

<8.> The poets of the new tragedies: Sosistratos, son of Sosistratos

<9.> The actors: Demetrios, son of Nikaios, of Miletus

<10.> The poets of the new comedies: Ariston, son of Timostratos, of Athens

<11.> Actor: Kleinagoras, son of Straton, of Mallos

<12.> Long race for boys: . . . (there follows a list of athletic events)

167. *SEG* 11.923, 33ff.; R. Sherk, *The Roman Empire,* no. 32. This inscription records the preparations for the six-day festival of the Kaisareia plus two days for the thymelic games of the Eurykleia at Gythion in Sparta in the year 15. Directions are given for performances in the theater immediately after the sacrifice to the emperor's family and also for thymelic contests. At line 33 there are some practical considerations.

The stage is obviously wooden, as it was at Sparta at this time too. The "four mime doors" are not easily explained.

> Let the ephors under Terentius Biadas while Chairon is general and priest of the god Augustus Caesar make available three images of the god Augustus and Julia Augusta and Tiberius Caesar Augustus and the scaffolding (*ikria*) in the theater for the chorus and four mimic doors (or "doors for mimes"?) and low podiums (?) for the symphony (i.e., the orchestra).

168. *IG* XI 9 189; *LS* 2.88. This is a law of 294–287 B.C. governing an extension of the athletic festival of the Artemisia in Eretria in Euboea to include musical events. There is no drama, but the details of payment to the participants are unique; only here is the *proagon* of a musical festival recorded outside of Athens. Compare the contemporary Euboean decree (162) where a choral piper gets 600 drachmas. It has been suggested that the parode here is in fact a piper or accompanist, since we should expect a prize for the pipes; but the amount seems low, and a parodist, the usual meaning, is likelier. The inscription records also that merchants may sell free of tax, obviously to encourage the market that went with this as with most festivals.

> The prizes are given as follows:
> For the rhapsode 120, second 30, third 20
> For the boy singer to the pipes 50, second 30, third 20
> For the men's kithara 110, second 70, third 55.
> For the singer to the kithara 200, second 150, third 100
> For the parode 50, second 10
> Maintenance expenses are to be given to the *agonistai* who come, at a drachma a day each, beginning not more than three days before the *proagon,* until the competition takes place.

169. *ID* 399A 49–52; cf. Sifakis, *Studies* 31; P. Bruneau, *Recherches sur les cultes de Délos* 73. Date: 193 B.C. After 200 B.C. the various sums handed on to the treasurers of the Apollo temple for the next year in Delos were kept in pots. Among those listed is the money for the two choral pipers (*choraulai*) for the boys' dithyrambs in the festival for Apollo. One can calculate that they get 1,500 drachmas each for coming, 205 each for maintenance, while the prize is astonishingly only 60; these amounts remained constant from 231 to 178 B.C. All this money could not come from the *choregoi.* The money was deposited at the end of the previous Delian year in the month Poseideon, then paid out for the Apollonia in Gamelion, the first month of the next year. We are made aware that *technitai* could charge huge sums merely to appear at a prestigious festival.

Another pot in which were 3,470 drachmas with the inscription "from the magistracy of Hellen and Mantineus under the archon Olympiodoros in the month Poseideon, Apatourios and Empedos deposited the payments for the pipers along with their expenses for upkeep and organization (*choregemata*)"; from this we took for Telemachos (the festival organizer) the salary and guest-gift and prize for winning and for the expenses of upkeep and organization: the total.

170. *IG* IX 1 694, 76ff. Date: 2nd c. B.C. This inscription now lost records the foundation by two private persons of a festival in Corfu. The interest from the gift is meant to pay for dramatic events in a festival of Dionysus. The foundation left 120 mnas, which is to be set at interest of 16 percent for three whole years, so as to reach 180 mnas (3 talents): only in the fourth year could the interest be touched.

...After the invested capital has increased to 180 mnas and the 180 mnas have been lent out, after a year has passed since the lending out of the 180 mnas, let the archons send to hire *technitai* according to the agonothetic law, and let the archons of the respective years do all the rest as has been written in the gift, unless there is a postponement by Council or Assembly because of war. When once a beginning has been made, <the city> is to hire every second year from the interest on the three talents, for 50 mnas three pipers, three tragedians (i.e., three companies), and three comedians, and the rest <is to be> according to the agonothetic law. Let the customary expenses for maintenance be given the *technitai* from the interest, apart from the 50 mnas. Those who manage the money at the times the *technitai* come, when they take in the money, are to hand over the 50 mnas pay for the *technitai* and the expenses they incur to the *agonothetes* in the month of Artemision before the sixth day, and the remainder to their elected <successors>.

171. W. Blümel, *Die Inschriften von Iasos,* no. 160. Date: about 200 B.C. This is typical of a number of distinctive inscriptions from the town of Iasos in Caria in Asia Minor (160–217 Blümel). They list donations from rich citizens toward the festival. Dymas is elsewhere honored as a wealthy poet of tragedy. The drachma is a nominal fee charged by the city for the use of the theater, while the *choregos* bears the cost.

Under the garland bearer Apollo, who followed Nemertes, the following gave their services: the *agonothetes* Apollodorus, son of

Charmos, <gave> Sosylos the comedian for two days, and the appearance cost a drachma, but the viewing was free. Dymas, son of Antipatros, because of the gift that he made as *choregos* in the preceding year, <gave> Sosylos the comedian, and the appearance cost a drachma, but the viewing was free; Nemertes, son of Theotimos, because of the gift that he made as garland bearer, <gave> Eualkes the kitharist, and the appearance cost a drachma, but the viewing was free; Menon, son of Artemon, as *choregos,* <gave> Eualkes the kitharist, and the appearance cost a drachma, but the viewing was free; Menedemos, son of Artemon, as *choregos,* <gave> Eualkes the kitharist, and the appearance cost a drachma, but the viewing was free; Hermodoros, son of Drakontides, because of the gift that he gave as *agonothetes* in the preceding year, <gave> 300 drachmas.

172. *IG* II² 3157. An honorary decree from the 1st c. This is rare evidence for drama at the Panathenaea.

...] himself was *choregos* and director with the cyclic choruses of men for the tribe Kekropis, and directed a brand new tragedy at the Great Panathenaea [...

173. Suetonius, *Domitian* 4.8–10. Written ca. 120 and referring to an event in 86. The emperor established the Capitolia at Rome, the most successful of the Greek games in Italy. He dresses as a Greek *agonothetes.*

He established also in honor of Zeus Capitolinus a quinquennial festival in three sections, musical, equestrian and gymnic, with somewhat more crowned victors than nowadays. For they competed also in prose oration in Greek and Latin and, besides kitharodes, choral kitharists and solo kitharists, and even girls in a race in the stadium. He presided over the contest with Greek shoes, dressed in a purple cloak in Greek style, wearing on his head a gold crown with the figures of Jupiter, Juno, and Minerva; seated with him were the priest of Jupiter and the College of the Flaviales in the same dress, save that their crowns carried his image also.

IIIC. The Roman World

The origins of native Roman drama are unclear. Augustan poets (175) are untrustworthy, as are the later grammarians (176), tending on the whole to repeat or vie with earlier Greek theorists. We can be more confident about the contribution and nature of Etruscan dancers, the Oscan-masked Atellan farce, and the role of young men in impromptu farce and native customs like Fescennine comic abuse, as in the only longer description (174) of the origins of Roman theater from the antiquarian Varro at the end of the Republic. But the Romans themselves had only limited information, e.g., they could not separate out their word *satura,* which meant "musical medley" and then "satire," from the Greek *satyroi.* Traditionally the drama of Rome began with the Greek Livius Andronicus from Tarentum, who introduced translations of Greek drama to Rome (178) probably at the Roman Games in 240 B.C., but even that date was not certain, and there had been many festivals of drama before. Our other principal pieces of evidence are descriptions of Roman processions (177), which again show the importance of Etruscan culture upon Rome.

It is uncertain that a college of poets (194, 195) existed in republican times, to match the Greek unions (IVAii); Greek actors often were brought to Rome (184, 185), but the Roman actors were less well organized. The republican troupes seem to have applied to the aediles for the right to play, and there was some selection process.

Fortunately we are better informed about the origins of the dramatic festivals (179–81). Games at Rome must be roughly divided into regular games (*ludi sollemnes*) and "honorary spectacles" (*munera;* singular *munus*), especially gladiatorial games (182). These in turn can be subdivided into their genres, i.e., scenic games (*ludi scaenici*), circus games (*ludi circenses*), etc. The *ludi sollemnes* are held regularly by the civic authorities as part of religious festivals or public celebrations, whereas the *munera* are essentially donated spectacles by the wealthy at funerals, triumphs, or other special occasions; these are irregular, though of course they could be attached to regular games by the presiding magistrates, who would then pay for them (183–84). The *ludi sollemnes* were entrusted to Roman magistrates even in imperial times. Four aediles had charge of games along with feasts, construction, and police duties from at least 367 B.C., though the games were transferred from the aediles to the praetors in 22 B.C. In imperial times the holding of these games could bankrupt members of the senatorial class (189–92); though Augustus had forbidden them to spend more than the same amount contributed by the state, a few years later he allowed three times as much, and such legislation was repeated and largely ineffectual. The main scenic games were instituted or attached to existing festivals in Rome all by about 200 B.C. The six major *ludi publici* follow:

1. Roman, in charge of the curule aedile, and then the praetor after Augustus, in September in the Circus Maximus, were regularized in 366 B.C.; three days of *ludi scaenici* (perhaps Atellan) appear to have been attached to these games in 366 B.C. In 214 B.C. the *ludi scaenici* were four days long (179). The Roman Games were later extended to ten days. They were also called *Ludi Magni* ("Great Games").

2. Plebeian, instituted in 220 B.C., in charge of the plebeian aedile in November in the Circus Flaminius, had plays by 200 B.C., and clearly was a counterpart to the Roman Games.

Only in these two is *instauratio* (see below) recorded. There were two games dedicated to Greek divinities:

3. Apollinares were instituted in 212 B.C., in charge of the urban praetor in mid-July, and had always a scenic component.

4. Megalenses, or Megalesia, were founded in 204 B.C. for the Great Mother (i.e., Cybele); the first scenic display was attached in 194 B.C. (Livy 34.54). The temple to the goddess on the Palatine was dedicated in 191 B.C., where the plays were then performed under the curule aedile.

There are two games for Roman divinities:

5. Floralia, celebrated from at least 241 B.C. for the goddess Flora, with regular annual scenic games from at least 173 B.C. in April/May, were particularly associated with mimes and celebrated by the city prostitutes.

6. Ceriales, for Ceres, in charge of the plebeian aediles in April, were celebrated from 202 B.C., but it is not known when dramas were attached.

It is notable that there are no games for Dionysus or his Latin equivalent.

The growth of drama and festivals was much favored by the politicians who sought to win votes by their expenditures on games. This zeal to entertain the masses, which authorities sought ineffectively to control until the end of the Roman Empire, exercised a decisive influence on the quantity and quality of the shows offered in Rome, and on the politicization of the theater. Games were theoretically a religious ritual holiday, and breaches of the ritual would require them to be repeated—whence the concept of *instauratio* (180). But the desire to repeat them was clearly politically useful to their political promoters, to whom the playwrights had to apply. Theoretically the state gave the funds for the games (181)—as originally it did to the religious institutions—but this was insufficient, and had to be supplemented from the magistrates' own funds and eventually, their political backers (196). After ca. 200 B.C. the amount was no longer fixed, and ambitious politicians were free to spend their own money or that of their backers on their games, despite varied attempts to limit these increasing expenditures. The religous element was subordinated to the political.

From the beginning, games involved horse racing, boxers, and such contests in honor of the gods, but musical shows were also offered; the dramatic games soon exceeded the days devoted to all other performances, but the Roman playwright was always in competition with other types of entertainment, and several theaters could be playing at the same time. It is difficult therefore to know how many days were available for drama in the course of a year, since though there may have been only 14 official drama days in 180 B.C., this number could be greatly increased by *munera* of which we know nothing, and by the repetition of festival days as a further donation at private expense by the presiding magistrates; this was called *instauratio,* and could at times lead to the number of days set aside for a festival being trebled. A reasonable guess is that, under the Republic, festival official days for drama were about 24 in 180 B.C. In 100 B.C., from about 36 regular festival days 28 were reserved for theater, and in 44 B.C. the figures are 42 out of 59. In 325, 101 days out of 176 are reserved for drama, which would then consist also of mimes and pantomimes; the remaining days would be for spectacles such as wild beast hunts (*venationes*) and gladiatorial games, all of these being supported by complex and expensive organizations. The increase is due to a number of new festival days to celebrate various emperors, such as the Palatini and Augustalia (cf. 200).

Gladiatorial contests are introduced as part of private funeral games in 264 B.C. (Livy, *Epitome* 16), but then by public figures, and held in the forum; they became irregularly attached as *munera* to the public *ludi,* but Claudius obliged the quaestors to offer them as a regular part of their office from 47. Irregular *munera* in imperial times were in the hands of representatives of the imperial family, and, afterward, appointed officials called *procuratores a muneribus* (206) from the time of Claudius. But the actual mounting and running of the massive theater industry that developed in imperial Rome is largely unknown to us, save from inscriptions and a few legal decisions. Around 100 A.D. a special ministry called the *summum choragium* (literally, "the highest stage apparatus") was created near the Colosseum for the stage apparatus and officals who looked after the imperial games (205). Its officers were senior civil servants, led by a procurator; a suboffice was that for stage material (*ornamenta*). About the beginning of the 3rd c. another senior official with the Greek title *logista thumelae* (*CIL* 13.1807) appears, perhaps responsible only for the scenic games.

We know little of the actual organization of the huge spectacles at Rome, let alone the minor versions in the cities of the empire, which were modeled on the structure in Rome. Our fragmentary evidence consists of epitaphs of the bureaucrats (201–4), and some legal documents. These are most valuable when they give a succession of posts held, enabling us to see the importance of the position from the order of ranking. The immense importance and expenditures attached to the smooth administration of the Roman games as a source of political power can be imagined from the fact that that position in the imperial civil service was more important than the procuratorship of Britain. But religious games continued even under Christianity.

Sources

174. Livy 7.2. Written ca. 20 B.C. Livy derives his discussion about games in honor of Jupiter from Varro's effort to systematize theater history in a series of artificial stages. Varro lived from 116–27 B.C.

> ... among other efforts to disarm the wrath of the gods, the Romans are said also to have instituted theatrical entertainment (363 B.C.). This ... was imported from abroad. Without any singing, without imitating the action of singers, clowns (*ludiones*) who had been brought in from Etruria danced to the strains of the piper and performed not ungraceful movements in the Etruscan fashion. Next

the young Romans began to imitate them, at the same time exchanging jests in uncouth verses and bringing their movements into a certain harmony with the words. And so the amusement was adopted, and frequent use kept it alive. The native professional actors were called *histriones* from *ister,* the Etruscan word for actor; these no longer as before threw out rude lines hastily improvised, like the Fescennines (a rural form of ritual abuse, especially connected with weddings), but performed *saturae* (medleys?), full of tunes with melodies written out to go with the pipes and with suitable movements. Livius <Andronicus> was the first some years later (240 B.C.?), to abandon *saturae* and compose a play with a plot. Like everyone else in those days, he acted his own pieces, and the story goes that when his voice, owing to the frequent demands made upon it, had lost its freshness, he asked and obtained the indulgence to let a boy stand before the piper to sing the monody, while he acted it himself, with a vivacity of gesture that gained considerably from his not having to use his voice. From that time on, actors (?of comedy) began to use singers to accompany their gesticulation, reserving only the dialogue parts for their own delivery. When this type of performance had begun to wean the drama from laughter and informal jest, and the play had been gradually developed into art, the young men abandoned the acting of comedies to professionals, and revived the ancient practice of refashioning their nonsense into verses and letting fly with them at one another; this was the source of what were later called *exodia,* and more usually mixed with Atellan farces. The Atellan was a kind of comedy acquired from the Oscans (cf. 187), and the young men kept it for themselves, and would not allow it to be polluted by the professional actors; that is why it is a fixed tradition that performers of Atellan plays are not disenfranchised (i.e., *infames* like other actors) but serve in the army as though they had no connection with the stage. . . . so it could be seen, how from a sane beginning the (theater) business has come to this insanity, scarcely to be supported even by wealthy kingdoms.

175. Horace, *Art of Poetry* 181 ff. Written ca. 10 B.C. We include this passage here to illustrate how the poets of the Augustan period are dominated by Greek theory.

[181] You will not bring on the stage what should be performed behind the scenes and you will keep much from our eyes, which the actors' ready tongue will soon narrate before us; so that Medea

is not to butcher her boys before the people nor impious Atreus cook human flesh on the stage...[189] Let no play be shorter or longer than five acts...Let no god intervene, unless a knot come suitable for such a deliverer, nor let a fourth actor try to speak... [193] Let the chorus sustain the part and strenuous duty of an actor and sing nothing between the acts that does not advance and blend suitably into the plot.

176. Diomedes, *Glossaria Latina* 1.492.2. This late Latin grammarian is not usually trustworthy, but here he may be.

But Latin writers (of tragedies) introduce several characters (i.e., more than three) into their stories to make them more impressive by the numbers.

177A. Etruscan influence. Appian, *Punic History* 66. Written early 2nd c., referring to 201 B.C.

There preceded the general himself (Scipio Africanus Maior), lictors with scarlet tunics, and a chorus of lyre players and *tityristai* (?satyrs), in imitation of an Etruscan procession, with waistbands and gold headbands; they marched in step and in order with singing and dancing.

177B. Fabius Pictor, *FGrH* 809 F 13b.26ff., cited by Dionysius of Halicarnassus, *Roman Antiquities* 7.72.5, describing "from what he knew at first hand" at the end of the 3rd c. B.C. the *pompa circensis*—the procession from the Capitol to the Circus Maximus—of the original Roman Games.

There followed the competitors' many choruses divided in three groups, first men, then young men, then boys, and there followed with them pipers blowing into old-fashioned short pipes, and lyre players strumming on seven-stringed ivory lyres and the so-called *barbita*. The dress of the dancers was purple tunics held in with brass belts and swords hung by them and spears shorter than the usual, while the men had brass helmets with conspicuous crests and wings. One man led each chorus, who led off the dance movements for the rest, being the first to illustrate the warlike and emphatic gestures in proceleusmatic rhythms for the most part. After the armed dances, the choruses of *satyristai* came in procession ("imitating the Greek *sikinnis*," adds Dionysius). Their costume was wooly tunics, and garlands of all kinds of flowers, and they had loincloths, goatskins and tufts of hair standing on their heads, and so on; they made jokes and imitated the serious movements, turning them into ribaldry. After these choruses came the lyre players in a body.

178. Cicero, *Brutus* 72, cf. Aulus Gellius 17.21.42 quoting Varro. This is written in 46 B.C. and strongly suggests that there was even then no consensus about the earlier history of Roman drama.

> Yet this <L.> Livius <Andronicus> first produced a play in the consulship (240 B.C.) of Gaius Claudius, son of Caecus, and M. Tuditanus, as late as the very year before the birth of Ennius, 514 years after the founding of Rome according to the authority I follow (probably Atticus), for there is a dispute among writers about the chronology.

179. Livy 24.43.7. Written ca. 20 B.C. and referring to 214 B.C.

> Tradition has it that at the festival given that year by the curule aediles, four days were devoted to dramatic performances for the first time.

180. Livy 25.2.8. Written ca. 20 B.C. and referring to 213 B.C.

> The generosity of the aediles consisted in celebrating the Roman Games splendidly for the resources of the time, and in repeating them (*instauratio*) for one day.... The Plebeian Games were repeated for two days.

181. Dionysius of Halicarnassus, *Roman Antiquities* 7.71.2. Written ca. 10 B.C. The Senate does not allow for inflation.

> <The Roman Senate> ordered this festival (the Roman Games) to be celebrated (in 364 B.C.)...; and they ordered 500 mnas of silver to be expended every year upon the sacrifices and the games, a sum the Romans laid out on the festival until the time of the Punic War (218 B.C.).

182. Livy 31.50.4. Written ca. 20 B.C. and referring to 200 B.C. Many games, not always dramatic, were donated by the wealthy as *munera*. In some towns an official called a *munerarius* was entrusted with the task of ensuring donations.

> Funeral games lasting four days were given in the forum in commemoration of the death of M. Valerius Laevinus by his sons Publius and Marcus, and a gladiatorial show was given by them.

183. Livy 36.36.1–2. Written ca. 20 B.C. and referring to 191 B.C. *Ludi* were often in the early Republic the result of vows. Here is a clear case of a dispute between state and individual over the costs.

> The other consul, P. Cornelius Scipio, who had been allotted the province of Gaul before he departed to the war... demanded of the Senate that money be voted to him for the the games, which, as praetor in Spain he had vowed in a critical moment of the battle. His request seemed unprecedented and unreasonable; they voted

that whatever games he had vowed on his own sole initiative, with no authorization from the Senate, he should celebrate either out of the spoils ... or out of his own pocket. The games were celebrated through ten days by P. Cornelius.

184. Livy 39.22.1–2. Written ca. 20 B.C. In this same year (186 B.C.) L. Scipio also collected Greek *technitai* from Asia for his triumphal games (Livy 39.22.10).

The Taurian games (irregular and otherwise unknown) were performed for two days for religious reasons. Then for ten days with great magnificence, M. Fulvius gave the games he had vowed during the Aetolian War (Livy 39.5.7 tells us that he had set aside from "donations" from the Aetolian cities a hundred pounds of gold, but the Senate only allowed him to spend 80,000 sesterces of it). Many *technitai* (Lat. *artifices*) came from Greece to do him honor. Also a contest of athletes (boxers?) was for the first time made a spectacle by the Romans, and a hunt of lions and panthers was given, and the games in number and variety were celebrated in a manner almost like that of the present time.

185. Polybius 30.14. Written ca. 140 B.C. about the events of 167 B.C. He is talking of musical and dramatic contests. There was also an orchestra built for these foreign players.

<L. Anicius> summoned the most distinguished artists (*technitai*) of Greece and constructed a very large stage in the circus.

186. Tacitus, *Annals* 14.20–21. Written ca. 115. Tacitus records the debate at the foundation by Nero of his Neronian games in the Greek style in 60. There were to be competitions for oratory and poetry as well.

Some recalled with approval the criticisms of Pompey, among his elders, for constructing a permanent theater, whereas previously performances had been held with improvised stage and auditorium, or to go back to a remoter past, spectators had stood, since it was feared seats might keep them idle for days on end. As for the shows, the objectors said, let them continue in the old Roman way, whenever it falls to the praetors to celebrate them, and provided no citizen is obliged to compete.... (On the other side it was argued:) But our ancestors too did not shrink from such public entertainment as contemporary resources permitted. *Histriones* were imported from Etruria.... Ever since the annexation of Greece (146 B.C.) and Asia, performances have become more ambitious. Two hundred years have passed since the triumph of Lucius Mummius (145 B.C.), who first gave that sort of show here, and during that time no upper-class Roman has ever demeaned himself by professional acting. As for a permanent theater, it was more economical than the construction and demolition of a new one every year at vast expense. If—as now suggested—the state pays for shows, it will save the purses of officials and give the public less opportunity to ask them for Greek contests. . . . . Certainly the display took place without any open scandal. Nor was there partisan rioting, since the pantomimes, though allowed back on stage, were banned from the sacred contests.

187. Strabo 5.3.6. Written late 1st c. B.C. The geographer is perhaps referring to Atellan plays. Rome was still trilingual at this time.

> Among the Romans . . . at the time of a certain traditional competition, poems in that dialect (i.e., Oscan) are brought to the stage and recited like mimes.

188. Note in *Codex Montecassinus* 1086, fol. 64, written in the 9th c. This is our only evidence for the last recorded Roman-performed tragedy by a living author, a well-known friend of Vergil and Horace, produced on the stage in 29 B.C.

> Lucius Varus Rufus produced on the stage at the games Augustus gave after the victory of Actium a tragedy *Thyestes,* which he had finished with great care; for this drama he got one million sesterces.

189. Cicero, *Letters to his Friends* 2.3. Written 53 B.C. His friend Scribonius Curio was going to give games anyway, and this high-minded philosophizing was at variance with the realities of politics.

> No one admires the capacity to give displays (*munera*), for that is a function of resources not native ability, nor is there anyone who is not already tired to death of them.

190. Plutarch, *Precepts of Statecraft* 822f. Written ca. 115.

> If <the statesman> is poor, he must not produce foot races, theatrical shows, and banquets in competition with the rich for reputation and power.

191. Martial 10.41. Written ca. 90. The poet is satirizing a wife who divorces her husband when she sees that he is going to be bankrupted by the games he must subsidize from his own pocket as magistrate. But theater was usually cheaper than the other kinds of spectacle.

> He was praetor. The purple robe (symbol of the *agonothetes*) of the Megalensian festival was going to cost 100,000 sesterces, even if you gave a pretty thin show, and the Plebeian festival would have run off with 20,000. That's not divorce, Proculeia, just good business.

192. Scriptores Historiae Augustae, *Marcus Aurelius* 11.4. Written late 3rd to early 4th c. and referring to the reign of Marcus Aurelius (161–80). Contrast Seneca, *Letters* 80.7, where the actor gets ten bushels of grain and five denarii. An emperor (Galba) who gave five denarii was a miser (Suetonius, *Galba* 12.3). An aureus was twenty-five silver denarii.

> <Marcus> reduced the cost of theatrical offerings also, decreeing that though an actor might receive five aurei, nonetheless no games sponsor (*editor*) was to exceed ten aurei.

193. Horace, *Satires* 1.10. Spurius Maecius Tarpa had been appointed to approve plays by Pompey in 55 B.C. for his new theater. But Horace's remarks (from ca. 35 B.C.) suggest something like a *proagon* in a temple, perhaps of the Muses.

> (While others write epic and tragedy, etc.,) I play at these poems that are never going to ring out in competition in the temple with Tarpa as judge, or return again and again as spectacles in the theaters.

194. Festus 466.29ff L. The lexicographer of the late 2nd c. is explaining unclearly and possibly incorrectly that the old Romans used the word *scriba* to mean poet as well as administrative clerk. He seems to be citing a decree of the Senate authorizing an official college of literary artists; but the temple was not for their exclusive use, and the artists are not the Artists of Dionysus.

> So when Livius Andronicus in the Second Punic War (ca. 207 B.C.) wrote a hymn that was sung by the virgins, because the state's affairs began to be conducted more successfully, the temple of Minerva (goddess of artisans) on the Aventine was officially granted, where the *scribae* and *histriones* might assemble and make offerings in honor of Livius because he used to write plays and to act in them.

195. Valerius Maximus, *Memorable Deeds and Sayings* 3.7.11. This unreliable author of the early 1st c. would be referring to a time ca. 90 B.C. The dramatist Accius would have been very old at the time. This is the only certain mention of a "college of poets," which cannot be connected with the preceding college, or documented after this date.

> <Accius> never got to his feet for Julius Caesar <Strabo> (an aristocratic writer of tragedies), distinguished and powerful though <Strabo> was, when <Strabo> came into the college of poets, not because he (Accius) was forgetful of his status, but because he was sure that in a comparison of the studies they shared, he was himself somewhat superior. Wherefore he could not be accused of arrogance, since they were occupied in a contest of books not ancestors.

196. Seneca, *On Benefits* 2.21.5. Written ca. 60. The reference is to the time of Caesar.

> Let's take the example of Graecimus Iulius, a man of distinction... When he was accepting money from his friends who were contributing to the expenses of his games, he did not accept a great sum sent by Fabius Persicus.

197. Philostratus, *Lives of the Sophists* 1.25, p. 535. Written between 217 and 238 and referring to mid-2nd c. An actor appeals personally to the emperor.

> Once when an actor of tragedy who had performed at the Olympic Games in Asia, over which Polemo (a wealthy orator) presided, declared he would prosecute him because Polemo had expelled him at the beginning of the play, the emperor asked the actor what time it was when he was expelled from the theater, and when he replied that it happened at noon,...

198. *Lex Coloniae Genetivae Iuliae* 70–71. This set of laws inscribed on a bronze tablet for a colony in Spain is in its original form probably to be dated about 44 B.C. for Italian cities.

> All *duoviri* (city magistrates)... shall during their magistracy at the discretion of the decurions (the city council) celebrate a gladiatorial show or dramatic spectacles to Jupiter, Juno, and Minerva (the usual Capitoline triad) and to the gods and goddesses, or such part of the said shows as shall be possible, during four days for the greater part of each day, and during one day games in the circus or forum to Venus; and on the said spectacles or shows each of the said aediles shall expend out of his own money not less than 2,000 sesterces, and from the public funds it shall be lawful for each several *duovir* to expend a sum not exceeding 2,000 sesterces, and it shall be lawful for the said persons to do so with impunity.... All aediles during their magistracy shall celebrate a gladiatorial show or dramatic spectacles to Jupiter, Juno, and Minerva or whatever portion of such shows as shall be possible during three days for the greater part of each day and during one-day games in the circus or forum to Venus; and on the said spectacles or shows each of the said aediles shall expend out of his own money not less than 2,000 sesterces, and from the public funds it shall be lawful to expend for each several aedile 1,000 sesterces; and a *duovir* or *praefectus* shall see that the said money is given or assigned.

199. Cicero, *For Milo 95*. Delivered 52 B.C. Cicero claims that Milo spent three patrimonies on shows in his attempts to become consul in 53 B.C.

> He reminds us that for your safety, he did his best . . . to use his three patrimonies as a means of mollifying them (the plebs and the mob); he has no misgivings lest, having appeased the plebeians with his shows . . .

200. *ILS* 154. Inscribed altar. Date: 18. The *duoviri* in Bracciano set up an altar for Augustus, Tiberius, and Livia.

> Decrees: . . . and that on the birthdays of Augustus and Tiberius, before the decurions come to eat, their *genii* (native spirits) be invited with incense and wine to dine at the altar of the *numen* (godhead) of Augustus. We had the altar constructed at our own expense; we had games celebrated for six days from the Ides of August.

201. *ILS* 5207. Inscribed gravestone. No date. Cf. *CIL* 6.10092. The organizing of games went through middlemen. This is the gravestone of a Roman *locator,* who hired out players.

> Quintus Gavius Armonius, players' agent, lived twenty-six years and six months.

202. *ILS* 5208. Inscribed gravestone. Date: 2nd c.? An ex-actor becomes an agent. The Greek word for "agent" (*promisthota*) is perhaps used for the expected Latin *manceps,* since the inscription comes from North Greece. For "archmimes" see V.

> Titus Uttiedius Venerianus, Latin archmime and public servant for 37 years, an agent (*promisthota*) for 18 years, lived 75 years . . .

203. *ILS* 5206. Inscribed gravestone. Date: late 2nd c.? An imperial freedman controls the hiring of actors, whose union he heads.

> For Marcus Aurelius Plebeius, freedman of Augustus, elected <players'> agent on a permanent salary (*diurnus*), scribe, and master for life of the corporation of the Latin players, with unmatched trustworthiness acting in the interests of the above named corporation . . .

204A. Officials. *ILS* 5268. Inscribed gravestone. Date: 1st c. Especially under the empire, specialists for stage productions came into existence, both public and private: they testify to a complex organization. We give only a few names.

> To the memory of Hermippus, freedman of Augustus, procurator for the stage (*scaenica*).

204B. *ILS* 5269. Inscribed gravestone. Date: 1st c. We can only guess what some of the officials did: this one is possibly an overseer.

Marcus Vipsanius Narcissus, *rogator* for the stage (*ab scaena*).

204C. *CIL* 6.10089 (cf. 3756); *ILS* 1766. Inscribed gravestone. Date: second half of 1st c.

Titus Claudius Philetus, freedman of Augustus, secretary to the office of scenic and gladiatoral clothing...

204D. *ILS* 5270.

Lucius Marius Auctus, *denuntiator* for the Greek stage.

204E. *CIL* 6.33775.

To the memory of Silvanus, house slave of Caesar, *dispensator* of *scaenica*, who lived 34 years.

205A. *Summum Choragium.* *CIL* 6.10083. Inscribed gravestone. Date: 2nd c. The *summum choragium* was the administrative offices for the imperial games. It was established by the mid-2nd c.

Farewell Marcus, dear soul, assistant procurator of the *summum choragium*.

205B. *CIL* 6.297. Inscribed offering. Date: 2nd c.

For Heracles and Silvanus because of a vow. Trophimianus, freedman of Augustus, procurator of the *summum choragium*, with his wife Chia.

205C. *CIL* 6.10084. Dedication by a financial officer. Date: 2nd c.

Bursar of the *summum choragium* of Augustus, gave <this> free to the college.

205D. *CIL* 6.10085. Inscribed gravestone. Date: 2nd c. Even a doctor was attached to the office; possibily looking after gladiators would be one of his tasks.

In memory of Publius Aelius Agathemerus, freedman of Augustus, doctor of the office (*ratio*) of the *summum choragium*.

205E. *CIL* 6.10086. Inscribed gravestone. Date: 2nd c. Another *tabularius* at *ILS* 3727 is quite wealthy.

In memory of Ulpia Synoris his wife, Tertius, freedman of Augustus, *tabularius* (accountant) of the *summum choragium*.

205F. *CIL* 3.348. Honorary decree. Date: 2nd c. The inscription comes from Phrygia, and shows that the offices the person honored had held previously were in ascending order of importance.

Marcus Aurelius Marcio, freedman of Augustus, assistant financial officer, procurator of marble quarries, procurator of Britain, procurator of the *summum choragium*, procurator of Phrygia...

206A. *ILS* 1567. Dedicatory inscription. Date: second half of 1st c. The office *a muneribus*, i.e., in charge of imperial shows, presumably often gladiatorial, was also a high administrative post.

Tiberius Claudius Bucolas, freedman of Augustus, pre-taster (of food for the emperor), head of the diningroom staff, procurator for *munera,* procurator of the water supply, procurator of the court...

206B. *ILS* 1738. Inscribed gravestone. Date: 217. This time the career is listed in inverse order, since Prosenes ended his days as imperial chamberlain.

For Marcus Aurelius Prosenes, freedman of Augustuses, chamberlain to Augustus (Caracalla), procurator of the treasuries, procurator of the personal property of the emperor, procurator of *munera,* procurator of vineyards, appointed by the God Commodus to the court: for their most devout and deserving patron his freedmen decorated this sarcophagus at their own cost.

207. Augustine, *City of God* 2.4. Written ca. 420. Augustine is recalling his youth (354–83) in North Africa, where drama was still connected closely with pagan religious festivals. This was a principal reason for the hatred of the theater by the Christian fathers.

I myself too in my youth sometimes went along to the spectacles and games of their irreligious ceremonies. I would watch the *arrepticii* (?dervishes), would listen to the musicians, would take delight in the shameful shows that were put on in honor of gods and goddesses, of the virgin Caelestis and the Berecynthian mother of all (i.e., Cybele), before whose couch on the anniversary of her washing were chanted publicly by the vilest players such tales as...were not fit for the very mothers of the players to hear.

IV. Actors and Audience

IVA. Actors and Acting

IVAi. Actors in the Classical Period

The history of the theater in the 5th and 4th c. B.C. is largely the history of the specialization and professionalization of its functionaries. From Aristotle on, the ancient tradition claimed that the early playwrights themselves performed their plays (1–3, 304). Allegedly Sophocles first broke the tradition because of a weak voice (3A). Some find independent confirmation of this tradition in the report that Sophocles was portrayed in the Painted Stoa playing the kithara as Thamyras (3A). We hear that a number of comic poets also began their careers as actors (4–6); perhaps for a time, like Sophocles, they practiced both professions simultaneously.

Nevertheless, the sources, particularly for the early period, must be approached with caution. The whole tradition is overschematic and smacks of Aristotelian teleological historiography, crediting major figures with decisive "discoveries," while the theatrical genres, like organisms, gradually attain their "proper" form. A good example is the "invention" of the conventions limiting the number of actors. The Greek word *hypokrites,* "actor," is used only of speaking performers. The number of mute performers who might appear on stage was in principle unlimited, but the number of (speaking) actors came to be fixed at three. The tradition is divided as to whether Aeschylus or Sophocles is to be credited with increasing the number of actors from two to three (7–9). It was probably neither. The extant playtexts show a much more complex development. Of Aeschylus' plays, *Persians* (472 B.C.) and *Suppliants* (ca. 463 B.C.) require only two actors, and *Seven Against Thebes* (467 B.C.) and all the plays of the *Oresteia* (458 B.C.) require three. In *Seven Against Thebes* a third actor may be required in the final scene, which is probably a late interpolation. But even if there are three actors on stage, three-way conversation is avoided; while two actors speak, the third remains silent.

This is also true of *Prometheus Bound, Agamemnon,* and *Libation Bearers* (apart from Pylades' three lines). *Eumenides* is the first play to make free use of the third actor.

The limitation of speaking parts to three was probably not the result of any single poet's overweening influence or a sudden general recognition of drama's ordained nature. Rather, the institution of an actors' competition at the Dionysia in 449 B.C. (11–12) and at the Lenaea ca. 432 B.C. (13) is more likely to have occasioned regulations of this sort, whether in the interest of fair competition, or because a three-actor limit balanced the need for poetic versatility with the desire to maximize the main actor's exposure to the audience. It is surprising to note that the "three-actor rule," though strictly observed in tragedy, is frequently violated in Old Comedy: of all of Aristophanes' plays, only *Knights* and *Plutus* can be performed without a fourth actor, while *Clouds* and *Acharnians* appear to require five. If the existence of an actors' competition placed a strict limit on actors in tragedy, it did not for comedy, for though the earliest positive evidence for a comic actors' prize at the Lenaea appears on a fragment of the Victor Lists for 375 B.C., the reconstruction of the monument shows that two columns preceded this fragment and that the list and the contest must go back to ca. 440 B.C. (cf. III 68). Note, however, that the use of fourth and fifth actors in comedy is generally limited to very brief appearances. By the time of Menander, comedy did strictly observe the three-actor rule. This may have some connection with the inception of a comic actors' contest at the Dionysia 328–312 B.C. (14). No actors' contests are attested for the Rural Dionysia.

The story of Sophocles' decision to abandon acting may be due to a recognition of new professional standards leading to a gradual separation of the functions of poet and actor and further encouraged by the establishment of actors' competitions. The sources for the earliest period attest poet actors and actors permanently associated with particular poets (9, 10). This ended by the time of the actors' contest, when the archon allotted actors to the poets (15). Concern for fair and equal competition led, by the mid-4th c. B.C., to a further attempt to separate the actor's contribution from the poet's, when each principal actor was allotted to one play of each tragic trilogy (16).

Another effect of the competitions was a standardization in the structure of acting troupes: each specialized in only tragedy or comedy (25) and each was composed of three actors, the protagonist, deuteragonist, and tritagonist, a hierarchy so rigid that it became archetypal and proverbial (18–22). In Greek literature the terms appear most frequently in metaphors, where "protagonist" is used for "star"; "deuteragonist" for "adjutant," "second-fiddle," and "sidekick"; and "tritagonist," a term of abuse meaning something like "third-rate." Another literary stereotype fixes upon the paradox that this hierarchy might be reversed on stage and the tritagonist might play the tyrant, the protagonist the slaves; the cliché may owe more to its attractive paradox than to any normal practice (20–22). Only the protagonists could form contracts with the archon, receive payment from the state, or win the actor's prize (15, 17). The tritagonist seems to have hired himself out directly to the protagonist (18, 21). For want of any ancient testimony, many scholars are content to suppose the deuteragonist a "partner" in the firm. Most troupes no doubt included family, apprentices, and hangers-on who could serve as mutes in the performance. The cost of keeping the actors and hiring extras apparently fell to the *choregos* (19, III 98).

The power and prestige of actors increased rapidly in the 4th c. B.C., when Athenian drama acquired an international market (26–28; IAi). While touring the Greek world, actors assumed many of the functions performed at Athens by archon, poet, and *choregos,* and other specialized functions, such as chorus director or stage manager. In remoter areas they must have become entirely self-sufficient, except perhaps for the provision of a chorus (26). Communities throughout Greece came to recognize actors' claims to sacred immunity and free passage, justified by drama's connection with religious ritual. This sometimes led to the employment of actors as ambassadors and go-betweens, particularly in the intrigues of the Macedonian monarchs (29–31). Athens appears to have been particularly free in granting citizenship to prestigious actors like Neoptolemos (30E) and Aristodemos (30F) in order to use them for international negotiations. It was the royal patronage of Philip and Alexander that had the greatest impact upon the profession. Following the tradition established by Archelaus (I 25–27), they patronized the arts, particularly theater, to enhance their international prestige. Philip and Alexander's active participation in the promotion of Greek culture went a long way toward reconciling other Greek states to their growing political hegemony, for the Greeks traditionally regarded the Macedonians as a foreign barbarian power. Particularly skillful was Alexander's use of theatrical extravaganzas to mark the major victories of his Asian campaign: not only did they help, during his absence, to concentrate the attention of the potentially rebellious Greeks upon his unfailing fortune, wealth, and power, they also helped color these conquests as Panhellenic, not merely Macedonian, triumphs (31C–E). These lessons in propaganda and public relations were not lost on Alexander's successors. Macedonian patronage was a major factor in severing the theater from its Dionysian past. Dramatic performances were incorporated with other entertainments in massive ad hoc festivals created for the celebration of secular events such as weddings and military victories (29, 31C–E). The growth in demand for actors with the internationalization of theater in the early 4th c. B.C. was increased tenfold with Alexander's conquests. Cities were forced to safeguard their interests by advancing large deposits on dramatic performances and imposing fines for failure to appear (30F–G, 31C, cf. III 40). Top actor's incomes grew from huge at mid-century (32) to legendary (33) by its end. These heady days saw the creation of the world's first international trade union, the Artists of Dionysus (IVAii): before the late 4th c. B.C. we hear only of small local associations that were probably designed for social and religious functions more than for the promotion of professional interests (23–24).

Sources

Poet/Actors

1. Aristotle, *Rhetoric* 1403b18–23. Written ca. 330 B.C.
   Study was first made of the aspect <of rhetoric> that naturally comes first, namely, the means by which persuasive arguments are to be gotten from the subject matter itself; next, stylistic organization; and third, that which is most important, but has never yet been the object of study, namely, delivery. Indeed, the study of delivery came late to tragedy and the art of epic recitation; the poets themselves first acted out their tragedies.

2A. Thespis. The "Parian Marble" 58. See III 45.

2B. Plutarch, *Solon* 29.6. Written ca. 115; the anecdote is set in the mid-6th c. B.C.
   Thespis and his followers had already begun to develop tragedy—an affair that, because of its novelty, attracted large crowds, though it had not yet been organized into a contest—when Solon, being by nature fond of entertainment, inquisitive, and in his old age especially given to leisurely activity, games, drink, and music, watched Thespis himself doing the acting, as was the custom among the ancients. After the performance he called to him and asked if he was not ashamed to tell such lies in front of so many people. When Thespis replied that there was no harm in speaking and acting as

he did in play, Solon banged the earth with his walking stick, saying, "if people so praise and admire it, we will soon find this play among our serious pursuits."

3A. Sophocles. *Life of Sophocles* 4.

<Sophocles> innovated a great deal in matters of performance. First, because his own voice was weak, he did away with the custom of poets acting; in earlier times the poet himself used to act. He also increased the number of choreuts from twelve to fifteen, and he established the third actor. They say that he even took up the kithara and only ever played kithara in the *Thamyras* (ca. 470–460 B.C.), whence he is painted holding a kithara in the Painted Stoa.

3B. Athenaeus 20e. Written ca. 200.

Sophocles was very attractive in his youth and had learned dance and music even as a child from Lampron. In any case, after the Battle of Salamis (480 B.C.), he danced around the victory monument anointed and nude with a lyre. Some say he wore a *himation*. And he himself played kithara while putting on the *Thamyras*. He showed himself an excellent ballplayer when he produced the *Nausi-caa* (ca. 470–460 B.C.).

4. *Suda*, s.v. *Chionides*. Written ca. 900. The word "protagonist" is emended by some editors to read "was the first competitor."

Chionides: an Athenian, writer of Old Comedy, whom they also say was a protagonist of Old Comedy; he directed eight years (486 B.C.) before the Persian Wars.

5. Scholion to Aristophanes, *Knights* 537. The treatise *On Comedy* also says Crates was an actor (cf. 6). Crates was active from ca. 450 to 430 B.C.

<Crates> was a comic poet, who first acted in the plays of Cratinus and later himself became a poet...

6. Anon., *On Comedy* 29 = *Prol. de Com. III* 9, p. 7 Koster.

<Pherecrates>, an Athenian, won in the archonship of Theodoros (437 B.C.). Being an actor (something has dropped out of the text; supply "at first, but by later becoming a poet,") he emulated Crates.

The Poets' Actors

7. Aristotle, *Poetics* 1449a15–19. See II 11.

8. Diogenes Laertius 3.56. Written first half 3rd c. The ascription of the third actor to Sophocles is found also in the *Suda*, s.v. *Sophocles,* and in 3A and 9.

Just as in ancient times in tragedy the chorus first performed the drama alone and later, in order to give the chorus a break, Thespis instituted a single actor, Aeschylus a second, and Sophocles filled up the complement of tragedy with a third, so too the subject of philosophy was formerly simply physics, later Socrates added ethics, and Plato added dialectic as a third and brought philosophy to its ultimate state of perfection.

9. *Life of Aeschylus* 15. Dicaearchus was a student of Aristotle, active from ca. 326 to 206 B.C.

As his actor, <Aeschylus> used first Kleandros, then he also added the second actor to him, Mynniskos of Chalkis. He himself introduced the third actor, but according to Dicaearchus of Messana, it was Sophocles.

10A. Sophocles' Actors. Scholion to Aristophanes, *Clouds* 1267.

Others say that Tlepolemos was the tragic actor who continually acted for Sophocles.

10B. Scholion to Aristophanes, *Frogs* 785. Callistratus and Apollonius (of Rhodes) were Alexandrian scholars of the 2nd and 3rd c. B.C.

(Commenting on Kleidemides, mentioned in the text,) Callistratus says that this is perhaps Sophocles' son, but Apollonius that he is Sophocles' actor.

10C. Istros in the *Life of Sophocles* 6. Istros was active in the mid-3rd c. B.C.

Moreover Istros says that <Sophocles> invented the white boots that actors and the members of the chorus wear. And he wrote his dramas with their (i.e., the actors') characters in mind.

Actors' Competitions

11. *IG* II² 2318. *Fasti*, fr. b2. This entry is for the Dionysia 447 B.C. The date is determined by the fragment's relative position on the monument. This is the earliest entry for a victorious actor in the inscribed lists. The entry for 458 B.C. is complete and makes no mention of actors. A line count between the fragments shows that the extra entry for the tragic actors' competition could only have been made twice before the present entry. Hence the contest must have been begun in 449 B.C.

...]n of Lamptres was *choregos*
Sophocles was *didaskalos*
the actor Her]akleides ...

12. *IG* II² 2325. Victor Lists, fr. p, listing victorious tragic actors at the Dionysia in order of their first victory and adding the total number of victories after the name (see I 102). Since the list begins with Herakleides, we must infer that Herakleides won the prize in both 449 and 447 B.C. (see 11).

Of Tragic Actors

Heraklei[des
Nikomacho[s
Mynniskos
Saondas [I]
Andron II
Ch]ai[r]estratos I
Menek]rates III
Lep]tin[es
Kleandro]s I

13. *IG* II² 2325. Victor List of tragic actors at the Lenaea, fr. r. The date of the beginning of the Lenaean tragic actors' contest depends upon comparison with the *Didaskaliai* and Dionysian Victor List. On the one hand, the *Didaskaliai* show that Kallippides won a Lenaean victory in 418 B.C. (III 74), and if Kallippides' name is correctly restored in the sixth entry on this list, then it can begin no later than 423 B.C., and possibly well before, since there is no reason to suppose that the victory in 418 B.C. was the first of Kallippides' Lenaean victories. On the other hand, the Dionysian Victor List (12) shows Chairestratos, Menekrates, and Leptines in sixth to eighth place, while in this list they appear in first to third. Chairestratos can have won his Dionysian victory no earlier than 443 B.C., but this is almost certainly too early since the Lenaean Victor List for comic poets is to be dated ca. 440 B.C. (III 68). If we assume that these actors won their first victories in both contests about the same time, then we are left with an outside range of ca. 440–423 B.C., with a highly probable midpoint date of ca. 432 B.C.

Of Tragic Actors

Chaires[t]ratos I
[Me]n[ekr]ates I
Leptin]es III
[—]

Mynnisk?]os II
Kallippi]des Π (i.e., five victories)
Nikostra]tos III

14. *IG* II² 2323a. The inscription contains *Didaskaliai* referring to the Dionysia of 312/1 B.C. The *Fasti* contain no reference to a competition for comic actors, indicating that no such contest existed down to 329 B.C. The competition for comic actors at the Dionysia is thus datable to 328–312 B.C. Note that Asklepiodoros acts in two comedies in 311 B.C.

actor Asklepiod]oro[s
Menander] fifth with *Charioteer*
actor Kal]lippos the elder
actor Kalli]ppos the younger won
In the archonship of Polem]on (312/1 B.C.) with old <comedy>
... with *T]reasure* of Anaxandrides
poet Philip]pides with *Initiate*
actor Ask]lepiodoros
Nicost]ratus second
with ...]*seer*
actor K]allippos the younger
Ameini]as third with *Woman who Ran Away*
this poet was allotted a chorus though still an ephebe
actor Ask]lepiodoros
Theophilo]s? fourth with *Pankratiasts*
actor ... ip]pos
Menander fifth with *C]hild*
[actor—]
actor Asklepiodoro]s won

15. Hesychius, *Suda,* and Photius, *Lex.,* s.v. *nemeseis hypokriton* ("assignment of actors"). Written 5th and 9th c.

The poets used to get three actors (*hypokritai,* i.e., protagonists) assigned by lot to act the dramas. Of these the winner was entered in the competition of the following year, bypassing the preliminary selection.

16. *IG* II² 2320. Fragment of the *Didaskaliai* listing contestants in the Great Dionysia of 341–339 B.C. The list gives only three letter abbreviations for poe(t), act(or), act(ed), sec(ond), thi(rd). We preserve the exact word and line order.

With ol]d <tragedy> Ne[optolemos
the *Iphige]nia* of Eur[ip]ide[s
poet] Astydamas
with *Achi]lles* acted Thettalos
with *Athamas* acted Neoptolemos
with *An]tigone* acted Athenodo[ros
Eu]aretos s[econd] with *Teucer*
ac]ted Athenodoros
with *Achi]lles* a[cted] Thettalos
with . . . ac[ted N]eoptolemos
Aphareus] third with *Peliades*
acted Neopt]olemos
with *Orestes* [acted Athenodoros
with *Auge* acted Thetta[los
actor Neoptolemos wo[n
In the archonship of Nikomachos (340) with satyrplay
Timokles with *Lycurgus*
with old <tragedy> Neoptolem[os
with the *Orestes* of Euripides
poet Astydamas
with *Parthenopaeus* acted Thet[talos
with *Lyca]on* acted Neoptole[mos
Timokles second with *Phrixus*
acted Thettalos
with *Oed]ipus* acted Neoptolemos
Euar]etos third
with *Alc]me[on]* acted Thetta[los
with . . .] acted Neopto[lemos
actor Th]ettalos won
In the archonship of Theo]phrastos (339) with sa[tyrplay
. . .] with *Daughters of Phorcys*
with old <tragedy> Nik]ostr[atos
. . . of Eu]ripi[des

Structure and Financing of Acting Troupe

17. Strattis, *Anthroporestes, PCG* F 1. Strattis was active from ca. 419 to 375 B.C. Euripides' "cleverest drama" is the *Orestes* produced in 408 B.C. Unfortunately this fragment is cited without context, so that we can only assume that the person criticized for hiring Hegelochos is the archon (cf. 15). "Artichoke," *kinnarou,* is a conjecture for the manuscript's *kyntarou* or *kinyarou:* artichokes were thought to be injurious to the voice.

> I don't care about the other songs, but he murdered Euripides' cleverest drama by hiring Hegelochos, son of Artichoke, to play the first part.

18. Demosthenes, *On the Crown* 262. See 165.

19. Demosthenes, *On the False Embassy* 199f. Delivered 343 B.C.

> Do these men not know that from the beginning you read the <sacred> books while your (i.e., Aeschines') mother performed initiation rites, and while still a child you wallowed about at revels among drunken men? And that afterward you served as an undersecretary for the civil service and could be bribed for two or three drachmas? That at last till recently you were nicely fed at the cost of other people's *choregiai,* provided you served as tritagonist.

20. Demosthenes, *On the False Embassy* 247. Delivered 343 B.C.

> Theodoros frequently acted the *Antigone* of Sophocles, as frequently did Aristodemos, in which <Aeschines> neglected those beautifully constructed and, for you <Athenians>, valuable iambs, which he himself frequently recited and knew backwards. For surely you know that in all tragic performances it is reserved as if a prerogative for the tritagonists to appear as tyrants and scepter bearers. Now consider what sort of things this Aeschines-Creon was made to say in this drama, and which he never said to himself for the benefit of the embassy.

21. Plutarch, *Precepts for Governing the State* 816f. Written ca. 115.

> It is absurd that the protagonist in tragedy, though a Theodoros or Polos, should frequently follow in the train of a hireling who speaks the third part (i.e., tritagonist) and that they should address him humbly, because he wears a diadem or holds a scepter.

22. Plutarch, *Lysander* 23.4. The passage draws a simile between tragic actors and the Spartan king Agesilaus in Asia with his more brilliant adviser, Lysander.

> Just as naturally happens with actors in tragedies where he who wears the mask of a messenger or servant gains glory and takes the lead (lit., "is the protagonist"), while he who bears the crown and scepter is not listened to when he speaks.

23. Istros in the *Life of Sophocles* 6. Istros was active in the mid-3rd c. B.C. The phrase "from the educated" may refer to the cultural élite or possibly to trained theater personnel.

From the educated (*ek ton pepaideumenon*), <Sophocles> composed a religious organization (*thiasos*) in honor of the Muses.

24. Phalaikos?, *Greek Anthology* 13.6. The poem purports to be an epitaph for the comic actor Lykon (see 31C–D) on a monument that appears to have been set up by some local *thiasos* or actors' club (probably not the *technitai*), as the poem suggests. Such honors were frequently paid to deceased members by professional associations in antiquity. Lykon probably died in the late 4th c. B.C.

> I, this splendid image of the comedian, ringed with ivy and garlands for the festal hymn to Dionysus, was set up so that a marker might stand over Lykon. How excedingly brilliant the man was! This is a memorial to the man who was charming at club gatherings and drinking parties and is laid down for future generations as a likeness of his traits.

25. Plato, *Republic* 395a. Written ca. 370 B.C. with a dramatic date of ca. 410 B.C. In Plato's *Symposium* 223d, Socrates argues against Aristophanes and Agathon that a tragedian could write comedy and vice versa. We do not in fact find actors who distinguish themselves in both comedy and tragedy until the end of the Hellenistic period.

> (Socrates speaks) " . . . the same people cannot even represent with equal success those forms of representation that are considered related, for example, those who write tragedy and comedy. Or did you not just say that both of these were representational artists?" "I did, and you are right that the same people are unable to do both." "Nor are the same people simultaneously reciters of epic and actors." "True." "Nor are the same people both actors in tragedy and in comedy, although both of these are representations."

The Rise of the Acting Profession

26. Plato, *Laws* 817a–d. See III 2.

27. Aristotle, *Rhetoric* 1403b31–35. Written ca. 330 B.C.

> Those who use their voices well carry off almost all the prizes from the contests. Just as in the theater the actors are now more important than the poets, so it is in the political contests, because of the degeneracy of the citizens.

28. Plutarch, *Famous Sayings of the Spartans* 212f. Written ca. 115 and referring to sometime before ca. 390 B.C. The Spartans were renown for their "laconic" but concise wit, and their king Agesilaus (444–360 B.C.) for the verbal rapier-thrusts with which he deflated the proud and pretentious. The local mummery to which Agesilaus refers may only have been performed by helots. The anecdote is of particular interest since it assumes that by the earliest years of the 4th c. B.C., a tragic actor might acquire international fame (cf. I 30). The same story is told in Plutarch's *Agesilaus* 21.

> He seemed not to notice the things that others marveled at. Once Kallippides the tragic actor, renowned and famous all over Greece and cultivated by all, encountered <Agesilaus> and greeted him for the first time. He then thrust himself in his train and kept making himself conspicuous, hoping that <Agesilaus> would initiate some friendly conversation with him. Finally he asked, "Your majesty, do you not recognize me, have you not heard who I am?" Agesilaus turned to look at him and said, "Aren't you Kallippides the mummer (*deikeliktas*)?" This is what Spartans call mimes.

29. Demosthenes, *On the False Embassy* 192f. Delivered 343 B.C., referring to 348 B.C. The use of the word *technitai* for performers is interesting but need not imply the existence of the actors' union (IVAii). Satyros was a very famous comic actor and won at least six victories beginning at the Lenaea, ca. 375 B.C.

> When Philip took Olynthus he held an "Olympic" festival. He invited all the performing artists (*technitai*) to the sacrifice and festivities. While feasting them and crowning the victors he asked Satyros, the comic actor, why he alone had no request to make of him. Was it because he perceived some stinginess or ingraciousness in him? They say Satyros replied that he had no need of what the others requested, but, though Philip could easily grant all that he would like to request, he was afraid he would not obtain it. When Philip asked him to speak and blustered something to the effect that there was nothing he wouldn't do, they say he explained that Apollophanes of Pydna was a friend of his and, when he was murdered, his relatives in fear sent his daughters, who were children at the time, away to Olynthus. "These girls were made captive when the city was taken and are your prisoners . . . I wish to give them a dowry and find husbands for them and will not permit them to suffer anything unworthy of myself or their father." When the guests at the party heard this, they gave such loud applause that Philip was somewhat moved and gave the girls to him.

30A. Aristodemos, Neoptolemos, and Philip. Second Hypothesis to Demosthenes, *On the False Embassy*. The hypothesis recounts the events leading up to the peace negotiations between Athens and Philip of

Macedon that led to the Peace of Philocrates in 347/6 B.C. For Neoptolemos, see also 16, and for Aristodemos, 20. The events referred to here took place before the fall of Olynthus in 348 B.C.

> When the Athenians and Philip had fought against one another for a long time, both sides eventually wanted to make peace, but thought it a disgrace to be first to make the proposal. Aristodemos and Neoptolemos were tragic actors. Because of their profession these men had safe-conduct to go wherever they wished, even into enemy territory. Now these men had come to Macedonia and displayed their art, and Philip received them so warmly that he added gifts from his own possession to their other remuneration. As he was aware that the Phoceans, Thessalians, and Thebans were about to send embassies to him, he wanted to deceive the Athenians. Seizing this opportunity, when Philip saw off Aristodemos and Neoptolemos he told them he was a friend of the Athenians.

30B. Demosthenes, *On the Crown* 21. Delivered 330 B.C.

> The first to mention peace was Aristodemos the actor.

30C. Demosthenes, *On the False Embassy* 315. Delivered 343 B.C.

> Now I wish to go over in summary the manner in which Philip conquered you by diplomacy by attaching these scoundrels to himself. It is well worthwhile to lay out and examine the entire deceit. From the very start he wanted peace because his country was being torn apart by pirates and commerce completely blocked so as to deprive him of all benefit from his resources. So he sent you those magnanimous spokesmen of his, Neoptolemos, Aristodemos, and Ktesiphon. Then we went as ambassadors to him, and he immediately bribed this fellow (Aeschines) to use his words and energy in support of the despicable Philocrates and to overpower those of us who wished to do what was right.

30D. Hypothesis to Aeschines, *On the False Embassy*.

> The Athenians fought a war with Philip, later they were persuaded by Aristodemos and Neoptolemos and Ktesiphon to make peace with him, and they sent two embassies, one to negotiate peace, the second to take oaths.

30E. Demosthenes, *On the Peace* 6. Delivered 345 B.C.

> Then again, Athenians, because I perceived that Neoptolemos the actor enjoyed the privilege of safe-conduct under guise of his profession, but was actually doing the greatest harm to the city and managing and governing your affairs for Philip, I came forward and addressed you, not on account of any personal enmity or malice,

as is evident from my subsequent deeds. And I will not this time accuse those who spoke on behalf of Neoptolemos, for there was no one, but I will accuse you yourselves. For if you were watching tragic players in the sanctuary of Dionysus, and it were not a question of <the city's> safety and national interests, you would not have listened to him with such favor nor to me with such aversion.

30F. Aeschines, *On the False Embassy* 15–19. Delivered 343 B.C.

About the same time, he took Olynthus and many of our citizens were taken prisoner inside the city, among them Iatrokles the brother of Ergochares and Eueratos the son of Strombichos. When their relatives proposed to supplicate on their behalf, they asked you to create a commission; Philocrates and Demosthenes came forward and spoke on their behalf, but not Aeschines. And they sent Aristodemos the actor as an ambassador to Philip because Philip knew him and was well disposed to him because of his artistry. When he returned from his embassy Aristodemos, due to some engagements, did not come to the Council before Iatrokles, released without ransom, returned from Macedonia. At that point many grew vexed that Aristodemos had not given a report of his embassy though they were hearing the same account of Philip from Iatrokles. In the end Demokrates of Aphidna came before the Council and persuaded it to summon Aristodemos. Demosthenes, my accuser, was one of the councillors. When Aristodemos appeared he reported that Philip had shown a great deal of good will toward the city and added that he even wished to become the city's ally. He said this not only in the Council but in the Assembly. And there Demosthenes said nothing against him; on the contrary he proposed a decree to crown Aristodemos. After this had been said, Philocrates proposed a motion to choose ten men as ambassadors to Philip to discuss peace with Philip and matters of common interest to Athens and Philip. During the election of the ten ambassadors, Nausikles put me forward as a candidate and Philocrates himself put forward Demosthenes, the very man who is now Philocrates' accuser. He was so keen on the matter that he proposed in Council that Aristodemos also be made an ambassador and relieved of any penalties <he might incur by his participation>, and that ambassadors be chosen to send to the cities in which Aristodemos was to perform in order to request that he be exempted from his fines. In confirmation of what I say, take these decrees and read the deposition of Aristodemos and call up those to whom he made the deposition so that the jurors may know who Philocrates' supporter is and who it is who claimed he would persuade the people to give gifts to Aristodemos.

30G. Scholion to Aeschines, *On the False Embassy* 19.

He means to say that Aristodemos had received deposits from some cities to secure his participation in their competitions. This is because he was a tragic actor and he was obliged either to compete or to pay up double the deposit. The ambassadors were needed to persuade the cities not to take twice the deposit but only the amount of the deposit itself.

30H. Diodorus 16.92. Written ca. 60–30 B.C. Diodorus records an ominous event that took place at the wedding of the daughter of Philip of Macedon, the evening before his assassination.

At the king's drinking party Neoptolemos the tragic actor, outstanding in his profession for the power of his voice and for his popularity, was ordered by Philip to present some of his most successful lines, and particularly something that would have reference to his <planned> expedition against Persia.... (Neoptolemos goes on to sing an unidentified tragic ode.)

30I. Suetonius, *Caligula* 57.4. Written ca. 120. Suetonius lists several "omens" portending Caligula's death. Josephus, *Jewish Antiquities* 19.94, says that Caligula was murdered when he was entering the theater to see a play called *Cinyras*. Cf. V 35.

Mnestor the pantomime danced the tragedy that Neoptolemos the tragic actor once performed at the contest at which King Philip of Macedon was killed (336 B.C.).

30J. John of Stobi, *Florilegium* 34.70. Probably written early 5th c.

Someone asked the tragic actor Neoptolemos what he found most striking in the words of Aeschylus, Sophocles, or Euripides. He said none of these, but something he himself had seen take place on a greater stage, when Philip, who had taken part in the procession at the wedding of his daughter Kleopatra and had been acclaimed the thirteenth god, and was murdered on the next day in the theater and laid out prostrate.

31A. Alexander-toadies. Plutarch, *Alexander* 8.2–3. Written ca. 115 and referring to events in 330–325 B.C.

<Alexander> was by nature fond of literature and reading.... Since no other books were available in central Asia, he ordered Harpalus to send some. Harpalus sent him the books of Philistus, several of

the tragedies of Euripides, Sophocles, and Aeschylus, and the dithyrambs of Telestes and Philoxenus.

31B. Plutarch, *Alexander* 10. Written ca. 115, referring to an event in ca. 337/6 B.C. Thettalos was one of the leading tragic actors of the age (cf. 16). The Aristokritos who served as Philip's envoy may also be the tragic actor of that name.

> When Pixodaros the satrap of Caria, in an attempt to maneuver a military alliance with Philip, proposed to give his eldest daughter in marriage to Philip's son Arrhidaeus and sent Aristokritos to Macedonia for the purpose, once more Alexander's friends and mother approached him with malicious gossip to the effect that Philip was preparing Arrhidaeus for the kingship with a brilliant marriage and powerful connections. Distraught by this, Alexander sent Thettalos the tragic actor to Caria to persuade Pixodaros that he should ignore the bastard and half-wit <Arrhidaeus> and make his connection with Alexander. Pixodaros greatly preferred this option. When Philip found out...he scolded Alexander harshly...and he wrote to the Corinthians to send Thettalos to him in chains.

31C. Plutarch, *Alexander* 29. Written ca. 115, referring to 331 B.C. The same story appears in Plutarch's *On Alexander's Luck* 334e.

> When he returned to Phoenicia from Egypt, Alexander held processions and sacrifices to the gods and arranged dithyrambic and tragic competitions that were famous not only for their lavish preparations but also for the high quality of the competition. The kings of Cyprus acted as *choregoi,* just as at Athens men chosen by lot acted as *choregoi* for their tribes, and they competed with amazing zeal. Nikokreon of Salamis and Pasikrates of Soli were especially competitive because they were allotted the most famous actors, Pasikrates getting Athenodoros, and Nikokreon Thettalos, of whom Alexander himself was a great fan. <Alexander> did not show his partisanship until Athenodoros was announced victor by the vote. Apparently he then approved the vote of the judges but said he would gladly have given up part of his kingdom sooner than see Thettalos beaten. And yet when Athenodoros was fined by the Athenians because he did not keep an appointment to appear at the Dionysia, he requested that the king <Alexander> write on his behalf, but instead of doing this <Alexander> paid the fine on his behalf. When Lykon of

Scarpheia was putting on a successful performance in the theater and inserted a line in the comedy with a request for ten talents, <Alexander> laughed and gave it to him.

31D. Chares, *Histories of Alexander,* book 10 (*FGrH* 125 F 4). Chares was Alexander's chamberlain and an eyewitness of the events here described. The weddings took place at Susa. Date: summer, 324 B.C.

When he overcame Darius he had a wedding for himself and for ninety of his friends besides ... The wedding lasted for five days and very many foreigners as well as Greeks entertained; especially noteworthy were the Indian conjurors and also Skymnos of Tarentum, Philistides of Syracuse, and Herakleitos of Mitylene. Afterward the rhapsode Alexis of Tarentum performed. There appeared also the kithara players Kratinos of Methymna, Aristonymos of Athens, Athenodoros of Teios. Herakleitos of Tarentum and Aristokrates of Thebes sang to the kithara. There appeared also singers to the accompaniment of pipes, Dionysios of Heraclea and Hyperbolos of Cyzicus. There appeared also pipers who first played the Pythian and afterward played for choruses; they were Timotheos, Phrynichos, Kaphisias, Diophantos, and Euios of Chalcis. And from that day those who previously were called Dionysus-toadies were called Alexander-toadies because of the extravagant gifts in which Alexander delighted. The tragedians Thettalos, Athenodoros, and Aristokritos and the comedians Lykon, Phormion, and Ariston performed. Phasimelos the harper was also present.

31E. Plutarch, *Alexander* 72.1. Written ca. 115, referring to late 324 B.C.

When <Alexander> came to Ecbatana in Media and dealt with urgent business, he once more occupied himself with theaters and festivals, as three thousand scenic artists (*technitai*) had arrived from Greece.

32. *FD* III 5.3.67. Date: 362 B.C. List of donations for the rebuilding of the Temple of Apollo at Delphi. No other private contribution on the list exceeds fifteen drachmas. Theodoros was the most famous tragic actor of the early 4th c. B.C. (20, 21; I 8A; III 92).

Theodoros the Athenian actor <contributed> seventy drachmas.

33. Pseudo-Plutarch, *Ten Orators* 848b. The anecdote is set before 322 B.C. The same story is told about Aristodemos by Gellius 11.9. Gellius identifies his source as Critolaus, who wrote in the first half of the 2nd c. B.C.

> Polos the actor once mentioned to <Demosthenes> that he earned a talent for two days' competition. He replied, "I have earned five talents in a single day for keeping quiet."

IVAii. The Artists of Dionysus

We have a great deal of information from inscriptions about the guilds of dramatic artists; here we can only translate a fraction of this complex and often fragmentary material that covers at least six centuries. The Artists of Dionysus first appear as an identifiable group of performers, not yet organized, about 330 B.C. (34); the Greek name is *technitai*, i.e., those practicing a skill or trade (*techne*), sometimes with the addition "of" or "in regard to Dionysus," and this becomes their official title certainly from the 2nd c. B.C.; the Latin term is *artifices*, i.e., those practicing a craft (*ars*). They call themselves a "commonweal" or "guild" (*synodos*) in the 3rd c. B.C. Even though the actual process of the formation of the guild is unknown, it is safe to say that it is connected with the organization of festivals, not only at Athens, and not solely with drama, but with the entire range of competitions for the stage, of which drama was usually the most complex part; in ancient terms the artists dealt with both "scenic," i.e., dramatic, and "thymelic," i.e., musical, contests. From the beginning the guild included musicians, costumers, and even mask makers (43B) as well as choral dancers and solo dancers—in short all the staff required to put on a festival. International travel was dangerous, and the safety of an actor would be better guaranteed by an association that could exert sufficient power to obtain for all (38) the rights only a few privileged individuals could normally extort (37). If a single impetus is to be sought for the birth of the guild, it would be the massive international sponsorship of the performers by the Macedonian kings who came to rule Greece and the Hellenistic rulers who followed them (30, 31). Some of the *technitai* achieved high political position by their oratorical abilities. These would be natural leaders for a guild, and we do in fact find that the Athenian ambassadors who negotiated the first known privileges with the authorities in Delphi for the Pythian games were two of the best-known tragedians of the day (39). Numerous inscriptions reveal the extraordinary variety of the guild members, though the terminology is not always clear to us (44). The actual dramatic personnel could be in a minority; but the guild members could assume various roles (44). Mimes appear to be excluded, and pantomimes and mimes were admitted perhaps only in the 2nd c. The appearance of a Guild of Fellow Competitors in addition to the regular Commonweal of Artists in Pergamum (*CIG* 1016), however, is an indication that not everyone in any festival belonged to the guild, but that the guild felt itself able to speak on their behalf (47B).

Throughout the guild's long history, we find it constantly reaffirming its privileges (46, 47), which implies that others sought to remove and limit them. The honors—called *philanthropa*—that actors regularly demanded were freedom of travel, freedom from taxation, and freedom from arrest, should the local authorities seek security for the debt of a fellow countryman of the actor (39). It was therefore to be expected that the guild would demand such privileges for all its members before they would perform. It is notable that they claim to be a religious body (39, 41) in the service of the gods, though there is a scarcely concealed threat that the services of the gods will not take place without freedom from taxation (44). This claim for exemption on religious grounds in turn explains why artists are recorded as having "donated" a performance for the god, for which the grateful community votes to thank them with a crown of a certain value. On the positive side, the guild also demanded the right to wear its insignia, specifically crowns, purple robes, and gold, which were of course the insignia of the god, his worshipers, and priests; we should remember that the guild was a highly distinct group in society, a fact that no doubt contributed to their reputation for arrogance (35).

In imperial times great artists are honored not only as citizens but as councillors of many cities. The Hellenistic kings appear frequently as champions of the guild and its privileges; clearly the services of the artists could be of great value to them. In Egypt we find that the name of the local guild has included the kings in its title (43), a testimony to the royal patronage, but also a recognition that the artists were devoted as much to the kings as to Dionysus. This attachment to the authorities led in time to the close ties with the Roman emperors.

But the guild, from its inception, could and did behave like a state, appointing not only administrative (*prytaneis*) and financial officers (*oikonomoi*) but even ambassadors—thus emphasising its supra- and international status—and official delegates (*theoroi*) to the major festivals (40). The artists therefore enjoyed a unique and indeed anomalous constitutional and legal status. On the other hand, it was still formally a religious organization, with priests acting as executives, dedicated to the worship of Dionysus. The guild celebrated Dionysia as their main feast day, with the usual procession, feasting, drinking, and sacrifice. The guild itself had its own laws and protocols (*diagraphai*); officers were appointed usually annually by the *technitai*, though the actual executive positions varied greatly with place and time. In the world organization, the chief officers were the archon, secretary, and legal expert, and a chief priest, who was priest of Dionysus and of the emperors at the same time.

The years of civil war that marked the end of the Roman republic led to a general decline in the power of the Greek *technitai,* though its members knew how to maintain influence (46, 47A). The first certain indication of a world organization is in a letter of the emperor Claudius (47B) addressed to the "World Artists of Dionysus, Sacred Victors in Crowned Contests and their Fellow Competitors"; it confirms the privileges awarded them by Augustus. The model for the close connection of rulers and *technitai* was given by Egypt and Pergamum, while Mark Antony, who was a sponsor of the *technitai* and who called himself "the new Dionysus," had assembled all the *technitai* he could for his wedding with Cleopatra in 32 B.C. At any rate the various guilds were organized into one world association with their seat eventually in Rome at least by the time of Hadrian (117–38), even though they and others might continue to exist as local associations. The high point of the guild and the related dramatic associations (V 7) is in the 2nd c., when the empire was filled with festivals, many officially named for the emperors. The emperor Hadrian, the greatest patron of Greek culture, is now, like Antony earlier, called "the new Dionysus" by the association, thereby achieving a coincidence of ruler and god; other emperors were also given this title. Soon after, in 142, the guild honors the imperial chamberlain, Aelius Alcibiades, from Nysa in Asia Minor, for his munificence toward them and their headquarters in Rome. The world guild is still found in Christian times, especially in Egypt and Asia Minor. In the 3rd c. it seems to have combined with the athletic world guild to assert its privileges in festivals.

It is worth noting the importance and popularity of Greek actors, or at least actors of Greek origin, in a Latin speaking area; Latin actors must have required their own organizations. The most important among the other guilds were the Parasites (of Apollo), who were primarily an association of pantomimes and mimes (V 6, 7). They existed from the 2nd c. B.C. but are attested mainly for the empire, by which time they are organized in close association with the world guild of the *technitai* without being part of it. There are other shadowy organizations, such as the Society of Greek Singers, the Corporation of Tragedians and Comedians, attested for the year 169, and various colleges (*collegia*) of pipers, harp players, Roman pipers, musicians, and mime artists. But an important group were the artists—slaves and freedmen—of the imperial household, whose job it was to give public performances as well as to entertain at state dinners and similar functions of the imperial family (IVBiii). These performers became numerous enough to develop into a separate part of the imperial administration by the 2nd c., called the *summum choragium*, which had its own support staff and wardrobe (III 205, 206). Since it was located not far from the Colosseum, it must have been primarily reponsible for the spectacles there, including the gladiatorial events. We may take this as a sign of the increasing control of all performers, including dramatic, by the imperial authorities. During the 3rd c. all evidence for the guilds disappears. The last title recorded (274/5) is also the longest (under the emperor Aurelian), "The Sacred Musical Traveling Aurelian World Great Guild of the Artisans of Dionysus, Sacred Crowned Victors, and their Fellow Competitors."

Sources

34. Aristotle, *Rhetoric* 1405a23. Written ca. 330 B.C. Possibly the first mention of the *technitai*. Cf. 31.

> Some call them "Dionysus-toadies," but they call themselves "artists" (*technitai*); both are metaphorical, the first sneering, the second the opposite.

35. Philostratus, *Lives of the Sophists* 2.16. Written sometime between 217–238 and referring to the end of the 2nd c.

> <Euodianos> was appointed also to supervise the Artists of Dionysus, a very arrogant class of men and hard to keep in order.

36. [Aristotle], *Problems* 956b11. Possibly written ca. 300 B.C.

> Why are the Artists of Dionysus generally bad characters? Is it because they participate least in reason and wisdom, since most of their life is spent in arts that they practice for a living, and because much of their life is spent in incontinence and sometimes in dire straits? Both these conditions are productive of meanness.

37. *SEG* 1.362; M. Schede, *AM* 1919, 16–20. This inscription is a decree of ca. 306 B.C. of the island of Samos, under political pressure to celebrate the kings appropriately. It honors one of the greatest actors of antiquity, Polos of Aegina (see 33, 62). It is obvious that the citizens can scarcely afford the fees that he commands, and it is to be supposed that this inscription represents a contract proposed by the great actor, or his agent. These are the rights to which actors aspired.

> For Polos, son of Sosigenes, of Aegina. It was decided by the people, and Demaretos, son of Demeas, moved: whereas Polos, son of Sosigenes, of Aegina, showed himself in times past devoted and

zealous in the city's interests and whereas now the people have voted for us to celebrate festivals for Antigonos and Demetrios at the good news (i.e., at the news of the victory of these kings) and whereas ambassadors have presented themselves before him and whereas he has agreed to act for lower fees for the people and has received the <income> from the theater and for the rest (of his fees) has granted a delay to the city as the people requested of him—it is agreed by the Council and the people: to have Polos praised for his excellence and zeal, which he has demonstrated for the people, and that he be accorded the same solicitude by the people; that he be granted the rights of citizenship on an equal and similar basis, and that he be alloted a tribe, a thousand, a hundred, and a clan, and registered like all other Samians; that he be a guest-friend of the people; that he have in war and peace right to sail in and out, free of reprisal and without any treaty; that if he needs anything he have access to Council and people first after the sacred or royal business; that he be given a front seat in all the contests that the city celebrates; that all these privileges be valid for himself and his descendants; that Polos be crowned with a crown of foliage at the tragic contests of the Dionysia; that the *agonothetes* along with the *demiourgos* take care of the proclamation; that this decree be inscribed on a stone slab and set up in the temple of Hera, and the Council's secretary take care for the allotment and writing up. He was allotted the tribe Cheseis, the thousand Oinopes, the hundred, and clan Helandridai.

38. *SIG*³ 460; *Festivals*² 282. Delphic Inscription. Date: soon before 279 B.C. Certain privileges are granted to the Isthmian guild by the Delphians. This inscription is the first mention of a guild. The privileges granted are those normally accorded to visiting dignitaries.

> Lord <Apollo>: The Delphians have granted to the Commonweal of the Artists Who Travel Together to the Isthmus and Nemea: right to prior consultation of the oracle, right to front seats and prior judgment. When Ainesilas was archon, and Deinon, Amunandros, Ornichidas were councillors.

39. *IG* I I² 1132 + *FD* 3.2.68; *SIG*³ 399; *Festivals*² 308, no. 2. Delphic decree, with copies found both in Athens and in Delphi. Date: ca. 278 B.C. The authorities in charge of the sanctuary and games at Delphi, the Amphictyons, confirm the privileges of the Athenian artists. This is the second certain attestation of the existence of a guild, whose representatives

to the Amphictyons are two of the best-known tragedians of the time (cf. 16, 30).

It was decided by the Amphictyons and the *hieromnemones* and the *agoratroi:* In order that for all time the *technitai* in Athens may have freedom from seizure (*asylia*) and from taxation, and that no one may be apprehended from anywhere in war or in peace or their goods <seized>, but that they may have freedom from taxation and have immunity accorded to them securely by all of Greece, the *technitai* are to be free of taxes for military service on land or sea and all special levies, so that the honors and sacrifices for which the *technitai* are appointed may be performed for the gods at the appropriate times, seeing that they are apolitical (*apolypragmoneton*) and consecrated to the <services> of the gods: let it be permitted to no one to make off with the *technitai* either in war or in peace or to take reprisals against them, provided that they have contracted no debt with the city as debtors, or are under no obligation for a private contract. If anyone acts contrary to this, let him be liable before the Amphictyons, both he himself and the city in which the offense was committed against the *technitai*. The freedom from taxation and the security that has been granted by the Amphictyons is to belong for all time to the *technitai* at Athens, who are apolitical. The secretaries are to inscribe this decree on a stone slab and set it up in Delphi, and to send to the Athenians a sealed copy of this decree, so that the *technitai* may know that the Amphictyons have the greatest respect for their piety toward the gods and are adhering to the requests of the *technitai* and shall try also for the future to safeguard this for all time and in addition to increase any other privilege they have on behalf of the Artists of Dionysus. Ambassadors: Astydamas, poet of tragedies, Neoptolemos, tragic actor.

40. *SIG*[3] 457; Feyel, *Contribution à l'épigraphie béotienne* 89–90; *Festivals*[2] 308. Boeotian inscription. Date: ca. 211 B.C. The Isthmian guild accepts an invitation to perform at the festival of the Muses at Thespiae in Boeotia.

The thymelic contest for crowns first took place while Hierokles was *agonothetes,* and Mnasion was priest of the Muses, and Aischylos represented the *technitai;* and <these are> the decrees concerning the contest of the Mouseia: <Decree of the> *technitai:* it was decreed by the *technitai* from the Isthmus and Nemea: whereas Hierokles appeared as ambassador from the city of the Thespians and the league of the Boeotians and presented resolutions and a letter, in which he invited the *technitai,* since the city of the Thespians has decided that the thymelic contest for the Muses in Helicon be for crowns (instead of as previously for less prestigious money prizes)—the contest of the pipers, the singers to the pipes, the lyre players, the singers to the lyre, and for the poet of epic—and that the year in which the festival is held may be changed (presumably so that the date of the four-yearly festival would agree better with older festivals), and that <the *technitai*> join in an embassy about this wheresover the city of the Thespians invites them, as in previous times, and that the *technitai* are to perform whatever other action is useful and noble [....] and whereas Hierokles made a presentation in accord with what was written in the resolutions, and discoursed on the mutual benefits that had existed from the beginning between the city of the Thespians and the *technitai:* In regard to all the above: Good Fortune: <resolved> that the *technitai* decide to applaud the city of the Thespians and the league of the Boeotians for the zealous regard that they hold toward the sanctuary of the Muses and the Commonweal of the Artists: and to answer them, that, understanding that the festival of the Muses was a common <venture> of the city of Thespiae and themselves, even in the past they displayed all possible zeal both in joint sacrifice and selecting a priest from among themselves, dispatching official delegates, making resolutions, and joining in embassies to proclaim the contest to the other Greeks, as the city of Thespiae invites <them to do>; and to make clear to them that now also they are the first to recognize the contest of the Muses as for crowns [... (the rest of the decrees is missing).

41. *FD* 3.1, no. 351 and p. 402; L. Robert, *OMS* 7.768, 11; *Festivals*[2] 309. Delphic decree. Date: ca. 220 B.C. This badly damaged inscription explains how the Amphictyons meeting at Delphi as the governing body reply to the *technitai* and the city of Thebes about the Theban festival of the Agrionia.

...the Amphictyons decreed: in order that the two-yearly festival for Dionysus and the contests that the city of Thebes celebrates and the Commonweal of the Artists Who Travel Together to the Isthmus and Nemea may be <graced> with the greatest splendor, the *hierom-nemones* who are in session when the biennial festival and the contests are celebrated in the Kadmeion at Thebes are to see to it that each <event> take place on the day on which the city of Thebes and the Commonweal of the Artists wish [it to....] and that there be security and freedom from seizure for all the *technitai* who are detailed for the sacrifice of the biennial festival, during the five days arriving and another five going, and for as long as the festival goes on, both for themselves and their fellow workers in all places. If anyone in defiance of these <instructions> makes off with someone or seizes him as security, let him be liable before the Amphictyons. The sanctuary of Dionysus the Kadmean at Thebes is to be an asylum for all, like the temple at Delphi. The sacrifice and the armistice are to be announced to the cities and the city of Thebes and the *technitai*. The final authorities are to be those administering the affairs of the sanctuary along with the priest of Dionysus, the managers (*epimeletai*) appointed by the *technitai,* and the *agonothetes* of the Thebans. The secretary is to write this resolution on two slabs and to set up one at Delphi in the sanctuary of Apollo, wherever seems to be the best location, and one in Thebes beside the tomb of Semele, but to set <a copy> up wherever appears to be the best location in the other sanctuaries. (Another decree follows.) In the archonship of Nikarchos at Delphi, at the autumn meeting, the Amphictyons decreed: whereas the city of Thebes and the Artists Who Travel Together to the Isthmus and Nemea have invited the Amphictyons to make the sanctuary of Dionysus an asylum and to take care of their security and the contest: in order that the sacrifice in the biennial festival may be celebrated with the greatest splendor for Dionysus the Kadmean, the Amphictyons decree: if any of the pipers or the choreuts or the tragedians or comedians detailed for the biennial festivals by the *technitai* do not perform at the biennial festival and the contests according to the law of the city of Thebes, but though in good health abandon the contest, neither he nor his fellow workers are to have security in war and peace; if he does not compete, and if he is fined by the *agonothetes,* let him also be liable to seizure anywhere; and if city or [. . .] takes the fine from the person fined[. . .

   42. *BCH* 46 (1922) 312; *SEG* II 580; Robert, *Études anatoliennes* 39ff.; *Festivals*[2] 314. Teian decree. Date: ca. mid-3rd c. B.C. This damaged inscription records that the city of Teos, which was part of the Attalid kingdom of Pergamum, arranged to buy land for the *technitai* of the Ionian guild, on favorable terms, presumably for their headquarters. In the lost beginning, the city has awarded them a crown to thank them for their services. One has the impression that hard bargaining has preceded this decree.

...resolved:] that the priest of Dionysus at the Dionysiac festival and the *prytanis* in the prytanic office and the sacred herald at the assemblies pray for prosperity also for the Commonweal of the Artists of Dionysus (i.e., as well as for the city); to buy for them a parcel of land in the city or territory to the value of six thousand drachmas, and to proclaim as sacred the land bought, which the people has dedicated to the Commonweal of the Artists of Dionysus, as being free of the taxes that the city imposes; to appoint two men, to buy property for referral to the people; in order that the money be available for the purchase, the treasurers in office are to give to the men to be appointed three thousand drachmas from the amount transferred from the fortification account, which was given for the payment of corn; let the incoming treasurers pay out the remaining three thousand drachmas from the first payments to be made to <the *technitai*> from the royal office (at Pergamum) for city administration; a stay of repayment is also to be granted to them for five years beginning in the month Leukatheon and the prytany of Metrodorus. In order that all may be aware of the decrees of the people, this resolution and the <award of the> crown is to be engraved on a stone slab and set up by the temple of Dionysus. Also there is to be engraved on the side wall of the theater entrance this decree and <the award of> the crown. Let the treasurers in office make payment for the inscription of the crowns and decrees and the erecting of the slab; the delegates who have been appointed are to hand over this decree to the Artists of Dionysus and commend them for the goodwill, which they continue to display toward the people of Teos. There were appointed to purchase land [...,] son of Epitimides, Thersion, son of Phanos.

43A. *OGIS* 50; *Festivals*[2] 310. Honorary decree from Egypt. Date: ca. 240 B.C. The local association of the Egyptian *technitai* at Ptolemais, organized like a small city, honor one of their benefactors, Dionysius.

The Artists of Dionysus and the Brother Gods (i.e., the Ptolemies) and those who administer the association decreed: to crown Dionysios son of Mousaios *prytanis* for life with an ivy garland according to the traditional ways because of his goodwill toward the city of the Ptolemaiites and toward the Artists of Dionysus the Great and of the Brother Gods: to proclaim the crown at the Dionysia; this decree to be written up on a slab and placed before the shrine of Dionysus. The financial officer (*oikonomos*) Sosibios is to meet the expense for the slab.

43B. *OGIS* 51; *Festivals*[2] 310f. Date: ca. 240 B.C. The same association honors Lysimachos. Note that the association contains nonperformers as well as a dancer (pantomime?).

> The Artists of Dionysus and the Brother Gods decreed: whereas Lysimachos son of Ptolemaios of the Sostratic deme, hipparch and *prytanis* for life, has shown goodwill toward our king and his parents even before, and more so still in the present time, and also happens to be of a pious and holy disposition toward Dionysus and the other gods, and in all things treats the *technitai* with consideration; and with zeal and energy he undertakes everything for individuals and the community, dedicating himself to the advancement of the association (*techniteuma*); and whereas it is good to honor with the appropriate honors such men who distinguish themselves; the Commonweal of the Artists of Dionysus, whose names are inscribed below, have voted: to honor Lysimachos with a crown of ivy in the traditional fashion on the 11th of the month Peritios at the Dionysia for his achievements and his piety toward the king and his parents and the *technitai*. Good fortune; and to dedicate also his carved likeness in the forehall of the prytaneum; and the secretary of the Commonweal Demarchos is to inscribe this decree on a slab and set it up before the temple of Dionysus; the financial officer Sosibios is to meet the expense for this. (At this point the inscription preserved originally a probably complete list of the association in three columns; noteworthy is the division of the tragic actors into one *tragoidos* and four *synagonistai,* while the six *komoidoi* form one group and appear not to have a piper.)

Zopyros in charge of the rites of the two yearly and annual festival, and his brothers (who are the two first named):

Dionysios	**tragic actor**	**tragic piper**
Taurinos	Metrodoros	Thraikides
tragic poets	**comic actors**	**trumpeter**
Phainippos	Telemachos	Thrasymachos
Diognetos	Agathodoros	**mask maker?** Baton
comic poets	Apollonios	**honorary guests**
Stratagos	Asklepiodorus Apol-	Demetrios
	loniou	

Mousaios	Apollonios	Phaidimos
epic poets	Diodoros	Artemidoros
Demarchos	**tragic synagonists**	Spoudias
Theogenes	Apollonides Ardonos	Dionysios
Artemidoros	Kleitos	***technitai*-supporters**
singer to lyre	Ptolemaios	Demetrios
Menippos	Zopyros	Stephanos
lyre player	**chorus director**	Leon
Herakleitos	[. . .]	Artemidoros
dancer		Demetrios
Ptolemaios		Aristonous
[. . .]		[. . .]

43C. *BGU* 6.1211; *Select Papyri* 2.208; *C.Ord.Ptol.* 29. Papyrus recording a decree of Ptolemy IV. Date: ca. 210 B.C. Ptolemy IV in this much discussed papyrus is exercising direct control over what seem to be mystic priests of Dionysus, by making them register in Alexandria; some of these must be associated with the artists' organizations, as later in Asia. But the cult of Dionysus already is aligned with the cult of the kings, both in Egypt and Asia.

> By decree of the king. Persons who perform the rite of Dionysus in the country shall sail down within ten days from the day on which the decree is published and those beyond Naucratis within twenty days, and shall register themselves before Aristoboulos at the registration office within three days from the day on which they arrive, and shall declare forthwith from what persons they have received the transmission of the sacred rites for three generations back and shall hand in the sacred book sealed up, each inscribing thereon his own name.

44. *SIG*³ 711; cf. Mette, *Urkunden* 72; Sifakis, *Studies* 86ff. Delphic honorary decree. Date: 105 B.C. The *technitai* sent large numbers of their members as part of an embassy to offer sacrifice and perform at Delphi for Pythian Apollo at, theoretically, eight-year intervals. This is the third Pythais, which attracted over 350 *technitai* as pilgrims. Here the Delphians honor the artists, thereby recording many members for posterity; but this was clearly done at the request of the association. The opening rituals were followed by a festival. Note that the tragic subdirector Diokles in fact directs the great chorus of hymns to Apollo and therefore performs the same function as the chorus director we meet elsewhere; he is a subdirector only because the chief actor or the poet was the main director. One of the chorus is also listed as a comedian. From such lists as these we can follow the careers of individuals, e.g., Praxiteles, son of Theogenes, is a comic synagonist here, but in the fourth Pythias of 97 B.C. a protagonist of tragedy; he also won a second victory as an actor of "old" comedy and the prize as herald at the Sarapieia of Tanagra afterward.

The archons of Delphi and the city greet the Artists of Dionysus. We have inscribed for you a copy of the answer given by us, so that you may know. Hail. Whereas the Artists of Dionysus in Athens and their officer (*epimeletes*) Alexandros son of Ariston, comic poet, show reverence toward the divinity, and honor their own people and desire to exalt their own relations with the gods because of the fact that they were the first to be benefactors of every art and founders of scenic contests; and are most mindful of everything that incites to fame, for which they have freedom from arrest and all the other honors affecting their safety and reputation from the Amphictyons and other Greeks and the Romans who rule: and whereas now, according to their ancestral traditions the Athenians have sent the Pythais, considered sacred, at a nine-year interval, according to the oracle of the god for the health and safety of all the citizens and their wives and children and friends and allies, and have made their ancestral sacrifices with great generosity to the god, and have celebrated the procession splendidly and in a manner worthy of the god and their own land and their association and of their own good reputation and excellence, and have performed far more sacrifices and offerings and duties than previously; they have sung their ancestral paean impressively, and at the first offerings of the competition they performed for the god with their unique skill, and honored the Apollo of our fathers with delightful and ever-to-be-remembered delights, by which means they exalted him who is the lord of our reverence to the best of their abilities, and they devoted honors to the god by means of their personal performances, sending as their administrative officer (*epimeletes*) and chief festival ambassador from their own number Alexander, son of Ariston, comic poet; and as festival ambassadors Diokles, son of Aischines, tragic subdirector (*hypodidaskalos*); Glaukias, son of Herakleides, comedian; Aristomenes, son of Aristomenes, tragic poet; Agathokles, son of Socrates, comedian; Ariston, son of Menelaos, tragic poet; Chairestratos, son of Philagros, tragic actor (*synagonistes*); and the director of the great chorus, Diokles, son of

Aischines, tragic subdirector; kithara players:...(five names) and those who are accompanists on the kithara (three names); and the pipers (six names) and those who were to sing the paeans and the chorus (42 names); and they sent also those who were to take part in the thymelic competition and the scenic contest in the days sacred to the god:

    epic poets (three names)
    rhapsodes (three names)
    singer to the pipes (one name)
    Pythian (i.e., solo) kitharist (one name)
    pipers (three names)
    comedians (four names)
    and those who competed along with them (six names)
    poets of satyrs (five names)
    tragedians (two names)
    and those who competed with them (seven names)
    poets of tragedies (two names)

In order that Delphians will remember and show appropriate thanks, be it resolved by the city of Delphi to praise the Commonwealth of the Artists of Dionysus and to award them a crown of gold of the god, with which it is the ancestral custom to crown our private benefactors, and they are to set up two golden statues of the association, one in Delphi in the most visible place of the temple, and one in Athens in the court of Dionysus, to request the Athenian people for the placement, and to write on the base of each of the statues, that the city of Delphi has dedicated <a statue> of the Commonwealth of the Artists in Athens for their excellence and reverence toward the divinity; the archons are to make the proclamation of the crowns in the athletic contest of the Pythia and the Soteria, in accordance with the decree. Likewise they are to give the same honors for their administrative officer and chief festival ambassador Alexander, and to crown also their chorus director Diokles and the ambassadors with the crown of the god (i.e., laurel), and they are to praise both the rest of the *technitai* who have visited us and have performed their sacred duties, for their behavior and zealousness; and there is to be to all the *technitai* in Athens freedom from arrest, right to prior consultation of the oracle, and rights of hospitality, both for them and their descendants, and they are to have the other honors and civil rights (*philanthropa*) from the Delphians as other benefactors have. In order that to all who come after us the zeal and goodwill of such men may be evident, this decree is to be inscribed in the temple of Apollo on [the treasury of the Athenians and its wording sent] to the Council and people of the Athenians, and likewise to the Commonwealth of the Artists in Athens.

45. *Festivals*[2] 316; Robert, *Études anatoliennes* 446ff. Decree of the Hellespontine Artists. Date: 2nd c. B.C. The city of Iasos in Asia Minor in bad economic times, like many others including Delphi, requested the *technitai* to help them with their festivals. The *technitai* duly subsidize the city by providing members free. But the group sent is so small that it was presumably meant only to subsidize the existing though inadequate resources of the Iasians.

> Resolution of the Commonweal of the Artists of Dionysus in Ionia and the Hellespont and those of Dionysus the Leader. Whereas the Iasians are friends and acquaintances and benefactors and maintain [their present goodwill] and friendship from ancient times toward the [*technitai* . . . and the] people <of Teos?>, and continue to uphold the privileges granted to the Commonweal of the Artists of Dionysus by the Greeks according to the [oracles] and by the Romans, our common benefactors and saviors, and have in former times also shown all possible zeal and pride with regard to the [celebration?] of their games [. . .] Good Fortune: it is resolved by the Commonweal of the Artists of Dionysus; in order that [. . . , to detail] for Dionysus and the Iasians <the following> from the registered *technitai* participating in our association for the competitions celebrated with them in honor of Dionysus, in view of our longstanding friendship: 2 pipers, 2 tragedians, 2 comedians, a singer to the lyre, and a lyre player, in order that they may celebrate their choruses for the god in accordance with their ancestral regulations; and to allocate their services [. . .]; and all those detailed are to celebrate the contests of the Dionysia at the defined times, providing everything according to the laws of Iasos. Whosoever of those detailed by the majority (of the *technitai*) does not show up in Iasos or does not celebrate the competitions, let him pay to the Commonweal of the Artists of Dionysus one thousand drachmas of Antiochos as sacred to the god and unavoidable, unless the failure is due to illness or bad weather. Such a person may excuse himself from the fine by making his defense before the assembled *technitai,* by producing clear proof and being acquitted by a vote according to the law. In order that the Iasians recognize the zeal of our gathering and the

devotion we have toward our friends in times of necessity, ambassadors are to be chosen, who on arrival at Iasos will transmit this decree to the executive and on appearing before the Council and the people will explain the honors that have been decreed them; renewing the privileges bestowed on each other by our ancestors, they will invite the Iasians to maintain their familiarity with the Commonweal of the Artists of Dionysus by adding to the friendship in accord with the goodwill that is inherited from our ancestors. There were chosen as ambassadors Ploutiades singer to the lyre, Lysimachos poet of tragedies, Nikostratos tragic synagonist. The following were detailed along with their support staff: pipers Timokles, Phaitas; tragedians (i.e., leaders of troupes) Poseidonios, Sosipatros; comedians Agatharchos, Moirias; singer to the lyre Zenotheos; lyre player Apollonios of Samos. Approved when Apollo was crown bearer for the third time after Menes son of Tyrtaios, on the 6th day of <the month> Apatourion.

   46. M. Segré, *Riv. di Filologia* 66 (1938) 253ff.; *Bull. Ép.* 1939, no. 263; R.K. Sherk, *Historia* 15 (1966) 211–16; *Rome and the Greek East*, no. 62. Inscription recording letters of Sulla. Date: ca. 80 B.C. The Romans had caused immense damage to Greece and the East in the years previous to this decree. The *technitai* however have managed to have their privileges continued as before. The dictator Sulla writes two letters, one to the people of Cos allowing the privileges to be advertised; the second was sent to the association of Ionia and the Hellespont confirming their privileges on the authority of the Senate.

   (To the Coans) Lucius Cornelius Sulla, son of Lucius, <called> the Fortunate, dictator sends greetings to the leaders of the people of Cos. To Alexander of Laodicea, lyre player, a gentleman and friend of ours, ambassador from the Commonweal of the Artists of Dionysus in Ionia and the Hellespont and of Dionysus the Leader, I have permitted that a slab be set up with you in the most conspicuous place, on which the privileges granted by me to the *technitai* will be set up. Since he has now gone as ambassador [to Rome], and the Senate has passed a resolution about this, I wish you to consider how [there can be indicated with you] a most conspicuous place, in which [the slab referring to the *technitai*] will be set up. I have subjoined [?a letter with the resolution of the Senate?...(To the Artists)...] along with the goodwill that you have toward us; I therefore wish you to recognize that I have published a decision based on a Council vote that all the benefits and honors and freedom from civic liabilities that the Senate and consuls and magistrates have given you for the sake of honoring Dionysus, the Muses, and your organization, they have confirmed, in order that you may have these and [just as before] you may be free of all civic duties and military service and that you may pay no [taxes] nor be disturbed by [anyone] for provisioning or [billeting], or that [you be compelled] to take in [lodgers.

47A. British Museum papyrus, ed. Kenyon, *CR* 7 (1893) 476; Sherk, *Rome and the Greek East,* no. 85. Date: 42/1 or 33/2 B.C. A number of copies of formal documents survive on papyrus, which deal with relations between Roman rulers and the Artists and the affirmations of their rights by emperors in the first two centuries A.D. We give two. The first is a much later copy of a letter from Ephesus by Mark Antony in 33 B.C. confirming the rights of the athletic guild, about which we are better informed. It must serve as a parallel for the kind of letter he must have sent also to the actors' guild.

Marcus Antonius, dictator and triumvir for the establishment of the republic, greets the Commonweal of the Greeks from Asia. Earlier Marcus Antonius Artemidorus, my friend and masseur, appeared before me in Ephesus, with Charopinus of Ephesus, eponymous priest of the Crowned Sacred Victors from the Whole World, in regard to the earlier existing rights of the guild remaining inviolable, and in regard to the other honors and privileges that he has asked of me: freedom from military service, freedom from imposition of liturgies, freedom from having soldiers billeted on them, the truce during the festival (probably the great festival of Artemis rather than the private festival of the organization), and their freedom from arrest and their right to wear purple, in order that I might agree to write forthwith to you:—I concede <these>, wishing to show favor to the dignity and the bettering of their guild both on account of my friend Artemidorus and for their eponymous priest. And now again that Artemidorus has come before me, in order to be allowed to set up a bronze plaque, and make an inscription on it with regard to the aforementioned privileges, I, choosing to impede Artemidorus in no way concerning his appearance before me, have authorized the establishment of the plaque, as he requests; I have written <this> to you about the matter.

47B. *BGU* 4.1074; cf. *Milet* III (1914) 156: Millar, *Emperor in the Roman World* 460ff.; Sherk, *Roman Empire,* no. 54. Date: 43. The second document is also a much later copy from Egypt of our first record of the actors' guild after the establishment of the empire. It formed part of a legal dossier of a local secretary of the guild claiming tax exemption in 275. This was doubtless the main reason why we now possess these records.

> Tiberius Claudius Caesar, tribune] for the second time, consul for the third, in the fourth year as emperor (i.e., 43) sends greetings to the Crowned Sacred Victors of Dionysus from the Whole World and their Fellow Competitors. [...] and the legal rights and privileges granted you by the God Augustus I confirm. The ambassadors were (there follow four Greek names, all beginning with Claudius).

48. Philostratus, *Lives of the Sophists* 85.15 Kayser. Written sometime between 217 and 238 and referring to mid-1st c. Inscriptions concerning the artists have been found in this place in Athens.

> <Philagros of Cilicia> came to the Council Chamber of the *technitai,* which is built near the gates of the Kerameikos not far from the knights' <grounds>.

IVAiii. Classical and Hellenistic Acting

Broadly speaking, the literature distinguishes two tragic acting styles, a "grand" and a "realistic" style, which compete with one another from the late 5th c. B.C. onward. The earliest critical description of these opposed styles appears in comedy (49–51, 57, 58); in particular the debate between Aeschylus and Euripides in Aristophanes' *Frogs* seems to have had a decisive impact on the later theoretical literature (see esp. 52). Aristophanes creates neat oppositions between the two dramatists in diction, dramatic purpose, staging, and costume: the obscure, poetic language of Aeschylus is opposed to the everyday speech of Euripides (49–51, 58); Aeschylus' transporting emotional impact is opposed to Euripides' clever intellectual argumentation (49–51, 58); Aeschylus' tableaux and the imposing silences of his characters contrasts with the petty chatter and busyness of Euripides' (50, 51); a particularly clear opposition is provided by the princely ornate costumes of Aeschylus and Euripides' penchant for dressing his fallen heroes in rags (51, 57).

Actors are praised or condemned by the criteria of these styles. The actor Kallippides was judged a typical representative of the new school of realism in the late 5th c. B.C. Mynniskos, who was associated with Aeschylus (9) and an actor of the old school, called Kallippides an ape (60): no doubt, in comparison with the stately mannerisms of earlier actors, Kallippides' gestures seemed twitchy and hyperactive, part of a pattern with the putative busyness of Euripides' characters. Aristophanes charges Kallippides' visual realism with a lack of dignity, in terms highly reminiscent of his ridicule of Euripides' costuming (59). Though Aristotle's interest in rhetoric caused him to admire naturalism in vocal delivery (61), his elitist sensibilities were affronted by gestural realism, and particularly the imitation of lower-class women (60). He resolved his ambivalent feelings for the new style by maintaining that verbalization was central to tragedy in a way that gesture and visual presentation were not (60, 63).

The two styles clearly depended upon one another for their effect: there was nothing particularly "real" about rags or prosaic speech in themselves; their effect lay in their implicit criticism of the grand style's artifice in the use of extravagant garments and phrases. While both styles necessarily coexisted, the realistic style dominated the tragic stage of the 4th c. B.C. When New Comedy adopted realism, however, the tragic stage appears to have reacted by becoming more grandiose and stylized. Hellenistic scholarship retrojected to the time of Aeschylus much that was peculiar to its own contemporary tragedy, such as the elevator boots (buskins), elongated stylized masks with the *onkos* (see I 142), elaborate stage designs, and machinery (52, 54–56). This tendency to regard Aeschylus as the inventor of all the garish accessories of Hellenistic theater was encouraged by a classicizing reperformance tradition (cf. the pageantry condemned in I 53) and by Aristotelian theory, which opposed tragedy "in itself" to the external adjuncts added "in performance" (63, but qualified by 170). It was convenient for the overall evolutionary scheme of Aristotelian cultural history to suppose that drama was originally burdened with superficial forms borrowed from other arts but gradually cast them off to find its own proper form. Spectacle (*opsis*) came to be thought of as one such primitive element. Aristophanes seemed to give convincing proof that Aeschylus distinguished himself from later poets by his use of spectacle. The influence of Aristotle and his school on later dramatic criticism was enormous and is exemplified among other things by the frequency with which the literature repeats the terms *ekplexis,* "a dazzled or stunned state" (and words with the same root: *ek/exe* + *plek-/plet-/plex*), and *teratodes,* "sensationalistic." This influence is nicely attested by the assumption on the part of later commentators that the visual aspects of drama are both vulgar and archaic (64, 65). Note in particular 64's apology for Sophocles' decision to stage Ajax' suicide: "Perhaps he wished to dazzle them (*ekplexai*). It is pointless and impious to condemn one of the ancients."

It is perhaps partly due to Aristotelian contempt for visual effects that our literary sources ignore this aspect of drama and generally limit their interest in acting to the rhetorical side of the actor's art (66–75). Apart from Old Comedy, almost all extant discussion of acting is to be found in the rhetorical literature, where the term *hypokrisis,* literally, "acting," is used for the aspect of rhetoric that we call "delivery" (66–70). There is indeed ample evidence to show the paramount importance of voice and verbal delivery on the ancient stage (69–75, cf. 30H), but our written sources are by nature inclined to downplay the visual. For this the artifacts provide the most reliable evidence (see IC). Peripatetic attitudes may also be responsible for the fact, attested by the artifacts, that from late Hellenistic times, as tragedy and comedy became less popular and more "classical" and "academic" forms of entertainment, acting styles really did become stiffer and more rhetorical.

The evidence for stage decoration and stage machinery helps counterbalance the traditional impression that ancient acting was something lifelessly static and statuesque. Our most important source is Pollux (app.

A), but Pollux is only reliable for the resources of the late Hellenistic theater, and the main features of the earlier theater must be reconstructed from other evidence. The introduction of the *skene* building cannot be placed any later than the production of the *Oresteia* in 458 B.C. (see I 126–27). The use of a low stage (about three feet above orchestra level) is amply attested by the comic pot illustrations (see I 131, 133), though modern classical scholars generally prefer to argue the point on the ambiguous literary evidence (e.g., 76). Despite Aeschylus' reputation for inventing stage machinery and gaudy effects, it is Euripides and Agathon who were associated with the use of the *mechane* and the *ekkyklema* (57, 77, 78). Despite the claims of the scholia (78B–C), we cannot be certain whether Aeschylus used either of these contraptions. The evidence of Old Comedy proves that the devices were commonplace in tragedy by ca. 435 B.C. Old Comedy appears to have used the devices exclusively in paratragic scenes involving gods or in spoofs on recognizable tragic heroes, or in the mock heroic appearances of contemporaries, usually the tragedians themselves (57, 77A–C, cf. *Birds* 1184ff., *Thesmophoriazusae* 1098ff., 78A, E, F). By the time of New Comedy's more realistic theater, the *mechane* was used only for prologue-gods, and the *ekkyklema* was used only rarely to create tragic modalities (as in *Dyskolos,* act 4), but both devices continued to be used (and overused) on the Hellenistic tragic stage (e.g., 78E). The exact nature of the *ekkyklema* is disputed because the sources are contradictory: it literally means the "roller-out," but many of the sources speak of it revolving. The *exostra* ("the thing pushed out") appears sometimes to be distinguished from, sometimes identified with, the *ekkyklema:* whatever its exact nature, it seems to have been a functional equivalent. By Hellenistic times highly elaborate scenic back-drops were used in various forms (80–82). To those mentioned below we should add the *pinakes* and *thyromata* attested in inscriptions (I 112) and the architectural remains of several Hellenistic theaters (see I 149, I 150, I 153). Later scholars attributed the invention of scene painting to Agatharchus (80B) at the invitation of Aeschylus, or to Sophocles (80A, possibly a late interpolation in Aristotle's text). No securely identifiable remains of the *scaena versilis* and the *scaena ductilis* (82) have been found at any theater, but among the devices mentioned by Pollux, the Charonian steps are perfectly preserved at the Hellenistic theater of Eretria and suited to such ghostly apparitions as that of Darius in Aeschylus' *Persians.*

Sources

The Grand Style

49. Aristophanes, *Clouds* 1366ff. See I 7.

50. Aristophanes, *Frogs* 907–26. Produced Lenaea, 405 B.C. From the contest between "Aeschylus" and "Euripides" for the "chair" of tragedy in the underworld. "Euripides" criticizes the Aeschylean style and is answered by Dionysus in his capacity as judge.

> EURIPIDES: I will characterize my own poetry in a moment, but first I wish to expose my adversary (Aeschylus) as a charlatan and a cheat and show the devices he used to hoodwink the audience of his day, fools nurtured by Phrynichus (the tragic poet, active 511 to after 476 B.C.) First of all <Aeschylus> would veil the head of some Achilles or Niobe, never showing their face, and sit them down alone, a mere pretense of tragedy, not uttering a syllable. DIONYSUS: No, by Zeus, not a syllable! EURIPIDES: Then the chorus would ram the audience with a chain of four successive odes sung without interruption. But the actors remained mute. DIONYSUS: I used to like the mute actors: they pleased me no less than do the chatterboxes nowadays. EURIPIDES: That's because you were simpleminded, you know. DIONYSUS: I agree. Why did that so-and-so do this? EURIPIDES: Because he's a fraud. So the audience would sit and wait to see when Niobe would say something; meanwhile the drama continued. DIONYSUS: The bastard! He really took advantage of me! [To Aeschylus] Hey, why are you writhing about like that? EURIPIDES: Because I'm exposing him. And then when he'd produce this nonsense and the drama would be half over, the actor would come out with a dozen ox-sized words, with beetling brows and plumes, something bogey-faced and unintelligible to the audience.

51. Aristophanes, *Frogs* 1058–69. Produced Lenaea, 405 B.C. Aeschylus defends himself against Euripides' criticisms.

> AESCHYLUS: But, you poor fool, it's necessary to produce words to suit great sentiments and ideas. Besides, heroes are semidivine and as such should use words that are larger than life. Moreover, they wear clothes that are much more opulent than our own. Mine was just the right style of presentation and you outraged it. EURIPI-

DES: How so? AESCHYLUS: First by bringing on kings wearing rags so that they would seem more pathetic to the audience. . . . Then you taught the audience to practice chatter and drivel.

52. *Life of Aeschylus* 2–14. This biography is drawn from late Hellenistic peripatetic sources.

<Aeschylus> began making tragedies when young and he greatly surpassed his predecessors in poetry, in the arrangement of the *skene,* and in the brilliance of the furnishings (*choregia*) and the costumes of the actors and the grandeur of the chorus, as Aristophanes also attests (*Frogs* 1004f.): "O first of the Greeks to fortify grandiose speech and adorn tragic blather . . ." The narrative structure of his dramas does not have many reversals and complications as in the later dramatists. For he alone was anxious to envelop his characters with gravity, judging archaic the magnificent and heroic, but considering rascality, wizardry, and sententiousness to be alien to tragedy, so that Aristophanes makes fun of the excessive gravity of his characters. In the *Niobe,* for example, she (Niobe) sits shrouded at the grave of her children without uttering a sound until the third act. In the *Ransom of Hector* Achilles, similarly enshrouded, makes no sound, except in the initial exchange with Hermes. Whence one can find very many passages in his plays that are outstanding for their arrangement, but maxims or pathetic passages or anything calculated to induce tears are rare. He employs spectacle and language for stunning sensationalism (*ekplexis teratodes*) rather than illusion. . . . Some say that in the performance of the *Eumenides,* he gave the chorus a scattered entry, which so stunned (*ekplexai*) the audience that children fainted and women miscarried. . . . Aeschylus first increased tragedy's stature by presenting the noblest sufferings and he adorned his stage and dazzled (*kateplexe*) the gaze of his audience with splendor, paintings, and devices (*mechanai*), altars and graves, trumpet blasts, apparitions, Furies, covering his actors with sleeves and long trains, giving the masks the *onkos* (swelling on top), and raising them (actors) aloft with larger buskins.

53. Athenaeus 21d. See IV 304.

54. Philostratus, *Life of Apollonius* 6.11. Written ca. 217. Apollonius' speech is very pompous and imprecise, but he appears to distinguish Aeschylus' poetic style from his performance art.

When I met the Indians their teachings made the kind of impression upon me they say Aeschylus' wisdom made upon the Athenians.

He was a tragic poet, who found the art unelaborate and as yet unadorned. And if he compressed the chorus that had previously been scattered (or prolix?) or if in eschewing long runs of monodies he invented the actors' dialogues, or contrived ways in which people might die behind the stage and not be slaughtered before the audience, he is not for all that to be considered any less a genius, but it must be allowed that a less clever poet could have come up with these ideas. But he strove to make his utterances worthy of tragedy and he also strove to make the art (in performance) <more worthy>, thinking it more suited to the grandiose than the abject and groveling: he developed masks resembling the appearance of heroes and shod his actors in buskins to allow them to walk like heroes, and first adorned them with costumes that conveyed the visual impression of heroes and heroines.

55. Philostratus, *Lives of the Sophists* 1.9.1. Written between 217 and 238.

Sicily produced Gorgias, to whom we think it right to attribute the art of the sophists, as if father of the profession. Just as we might remember Aeschylus for his great contribution to tragedy in fashioning its costume and high buskins and the style of its heroes and its messengers (*angeloi*) and messengers from inside the palace (*exangeloi*) and what could be done on the stage (*skene*) and in front of it—all this is (comparable to) what Gorgias represented to his colleagues.

56. Cramer, *Anecdota Parisiensia* 1.19. Note that the list, though less full, lists the stage devices in the same order found in Pollux, the garments nearly so. For descriptions of some of the garments see Pollux, app. A.

If someone wishes to attribute to Aeschylus all the inventions of the stage—*ekkyklemata* ("rollers-out"), *periaktoi* ("revolvers-about"), *mechanai* ("machines," i.e., the crane, stage machine par excellence), *exostra* ("out-shovers"), *proskenia, distegia* ("second stories"), lightning observatories, thunder machines, *theologeia* ("places where the gods talk"), and *geranoi* (literally, "cranes," but it is unknown if or how these differed from the *mechanai*), and of course also the *xystides, batrachides,* masks, and buskins, and those *poikila, syrmata,* the *kaluptra, kolpoma, parapechu,* and *agrenon,* and the third actor added to the second—or if Sophocles also devised and invented some of these things; those who wish can argue about this and drag the credit in either direction.

The "Realistic" Style

57. Aristophanes, *Acharnians* 404–34. Produced Lenaea, 425 B.C.
DIKAIOPOLIS (knocking at Euripides' door): Euripides! Dear little
Euripides! Hear me, if ever you heard any man! I, Dikaiopolis of
the deme Cholleis, call you. EURIPIDES: I'm busy. DIKAIOPOLIS:
But roll out on the *ekkyklema*! EURIPIDES: Impossible! DIKAIOPO-
LIS: But do it anyway! EURIPIDES: All right, I'll roll out on the
ekkyklema but I've no time to come down. DIKAIOPOLIS: Euripides . . . EURIPIDES: What utter you? DIKAIOPOLIS: Do you write
up there, when you could come down? No wonder you produce
lame heroes. But why are you dressed in rags from your tragedy,
such pathetic clothes? No wonder you produce beggars. I beseech
you, Euripides, by your knees, give me some rag from one of your
old plays. I have to make a long speech to the chorus, and if I
don't do a good job, the penalty is death. EURIPIDES: What tatters?
Do you mean the ones with which the unlucky old Oeneus here
competed? DIKAIOPOLIS: No I didn't mean Oeneus, but someone
even more wretched. EURIPIDES: Those of blind Phoenix?
DIKAIOPOLIS: No, not Phoenix. Some other more wretched than
Phoenix. EURIPIDES: What scraps of dress does this guy want?
Do you mean those of Philoctetes the beggar? DIKAIOPOLIS: No,
someone much much more beggarly. EURIPIDES: Well then you
want the squalid garb that the lame Bellerophon here wore?
DIKAIOPOLIS: Not Bellerophon. But the one I'm thinking of was
also lame, beggarly, babbling, and eloquent. EURIPIDES: I know
the man! Mysian Telephus. DIKAIOPOLIS: Yes, Telephus. Please
give me his wraps, I beg you. EURIPIDES: Slave, give him Telephus'
rags! They're just above Thyestes' rags, between those and Ino's.

58. Aristophanes, *Frogs* 959–67. Produced Lenaea, 405 B.C. Euripides
defends his art against Aeschylus.

I brought on stage the things of everyday life that we use and are
in constant contact with and that would lay me open to criticism
since the audience had the requisite familiarity to detect any errors
in my artistry. But I didn't bluster them out of their senses or
dazzle them (*exepletton*), producing Cycnuses and Memnons
mounted on horses with bells and cheek-guards (literally, "bellcheek-
guardmounted," a parody of Aeschylean compounds). You will tell
his students from mine: his are Phormisios and Megainetos *alias*
Manes (the significance of the nickname is unclear), trumpet-lance-

beardians, flesh-ripping-pine-benders, but mine are Kleitophon and the suave Theramenes.

59. Aristophanes, *Women Who Pitch the Tents* (*Skenas Katalambanousai*), *PCG* F 490. Date: late 5th to early 4th c. B.C. Kallippides was active from ca. 430 to 390 B.C. (see 13, 28; I 29, 30).

Like Kallippides I am sitting upon the floor-sweepings.

60. Aristotle, *Poetics* 1461b26–62a14. Written ca. 330 B.C. For Mynniskos see 9, 12, 13.

One may well be at a loss to decide whether epic imitation is better than tragic. For if the less vulgar is the better—the less vulgar being always that which is directed to the better part of the audience—it is only too clear that the vulgar art is that which imitates everything. Supposing that their audience will understand nothing unless they incorporate it in their representation, some artists will produce any gesture, like bad pipers who will circle about if imitating the throwing of a discus or drag along the leader of the chorus if they are playing a *Scylla*. Now tragedy is just this sort of art. So too the older actors perceived the younger generation of actors: Mynniskos used to call Kallippides an ape because he overdid everything; the same opinion might be held of Pindaros. The relation of these actors to their older contemporaries is arguably the same as tragedy generally is to epic. Epic, so the argument goes, is directed to a superior audience that has no need for such gestures and postures, but tragedy is directed toward an inferior. If then tragedy is vulgar, clearly it would be worse. We may answer, first of all, that this charge has nothing to do with poetry but with acting, since one can overdo gestures even in an epic recitation, as did Sostratos, or in song, as did Mnasitheos of Opous. Secondly, not all movement is objectionable—one would not condemn dance, for example—but only that which is in imitation of inferior people: Kallippides was censured, as are others today, for representing lower-class women. Tragedy does its work even without movement, just like epic: by reading it you can tell what kind of tragedy it is. If then tragedy is superior in other respects, it is not necessarily subject to this fault.

61. Aristotle, *Rhetoric* 1404b18–25. Written ca. 330 B.C. Theodoros was active from at least ca. 390 to ca. 359 B.C. (see 20, 21, 32).

Therefore one must conceal careful composition and take care not to appear to speak artificially but naturally; the latter is persuasive, the former the opposite, for when people detect artifice they suspect they are being tricked, just as they distrust mixed wines. Consider, for example, the difference between Theodoros' voice and that of other actors: his seems the voice of natural speech, theirs artificial. The deception succeeds when one composes from a vocabulary chosen from normal conversation. Euripides was the first to do this and showed the way.

62. Aulus Gellius 6.5. Written ca. 180, referring to the later 4th c. B.C. or very early 3rd c. B.C. On Polos see 33, 37.

There was a very famous actor in Greece who excelled in the brilliance and charm of his voice and gestures. They say his name was Polos. He performed the tragedies of great poets with ingenuity and dedication. This Polos lost his son, whom he loved exceedingly. When he felt he had his fill of mourning, he returned to his artistic endeavours. At the time, he was to act the *Electra* of Sophocles at Athens and was supposed to carry an urn as if it held Orestes' remains. The tragedy's plot has Electra carrying what she thinks are the remains of her brother and mourning and lamenting his supposed death. Polos therefore, dressed in the sombre robe of Electra, took his son's urn from the grave and, embracing it as the urn of Orestes, filled everything about him not with representations and imitations, but with real living grief and lamentation. The audience was deeply moved to see the play acted this way.

Aristotle and the Scholarly Tradition on Visual Effects

63A. Aristotle, *Poetics* 1449a8–9. Written ca. 330 B.C. See context in II 11.

...and to judge tragedy in itself or in relation to its audience...

63B. Aristotle, *Poetics* 1450b16–20. Aristotle claims that tragedy has six necessary elements: plot, character, diction, thought, visual effect (*opsis*), and music.

Visual effect is highly emotive, but is least a matter of art and least specific to poetry: the effect of tragedy is felt even without performance and actors. The production of visual effects sooner falls in the province of the art of the mask maker than of the art of poets.

63C. Aristotle, *Poetics* 1453b1–10.

It is possible to produce fear and pity through visual effects. It is also possible to do so from the composition of the action itself. The latter is superior and the sign of a better poet. The plot should be so constructed that even without seeing it, but merely listening to the events unfolding, one will shudder and feel pity from the circumstances, as experienced when listening to the myth of Oedipus. To manage this through visual effect is less professional and incurs production costs (*choregia*). Those who use visual effects to create only sensation (*to teratodes*), not fear, have nothing to do with tragedy.

64. Scholion to Sophocles, *Ajax* 815. See I 54B.

65. Scholion to Sophocles, *Electra* 1404.

Messengers customarily report what has happened within to those outside. In this case, however, <Sophocles> didn't compose <in the normal fashion> in order not to waste time in the drama, since the subject at hand is the suffering of Electra. In this case the audience hears her shouting at the time of the killing of Clytemnestra and the deed appears more vivid than if it were reported by a messenger. In addition the vulgarity of visual presentation (*opsis*) is avoided, but the scene is made no less vivid because of the shout.

Voice, Expression, Enunciation

66. Aristotle, *Rhetoric* 1403b26–33. Written ca. 330 B.C. Aristotle explains that there are three branches of the study of rhetoric: argument, arrangement, and then delivery. "Delivery" translates the Greek *hypokrisis,* which literally means "acting."

<Delivery> (*hypokrisis*) is concerned with the way the voice is to be used to match each emotion, when loud, soft, or middling, and when to use a high, low, or middling pitch, and what are the rhythms suited to each situation. There are three objects of investigation: volume, pitch, and rhythm. Those who know how to use their voices almost always walk away with the prizes; just as in the theater actors are more important now than poets.

67. Aristotle, *Rhetoric* 1413b14–28. Date: ca. 330 B.C. Aristotle distinguishes the style of works intended to be read and speeches intended for delivery.

And when compared, the works of prose authors seem thin in debate, and the speeches of orators, though they sound good when spoken, look amateurish when examined on the page. The reason for this is that histrionics (*ta hypokritika*) are suited to debate. Thus speeches do not have their proper effect if the histrionics (*hypokrisis*) are removed, but they appear silly, without conjunctions and with frequent repetition, which are rightly censured in written work but not in spoken delivery, and they are used by orators, because they are histrionic (*hypokritike*). It is nonetheless necessary to vary the manner of delivery when repeating something: this, as it were, paves the way for histrionics (*to hypokrinesthai*). "This is the man who robbed you, this is the man who deceived you, this is the man who in the end dared betray you"; or as Philemon the actor did in Anaxandrides' *Crazy for Old Men,* when he said, "Rhadamanthys and Palamedes," and in the prologue of *The Pious Ones,* when he said, "I." But if he doesn't act it, it sounds stiff as a board. The same is true of phrases without conjunctions: "I came, I met, I pleaded." One must act and not say it as one phrase in the same manner and tone.

68. Demetrius, *On Style* 193–95. This rhetorical handbook is traditionally ascribed to Demetrius of Phaleron (ca. 350–280 B.C.), but is almost certainly late Hellenistic in date.

The lax style is perhaps more dramatic. It is also called the histrionic style (*hypokritike*), since its loose structure provokes histrionics (*hypokrisis*). The graphic style is easy to read: it is that which is connected and, as it were, made secure with conjunctions. For this reason also they perform Menander, which is loose for the most part, but they read Philemon. Let this one example suffice to show that the loose style is histrionic (*hypokritikon*): "I took up, I begat, I will nourish, friend." So loose is the phrase that it forces even the unwilling to act it because of its looseness. But if, conjoining the clauses, you were to say, "I took up and I begat and I will nourish," you would insert a great lack of emotion with the conjunctions. Emotionlessness is very unhistrionic (*anhypokriton*). There are also other rules for histrionics (*hypokritika*): take Ion, for example, in Euripides' play (*Ion* 154ff.), who grabs his bow and arrows and threatens the swan that is defecating on the statues, for much movement is required of the actor by running for the bow and arrows and looking up in the air while the character converses with the swan, and doing all the other posturing demanded of the actor. But our present discussion is not about acting.

69. Pseudo-Plutarch, *Ten Orators* 844f–45b.

Since <Demosthenes> was short of breath he paid the actor Neoptolemos ten thousand drachmas to learn how to deliver long sentences (lit., "whole periods") without taking a breath.... Once <Demosthenes> was hissed out of the assembly and walking home in despair. Eunomos of the deme Thriasia, already an old man, met him and encouraged Demosthenes, but the actor Andronikos encouraged him most of all by telling him that his speeches were good, but that his delivery (*hypokrisis*) was defective, and he repeated from memory what he had said at the assembly. Demosthenes was convinced by this and put himself under Andronikos' tutelage. As a result, when someone asked him what was most important in the science of rhetoric, he said, "Delivery" (*hypokrisis*); and what second, "Delivery"; and what third, "Delivery."

70. Pseudo-Plutarch, *Ten Orators* 848b.

<Demosthenes> said, "One should judge actors by their voice, but orators by their good sense."

71. Diogenes Laertius 7.21. Probably written first half of 3rd c. Zeno lived from 335 to 263 B.C.

<Zeno> said that one should converse forcefully, like the actors, with a loud and powerful voice, but not open one's mouth wide.

72. Pollux 4.114. Date: 2nd c. Cf. IV 165. Pollux lists six terms of abuse for actors who shout.

You would say "deep-groaning actor," "roaring," "roaring about," "oil-flasking" (for a "hollow voice," as if speaking into an oil flask), "larynxing," "pharynxing."

73. [Aristotle], *Problems* 11.22. Probably written ca. 300 B.C.

We see that all those who train their voices, such as actors, choreuts and the like, perform their exercises early while fasting.

74. Cicero, *Against Quintus Caecilius* 48. Date: 70 B.C.

Just as among Greek actors, we see that the deuteragonist and tritagonist often hush their voices, though they are better able to project them than the protagonist, so that the protagonist will stand out as much as possible.

75A. Hegelochos. Scholion to Euripides, *Orestes* 279, "After the storm once again I see the calm." There is some doubt as to the exact nature of Hegelochos' pronunciation error. In Greek verse a final vowel drops out before an initial vowel, a phenomenon known as elision. Hellenistic grammarians indicate that the syllable preceding the elided final vowel was joined, without pause, to the initial vowel of the following word, but Hegelochos chose an unfortunate moment to take a breath. This may also have been compounded by an error in rendering tonic accent, since the proper pronunciation of "weasel" requires the final syllable to be pronounced with a rising and a falling tone (marked by a circumflex accent), but the elided word, "calm," has only a rising tone (or no tone at all, cf. IV 278). Hegelochos may have produced a mechanical error because of a large number of circumflex accents in the line surrounding the syllable in question. Date: 408 B.C.

> This line is ridiculed in comedy because of Hegelochos the actor. As he was not able to separate the syllables of the the elision when his breath failed him, he seemed to the audience to say the animal "weasel" (*galen*), but not the "calm" (*galena*). (One translator suggests "After the storm the sea(l) looks calm again," which unfortunately inverts the error made in Greek.)

75B. Aristophanes, *Frogs* 303. Produced Lenaea, 405 B.C.

> It's possible for us to say like Hegelochos, "After the storm once again I see the weasel."

75C. Strattis, *Anthroporestes, PCG* F 1. See 17.

75D. Sannyrion, *Danae, PCG* F 8. The lines are probably spoken by Zeus as he contemplates how best to penetrate into Danae's underground chamber. Date: late 5th or early 4th c. B.C.

> What shall I become in order to go down into this opening? Let's see. I know, I'll become a weasel. But no, Hegelochos the tragedian, if he spotted me, would immediately denounce me, shouting aloud, "After the storm once again I see the weasel."

Stage, Stage Decoration, and Stage Machinery
(See Pollux, app. A)

76. Aristophanes, *Wasps* 1342–44. This passage is probably the best verbal evidence that can be cited for the existence of a low stage. The aged hero, Philokleon, marvelously rejuvenated, abducts a pipe-girl from a party and brings her home. It appears that he mounts the stage, then offers his *phallos* to help her up. The value of the passage is unfortunately compromised by its deliberate ambiguity. The meaning of "climb up" is arguably restricted to the sexual innuendo and has no reference to theater topography, but it is difficult then to see what the surface meaning of the double entendre might be. Strings were attached to the legs of beetles, and they flew about in circles.

> Grab hold of this rope and climb up here, my little golden beetle. Hold on! Watch out, though, the rope is rotten with age. Nonetheless it doesn't mind a bit of rubbing.

77A. *Mechane.* Aristophanes, *Peace* 173–76. Produced Dionysia, 421 B.C. The Athenian farmer Trygaios flies to heaven on the back of a dung beetle in order to rescue the goddess Peace and bring her back to war-torn Greece. The flight to heaven is an overt parody of Euripides' *Bellerophon,* in which the hero, Bellerophon, flies to heaven on the winged horse, Pegasus. While riding the beetle the actor breaks the illusion and speaks to the machine operator.

> I'm scared dammit, and I'm not joking anymore either. Watch out for me, machine operator (*mechanopoios*)! I can feel my bowels getting loose, and if you don't watch out I'll feed the dung beetle.

77B. Aristophanes, *Daedalus, PCG* F 192. The text is corrupt and the translation very uncertain.

> O machine operator, whenever you wish to raise me aloft with the wheel, say, "Hello light of the sun."

77C. *POxy* 2742.3–19. Written 2nd c. The papyrus seems to be a commentary on a comedy, possibly the *Seriphioi* of Cratinus. Strattis' *Atalantos* and *Phoenician Women* were produced in the late 5th or early 4th c. B.C. The citation from the *Phoenician Women* parodies the opening lines of Euripides' *Hypsipyle* and appears to be spoken, as in Euripides' play, by Dionysus. The *Gerytades* was probably produced ca. 407 B.C.

> They called so (i.e., *krade* = "fig branch") [a] long [device] from which they [appeared? hung? flew?] above? [...] men tied to. In the *Atalantos* of Strattis: "From the *krade*, for I've now become a fig, let the machine operator (*mechanopoios*) pluck me down at once!" And in the *Phoenician Women*: "Dionysus, who with *thyrsoi* the pipers [...] ensnared through the wickedness of others I come hanging like a fig from the *krade*." Aristophanes in the *Gerytades*: "the machine operator (*mechanopoios*) should turn the *krade* about at once."

77D. Zenobius, *Proverbs* 3.156 (= Pseudo-Plutarch, *Proverbs* 2.16). Hesychius and the scholia on Aristophanes give abbreviated versions. Compare Pollux' remarks, app. A.

> "A broken *krade*." Now *krade* is not the fig branch, but the hook from which the actors on the tragic stage hang, attached by waistbands and ropes, when they represent appearances of the gods.

77E. Bekker, *Anecdota Graeca* 1.232

> the gaff (*harpax*) ... from which the prepared actor performed tragedy.

77F. Plato, *Cratylus* 425d. Date: ca. 385 B.C.

> We can refer to nothing better than this for the truth about the first names for things, unless, like the tragic poets, who whenever they are stuck take refuge in machines and raise up gods, you wish that we should get off this way, saying that the gods established the first names for things.

77G. Antiphanes, *The Art of Poetry*, *PCG* F 189. From a comedy, possibly the prologue, written sometime from ca. 380 to 300 B.C. The simile in this passage is to be explained with reference to the practice of athletes in competition who raised their fingers as a signal of giving up.

> Tragedy is a lucky genre in every respect...and then whenever <the tragedians> have nothing more to say and have altogether given up on their plays, they raise the machine like a finger and this is enough for the audience.

77H. Aristotle, *Poetics* 1454a36–b5. Written ca. 330 B.C.

> It is evident then that the resolution of the plot should arise out of the plot itself, and not from the machine as in the *Medea* and in the episode about sailing home in the *Iliad*. But one should make use of the machine for things external to the drama, or for things that happened beforehand and of which no human could have knowledge, or for things that will happen afterward that need to be foretold and reported, for we concede that the gods see all.

77I. Scholion to Lucian, *Lover of Lies* 7.

> "God from the machine." In the theater, whenever something unexpected and credible had to be performed, up above the doors on either side of the middle of the theater....Of the two machines suspended in the air the one on the left makes gods and heroes appear suddenly, as bringing solutions to hopeless problems.

78A. *Ekkyklema*. Aristophanes, *Thesmophoriazusae* 95f. and 264f. Produced 411 B.C. Euripides and his kinsman go to visit Agathon to persuade him to infiltrate the women's assembly at the Thesmophoria; failing in this they borrow feminine garments with which to disguise Euripides' kinsman. Agathon emerges from his house spouting verse and riding the *ekkyklema,* as the following lines show.

> EURIPIDES: Quiet! KINSMAN: What is it? EURIPIDES: Agathon is coming out. KINSMAN: What does he look like? EURIPIDES: It's this man, the one being rolled out (*ekkykloumenos*)....(Then at the end of the episode:) AGATHON:...Well, you have what you need. Someone roll me back in (*eiskyklesato*) quick as can be!

78B. Scholion to Aeschylus, *Libation Bearers* 973.

> The *skene* opens and the bodies, which he calls "double tyranny," are seen upon the *ekkyklema*.

78C. Scholion to Aeschylus, *Eumenides* 64.

> The device has turned around to make visible how things appear inside the shrine.

78D. Scholion to Sophocles, *Ajax* 346. Teucer says, "Look here! I am opening the doors. You can gaze upon his deeds, and how he himself fares."

> There is an *ekkyklema* so that Ajax can appear amidst the sheep. For these things also shock the spectator; spectacle is deeply emotive. He is shown carrying a sword, covered in blood, sitting among the sheep.

78E. Scholion to Euripides, *Hippolytus* 171. The scholion claims to report some difficulty Aristophanes of Byzantium had with the passage in the *Hippolytus* where the lovesick Phaedra is brought outside the palace by her nurse and attendants. Unfortunately there is corruption in the first sentence, allowing for two interpretations. Aristophanes either complained that Euripides used the *ekkyklema* to bring Phaedra out, but should not have, or he complains that Euripides did not use the *ekkyklema,* but should have so as to show her inside the palace and not have recourse to the unrealistic expedient of bringing her outside on her sickbed. The first alternative appears more likely and best explains the corruption. There is no reason to believe that Aristophanes knew anything about the staging of the original production.

> Aristophanes marked this passage because, to be precise, the *ekkyklema* [contradicts] (or possibly "[suits]") the action. This is so because onstage interior action is <normally> shown <by the *ekkyklema*>, yet <Euripides> presents <Phaedra> as coming outside.

78F. Scholion to Aristophanes, *Clouds* 184.

> He sees them primping themselves as philosophers, when the *ekkyklema* turns about.

78G. Stage direction in text of Aristophanes, *Thesmophoriazusae* 277.

> The sanctuary is pushed out.

78H. Scholion to Aristophanes, *Thesmophoriazusae* 277.

> The Thesmophorion is rolled out to the outside.

78I. Scholion to Aristophanes, *Acharnians* 408.

> The *ekkyklema* is said to be a wooden contraption on wheels, which, when it turns about, shows actions supposed to be taking place inside, as if in the house, to those outside as well, I mean to say the audience.

78J. Scholion to Clement of Alexandria, *Stromateis* 4.97.

> <The *ekkyklema* is> a device on wheels on the outside of the *skene;* when it turns about, the interior seems to become visible to those outside.

78K. Eustathius, *Commentary on Homer's Iliad* 976.15. "Device" is obviously a corruption for *skene,* which has been incorporated into the text copied by Eustathius along with the correct wording.

> The *ekkyklema,* which is also called the *ekkyklethron,* is a contraption on wheels, by which things in the device (*skeue*) or *skene* are shown.

79A. *Exostra.* Hesychius, s.v. *exostra.* Written 5th c. Compare Pollux, app. A: "People think the *exostra* is the same thing as the *ekkyklema.*"

> *Exostra:* the *ekkyklema* on the *skene.*

79B. *IG* XI 199 A 95–96. Inscription giving accounts from Delos. Date: 274 B.C.

> To Epikrates, who contracted to plane and reconstruct the old stages and make the two new stages above and make the two new *paraskenia* above and to surround them with the old paintings of the *paraskenia* and to reconstruct the *exostra* and the ladder and the altar: 337 drachmas.

79C. Polybius, *Histories* 11.6.8. Written ca. 145 B.C. The orator Thrasykrates attempts to persuade the Aetolians to remain neutral, ca. 207 B.C., during the First Macedonian War. The Aetolians' pact with the Romans betrayed Greece to a barbarian enemy, as became clear when Sulpicius Galba took Oreos in Northern Euboea and Aegina.

> And these previous events went unnoticed, but now through Oreos and the poor Aeginetans, you have been exposed to all, since Fortune, as if by design, has mounted your misconduct upon the *exostra.*

79D. Cicero, *On the Consular Provinces* 14. Delivered late June or early July, 56 B.C.

> And so that other fellow (Piso) is either himself well-instructed and finely educated by his Greeks, with whom he now carouses on the *exostra,* though formerly he did so behind the *siparium* (a stage screen or curtain normally associated with mimes), or he has friends who are more cautious than Gabinius, since none of his letters have come forward.

79E. Vegetius, *Epitomy of the Science of Warfare* 4.21. Written ca. 390. The soldiers and their equipment appear to be mismatched in the first sentence.

> Once the siege towers have been brought up to the wall, slingers with stones, archers with javelins (*sic*), *manuballistarii* or *arcuballistarii* with arrows (*sic*) and javelin throwers with lead shot and missiles (*sic*) clear men from the walls. Once this is done ladders

are brought to the wall and they occupy the city. But those who
rely on ladders frequently incur danger.... For that reason besiegers
break into the walls of the enemy with the *sambuca* ("harp"), the
exostra, and the *tolleno* ("swing-beam")...The name *exostra* is
given to a bridge...because it is suddenly thrust forward from the
siege tower onto the wall.

80A. Scene Painting. Aristotle, *Poetics* 1449a18. See II 11.

80B. Vitruvius, *On Architecture* 7, preface 11. Written ca. 25 B.C.
Little is known about Agatharchus of Samos. Vitruvius' words seem to
indicate that he was active about 458 B.C. (time of the production of the
Oresteia), and an anecdote in Plutarch has Alcibiades imprison him in
his house and compel him to decorate it, ca. 430–420 B.C. The philosophers Anaxagoras and Democritus lived from ca. 500 to ca. 428 B.C. and
ca. 460 to 355 B.C., respectively.

> For Agatharchus first produced a scene painting at Athens when
> Aeschylus was directing tragedy, and he left behind a commentary
> about it. Democritus and Anaxagoras made use of his work when
> they wrote on the same subject to show how, if a fixed point is
> taken as the center for the direction of the gaze and the projection
> of the radii, we necessarily follow these lines by some natural law,
> so as to make indistinct images from an indistinct object yield the
> appearance of buildings in the scenery of the stage, and figures
> painted on a vertical and flat surface appear to recede in one
> direction and project in another.

80C. Vitruvius, *On Architecture* 5.6.

> There are three categories of scene painting: one called "tragic,"
> the second "comic," the third "satyric." Now, of these, the subjects
> are completely different. The tragic are laid out with columns,
> pediments, statues, and other royal accoutrements. The comic have
> the appearance of private houses and balconies and projections fitted
> with windows in the manner of ordinary houses. The satyric are
> painted with trees, caves, mountains, and features of the countryside
> formed in the manner of a landscape painting.

81. Vitruvius, *On Architecture* 5.6.8. Written ca. 25 B.C. For the
conventions governing the wing entrances, cf. IV 308–9.

> The stage has its system of organization designed in such a way
> that the central doors are decorated like the gates of a palace, and
> to the right and left are guest quarters. Next there are spaces
> prepared for scenery, which the Greeks call "turnabouts" (*periaktoi*)
> from the fact that there are triangular machines here that can be

turned and have three types of scenery, one on each side. When the
the plays are about to change or gods are about to appear with
sudden thunderclaps, they turn them and change the scene presented
to the audience. Next after these places there are projecting angles
that constitute the entrances to the stage, one from the marketplace
and one from abroad.

82. Servius, *Commentary on Vergil's Georgics* 3.24. Written 4th c.
"Or to see how the scenery divides when the side-scenes are turned."
Scenery was made either to be turned (*versilis*) or to be drawn apart
(*ductilis*). It is "turnable" when suddenly the entire scene is changed
by certain machinery, and it presents a new scene painting; it is
"drawable" when panels are drawn from either side to uncover a
new scene painting beneath it.

IVAiv. Republican and Imperial Actors and Acting

Legally the acting profession in Rome brought with it a reduction of civilian rights (84), so that an actor was technically *infamis*. The Romans recognized that their attitude to acting was different (83) from that of the Greeks, but even in republican times great actors (92) could rise to the status of knights, whereas honors were later showered on the imperial freedmen and others who attained prominence on the stage. Not only the emperor but private individuals kept troupes of mimes (107) and actors (101) for their own and their friends' entertainment, so that there resulted a privatization of drama, which was suited to the taste of the wealthy; but these actors would also prove valuable for those required to provide games because of their political position (98). The increase in the size of stage spectacles that can be documented from the 1st c. B.C. (114) is matched by the proliferation of private drama (102), whereby gardens and courtyards could be adapted as temporary theaters.

Slaves who displayed acting talents could become a valuable investment. It seems to have been normal (100) for owners to turn over a gifted slave to a known actor for training, who in return could take, e.g., a half share in his new apprentice. If the investment was successful, the slave would perhaps buy his freedom at a handsome profit (95) to his former owner, while still being obligated as a freedman (98) to perform duties for him. The imperial, and even some private, households would be presumably large enough to provide their own acting school. However the fact that actors and all other performers, even those who were free citizens, could be publicly whipped (86) at games both in imperial and in republican Rome suggests that the status of the profession remained lower than it had ever been in classical Greece. It may seem therefore strange that many laws (113) were passed to prevent members of the higher orders appearing on the stage, not always under compulsion.

Finally we offer some examples that reveal the kinds of criticisms made by the ancients of their actors. Acting was always important in the study of rhetoric, and the ancient audience was not without acumen (116). Yet the profession is accused (115) by the more sophisticated, with reason, of seeking vulgar ostentation.

Sources

Status of Actors

83. Cornelius Nepos, *Preface* 5. Written ca. 34 B.C. The Romans recognized that their attitude to acting was fundamentally different from Greek.

> <In Greece> to go on the stage and be a spectacle for the people was not a dishonor; all these activities with us are considered to bring *infamia,* or to be vulgar and alien to decent behavior.

84. *Digest* 3.2.2.5 (Ulpian). An imperial lawyer ca. 200, comments on a republican ruling.

> The praetor rules: "whosoever goes on stage is *infamis.*" The stage, as <Antistius> Labeo (ca. 10) defines it, is a thing that, for the purposes of putting on games in any place, where anyone stands or moves to make a spectacle of themselves, is placed in public or private or in a street, in whatever place people are admitted for the sake of spectacle.

85. *Lex Iulia Municipalis* 123 (= *FIRA* 1.18). This Spanish law is based probably on a law of Caesar's of ca. 46 B.C.

> (A long list is given of all those who may not hold office or vote: those convicted of theft or breach of trust, gladiators, bankrupts, exiles, criminals, cashiered soldiers, prostitutes.... The list con-cludes:) ... or those persons who have been or shall be trainers of gladiators or who have or shall have performed in public games (*ars ludicra*) or maintained a brothel.

86. Suetonius, *Augustus* 45.3. Written ca. 110. It is obvious that actors during the Roman republic could be struck with impunity; note that they may still be struck during their performance. The reference is to ca. 10 B.C.

> <Augustus> deprived the magistrates of the power allowed them by an ancient law of punishing actors everywhere and anywhere, restricting it to the time of the games and to the theater.

87. Tacitus, *Annals* 1.77. Written ca. 115. Under Tiberius in 15 it was proposed to bring the lash back for pantomimes, presumably even outside the theater.

> The riot was discussed in the Senate, and proposals were mooted that the praetors should be empowered to use the lash on actors (*histriones*).

88. Lucian, *Fisherman* 33. Written ca. 170. He is referring to games of the 2nd c. The whip carriers, usually twenty in number, were citizens usually under the control of officials called *athlothetai;* ultimately the agonothete was responsible for their conduct. They could whip performers or spectators. The Roman magistrates had also their lictors, and emperors had a cohort of the praetorian guard stationed in the theater. Theater police (rod holders: in Greek *rhabdouchoi*) had existed from the beginning (cf. 172, 173).

> Certainly the officials of the games (*athlothetai*) always flog an actor if he takes the part of Athena or Poseidon or Zeus and does not play it well and in accordance with the dignity of the god.

89. *Digest* 50.4.18. This is a legal ruling of the 2nd c.

> Also whip carriers who accompany the *agonothetes* in the contests and the scribes of a magistrate are personally responsible to them in their public duties.

90. Plutarch, *Brutus* 21.3. Written ca. 115. Brutus is finding artists for his Ludi Apollinares in 44 B.C. Clearly, friendship with star actors was politically essential.

> And he himself went down to Naples and conferred with a very large number of actors; and regarding Cannutius, an actor who enjoyed a great reputation, he wrote to his friends that they should persuade him to go to Rome; for no Greek could properly be compelled to go.

91. Cicero, *For the Comedian Roscius* 23. Delivered 66 B.C. The most famous comic actor of his day is defended by his friend Cicero. Roscius had become so wealthy and powerful that he became a knight, and thereafter refused to take any salary, which would have arguably rendered him *infamis*.

> Was <Roscius> in want? No. He was wealthy. Had he any debts? No, he had plenty of money. Was he a miser? No, even before he became rich, he was always most liberal and generous. Heavens, a man who refused to make a profit of 300,000 sesterces—for certainly he could and ought to have earned that amount if Dionysia (a mime actress) can earn 200,000. . . . In the last ten years, Roscius could have made 6,000,000 sesterces; he would not. The labor that could earn a fortune, he undertook; the fortune it might have brought, he rejected.

92. Macrobius, *Saturnalia* 3.14.13f. Written in the 5th c. about the great actor Roscius of the time of Cicero. The privilege of a "daily

salary," i.e., a regular salary, is one often proudly proclaimed by artists, but it may not have meant much sometimes.

> This is the Roscius who was also a great friend of L. Sulla and was presented by the dictator with the gold ring of knighthood. Moreover, such was his popularity and fame that he received a daily salary of a thousand denarii from the public funds for himself alone apart from payments made to his company of players. And as for Aesopus, we know that he bequeathed two million sesterces to his son from the proceeds of an equal professional skill.

93. Cicero, *Letters to His Friends* 10.32.2. Written, June 8th, 43 B.C. Asinius Pollio, who wrote Roman tragedies himself, tells Cicero about the outrageous behavior of the quaestor Balbus in Spain, who behaved as Caesar had with Laberius (cf. V 2).

> At the games that he gave in Cadiz, he presented on the last day the actor Herennius Gallus with a gold ring and brought him into the fourteen rows, for that was the number of the rows of equestrian seating he had created.... In the course of the games, he staged a Roman drama (*praetexta*) all about his own expedition to tamper with the loyalty of the proconsul L. Lentulus and—would you believe it?—he was so much affected by the representation of his own adventures that he burst into tears.

94. Dio Cassius 56.47.2. Written ca. 240, this refers to the first of the great pantomime riots in the year 14 under Tiberius, but it is also a rare example of a wildcat strike or impromptu extortion (cf. 87).

> Meanwhile the populace fell to rioting because at the Augustalia one of the dancers (i.e., pantomimes) would not enter the theater for the stipulated pay; and they did not cease their disturbance until the tribunes who were in charge convened the Senate that very day and begged it to permit them to spend more than the amount allocated.

95. Pliny, *Natural History* 7.128. Written mid-1st c. He is talking about the prices of slaves.

> This sum (700,000 sesterces) has been exceeded by the pantomimes (*histriones*) by a considerable amount in our time, but they bought thereby their freedom. Even in the time of our ancestors, the actor Roscius is said to have earned 500,000 sesterces annually.

96. Lucian, *Icaromenippus* 29. Written ca. 150.

> If you take away their (tragedians') masks and their gold embroidered robes, nothing is left but a funny little man hired for a competition for seven drachmas.

97. *Digest* 28.1.25. This ruling is attributed to the time of Hadrian. Here a distinction is made between the wealthy, like Pliny, who kept actors for their own amusement at dinner, and those who were professional *locatores* (dealers) and made money out of them. Of course one could do both.

> For if anyone has a pantomime or an archmime as freedman, and is of such modest substance as to have no other means of using their services but by hiring them out...

98. *Digest* 28.1.27. Date: time of Hadrian (117–38). This ruling reminds us that a freed slave was still by law under strict obligation to his former master; here he may also be compelled by his former master to perform for the benefit of his political friends, a severe additional burden.

> If a freedman exercises the art of a pantomime, it is true that he ought to provide his services free not only for his patron but also for the games of his friends.

99. Plutarch, *On Tranquillity of Mind* 13, 473b. Written ca. 115. The stars enjoyed immense popularity at all times.

> Free men and patricians regard with wondering admiration and envy successful comedians in the theater and dancers and servants at the courts of kings.

Training

100. Cicero, *For the Comedian Roscius* 27–28. Delivered 66 B.C. Roscius, as an investment, took on slave pupils who showed ability; he was a good teacher (cf. *ORF* 21, fr. 30; Cicero, *On the Orator* 1.129). In this case, a legal dispute had arisen about the financial disposition of the successful "investment," whose name was Panurgus (Greek for "rascal").

> "Panurgus," says he, "was the slave of Fannius, and became the common property of Fannius and Roscius."... You assert, Saturius, (the opposing lawyer) that Panurgus was the private property of Fannius.... What belonged to Fannius was worth not more than 4,500 sesterces; what belonged to Roscius was worth more than 100,000 sesterces, for no one judged him by his body but valued him for his skill as a comedian.... What hopes, what expectations, what enthusiasms, what favor accompanied Panurgus on the stage because he was the pupil of Roscius!

101. Pliny, *Epistles* 5.19. Written ca. 100. Not all the wealthy will have cared for the actors in their service so well as Pliny did.

<My freedman Zosimus'> profession . . . is that of comedian, wherein he highly excels. He speaks with great emphasis, judgment, propriety, and a certain gracefulness; but also plays the lyre more skillfully than a comedian needs to do. To this I must add that he reads history, oratory, and poetry. . . . Some years ago he strained himself so much by too vehement an exertion of his voice that he spat blood, upon which account I sent him to Egypt.

102. Pliny, *Epistles* 9.36. Written ca. 100. He describes how someone like Zosimus was useful to a country gentleman.

At supper, if I have only my wife with me or a few friends, some author is read to us, and after supper <there is> a comedy or a lyre player.

103. Lucian, *On Dancing* 27–29. Written mid-2nd c. The satirist is criticizing drama one-sidedly in order to praise pantomime by comparison. In the process, he gives us our best picture of a tragedian of his day. Cf. I 142.

What a repulsive and at the same time frightful spectacle is a man tricked out to disproportionate stature, mounted on high clogs, wearing a mask that reaches above his head with a mouth set in a vast yawn as if he meant to swallow up the spectators. I forbear to speak of pads for the breast and pads for the paunch, detachable fat that he puts on so that the grotesqueness of his height won't be more obvious for his skinniness. Then too inside all this you have the man himself bawling and bending over backward and forward, sometimes even chanting his iambics and—most disgraceful of all—melodically singing the <reports of the> disastrous events and making himself answerable for his voice alone since the poets who lived long ago prescribed everything else. . . . (Lucian then contrasts the pantomime.) The dancer's mask is most beautiful and suited to the drama that forms the theme; its mouth is not wide open as in tragedy and comedy, but closed, for he has many people who do the shouting for him.

104. *Inschriften von Olympia* 237. Honorary decree. Date: 140. Heralds were often also actors and were, since the time of Aristotle, the product of voice training, necessary in the huge theaters.

Publius Aelius Artemas of Laodicea (in Asia Minor), who won the 229th Olympiad in the heralds' competition and the following competitions: Capitolia in Rome, Aktia, Isthmia five times, Pythia, Panathenaia, at Smyrna the common games of Asia, at Pergamum the sacred [?] twice . . . (the list continues) . . . and 250 other competitions with money prizes, under the voice training of Lucius Tyrronius Longus of Ikonium and Laodicea.

Private Troupes

105. Sallust, *Jugurtha* 85.39. Written ca. 40 B.C. and referring to 107 B.C. Cf. Polybius 31.25.4; Apuleius, *Apology* 13.20.

> (Marius speaks:) "They say that I am common and of rude manners because I cannot give an elegant dinner, and because I pay no actor or cook higher wages than I do my overseer."

106. Petronius, *Satyricon* 53.13. Written ca. 60. The satirist makes fun of the rich Trimalchio, who not only buys Greek comedians to do Latin plays but reveals his vulgarity in that he prefers the low Atellan to Menander. The piper should of course not sing.

> "Why," said <Trimalchio>, "I once bought Greek comedians, but I preferred them to do Atellans; and I told my choral piper (*choraules*) to sing in Latin."

107. Pliny, *Epistles* 7.24.4–5. This famous example refers to ca. 100. But we know that the old lady's forebears had also kept mimes.

> <Ummidia Quadratilla> used to keep pantomimes and was much fonder of them than was appropriate to a woman of high rank.

108. *ILS* 5216. Inscribed gravestone. Date: ca. 30 B.C.

> For Ecloga, mime of King Juba (of Mauretania), who lived eighteen years.

109. *ILS* 5205. Inscribed monument. Date: mid-1st c. This stone from Arelate in southern France records a large troupe called Asiaticiani. These were almost certainly the private actors and mimes of the famous and wealthy senator from Vienne, Asiaticus, who was killed by Claudius. One suspects that mimes could be politically useful to such an owner.

> Stage actors of Asiaticus and those who are in the same corporation set this up for themselves.

Aristocrats on Stage

110. Suetonius, *Nero* 4. Written ca. 110, referring to 16–19 B.C. This was one of the first appearances of the upper classes on the stage.

> While holding the office of praetor and consul, L. Domitius Ahenobarbus brought Roman knights and married women onto the stage to act a farce.

111. Suetonius, *Tiberius* 35.2. Written ca. 110, referring to ca. 15. Perhaps the aristocracy had other reasons for wanting to be degraded from their rank.

> The most profligate young men of both orders voluntarily incurred degradation from their rank so as not to be prevented by the decree of the Senate from appearing on the stage and in the arena. All such . . . <Tiberius> punished with exile.

112. Tacitus, *Histories* 2.62.2. Written ca. 115.

> Under Otho (in 69), strict measures were taken to prevent Roman knights from degrading themselves in games or arena. Former emperors had driven knights to such actions by money or more often by force.

113. Inscription recording a decree of the Senate, from Larinum, ed. B. Levick, *JRS* 73 (1983) 98; W.D. Lebek, *ZPE* 81 (1990) 59. Date: 19. We know that the legislation of the year 11 mentioned here was ineffective.

> Whereas M. Silanus and L. Norbanus Balbus the consuls declared that in accordance with the commission given them, they had drawn up a memorandum on senatorial decrees pertaining to [descendants of senators] or to those who, contrary to the dignity of the order to which they belonged, were appearing on the stage or at games[; and young people behaved] as forbidden by the Senate decree that had been passed on that subject in previous years, employing fraudulent evasion [to the detriment of] the majesty of the Senate; [what measures were to be taken in this matter?—The Senate recommends] that it pleased them that no one should bring onto the stage a senator's son, daughter, grandson, granddaughter, great-grandson, great-granddaughter, or any male who [himself or his father or grandfather,] whether paternal [or maternal, or brother] had ever possessed [the right] of sitting on the seats reserved for the knights, or a woman whose husband or father or grandfather on mother's or father's side or their brother has ever had the right to be a spectator on the knights' seats; [no one should enter a gladiatorial agreement with] them by means of a fee [or contract with them to kill wild beasts] or to snatch the plumes of gladiators or lift the staff (? be a gladiatorial umpire) or to take part in any way in a similar subordinate capacity. . . . (The decree quotes an earlier decree of 11:) . . . [In the Senate decree] that was passed on the motion of the consuls Manius Lepidus and T. Statilius Taurus [. . .]. viz., that it should be permissible for no female of less than twenty years of

age and for no male of free birth of less than twenty-five to pledge themselves a gladiator or hire out their services [for arena or stage...] except any of those who had been consigned by the deified Augustus or by Tiberius Caesar Augustus to [their creditor in servitude] etc. (i.e., those who have got themselves so far in debt that their only hope is to gain money on the stage or in the arena)...

Comments on Acting

114. Cicero, *Letters to Friends* 7.1. Cicero describes maliciously the great show at the opening of Pompey's theater in 55 B.C. in a letter to an elderly friend who was not there. Sensational spectacle was already offensive to cultivated people.

> If you ask me, of course the games were magnificent, but they wouldn't have been to your taste; I go by my own feelings. For in the first place those actors had made a comeback on the stage out of respect (for Pompey) who had, I imagined, left it out of <self> respect. Indeed your favorite, our friend Aesopus (a tragic actor), was such a failure that nobody on earth would have regretted his quitting. When he began to swear an oath (in some tragedy), his voice failed him at the crucial point: "If I willingly deceive...." No need to say more; you know what the rest was like. They didn't even have the attractiveness that middling quality games usually have. For any feeling of cheerfulness was extinguished by the spectacle of such magnificence.... For what pleasure can there be in the sight of six hundred mules in the *Clytemnestra* or three thousand craters in the *Trojan Horse* or the various accoutrements of foot and horse in some big battle. All of which excited the admiration of the people.... I don't think you were sorry to miss the Greek and Oscan plays (i.e., comedies and Atellans)...

115. Horace, *Epistles* 2.1.182–207. Written ca. 10 B.C. The poet also laments the decline of taste and the emphasis on tragic spectacle. The satirist Lucilius probably had done the same a hundred years earlier. The point about the volume of noise is important.

> Often even the bold poet is frightened and put to rout, when those who are stronger in number, but weaker in worth and rank, unlearned and stupid, and ready to fight it out if the knights (who had the first fourteen rows) dispute with them, call in the middle of a play for a bear or boxers; in such things the rabble delights. But nowadays all the pleasure even of the knights has passed from

the ear to vain delights of the wandering eye. For four hours or more the curtains are kept down (i.e., open) while troops of horse and files of foot sweep by; then kings are dragged on, once fortune's favorite, now with their hands bound behind them. With hurry and scurry come chariots, carriages, wagons, and ships; and borne in triumph are spoils of ivory, spoils of Corinthian bronze.... For what voices have ever prevailed to drown the din with which our theaters resound? One might think it was the roaring of the Garganian forest or the Tuscan sea; amid such clamor is the entertainment viewed, the works of art and the foreign finery, and when, overlaid with all of this, the actor steps on the stage, there is huge applause.

"Has he said anything yet?"

"Not a word."

"Then what are they applauding?"

"The woolen robe that imitates violets with its Tarentine dye."

116. Cicero, *Orator* 173. Written 46 B.C. Despite the noise of the spectacles, plenty of evidence exists that the public demanded a high standard of acting.

People do in the case of poetry, for the whole audience will hoot at one false quantity (in meter). Not that the masses know anything of feet or understand about rhythm.

117. Quintilian, *Institutes of Oratory* 6.2.35. Date: ca. 100.

I have often seen actors both in tragedy and comedy leave the theater still drowned in tears after concluding the performance of some moving role.

118. Quintilian, *Institutes of Oratory* 2.10.13. Date: ca. 100.

I may cite the practice of some comic actors whose delivery is not exactly that of common speech, since that would be inartistic, but is on the other hand not far removed from the accents of nature, for, if it were, their mimicry would be a failure; what they do therefore is to exalt the simplicity of ordinary speech by a touch of stage direction.

119. Quintilian, *Institutes of Oratory* 11.3.91. Date: ca. 100. The rhetorician takes his examples oddly from the plays of Menander, and not their Latin adaptions. One wonders if these are not school examples.

For even comic actors seem to me to commit a gross offense against the canons of their art, when, if they have in the course of some narrative to quote either the words of an old man, as, e.g., in the *Hydria* prologue, or of a woman, as in the *Georgos,* they utter

them in a tremulous or treble voice, notwithstanding the fact that
they are playing the part of a young man.

120. Quintilian, *Institutes of Oratory* 11.3.11. Written ca. 100 and
referring to actors of the late republic. The orator could never have heard
any of the actors he mentions.

> The slower the delivery, the greater the emotional power. Thus
> Roscius was rapid and Aesopus weighty because the former was a
> comic and the latter a tragic actor. The same rule applies to
> movements. Consequently, on the stage, young men and old soldiers
> and married women all walk sedately while slaves, maids, parasites,
> and fishermen are more lively in their movements.

121. Aulus Gellius 1.5. Written in the 2nd c. about Hortenius who
was consul in 69 B.C. This is interesting evidence that orators used more
restrained gestures than actors.

> Hortenius, quite the most famous orator of his time . . . because he
> dressed with such extreme foppishness . . . and in talking used his
> hands excessively in lively gestures, was attacked with jests and
> taunts . . . for appearing like an actor.

IVB. The Audience

IVBi. The Athenian Audience in the Fifth and Fourth Centuries B.C.

Plato estimated the size of the theater audience in Athens at 30,000 (122), but modern estimates of the capacity of the Theater of Dionysus vary between 15,000 and 20,000. This figure is roughly five to seven percent of the total population of Attica, which for 431 B.C. is estimated at 310,000, including 110,000 slaves and 28,500 metics. Not surprisingly, a number of sources attest fierce competition for seats (136, 137, 152). If Athenians were always the avid theatergoers Herakleides claims (157), then it is so much the more remarkable that we have no record of any attempt to restrict attendance. On the contrary, attendance at the theater was not only considered a right and privilege of Athenian citizenship (see on the *theorikon,* below), but the sources give ample evidence for the participation of all Athenian residents, whether metics (123) or slaves (124, 127, 129, 172), as well as large numbers of foreigners (122–25, 135A, 136, 155).

From 1796 to the present day, several classical scholars have argued for the exclusion of women and children from the festival. In our opinion, the testimony of ancient authors shows clearly that women (and boys) were present in the audience (124, 126–29, 155, 156, 172). The contrary argument rests mainly upon the comic poets' habit of addressing the audience as "gentlemen." This fails to distinguish physical from ideological forms of exclusion. Addresses to "gentlemen" show only that the notional audience was composed of male citizens. Athenian rhetoric was developed in the Assembly and the law courts, where the audience was entirely composed of adult males. When comic characters address the audience as "gentlemen," this is only a social and rhetorical reflex. The fact that the Assembly often met in the theater or that a mock trial (*agon*) usually lies at the heart of an Old Comic plot no doubt did much to reinforce this linguistic habit. Something more can be made of the habit of addressing the crowd as "men of Athens"; this reflects the speaker's desire to appeal to the segment of the audience that was generally deemed capable of formulating or influencing a judgment. The most comprehensive address to a Greek audience is "men and boys": evidence only of the conceptual invisibility of women in the theater, not of their actual exclusion. Possibly the number of women in the audience was disproportionately small, and 130 and 144A are frequently cited to show that "respectable" women normally stayed home, but 129 and 128 contradict this view.

Some important developments affected the composition of the audience in the 5th and 4th c. B.C. The Athenian Dionysia grew in international prestige and popularity until it became a major Greek festival, by the late 5th c. second only to the Olympics. The increasingly international character of the audience at the Dionysia and (to some extent also) the Lenaea (see IIIAib) contributed to the gradual obsolescence of the political satire that dominated Old Comedy from ca. 430 to 410 B.C. The anecdote preserved by Aelian (125), though doubtless fiction, nevertheless illustrates the difficulty foreigners had in appreciating its parochial references. More important in the late 4th c. B.C. was the Macedonian support for the oligarchic faction in Athens, which culminated in the restriction of Athenian citizenship to the wealthier classes in 322 and 317 B.C. (131–33). The new oligarchy dismantled several democratic institutions, among them the *choregia* (IIIAiia) and the festival fund (*theorikon*), through which the lower classes were ensured a place in the theater both as participants and spectators. The bourgeois character of New Comedy amply reflects the values of the dominant constituency in the late 4th-c. B.C. theater (cf. IIIAiic).

The origin of the festival fund is highly controversial. No ancient sources before 343 B.C. refer to the festival fund, but some of these trace the institution back as far as Pericles' democratic reforms before 449 B.C. (134, 135). The *theorikon* was a dole of money given to all Athenian citizens for the purpose of paying the cost of tickets to the theater (134, 136, 137), allegedly to give poorer citizens an equal opportunity to attend the theater. But there is also controversy over the function and nature of the *theorikon*. The ancient sources allege that seats were first sold in order to quell disturbances that erupted in the fierce competition for seats and that the dole was then introduced to allow poor citizens an equal chance of getting theater tickets (134–37). If this was its sole function one might have expected a distribution of tickets rather than the cash dole indicated by the texts, since this would simply have moved the site of disturbances from the theater to the ticket booth. Moreover the real obstruction to accessibility to the theater was limited space, not the high cost of tickets, which seems never to have exceeded two obols (142, cf. 136). It could hardly have been expected that all recipients would use the money to buy tickets, when the number of adult male citizens alone was at least twice the theater's seating capacity. It is clear however that the money was intended for use at the festival since the law restricted the *theorikon* to citizens actually present in Athens at the time of distribution (138). Doubtless the money could be used for general festivities and was not specifically tied to the theater (134 and 137 allow for wider usage). The sum distributed is normally given as either 2 obols or 1 drachma (see 136; 6 obols = 1 drachma). But by the late 4th c. B.C. the amount was 5 drachmas, an increase that cannot be entirely due to inflation (138). Perhaps the most important consequence of the institution of the theoric fund was to give the state a direct interest in stabilizing admission costs, and this was probably more important than the dole itself in guaranteeing universal eligibility, though the theater's size denied universal accessibility.

The practice of leasing the theaters to management corporations probably predates the introduction of the *theorikon,* since the latter seems to presuppose admission charges paid to a third party: the system would make little sense if the state merely collected the cash at one end that it distributed at another. Ulpian's reference to the theater manager (*architekton*) seems to point to this conclusion (137). Possibly the leasing arrangements and the *theorikon* were introduced simultaneously. One ancient account associates the origin of the *theorikon* with the first attempt to sell seats in the theater (136). If this connection is sound, then the references to theater lessees would support an early date for the *theorikon* (139–41). Of great interest is a fragmentary inscription recording the details of a contract for the lease of the theater of Piraeus for a sum of 3,300 drachmas, which we are told is 300 drachmas more than the deme expected from the contract (141). Unfortunately, we do not know how long the lease was for. It appears that the cost of seats was stipulated, doubtless 2 obols. The contract further stipulates that the lessees are to build benches for the audience and give free admission to all those granted *prohedria* (see below). From 330 B.C. (142) frequent reference is made to an official called the architect (*architekton*). His full title is the "architect in charge of sanctuaries." Inscriptions show that he is an elected magistrate by 270 B.C. His appearance seems to indicate direct assumption of the management of the theater by the state, a possible consequence of the construction of a permanent stone auditorium under Lycurgus. Leasing arrangements continued at Piraeus because it was a wooden theater and the auditorium, if not the stage house, had to be reconstructed for each festival (141), but by 307/6 B.C. an inscription attests an *architekton* for the theater at Piraeus. This perhaps reflects the increase in direct state control of the theater under Demetrius of Phaleron (the regent imposed by the Macedonians in 317–307 B.C.) rather than the rebuilding of the Piraeus theater in stone.

Seating arrangements also appear to have been regulated directly by the state. They reflect Athens' most important political and social divisions. The first few rows bordering the orchestra were reserved for various officials, foreign dignitaries, and such public benefactors and culture heroes as victorious generals or athletes (143–50). The privilege, called *prohedria* ("front-seating"—the term is used both of the privilege and the place), could be a perquisite of public office or a special honor conferred by a vote of the Assembly. The marble *prohedria* of the theater of Lycurgus can still be seen in the theater today. At the center of the first row is the highly ornate throne of the priest of Dionysus Eleuthereus with marble seats for other sacerdotal figures on either side. This arrangement doubtless carries on the tradition of the earlier theater where the priest of Dionysus was easily accessible to the actors (143 and I 131). Literary sources attest permanent sections of the theater reserved for the members of the Council (144, 145), young men on military service (*epheboi*, 144B), the archons, the *nomophylakes* (146), and the generals (147–49). Apparently nothing prevented ordinary citizens from occupying seats in the front rows. *Prohedria* only conferred the right to oust other occupants from front-row seats (151), though exercising that right could sometimes be problematic (152). Honorary grants of *prohedria* sometimes involved an escort by state officials (cf. 159).

Behind the *prohedria* the common people sat on wooden benches until Lycurgus (130, 136B, 137, 153, 154, 169, cf. 141). From Roman times three statue bases dedicated by the tribes Erechtheis, Akamantis, and Oineis were found at the foot of the first, sixth, and eighth wedges of the thirteen *kerkides* of the Theater of Dionysus, and these correspond to the traditional order of the ten tribes if the central wedge is given to the Council and ephebes and the outer wedges to noncitizens and perhaps also citizen women (155, 156). This can be taken together with epigraphic evidence for tribal seating at other Greek theaters and Athenian tokens, identified as theater tickets, stamped with tribal names, to argue that an ideal tribal division was maintained at the Theater of Dionysus. This would have been particularly useful to stimulate rivalry for the tribal dithyrambic competition; perhaps also to control excessive rivalry. There is, however, no reason to think that this division was ever strictly maintained or even voluntarily observed for drama, which had no tribal basis, though even here partisanship could run high (III 112).

The sources all depict Athenians as a demanding, unruly audience, and anything but passive in expressing approval or disapproval. The festival atmosphere did not have the polite tone of modern theater audiences. Part of the expense incurred by a comic *choregos* went to the distribution of food and wine to the spectators (126, 161–64). A much underestimated part of the Old Comic poet's art was to keep the audience actively participating in the performance and to cue it continually for outbursts of approval not only to impress the judges (IIIAiib) but also to control its energy and prevent it from overtaking the performance. Tragedy stood in a much more precarious position: the slightest awkwardness could result in outbursts of disapproval, shouting, hissing (or whistling, 166, 168, 171, 172), clucking (166, 168), heel banging (153, 169), and, possibly, food throwing (165). Prolonged disturbances were frequently resolved only when the actors and chorus abandoned the performance, a calamity that befell even the best tragedians of the age (170, 171, cf. III 40). Crowd control appears to have necessitated a special force of theater police, called "rod holders" (*rhabdouchoi*, 88, 172, 173).

Sources

Composition of the Audience

122. Plato, *Symposium* 175e. See III 70A.

123. Aristophanes, *Acharnians* 501–8. See III 69A.

124. Theophrastus, *Characters* 9.5: "The Shameless Man." Written ca. 319 B.C.

> He buys places at the theater for his foreign guests, then does not give them the seats. Instead he brings his sons as well as the pedagogue the next day.

125. Aelian, *Varia Historia* 2.13. Written in the late 2nd and early 3rd c. The passage purports to relate an event that took place during Aristophanes' production of the *Clouds* in 423 B.C.

Since it was the Dionysia, an enormous crowd of Greeks arrived
<in Athens> for the sake of the spectacle. A certain "Socrates" was
being bandied about on the stage and frequently being named and
I wouldn't be surprised if he were actually visible among the
actors—for clearly the mask makers made him as like the real
Socrates as possible. But a murmur arose among the foreigners, for
they had not heard of the man who was being ridiculed, and they
began to inquire who this Socrates was. So when the real Socrates
became aware of this—he was present not by chance, but, knowing
that the comedians would ridicule him, he made a point of sitting
in a good section of the theater—in order to relieve the foreigners
of their perplexity, he stood up and remained visible standing for
the duration of the comedy. So great was Socrates' contempt for
comedy and the Athenians.

126. Aristophanes, *Peace* 962–67. Produced Dionysia, 421 B.C. There
is a mock sacrifice in the play, in preparation for which the slave
distributes "barley groats" (normally thrown at the sacrificial animal
before it is killed). It is likely that these "barley groats" are the fruits
and nuts usually tossed out to the audience (see 161–64 below). This
passage is sometimes cited as proof that women did not attend the
theater. It seems to us to demonstrate the opposite.

> TRYGAIOS: And throw the audience some barley. SLAVE: Done!
> TRYGAIOS: You've already distributed it? SLAVE: Yes, by Hermes.
> There isn't a man in the audience who doesn't have barley (slang
> for penis). TRYGAIOS: But the women didn't get any. SLAVE: The
> men will give it to them tonight.

127. Plato, *Gorgias* 502d. Written ca. 390 B.C. and set in 427 B.C.

> SOCRATES: Or don't you think the poets practice rhetoric in the
> theaters? KALLIAS: I do. SOCRATES: So now we've discovered a
> kind of rhetoric directed at a public composed of children together
> with women and men, slave and free.

128. Plato, *Laws* 658c–d. Written ca. 360–347 B.C.

> ATHENIAN: If the very young children were to judge <the best
> performance> they would choose the magician; . . . if the older chil-
> dren, the comic poet; the educated among the women, the young
> men, and just about the bulk of the crowd would choose tragedy.

129. Plutarch, *Phocion* 19.2–3. See III 98.

130. Aristophanes, *Thesmophoriazusae* 390–97. Produced 411 B.C.
From the *agon;* the "First Woman" complains about Euripides' misogyny.

Where has he not slandered us women, if only there are spectators, tragedies and choruses, calling us adulteresses and man-crazy, wine tipplers, traitresses, chatterboxes, good-for-nothings, the scourge of husbands. As soon as they come home from the wooden bleachers they give us suspicious looks and immediately start searching the house for a hidden lover.

131. Diodorus 18.18.4–5. Written ca. 60–30 B.C. After the sudden death of Alexander in Babylon in 323 B.C., several of the mainland Greek states under the leadership of Athens revolted against the Macedonians. Antipater, viceroy of Macedonia, crushed the rebellion, which came to be known as the "Lamian War," by early 322 B.C. Diodorus describes the terms of peace dictated by Antipater to Athens at the end of the war.

<Antipater> dealt humanely with <the Athenians> and conceded that they retain possession of their city, their property, and everything else, but he altered their constitution from the democracy and commanded them to adopt a system of government based on the assessment of wealth and to reserve citizen rights and the franchise for those owning more than 2,000 drachmas. Those who were assessed below this amount he drove out of the state alleging that they were troublemakers and warmongers. To those who wanted it he gave land for settlement in Thrace. Now these latter numbering more than 12,000 (a generally accepted correction of the manuscripts reading of 22,000) emigrated from their homeland; the former, those who were above the census limit, numbering about 9,000, were set in charge both of the city and its territory and they governed themselves in conformity with the constitution of Solon.

132. Plutarch, *Phocion* 27.5 to 28.7. Written ca. 115 and referring to the aftermath of the Lamian war.

After dialogue with the embassy headed by Phocion, Antipater replied that he would have friendship and alliance with the Athenians, provided they surrender Demosthenes, Hyperides, and their supporters, that they adopt the ancestral (i.e., "Solonian") constitution based on an assessment of wealth, that they receive a garrison at Munychia, and that they pay the cost of the war plus an indemnity. . . . The garrison under the command of Menyllos did no harm to anyone, but of those, numbering more than 12,000, who had been disenfranchised through their poverty, some remained and chose to suffer hardship and disgrace, but the rest, who left Athens because of this and resettled in Thrace, when Antipater provided land and a city, resembled a population reduced by siege.

133. Diodorus 18.74.3. Written ca. 60–30 B.C., referring to 318 B.C. After the death of Antipater in 319 B.C., the regency fell to Polyperchon. A group of Alexander's successors, plotting to carve up the empire, went to war with the regent. Polyperchon, wishing to secure his hold on the Greek cities, promised to overthrow the oligarchies introduced by Antipater. Democratic revolutions subsequently took place in several cities, notably Athens, but the oligarchic constitution was restored when Athens was forced to come to terms by the arrival of Cassander in 318 B.C.

> After several embassies they agreed on a peace on condition that the Athenians retain their city, territory, income, and ships and everything else as friends and allies of Cassander, but that Cassander temporarily hold Munychia until he should complete his war against the kings, and that the government be managed by those with wealth assessed above 10 mnas (1,000 drachmas), and that Cassander appoint a single Athenian of his choice as overseer of the state. Demetrius of Phaleron was chosen.

Theorikon and Entrance Fees

134. Harpocration, s.v. *theorika*. Written probably 2nd c. Philochorus lived from ca. 340 to 261 B.C. *Atthis* covers Athenian history to shortly before his death (see also 135). Philinos was an orator who unsuccessfully opposed Lycurgus' proposal to place statues of Sophocles and Euripides in the theater ca. 335 B.C.. Eubulus was a prominent politician from 355 to 342 B.C. On Hyperides see 138A. The ascription of the creation of the fund to Agyrrhios may be the result of confusion with his institution of Assembly-pay.

> The festival money was public money collected from the city's revenue. Earlier this money was kept for the needs of war and called military money; later it was made available for public activities and doles. Agyrrhios the demagogue first started it. Philochorus says in the third book of the *Atthis*: "the festival money (*theorika*) was first conceived to be the drachma for the spectacle (*thea*), whence it got its name," and so on. Philinos in his speech *Against the Statues of Sophocles and Euripides* says about Eubulus that "it was called 'festival money' because when the Dionysia was nigh Eubulus made a dole for the festival so that all could participate and none of the citizens would be excluded from watching the celebration through poverty." Elsewhere, however, it is otherwise defined as that given out for the spectacle and for the holidays, and this is clear from

Demosthenes' *First Philippic* (351 B.C.). Hyperides makes it clear in the speech *Against Archestratides* that anyone who was abroad did not receive the festival money. There was a magistracy in charge of the festival money, as Aeschines shows in the speech *Against Ktesiphon* (i.e., ch. 24, 330 B.C.).

135. Plutarch, *Pericles* 9. Written ca. 115. Pericles was prominent in Athenian politics from ca. 463 to 429 B.C. Plutarch's source for Pericles' introduction of the *theorikon* was probably Philochorus' *Atthis,* book 3 (see 134), which ended with the year 449 B.C.

> Though Thucydides characterizes Pericles' policies as aristocratic— "in word it was democracy, in fact it was the rule of the foremost man"—many others say that he promoted the interests of the people by distributing colonial lands, setting up the festival fund (*theorika*), and instituting pay for public service.

136A. Lucian, *Timon* 49. Written 2nd c.; the fictional date is the late 5th c. B.C.

> ... then when the lot fell upon him to distribute the festival money to the tribe of Erechtheis and I approached asking for my share, he said he did not recognize me to be a citizen.

136B. Scholion to Lucian, *Timon* 49. This is one of the fuller versions of an account that appears also in Ulpian (137), Libanius (*Hypothesis to Demosthenes' First Olynthiac*), and the Byzantine lexicographers, with slight variations: all other sources set the cost of admission to two obols, although Photius also has a version with one drachma; the *Etymologicum Magnum* (s.v. *theorikon argyrion*) and Photius (s.v. *theorikon kai theorike*) make the initial disturbance the contention for seats between foreigners and citizens, though elsewhere Photius (s.v. *theorika*) follows the opposition between rich and poor. All of these authors draw upon a common source, very likely Philochorus' *Atthis* (see 134, 135).

> In ancient times the Athenian state was devoted to spectacles and in particular to attending the Dionysia since tragedy at that time was at the height of popularity due to the excellence of the playwrights and the competitive zeal of the *choregoi*. Since the theater had not yet been built in stone and people would rush for seats and even occupy places during the night before the performance, there were shoving matches, battles, and beatings. They decided then to sell seats so that each spectator would have his own seat and not cause a disturbance by guarding places or occupying them in advance and so that those who came late would not be deprived of a spot. Then, since the poor were at a disadvantage compared

to the rich, who could buy tickets at high prices and for ready cash, the state began to provide the cost of admission for each citizen from public funds. The dole amounted to a drachma, and it was not permitted to pay more or less than a drachma. In this way the rich gained no advantage from their wealth and the poor were not constrained by their poverty.

137. Ulpian on Demosthenes, *Olynthiacs* 1.1. Written early 3rd c.

When the Athenians got hold of military money they immediately turned it into festival money (*theorika*), so that each citizen received two obols for the festival, one to provide himself with food, the other to have something to give to the theater manager (*architekton*): they did not have a theater built in stone in those days. Then when Demosthenes wished to turn this into military money, as the war against Philip was upon them, he took care not to appear offensive to the Athenians right at the beginning (of his speech), as one who indeed intended to deprive them of their two obols. While at the beginning he puts off saying this clearly, but allows them to suspect it by saying that one must pass judgment on the proper disposition of the monies.... It is important to know that Pericles originally made this public festival money for the following reason. When there were many wishing to get into the theater and there was fierce competition for places both among citizens and foreigners, and then when the rich bought up all the seats, Pericles wanted to please the people and the poor and decreed that the city's income be turned into festival money for all citizens so that they too could have the means to buy seats. When a certain Apollodoros wanted to turn it back into military money, Eubulus, who was influential in government and a demagogue, saw the opportunity of increasing his popularity among the people and passed a law exacting the death penalty for anyone who tried to convert the festival money into military money. Therefore, as often as Demosthenes mentions it in the *Philippics*, he only advises them to release it, but does not speak for the record, which would be dangerous. Nevertheless, he did not persuade them, except perhaps afterward when they were forced to do this by the war.

138A. Hyperides, *Against Demosthenes* 26. Delivered probably early 323 B.C. Both of the following passages are from the prosecution of Demosthenes for taking bribes from Harpalus, whom Alexander put in charge of the Persian treasures of Ecbatana, and who absconded with the money in 324 B.C. The two passages may refer to the same event.

Note that the offense was not collecting the money on someone else's behalf, but collecting money for someone who was not present in Athens.

> Konon of the deme Paiania took the *theorikon* on behalf of his son, though his son was abroad. For five drachmas he owed a fine of a talent (6,000 drachmas), though he pleaded with you.

138B. Dinarchus, *Against Demosthenes* 56. Delivered 323 B.C.

> Again, when someone thought fit to take the five drachmas in the name of someone who was absent <the Council merely> reported him to you.

139. Pollux 7.199 (= Aristophanes, *PCG* F 575). Written 2nd c. Aristophanes' *Phoenician Women* was written sometime between 411 and 388 B.C.

> Just as in the *Phoenician Women* (of Aristophanes), a theater seller (*theatropoles*) is one who contracts to sell a spectacle.

140. Theophrastus, *Characters* 30.6: "The Greedy Man." Written ca. 319 B.C.

> And he goes to the theater with his sons only when the theater-lessees (*theatronai*) give free admission.

141. *IG* II² 1176 with the addition of two new fragments published in 1960 (EM 13447) and 1961/3 (EM 13446). The text is that of *The Athenian Agora*, vol. 19 (Princeton 1991), L. 13. Inscribed decree. Date: ca. 324/3 B.C. The deme of Piraeus makes a contract with a firm of theater managers. The theater in Piraeus probably seated around 5,000. At 2 obols a head, a single day of performance could bring in 1,666 drachmas. This means that roughly two days of capacity audiences are required to cover the cost of the lease, let alone further investments in material and labor. It seems reasonable to assume therefore that the lease was to last for more than one year. The inscription is probably not the lease itself, but the text of the decree ratifying it in the Assembly at Piraeus. Though a copy on stone is mentioned in the inscription, that copy was to be erected in the marketplace of Piraeus, while the fragments of this inscription were found in Athens. More significantly, this inscription does not have the name of the individual who is to keep the actual document. The lessees seem to have paid 300 drachmas more than the contract was worth. Perhaps Theaios persuaded the contractors to pay something extra as a public benefaction and, no doubt, as an advance on the civic honors they are granted at the end of the decree.

> ... the] stage-building [... i]f they want something [with res]pect to the construction. The lessees shall be permitted to use stones and earth from the sanc[tuary] of Dionysus. When the lease expires the

lessees are to re[turn] everything in good repair. I[f they should (alter anything?)] on the stage-building, he (one of the lessees?) may take away a[ll] the ti[le and w]ood when the contract expires [. . . The] lease is to take effect in the archonship of Hegesias (324/3 B.C.). Demesmen will pay cash to enter the theater, except those to whom the demesmen have granted *prohedria*. These are to be register[ed with the l]essees of the theater. The mayor, [the priests? and the he]rald are to ha[ve *prohedria]* and anyone else to whom [the demesman have granted] *prohedria*. But all those who [(two lines are missing here). . . . The lessees] are to fu[rnish] the auditorium with benches [for the demesm]en [according to] local custom. If they do not act in accordance with the agreement concerning the theater, the people of Piraeus will build what is necessary, and the lessees of the theater will bear the expense. The people of Piraeus will choose three men from Piraeus to act as overseers when they hand over the theater. The mayor and the treasurers will have copies of the agreement inscribed on a stone stele and placed in the marketplace of the deme. Beside it will be written the name of the man with whom the lease is deposited. The lessees are Aristophanes, son of Smikythos—600 <drachmas>; Melesias, son of Aristokratos—1,100 <drachmas>; Arethousios, son of Aristoleos, of Pelekes—500 <drachmas>; Oinophon, son of Euphiletos, of Piraeus—1,100 <drachmas>. Kalliades spoke. It was ratified by the people of Piraeus. Since Theaios (probably the negotiator for Piraeus) showed zeal for his fellow demesmen both now and on former occasions and has made the theater earn 300 drachmas more (than expected? than previously contracted?), he should be crowned with a crown of olive branches because of his virtue and justice toward his fellow demesmen. The lessees of the theater should also be crowned, Aristophanes of Piraeus, Melesias of Lamptrai, Oinophon of Piraeus, Arethousios of Pelekes.

142. Demosthenes, *On the Crown* 28.5. Delivered 330 B.C. He speaks of the ambassadors from Phillip, who came to Athens in 346 B.C.; the event is also mentioned below in 159.

But what should I have done? Proposed a bill not to receive in the Assembly men who had come for the express purpose of negotiating with you. Should I have required the theater manager (*architekton*) not to assign them seats? But they would have watched the plays from the two-obol seats, if I had not passed this bill.

Seating Arrangements

143. Aristophanes, *Frogs* 297. Performed Lenaea, 405 B.C. As they enter the underworld, Dionysus is frightened when Xanthias claims to see a monster and runs to take refuge by the priest of Dionysus in the front row of the *theatron.*

> Protect me, priest, so I can be your drinking buddy.

144A. Aristophanes, *Birds* 793–96. Performed Dionysia, 414 B.C. From the *parabasis,* in which the birds argue that the spectators would benefit by joining them, and, in particular, by having wings.

> If any among you happens to be having an affair and were to see the husband of his mistress in the seats for the Council *(bouleu-tikon),* this fellow would again flap his wings and fly off from the audience to return once more after he has had a screw.

144B. Scholion to *Birds* 794 (= *Suda,* s.v. *Bouleutikos).* "Ephebes" are young men beginning their military service. The same information is given by the lexicographers Pollux, Hesychius, and the *Suda,* the only significant variation being that the earlier lexicographers, Pollux and Hesychius, call the areas *bouleutikon* and *ephebikon.*

> "In the seats for the Council": this is the part of the theater reserved for the members of the Council just as the *ephebikos* is reserved for the ephebes.

145. Aristophanes, *Peace* 887–908. Performed Dionysia, 421 B.C. The hero, Trygaios, rescues Peace and her companions, including Festival, who are personified. Trygaios presents Festival (who was probably represented in the play by a female slave or prostitute) to the Councillors sitting in the *bouleutikon.*

> Councillors, presiding officers (of the Council), look at Festival; look at all the good things I'm about to give you (there follows a long passage full of double entendres playing the concept of "festival" against the actress/sex-object representing it). . . . But O presiding officers, take Festival. See how eagerly the presiding officer received her! But he wouldn't have, if he expected no profit by it. Rather I would have found him holding out the pretext of a legal holiday (puns on "holding out his palm" for a bribe).

146. Philochorus, *FGrH* 328 F 64b. Written ca. 261 B.C. The fragment is reconstructed by a comparison of passages with nearly identical wording from the Lexicon Cantabrigiense, Photius, and the *Suda* (cf. 136B). It deals with officials called "guardians of the laws" *(nomophylakes).* Only the passage relating to their reserved seats in the Dionysia is quoted.

... at spectacles they sit in chairs opposite the nine archons.

147A. Aristophanes, *Knights* 573–77. Performed Lenaea, 424 B.C. In the *parabasis* the knights maintain that, unlike modern generals, they expect nothing for their service to the country. Kleainetos is the father of Cleon. Cleon was given the honor of receiving meals in the town hall and of *prohedria* after his victory at Pylos in 425 B.C. For the latter's relationship with Aristophanes, see IIIAiic.

> And none of the generals of earlier days would apply to Kleainetos for free meals (in the Prytaneion), but nowadays if they don't get meals and *prohedria* they say they won't fight.

147B. Aristophanes, *Knights* 702–4.

> CLEON: By the *prohedria* I got from Pylos (I swear) I'll destroy you. SAUSAGE SELLER: Go on! *Prohedria*! I'd love to see you moved from your *prohedria* and sitting in the farthest row.

148. *IG* II^2 500.20–36. A decree of the Council honoring the taxiarchs (elected military officials subordinate to the generals) of 305/4 B.C. for "having completed all their tasks with great care and led the citizens with distinction." Athenian documents granting *prohedria* are frequent after ca. 330 B.C. but not found before, possibly because it is assumed in the etcetera-clauses that end the lists of more important grants in earlier honorary decrees.

> ... the Council... proposes to praise the taxiarchs who held office under the archonship of Euxinippos and to crown them with golden crowns according to custom for their excellence and conscientiousness toward the Athenian people, and that they should have *prohedria* in all the competitions produced by the city and that the theater manager (*architekton*) should assign them permanent seats beside those that are assigned to the generals.

149. Theophrastus, *Characters* 5.7: "The Obsequious Man." Written ca. 319 B.C.

> And whenever there is a spectacle he sits in the theater close to the generals.

150. Aeschines, *Against Ktesiphon* 154. See III 36B.

151. Scholion to *Knights* 573–77. Cf. 147A.

> "Nowadays if they don't get *prohedria*": this is a manner of distinction. It was permitted to those who attained this honor to oust anyone already occupying a seat, no matter who they were, and take their place whether in the Council Chamber, the Assembly, the theaters, or all other gatherings.

152. Demosthenes, *Against Meidias* 178–79. Written in 346 B.C., Demosthenes refers to an event in 362 B.C. The archon eponymous, the king archon, and the polemarch each had the right to choose two assistants, including here, as elsewhere, a relative. The legal procedure described in this passage, *probole,* was restricted to offenses committed at festivals and consisted of a pre-judicial prosecution at the first meeting of the Assembly following the festival (see III 15). It appears that the matter had still to be taken before a regular jury if the proceding was to have any effect.

> There was another person whom you <Athenians> deemed to have committed an offense concerning the Dionysia and you found him guilty, though he was assistant to the archon <eponymous>, his son, because he laid hands upon someone who had occupied a seat and expelled him from the theater.... The prosecutor seemed to you to have an important and fair argument when he said <to the defendant>: "If I took a seat, sir, if I paid no attention to the announcements, as you say, what course of action did the law permit you and the archon himself? To ask the <archon's> attendants (*hyperetai*) to oust me, not to strike me yourself. And if I don't obey even then, to impose a fine, to do anything rather than lay your hands on me. The laws provide many sanctions against the violation of the person <of a citizen>." So he spoke, and you found the defendant guilty. However, the defendant did not go to court, but died before that.

153. Scholion to Aristophanes, *Thesmophoriazusae* 395. See 130.
> Since there were still wooden bleachers in the theater and they sat on wooden benches in the Assembly. Before the theater was built (i.e., in stone), they nailed together benches and watched the entertainment in this way.

154. Cratinus, *PCG* F 360. From an unknown play, probably the *parabasis.*
> Hail, O greatly-laughing-at-stupidities crowd, best of all judges of our wisdom on the days after the festival. Blessed bore you your mother, the noise of the wooden bleachers.

155. Scholion to Aristophanes, *Ecclesiazusae* 22. The scholion refers to a politician mentioned in the *Ecclesiazusae,* performed 392 B.C.
> Phyromachos introduced legislation assigning separate seats to women and men and separating prostitutes from free women.

156. Alexis, *Gynecocracy, PCG* F 42. Performed ca. 350–275 B.C.

You women must watch the festival sitting in the furthest *kerkis* like foreign women.

Behavior

157. Herakleides, *On the Greek Cities* 1.4. This is a travel book written in the mid-3rd c. B.C.

Genuine Athenians are keen (or shrewd) students of the arts and untiring theatergoers. In general, Athens differs from the other cities as much as the other cities differ from the farm in the pleasures and refinements of life.

158. Xenophon, *Oeconomicus* 3.8. Written early 4th c. B.C. and set in the later 5th c. B.C.

(Socrates speaks to Kritoboulos.) As it is, I've known you to get up very early in the morning and walk a very long way to see a comedy and eagerly urge me to go along and see it with you.

159. Aeschines, *Against Ktesiphon* 76. Delivered 330 B.C. and referring to 346 B.C. The same event is referred to in Aeschines' *Embassy* 111.

It remains for me to describe <Demosthenes'> sycophancy. For Demosthenes, men of Athens, though on Council for a year, can never be shown to have invited an embassy to take the front seats (*prohedria*), but only on that occasion (the visit of an embassy from Philip of Macedon) for the first time did he invite an embassy to take front seats, and he put cushions on the seats and spread a purple carpet over them, and at the break of dawn he led the ambassadors into the theater, causing people to hiss at the disgrace.

160. Theophrastus, *Characters* 2.11: "The Toady." Written ca. 319 B.C.

And in the theater, grabbing the cushions from the slave, he himself spreads them out (for his patron).

161. Philochorus, *Atthis* in Athenaeus 11.464. Written ca. 261 B.C.

At the time of the contests of the festivals of Dionysus, the Athenians first, after taking breakfast (or brunch) and drinking wine, walk to the spectacle and watch it with garlands on their heads. Throughout the contest wine is poured out for them and dried fruit and nuts are passed around. They poured out wine when the choruses were entering the theater and then again after the play, when the choruses were exiting. Pherecrates the comic poet (active ca. 440–400 B.C.)

bears witness to this when he says that to his day the audience was never left unfed.

162. Aristotle, *Nicomachean Ethics* 1175b. Written ca. 330 B.C.

And so, when we take great pleasure in any one thing, we cannot really do another, and when we take slight pleasure in some activity, we engage in another; for example, those who eat nuts and dried fruit in the theater munch most when the acting is bad.

163A. Aristophanes, *Wasps* 56–59. Performed Lenaea, 422 B.C.

Expect nothing overambitious from us, not even a joke stolen from Megara. We don't have a brace of slaves to throw nuts from a basket to the audience.

163B. Scholion to Aristophanes, *Wasps* 58.

Because other poets through the frigidity of their poetry mitigated the poverty of the drama by tossing out nuts.

164. Aristophanes, *Plutus* 788–801. Produced 388 B.C. The god of wealth, cured of his blindness, is brought home by the hero and is greeted in front of the house by the hero's wife. She offers to receive him by showering him with dried fruit and nuts, as was customary in welcoming a new bride or a new slave to the household.

WIFE: O dearest of men! Greetings to you and you. Come, as is the custom, I'll shower you with these fruits and nuts as I receive you. WEALTH: Please don't, because the moment I've entered a house, and especially now that I can see, it is not proper that I diminish its contents, but rather that I increase them. WIFE: Then you won't receive the fruits and nuts. WEALTH: Yes, inside by the hearth, as is customary. That way we can avoid bad taste, since it isn't proper for a comic poet to throw figs and nuts out to the audience and then make them laugh at it.

165. Demosthenes, *On the Crown* 262. Delivered 330 B.C. and refer- ring to ca. 370–360 B.C. It is not entirely clear whether we are to imagine Aeschines pilfering fruit and vegetables from the fields or collecting them from the stage after an unsatisfactory performance. The produce is in any case an allusion to the rustic audiences of the rural Dionysia (see III 53).

(to Aeschines.) ... you hired yourself out as a tritagonist to Simykas and Sokrates, the "deep-groaners" as they were called, and collected the figs, grapes, and olives of other people's farms like a fruit seller, earning more from this than from the contests, where your very life was at stake, since there was a truceless and undeclared war between you and the audience, from whom you took so many wounds that anyone unacquainted with such perils you rightly mock as a coward.

166. Demosthenes, *Against Meidias* 226. Date: 346 B.C.

Those of you who were in the audience at the Dionysia hissed and clucked at this man (Meidias) as he entered the theater, and you gave every existing sign of hatred, though you had not yet heard anything about him from me.

167. Theophrastus, *Characters* 11.3: "The Disgusting Man." Written ca. 319 B.C.

In the theater he claps whenever the others stop, and he hisses at those which the rest of the audience watch with pleasure. When the auditorium is silent, he stands up and burps in order to make them turn around and look at him.

168. Harpocration, s.v. *eklozete*. Probably written in the 2nd c.

They called "clucking" a sound made by the mouth that they used for the purpose of driving off stage performers that did not please them.

169. Pollux 4.122. Written 2nd c. See app. A.

170. Aristotle, *Poetics* 1455a21–29 and 1456a10–19. Date: ca. 330 B.C. Carcinus was a prominent tragedian of the 4th c. B.C.; Agathon was an important tragedian of the last two decades of the 5th c. B.C. The flaw in Carcinus' production is unclear: one suggestion is that the central *skene* door was designated a temple door and then made to serve as a tomb without adequate forewarning.

One should try as much as possible to envision the stage action in composing plots and shaping the dialogue. For the author that sees the action most clearly as if in its midst will find the right expression and will be least vulnerable to incongruities. The fault found with Carcinus is evidence of this. He had Amphiaraus come up out of the sanctuary, something that would not trouble a reader, but in performance he was expelled because the audience was annoyed by it. . . . One should remember what I have said frequently and not make a tragedy an epic composition—by epic I mean that which contains many myths—as if one were to write the entire story of the *Iliad*. There (in epic) because of its length each section is of the appropriate size, but in drama the result would be far from what was intended. Evidence of this can be found in the fact that all the poets who wrote tragedies on the entire fall of Troy, and not just a part of it like Euripides, or <the whole myth of> Niobe, and not <just a part of it> like Aeschylus, either were expelled or did badly in the competition, since even Agathon was expelled for this reason alone.

171. Demosthenes, *On the False Embassy* 337. Delivered 343 B.C.

Perhaps it is also necessary to say something about <Aeschines'> voice. It is very loud and I hear that he is proud of it as if overwhelming you with his histrionics. You would seem to me to perpetrate the greatest of all absurdities if, when he performed the saga of Thyestes and the Trojan War badly, you hissed and expelled him from the theater and all but stoned him so that he ended up giving up bit-acting ("playing the tritagonist"), but then when he is no longer on stage, but has made a mess of a thousand things in matters of the greatest public importance, you then pay attention to him because he resonates well.

172. Plato, *Laws* 700c–701a. Written ca. 357–347 B.C. The Athenian interlocutor speaks of the good old days when each kind of music had its own proper form and genres were not mixed. For the musical developments see IVC.

The authorities knew these forms, and knowing them, at the same time judged them. Moreover they punished anyone who did not conform. There was no whistling nor any rude shouting from the crowd, as we have now, nor any applause. Educators believed that one should listen in silence till the music ended, while the punishment of the disciplining rod was reserved for children and pedagogues and for the majority of the crowd. In this the majority of citizens wished to be governed in so orderly a fashion, and not to judge by creating a disturbance. Afterward, however, as time passed, poets who were poetic by nature, but ignorant of the justice and laws of the Muses, started this unmusical perversity by reveling and allowing themselves unduly to be possessed by the pleasure of music. They mixed lamentations with hymns and paians with dithyrambs and imitated the music of pipes with the kithara, mixing everything with everything else. Unintentionally, through musical ignorance they trumped up evidence against music saying that it had no correct standards and that it was most correctly judged by the pleasure of whoever enjoyed it, be he good or bad. By writing such poems and saying such things they imposed musical perversity on the majority and instituted the audacity that made people think themselves capable of passing their own judgment. This then is how the audience, once silent, became vocal, pretending to know what is good music and what not, and instead of aristocracy in music a degenerate theatrocracy came into being. Now if it had even been a democracy only of free men, it would not have been such a terrible thing. As it is, the perverse opinion that everyman is an expert on everything rules over us, and liberty has gone along with it. They have become fearless in the opinion that they are knowledgeable and this license has given birth to shamelessness.

173A. Aristophanes, *Peace* 734–47. Performed Dionysia, 421 B.C. The passage is from the *parabasis,* also called "the anapests," where it is normal for the poet to address the audience through his chorus and praise himself. We hear of "rod holders" whipping a competitor on the racecourse at the Olympic games in 419 B.C. (Thucydides 5.50.4). Note also the reference to the "disciplining rod" in 172. These theater police are distinct from the archon's attendants in 152—one might sooner have expected a reference to the rod holders there.

> The rod holders (*rhabdouchoi*) should beat any comic poet who comes forward during the anapests and praises himself in front of the audience, but if, daughter of Zeus, it is all right to praise someone who has become the best and most famous of all comic poets, then our poet says he is worthy of great praise.

173B. Scholion to Aristophanes, *Peace* 734.

> There were rod holders in the theater who were responsible for keeping order among the audience.

IVBii. Roman Audience and Society

Even from the earliest times until the end of antiquity we find a concern for order in the theater. In Greece there had been reserved seats for not only distinguished magistrates and priests, or groups of magistrates, but also ephebes, the tribal divisions of a state (143–56), and later even singers, tradesmen, and ethnic groups. In the Roman republic (175) there had been reserved places in the public squares for privileged families to watch the shows performed there. In the theatrical games (177) the senators quickly obtained the right to sit at the very front, in what would be in Greece the orchestra, while the knights (180), a census class with a property requirement of four hundred thousand sesterces (181, 182), soon gained the right to sit behind them in the first fourteen rows, which would amount in the theater of Pompey to about two thousand places. The theater then tended physically to become representative of the hierarchy of the state (188) itself. We find that such arrangements were also included in Caesarean municipal ordinances of the towns and colonies (176, 183), it being self-evident that this symbol of hierarchical order should be publicly manifested. But Augustus, and later emperors also, introduced even greater order in the appearance of theater seating by insisting on a dress code (184–186), and apportioning seats to bodies of magistrates (190), priests (187), and professional groups. The theater then could become even more clearly a visual symbol of law and order, and the word *ordo* means a "row of seats" and a "social class," as well as "order" generally. Correct public seating is, for the Romans, of central importance to the state, but we are ill informed about specific seating arrangements (189).

However we have plenty of evidence that the theater could be a disorderly place (198). Actors were booed off (192), plays had to be broken off (199), and noise and shouting were common. Likewise the crowd was easily moved to wild approval or emotion (193–96), waving their clothing and hands (200). This could be exploited by the actors' supporters for their profit, and some of the worst riots are caused by theater factions, who are attested from the 2nd c. B.C. (201), and who must have developed the techniques of rhythmic clapping and shouting (*acclamatio;* 202, 203), which were eventually applied to politics and even the courts (204).

In the Greek world many communities held their political gatherings in the theater (205, IVBi). In Roman areas, for different reasons, performances in the theater—or amphitheater or circus—could allow the people to raise matters of social importance (206, 207). Theater became a touchstone for the mood of the people (209), a substitute for opinion polls and newspapers, and politicians of the Republic could think of the theater as power (208). All the techniques of populist vote seekers could be effectively applied there, and there is no sign of libel laws (210). See further IVBiii.

Sources

Seating and Dress

174. Juvenal, *Satires* 3.171. Written ca. 120. This is one of a number of somewhat idealized pictures of life before the great theaters.

> There are many parts of Italy where no one puts on a toga until dead. Even on days of festival, when a brave show is made in an earth theater, and the well-known *exodium* (probably an Atellan farce) comes again on the stage, when the country infant on its mother's breast shrinks back in fear at the gaping of the pallid masks, you will see the orchestra and people dressed alike, and the worshipful aediles content with white tunics in their high office. In Rome everyone dresses smartly.

175. Cicero, *Philippics* 9.16. Delivered 43 B.C. In the forum, where gladiatorial games had long been held, places had been reserved for distinguished families.

> \<I propose that the Senate decrees\> that a bronze statue on foot be erected to Servius Sulpicius on the rostra (in the forum) and that round that statue there be a space of five feet on all sides reserved for his children and descendants to view the shows and gladiatorial games.

176. *Lex Coloniae Genetivae Juliae, FIRA* 1.28.126–27. This is a part of a set of laws governing the town of Urso in Spain, founded by Caesar. The text is originally from ca. 46 B.C. but has been reedited. The theatrical games and the order of seating are clearly of fundamental importance to the sense of social organization; there is a separate section in the law for the circus games.

> Every *duovir*, aedile, or *praefectus* of the Colony or any other person in the said Colony celebrating dramatic spectacles shall accommodate the colonists of the Colony, resident aliens, guests, and strangers in such a manner as the decurions shall have decreed

and determined in all good faith, not less than fifty decurions being present when the said matter is discussed. Whatsoever shall be so decreed and determined by the decurions shall in accordance with this law be legal and valid. Nor shall the person celebrating the games accommodate the aforesaid nor order the same to be accommodated otherwise or in another manner, nor give nor apportion nor assign places nor order places to be given apportioned or assigned in other manner, nor shall he do anything or order anything to be done whereby the said persons shall sit otherwise or in another manner than in the places given, apportioned, or assigned nor whereby any knowingly and with wrongful intent shall sit in a place reserved for others . . . (there follows the penalty).

Respecting any dramatic spectacles in the Colony, no person shall sit in the orchestra to view the performance, save a magistrate or promagistrate of the Roman people, or a Roman official charged with jurisdiction or one who is or has been a senator of the Roman people, or the sons of such a senator, or a prefect of engineers or the magistrate or promagistrate holding the province of further Spain, or Baetica, or those persons who are or shall be allowed by this law to sit in the place assigned to the decurions. Nor shall any person introduce into the said place nor allow to sit therein any persons other than the aforesaid.

177A. Livy 33.44.5. Written ca. 20 B.C. and referring to 194 B.C. The Roman Senate gets itself the best seats, long before a permanent theater existed.

<The censors> made themselves very popular with the Senate, when at the Roman games they ordered the curule aediles to separate the seats of the senators from the people; for before that, the audience had their seats all mixed.

177B. Livy 34.54.4. This causes controversy.

The curule aediles . . . were the first to give dramatic games at the Megalensia. At the Roman Games of these aediles it was the first time that the Senate was separated from the audience as spectators, and that caused talk, as with any innovation.

178. Dio Cassius 58.4.4. Cf. Suetonius, *Augustus* 43.5. Written ca. 240 and referring to the year 30. The emperors and their favorites maintained special seats in the orchestra. For some events the seats of honor would be in the tribunalia or in a loge at the center front.

. . . they set up bronze statues to <Tiberius and Sejanus> . . . and brought gilded chairs into the theater for both.

179. Cicero, *Letters to Atticus* 2.1.3. Written 60 B.C. Cicero jokingly quotes his enemy Clodius, whose sister was married to a consul, complaining that he was not given sufficient place by him. We see that the consuls—and other officials—also had seats for their wives and relatives too. Note that these were at Rome measured in (Roman) feet, ca. 29 centimeters. The marks in Greek theaters allow ca. 43 centimeters per seat.

> "My sister who has so much room as a consular only gives me one foot."

180. Plutarch, *Cicero* 13. Written ca. 115 and referring to 67 B.C. The knights under the Roscian Law also get their earlier right to good seats formally confirmed, possibly after they had been removed by Sulla, but this was not popular either.

> Marcus (rather, Lucius Roscius!) Otho was the first to separate in point of honor the knights from the rest of the citizens, which he did when he was praetor (this is wrong; he was tribune in 67 B.C., praetor in ca. 63 B.C.), and gave them a particular place for viewing, which they still retain. The people took this as a mark of dishonor to themselves, and when Otho appeared in the theater, they hissed him insultingly while the knights received him with loud applause. The people renewed and increased their hisses, and then the knights their applause. After this they turned on one another with abuse, and disorder reigned in the theater.

181. Cicero, *Philippics* 2.44. Written 44 B.C. But it appears that the Roscian law contained more special provisions, defining who was a knight. Here Cicero is attacking Antony.

> Yet it was typical of your impudence, that you sat in the fourteen rows, when by the Roscian law there was a specific place set aside for the bankrupt knights, though for those who went bankrupt by the fault of fortune not their own.

182. Suetonius, *Augustus* 44.1. Written ca. 110 and referring to ca. 20 B.C. A knight's status was determined, among other things, by his financial assets.

> Since many knights whose property was diminished during the civil wars did not venture to view the games from the fourteen rows through fear of the penalty of the law regarding theaters, <Augustus> declared that no one was liable to its provisions if they themselves or their parents had ever possessed a knight's estate.

183. *Lex Iulia Municipalis, FIRA* 1.13.135ff. This law was operative in Italy from about 46 B.C.

It shall not be lawful for any persons who within a municipality, colony, prefecture, forum, or *conciliabulum* are forbidden by this law to be senators or decurions or *conscripti* (councillors) to stand for or to hold the office of *duovir* or *quattuorvir* or any other magistracy or competence from which he would pass into the said order, nor to sit in the space assigned to senators, decurions, or councillors at the games or gladiatorial contests, nor to be present at a public banquet.

184. Suetonius, *Augustus* 44.1. Written ca. 110. Augustus, in imposing order on the seating everywhere about 20 B.C., was following in part previous legislation.

He put a stop by special regulations to the disorderly and indiscriminate fashion of viewing the games, through exasperation at the insult to a senator to whom no one offered a seat in a crowded house at some well-attended games in Puteoli. In consequence, the Senate decreed that whenever any public show was given anywhere, the first row of seats should be reserved for senators; and at Rome he would not allow the envoys of the free and allied nations to sit in the orchestra, since he was informed that sometimes even freedmen were appointed. He separated the soldiers from the people. He assigned special seats to the married men of the commons, to boys under age their own section, and the adjoining one to their praeceptors; and he decreed that no one with a dark coat (*pullatus*, i.e., lower class) should sit in the middle rows. He would not allow women to view even the gladiators except from the top seats, though it had been the custom for men and women to sit together at such shows. Only the Vestal Virgins were assigned a place in the theater to themselves, opposite the praetor's tribune.

185. Dio Cassius 59.7.8. Written ca. 240 and referring to the innovations of Caligula in 37. The senators had to wear their uncomfortable togas even in the heat of summer.

Any who wished might come without shoes to the games. . . . It was at this time that the senators first began sitting on cushions instead of bare boards, and that they were allowed to wear hats in the theater in the Thessalian fashion, to avoid discomfort from the sun's rays. And at any time that the sun was particularly hot, they used the *Diribitorium,* which was furnished with tiers of benches, instead of the theater.

186. Martial 5.23. Written ca. 90. Domitian had reimposed stricter legislation regarding seating and dress in the theater. The aim here was to be able to identify the knights by their dress.

> You were clad, Bassus, in the color of grass as long as the rules about seating in the theater were not listened to. After the carefulness of Our Serene Censor (Domitian) has ordered them to be renewed, and more authentic knights hearken to Oceanus (the usher), it is only in scarlet- or purple-dyed clothes that you are resplendent.

187. *ILS* 5049. This is one of a number of inscriptions engraved on the seats of the great amphitheater in Rome later called the Colosseum, finished about 80. This one reserves a space for the Arval Brothers, a priestly college of twelve. There are sixteen "finger breadths" in a Roman foot, so that they have a meter each.

> For the Arval Brothers in the first *maenianum* (the lowest section) in the twelfth *cuneus* (the wedge-shaped section, bounded by the aisles) on eight marble steps (as opposed to the wooden seats toward the top); on the first step 5.5 feet (= 1.54 meters), on the eighth 5.5 feet: sum 42.8 feet (12.32 meters).

188. Tacitus, *Annals* 13.54. Written ca. 115 and referring to 56. The theater visibly represented the social order, as we see from this anecdote about visiting German leaders.

> ...they visited the usual places shown to barbarians, and among them the theater of Pompey, where they were to contemplate the size of the population. There, to kill time—they had not sufficient knowledge to be amused by the play—they were putting questions as to the crowd seated in the auditorium, the distinctions between the orders, as to which were the knights, where was the Senate, when they noticed a few men in foreign dress in the senatorial seats.

189. Suetonius, *Caligula* 26.4. Written ca. 110 and referring to ca. 35. We do not know why some seats were free and desirable.

> Being disturbed by a noise made by those occupying the free seats in the circus in the middle of the night, <Caligula> drove them all out with cudgels; in the confusion more than twenty Roman knights were crushed to death, with as many matrons and countless numbers of others. At the plays in the theater, sowing discord between plebs and knights, he gave out the *decimae* (free tickets?) far ahead of time, so that the knights' places would be occupied by the rabble also.

190. Tacitus, *Annals* 16.12.1. Written ca. 115 and referring to 65. There must have been many more reserved places in the theater, of which we know nothing.

...as a prize a place was given them in the theater among the tribunes' agents.

Audience Reaction

191. Cicero, *On Friendship* 40. Written 45 B.C., but referring to the time of the early 2nd c. B.C. Even then it was useful for politicians to have friends in the theater.

> What shouts recently rang through the entire theater during the performance of the new play, written by my guest and friend Marcus Pacuvius, at a scene where, the king being ignorant which of the two was Orestes, Pylades—who wished to be put to death instead of his friend—declared, "I am Orestes," while Orestes continued steadfastly to assert as was the fact, "I am Orestes." The people in the audience rose to their feet and cheered this incident in fiction.

192. Cicero, *For Roscius the Comedian* 30. Delivered ca. 65 B.C.

> The same thing happened recently with the comedian Eros. Driven off the stage, hissed and even insulted, he took refuge as at an altar in the house of Roscius.

193. Cicero, *Stoic Paradoxes* 3.26. Written ca. 50 B.C.

> If an actor makes a movement that is a little out of time with the music or recites a verse that is one syllable too long or short, he is hissed and booed off the stage.

194. Epictetus, *Dissertations* 3.4.4. Written ca. 100 and referring to a comic performance in Epirus in imperial times, in which the governor is strongly partisan.

> "See," says one, "how the procurator of Caesar acts in the theater. He shouts; well, I'll shout too. He jumps up and down. His slaves sit around and shout, whereas I haven't any..."

195. Cicero, *Tusculan Disputations* 1.16.37. Written ca. 45 B.C.

> The crowded concourse of the theater with its contingent of silly women and children is stirred by the sound of such a splendid line as "I am present and come from Acheron."

196. Cicero, *On Laws* 2.39. Written 52 B.C.

> Yet I do observe that audiences that used to be deeply affected by the music of Livius <Andronicus> and Naevius now leap up and twist their necks and roll their eyes in time with our modern tunes.... Ancient Greece used to punish such offenses severely.

197. Ovid, *Fasti* 3.535–36. Written ca. 8. The poet is describing the folk festival of Anna Perenna.

> There they sing whatever they have learned in the theater, and move their hands easily to the words.

198. Plautus, *Poenulus* 1–35 (Prologue). This is apparently a later addition to the play, but presumably illustrates accurately the problems of dealing with the unruly audience in the 2nd c. B.C.

> I have in mind to imitate the Achilles of Aristarchus (a tragedian). From there I shall take my prologue: "Be quiet! Be silent! Pay attention! The general bids you listen!"—the general director, I mean—and sit on your benches cheerfully, you who have come both hungry and full. You who ate were much smarter; you who didn't—get stuffed on our plays (a pun on *fabulis,* "little beans"). For it's pretty stupid for someone who has something to eat all ready for him, to march in here for our sake and sit lunchless. Rise, crier, and get the people to listen. I've been waiting a long time to see if you know your duty; exercise the voice by which you live. For unless you roar, starvation will make off with you and your silence. (The crier announces the play.) There: now sit down, so that you can get double pay. Well done of you to keep my edicts. Let no elegant tart take a seat on the edge of the stage (*proscaenium*); let neither lictor—or his rods—speak at the wrong time, nor the usher (*dissignator*) wander in front of people's faces, or show them their seat while an actor is on stage. Those who have stayed too long at home in idle slumber should now stand and wait patiently, or else refrain from sleeping in. Let no slaves crowd in but leave room here for free men, or else pay cash for manumission; if they cannot, let them go home and avoid a double misfortune of getting welts here and at home too, if they have been slacking off when their masters come home. Let nurses attend to their pretty brats at home, let no one bring them to this play, for the nurses may go dry and the children starve to death or go wailing here for food like so many young goats. Married women are to view this play in silence, laugh in silence, temper here and there their tuneful chirping, take their prattle home, and not be a nuisance to their husbands there as well as here.

199. Terence, *Hecyra* 29ff. (Prologue). This is spoken by the director Lucius Ambivius, after the play had previously twice been broken off. Date: ca. 160 B.C.

I present to you the *Hecyra,* which I have never been allowed to put on in silence, for such was the disaster that overwhelmed it. That disaster will abate through your understanding. When I started on the first presentation, the boasting of the boxers (an alternative entertainment)... the gathering of their supporters, the din, the shouting of the women, caused me to leave the stage before time. With the new play I started to employ my old habit, to continue with the experiment. I put it on again. The first act went well, but when there was a cry that gladiators were going to be put on, the people poured in and created chaos by shouting and struggling for seats. I could not meanwhile keep my ground. But now there is no mob, just peace and quiet. I have time to present the play, and you have the power to join in gracing the theater games.

200. Dio Cassius 62.20.3. Written ca. 240 and referring to the time of Nero (54–68). These are the standard ways of demonstrating approval.

They would wave their hands and shake their togas at every utterance of <Nero's> and lead others to do the same.

Claques

201. Plautus, *Amphitruo* 65–85 (Prologue). This is the first clear mention of paid theater claques at Rome or indeed anywhere else, cf. *Poenulus* 36–39. The prologue, spoken by the god Mercury, is probably later than Plautus himself, ca. 150 B.C. The language is highly legal. Competition seems envisaged.

Let inspectors go from seat to seat through all the auditorium, and if they chance to see claqueurs (*fautores*) assigned, let them seize their togas in the auditorium as a pledge; those who have canvased the palm for the actors or for any *artifex* (i.e., *technites*)—whether through written language or canvased in his own person or through an intermediary—or further, those aediles who have given <the prize> treacherously to anyone—Jupiter has ordered that for them the same law hold good, as if they had canvased a magistracy for themselves or someone else. He said that you lived as victors by valor not by intrigue and treachery. Why should there be any less the same law for the actor than for the chief citizen? One should canvas by valor not by claqueurs. The person who does right always has enough claqueurs, if those can be trusted who have the matter in hand. Jupiter also gave me this instruction, that there be inspectors for the actors. Whoever has organized specific people to applaud him, or acted to prevent another winning approval, the inspectors are to flay his costume and his hide.

202. Ovid, *Art of Love* 1.113. Written ca. 5 and referring to the times of early Rome.

> In the middle of the applause—at that time there was no art of handclapping—...

203. Tacitus, *Annals* 1.16.3. Written ca. 115 and referring to 14. Apparently the technical term for the leader of a theatrical claque was *dux,* or *signifer* ("standard-bearer"), or "head of faction." The term "operations" is a euphemism.

> Percennius...who had once been the leader of theatrical operations, then a common soldier, voluble and skilled in stirring up gatherings with his histrionic training...

204. Pliny, *Epistles* 2.14.4. The orator writing in 100 is talking about lawyers; they began using claques about 60, presumably imitating the organization in the theaters.

> The listeners who follow them are like actors, hired and bought; they get together with the contractor; in the middle of the courthouse their meal tickets are handed out to them openly as in a dining room. They run from one court to another at a like salary. Hence these people are wittily called "Sophocleses" from *sophos* and *kaleisthai* (i.e. Greek "bravo" + "cry"); in Latin the name for them is *laudiceni* ("applaud-dinner").

Theatrical Politics

205. *Acts of the Apostles* 19.29 and 32–34. In ca. 50, Paul in Ephesus caused an uproar among the craftsmen and the people. Note the use of acclamation.

> And the whole city was filled with confusion.... They rushed with one accord into the theater.... Some therefore cried one thing and some another: for the assembly was confused; and the more part knew not wherefore they were come together.... But when they knew that he was a Jew, all with one voice about the space of two hours cried out, "Great is Diana of the Ephesians!"

206. Cicero, *Letters to Atticus* 2.19.3. Written 59 B.C. Cicero reports to his friend on political sentiment in the theater.

> Popular sentiment has been most manifest at the theater and spectacles.... At the Games for Apollo, the tragedian Diphilus attacked poor Pompey (who was not there) quite brutally. "By our misery

you are great." There were a dozen encores. "But that same manhood bitterly / in time to come shall you lament." The whole audience bellowed applause as he spoke that, and likewise with the rest.... When Caesar entered, the applause was nonexistent. He was followed by Curio Junior, who received the sort of ovation that Pompey used to get in the days before freedom fell. Caesar took it badly.... They hate the knights, who stood up to applaud Curio.... They threaten the Roscian Law.

207. Cicero, *For Sestius* 118. Delivered July, 57 B.C. Cicero describes how the theater applauds the senators and consul but abuses Clodius.

For when a Roman comedy (*togata*) *Simulans* (by Afranius) was being performed, the whole company (*caterva*) in a loud chorus chanted theateningly into the face of the accursed wretch: "This, Titus, is the sequel, the end of your vicious life!" He sat lifeless, and the man who used to celebrate his gatherings with the abusiveness of his claqueurs (*cantores*) was booed out by the voice of real *cantores,* (i.e., singing actors).

208. Cicero, *For Sestius* 115. Delivered 56 B.C. This speech of Cicero's expresses a belief in the theater as "the true and incorruptible judgment of the whole people" (119); he even uses the expression *theatrum populusque romanus* (116). Political claques are mentioned for the first time.

Expressions of public opinion at assemblies and at meetings are sometimes the voice of truth, but sometimes falsified and corrupt; at theatrical and gladiatorial shows it is said to be common for some feeble and scanty applause to be started, purchased by the frivolity of some people, and yet, when that happens, it is easy to see how and by whom it is started.

209. Appian, *Civil Wars* 3.24. Written 165 about the scene after the murder of Caesar in 44 B.C.

They showed their feelings clearly while Brutus' games were in progress, lavish as these were. Though a certain number, who had been hired for this purpose, shouted that Brutus and Cassius should be recalled, and the rest of the spectators were thus wrought up to a feeling of pity for them...

210. Cicero, *On the Republic* 4.12. Written 51 B.C. There is some uncertain republican evidence that it was forbidden to libel someone by name on the stage.

On the other hand our Twelve Tables, though they provide the death penalty for only a few crimes, did provide it for any person who sang or composed a song that contained a slander or insult to anyone else. . . . The early Romans did not desire that any living man should either be praised or blamed on the stage.

IVBiii. Emperors and Theater

The late Republic saw nobles bankrupt themselves in giving games for the people, to curry popular favor. Emperors such as Galba and Tiberius who did not show such lavishness could incur a dangerous hostility. There was even a tradition that the emperor would grant wishes expressed by the people in concert; failure to do so incurred their ill will (212). Tiberius allegedly refused to attend the games after the theater crowd "forced" him to do things against his will. It was, if not a duty, at least a wise act, for an emperor to attend games and appear to be enjoying them with his people (213, 214). Claudius could make himself popular by merely standing in for Caligula. An emperor was in a sense an actor in an imperial ceremony, where the theater represented the visual organization of society (IVBii). It was a burden for those emperors who felt that they had better things to do; even Julius Caesar was criticized for doing his correspondence at the games.

The theater—perhaps even more than the Circus or amphitheater, which did not exist in most places and is also often confusingly called "theater" in our sources—was the only place where loss of political liberty under the empire was not complete, for there the mass audience could still express its feelings with some freedom. The theater gained thereby immense political importance, becoming inevitably itself politicized as the place where the imperial authority and people could communicate directly. Despite its size, it was still potentially of an intimacy that enabled the people or even individuals (215) to be heard. The people and performers could express themselves forcefully (216), and could either be tolerated (218) or suppressed (222) or controlled by force (229) or by manipulation of the crowd (231). Direct control of the program for propaganda is rarely attested (224).

We know that the theater claques had become a powerful force by 14 (226), though they had existed even in the Republic (201, 207). Many emperors (227) tried to control them and the disorder frequently associated with them by banishment, passing (largely ineffectual) laws, and keeping enough soldiers at hand; Nero, one of the most popular emperors with the crowd, attempted to do without these (232), but he was forced soon afterward to bring them back (233). Riot in the theater was due primarily to the excesses of the fan clubs, especially the supporters of the pantomime artists, though with possible political and social influences. The only cure was to exile the pantomimes, and this was indeed done by various emperors, though inevitably the performers soon returned and with them their claques, due to popular demand (233, 236).

Claudius tried to reduce the excesses of the claques (240), but his successor Nero himself organized a large claque (five thousand is mentioned) of trained and burly youths with officers from the upper class (230, 231). These so-called Augustiani were intended to drown out protest and sing approval with rhythmic clapping; we are told that the origin of this fashion was in Alexandria. This was an enterprising solution by an emperor who was knowledgeable about theaters and theatrical effects. The so-called *acclamationes*–the chanting of long slogans by groups— whether official (*ovationes*), unofficial, or even spontaneous, are thereafter one of the features of all imperial appearances and of mass gatherings (231, 241), where the Senate itself was required to join in (242).

We know that pantomimes were attached to the horse-racing factions, and that they performed in the Circus (246); we do not know exactly when and why the claques and the factions combined, but they became a serious threat to law and order in the later empire, even after the emperor started to pay for the pantomimes and eventually the claques himself. Some emperors were supported by specific factions, and themselves supported specific pantomimes or charioteers; but on the whole emperors tried sometimes in vain to control the clubs, whose behavior to an unknown extent will often have been sheer hooliganism caused by rivalry; most of their members were youthful (244), highly mobile, and an indispensable part of the theater.

The practice of deliberately applauding at politically sensitive remarks is well known from Cicero, who makes it clear that in the Republic the reaction of the crowd to the remarks of mimes and actors was a barometer of political success (206, 207). As it was sometimes unwise in the empire to be openly political, so the theater itself, like the schools of rhetoric, could only express itself indirectly. Tragedy, with its often sensational depictions of bloody tyrants, could lend itself only too easily to an anti-imperial interpretation (221, 222). Even easier would it be for mimes and pantomimes to make political points, which would be signaled by the audience (218). But by the end of the 3rd c. the crowd could outmaneuver the acclamations of the Senate and knights together. Trajan first published the acclamations, showing that they were more than ever regarded as a popular barometer.

The cultural policies of the later Christian emperors are particularly interesting since they show that the emperor was unwilling to abolish mimes as the church wanted; yet he did try to enforce a ban on Sunday games (249) since, as Augustine complained, the parishioners, if offered a choice, preferred the theater to church. Decrees are even issued against the luxurious dress of these mime actresses, who are clearly the theatrical stars of their time (253), and banning the general display of pictures showing theatrical and pantomime favorites (250). On the one hand, the emperor is dependent on artists for his cultural politics in managing the masses; on the other hand, he cannot permit them to achieve the social status that would make their popularity a political risk.

The number of days in the calendar devoted to theater continued to rise until at least 350, and we must remember that in a sense the last century of the Roman Empire was also the highpoint of "the civilization of the spectacle," if not of drama.

Sources

211. Cicero, *For Sestius* 106. Delivered 56 B.C.
There are three places above all where the will of the people makes itself known; public assemblies, elections, and gatherings for games and gladiators.

212. Fronto, *Principles of History* 20, p. 213.9 van den Hout. Written 165. The orator gives another version of the Juvenalian "bread and circuses" (*panem et circenses*), an idea that probably derives from Alexandria; cf. Josephus, *Jewish Antiquities* 19.30; Dio Chrysostom *Orations* 32.31.
The emperor did not neglect even actors (i.e., pantomimes) and the other performers of the stage, the Circus, or the amphitheater, knowing as he did that the Roman people are held fast by two things above all, the corn dole and the shows; that the success of a government depends on amusements as much as on more serious things. . . . by shows <the whole populace is kept in a good mood.>

213. Suetonius, *Augustus* 45. Written ca. 110 and referring to 27 B.C. to 14. From the beginning, emperors took a very personal interest in the theater.
Augustus himself usually watched the games in the Circus from the upper rooms of the houses <overlooking the Circus> of his friends and freedmen, but sometimes from the imperial couch (*pulvinar*) and even in company with his wife and children. . . . He used to offer special prizes (*corollaria*) and numerous valuable gifts from his own purse at games given by others . . .

214. Suetonius, *Claudius* 21.5. Written ca. 110 and referring to 41–54. The emperor jokes with the people in the theater.

> Claudius would address the audience, and invite and urge them to merriment. . . . For example, when they had called for Palumbus (a gladiator) . . .

215. Tacitus, *Annals* 3.23. Written ca. 115. The place is Pompey's theater, where a real-life drama is enacted in 20.

> The trial was interrupted by games. While they were on, Aemilia Lepida, accompanied by other distinguished ladies, entered the theater and with loud lamentations called on her ancestors, including Pompey himself, whose memorials and statues stood before everyone's eyes. The crowd was sympathetic and tearful, and howled savage curses on Quirinus (the prosecutor) . . .

216. Tacitus, Annals 11.13.1. Written ca. 115 and referring to 47. Claudius had assumed the office of censor, which had been neglected. Pomponius is the last recorded writer for the Roman stage and the leading tragic playwright of his time, being author of an *Atreus*.

> Claudius . . . reprimanded in austere edicts the license shown in theaters by the populace, which had directed insults at the consular P. Pomponius <Secundus>—he composed songs (i.e., tragedy) for the stage—and at several women of rank.

217. Suetonius, *Claudius* 34.2. Written ca. 110 and referring to 41–54. We get an interesting sidelight on what the same Claudius did when the complex stage machinery for his spectacles did not work.

> In addition to the appointed combatants, he would for trivial and hasty reasons, improvise other matches even between the carpenters and men of that class if any *automatum* (a surprise effect?) or *pegma* (stage machine) or anything else of that kind had not functioned well.

218. Suetonius, *Nero* 39.3. Written ca. 110 and referring to ca. 65. The emperor had to put up with very pointed jibes from the stage. Nero is reminded of his murder of his parents.

> An actor of Atellan farces in some song "Hello Mother, Hello Father" made gestures to imitate a drinking and drowning person, that is, hinting at the deaths of Claudius and Agrippina.

219. Suetonius, *Augustus* 53.1. Written ca. 110 and referring to sometime between 27 B.C. and 14. Plays could come to a halt to allow political posturing.

> When the words "O just and gracious Lord" were uttered in a mime at which <Augustus> was a spectator, and all the people

sprang to their feet and applauded as if they were said of him, he at once checked their unseemly flattery.

220. Suetonius, *Augustus* 68.1. Written ca. 110 and referring to some time between 27 B.C. and 14. The audience could also see political references where presumably none was intended.

> One day when there were plays in the theater, all the people took a line as intended to offend him and loudly applauded it, as it was spoken on the stage referring to a castrate priest of Cybele, beating his tambourine: "See you how a catamite controls the globe with his finger."

221. Suetonius, *Domitian* 10.4. Written ca. 110 and referring to 93. But it could be dangerous for an author when an emperor saw political references, even if none were intended.

> He executed the younger Helvidius, alleging that in an *exodium* (a mime) composed for the stage, he had, under the characters of Paris and Oenone, censured Domitian's divorce from his wife.

222. Dio Cassius 58.24.3–4. Written ca. 240 and referring to 34. Cf. Tacitus, *Annals* 6.29.4; Suetonius, *Tiberius* 61.3.

> Mamercus Aemilius Scaurus...was convicted because of a tragedy he had composed and fell a victim to a worse fate than that which he had described. *Atreus* was the name of the drama, and in the manner of Euripides it advised one of the subjects of that monarch to endure the folly of the reigning prince. Tiberius, on learning of it, declared that this had been written with reference to him, claiming that he himself was Atreus because of his bloodthirstiness, and remarking, "I will make him Ajax," he compelled him to commit suicide. The above, however, was not the accusation that was brought against him, but indeed he was charged with adultery.

223. Suetonius, *Vespasian* 19. Written ca. 110 and referring to 69–79. Mimes also took part in the funerals of emperors, and even there politics were not absent.

> At the plays with which Vespasian dedicated the new stage of the theater of Marcellus, he revived the musical entertainments. To Apelles the tragic actor he gave 400,000 sesterces; to Terpnos and Diodorus the lyre players 200,000 each; to several 100,000, while those who received least were paid 40,000, and numerous gold crowns were awarded besides.... At <Vespasian's> funeral, Favor, a leading actor in mimes, wore <Vespasian's> mask, and, according to the usual custom, imitated the words and actions of the deceased during his lifetime. When he asked the procurators in a loud voice

how much his funeral procession would cost and received the reply
"10,000,000 sesterces," he cried out: "Give me 100,000 and fling
me even into the Tiber."

224. Pliny, *Panegyricus* 54.1. Written 100. Pantomimes could be
agents of imperial propaganda, at least in the time of Domitian (81–96).
Trajan (98–117) is praised openly for allegedly stopping the practice,
which may have been more widespread than we are aware.

> And what place remained ignorant of wretched flattery, when the
> praises of emperors even at games and opening events were cele-
> brated, or danced (i.e., in pantomime) and corrupted into every
> kind of low theater by effeminate voices, rhythms, and gestures?
> What was disgraceful was that they were praised at the same time
> in the Senate and on the stage, by actor and consul. You (the
> emperor Trajan), on the other hand, have removed the arts of the
> theater from your worship. Thus serious poetry and the everlasting
> glory of our historic past pay you tribute in place of a moment's
> disgraceful publicity; furthermore the whole theater audience will
> rise to show its respect with all the more unanimity now that the
> stage is to say less of you.

225. Tacitus, *Annals* 1.54. Written ca. 115 and referring to 14. This
is the first report of the troubles caused by the pantomime claques.

> The Augustal Games, now first instituted, were marred by a distur-
> bance due to a competition of pantomimes. Augustus had counte-
> nanced these theatrical exhibitions to please Maecenas, who had
> fallen violently in love with Bathyllos (a famous pantomime).

226A. Tacitus, *Annals* 1.77. Written ca. 115 and referring to 15. The
fan clubs of the pantomimes are now a serious menace.

> The disorderliness of the stage that had become apparent the year
> before now broke out on a more serious scale. Apart from casualties
> among the people, several soldiers and a centurion were killed and
> an officer of the Praetorian Guard wounded in the attempt to repress
> the insults leveled at the magistracy and the dissension of the crowd.
> The riot was discussed at the Senate and proposals mooted that the
> praetors be empowered to use the lash on actors. . . . (Actions taken
> included:) No senator was to enter the houses of the pantomimes.
> If they came out, Roman knights were not to gather round, nor
> were their performances to be followed except in the theater; while
> the praetors were to be authorized to punish with exile any disorder
> among the spectators.

226B. Dio Cassius 57.14.10. Written ca. 240. Dio sheds more light on the affair. The pantomime factions are connected with and protected by wealthy young men.

> <Drusus, Tiberius' son,> was so friendly with the pantomimes that they rioted and did not come to order even under the laws that Tiberius brought in to control them.

227A. Tacitus, *Annals* 4.14.3. Written ca. 115 and referring to 23. Cf. Dio Cassius 57.21.3. Tiberius in particular found the pantomimes and their fans insupportable, but here they seem surprisingly to be connected with a development of the Atellan farce with political overtones. The solution of exile was to be often repeated.

> Tiberius at last brought up the question of the effrontery of the actors (*histriones,* i.e., probably the pantomimes), <saying> that they were frequently the fomenters of sedition against the state and of debauchery in private houses; the old Oscan farce (Atellan), a most trivial pleasure with the crowd, had come to such a level of indecency and influence that it needed the authority of the Senate (i.e., not just praetors) to restrain it. The actors were then banished from Italy.

227B. Suetonius, *Tiberius* 37.2. Written ca. 110.

> When a quarrel in the theater ended in bloodshed, he banished the leaders of the factions (*factiones*) as well as the actors who were the cause of the dissension; and no entreaties of the people could ever induce him to recall them.

228. Dio Cassius 59.2.5. Written ca. 240 and referring to 37.

> Caligula lavished boundless sums upon actors, whose recall (i.e., after their banishment by Tiberius) he at once brought about.

229. Tacitus, *Annals* 6.13. Written ca. 115 and referring to 33.

> In the same year the high price of corn nearly caused riots. In the theater for several days sweeping demands were shouted with a presumption rarely displayed to emperors. Upset, Tiberius reproved the officials and Senate for not using their authority to restrain popular demonstrations.

230. Tacitus, *Histories* 1.72. Written ca. 110 and referring to 69.

> All Rome gathered to the Palace and the squares and, overflowing into the Circus and theaters, where the mob can demonstrate with the greater impunity, raised a seditious clamor. (The people demand—successfully—the death of the hated Tigellinus.)

231A. Suetonius, *Nero* 20.3. Written ca. 110. Nero in 59 founds his own huge claque, which could also function as a bodyguard.

Greatly taken with the rhythmic laudations of some Alexandri-
ans...he summoned more men from Alexandria. Not content with
that, he selected some young men of the order of knights and more
than five thousand sturdy young commoners to be divided into
groups and learn the Alexandrian styles of applause—they called
these *bomboi* ("boomings") and *imbrices* ("rooftiles") and *testae*
("bowls")—and practice them when he sang....the leaders were
paid four hundred thousand sesterces each.

231B. Dio Cassius 62.20.4–5. Written ca. 240.

Nero had got ready a special corps of about five thousand soldiers
called "Augustiani"; these would lead the applause, and all the rest,
however loath, were obliged to shout with them....Especially the
prominent men...joined in all the shouts of the Augustiani, as if
they were delighted. And one might have heard them exclaiming:
"Glorious Caesar! Our Apollo! Our Augustus! The only Pythian!
We swear by you, O Caesar! None surpasses you!"

232. Tacitus, *Annals* 13.24. Written ca. 115 and referring to 55. Nero
tries unsuccessfully to do without soldiers in the theater.

At the end of the year the cohort usually present on guard at the
games was withdrawn, the object being to give a greater appearance
of liberty, to prevent the troops from being corrupted by too close
contact with the license of the theater, and to test whether the
populace would continue its orderly behavior when its custodians
were removed.

233. Tacitus, *Annals* 13.25.3. Written ca. 115 and referring to 56.
Nero's experiment fails.

Even the license of the players and the fans of the actors Nero
converted into something like pitched battles by waiving penalties,
by offering prizes, and by viewing the riots himself, sometimes in
secret, very often openly, until with the populace divided against
itself and still greater commotions threatened, no other cure offered
itself but to expel the actors (pantomimes) from Italy, and to have
the soldiers again take their place in the theater.

234. Tacitus, *Annals* 14.20–21. Written ca. 115 and referring to 60.
In the consulate of Nero—his fourth term—and Cornelius Cossus,
a quinquennial competition on the stage in the style of a Greek
contest was introduced at Rome (the "Neroniana")....The spectacle
in fact passed over without any glaring scandal; and there was no
outbreak, however slight, of popular partisanship, since the pantomime actors, though restored to the stage, were debarred from the

sacred contests. . . . The Greek dress, which in those days most people wore at the festival, became at that date obsolete.

235. Suetonius, *Galba* 13. Written ca. 110 and referring to 69. The public seizes on a chance to express its opinion of the emperor's meanness.

. . . when the actors of an Atellan farce began the familiar lines: "Here comes Onesimus from the farm," all the spectators finished the song in chorus and repeated it several times with appropriate gestures.

236. Suetonius, *Domitian* 7.1. Written ca. 110 and referring to ca. 90. Pantomimes continue to cause trouble.

He forbade the appearance of pantomimes on stage but allowed the practice of their art in private houses.

237. Dio Cassius 68.10.2. Written ca. 240 and referring to 103.

Trajan celebrated a triumph . . . and he brought the dancers of pantomimes back into the theater, being enamored of Pylades, one of their number.

238. Suetonius, *Titus* 7.3. Written ca. 110 and referring to ca. 80. Many emperors had remarkably close relations with performing artists, possibly resulting from their joint activity as "young men."

Some of Titus' favorite boyfriends, though they were such skillful dancers that they later became stage stars, he ceased not only to cherish any longer but even to witness their public performances.

239. Suetonius, *Domitian* 13.1. Written ca. 110 and referring to 81–96. Some emperors enjoyed acclamations.

He delighted to hear the people in the amphitheater shout on his feast day: "To our Lord and his Mistress good luck!"

240. Dio Cassius 60.5.4. Written ca. 240 and referring to ca. 41. Other emperors found it excessive.

Claudius checked the many excessive acclamations accorded him.

241. Dio Cassius 62.20.5. Written ca. 240 and referring to ca. 59. These are acclamations accorded to Nero in public places.

The whole population, the senators themselves most of all, kept shouting in chorus: "Hail Olympic victor! Hail Pythian victor! Augustus! Augustus! For Nero Heracles! For Nero Apollo! The only total victor! The only one in history! Augustus! Augustus! Divine Voice! Blessed are they that hear you!"

242. Dio Cassius 73.20.2. Written ca. 240 and referring to 192. But the senators did not have much choice, as the senator Dio reports, who was obliged to watch the emperor Commodus killing animals in the amphitheater.

We would shout out whatever we were commanded and especially the words continually: "You are Lord! You are first! Of all men most fortunate! You are victor! You will be victor! Forever, Amazonian, you are victor!"

243. Dio Cassius 74.2.3. Written ca. 240 and referring to 194. A year later, after the death of Commodus, the crowds shouted other slogans.

The crowd shouted to those senators who had been particularly afraid of Commodus: "Hooray hooray! You are saved! You are victorious!" All the shouts that they had been in the habit of uttering in a sort of rhythmic way out of obsequiousness to Commodus in the theaters, they then chanted with alterations to make them ridiculous.

244. *Digest* 48.19.28.3. This legal ruling dates to the early 3rd c.

Some, who call themseves commonly "young people," are in certain cities in the habit of participating in the turbulent *acclamationes* of the mob. If they have not committed anything worse and have not been previously warned by the authority, they are sent off with a beating or else the spectacles are forbidden them.

245. Julian, *Letters* 304c. Written mid-3rd c. Cf. *Misopogon* 340A. The emperor Julian, though a pagan, disliked the theater generally.

Let no priest go into the theater, nor make a friend of any actor or charioteer; and let no dancer or mime approach his door. I permit him, should he wish, to attend only the sacred games, in which women (i.e., their wives) are forbidden to participate, not only as competitors but also as spectators. As for the hunts that the city organizes in the theaters, do I have to add that they are forbidden to not only priests but also their children?

246. Cassiodorus, *Variae* 1.32.2. In ca. 538 Cassiodorus edited letters and edicts he had written for the Gothic kings. In 507/8, Theodoric held the city prefects responsible for the troubles caused by pantomime factions, in which senators were insulted and citizens killed.

You must see to it that no cause for uprisings occurs in the spectacles, for your best advertisement is a quiet people. Let the custom of insulting people be restrained, so that liberty not be denied a certain freedom of expression, or manners want discipline.... Indeed, so that no mad contention may again arise, let Helladius (a pantomime) come forward, to provide pleasure to the populace, and gain himself equality of monthly salary with the other pantomimes of the factions. However in the matter that causes frequent uprisings among them, we decree as follows: the fans (*amatores*) of Helladius, whom we instructed to dance in the center (*de medio*) without favoring either side, are to have a free choice to be spectators from wherever they wish.

247. Cassiodorus, Variae 1.27.4. But the abuse of important people by the public continued. In 509 Theodoric decreed that not all the offenses offered to the magistrates by the people in the Circus should be taken seriously.

But lest perhaps the popular talk offend important people, there has to be a distinction in its assumption. Is everyone to be held guilty, who has intemperately committed an offense on some distinguished senator passing by, by cursing when he should have spoken fair? Who asks for solemn manners in the spectacles? Catos are not in the habit of collecting in the Circus. Whatever is said by a joyous people there, is not held to be offensive. The place itself prevents excesses. If their freedom of speech is patiently accepted, it is shown to be an ornament to princes themselves.

248. *Theodosian Code* 15.9.2. A decree of Honorius and Theodosius. Date: 409. Even at this late date, governors could ruin themselves and the taxpayers by putting on games with rich prizes and paid applause, in an effort to win popular approval.

We advise all provincial governors to attend the festivities of the traditional games and take pleasure in winning the approval of the people, but not to exceed in expenditure the disbursement of two *solidi* (gold coins), and not to let the thoughtless craze for claques ruin the power of the magistrates, the wealth of the citizens, the houses of the wealthy, the riches of the affluent, and the strength of the province.

249. *Theodosian Code* 2.8.23. Decree of 399. The emperors repeatedly demand that games not be held on Sundays, with limited success.

On the Lord's day, which is given its name to revere him, neither theater games nor horse contests nor any spectacle, which has been invented to gladden the spirits, is to be celebrated in any city. The birthday of the emperor, however, if it falls on a Sunday, is to be celebrated.

250. *Theodosian Code* 15.7.12. Decree of 394. The emperor is annoyed that pictures and advertisements for leading actors and pantomimes are everywhere.

Wherever in the public porticos or the places in cities, where images of us are wont to be consecrated, a picture shows a pantomime in mean dress or a charioteer with wrinkled pleats or a cheap actor, let it be there removed, nor anywhere after that let it be allowed to advertise dishonorable persons in an honorable place; however, in the entrance to the Circus or the forecourts (*proscaeniis*) of the theater we do not forbid them to be placed.

251. *Theodosian Code* 15.7.12. Decree of 394. Mime actresses are not to dress as nuns, but it is not clear whether this is on or off the stage; probably both.

We further add that mime actresses and those who make a profit from bodily entertainment (i.e., prostitution) are not to use publicly the dress of those virgins who are dedicated to God.

252. *Theodosian Code* 15.7.8. Decree of 381. Cf. *ibid.* 7.4, 7.9, etc. Mime actresses, in particular, tried regularly to escape from their profession, whose practice legally forced them and their children into a low status, and they had to be forced back to the stage with unpleasant threats.

If a woman of the stage demands freedom in the name of religion (i.e., because she is a Christian), with respect to her petition let permission not be denied her. However, if it is later discovered that she has indulged in disgusting embraces, and betrayed the religion that she sought, and practices as an actress in her heart what she has offically abandoned, let her be hauled back to the stage without hope of absolution and remain there until she is an old woman deformed with age; and let her not even then gain absolution, when she cannot be anything but chaste.

253. *Theodosian Code* 15.7.11. Decree of 393. The emperor tries to limit display of wealth by the mime actresses.

No mime actress is to wear gems or silken brocade or cloth of gold. Let her know that she is to abstain also from those clothes, which are called in Greek *alethinocrustae* (true-colored), in which pure crimson dominates mixed with another color. We do not forbid them to wear the same clothes with check patterns or other colors of silk or gold without gems on neck, arms, or belt.

254. Cassiodorus, *Variae* 4.51.3–4. In 507 or 511 Theodoric orders that the prefect of the city is to repair the theater of Pompey now falling into decay, despite the depraved tastes that had been displayed in it.

We believe that the fabric of the theater that is collapsing under its great weight must be reinforced by your plan.... The ancients made a place to contain such a large people, so that they, who seemed to have obtained the sovereignty of the world, could have their own spectacle.

255. *Theodosian Code* 6.4.13. Decree of 361. The emperor decrees who is reponsible for the conduct of the city games.

Out of the three praetors who, being formally designated, are wont to produce a show, three are to devote themselves to the needs of the show and the pleasures of the people, while two are to provide the funds to be available in sufficient amount for the workshops of the said city.

IVC. Music

The music of Greek drama is all but lost, and we depend heavily on the testimony of comic writers, philosophers, and grammarians to gain some impression of this very important aspect of ancient performance: not only was music as integral to ancient drama as it is to modern musicals, but a close causal relation exists between the development of Greek music and the diachronic changes in the form, style, and content of Greek drama. In particular, dramatic evolution in the classical period is characterized by a shift of the musical element from chorus to actor (286–88), and by an overall diminution of musical content from about two-thirds of the performance in the early 5th c. B.C. to mere interludes by the late 4th c. B.C. (IVD). Evidence for later periods is less clear, but Hellenistic drama seems generally to have reinserted the musical element: Plautus' practice of rewriting early Hellenistic comic monologues and dialogues as solos and duets may reflect general trends in performance, not only in Rome but throughout the eastern Mediterranean world in the later 3rd and early 2nd c. B.C. (see 258; V 48, 49).

Virtually all the dramatic texts are written in verse. Of verse rhythms, we can distinguish three species, each with its own proper style of delivery. Iambic trimeters, basically six "feet," each with one short syllable followed by one long syllable, comprise most of the monologues and dialogues in drama, and it is the preferred meter for the exposition of the plot and the presentation of dramatic action. This meter was felt to approximate most closely to the natural rhythms of Greek speech and was delivered in a speaking voice (256–58). Opposed to the iambic trimeter are the so-called lyric meters, which are combinations of complex rhythmic phrases. These lyrics were invariably sung, usually to the accompaniment of pipe music (e.g., 259), though the kithara and other instruments were occasionally used (3A). Song was generally the medium for reflective and highly emotional utterances. Between trimeter and lyric are a number of longer lines of regular meter, principally, iambic tetrameter (with one and a half more feet than trimeter); trochaic tetrameter (like iambic, but reversed, with long preceding short syllables); and anapestic tetrameter (seven and a half feet, each basically composed of two short syllables followed by a long). The evidence suggests that these meters were normally chanted to the music of the pipes (260–64). The chanting or recitative was used for moments of growing excitement (264), or for passages transitional between speech and song, especially those associated with major spatial movements of the chorus: the *parodos,* or entrance of the chorus as it moves from the wing entrance (also called *parodos),* normally to break into song once it has arrived in the orchestra (309B); the *parabasis* in comedy, where the chorus turns and moves toward the spectators chanting anapests followed by alternating song and recitative (263, 308, 311; app. A); the *exodos,* or departure of the chorus, which frequently combines elements of song and elements of recitative, especially in comedy (265). This tripartite division of verse rhythms and corresponding modes of delivery represents only a general norm that invited variation and innovative combination: 266, for example, gives evidence of a form of delivery between song and recitative.

The most important development in ancient music is the gradual emergence of what was called the "New Music" over the course of the 5th c. B.C. (267–80). New Music was largely a symptom of the professionalization of the music industry. In the case of theatrical music the situation is in many ways analogous to the rise of the actors' profession. Though there was never a prize for pipers, as there was for actors, the musicians' contribution to the competition was important enough that pipers became subject to the same regulatory institutions that eventually severed the link between poets and actors (IVAi). Like actors, pipers were originally hired and paid by the poets (267), but by the later 5th c. B.C. the state seems to have assumed the cost, as it did for the actors. We know at any rate that the *choregoi* drew lots for the order of choice for the piper as they did for the actors (III 84). Nevertheless dramatic poets still regularly composed their own music and taught their own choruses (275–77, 303–5, 307) until late in the 4th c. B.C., long after they gave up acting. Yet few could afford to ignore new musical fashions or to leave untapped the resources of the musical virtuosity provided by the newly specialized pipers' and actors' professions. Dramatic music grew increasingly autonomous in various ways, so that already by ca. 467 B.C. Pratinas felt it necessary to assert the primacy of the poetry over the music (268); by ca. 380 B.C. Plato writes of this primacy as a conservative ideal (282); but by Hellenistic times it is a truism that words are subordinate to music, not music to words (278). At the end of the 5th c. B.C. it is not surprising to find Euripides and Agathon experimenting with New Music and adapting tragic form to its requirements (270, 275–80).

The dithyrambic poets Melanippides, Cinesias, Phrynis, Timotheus, and Philoxenus were the first to develop the New Music; dithyramb, a choral song with accompaniment, was more purely musical than drama (267, 269–74, 283). New Music's main characteristics were a large increase in music's range and complexity and a wide-scale rejection of traditional music's conventional constraints. The former is reflected in the critics' frequent metaphors of twisting, turning, wandering, perforations, and anthills (267, 274, 280); the latter by metaphors of looseness, laxness, slackness, softness, and effeminacy, by which the critics added a moral dimension to their assault on New Music, pretending that its innovations were at once both cause and effect of self-indulgence and spiritual degeneracy (269, 271–73, 276, 277, 281–85).

Dionysius shows how New Music ignored the natural tonal accent and the vowel quantities of spoken Greek, thereby liberating itself from the hegemony of the poet's words (278). It is very fortunate that, of some fifty scraps of ancient musical notation, the two oldest, dated 3rd to 2nd c. B.C., are choral odes from Euripides' *Orestes* and *Iphigenia in Aulis*. They show many of the features Dionysius identifies in the *parodos* of *Orestes* and probably preserve Euripides' original scores (279).

In addition, New Music added several new notes and intervals to the traditional scales (267, 271–73, 280, 282), introduced new octave species or "modes" (based on relative sequences of intervals; 267, 280), used modes associated with other kinds of music (172, 280), allowed modulations or movements from one mode to another within a single piece (267, 269, 282, 283, 288), and added to the traditional enharmonic genus (a system of scales) two new genera, the diatonic and the chromatic (276, 280, 284). The old rhythmic patterns of choral song with their more or less regular metrical patterns and strophic responsion (*strophe* corresponding exactly to *antistrophe*) were rejected in favor of a kind of polymetric "free" stanza (268, 287, 288). The metrical innovations are most clearly detectable in *Trojan Women* (415 B.C.) and later plays. Euripides seems to have been particularly free with the music of arias delivered by actors, e.g., *Ion* 112ff. and *Orestes* 1369ff. The complexity of the New Music was a major factor in the diminution of the chorus' role in drama, since it was better suited to delivery by soloists with professional training than by a nonprofessional citizen chorus (286–88).

From the very beginning, critics of the New Music construed these developments as a direct assault on traditional values. The ideological opposition of New Music vs. traditional music came to be aligned with several other loaded ideological oppositions, among them foreign vs. Greek (implicit in the preference for the "Dorian" mode—in *Laches* Plato calls it "the only true Greek mode"), female vs. male (276, 281–85, implicit also in the word translated as "soft," which can mean "effeminate"), self-indulgence vs. self-control (269, 271, 276, 281–85), vulgar vs. noble (267, 281B), and, ultimately, democratic mob vs. oligarchic elite (172, 286). It is important to keep in mind that, however far-fetched, these associations were very real to contemporary reception. One must also keep in mind that almost all of our sources are hostile; most philosophers and theorists were in fact members of the conservative elite. These very sources make it clear that the bulk of the audience embraced the New Music with enthusiasm—no doubt attracted in part by its opposition to conservative values. In any case, New Music's enormous éclat and the degree of partisanship and hostility that it inspired show that the issue had a resonance far beyond mere music.

Sources

Speech, Song, Recitative

256. Aristotle, *Poetics* 1449b24ff. Written ca. 330 B.C.

Tragedy then is an imitation of a serious and complete action, which has duration, in sweetened speech without each species of sweetening in all of its parts. . . . By "sweetened speech" I mean that which has rhythm and music; by "without each species of sweetening" I mean that some parts are delivered with meter alone and again that others are delivered with song.

257. Aristotle, *Rhetoric* 1408b33ff. Written ca. 330 B.C. Compare Aristotle's statements in II 11.

Iambic rhythm is the very speech of the masses, which is why, of all meters, men in conversation (spontaneously) utter iambics.

258. Lucian, *On Dance* 27. See 103. Lucian speaks of actors chanting iambic trimeters and singing messenger speeches.

259. Aristophanes, *Ecclesiazusae* 890ff. Produced ca. 392 B.C.

OLD WOMAN: . . . But you, you darling little piper, grab your pipes and pipe me a tune worthy of me and yourself. (She begins to sing a duet with the YOUNG WOMAN.)

260. Pseudo-Plutarch, *On Music* 1140f–41a. The iambics mentioned here are probably tetrameters and iambic metra in polymetric songs.

Archilochus (lyric poet of late 7th c. B.C.) invented the rhythm of the iambic trimeter and the combination of rhythms of different species and recitative (*parakataloge*) along 'with its instrumental accompaniment. . . . Moreover, they say Archilochus demonstrated how some iambics could be spoken to musical accompaniment and others sung, and that the tragic poets later took over this practice.

261. Xenophon, *Symposium* 6.3. Written ca. 390 B.C. with a dramatic date of ca. 422 B.C. Nikostratos was a tragic actor prominent in the late 5th and early 4th c. B.C. (see 13; I 30).

(At a party at Callias' house, Socrates and Hermogenes continue their conversation when the piper is asked to provide entertainment.) And Socrates said, "Callias, can you give some help to a man who is being defeated in argument?" "I can," he said, "but while the piper pipes, we should be completely quiet." Hermogenes said, "If you like, I can converse with you to pipe music, just like Nikostratos the actor chanted (*katelegen*) tetrameters to the pipes."

262. [Aristotle], *Problems* 19.6. Date: Hellenistic.

Why is recitative (*parakataloge*) <inserted?> in the songs tragic? Is it because of the contrast involved? Contrast is emotive in situations of great misfortune or grief; regularity is less conducive to lamentation.

263A. Aristophanes, *Birds* 665–84. Produced at the Dionysia, 414 B.C. In mythology, Prokne was turned into a nightingale and her husband Tereus into a hoopoe. In *Birds* she is made to appear just before the chorus performs the *parabasis* in anapestic tetrameters. It is clear from the jokes made after her appearance that Prokne is represented by the piper in his ordinary costume, which included the halter (*phorbeia*) that held the two pipes, here likened to a bird's beak; see e.g., I 125. The joke is further reinforced by reference to the gold thread on the piper's robes as a maiden's "gold" (elsewhere used of female genitals; e.g., III 26). The piper has to come forward here to accompany the *parabasis* and Aristophanes metatheatrically motivates this action and draws attention to this conventionally "invisible" presence.

HOOPOE: Prokne come out and show yourself to our guests.
PISTHETAIROS: Great Zeus, how beautiful the birdie is! How

delicate! How white! EUELPIDES: You know what, I would happily part her thighs! PISTHETAIROS: What gold she has, like a maiden! EUELPIDES: I think I would even kiss her. PISTHETAIROS: But, poor friend, she has a beak made of roasting spits. EUELPIDES: You just have to peel off the wrap from her head, as from an egg, and then kiss her. HOOPOE: Let's go! PISTHETAIROS: You lead us and good luck to us! (The actors leave the theater. The birds sing a few lyric lines before the anapestic tetrameters of the *parabasis*.) CHORUS (addressing "Prokne"): My dear one, my tawny one! O dearest of all birds, companion of my hymns, sister nightingale! You've come! You've come! I've laid eyes upon you bringing me your sweet note. But O you who play the lovely-voiced pipe with sounds of spring, begin our anapests!

263B. Scholion to Aristophanes, *Birds* 682.

They frequently speak the *parabases* to the accompaniment of pipes.

264. Menander, *Dyskolos* 880. Produced Lenaea, 316 B.C. The lines follow a stage direction (*parepigraphe*, see I 49): "the piper pipes," and the meter changes from iambic trimeter to iambic tetrameter.

GETAS: Hey you wretch, why are you playing pipes at me? I don't have time for you yet. They've sent me here to the sick man. Stop!

265A. Aristophanes, *Wasps* 581f. Produced Lenaea, 422 B.C. Philokleon lists the perks enjoyed by jurors.

And if a piper should win his case, in payment for it he pipes for the jurors as they leave <the court> wearing his halter (*phorbeia*).

265B. Scholion to Aristophanes, *Wasps* 582.

It was the practice in the *exodoi* for the piper to go in advance of the members of the chorus of tragedy, so as to lead the procession while playing the pipes.

266. Michael Psellos?, *On Tragedy* 61–66. The manuscript is dated ca. 1300 but contains information derived from Hellenistic authors.

There are some other things classified along with tragic music and meter, such as . . . *anaboema* (literally, "shouting out") . . . *anaboema* is very nearly like singing but something between song and recitative (*kataloge*).

Old Music and New Music

267. Pseudo-Plutarch, *On Music* 1141c–42c. The passage from Pherecrates puns continuously on terms that have both a musical and a sexual meaning. Needless to say, the translation cannot do it justice.

By adapting his rhythms to the tempo of the dithyramb and by employing a greater number and range of notes in imitation of the pipe's many tones, Lasus of Hermione (late 6th to early 5th c. B.C.) revolutionized traditional music. Similarly, the later composer Melanippides (ca. 480 to ca. 415 B.C.) did not stick with the music that preceded him, nor did Philoxenus (ca. 435 to ca. 380 B.C.), nor Timotheus (ca. 450 to ca. 360 B.C.). The latter divided the lyre, which had seven notes as far back as the time of Terpander of Antissa (mid-7th c. B.C.), into a larger number of notes. Even pipe playing went over from simpler to more intricate music. In antiquity, up to the time of Melanippides the dithyrambic poet, it happened that pipers received their wages from the poets, since poetry took the leading role, and the pipers were subordinate to the poet/ directors (*didaskaloi*). Later, even this custom perished, as attested by Pherecrates the comic poet (active ca. 440 to late 5th B.C.), who brings Music on stage in the form of a woman, with her entire body disfigured. He has Justice ask her the cause of her injury and Poetry (i.e., Music) says (*PCG F 155*):

> MUSIC: I am not unwilling to tell you for your indignation will find comfort in hearing, mine in telling. Melanippides was the start of my injuries. He first grabbed me, pulled me down, and loosened me up with his dozen (hyperbole for eleven) strings. But nevertheless the man [would have been satisfactory] compared to what I suffer now. And Cinesias (ca. 450 to ca. 390 B.C.), that damned Athenian, by making extramodal twists (modulations from mode to mode) in my shifts (*strophai,* a pun on "strophes" and *strophoi?* = "breast band") so ruined me that the left side of dithyrambic poetry seems right, just as in shields (in pyrrhic dances with shields? in the reflections on polished shields?). Nevertheless I could have put up with this man. And Phrynis banged his own whirler (*strobilos,* the musical meaning is disputed) into me and completely ravished me, bending and turning me in five modes with his dozen strings. But even this man might have been satisfactory; though he wronged me, he made up afterward. But Timotheus, my friend, dug me under and ground me down most disgracefully. JUSTICE: Who is this Timotheus? MUSIC: A redheaded Milesian. He did me a lot of damage. He outdid all the others I mentioned, bringing winding paths of anthills. And if he met me somewhere walking alone (with-

out words or dance), he stripped me and undid me with his dozen strings.

And Aristophanes the comic poet mentions Philoxenus and says that he brought lyrics [...] to the dithyrambic choruses (the text is corrupt). And Music says this (about Philoxenus):

> MUSIC: [...] extramodal and impious overshooting and trills, he filled me entirely with caterpillars (*kampai,* also "twists" and the musical term for "modulations") like a cabbage.

And many other comic writers pointed out the outlandishness of those who chopped music up into little pieces afterward. Aristoxenus (fr. 76 Wehrli) made it clear that proper mastery or misuse (of music) comes from training and instruction. He says that of his own contemporaries (4th c. B.C.), Telesias of Thebes happened to be trained in the best music while young and to study the compositions of famous composers and in particular those of Pindar, Dionysius of Thebes, Lampros, Pratinas, and all the other lyric poets who were good composers of melodies. He learned to play the pipes well and made satisfactory progress in the other areas of music generally. When he was already past his prime he was so completely hoodwinked by the elaborate music of the theater that he began to despise the noble models on which he had been trained and to devote close study to the works of Philoxenus and Timotheus, with a preference for their most elaborate and innovative compositions. Eager to attempt both styles in composing music, that of Pindar and that of Philoxenus, he was unable to gain proper mastery in the style of Philoxenus and the reason for this was his excellent training from childhood.

268. Athenaeus 617b. Written ca. 200 and referring to ca. 500–467 B.C. Pratinas' *hyporcheme* probably comes from a satyrplay.

When professional pipers and choreuts began to take control of the orchestras, Pratinas of Phlious was annoyed by the fact that the pipers did not play to accompany the choruses in the traditional manner, but that the choruses sang to accompany the pipers. Pratinas reveals his anger for those who did this in the following *hyporcheme* (*TrGF* 4 F 3): "What's this ruckus? What dances are these? What outrage has come to the much-clattering altar of Dionysus? Dionysus is mine, mine; it's for me to sing, for me to raise a clatter, as I speed over the mountains with the nymphs, like a swan leading a motley song! The Muse made song queen; let the pipes dance in her train! The pipe is a servant! Let it be content to lead only the revel (*komos*) and door-bashing fistfights of drunken young men! Hit the speckled-toad-breathed bastard! Burn his spit-wasting reed, the deep-voiced chatterbox, the tune-spoiling rhythm-wrecker, [peasant-slave] wrought by a hole-punch! Here! Look at me, my ivy-haired Lord Dithyrambtriumph (i.e., Dionysus), these are hand and foot tosses for you! Listen to my Dorian dance-song!"

269. Aristophanes, *Clouds* 966–72. Produced Dionysia, 423 B.C. The Greater Argument speaks of musical education in the good old days.

Then <the traditional education> taught boys to sit and memorize songs without pressing their thighs together . . . intoning in the mode that their fathers passed down to them, and if any one of them played the fool or tried some modulation like the modern poets, those hard-modulated modulations à la Phrynis, he was soundly thrashed for annihilating the Muses.

270. Satyrus, *Life of Euripides, POxy* 1176, fr. 39, col. 22. Written 3rd or early 2nd c. B.C. and referring to 412–408 B.C. Plutarch also repeats the anecdote.

[They say that] when Timotheus [was hissed?] by the Greeks because of his musical innovation and was in such deep despair that he decided to lay hands upon himself (i.e., commit suicide), Euripides alone ridiculed the audience in turn and, perceiving the greatness of Timotheus' art, he consoled him with the most encouraging words he could find, and in particular he collaborated with Timotheus in writing the proemium of the *Persians* and, upon winning, Timotheus [immediately] ceased to be despised.

271. *Suda*, s.v. *Timotheus*. Written ca. 1000.

Milesian lyric poet who added the tenth and eleventh string and turned ancient music toward the softer (*malakoteron*).

272. Nicomachus of Gerasa, *Manual of Harmony*, p. 274.5 (Jan). Written ca. 100.

Timotheus of Miletus <added> the eleventh <string> and afterward others <did so>. Then the number of strings was brought up to eighteen by them. Just as Pherecrates the comic poet, in the play entitled *Cheiron* (267), appears to fault them for their self-indulgence with respect to melodies.

273. Pseudo-Plutarch, *On Music* 1135c.

Krexos, Timotheus, and Philoxenus and the poets of that generation, became more vulgar and innovative, pursuing what is now called the "popular" and "thematic" (i.e., in the style of the cash-prize contests; see IIIB). The restricted number of notes, the simplicity, and the solemnity of music has come to be altogether old-fashioned.

274. *Suda,* s.v. *Philoxenus.* Written ca. 1000.

He was called "Ant."

275. Aristophanes, *Thesmophoriazusae* 99f. Produced 411 B.C. Euripides and his kinsman stand outside the house of Agathon. As Agathon is about to appear singing on the *ekkyklema* (see 78A), the piper plays a prelude. This is one of Aristophanes' parodies of the New Music (cf. esp. *Frogs* 1309–64).

> EURIPIDES: Be quiet! He's getting ready to sing. KINSMAN: The winding galleries of an ant! Or what's that twittering?

276. Plutarch, *Convivial Questions* 645d–e. Written ca. 115.

> The party was in Athens. Erato the music theorist had made sacrifice to the Muses and was feasting several guests. After dinner, garlands of all sorts were brought around and Ammonios mocked us for tying roses around our heads rather than laurel leaves, because garlands of flowers are girlish and generally better suited to maidens and women at play than the company of philosophers and men of culture: "I am especially surprised at Erato here, who expresses revulsion at the use of the chromatic genus and condemns the noble Agathon, who, he says, first inserted the chromatic as a new ingredient in tragedy, and look how he himself has woven bright flowery colors into our dinner party . . ."

277. *Suda,* s.v. *Agathoneion aulesis.* "Agathonian pipe music" is cited as a proverbial expression. Written ca. 1000.

> "Agathonian pipe music": music that is soft and loose.

278. Dionysius of Halicarnassus, *On the Arrangement of Words* 11. Written last quarter of the 1st c. B.C. At times Dionysius appears to imply three pitches, but there were only two, a raised pitch for acute syllables (or half-syllables in circumflexed long vowels) and the regular pitch of all other syllables. Dionysius illustrates his claims about the divorce of musical tones from word pitch with a passage from the *parodos* of Euripides' *Orestes,* an odd choice since the passage is part of a strophic pair and the music of strophic pairs does not, as a rule, respect word accents (this would make versification far more complex).

> The melody of spoken <Greek> is measured by a single interval that is very nearly that termed a "fifth." And it does not rise more than three tones and a semitone to the acute, nor fall more than this interval to the grave. The whole utterance of a single word is not spoken at the same pitch, but part is set at the acute, or part

at the grave, or part at both. Of the words that have both pitches, some have the grave fused with the acute on a single syllable, which we call "circumflexed," others have the different pitches on separate syllables and each retains its own quality. In bisyllabic words there is no pitch intermediate between grave and acute; in polysyllabic words of whatever length, the syllable that has the acute is but one among the many remaining grave syllables. Instrumental and vocal music employs a greater number of intervals, not only fifths, but starting with the octave it employs fifths, fourths, [thirds], tones, semitones, and some think that even the quarter-tone is used perceptibly. <Music> considers it proper to subordinate the words to the tune and not the tune to the words. There are many examples to illustrate this claim, but none so good as the lyrics of Euripides that he has Electra sing in the *Orestes* to the chorus (140ff.; the manuscripts give the first part of this, 140f., to the chorus): "Hush! Hush! Lighten your boot tread! Go away over there! Keep away from the bed!" In these verses, *"síga síga leukón"* are sung to the same note, although each of the three words has a grave and an acute pitch. Moreover, the third syllable of *arbýles* is sung to the same note as the second, though it is impossible for a single word to have two acute accents. Furthermore, the first syllable of *títhete* is sung to a lower note and the two following syllables share the same high note. Still further, the circumflex of *ktypeîte* disappears, since both syllables are sung at the same pitch. Finally, *apopróbate* does not receive an acute accent on its middle syllable, but the pitch of the third syllable has been transferred to the fourth. The same thing happens with regard to the rhythm. Prose diction does not violate or interchange the quantities of any noun or verb but keeps syllables long or short just as it finds them to be by nature; but musical rhythm changes them by shortening or lengthening them, till they are fequently converted into their opposites, for it does not regulate time in accordance with the quantity of the syllables but regulates the quantity of the syllables in accordance with the time of the music.

279A. Transcription of the music from Euripides, *Orestes* 338–44 (first *stasimon*), after M.L. West, *Ancient Greek Music* (Oxford 1992) 284. See Plate 21A. The music was found on a papyrus written in the 3rd or 2nd c. B.C. (*PWien* G 2315). The *Orestes* was produced at the Dionysia, 408 B.C. The score reveals the same kind of musical violation of natural rhythm that Dionysius found in the *parodos* of the same play:

e.g., in the final bar the Greek word *en* has two notes given to its initial syllable and hence is written *een* in the papyrus: we find a similar doubling of syllables in the Aristophanic parody of Euripides' music in *Frogs* 1301ff. and also in our manuscripts of the first *stasimon* of Euripides' *Electra,* in both cases notably on the word for "winding," a good example of the imitative expressionism typical of the New Music. On the whole, however, the music seems to respect the linguistic norms and does not reflect the kind of wild abandon projected by the conservative theorists. The notes in brackets are written for the pipes. The divergence of the instrumental from the vocal line (heterophony) also appears to be a feature of the New Music. The piece appears to be written in the enharmonic genus and the Dorian or Phrygian mode.

279B. Transcription of the music from Euripides, *Iphigenia in Aulis* 784–92, after M.L. West, *Ancient Greek Music* (Oxford 1992) 286. See Plate 21B. The music was found on a papyrus written in the 3rd c. B.C. The play was produced in 405 B.C., a year after Euripides' death, by his son, Euripides the Younger. The fragment is from the second *stasimon,* but is not strophic. The score reveals several incongruities between word pitch and musical tone. The genus is enharmonic and the mode probably Mixolydian.

280. Michael Psellos?, *On Tragedy,* Browning 5.39. The treatise uses the terminology of the Aristoxenian system, in which octave species or modes (based on a relative internal sequence of intervals) were played in different absolute pitches or keys (*tonoi*). Systems of variations in the octaves were called genera. In some writers, as here, *tonoi* and modes (*harmoniai*) are equated.

> Old tragic music employs the unmixed enharmonic genus and a genus formed by a mixture of the enharmonic and diatonic genera, but none of the tragedians appears to have made use of the chromatic genus until Euripides. The character of this genus is soft. Of the modes (*tonoi*) ancient tragedy mainly uses the Dorian and Mixolydian, the former because it is suited to solemnity, the Mixolydian because it is conducive to mourning. It also used the so-called free (or loose) modes (*harmoniai*), the Ionian and the free Lydian. Sophocles was the first to take up the Phrygian and the Lydian. Old tragedy also used the Phrygian in more of a dithyrambic style. The Hypophrygian and Hypodorian are rare in old tragedy as ... they are suited to dithyramb. Agathon first introduced the Hypodorian and the Hypophrygian mode (*tonos*) to tragedy. The Lydian is more suited to the style of singers to the kithara. The ancients made use of small scale

systems; Euripides first used a large range of notes. This style of
music was called "perforated" by the ancient musicians. And, generally
speaking, Euripides uses many more genera and has much more
variety than his predecessors.

The Ideology of Modes and Genera

281A. Damon. Philodemus, *On Music* 1.13 (Kemke). Philodemus, an
Epicurean philosopher of ca. 110–35 B.C., reports on Damon's musical
theories, developed in Athens sometime in the third quarter of the 5th
c. B.C. Damon was one of the most celebrated intellects of his day. He
was tutor, close personal friend, and adviser to Pericles. Damon developed
the theory that music has a direct ethical effect upon its listeners and
that these effects are positive or negative in different varieties of music.
Some of his theories were published in a speech to the court of the
Areopagus, where he warned that the New Music would lead to moral
degeneracy and insurrection and advocated that it be banned. Damon's
political influence was sufficiently threatening to merit ostracism sometime
from 450 to 440 B.C. but he was again active in Athens until the 420s B.C.
    When someone inquired whether music led to all virtues or <only>
    some, Diogenes of Seleucia (cf. 285) says that Damon the music
    theorist thought that it led to just about all and that he said that
    a boy singing or playing the kithara ought to reveal not only
    manliness and self-control but also justice.
281B. Athenaeus 628c. Written ca. 200.
    Damon of Athens and his followers do not put it badly when they
    say that songs and dances necessarily come into being as a result
    of some motion of the soul and that free and noble souls produce
    songs and dances of the same quality, and souls of the opposite
    character produce songs and dances of the opposite quality (or "free
    and noble songs produce souls of the same quality," etc.).
281C. Aristides Quintilianus 2.14. Written possibly 3rd c. Damon
attributed ethical qualities to individual notes and seems to have characterized them as male or female.
    <The character of> the modal scales (*harmoniai*) resembles either
    their commonest intervals or the notes that serve as their upper and
    lower limits, and <the character of> these notes resembles the
    movements and emotions of the soul. Damon and his followers
    have demonstrated that the notes of a continuous melody, through
    their resemblance <to movements of the soul>, both instill character-

istics previously absent in children and even in older people, and draw out characteristics previously latent. At any rate, in the scales handed down by him, one can see that, of the moveable notes, sometimes the female and sometimes the male predominate or are used less or omitted altogether. It is clear that the utility of a mode is in accordance with the character of each soul.

281D. Plato, *Republic* 424c. Written ca. 380–370 B.C.; set in ca. 410 B.C. Socrates speaks.

One must beware of changing to a new form of music, since this puts at risk the entire <social structure>. For the forms of music are never disturbed without unsettling the very constitution of the state. So says Damon and I believe him.

282. Plato, *Republic* 398d–99d. Written ca. 380–370 B.C.; set in ca. 410 B.C. In his writings, Plato makes several complementary references to Damon. Plato is said to have been taught music by Damon's student Drakon. Damon's influence is palpable in this discussion, by Socrates and Glaucon, of music censorship in the model state. Cf. 172.

"Insofar as <a song> is words, it certainly does not differ from unsung words as regards being said in the same forms and manner as we prescribed just now?"—"True," he (Glaucon) said.—"And the music (*harmonia*) and rhythm are to follow the words?"—"Of course."—"But then we said we had no need for dirges and lamentations among our words."—"Certainly not."—"What are the dirgelike modes (*harmoniai*)? Tell me, since you are musical."— "Mixolydian," he said, "and Tense Lydian and suchlike."—"Then are these," said I, "to be excluded? They are useless even to women who are to be respectable, let alone to men."—"Right."—"And again drunkenness, softness, and idleness are most unsuited to our guardians (the governing class of the model state)."—"Certainly."— "So which are the soft and convivial modes?"—"Some Ionian and Lydian modes are called lax," said he.—"Is there any way you would use these for warlike men?"—"Not at all," he said, "but it appears that only the Dorian and Phrygian are left to you."—"I am unfamiliar with the modes," I said, "but see you leave me the mode that imitates the utterances and intonations of a man brave in war and in all activities that are engaged in under constraint, and who, when he has fallen into misfortune and confronts wounds, death, or some other misfortune, stands up to his fate in all these circumstances with a steadfast and enduring spirit. And <see you leave me> another mode for one engaged in peaceful and not constrained but voluntary action, either persuading someone of something or requesting something of someone, whether of a god by prayer, or of a man by instruction and admonition, or on the contrary attending to another, who is requesting or instructing or persuading, and in consequence acceding to his wishes and not bearing himself with arrogance but acting with self-control and moderation in all these circumstances and acquiescing in the results. Leave me these two modes, constrained and voluntary, which best imitate the utterances of those in good fortune or in bad fortune, acting with self-control and with courage."—"But," said he, "you ask me to leave you none other than those I just mentioned."—"Then," said I, "we will not need multistringed instruments or instruments capable of playing in all modes."—"I think not."—"So we won't employ the makers of spindle harps (*trigona*) and open and pillar harps (*pektides*) and all the other instruments that have many strings and can play many modes."—"It seems we won't."—"Well then, will you allow pipe makers and pipers into the state? Or is this not the most "many-stringed" of instruments and <is it not true that> even the instruments that play all modes are mere imitations of the pipes?"

283. Aristotle, *Politics* 1342a32–b14. Written ca. 330 B.C. The reference to Philoxenus' failure is misleading and probably refers to a modulation from Dorian to Phrygian mode (cf. 267).

Socrates in the *Republic* <of Plato> makes a mistake in allowing the Phrygian mode alone to be kept along with the Dorian and this even though he earlier rejected the pipe as an instrument. Of all modes the Phrygian has the same effect as the pipe among instruments: both are orgiastic and emotional. Poetry shows that this is so. All Dionysiac revels and other such activities are especially associated with pipes among instruments, and among modes find their proper expression in the Phrygian. For example, the dithyramb is generally agreed to be a Phrygian thing. The experts give many illustrations of this fact and particularly note that Philoxenus tried to write the dithyramb *Muses* in the Dorian mode but failed and fell naturally back into the Phrygian as that suitable for his composition. As for the Dorian mode, all agree that it is steady and most expressive of a manly character.

284. *PHibeh* 13.1–22; M.L. West, *ZPE* 92 (1992) 16. A 3rd-c. B.C. papyrus preserves an anonymous diatribe, perhaps by the sophist Alcidamas, against music theoreticians, particularly Damon and his followers. For reasons of style, and because of the reference to tragedy's use of the enharmonic genus, it is generally assumed that the speech was written in the early 4th c. B.C. If so it is the earliest mention of the three genera, the traditional enharmonic genus, and the chromatic and diatonic associated with the New Music. Though the author denies the ethical effects attributed to music by Damon and his followers, the discussion here focuses on musical genera and not on modes and rhythm as in Damon, Plato, and Aristotle. The focus on genus reappears in the writings of Diogenes of Seleucia (285).

> Men of [Athens], I have often had occasion to marvel at your failure to perceive that certain men lecture you on arts beyond their competence. Calling themselves "harmonicists" (*harmonikoi*), they select and compare [a number of songs], randomly condemning some, and unmethodically praising others. They say that one should not regard them as instrumentalists or singers. They claim to leave these matters to the others, while reserving the theoretical part as their own special province. Yet not only do they appear to have devoted no small effort to the matters they pretend to leave to the others, but in the areas where they claim expertise, they appear mere improvisers. They claim that some melodies make people disciplined, others make them sensible, others just, others manly and others cowardly. They are hardly conscious of the fact that the chromatic genus could not produce cowards any more than the enharmonic could make its users manly. Who does not know that the Aetolians, the Dolopes, and all those [who sacrifice at Thermopylae (i.e., members of the Delphic Amphictyony)], though they employ music in the diatonic genus, are nevertheless much more manly than the singers of tragedy who have always been accustomed to singing in the enharmonic genus? So clearly neither does the chromatic genus make men cowardly nor the enharmonic manly.

285A. Philodemus, *On Music* 4.15 (Neubecker). Philodemus, writing in the 1st c. B.C., criticizes the stoic philosopher Diogenes of Seleucia (ca. 240–152 B.C.), and through him the 4th-c. B.C. Platonist Heraclides of Pontos.

> With respect to what Diogenes says—that once we have grasped the writings of Heraclides about appropriate music and inappropriate music and about manly and soft (tone-) character and about actions (?) that fit or do not fit a given person, we will consider music not far removed from philosophy insofar as music is useful for most aspects of life and the pursuit of it gives us the proper

disposition for acquiring many, or rather all, virtues—<all this>
we discussed in the third book of our commentary and have shown
to what degree it, along with other similar statements, is pure
nonsense. Moreover, the concept some people have of justice is
ridiculous. For it is unimaginable that sounds affecting only the
sense of hearing, which is irrational, should contribute something
to the disposition of the soul, which gives insight into what is
profitable and what unprofitable for community life and causes us
to choose the former and avoid the latter . . .

285B. Philodemus, *On Music* 4.8 (Neubecker).

Music in itself does not produce the effects that <Diogenes> asserts
as if an absolute certainty, and it does not tempt men or women
to disgraceful forms of intercourse nor adolescent youths to adopt
the female role. Neither he nor the comic poets have shown anything
of the sort in the music of Agathon or Demokritos; they merely
allege it.

Choral Song to Actor's Monody

286. [Aristotle], *Problems* 922b10–28. Date: Hellenistic. The *Geryone*
mentioned may be that attributed to the 3rd-c. B.C. tragedian Nikomachos
of Alexandria (*TrGF* 127 F 3).

Why do tragic choruses not sing in the Hypodorian or in the
Hypophrygian mode? Is it because these modes have least melody,
which choruses most need? The Hypophrygian has an active character, which is why both the *exodos* and the arming scene in the
Geryone are written in this mode. The Hypodorian is grandiose
and steady and therefore of all modes most suited to the kithara.
Both of these are unfit for the chorus; they are suited rather to the
actors. This is so because the latter represent heroes, and in ancient
times only leaders were heroes, while the ordinary people were
(mere) men and they made up the chorus. A mournful and quiet
character and melody therefore suits them, since they are human.
Though the other modes have this, the Phrygian has it least of all:
it is inspired and bacchic. In this mode we become emotional and
the weak are more emotional than the powerful, which is why even
this mode suits choruses, but in the Hypodorian and Hypophrygian
modes we are moved to action, which does not suit a chorus. The
chorus shows inactive concern; to those it attends it provides nothing
but good will.

287. [Aristotle], *Problems* 920a. Date: Hellenistic.

Why are the Hypodorian and Hypophrygian mode not used by choruses in tragedy? Is it because they do not permit an antistrophe? But they are suited to actors' monodies because they are mimetic.

288. [Aristotle], *Problems* 918b. Date: Hellenistic.

Why are the songs called *nomoi* not composed with strophic responsion while other choral odes are? Is it because the *nomoi* were performed by professional artists (*agonistai,* literally, "competitors") whose song became long and varied since by that time they were capable of imitation (*mimesis*) and prolonged delivery. Just like the words, the music must always keep changing as it follows the imitation: in fact it is more important to imitate with music than with words. By the same token, dithyrambs also ceased to have responsion when they became mimetic, although they had it previously. The reason is that in ancient times free citizens themselves formed the choruses and it was difficult for a large number to sing like professionals, so they sang songs keeping to a single mode: it is easier for a single person to perform many modulations (from mode to mode) than for a large number, and easier for a professional than for those adhering to usual practice. This is why they composed simpler music for them. Strophic responsion is a simple thing: there is a single rhythm and meter. For the same reason, songs sung by stage actors have no strophic responsion, but the songs of the chorus do: the actor is a professional and an imitator; the chorus is less capable of imitation.

IVD. The Chorus

The history of the dramatic chorus is one of decline both quantitatively and qualitatively. In quantative terms, Aeschylean tragedy averages 40 to 50 percent choral participation, while no extant tragedy earlier than 425 B.C. (except? *Prometheus Bound*) is less than 20 percent choral. But later tragedies are considerably less; the *Orestes* of Euripides (408 B.C.), for example, is only 10.5 percent choral. Note, however, that our two latest tragedies, *Bacchae* (405 B.C.?) and *Oedipus at Colonus* (401 B.C.), with 27 percent, and 22 percent, respectively, are exceptions to a nonetheless clear trend. In qualitative terms, the chorus undergoes a similar decline, from a role central to the action, as in *Suppliants* and *Eumenides,* to one merely marginal, as in the late plays of Euripides, where its comments, even its presence, are often ignored by the main characters, and its persona is often distant and abstract (in *Iphigenia in Aulis,* mere sightseers). Aristotle tells us that Agathon began writing generic choral songs (*embolima*) suited for insertion in any drama; he implies that they became the fashion in 4th-c. tragedy, robbing the chorus of every vestige of personality or relevance (289).

Comedy provides a clearer, if slightly different, picture. Aristophanes' *Acharnians,* our earliest extant comedy (425 B.C.), is 24 percent choral song or recitative, and the percentages remain about the same until *Ecclesiazusae* (392 B.C.) and *Plutus* (388 B.C.), when they drop suddenly to 8.5 and 3.2 percent, respectively. Though one choral ode has dropped out of *Ecclesiazusae* and six from *Plutus,* full choral participation would not have exceeded 10 percent. The manuscripts mark the omission of the odes with the tag "choral ode" (*chorou*), possibly indicating the use of *embolima.* In *Plutus* the chorus has no narrative function, they simply appear and exchange a few lines in recitative, then song, with an actor; for the remainder of the play, they deliver no more than thirteen lines at six different intervals in the action, and finally a two-line ditty to mark their *exodos*. The chorus interacted with the actors at least until the late Middle Comic period, ca. 340 B.C. (290, 291). Plautus' Latin adaptation of a Greek comedy by Diphilus probably preserves the *parodos* of a chorus of fishermen followed by a short exchange with an actor and the chorus' apparent departure (291). In New Comedy the actors generally left the stage at the first approach of the chorus, sometimes with a formulaic announcement, "Here come a bunch of drunken rowdies" (292). There is no certain instance of dialogue between actors and chorus in New Comedy. The tag "of the chorus" in the manuscripts indicates an unrecorded song-and-dance routine, probably *embolima,* at each of the act breaks. It is not clear if it departed or remained silently in the orchestra after each entr'acte performance. Inscriptions attest the use of the chorus in drama until at least 180 (293), though with numbers considerably diminished: we hear of groups of eight and seven comic choreuts at the Delphic Soteria in the mid-3rd c. B.C. (293B) and only four comic choreuts a century later (293E). The remains of a Hellenistic (perhaps 3rd-c. B.C.) tragedy, *Exagoge* (the *Exodus*), by the Jew Ezekiel suggest a chorus of sisters of Sepphora and some integration of the chorus into the main narrative. The anecdote in Plutarch (294), though doubtless pure fiction, presupposes the survival of some form of choral accompaniment in performances of "old tragedy."

In comparison with tragedy, the comic trend shows an apparent lateness and suddenness in choral decline. Many isolate the comic development and associate it with the financial and spiritual exhaustion of Athens after the Peloponnesian War. It seems shortsighted, however, to explain the comic trend without reference to the parallel decline in the tragic chorus, which is steady and systematic and cannot be attached to specific political events of the late 5th c. B.C. Moreover, the lateness and suddenness of the comic decline may be more apparent than real, due to our reliance on the oeuvre of a single and atypical author. In its heyday Aristophanes' political comedy succeeded in satisfying the growing taste for coherent plots (cf. II 12) without sacrificing comedy's traditional choral architecture. It took its departure from major political and social issues; of these, its zany hero was little more than a residue; his/her wild program of reform required little more than the support of the chorus: the major choral structures of *parodos, agon, parabasis,* and *komos* were thus easily integrated into a narrative of obstruction, persuasion, comment, and victory. But other contemporary comic writers developed more coherent and complex plots at the direct expense of the chorus; it was these styles that prevailed by the end of the century. Moreover the choral structure of Aristophanic comedy already shows signs of disintegration in *Lysistrata* (411 B.C.), *Thesmophoriazusae* (411 B.C.), and *Frogs* (405 B.C.)

A primary cause of the decline is the growth of professionalization in the theater and the development of new standards in acting (see IVAiii), music (see IVC), and dance, rather than changes in the constitution of the chorus itself. The chorus continued to be drafted from citizen amateurs until the abolition of the *choregia* in the late 4th c. B.C. (III 110), while music tended to ever-greater rhythmic and melodic complexity, better suited to a single voice. In contrast with highly trained actors, the amateurishness of the chorus became an embarrassment. In addition, the growing taste for realism and more complex plots tended to favor actors over chorus. The latter was an unnatural and awkward participant in the drama, severely limited in its ability to participate in the action, since that would entail either breaking the unity of the group or creating narrative and choreographic absurdities: though superior in numbers, privy to all secrets, the chorus witnessed the most heinous crimes with passive resignation, hemmed in by awkward conventions, never to do or say anything of consequence.

In defiance of the general trend to professionalization and internationalization, Athenian law demonstrates a strong desire to retain the traditional chorus of citizen amateurs. Membership in choruses at the Great Dionysia was strictly limited to Athenian citizens; the Lenaea was sufficiently relaxed to allow the participation of resident foreigners (see III 72). *Choregoi* who admitted foreign choreuts or disenfranchised Athenians were fined one thousand drachmas (295). The seriousness with which Athenians regarded any infringement of this rule can be gauged by the right granted any citizen of physically ejecting a suspected foreigner from a chorus even during performance (296, 297). Since the law was subject to abuse by *choregoi* eager to spoil their rivals' performances, a financial risk was imposed on any who ejected choreuts (298): ejectors were required to pay one thousand drachmas to the state treasury, and fifty drachmas for merely interrogating a choreut. The sum was presumably recovered from the fine imposed on the *choregos,* if he was found guilty, but forfeited if the prosecution failed or was abandoned. The numerous occasions on which *choregoi* willingly risked disaster in hiring foreigners is impressive testimony to the value of skilled choreuts and chorus directors (295–97).

To ensure a supply of citizen choreuts, *choregoi* were endowed with extraordinary powers of compulsion, of imposing fines, and of seizing

the property of anyone unwilling to serve in a chorus (299, 300). Unless
these rules apply only to the recruitment of boys' dithyrambic choruses,
they are evidence against the existence of a choreutic profession in Athens,
at least in the 5th and early 4th c. B.C., from which a *choregos* could
draw a supply of willing recruits; rather they indicate that many or most
citizens regarded chorus duty as a burden. We know very little about the
customs and regulations governing the recruitment of choruses. Attic
iconography normally shows choreuts to be young and beardless, normally the sign of adolescence (I 137): this has recently given rise to a
theory that choruses were composed of ephebes, young men undergoing
military training. To be sure, choreuts were normally enlisted from the
young, since the service was strenuous—Plato could not imagine anyone
over thirty taking part in a dramatic chorus (*Laws* 665b). But the sources
do not support the interpretation of chorus service as an official ephebic
duty. If it were, it would be difficult to explain why extra compulsion
had to be exercised in enlisting choruses. More particularly, one could
scarcely explain the procedure for granting choreuts an exemption from
military service (301), if chorus duty were itself part of military training.
Some feel that 302 is evidence against such exemption, but the case seems
to arise from the failure on the part of the *choregos* to make formal
application to the archon (cf. 313). The abolition of the *choregia* under
Demetrius of Phaleron probably signaled the end of the amateur citizen
chorus: the festival inscriptions of the Hellenistic period refer to professional choreuts (293).

   A class of professional chorus directors (*chorodidaskaloi*) did develop
by the the late 5th c. B.C. (301, cf. 297) and perhaps much earlier (307),
keeping pace with specialization in acting and music. In the 5th c. B.C.
the poets normally arranged their own songs and dance and taught them
to the chorus (303–5, 307). The chorus of *Peace* (421 B.C.) still refers to
Aristophanes as its *didaskalos* (738), though this may be a purely conventional way of saying "poet," as it is in *Acharnians* 628ff., which we
know was directed by Callistratus. By 412 B.C. dithyrambic chorus directors were allotted to *choregoi* and presumably paid by the state; it is
tempting to suppose that the same may have been true of tragic and
comic chorus directors, since the state also paid and allotted actors and
pipers, but 297 specifically states that Theozotides *hired* a tragic chorus
director, one, moreover, who would not have been selected or approved
by any archon. Note Demosthenes' reference to the desire to remove
Sannion the tragic chorus director during performance in the theater

(314): this seems to imply that Sannion also served as the chorus' lead singer and dancer, *koryphaios.*

The report that Aeschylus worked with a chorus of 12 (306) seems confirmed by the distribution of lines in *Agamemnon* 1346–71 to 12 individual choreuts. For satyr play the evidence is less clear (see I 137). The ascription of 24 members to the comic chorus (308; app. A) likewise appears confirmed by the enumeration of 24 birds at Aristophanes' *Birds* 297ff. It seems likely that the tragic chorus was increased soon after 458 B.C., the date of *Oresteia,* and this agrees with the ancient tradition that Sophocles increased the chorus to 15 (306). An inscription dated to ca. 440 B.C. lists 14 tragic performers (307): these must be choreuts, as honorary decrees of this sort normally only mention citizen volunteers (and not paid performers such as actors or pipers). The fact that only 14 names appear may best be explained by the hypothesis that the *koryphaios* was a hired professional, like Sannion in 297, and therefore did not merit mention. This could also explain the appearance of only 11 choreuts on the Pronomos vase (but see on I 137), though there the piper Pronomos is not only present but central to the composition.

The chorus was organized in a strict hierarchy on the analogy of a hoplite battle line (309, 313A). Rectangular in formation (as opposed to the round dithyrambic choruses; cf. I 125), the best dancers stood in the left row (309, 313), in full view of the audience, with the *koryphaios* in the center, flanked by the next best dancers (315, 316). Less accomplished dancers stood in the rear, the worst in the center row(s) (314). The hierarchical arrangement is consistent with the claim that the chorus always entered through the *parodos* on the audience's right (western entrance in the Theater of Dionysus). Pollux claims that they could enter either by rows or by files (app. A). Various typical movements are reported for antistrophic choral odes and comic *parabaseis,* perhaps in essence correct, though all the accounts of choral movements are late and no doubt extremely reductive (308, 310, 311). Not all entrances were in formation, e.g., the *parodos* of *Birds.* The claim that the main movements of the chorus from one part of the orchestra to another (*parodos, parabasis, exodos*) were executed by marching in formation receives general confirmation from our texts where the lines are written in tetrameter (recitative) meters (IVC). It is probable that all choral songs (even actors' monodies) were accompanied by rhythmic dancelike movements. Of dance, little is known: written sources provide a few typical names of dances and dance figures, and fewer descriptions (317–26); the iconographic evidence is more informative. The theoretical and philosophical discussions are of particular value in that they disclose ideological reactions to changes in dance that parallel those of the music critics (IVC). In particular, one should note the binary division of dance forms into noble and base, self-controlled and self-indulgent, warlike and decadent, orderly and anarchic, manly and effeminate, masterful and servile (325 and esp. 326). Like music, dance appears to have shifted its *locus* from the chorus to the actors, so that where, in the days of Phrynichus, choral dance might be compared to the varied rhythms of the sea (303), by the late 5th c. B.C., Plato, the comic poet, describes them standing stock-still and howling (325). Still more disturbing to the political conservative's concept of traditional order was the fact that dance, like music, appears to have liberated itself from the hegemony of the text, a development construed by the philosopher Plato as a revolt against *logos* (both "word" and "reason") by the physical appetites (326).

Sources

History

289. Aristotle, *Poetics* 1456a25–32. Written ca. 330 B.C. Agathon produced tragedies from ca. 416–401 B.C.

> It is necessary to consider the chorus as one of the actors, a part of the whole and a participant in the action, not as in Euripides, but as in Sophocles. The songs of the later tragedians have no more connection with the story than they do with any other tragedy, and so they sing *embolima* ("throw-ins"). Agathon was the first to produce this sort of thing. And yet what difference does it make if they sing *embolima* or insert a speech or a whole episode from one drama to another?

290. Aeschines, *Against Timarchus* 157. See III 53C.

291. Plautus, *The Rope* (*Rudens*) 284–324. Written ca. 220–184 B.C. The *Rudens* is an adaptation of a play by Diphilus, the Greek late Middle/New Comic poet (ca. 335 to ca. 300 B.C.). The chorus of fishermen in this passage should be compared with the chorus of witnesses in Plautus' *Carthaginian* (*Poenulus*) 515–816, of which the Greek model is probaby the *Carthaginian* (*Karchedonios*) of Alexis (active ca. 350–275 B.C.). The two characters described by Trachalio are the "excellent youth" and the pimp (see app. A, New Comic masks, nos. 8 and 10).

> AMPELISCA: Please, is this the temple of Venus? PTOLEMOCRA-
> TIA: It is. I am known as the priestess of this shrine. But whatever

you wish I will do gladly as far as I am able. Come with me this way. PALAESTRA: You have our most heartfelt and gracious esteem, Mother. PTOLEMOCRATIA: So it must be.

Act 2

FISHERMEN: Poor men live lives wretched in every way, especially those who have learned no trade or skill: whatever one finds at home must necessarily satisfy. You can pretty well tell how rich we are just from our clothes: these hooks and these fishing rods serve us as trade and finery. Every day we come from the city here to the sea in search of food. This we have in place of exercise in the gymnasium or wrestling grounds. We hunt for urchins, limpets, oysters, *balani* (some kind of shellfish), seasnails, sea-anemone (?), mussels, fluted *plagusiae* (a shellfish). Afterward we go fishing with hooks and stones. We hunt for food from the sea. If we chance upon no chance, and no fish is caught, we return home quietly, washed and salted, and go to bed without dinner. But we have no hope, now that the sea is surging wildly. Unless we can find some seasnails, we will be totally dinnerless. Now we pay our respects to Venus here, so that she will aid us nicely today. TRACHALIO (just entering): I've kept my eyes wide open so as not to pass master by. When he came out, he said he was going to the port and ordered me to come meet him here at the shrine of Venus. But I see some people standing here that I can conveniently question. I'll go up to them. Greetings sea-thieves, snailmen and hookmen, famished race of men. What are you about? About to die? FISHERMEN: Aye, of hunger, thirst, and false hopes, as befits a fisherman. TRACHALIO: While you were standing here did you see a young man come by in a hurry with a powerful demeanor, ruddy, strong, leading three supermen with cloaks and swords? FISHERMEN: We know of the approach of no one of the aforesaid description. TRACHALIO: How about an old man, bald as a silen, well-dressed (? *statutus*), potbellied, twisted brows, wrinkled forehead, fraudulent, despised by gods and men, evil, full of evil and disgraceful vice, who was leading along two considerably beautiful women? FISHERMEN: Any one with such virtues and accomplishments would be better to go to the hangman than to Venus. TRACHALIO: But tell me if you saw him. FISHERMEN: No one came here at all. Goodbye! TRACHALIO: Bye...(The fishermen go off and appear nowhere else in the play.)

292A. Alexis, *Hairdresser, PCG* F 112. Written ca. 350–275 B.C.

As a matter of fact I see a [large] mob of men carousing and heading this way on the assumption that the nobility are assembled here. (He addresses the mob.) May I never meet you when I'm alone at night and you've come from a good time dancing. I'd never get away with my cloak unless I sprouted wings.

292B. Menander, *Dyskolos* 229ff. Produced Lenaea, 316 B.C.

DAOS: I think I'd better go and do this now. As a matter of fact I see some drunken devotees of Pan here coming this way to the sanctuary. I think it not a good moment to stand in their way.

OF THE CHORUS (*chorou*)

(The beginning of act 2 follows immediately after this.)

292C. Menander, *Aspis* 245ff. Date: ca. 321–292 B.C.

DAOS (speaking to the waiter, who, along with the cook, has been dismissed): Get away from this door. As a matter of fact I see this other gang here of drunken men approaching. (To the drunks.) You're smart. What fortune will bring is uncertain. Enjoy yourselves while you can!

OF THE CHORUS (*chorou*)

(Act 2 follows immediately.)

292D. Menander, *Perikeiromene* 261ff. Date: ca. 321–292 B.C.

<DAOS> . . . A bunch of drunken youths are approaching. I give my mistress high praise. She's brought the girl to our house. That's a real mother for you! I've got to find my young master. It seems a good moment for him to come home on the double, I'd say.

OF THE CHORUS (*chorou*)

(Act 2 follows immediately.)

292E. Menander, *Epitrepontes* 168ff. Date: ca. 321–292 B.C.

CHAIRESTRATOS: Let's go, since, as a matter of fact, I see a gang of drunken teenagers coming to this place. I think it not a good moment to stand in their way.

[OF THE CHO]R[US] ([*ch*]*o*[*rou*])

(Act 2 follows immediately.)

292F. Plautus, *Bacchides* 105–8. Produced ca. 200 B.C. Plautus' play is a Latin adaptation of Menander's *Twice Deceived*. The Latin plays had no choral interludes: passage of time appears generally to have been marked by musical interludes by the piper. Comparison with the passages cited above makes it clear that Plautus has translated the Greek formula that introduced the chorus and ends the first act.

BACCHIS: . . . Let's go away inside so that you can wash. In any case let's get out of the way of whoever it is here who's coming to raise a commotion. As you came by ship, I expect your nerves are a bit unsteady. SISTER: A little, sister. BACCHIS: Then follow me inside so that you can rest your fatigue on the couch. (The stage is left empty momentarily.)

293A. Euboean Festival Decree (*IG* XII 9, 207 and p. 176, etc.). See III 162.

293B. Soteria Victor Lists (*SIG*³ 424A). See III 165A.

293C. Decree of *Technitai* at Ptolemais (*OGIS* 50–51). See 43A–B.

293D. Delphian Pythais Decree (*SIG*³ 711). See 44.

293E. Isthmian/Nemeans at Winter Soteria (*SIG*³ 690). See III 165B.

293F. Serapieia Accounts (*SEG* 19.335). See III 161.

293G. *SEG* 11.923. See III 167.

293H. *MAMA* 8.85–86, no. 420. See III 159B.

294. Plutarch, *Crassus* 33.3. Written ca. 115 and referring to 53 B.C. The passage purports to describe events immediately following the battle of Carrhae, in which the triumvir Crassus was killed. The *exodos* from Euripides' *Bacchae,* where Agaue appears with the head (i.e., mask) of Pentheus and sings an exchange with the chorus, was put on as a dinner entertainment at the Parthian court.

Meanwhile Hyrodes happened to have made his peace with Artavasdes of Armenia and agreed to accept <Artavasdes'> sister as a wife for his son Pakoros. They hosted each other at banquets and drinking parties and brought in many Greek entertainments, as Hyrodes was not ignorant of Greek language and literature and Artavasdes wrote tragedies, speeches, and histories, some of which are extant. The tables had been removed (after dining) when the head of Crassus was brought to the door, and the tragic actor named Jason of Tralles was singing the part of Euripides' *Bacchae,* which deals with Agaue (1168ff.). While the audience was showing its approval, Sillakes, who had been standing at the door of the room and making his obeisance, threw the head of Crassus into the center of the group. When the Parthians lifted it up with applause and shouts of joy, the servants, at the king's request, had Sillakes lie down (on one of the dinner couches), and Jason gave the mask of Pentheus to one of the choreuts, took up the head of Crassus, and, working himself into a bacchic frenzy, began to sing those songs (just performed) with inspiration and <the lines> from the song "We carry from the mountain to the palace a fresh cut tendril, a wondrous prey." And this delighted everyone. But when the exchange with the chorus that follows was being sung—

> CHORUS: "Who killed him?"
> AGAUE: "Mine is the honor."

—Pomaxathres, who happened to be at the banquet, jumped up and took the head away from him, claiming that it was more appropriate for him to say this than Jason. The king was delighted and gave Pomaxathres the customary gifts and Jason a talent. They say that Crassus' expedition came to such a close, ending like a tragedy.

Regulation

295. Plutarch, *Phocion* 30. Written ca. 115 and referring to ca. 350–319 B.C. The anecdote may preserve accurate details of the law cited, though the rest is probably pure fiction.

> Demades prided himself on his wealth and lawlessness, and since there was a law in Athens at the time that a foreigner was not to be a member of a chorus or else the *choregos* would pay a penalty of one thousand drachmas, he brought one hundred foreigners into the orchestra as choreuts and simultaneously brought into the theater a fine of one thousand drachmas for each of them.

296. Pseudo-Andocides, *Against Alcibiades* 20–21. See III 105.

297. Demosthenes, *Against Meidias* 58–61. See III 107.

298. Demosthenes, *Against Meidias* 56. Date: 349/8 B.C.

> Moreover you are aware of the fact that, though you do not wish any foreigner to be part of the competition, you did not permit any *choregos* simply to accost and interrogate the choreuts, but rather you imposed a fine of fifty drachmas on anyone who accosted a choreut and one thousand drachmas on anyone who ordered a choreut to sit <among the spectators>. Why did you do this? So that no one would deliberately accost, obstruct, or violate someone who is garlanded and in the service of the god that day.

299. Antiphon, *On the Choreut* 6.11. See III 94.

300. Xenophon, *Hieron* 9.4. Written ca. 360 B.C. and set in dialogue form with a dramatic date of 476 B.C. The constraint referred to may possibly be that exercised by *choregoi* (cf. III 94), but the syntax suggests that the chorus director at least shares in some legal power over the choreuts.

Whenever we want choruses to perform in competition, the archon
sets up prizes, but the actual recruitment of the choreuts is assigned
to the *choregoi,* and to others to direct them and to apply constraint
to any whose performance is in any way deficient.

301. Demosthenes, *Against Meidias* 15. See III 106.

302. Demosthenes, *Against Boiotos* I 16. Delivered ca. 348 B.C. The
speech is a prosecution by a man named Mantitheos whose father was
allegedly forced into acknowledging Boiotos as his son. Boiotos subsequently changed his name to Mantitheos, and the prosecutor Mantitheos
claims that this has led to confusion and hardship, since in Athens citizens
were identified by their name, father's name, and deme, all of which are
shared by prosecutor and defendant in this case.

Who in the general populace would know which of us this man is,
given that there are two Mantitheoses with the same father. Now
suppose that he were prosecuted for evasion of military service and
that he was a member of a chorus when he should have been on
campaign? It so happens that just recently when the others went
off to Tamynai (in Euboea) he stayed behind to celebrate the Festival
of the Cups (see III 78) and remained here to dance in a chorus at
the Dionysia, which all of you saw who were in Athens. And after
the soldiers left Euboea he was arraigned on a charge of desertion,
and I, though I was a *taxiarch* of my tribe, was forced because of
my name and patronymic to receive the summons.

303. Plutarch, *Convivial Questions* 732ff. Written ca. 115. Phrynichus
wrote tragedies in the early 5th c. B.C., but this epigram is doubtless
Hellenistic.

Indeed Phrynichus the tragic poet says about himself that (*TrGF* 3
T 13): "Dance provided me with as many figures as baleful night
produces waves on the sea in a storm."

304. Athenaeus 21d–22a. Written ca. 200.

And Aeschylus not only invented the comeliness and magnificence
of dress that the (Eleusinian) priests and torchbearers emulate, but
he also used to invent many dance steps and imparted them to his
choreuts. At any rate, Chamaeleon (peripatetic philosopher, ca.
350–280 B.C.) says (fr. 41 Wehrli) that first <Aeschylus> himself
arranged his choruses without the use of chorus directors (*chorodidaskaloi*), himself creating the dance movements for the choruses
and generally taking upon himself the entire direction of the tragedy.
At any rate, he seems to have acted in his dramas. Anyway Aristophanes—and credible information about tragedy is to be found in the

comic poets—makes Aeschylus say (*PCG* F 696), "I myself used to create the movements for the choruses," and again, "I know about <Aeschylus'> *Phrygians;* I was in the audience when they came with Priam to ransom his dead son, making a lot of movements that way and that way and this way." And Telesis, or Telestes, the dance director (*orchestodidaskalos*) invented many dance movements, masterfully describing the lyrics with his hands.... Aristokles (2nd c. B.C.) says that Telestes, Aeschylus' dancer, was such a consummate artist, that in dancing the *Seven against Thebes* he was able to communicate the events with his dancing. They also say that the ancient poets Thespis, Pratinas, Cratinus, and Phrynichus were called dancers not only because they consigned their dramas to the dancing of the chorus, but also because, quite apart from their own poetry, they gave dance lessons to any who wanted.

305. Plutarch, *On Listening to Lectures* 46b. Written ca. 115, referring to 5th c. B.C.

Now when Euripides the poet was teaching his choreuts how to sing an ode composed in a given mode, one of them laughed. He said, "If you weren't insensitive and ignorant, you would not laugh at me singing in the Mixolydian mode."

Formation and Movement

306A. *Suda,* s.v. *Sophokles.*

Sophocles ... first introduced a chorus composed of fifteen youths; previously it was composed of twelve.

306B. *Life of Sophocles* 4. See 3A.

307. *SEG* 23 (1968) 102. Dedicatory inscription on a statue base found at Varkiza, the ancient deme of Anagyros. Date: ca. 440 B.C. It is uncertain whether this inscription refers to one of the Athenian festivals or the Rural Dionysia at Anagyros (III 59). The word *tragoidos* in this period can mean a member of a tragic chorus, a tragic actor, or a tragic poet. Here the first meaning alone seems to fit, but the fact that there are only fourteen choreuts listed is puzzling, and may suggest that the *koryphaios* is reckoned in a category apart. "Euripides" is generally taken to mean the famous tragedian.

Sokrates set this up
Euripides was *didaskalos*
Tragic performers (*tragoidoi*)   Amphidemos

Python	Euthydikos
Echekles	Lysias
Menalkes	Son
Philokrates	Kritodemos
Echyllos	Charias
Meletos	Phaidon
Emporion	

308. *Prolegomena,* Xa (Koster). This passage is repeated by Tzetzes, and from Tzetzes copied by the *Anonymus Crameri* II. The perspective is that of an actor facing the audience.

> The comic chorus was composed of twenty-four men. And if it was supposed to come to the theater from the city, it entered through the archway on the left, and if supposed to come from the country, it entered through the right in rectangular formation looking away from the audience at the actors. When the actors left (for the *parabasis*) the chorus turned seven times, facing both parts of the theater.

309A. Aelius Aristides, *On Behalf of the Four* 154 (Behr/Lenz). Written mid-2nd c. A rhetorical exercise in which Aristides defends Miltiades against Plato's charges. The choral changes easily into a military metaphor.

> Where in the chorus should we put Miltiades the hero of Marathon, or what rank shall we give him? Or is it clear that we should give him the rank that faces the audience and is in clear view of everyone? Although he is not so much a leftstander as a man of the Greek right wing (of battle formation).

309B. Scholion to Aristides, *On Behalf of the Four* 154 (Dindorf 3.535ff.)

> When the choruses entered they sang their hymns moving transversely and kept the audience on their left, and the foremost of the chorus kept to the left side ... since the left side in choruses is more distinguished, though in battle <lines> it is the right.... When entering they placed the good choreuts on their left side in order that they might be located facing the people.

310A. Scholion to Euripides, *Hecuba* 647.

> One must realize that the choreuts sang the strophe while moving to the right, the antistrophe while moving to the left, and the epode while stationary.

310B. Atilius Fortunatianus, *Grammatici Latini* 6. 294ff. Written 4th c.

... In lyric songs properly written, one should find these three things: strophe, antistrophe, epode. Once long ago, songs dedicated to the gods were composed of these three movements: going around the altar from the right they called "strophe" (literally, "turning"); returning from the left "antistrophe" ("turning the other way"); later, when standing in the sight of the god (i.e., cult-image) they performed the rest with song, epode ("added song"), because they sang in addition to the strophe and antistrophe.

310C. *Etymologicon Magnum,* s.v. *prosodion.* Written 12th c.

Note that of songs and hymns some are called *prosodia* ("processional"), others *hyporchemata* ("dances to"), and others *stasima* ("stationary"). *Prosodia* are the songs uttered while the sacrifice is being brought to the altar. . . . *hyporchemata* are things uttered again while they danced and ran in a circle around the altar while the sacrifices were being burned. *Stasima* are what they uttered afterward while standing and taking a rest after encircling the altar. When they ran around the altar they moved from the left side to the right in imitation of the movement of the zodiac, since it also makes a movement opposite to that of the sky, moving from west to east. Later they went again from right to left in imitation of the sky. In the end they ran around the whole altar.

311. Hephaistion, *Enchiridion* p. 72 (Consbruch). Written ca. 150. The work underwent several abridgements and the contradictions may perhaps be attributed to this process.

There is in comedy also the so-called *parabasis,* to which, if written in its fullest form, there are seven parts. It is called *parabasis* when the choreuts, having entered the auditorium and faced each other (this should perhaps be emended to "them," meaning the audience), would "move up" and say something while they looked toward the auditorium.

312. Hesychius, s.v. *grammai.* Written 5th c.

Lines (*grammai*): they were in the orchestra, so as to set the chorus in file.

313A. Photius, *Lex.,* s.v. *tritos aristerou.* Written ca. 850. Cf. app. A.

In the tragic chorus there were three rows and (five) files. The leftmost row was the one on the side of the auditorium; the rightmost on the side of the *proskenion.* Consequently the center of the leftmost row held the most distinguished place and position, like that of the commander (of a military unit, *protostates*).

313B. Photius, *Lex.*, s.v. *aristerostates*. Written ca. 850. Cratinus' *Men of Seriphos* was produced ca. 424 B.C.

"Left-stander" (*aristerostates*) is an appellation in the comic chorus, but in the tragic "middle of the left." Cratinus in *Men of Seriphos* (= *PCG* F 229).

313C. Hesychius, s.v. *aristerostates*. Written 5th c.

"Left-stander" (*aristerostates*): the commander (*protostates*) of the chorus.

313D. Pollux 2.161. Written ca. 180.

Perhaps the left-stander in the chorus would suit the left side, as the right-stander the right.

314A. Photius, *Lex.*, s.v. *laurostatai*. Written ca. 850. Cratinus was active from ca. 450 to ca. 420 B.C. This fragment could be from *Men of Seriphos;* cf. 313B.

"Alley-standers" (*laurostatai*): the men in the middle of the chorus, as if they were in a narrow passageway. They are more worthless. So Cratinus.

314B. Hesychius, s.v. *laurostatai*. Written 5th c.

"Alley-standers" (*laurostatai*): the rows in the middle (this should be "the middle file[s]"), because in some narrow passageways they are not visible. Those who are worse stand in the middle; their superiors are first and last.

315. Aristotle, *Politics* 1277a1–12. Written ca. 330 B.C.

There would not be a single virtue for the citizen and the good man. For the virtue of a proper citizen must be common to all (it is necessarily in this way that the state is best), but the virtue of the good man cannot be, unless all citizens must necessarily be good in a proper state. Further, the state is composed of unlike elements, just as an animal is composed of mind and body, and mind of reason and appetite, and a household out of man and woman, and a property of master and slave; and since in the same way a state is composed of all of these and other unlike elements besides, there is necessarily no single virtue common to all citizens, just as among choreuts there is no single virtue for the *koryphaios* and the man standing beside him (*parastates*).

316. Aristotle, *Metaphysics* 1018b26–29. Written ca. 340–330 B.C. Aristotle discusses various senses of "priority." In Greek music, *nete* and *paranete* are the two highest notes on the scale; the "middle note" (*mese*) tended to serve as the tonal center of a composition (and the physical center of a heptachord). Cf. app. A.

<Things can be said to be "prior"> in respect of order: this includes everything that is positioned systematically in relation to some one determinate object, as the beside-stander (*parastates*) is prior to the third-stander (*tritostates*) and the seventh note (*paranete*) is prior to the eighth (*nete*), for in the first case the *koryphaios* is the starting point, in the second the middle note (*mese*).

Dance

317A. Becker, *Anecdota Graeca* 1.101.17 (= Aristoxenus fr. 104 Wehrli). Aristoxenus was a Pythagorean and Peripatetic philosopher of the 4th c. B.C. and the most influential writer on music in antiquity. Aristoxenus' comment here is frequently repeated by ancient writers. Cf. app. A.

> That the *kordax* is a type of dance Aristoxenus demonstrates in *On Tragic Dance* thus: "The so-called *emmeleia* is a type of tragic dance, just as the so-called *sikinnis* is satyric and the so-called *kordax* is comic."

317B. Michael Psellos?, *On Tragedy* 77 Browning. The manuscript is dated ca. 1300 but contains information derived from Hellenistic authors. The treatise repeats the information cited from Aristoxenus in 317A and adds a description of the *emmeleia,* probably also derived from Aristoxenus.

> The form of the dance was solemn and grandiose, with many long pauses between movements.

318. Athenaeus 630c–e. Written ca. 200.

> The satyric dance, as Aristokles says in the first book of *On Choruses* (2nd c. B.C.), is called the *sikinnis* ... Skamon in the first book of *On Inventions* says that the *sikinnis* is derived from the verb "to shake" (*seiesthai*). ... There are some who say that *sikinnis* is named poetically from "movement" (*kinesis*), which the satyrs make as quickly as possible when they dance. For this dance has no depth of feeling and therefore never slows down. In ancient times all satyric poetry was choral, as tragedy was also at the time; and so they had no actors. There are three dances for theatrical poetry: the tragic, the comic, and the satyric. In the same way there are three dances for lyric poetry: the *pyrriche,* the *gymnopaidike,* and the *hyporchematike.* The *pyrrhiche* is like satyric dancing be-

cause both are danced very quickly.... The *gymnopaidike* is something like the tragic dance that is called *emmeleia* ("harmonious"); in both, gravity and solemnity is visible. The *hyporchematike* resembles the comic dance that is called *kordax;* both are playful.

319. Athenaeus 629f. Written ca. 200. The list has several items in common with Pollux (app. A). All or most of these names were probably collected from the texts of classic dramatists such as we find cited here.

Dance figures are sword-dance, basket, *kallabides* (see 320), owl (*skops*), owling (*skopeuma*). The owl was a figure imitating men gazing into the distance (*aposkopounton*) and curving their hand high over their foreheads. Aeschylus mentions it in (his satyrplay) the *Ambassadors* (*TrGF* F 79): "Behold these ancient owlings." And Eupolis in the *Toadies* mentions *kallabides*: "He walks *kallabides;* he shits sesame cakes." <Other figures are> tongs (*thermaustris*), alternate hands (or feet, *hekaterides*), lookout (*skopos*), recumbent hand, snubhand, twofoot (*dipodismos*), woodtheft, elbows out, basket, whirlwind.

320. Photius, *Lex.*, s.v. *kallabides*. Written ca. 850.
Kallabides: to walk disjointedly and tug at one's haunches with one's hands.

321A. Pollux 4.103. Written ca. 180.
(Listing various dances.) There was also a certain "owl" (*skops*), also called *skopias,* which was a dance form with a twisting about of the neck in imitation of the bird, which is caught when mesmerized by dancing.

321B. Athenaeus 391a. Written ca. 200. Cf. Aelian, *Nature of Animals* 15.28.
Elsewhere again Aristotle says (293 Rose): "The *otos* is similar to the owl, but is not nocturnal.... It imitates men. At any rate it is caught when it imitates dancing.... in hunting them the most skillful dancer stands directly in front of them, and the animals, looking at the dancer, move like marionettes. Another hunter stands behind them and stealthily grabs hold of them while they are entranced by the pleasure of the imitation. They say that owls (*skops*) do the same... and a kind of dance is called 'owl' (*skops*) after the variety of movements observed in the animal."

322. Hesychius, s.v. *hyposkopon chera*. Written 5th c.
The gaze-under hand (*hyposkopon chera*): Aeschylus (*TrGF* F 339). He bids hold the hand as do people gazing at things in the distance,

just like Pans (mythological goat-men) do. The "lookout" (*skopos*) is a dance figure.

323. Eustathius, *Commentary on the Odyssey* 1601.28. Eustathius cites Critias, the 5th-c. B.C. Athenian philosopher and tragedian.

> *Thermaustris:* a dance with energetic foot movements. Critias (88 B 36 Diels-Kranz) at any rate writes as follows: "They leapt high into the air and crossed their feet several times before hitting the ground again."

324A. Pollux 4.102. Written ca. 180.

> "Alternate hands" (*hekaterides*) and "tongs" (*thermaustrides*) are energetic dances: the former exercises movement of arms; the latter involves leaping.

324B. Hesychius, s.v. *hekaterein*. Written 5th c.

> "To alternate" (*hekaterein*): to kick at ones haunches with both heels in alternation.

325. Athenaeus 628c–f. Written ca. 200. This passage gives us some insight into the historical development of the dance in drama and how conservative theorists interpreted these changes. Damon was a music theorist of the second half of the 5th c. B.C., whose moral interpretation of dance and music in terms of a binary class division between "noble" and "base" souls had a powerful influence upon right-wing music and dance theory, and particularly upon Plato. Chamaeleon wrote in the late 4th or early 3rd c. B.C., Plato (the comic poet) in the late 5th or early 4th c. B.C. Socrates, the philosopher, composed his poems while in prison in 399 B.C.

> Music contributes to the exercise and the sharpening of the intellect . . . The students of Damon the Athenian put the case well when they say that songs and dances necessarily result when the soul is somehow in motion and that those ("songs and dances," or "souls") that are freeborn and noble produce similar ("souls," or "songs and dances"), and the opposite produce the opposite. . . . For in dance or movement in general, decency and good order are beautiful, disorder and vulgarity ugly. This is why from the very beginning the poets arranged dances for free men and made use of dance-figures only to represent what was being sung, taking care always to preserve nobility and manliness in their movements, which is why they called these dances *hyporchemata* ("dances subordinate to"). But if anyone arranged the dance movements beyond measure or in writing the songs said something that was not expressed in the dance, he suffered disgrace. Thus, according to Chamaeleon (fr.

42 Wehrli) Aristophanes or Plato in *Costumes* (*Skeuai*) spoke in this way (Plato, *PCG* F 138): "so that if anyone danced well (in the old days), it was a good show, but now they don't do anything but stand stock-still as if stunned and howl." Back then the kind of dance performed by the choruses was decorous and dignified and like an imitation of the movements of men in arms, and Socrates in his poems says that the finest dancers are the best warriors. He writes: "Those who honor the gods most beautifully with choruses are best in war." For dancing is virtually like military maneuvers and a display both of discipline in general and of a concern for bodily health.

326. Plato, *Laws* 814d–16e. Written ca. 350 B.C.

...but about other movements of the whole body, the greatest portion of which one would rightly identify as some sort of dance, one must necessarily suppose that there are two types of dance, that which imitates more beautiful bodies tending toward solemnity, and that of uglier bodies tending toward the worthless, and again there are two types of the worthless and two types of the serious. Of the serious the one has to do with war and beautiful bodies engaged in violent struggle but of manly soul, the other of a soul in prosperous circumstances that is sensible amidst moderate pleasures...One would rightly call the warlike of these...the *pyrrhiche*...That of the unwarlike Muse, in which men honor the gods and the children of the gods in dance, could as a whole be considered a kind of dance performed in the confidence of prosperity. We could divide this into two varieties: a more pleasurable kind in which people find happiness after ridding themselves of a condition of hardship and danger; another more mellow variety connected with the preservation and increase of goods already acquired. In such circumstances everyone moves their body more the greater the pleasure, and less the smaller the pleasure. Moreover, the person who is more controlled and better trained in courage will make smaller movements, while the coward and the person untrained in temperance will provide greater and more violent changes of motion. And, generally speaking, no one using their voice in song or speech is able to keep their body altogether still. This is why the gestural representation of things said produced the entire art of dance. In all of these instances one person moves in tune (*emmelos*), another out of tune (*plemmelos*) <with what is said>. Anyone who gives consideration to the many ancient names for things handed down to us must praise them as well founded and true to nature, but this is especially true in the case of the dances of people in prosperity who are moderate in their pleasures: how correct and erudite the names, whoever it was gave them, and how rational the application of the label to all together, when he named them *emmeleiai,* and established two kinds of beautiful dances, the warlike *pyrrhiche* and the peaceful *emmeleia,* giving each its appropriate and harmonious name.... We have dealt with the questions concerning the comportment of beautiful bodies and noble souls toward dancing. We must now consider and come to an understanding of those questions that concern ugly bodies and mentalities and those inclined toward comic laughter, with respect to speech, song, and dance, and with respect to those comic representations that employ all of these. It is impossible to learn what is serious without the ridiculous or to learn any opposite without its opposite, if one is to be sensible; moreover it is not possible to actually do both, if one is going to have even a small share in virtue, but we have to learn <the ridiculous> for the sake of never doing or saying anything ridiculous through ignorance, as we must not, but we must order slaves and payed foreigners to imitate such things, and never make anything of them at all, nor permit the appearance of any free citizen, whether man or woman, who has learned them, but it should always appear that there is something strange about these representations.

V. Mime and Pantomime

As early as 336 B.C. the great tragedian Neoptolemos is alleged to have sung at a banquet of Philip of Macedon an aria adapted from a tragedy (IV 30H); and it is clear that the term "tragedian" (*tragoidos*), which had meant chief actor/director, in imperial times denoted principally but not always a solo performer, e.g., Nero, who sang a tragic role sometimes with the help of one or more assistants—who were at least later called *hypokritai* (51)—and a musical accompaniment. The tragedian performed with a mask, and sometimes a chorus (45) sang along with him. This operatic role could present a dramatic story by the selection or adaption of different texts from earlier works. There developed a general distinction between "sung tragedy" (46), i.e., operatic arias, and "danced tragedy" (39), i.e., the pantomime. In addition, tragic arias, adapted from the lyric or nonlyric parts of tragedy (48) or from early choral music, could be sung by a kitharode (47) to the lyre, or sung by choruses under a *choraules* (49); these choruses could function as a background to pantomime, in keeping with the traditions of choral and lyric poetry of classical times. In later Greek, the verb *tragodeo* means little more than "to sing." These are all further developments of the experiments of Hellenistic theater.

It is extremely difficult to trace the impact of native Roman drama, since most of it is lost, and what survives is very much influenced by Greek drama. It would appear that native Roman music and dance, such as the so-called *ludus talarius* (24), could have been adapted for mime and pantomime, while the old Atellan farce persisted well into imperial times in changed form, also influencing mime and even pantomime. In fact the earliest public dramatic dancing at Rome came from the Etruscans. These subliterary forms of drama achieved respectability in late republican times.

The two principal forms of drama that dominated the public stage in imperial times, and were important also in private performance, were mime and pantomime (25). Though both existed in a great variety of forms, we can say generally that mimes acted, sang, and danced without masks, either individually or in a troupe, whereas pantomimes wore masks, acted, and danced, but did not sing, being accompanied by a musical group or a chorus or soloist (23) who could explain the background. Again very generally speaking, mimes dealt in a realistic, comic, sententious, and often outrageously vulgar way with any theme whatsoever, while pantomime was a ballet enactment of a usually mythical story; it may have tended to appeal to higher tastes with tragic themes but could be erotic and comic as well; it was particularly popular when given as a spectacle in the great theaters. But since both forms could range from solo performances to wild extravaganzas, it needs to be remembered that these are generalizations.

Both forms had existed from the earliest times. Xenophon describes a private performance (ca. 420 B.C.) that was largely pantomimic, based on the myth of Dionysus and Ariadne, but apparently without masks. As for mime, we do not know if its real ancestors are the so-called mimes of the Sicilians Epicharmus (5th c. B.C.) or Sophron and his son (5th–4th c. B.C.), since only fragments survive.

The sponsorship of mime and pantomime by wealthy princes of the Hellenistic period (4th–1st c. B.C.) for their private entertainment was of great importance to their development. This trend was taken up by the Roman dictator Sulla (3) in the 1st c. B.C., and copied by the republican elite. But the ancients attributed to Augustus and his circle the introduction of pantomime and its famous performers Bathyllos and Pylades to Rome (23) from the east. Whatever the truth, the Romans generally felt that mime and pantomime had come to them from the greatest city of the Hellenistic world, Alexandria. Probably the pantomime in the grandiose form known to the Romans is a creation of these eastern artists at Rome. Both Pylades (28) and Bathyllos—stage names (32)—started schools to train others in their methods (31).

The first testimony to public mime performance is a late 3rd-c. B.C. relief with an inscription on a terra-cotta lamp from Athens (10). This is long before we know that mimes were performed regularly at the festival of the Floralia (1) in Rome, which was founded about 170 B.C. They became increasingly popular and more sophisticated, reaching a literary peak in the mid-1st c. B.C. with the famous writers Laberius, a knight, (2) and Publilius Syrus, a freedman from Syria.

The first certain pantomime is from a small town in Asia Minor (22) in about 75 B.C. and came to entertain at a festival, apparently as a solo artist. But this could be misleading because the Greek word *pantomimos* ("all-mime") is very rare in Greek, but it is the common word used in Latin. The normal Greek word (22) for a pantomime is the general word "dancer" (*orchestes*) or later in imperial times the more grandiose "actor of tragic rhythmic dancing" (23A), which was meant to distinguish the prestigious pantomime dancing from ordinary dancing. In Latin the word *histrio,* generally "actor," also comes to mean primarily a pantomime.

Mime was for a long time considered as an inferior form of drama by the Artists of Dionysus, who excluded mime actors from their association and from Greek festivals for most of their history; but in Rome at least the mime actors formed their own professional association (7). Nonetheless on occasion its male and female practitioners (18) could attain great influence and personal popularity. The mime appealed to the populace because of the freedom of expression allowed in it, so that it could indulge in political remarks even under a repressive regime. It also appealed because of the pithy quotations in which it abounded, and the songs that were quickly taken up by the audience. Not surprisingly a number of stock themes, all of them essentially folk motifs, were the staple of the popular mime, though our material is insufficient to say how great the variety was (16). The main themes we hear of are the cuckolded husband, myth travesties (21), and the "historical" mime Laureolus, but we have only vague notions of the shipwreck mime or the stupid-king mime. Some papyrus fragments of mime plots survive, which show there was a greater variety than we could have guessed. Parodies by mime actors of Christian baptisms have their origin in the parodies of ancient ritual initiation in old comedy seven hundred years earlier. It would seem that mime was roughly divided (19, 20) into longer versions with plots and acts, called "hypotheses," and shorter skits called "merriments" (*paignia*), which could be entr'actes for other entertainments, in public or private or in village feasts. Indeed the mimes appeared in musical skits both in between acts of drama—so called *embolima/ embolia*—and at the end of dramas—*exodia*—in which role they replaced the earlier Atellan farce, about the middle of the 1st c. B.C. At the lower end of the dramatic scale, mimes could specialize in everything from imitating animal noises to takeoffs of lawyers; a popular speciality of the mimes known as Homerists (9) was imitation of Homeric battles, sometimes comic.

Though mimes might act anywhere, on the formal stage they are associated with the *siparium,* a linen screen that is not to be confused with the *aulaeum,* the curtain proper. It is supposed that the mimes, during their entr'actes, performed at the front of the *proscaenium* against

the background of these plain *siparia,* which were unfolded across the
stage to hide the main scenery and through which the actor appeared
and disappeared quickly. The mime could be performed apparently sometimes on a temporary stage with as many as four doors (*SEG* 11.923.36),
or in a theater where stage properties could go into the orchestra. The
performers might wear any suitable costume (17), and masks and *phalloi*
when appropriate, and they appear to have been either barefooted or
sandaled. They classified themselves as archmimes (*archimimi*) or according to fixed "parts," of uncertain meaning (4, 5).

Since mime aimed mostly but not always at laughter, it was given to
extemporization and ad-libbing, pratfalls and beatings, and illogic of all
sorts (11–15); the favorite characters and themes were known and easily
recognized. Swift entrances and exits and an infinite variety of characters
added to the surprises in which mime delighted. There could be a small
band as well, giving a music-hall flavor, since mimes sang and danced,
and were often the source of popular songs. Perhaps there was a difference
between Greek and Roman mime (6), and certainly there were constant
developments in the protean form of the popular mime during its thou-
sand-year-long history. By the year 200, probably because of the favor
shown by emperors, inscriptions can record mime as well as pantomime
artists boasting that they were "winners of the sacred contests" (cf. IIIB),
e.g., at the festival of the Eusebeia at Puteoli, and were therefore on the
same level as Olympic victors (33); but competitions had existed earlier
(30).

If mime was the successor to comedy, pantomime was the natural
successor to tragedy (34, 35), especially after the comic and sometimes
erotic ballet of Bathyllos lost ground to the tragic ballet of the school
of Pylades. The ballet artists became famous above all as exponents of
myth (26), though the libretti, called "stories for dancing"—*fabulae
salticae*—were considered to be often vapid. In fact a later author (42)
can affirm that ordinary people know their myths largely from watching
pantomime. The action of the principal or occasionally principals as they
acted out a myth was all-important; frequent mention is made of twisting
(37), leaping, versatility (40), and sudden "freezing." Particular attention
was paid to the use of hand language (*cheironomy*), and to the use of
the mantle (*pallium*) to suggest items in the myth (38). Very early the
pantomime suffered additions that turned it increasingly into a spectacle,
like the Bacchic one Apuleius (41) describes in the theater at Corinth,
our only full description of a spectacle-pantomime. We hear much of
female dancers and later of female pantomime artists, who were enor-

mously popular, especially in Byzantium; perhaps they did not wear the usual mask. But pantomimes had a morally dubious repute (36).

Likewise the *pyrrhiche,* originally a solo or group dance for young men practicing martial movements, especially with the shield, became little more than a mass dancing show, often with a Bacchic theme and notable for the splendor of the costumes, and could serve as an opener or in the interval at the arena or theater. It obviously could overlap with pantomime. To this kind of pantomimic spectacle belongs presumably the report of the numerous dancing girls with accompanying choruses and dancing masters late in imperial Rome (57). At the Colosseum, at its opening in 80, animals (and even trees) followed Orpheus as he played on his lyre, though—in what was doubtless a surprise ending—they eventually ate him. Pantomime has begun to include gladiatorial elements. All of this indicates that enormous resources were consumed not only in the training of artists and animals, but in the construction of mechanical marvels (55) and ingenious effects (52), not to mention the huge arenas in which these engineering feats were to be displayed. It is remarkable that the Renaissance artists and engineers also found themselves putting their skills to use in animating the symbolism of classical myth, and thereby elaborating the trappings of imperial power as well as entertaining the people.

As a finale, we give a few of the passages that illustrate how the Romans developed massive organized spectacles with engineered effects. These summoned all possible resources and included the deaths of criminals (53, 56) and wild animals in a mythological context. The name *pyrrhiche* (54) was used when massed dancers were involved. It was for this that the great amphitheaters were constructed. But it too was theater.

Sources

Mime

1. Valerius Maximus 2.10.8. Written ca. 32, referring to mid-2nd c. B.C.

> While Cato was watching the Floralia, the populace was ashamed to demand that the mime actresses strip off. When he learned this from his good friend Favonius, who was sitting next to him, he left the theater, so that his presence would not hinder the traditional course of the show.

2. Macrobius, *Saturnalia* 2.7.1. Written late 4th or early 5th c. The reference is to 46 B.C. Laberius was one of the best-known writers of mimes. Being a knight, he was forced to become *infamis* and lose his status by going on the stage (IVAiv). Caesar wanted to have a competition of the best mimes of his time for his triumphal celebrations.

> Laberius, who was a Roman knight free with his opinions, was invited by Caesar for five hundred thousand sesterces to appear on the stage and himself act the mimes he wrote. But power can force, even when it invites and begs, and as a result Laberius proves that he was forced by Caesar in these verses from the prologue . . . In this performance also he revenged himself as best he could, by putting on the clothes of a Syrian slave, who bawls out, apparently badly beaten and like someone in a great hurry: "Up citizens: we lose our freedom."

3. Plutarch, *Sulla* 36. Written ca. 115, referring to first half of the 1st c. B.C.

> For these were the men who had most influence with <Sulla> now: Roscius the comedian, Sorex the archmime, and Metrobius the lysiode (impersonator of women).

4. *CIL* 6.1063. A list of Latin members of a mime troupe performing at a military festival. Date: April 11, 212. It is obvious that the chief mime is not automatically player of first roles; nor is the *stupidus* allocated to a particular role level; perhaps *archimimus* means little more than professional mime. Lucilius Marcianus, an *archimimus* here, appears in a list, *CIL* 6.1064, as *stupidus graecus*.

> Cluvius Glaber *archimimus,* Caetenius Eucarpus *archimimus,* Volusius Iuventus *stupidus,* Suellius Secundinus *stupidus,* Lucilius Marcianus *archimimus,* Vindicius Fel[ix . . .], Flavius Saturninus *scurra.*

5A. Parts and Roles. Festus 438.22 L. Written late 2nd c., referring apparently to the year 211 B.C. "Of second parts" seems to be usually the parasite, but could apparently be the *stupidus*. First and third roles were antagonists. There could, however, be more mimes involved.

> Volumnius, who danced to the pipes, was an actor of second roles, who is introduced in nearly all mimes as a parasite.

5B. Horace, *Epistles* 1.18.10–4. Written 20 B.C. This passage shows surprisingly what (some?) mime actors "of second parts" did, and why they often played parasites as Festus says.

> Another man, overprone to servility, a jester on the lowest couch (i.e., a parasite), so reveres the rich man's nod, so echoes his speeches and picks up his words as they fall, that you would think a

schoolboy was repeating his lessons to a stern master, or a mime player acting second parts.

6A. *ILS* 5201. Stele from Rome. Date: imperial period.

Praised by the people, wont to carry out their wishes, appointed to the stage (i.e., to the actors' college), parasite of Apollo, likewise a useful actor of fourth <parts> among dancing mimes.

6B. *ILS* 5209a. Gravestone from Praeneste. Date: imperial period.

Marcus Iunius Maior, freedman of Marcus, *archimimus,* member of the Parasites of Apollo.

6C. *ILS* 5211. Gravestone from Rome. Date: 2nd–3rd c.

Sleep on. To Claudia Hermiona, first *archimima* of her time. By her heirs.

7. *CIL* 14.2408; *ILS* 5196; E.J. Jory, *Philol.* 109 (1965) 307–8. Marble statue base. Date: 169. This monument from Bovillae in Italy honors a wealthy mime actor for his services toward the theatrical guild. This is not the *technitai* guild, but some lower and local body. The prestigious association called "The Parasites of Apollo," which contained also pantomimes, was clearly related to but not the same as the Mime Association. The monument gives an insight into the complexity of local theatrical organizations.

For Lucius Acilius Pompteius Eutyches, son of Lucius, noble archmime, appointee on daily salary (*diurnus*) in the Commune of Mimes, Parasite of Apollo, honored by tragic, comic, and all corporations to do with the stage, decurion at Bovillae, whom the appointed members (of the Commune of Mimes) have named "Father" for the first time ever:—the appointed members of the theatrical <guild> (*scaenici*) <set this up> from funds they collected because of his donations and his service to them. Because of this dedication of him (i.e., of this monument to him) he gave to the appointed members a donation of twenty-five denarii each, to the decurions of Bovillae a donation of five denarii each, to the Augustales three denarii each, to wives of those honored(?) and the people a denarius each. (There follows the date and a list of sixty of the *ordo adlectorum* <*scaenicorum*>, i.e., "organization of appointed performers on the stage," the local theatrical guild.)

8A. *ILS* 5224. Gravestone. Date: possibly 2nd c.

To the memory of Aemilia Irene, who lived twenty-six years, thirteen days; Aurelius Eutyches, *stupidus* of the urban troupe <set this up> for his dearest wife.

8B. *ILLRP* 804. This is the oldest epitaph for a mime. Date: probably first half of the 2nd c. B.C.

Protogenes Cloel(ius?) the delightful mime lies here, who by his nonsense gave much pleasure to the people.

9. *POxy* 1025. A letter from Oxyrhynchus in Egypt. Written late 3rd c. Roman citizenship was given to the whole empire under the emperor Aurelius Antoninus (Caracalla) in 212, and all those who acquired it took on the name Aurelius.

Aurelius Agathos gymnasiarch, *prytanis* in office, Aurelius Hermannobammon exegete, Aurelius Didymus chief priest, and Aurelius Koprias *kosmetes* of the city of Euergetis greet Aurelius Euripas mime artist and Aurelius Sarapas Homerist. Come again as is your wont, to celebrate the feast, making merry in our ancestral festival on the anniversary of the great god Kronos.

10. Watzinger, *MDAI* 26 (1901) 1ff. Inscription on a terra-cotta lamp from Athens with relief of three male figures including a *stupidus,* center. Date: ca. 225 B.C.

Mime speakers: plot (*hypothesis*): Mother-in-law.

11. Cicero, *Philippics* 2.65. Written 44 B.C.

He jumped for joy like a character in a mime, starving one moment, then suddenly rich.

12. Varro, *Antiquities* fr. 3 Cardauns (cited by Augustine, *City of God* 4.22). Written mid-1st c. B.C.

For this way we shall know what god we are calling and ought to invoke and for what reasons, so that we don't do what the mime artists do, and beg water from Bacchus and wine from the Nymphs.

13. Seneca, *Moral Letters* 114.6. Written ca. 56 and referring to the end of the 1st c. B.C.

\<Maecenas\> appeared with his cloak wrapped round his head, leaving only his ears exposed, like the millionaire's runaway slave in mime.

14. Cicero, *For Caelius* 65. Delivered 56 B.C. Cicero refers to the sudden changes and illogic of mime. The "clapper" (*scabillum*) was fastened to the mime's foot and used to mark time or prompt the stagehands.

So, the finale of a mime, not a play; there, when they can't find an ending, someone escapes from their hands, then the clappers go off, and the curtain is pulled.

15. Petronius, *Satyricon* 80. Written mid-1st c. This perhaps refers to a plot where treasure is discovered.

The troupe puts on a mime on the stage; one is called father, the other, son; another gets the name millionaire.

16. Choricius of Gaza, *Apology for Mimes* 110. Written beginning of 6th c.

Who would not give up an attempt to enumerate all <mimes> imitate? Master, servants, merchants, sausage sellers, bakers, restaurateur, banqueters, contract makers, stammering child, youth in love, another one angry, another quieting the other's anger.

17A. Costume. Scholion to Juvenal 3.177.

You will see the performers of mime just like the spectators; they wear the same clothes.

17B. Apuleius, *Apology* 13.5. Written 158. Apuleius suggests that a patchwork tunic was typical of mimes.

If I possessed a theatrical wardrobe (*choragium*) would you argue also from that, that I normally wore the trailing robe (*syrma*) of tragedy, the yellow gown (*crocota*) of pantomime, ... the patchwork tunic (*centunculus*) of mime?

18. *IG* XIV 2342 (= *GV* 675). A memorial epitaph from the amphitheater of Aquileia for a mime actress known for her singing. Date: ca. 220.

She won resounding fame on the stage earlier among many peoples and many cities for manifold excellence among mimes, later among choruses, often in musical contests. Herakleides, a good speaker and character mime, set up <this> memorial to the mime actress Basilla, the tenth Muse, thus not dead; though she is a corpse, she has won life as her fair reward, having found a resting place for her body in the soil of the Muses. That's life. Your fellow performers say to you: "Take heart Basilla: nobody is immortal."

19. Plutarch, *Convivial Questions* 712e. Written ca. 115. Plutarch describes the kinds of mimes suitable for entertainment at dinner around 100.

"Well," I replied, "there are certain mimes they call *hypotheseis* ("basic plots") and some that they call *paignia* ("merriments"), but I do not suppose that either kind is suitable for a dinner party. The *hypotheseis* have too prolonged an action and demand too much equipment; and the *paignia,* which are packed with scurrilous and trivial low comedy, ought not even to be seen by the slaves that fetch our shoes, if their masters are prudent. Even when women and young people are in the dinner company, most people put on imitations of actions and stories that are far more disruptive of an orderly mind than any drinking."

20. *P.Berol.* inv. 13927, ed. Wiemke, p. 192ff. List of stage requisites for mimes, apparently *paignia* and a *hypothesis*. Date: 4th/5th century.

(Titles) 1.<The plundered City>
         2.<The Ship?>
         3. No Need for Words
         4. <merriment> of the Softies
         5. <merriment> of the Sun
         6. Why Violence with Meat?
         <7>. <merriment> of the Goths.

———

Memo for the production of "Leukippe."
        barber's workshop
        barber's instruments
        mirror
        ribbons
        three jugs for the old wife
        moneybelt
        letterbox
        smith's instruments
        hammer, spatula
        the picture
        linen tunic

21. *Inschriften von Ephesos* 2091. Date: 2nd c. This theater inscription is accompanied by incised drawings of various scenes from mythological mime. The following characters are identified: Heracles, Thetis, Pileous (= Peleus), Hephaestus. The comic story was the birth of Hephaestus, his upbringing by Thetis and revenge on his mother Hera, and the attempts of Ares and Dionysus to free her, and finally the Return of Hephaestus drunk to Olympus. It occurs already on a Corinthian vase seven hundred years earlier as a comic dramatic theme (II 3). The presence of Heracles suggests another version.

Pantomime

22A. Greek Origins of Pantomime. *Inschriften Priene* 113.65. This inscription describes an *akroama* ("musical act"), which was part of a festival about 80 B.C. These inscriptions record only the use of the word "pantomime," but mimic dancing was from prehistoric times part of cult practice and was already an entertainment in classical Greece. For possible Etruscan origins, cf. III 177.

> (Zosimos, a benefactor of the city,) hired also a pantomime (*pantomimos*) Ploutogenes, able to charm by his art.

22B. Dioscorides, *Palatine Anthology* 11.195. Written ca. 220 B.C. This poem pretends to be the complaint of a dancer who has made a miserable impression in the female role of Hyrnetho in the "Temenidai," a plot probably based on a classical tragedy. Notable is that the successful opposition (in a competition?) danced the exotic and nonclassical role of the self-castrating priest of the Great Mother.

> Aristagoras danced "Gallus": I with much trouble got through the "Temenidai," lovers of war. He was sent off with applause, but one rattle of the clappers (sc., accompanying my dance) dispatched poor Hyrnetho. To blazes you deeds of heroes; for among philistines a lark would sing more musically than a swan (which conventionally but falsely was thought to sing most beautifully).

22C. Varro, *Menippean Satires* fr. 513 Astbury. Written ca. 60 B.C., but perhaps taken already from Menippus in the beginning of the 3rd c. B.C.

> Believe me, servants have devoured more masters than dogs have; if Actaeon had got in first and eaten up his dogs himself, he wouldn't be a joke for pantomimes in the theater.

23A. Pylades and Bathyllos. Athenaeus 20d. Written ca. 200. Ancient scholars were firmly convinced that pantomime in the sophisticated form popular in the Roman Empire was the invention of Syrian and Alexandrian artists who came to Rome in the second half of the 1st c. B.C.; Pylades (a stage name) invented tragic pantomime, while Bathyllos (also a stage name) invented comic.

> Of the so-called "tragic dancing" the first exponent was Bathyllos of Alexandria, who, says Seleucus (a grammarian of the mid-1st c.), danced pantomimes. Aristonicus (about the same time) says that this Bathyllos together with Pylades, who wrote a treatise on dancing, developed the Italian style of dance.... Now Pylades' dancing was solemn, expressing passion and variety of character, whereas Bathyllos' was more jolly.

23B. Plutarch, *Convivial Questions* 711e. Written ca. 115.

> As for dances, I should disqualify <from private parties> the Pyladic, as pretentious and emotional and requiring a large cast; but...I will accept the Bathyllic. It is a straightforward unaccompanied

dance, verging on the *kordax,* and presents a danced interpretation of Echo or some Pan or Satyr reveling with Eros.

23C. Jerome, *Chronicle* 2.143 Sch. Written 381.

In the year 22 B.C.: Pylades of Cilicia the pantomime, though earlier <performers> sang and danced themselves, at Rome first made a chorus and pipes accompany him.

24A. *Ludus Talarius.* Cassiodorus, *Chronica* 2, p. 131 M. Written in the 5th c. and referring to 115 B.C. The *ludus talarius* is a simple and possibly vulgar dance in long dress with castanet and cymbal accompaniment, probably Etruscan in origin and sanctioned by ritual. It may be connected with the later pantomime. We do not know if these two incidents are connected. The statement is unfortunately ambiguous.

When M. Metellus and M. Scaurus were consuls, L. Metellus and G. Domitius the censors banished the theater arts (*artem ludicram*) from the city except for a Latin piper with singer, and the *ludus talarius* (the manuscripts have *talanum*).

24B. Fronto, *On Speeches* 10. Written 163.

I praise what the censor did, who closed down the *ludi talarii* because he claimed that he himself, when he went past those things, maintained his dignity only with difficulty, avoiding tapping his feet to the strains of the clappers and cymbals.

25. Tacitus, *Dialogus* 29. Written ca. 80.

Indeed the proper and peculiar vices of this city seem to me to be almost begotten in the mother's womb, the craze for actors (pantomimes?) and the enthusiasm for gladiators and horses.

26. *Inscriptiones Creticae* 4.222A. From Crete. Date: 1st c. Artists were not only freedmen and slaves, though most were.

Lucius Furius Celsus, son of Lucius of the Falernian tribe, dancer of myths. Crowned in the theater with a golden crown, the greatest according to law, *proxenos* (i.e., representative) of the [Gortynians], a citizen himself and his descendants.

27. *ILS* 5210a. Gravestone. Pantomimes as young as six are known.

Hellas the pantomime lies in peace here, fourteen years old.

28. *CIL* 10.1074. Inscription from Pompeii. Date ca. 20 B.C. This is the first use of the word *pantomimus* in Latin, and the Pylades mentioned as a star attraction must be the famous Pylades. Some of the other entertainments mentioned are unknown from any other source. Note that the games are held in the forum, as often at this time, and not in the theaters.

Aulus Clodius Flassus, son of Aulus, thrice *duumvir,* five times elected military tribune by the people, <gave> in his first duumvirate at the Apolline games in the forum: a procession, bulls, matadors, escape artists, bridge fighters (i.e., gladiators; "bridge" was a type of scaffolding) three pairs, boxers in teams and fighters, games with every entertainment and with all the pantomimes and Pylades.

29. *ILS 5252.* This is the gravestone of the musical accompanist of the pantomime Paris.

Titus Claudius Corinthus, accompanist (*musicarius*) of Paris, for himself and his family.

30. *CIL* 6.10115. Inscription from Tivoli. Date: end of the 1st c. B.C. The inscription attests for the first time that competitions of some sort took place among these leading pantomimes, though the first official pantomime competitions were not until later at Naples. In Greece the pantomimes are not agonistic until the 2nd c. The palm branch that decorates this inscription is a symbol of competition in Italy. It is uncertain if Theorus is the original name of the famous Bathyllos.

Gaius Theorus, star, victor in pantomime.
If god himself is now captured by your [art], Theorus,
do [men] doubt that god wants to imitate <you>?
[You defeated] Pylades of Cicilia, Nomius of Syria, Hylas of
Salmakis, Pierus of Tivoli.

31. Seneca, *Nature Questions* 7.32.3. Written 62–65. This kind of philosophic abuse was picked up gladly by the church.

What effort is expended in case any pantomime name dies out! In their successors the edifice of Pylades and Bathyllos is preserved; of these arts there are many pupils and many teachers. The private stage rings loud in the whole city; on it men gambol, women too. Husbands and wives vie to see which can offer the more voluptuous(?) pose. Then when under the mask shame has long since been rubbed off their face, they turn to the helmet of the gladiator. No one cares for philosophy.

32. *ILS 5185.* Date: second half of 2nd c. This may be at least the third pantomime named "Pylades."

Publius Aelius Pylades, freedman of Augustus, pantomime, victor in the sacred contests, began <this monument>; Lucius Aurelius Pylades, freedman of the Augusti, his pupil, victor in the sacred contests, finished it.

33A. *ILS* 5186. Date: ca. 190. Imperial pantomimes could be both wealthy and influential, and could from the time of the original Pylades afford to put on public entertainments from their own resources. They were even awarded municipal offices.

> For Lucius Aurelius Pylades, freedman of Augustus, first pantomime of his time, crowned four times in the sacred games, patron of the *Parasiti* of Apollo, priest of the association, honored at Puteoli with the grant of decurion and duumviral honors, augur, on account of his love for his country and his extreme generosity in producing a gladiatorial show with a public hunt, at the pleasure of the most holy emperor Commodus, the Cornelian tribe <set up this monument>.

33B. *ILS* 5193. Honorary inscription. Date: 187. Septentrio started as an alumnus of Faustina the Younger, becomes an imperial freedman under Marcus or Commodus, and is "launched" (*productus*) by Commodus. The inscription is set up by the people of Lanuvium, to record his adoption into the usually exclusive club of the "young men" (*ordo iuvenum Lanuvinorum*); we find these clubs of "young men" (Greek *neoi,* Latin *iuvenes*) associated elsewhere with the theater and claqueurs, probably because they were themselves an indispensable part of public processions and spectacles.

> For the freedman of M. Aurelius Augustus, Agilius Septentrio, pantomime, first of his time, priest of the *synodus,* Parasite of Apollo, alumnus of Faustina, launched by M. Aurelius Commodus Antoninus Pius Felix Augustus, decorated with the *ornamenta* of a decurion by decree of the order, and adopted into the *iuvenes.* By order of the Senate and people of Lanuvium.

34. *TrGF* 1, p. 344 *ad* 14a. Inscription from Tivoli. Date: 199. This gives an important list of titles of pantomimes, nearly all adaptions of tragedies by Euripides. They represent his victorious roles, presumably to a choral background adapted from these plays. "In the general contest" indicates that he was overall victor in the festival as well.

> *Heracles, Orestes, Tympanistae* (of Sophocles) in the general contest, *Trojan Women, Bacchae, Hippolytus* in the general contest: for L. Aurelius Apolaustus Memphius, freedman of Augusti, pantomime, three times sacred victor, first of his time, . . .

35. Suetonius, *Gaius* 57.9. Written ca. 120, referring to 41. The passage shows clearly how classical tragedy was considered to be the ancestor of imperial "tragic" pantomime.

The pantomime Mnester danced a tragedy, which the tragic actor Neoptolemus had once acted at the games at which Philip king of Macedon was killed.

36. J. Bayet, *Libyca Arch. Epigr.* 3 (1955) 104. This is an inscription from Timgad in North Africa, ca. 200, in flawed iambic senarii. The emphasis on the moral uprightness of the deceased pantomime is found in other inscriptions, and is presumably a reaction against their generally dubious reputation as long-haired effeminates of ambivalent sexuality.

Here is Vincentius, the glory of pantomimes, living forever on the lips of the public, not only by theatrical skill, as they usually do. He was loved (?) by every decent and good person; toward all <he was> without malice and gentle. When often he danced the well-known stories, he held the theater until the evening stars rose. Here now under the earth he rests before the ramparts. He lived and flourished twenty-three years, but he was even more eloquent in the sanctity of his life than in his gestures.

37. Philostratus, *Life of Apollonius* 4.21. See III 81. It would appear that theological pantomimes were now being acted at the old Dionysiac festivals. One may suspect the influence of old cult traditions as well as more recent spectacles.

38. Fronto, *On Orations* 5, p. 150.16 van den Hout. Written mid-2nd c.

As actors (i.e., pantomimes), when they dance clad in their mantles, with one and the same mantle represent a swan's tail, the tresses of Venus, a Fury's scourge, so...

39. Suetonius, *Nero* 54. Written ca. 120, referring to 68.

<Nero> had publicly vowed...that on the last day he would appear as an actor (i.e., pantomime) and dance Vergil's Turnus.

40. Lucian, *On the Dance* 67–68. Perhaps influenced by the emperor L. Verus' love of pantomime, the sophist Lucian in the 160s composed an entire tract on the subject, listing the many subjects used, but not, unfortunately, details of production. Here, however, he usefully indicates the stage accompaniment.

The Greeks of Italy quite appropriately call the dancer a pantomime (= who mimes everything)....In general, the dancer undertakes to present and enact characters and emotions, introducing now a lover, now an angry person, one man afflicted with madness, another with grief, and all this within fixed bounds. Indeed the most surprising part of it is that within the selfsame day, at one moment we are shown Athamas in a frenzy, at another Ino in terror;

presently the same person is Atreus, and after a little Thyestes; . . . yet they are all but a single man. . . . The dancer has everything at once, and that equipment of his is varied and comprehensive—the pipes, the panpipes, the tapping of feet, the clash of cymbals, the melodious voice of the actor (a secondary role), the harmony of the singers.

41. Apuleius, *Metamorphoses* 10.29. Written second half of the 2nd c. Apuleius' novel describes a pantomime spectacle of the "Judgment of Paris" in the theater of Corinth, which followed a *pyrrhiche*. It is the only description of such a scene in antiquity. Both spectacles took place on the actual stage, which was about 50 by 8 meters. In between, the main curtain (*aulaeum*) was drawn up from its position on the floor, so as to block the view; it is not certain what the *siparia* were—perhaps side curtains here. They must have been lowered again, but this is not mentioned.

The day for the performance arrived. . . . Since the first part of the spectacle was devoted to choral festivities, I stood outside . . . and delighted my curious eyes through the open door at the sight of the spectacle. Girls and boys in the youthful prime of life, preeminent in beauty, in shining clothes, with expressive step, in order well disposed, wandered in graceful patterns, ready to dance a Greek *pyrrhiche,* now bending into a moving circle, now lining up in an oblique row and forming a hollow four-sided wedge, then separating into two groups. But as soon as the final blare of the trumpet brought an end to the intricate twists and turns of their to-and-fro movement, the curtain was drawn up; the *siparia* were folded together and the stage-building set up. It was a wooden mountain, on the model of that famous mountain that the prophet Homer hymned as Idaean, constructed on a high scaffolding, planted with bushes and live trees, pouring out a stream of water from the very top, a fountain flowing by the workmanship of a carpenter. A few goats grazed on the grass, and a young man, nicely tunic-clad in the manner of Paris, the Phrygian shepherd, a foreign cloak flowing from his shoulders, played the master of the flock, his head covered with a golden tiara. A handsome boy was there—his only covering an ephebic tunic over his left shoulder, notable for the yellow hair that fell all around, and among his hair stuck up little wings of gold, joined by a similar bond; caduceus and rod showed him to be Mercury. He danced forward with a gold-plated apple in his right hand, and offered it to him who looked to be Paris, while he indicated the wishes of Jupiter with a head movement; then he

withdrew elegantly and disappeared from sight. There followed a
girl with noble features, in appearance like the goddess Juno, for a
splendid diadem bound her head, and she carried a scepter. Another
girl burst in, whom you would take for Minerva, her head covered
with a brilliant helmet, and the helmet itself was covered with an
olive wreath; she lifted her shield and swung her spear, and was
just like she shows herself when she fights.

42. Libanius, *For the Dancers* 64.112f. Written 361.

> ... some god taking pity on the illiteracy of ordinary people, brought
> on dancing as a substitute kind of instruction for the masses about
> deeds of old; and now the goldsmith will keep up a decent conversa-
> tion with the product of the schools about the house of Priam or
> Laius.

Tragic Arias

43. Philodemus, *On Music* 70 (Kemke). Written ca. 50 B.C. The passage
is taken to mean that dancing has been eliminated from Greek tragic
acting.

> ... because we lose nothing when dancing has been excised from
> the dramas, since there was never anything in any dance that was
> of help toward the good and the noble.

44. Lucillius, *Palatine Anthology* 11.11. Date: 65. This is an epigram
on a character who brought too many friends to dinner.

> I didn't know you were a *tragoidos,* Epikrates, or a *choraules* (i.e.,
> a pipe playing director of a chorus), or anyone else at all that is
> supposed to keep a chorus; I only invited you.

45. Plutarch, *How to Tell a Flatterer* 63a. Written ca. 115.

> Just as the *tragoidoi* need a chorus to sing along with them, or a
> theater to join in applauding them...

46. Suetonius, *Nero* 21. Written ca. 120, referring to mid-1st c. Nero
was not only a pantomime and lyre player but also a tragedian, as here,
and singer to the lyre, all forms indebted ultimately to Greek tragedy.

> <Nero> also put on the mask and sang tragedies (i.e., tragic solo
> arias) representing gods and heroes and even heroines and goddesses,
> having the masks fashioned in the likeness of his own features or
> those of the women of whom he chanced to be enamored. Among
> other themes, he sang Canace in Labor, Orestes the Matricide, The
> Blinding of Oedipus, and the Frenzy of Hercules.

47. *Hesperia* 22 (1953) 192. An inscription found near Corinth honors a citizen of Miletus who was probably a kitharode rather than a tragedian. Date: first half of 2nd c.

> The Council and the people of Miletus <honor> Gaios Aelios Themison, son of Theodotos, who won the Isthmian and Nemean games, the joint games of Asia five times, and the other games ninety-four times, and was the first and only one to arrange lyrics for himself from Euripides and Sophocles and Timotheus. By decree of the Council.

48. Dio of Prusa 19.5. Written ca. 100. The arias that survived from tragedy were adapted from the iambic spoken parts of classical tragedy and not the earlier monodies or choral lyrics.

> In the case of comedy (presumably New Comedy) everything is kept; in the case of tragedy only the powerful parts remain, i.e., the iambics, and portions of these they still perform in the theaters, but the more delicate parts have fallen away, i.e., the lyrics.

49. W.E.H. Cockle, *Proceedings of the XIV Congress of Papyrologists* (London 1975) 59. A damaged papyrus from Oxyrhynchus in Egypt, of ca. 100, gives a list of musical scores adapted largely from tragedy for performance by a choir to the accompaniment of pipes. The adaptation would have meant rewriting a text, writing the choral accompaniment with pipe music. Epagathos is technically a *choraules* for whom there were special competitions.

> (Column 1:) Odes of Epagathos the piper for choirs: 40; from 6 plays: from *Hypsipyle* 6, from *Deidameia,* from the *Hermaphrodite,* from the *Ransoming of Hector,* from *Medea,* from *Antiope;* equals odes of his own: 40. (Column 2:) Odes [...] 2; _ Odes of Canopus (a piper?) 2; _ Dramatic Odes, Odes of the tragic actor 3; _ [...] of the tragic actor <total> 10; _ <Odes?> of Pamphylos the piper for choirs 6...

50. *Excavations at Dura-Europos: Preliminary Report of the 9th Season,* 1935–36, Part 3: *The Palace Inscriptions,* ed. C.B. Wells (Yale 1952), p. 31, no. 945. This is from a number of graffiti left by a theater company on a wall of the palace of this border fortress in Syria. Date: mid-3rd c.

> To remember Elpidephoros the tragedian of Byzantium, foster child of Domitius Pompeianus, the holy and just Dux Ripae (i.e., Governor of the Euphrates border), along with Probus his *hypokrites* (i.e., synagonist).

Spectacles

51. Suetonius, *Nero* 11.2. Written ca. 120, referring to 66. This is the last named performance of a comedy at Rome. But here it is sensationalized as a spectacle. The gifts thrown as a regular part of *munera* were called *missilia*.

> At the plays that <Nero> gave for the eternity of the empire, which by his order were called the *ludi maximi* ("greatest games"), parts were taken by several men and women of both orders (senatorial and equestrian).... A Roman play, too, of Afranius was staged entitled *The Fire* and the actors were allowed to carry off the furniture from the burning house and keep it. Every day thousands of presents were thrown to the people: these included a thousand birds of every kind each day, various kinds of food, tickets for grain, clothing, gold and silver, precious stones, pearls, paintings, slaves, beasts of burden, and even trained wild animals; finally ships and blocks of houses and farms. These plays he viewed from the top of the *proscaenium*.

52. Seneca, *Epistles* 88.22. Date: 64. Cf. Apuleius, *Metamorphoses* 13.5 for the complexity of buildings for *venatio*. Stage constructions belong in the circus and in the amphitheater and could be used for mime or pantomime or more dubious purposes.

> Games arts are those that aim to please the eye and ear. To this class you may assign the stage machinists (*machinatores*) who invent scaffolding (*pegmata*) that rises of its own accord, or platforms that silently tower up high, and many other surprising devices, as when objects that fit together then fall apart, or objects that are separate then join together automatically, or objects that stand erect then gradually collapse.

53. Strabo 6.272. Date: ca. 35 B.C. Already in republican times it had been possible to make a spectacle out of the condemnation of criminals: note that this is, as usual, in the forum, and part of a gladiatorial *munus*.

> And recently in my own time, a certain Selurus, called son of Etna, was sent up to Rome because he had put himself at the head of an army and for a long time had overrun the environs of Etna with frequent raids. I saw him torn to pieces by wild animals at an organized gladiatorial fight in the forum. He was put onto a tall contraption as though on Etna and it suddenly broke up and collapsed; he went down with it into fragile cages of wild beasts that had been set up beneath for that purpose.

54. Plutarch, *On the Delay of Divine Vengeance* 554b. Written ca. 115. The Romans had managed to convert the war-dance *pyrrhiche* into a method of disposing of criminals wearing the so-called *tunica molesta*. Elsewhere Plutarch (*Mor.* 997b) contrasts the decency of pantomime and *pyrrhiche* with gladiatorial combat, but he also (*Mor.* 802d) puts them all together as vulgar ways of entertaining the people.

> Yet some there are no wiser than little children, who see criminals in the amphitheater clad often in tunics of cloth of gold and purple mantles, wearing chaplets and dancing the *pyrrhiche,* and are struck with awe and wonderment, supposing them supremely happy, till the moment when, before their eyes, the criminals are stabbed and scourged and that flowery and sumptuous apparel bursts into flames.

55. Phaedrus, *Fables* 5.7. Written ca. 40, referring to the time of Augustus, ca. 10 B.C.

> Princeps, the piper, was quite well known, since he usually accompanied Bathyllos with his music on the stage. It happened at one of his shows ... that as the *pegma* was being pivoted through the air, he accidentally had a bad fall, and broke his left shin ... then the curtain went down, the sound of thunder rolled through the theater, and the gods spoke in the traditional way. Then the chorus struck up a song.

56. Philo, *Against Flaccus* 85. Philo alleges that the governor of Alexandria put on a show on the birthday of Caligula as part of his pogrom, probably in 39. Note that the brutalities take place in the theater, as often in the east.

> The show had been arranged in parts. The first spectacle, lasting from dawn to the third and fourth hour, consisted of Jews being scourged, hung up, bound to the wheel, brutally mauled, and hauled off through the orchestra to their death. After this fine exhibition came dancers and mimes and pipers and all the other amusements of theatrical contests.

57. Ammianus Marcellinus 14.6.19. Written late 4th c. It is difficult to know if the historian is exaggerating in his indignation, but the passage very interestingly shows how the *pyrrhiche* described in 41 by Apuleius, now accompanied by a choir, had become a major theatrical event in itself, a blend of Verdi and Place Pigalle.

> Not long ago (383) when there was a shortage of food <foreigners and intellectuals were driven out>, yet the genuine attendants upon actresses of the mimes, and those who for the time pretended to be such, were kept with us, while three thousand dancing girls,

without even being questioned, remained here with their choruses, and an equal number of dancing masters. And wherever you turn your eyes, you may see a throng of women with curled hair ... sweeping the mosaic floor with their feet to the point of weariness, and whirling in rapid gyrations, while they represent the innumerable figures that the stage plays have devised.

Appendices

Appendix A: Pollux, *Onomasticon* 4.99–154

Pollux was professor of rhetoric in Athens in the second half of the 2nd c. The *Onomasticon* is a kind of thesaurus organized by topics, and a large part of the fourth book is devoted to theater terminology. Pollux did not do original research but compiled the *Onomasticon* from often much older sources. One should remember that he is primarily concerned with the listing and explanation of individual words, many of which will be derived ultimately from very different and sometimes highly poetical sources from various periods; some terms are very rare, and he could be, and often is, wrong. Its value for stage production in the classical period is extremely limited: the information is derived mainly from Hellenistic scholars who often draw questionable inferences from passages of ancient authors, frequently ripped out of context. The lexicon itself has come to us in a shortened form, which increases the disorganization and confusion. But it does contain useful and often reliable information about Hellenistic theater production. Particularly useful and reliable is Pollux' list of New Comic masks at the end of this section. Artifacts show that the canon of masks was limited and highly codified, though probably not quite so rigid as Pollux' list suggests, and most of the mask descriptions correspond easily to the types illustrated (cf. I 139–41, 143, 144). Pollux' direct source (the encyclopedic dictionary of Pamphilus?) was probably a compilation from the works of Didymus, Tryphon (both later 1st c. B.C.), and the seventeen-volume *History of the Theater* by King Juba of Mauretania (active as late as 25). It has been conjectured that the ultimate source is Aristophanes of Byzantium's *On Masks* (before ca. 180 B.C.).

The Chorus (99–112)

Forms of dancing: *emmeleia* tragic, *kordax* comic, *sikinnis* satyric (cf. IV 317, 318).... Here are tragic dance figures (cf. IV 319, 323): snubhand, basket, recumbent hand, woodtheft, double, tongs, acrobatics, crossing the four.... Appropriate to these would be <the words> chorus, choreut, chorus making, chorus placing, choral song, *choreusai* ("to sing and dance"), fellow-choreut, *choregos, choregia,* and *choregion* is the place where the chorus does its preparation.... Leader of the chorus (*hegemon chorou*), *koryphaios,* chorus selector (*chololektes*), chorus maker (*choropoios*), director (*didaskalos*), assistant director (*hypodidaskalos*), chorus director (*chorodidaskalos*), right-stander (*dexiostates*), left-stander (*aristerostates*), third-stander (*tritostates*) (see IVD, esp. 313–16), and Aristophanes calls the woman "third-standress" (PCG F 503).... When a chorus is divided into two, the action is called a *dichoria,* each part is a *hemichorion,* and what they sing against one another are *antichoria....* And the entry of the chorus is called *parodos,* a necessary exit if they come in again *metastasis,* the entry after this *epiparodos,* and the last exit *aphodos* (despite Pollux this is normally *exodos*). An *epeisodion* (i.e., episode) is an action in drama linked to another action. A song that they sang as they went out (*exodion*). The parts of the chorus are (cf. IV 313): row (*stoichos*) and file (*zygon*). There are five files of three in the tragic chorus, and three rows of five, for there were fifteen in a chorus. They came in in threes, if the entrance was by files. If the entrance was by rows, then they entered by fives. Sometimes the *parodos* was one at a time. The comic chorus was of twenty-four choreuts with six files, and four to a file; there were four rows, with six in each row. Whenever one of the choreuts had to sing in a song as if playing the part of a fourth actor, the action is called *paraskenion,* as in the *Agamemnon* of Aeschylus. If a fourth actor utters something, this is called a *parachoregema,* and they say that this happens in the *Memnon* of Aeschylus. In ancient times the tragic chorus was of fifty (not true!), until the *Eumenides* of Aeschylus, when the public took fright in view of their size, and the law reduced the number of the chorus (cf I 23A). A special kind of comic choral song is the *parabasis,* when the chorus comes alongside <the *theatron?*> and says what the poet wants to say to the audience. It is reasonable for the comic poets to do this, but it is not tragic. Yet Euripides did this in many plays. For in the *Danae* he made the chorus of women sing something irrelevant on his own account, and out of forgetfulness he made them speak as men in form but in language as women. Sophocles does the same thing sometimes out of rivalry with Euripides, as in the *Hipponos*. There can be seven parts to the comic parabasis: *kommation, parabasis, makron, strophe, epirrhema, antistrophos* (usually called "antistrophe"), *antepirrhema*. Of these the *kommation* is the introduction of a short song, the *parabasis* is for the most part in anapests, but even if it is in another meter, it keeps the appellation "anapests." The so-called *makron* that follows the *parabasis* is a short lyric song sung without drawing breath. After the *strophe,* sung in lyric verses, comes the *epirrhema* in tetrameters. The *antistrophe* is a song corresponding to the *strophe.* The *antepirrhema* being the last part of the *parabasis* is in tetrameters, the same length as the *epirrhema.* . . .

Costume and Props (115–20)

. . . footwear in tragedy are buskins (*kothornoi*) and *embades* ("step-ins"); while *embatai* are comic. Tragic clothes are the *poikilon* ("embroidered")—so the *chiton* was called—and the overgarments are the *xystis, batrachis* ("frog-colored"), *chlanis,* gilded *chlamys,* gilt-edged, the *statos, phoinikis* ("scarlet cloak"), <and tragic headgear are the> tiara, *kalyptra* (veil), *mitra.* The *agrenon* was a woven woolen netlike shawl that covered the body, which Teiresias put on or some other soothsayer. The *kolpoma* was what Atreuses or Agamemnons or that sort put on over their *poikila;* the *ephaptis* was a sort of red or scarlet binding that warriors or hunters wore on their hand. The *krokotos* ("crocus dress," i.e., saffron-colored) is a *himation* (i.e., overdress). Dionysus used it and a flowery *maschalister* (breast-strap?) and a thyrsus. Those in distress wore dirty white clothes, especially fugitives, or gray or black or yellowish or bluish gray. Philoktetes and Telephus are dressed in rags. Also fawn skins, leather jackets, cutlasses, scepters, spears, bows, quivers, messengers' staffs, clubs, lion skins, and suits of armor are all part of the tragic male costume. Female is the purple *syrtos* (dress with a train), the white *parapechy* (a garment that covers the forearms and has a purple border on each side) of the queen. The *syrtos* of a woman in distress is black, the throwover blue gray or yellowish. The satyric costume is the fawn skin, the goat skin, which they call also the *ixale* and the *trage,* and also possibly the woven leopard skin, and the Dionysiac *theraion,* and the flowery *chlanis,* and the scarlet *himation,* and the *chortaios,* a shaggy *chiton,* which the silens wear. Comic costume is the *exomis:* it is an unfinished white *chiton* without markings, not sown together on the left side. Old men wear a *himation,* and *kampyle;* young men a *phoinikis* or dark purple *himation*. For peasants there are doublet, stick, and leather jacket. Young men use a purple dress, while parasites wear black or gray, except white in the *Sicyonians* of Menander, where the parasite is going to get married. Over the *exomis* of the slaves there is a sort of little white *himation*, which is called an *enkomboma* or *epirrhema*. The costume for a cook is an unfinished *diple*. The costume for comic women is, for old women, yellowish or pale blue, except for priestesses; they wear white. Bawds and mothers of prostitutes have a sort of scarlet ribbon round their head. The costume of young women is white or semitransparent, of heiresses a white-fringed dress. Pimps take pleasure in a dyed (i.e., brightly colored) *chiton* and a flowery wrap, carrying a straight crop; the crop is called an *areskos*. As well, the parasites have a strigil (i.e., body scraper) and oil bottle (I 139), while the peasants have a throwing stick for hares. Some women have a *parapechy* and a *symmetria*, which is a *chiton* down to the feet, purple-dyed all round.

The Theater, Stage, and Stage Properties (121–32)

Since the theater also is no small part of the arts . . . The first bench is the honor seating (*prohedria*, see IV 143–51) . . . They called banging their heels against the bleachers "heel-banging" (*pternokopein*); they did this whenever they wanted to chase someone off the stage (IV 170, 171); for the same reason they also clucked (*klozein*, IV 166, 168) and hissed (*syrittein*, IV 166, 168, 171, 172). There were sections of the theater called *bouleutikon* ("seats for the Council," IV 143–45) and *ephebikon* ("seats for the ephebes," IV 144B). . . . Parts of the theater are *pylis* (southernmost section of the theatron of the Theater of Dionysus?) and *psalis* (middle section?) and *katatome* ("rock-cutting"?, perhaps referring to northernmost section of Theater of Dionysus, which was cut into the acropolis rock in early Hellenistic times), *kerkides, skene*, orchestra, *logeion, proskenion, paraskenia, hyposkenia* (I 148–50). The *skene* is reserved for actors, the orchestra for the chorus; in it are the *thymele*, either some sort of podium or an altar. On the *skene* there was situated a street altar before the doors, and a table with cakes, which was called a *theoris* or *thyoris*. . . . The *hyposkenion* below the stage was decorated with pillars and reliefs facing the audience. Of the three doors of the stage building, the middle one is a palace or cave or distinguished house or entirely belongs to the protagonist of the drama, while the right-hand one is the lodging of the deuteragonist, and the left-hand one contains the lowest character or a remote temple or is uninhabited. In tragedy the right-hand door is for guests; the left is closed up. The *klision* ("shed") in comedy stands beside the house, indicated by curtains. It is a pen for animals, and its doors seem bigger, called *klisiades,* for driving in wagons and things carrying gear. In the *Sempstress* of Antiphanes it becomes a workshop. . . . By each of the two doors on either side of the middle one there could be another two doors. On either side were *mechanai* (IV 77) to which are fixed the *periaktoi,* the <stage>right one showing what is outside the city, the other things from the city, especially the harbor (IV 81). And it brings on sea gods, and all the heavier items that the *mechane* cannot carry. If the *periaktoi* are turned, the right one changes the place, but both change the country. Of the *parodoi,* the right-hand one (i.e., stage right) leads from the fields, the left-hand one (i.e., stage left) from the harbor or the city (IV 80D, 308). Those who arrive on foot from somewhere else come in through the second. When they come in through the orchestra onto the stage, they climb up on ladders (I 131). The steps of the ladder are called *klimakteres.* Items from the theater would be *ekkyklema, mechane, exostra,* lookout, wall, tower, signal beacon, second story, lightning observatory, thunder machine, *theologeion,* crane, swings, *katablemata* (drop-scenes?), hemicycle, *stropheion,* Charonian steps, trapdoors. The *ekkyklema* is a high podium on beams, on which rests a throne; it looks down on unspeakable deeds committed behind the *skene* in the houses (IV 78). The thing on which the *ekkyklema* is introduced is called an *eiskyklema.* One must assume this for each door, i.e., for each house. The *mechane* shows gods and heroes that are in the air like Bellerophon or Perseus, and it stands beside the left *parodos,* higher than the stage-building (IV 77). What is called a *mechane* in tragedy is called a *krade* in comedy (IV 77C–D). Clearly <the *krade*> is an imitation of a fig tree, for the people of Attica call a fig tree a *krade.* People think the *exostra* (IV 79) is the same thing as the *ekkyklema.* The lookout is made for lookouts or anyone else who keeps lookout. The wall and tower are so as to see from a height. The signal beacon indicates the action by its name. The second story was sometimes an overbuilding in a royal palace, like the one from which Antigone sees the army in the *Phoenician Women* (Euripides, *Phoenician Women* 90), and sometimes a tile roof, from which tiles are thrown. In comedy the pimps spy something from the second story or old crones or women look out. Lightning observatory and *bronteion*: the first is a high *periaktos*; the *bronteion* is bags filled with pebbles and blown up, which are knocked against bronze vessels below and behind the stage. From the *theologeion* above the stage, gods appear on high, like Zeus and the rest in the

Psychostasia (of Aeschylus). The crane (*geranos*) is a machine that moves in midair to pick up a body, which Dawn uses to snatch up the body of Memnon. "Swings" you could call the cables that hang down from above to support the gods and heroes who seem to move through the air. The *katablemata* were hangings or flats that contained pictures suitable for use in dramas. They were set down upon the *periaktoi,* and showed a mountain or a sea or a river or some such thing. The name of the hemicycle gives its appearance; its position is in the orchestra; its use is to show some place far from the city, or people swimming in the sea, like the *stropheion* also, which contains the heroes who have migrated to the divine world, or those dying in war or at sea. The Charonian steps, which lie at the bottom of the steps down from the *theatron,* allow ghosts to rise. The trapdoors are either on the stage to draw up a river or some such character, or by the steps, and the Furies come up from them.

Tragic and Satyr Masks (133–42)

Now these would be the tragic masks: shaven man, white, graying, black, blond, blondish. (OLD MEN.) These are old men: (1) The shaven man is the oldest, with white hair; the hair is attached to the *onkos*. The *onkos* is the bit above the face of the mask rising to a peak. The shaven man has a clean-shaven chin. (2) The white man's hair is entirely gray, and he has curls around the head, a firm chin, and jutting eyebrows and off-white complexion. The *onkos* is short. (3) The graying(?) man represents people who are naturally going white, and he is black and sallow. (4) The name of the black man comes from his complexion, and he is curly around the chin and head; the face is rough, and the *onkos* big. (5) The blond man has blond curls and a smaller *onkos* and has a good complexion. (6) The blondish man is otherwise similar save that he is sallower, and he represents sick characters.

(YOUNG MEN.) The masks of young men are the excellent, the curly, the partly curly, the delicate, the squalid, the second squalid, yellowish, the partly yellowish. (7) The excellent is viewed as oldest of the young men, beardless, well-complexioned, but getting dark (around the chin); his hair is thick and black. (8) The curly is blond with an excessive *onkos*. The hair is attached to the *onkos*. His eyebrows are raised, his appearance vigorous. (9) The partly curly, in other respects like the previous, is younger. (10) The delicate is blond with ringlets, white-complexioned, cheery, a model of a handsome god. (11) The squalid has a large *onkos,* is somewhat livid, downcast, grubby, with long blond hair. (12) The second squalid is as much thinner than the previous one as he is younger. (13) The yellowish has puffy flesh and lots of hair, slightly blond, with a sickly complexion, such as suits a ghost or a wounded man. (14) The partly yellowish is in other respects like the excellent but is yellowish to denote sickness or love.

(SLAVES.) The masks of the servants are the goatskin wearer, spade-beard, *anasillos* (= with Persian haircut). (15) The goatskin wearer has no *onkos,* but has a cap and long, combed-out white hair, and a yellowish, whitish face, a harsh nose, high forehead, and glowering eyes. He is yellowish, with a prominent jaw. (16) The spade-beard is in his prime and has a high broad *onkos,* with a furrow around the periphery <of the *onkos*>. He is blond, rough, ruddy-complexioned, suitable for a messenger. (17) The *anasillos* is blond with an excessive *onkos.* His hair is drawn back from the center; he has no beard and is slightly ruddy. He too is a messenger.

(WOMEN.) The masks of women are the gray long-haired, the old free woman, the old servant woman, the old woman shaven in the middle, the woman in goatskin, the long-haired yellow woman, the shaven-in-the-middle yellow, the shaven-in-the-middle fresh, the shorn girl, the second shorn girl, the maiden. (18) The gray long-haired is greater in age and prestige than the rest, white-haired with moderate *onkos,* sallow. In old times she was called partly yellow. (19) The old free woman is rather golden in complexion with a small *onkos.* Her hair comes down to the shoulders; she hints at misfortune. (20) The old servant woman has a cap of lambskin instead of an *onkos,* and has a wrinkled skin. (21) The old servant woman shaven in the middle has a short *onkos,* white skin, partly yellow complexion, and is not altogether gray. (22) The woman in goatskin is younger than her and has no *onkos.* (23) The long-haired yellow woman has black hair, a disagreeable look, and her complexion is as her name suggests. (24) The shaven-in-the-middle yellow woman is like the long-haired one, except for the bit shaven from the middle. (25) The fresh shaven-in-the-middle woman has her hair cut like the one before, but no longer the yellowness. (26) The shorn girl has instead of an *onkos* a parting in her brushed-down hair, and it is cut short all round; her complexion is sallow. (27) The second shorn girl is like the first except for the parting and the curls all round, as if she had been long in distress. (28) The maiden is a young mask, like Danae or another young girl.

The supplementary masks: Actaeon horned, or Phineus blind; Thamyris with one eye blue and the other black; Argos with many eyes; Euhippe daughter of Cheiron changing into a horse in Euripides, or Tyro with livid cheeks in Sophocles—she has got this from being beaten by her mother-in-law Sidero—; Achilles shorn in mourning for Patroclus; Amymone; or a river or a mountain; Gorgon or Justice, Death, Fury, Rage, Madness, Hybris, Centaur, Titan, Giant, Indus, Triton, perhaps also Polis, Priam (?), Persuasion, Muses, Hours, Nymphs of Mikathos (?), Pleiades, Illusion, Drunkenness, Dread, and Envy. Well, while these could also be comic, satyric masks are gray-haired satyr, bearded satyr, beardless satyr, grandfather Silenus (= Papposilenus). The masks are alike in all respects, except for the variations indicated by their names, e.g., the Papposilenos is more bestial in appearance.

New Comic Masks (143–54)

The comic masks, first, those of Old Comedy for the most part copied the faces of those they ridiculed or were fashioned with comic distortion. The masks of New Comedy are: (OLD MEN:) first grandpa (*pappos*), second grandpa, leading old man, the long-bearded or floppy-haired old man, the Hermonios, the spade-beard, the Lycomedean, the pimp, the second Hermonios. These are old men. (1) The first grandpa is the oldest, close-cropped, with a most gentle cast to his brows, well-bearded, with sunken cheeks, lowered gaze, white skin, a more or less cheerful brow. (2) The second grandpa is leaner with a more intense and irritated look, sallow skin, well-bearded, reddish hair, cauliflower ears. (3) The leading old man has a ridge of hair around his head, is hook-nosed, broad-faced and has a raised right eyebrow. (4) The long-bearded old man with a streaming beard (?) has a ridge of hair around his head, is bushy-bearded, and does not have raised eybrows; he has a sluggish look. (5) The Hermonios has a receding hairline, a bushy beard, and raised eyebrows; his look is fierce. (6) The spade-beard has a receding hairline, raised eyebrows, a beard coming to a point, is somewhat disagreeable. (7) The Lycomedean has curly hair, a long beard, one raised eyebrow; the mask denotes a busybody. (8) The pimp resembles the Lycomedean in all other respects, but that his lips are parted with a slight sneer and his brows are contracted and he has a receding hairline or is bald. (9) The second Hermonios has a clean-shaven scalp and is spade-bearded.

(YOUNG MEN.) The masks of the young men are the excellent youth, the dark youth, the curly-haired youth, the delicate youth, the rustic, the floppy-haired youth, the second floppy-haired youth, the toady, the para-site, the statuesque (? *eikonikos*), the Sicilian. (10) The excellent youth is ruddy, gymnastic, has a high complexion, a few wrinkles on his forehead and a ridge of hair around his head, and raised eyebrows. (11) The dark youth is younger, with relaxed brows, and appears cultured rather than given to sports. (12) The curly-haired youth is still younger, with a ruddy complexion and hair in conformity with his name; his eyebrows are raised and he has one wrinkle on his forehead. (13) The delicate youth has hair like the excellent youth but is youngest of them all; white-skinned, unsunned, he gives signs of delicacy. (14) The rustic has dark skin, broad lips, a snubnose and a ridge of hair around his head. (15) The floppy-haired youth is a soldier and a braggart, with dark skin and hair; his hair flops about, just as does the hair of (16) the second floppy-haired youth, who is more delicate and has blond hair. (17) The toady and (18) the parasite are dark, for they hang around the wrestling grounds, they are hook-nosed and easygoing. The parasite has more battered ears and is more cheerful, just as the toady has his eyebrows raised more malevolently. (19) The statuesque (? *eikonikos*) has patches of gray in his hair and shaves his chin, is grandly dressed and a foreigner. (20) The Sicilian is a third parasite.

(SLAVES.) The comic masks of slaves are the grandpa, the leading servant, the low-haired, the curly servant, the Maison servant, the cicada servant, and the floppy-haired leading servant. (21) The grandpa (*pappos*) is the only servant with gray hair, and this shows that he has been freed. (22) The leading servant has red hair braided in a roll, has raised brows and a screwed-up forehead. He is to slaves what the leading old man is to free men. (23) The low-haired has a receding hairline and is red-haired, with elevated eyebrows. (24) The name curly servant reveals the nature of the hair; it is red just like his skin; he has a receding hairline and is skew-eyed. (25) The Maison servant is bald and red-haired. (26) The cicada servant is bald and dark-skinned, with two or three black braids on his head; his beard is also black; he is skew-eyed. (27) The floppy-haired servant would resemble the leading servant except as regards his hair.

(OLD WOMEN.) The masks of women would be the following: the shriveled-up old woman or little she-wolf, the fat old woman, the old housekeeper or domestic or sharp old woman. (28) The little she-wolf is longish, has many fine wrinkles, is white, sallow, with twisted eye. (29) The fat old woman has wrinkles of fat in corpulent flesh and a band tying together her hair. (30) The old housekeeper is snubnosed; in each jaw, she has about two teeth.

(YOUNG WOMEN.) The masks of young women are the chatterbox, the curly-haired woman, the maiden, the false (i.e., violated) maiden, the second false maiden, the chatterbox with strands of gray hair, the concubine, the mature prostitute, the voluptuous little prostitute, the prostitute adorned with gold, the prostitute with a *mitra,* the little torch, the favorite handmaid with the shorn hair, the smooth-haired slave girl. (31) The chatterbox has flowing hair, carefully brushed to the side, straight brows, and white skin. (32) The curly-haired woman differs from the chatterbox in her hairstyle. (33) The maiden has a part in the middle of her hair that is brushed to the side, straight black eyebrows, and a pale white complexion. (34) The false maiden has whiter skin and her hair tied at the front; she looks like a recent bride. (35) The second false maiden is only distinguishable by not having a part in her hair. (36) The chatterbox with strands of grey hair reveals her appearance by her name; the mask indicates a retired prostitute. (37) The concubine resembles the previous mask but has flowing hair. (38) The mature prostitute is rosier than the false maiden and has braids about her ears. (39) The <voluptuous> little prostitute is unadorned; her hair is girt in with a ribbon. (40) The prostitute adorned with gold has lots of gold about her hair. (41) The prostitute with a *mitra* has her head wound about with a multicolored *mitra.* (42) The little torch is a style of binding the hair so that it comes to a point, whence the mask also gets its name. (43) The favorite handmaid with the shorn hair is a little slave with her hair cut short, who wears only a white *chiton* with a belt. (44) The smooth-haired slave girl has a part in her hair, is somewhat snubnosed and a slave of prostitutes; she wears a scarlet *chiton* with a belt.

Appendix B: Chronological Tables

Epochs of Greek and Roman History

	Greece		Rome	
Bronze Age	2800–1125 B.C.	Republican	509–31 B.C.
Geometric	1125–700 B.C.	Imperial	31 B.C.–493
Archaic	700–479 B.C.		
Classical	479–323 B.C.		
Hellenistic	323–86 B.C.		
Roman	86 B.C.–395		
Byzantine	395–1453		

Early Greek Drama

ca. 680 B.C.	Archilochus of Paros "leads off dithyramb" drunk.
ca. 600 B.C.	Arion said to "have invented the tragic mode and first composed a stationary chorus and sung a dithyramb and named what the chorus sang and introduced satyrs speaking verses."
ca. 580 B.C.	Cleisthenes of Sikyon "gives choruses to Dionysus."
before 534 B.C.	Institution of City Dionysia at Athens.
ca. 534 B.C.	"Thespis" said to have produced first tragedy.
ca. 502 B.C.	Athenians start to keep offical records of tragic and dithyrambic victories.
ca. 500? B.C.	Epicharmus begins to write comedy in Sicily.

Attic Tragedy and Comedy

486 B.C.	Comic contests introduced to City Dionysia.
484 B.C.	Aeschylus victorious for the first time.

468 B.C.	Sophocles wins for the first time.
458 B.C.	Aeschylus wins with *Oresteia* tetralogy.
456 B.C.	Death of Aeschylus.
455 B.C.	Euripides competes for the first time.
ca. 440 B.C.	Contests introduced to the Lenaea festival also.
427 B.C.	Aristophanes has his first play produced.
407 B.C.	Death of Euripides.
406 B.C.	Death of Sophocles.
ca. 385 B.C.	Death of Aristophanes.
ca. 380–320 B.C.	Middle Comedy.
ca. 330 B.C.	Aristotle's Poetics.
323 B.C.	Death of Alexander the Great.
322 B.C.	End of Athenian democracy.
ca. 320 B.C.	Beginnings of New Comedy.
316 B.C.	Menander produces *Dyskolos*.
291 B.C.	Death of Menander.

Roman Drama

ca. 240 B.C.	Translations of Greek tragedy and comedy produced at Rome.
ca. 230–184 B.C.	Plautus active in comedy.
ca. 173 B.C.	First offical mimes at the Floralia.
166–160 B.C.	Terence active in comedy.
53 B.C.	Construction of the Theater of Pompey.
31 B.C.	Battle of Actium: end of the Republic.
22 B.C.	Pantomime officially sponsored at Rome.
ca. 13	Vitruvius writes on architecture.
ca. 41	Seneca begins to write tragedies.
80	Dedication of the Colosseum.
ca. 170	Pollux writes on drama.
568	All shows banned at Rome.
692	Shows banned at Byzantium.

Dramatic Performance at Athens

533 B.C.	First performance of tragedies at the Dionysia; by 499 B.C. there are three competitors with three tragedies and a satyrplay each; by 341/40 B.C. this became a

satyrplay, an "old" tragedy, and one or two "new" tragedies.

508 B.C.   First alleged performance of dithyrambic "choruses of men" at the Dionysia; the "choruses of boys" are certain only from 480 B.C., but may also go back to 508 B.C.

486 B.C.   First performance of comedies at the Dionysia; there are five competitors with a comedy each, except for most of the Peloponnesian War (431–404 B.C.), when there may have been only three. After 300 there is evidence for six competitors.

449? B.C.   First competition for tragic actors at the Dionysia.

440–30 B.C.   First competition for comedies at the Lenaea, and possibly first competition for comic actors there. There were five competitors with a comedy each until at least 284 B.C.

First performance of tragedies at the Lenaea and possibly the first competition for tragic actors there. For the year 419/8 B.C. there are two competitors with two tragedies each; in 364/3 B.C. there are three competitors with two tragedies each.

348/7 B.C.   The *choregia* for comedy is transferred to the tribes.

318–307 B.C.   The *choregia* at Athens is abolished and replaced by the *agonothesia*.

275 B.C.   At some time before this date there was a special combined performance of three "old" comedies, three "old" tragedies, and three "old" satyrplays.

Chronology of Dionysia and Lenaea

Dionysia
    Contest of tragic poets: "Thespis" ca. 534 B.C.
    Contest of comic poets: Chionides ?486 B.C.
    Contest of tragic actors: ? ca. 449 B.C.
    Contest of comic actors: between 329–312 B.C.
    Performance of "old tragedy": irregular 386 B.C.; official by 341 B.C.
    Performance of "old comedy": irregular 339 B.C.; official by 311 B.C.
    Performance of "old satyrplay": before 341 B.C.; one only.
    Performance of dithyramb: unknown; official before 473 B.C.

Lenaea

    Contest of tragic poets: between 440–430 B.C.

    Contest of comic poets: ca. 440 B.C.

    Contest of tragic actors: ca. 432 B.C.

    Contest of comic actors: ca. 432 B.C.

    Contest of satyrplays: unknown

    Contest of "old drama": unknown

    Performance of dithyramb: known for early 3rd c. B.C.

Bibliographical Notes

General

J.R. Green, "Theatre Production: 1971–1986," *Lustrum* 31 (1989) 7–95, is the most complete recent survey of books and articles relating to the contexts of ancient theater. For the Greek theater the standard work is A. Pickard-Cambridge, *The Dramatic Festivals of Athens,* second edition by J. Gould and D.M. Lewis (Oxford 1968) and reissued with a short supplement in 1988: the book is highly reliable but dated and presupposes a classical background and a knowledge of Greek. M. Bieber, *History of the Greek and Roman Theater*[2] (Princeton 1961), is the largest collection of illustrations of artifacts and architectural remains, plans, and reconstructions. Unfortunately Bieber's text is not always reliable and is now very much out of date. E. Simon, *The Ancient Theater* (London/New York 1982), is unparalleled for clarity and concision, surveying both Greek and Roman theater contexts in 38 pages.

IAi. Dissemination of Athenian Drama and the Survival of the Texts to Hellenistic Times

The growth of the book trade in Classical Greece is described by E.G. Turner, *Athenian Books in the Fifth and Fourth Centuries* B.C. (London 1952), and, more recently, by B.M.W. Knox, "Books and Readers in the Greek World: From the Beginnings to Alexandria," in P.E. Easterling and B.M.W. Knox, *The Cambridge History of Classical Literature,* vol. 1, *Greek Literature* (Cambridge 1985) 1–16. E.G. Turner, *Greek Papyri: An Introduction* (Oxford 1968), and N. Lewis, *Papyrus in Classical Antiquity* (Oxford 1974), are useful sources of information about ancient books and the reconstruction of the texts from papyri. E. Pöhlmann, *Beiträge zur antiken und neueren Musikgeschichte* (Frankfurt 1988) 23–

40, examines the transmission of dramatic texts specifically: he is more confident than we are about the reliability of the early transmission and its dependence on the poets' autographs. J. Herrington, *Poetry into Drama: Early Tragedy and the Greek Poetic Tradition* (Berkeley/Los Angeles/London 1985), argues that the transmission of the 5th-c. B.C. dramatic texts was predominantly through reperformance and through popular song. The corruption of the texts by actors is the subject of D.L. Page, *Actors' Interpolations in Greek Tragedy* (Oxford 1934), and more recently of A. Garzya, "Sulla questione delle interpolazioni degli attori nei testi tragici," in I. Gallo, ed., *Studi salernitani in memoria di R. Cantarella* (Salerno 1981) 53–75. Taplin (see Artifacts, below) 2–6, 89–99, surveys the evidence for the expansion of the market for Athenian drama, particularly in the West.

IAii. Legacy of Ancient Scholarship

The basic work on ancient scholarship is still R. Pfeiffer, *History of Classical Scholarship: From the Beginnings to the End of the Hellenistic Age* (Oxford 1968), which paints, however, much too rosy a picture of both the quality of ancient scholarship and the quantity of our knowledge of it; it is also too interested in personalities and not in scholarly method. Far better in judgment is N.G. Wilson, *Scholars of Byzantium* (Oxford 1983), though there is as yet no similar survey of Roman scholarship. L.D. Reynolds and N.G. Wilson, *Scribes and Scholars*[3] (Oxford 1991), give a superb picture of manuscripts and their treatment by scholars through to modern times, with many illuminating examples. This has been revised and updated in new editions, sometimes in other languages, but particularly useful are the up-to-date bibliographies at the end of *Scribes and Scholars,* since they provide detailed information on many of the questions raised in IAii and IAi, and on matters that are not discussed here, such as the influence of the Church on scholarship. In addition to Turner's *Greek Papyri* (see Dissemination of Athenian Drama, above) a useful summary of the ancient book industry and scholarship in Hellenistic and later times can be found in P.E. Easterling, "Books and Readers in the Greek World: The Hellenistic and Imperial periods," in Easterling and Knox (see Dissemination, above) 16–41. On the use of literature in ancient education and the influence of rhetoric the standard work is H.-I. Marrou, *Histoire de l'éducation dans l'antiquité*[6] (Paris 1964), with important addenda, but it too ignores many practical questions, which would affect the teaching of drama, such as school performance.

IB. Inscriptions

There is no work dealing with only the theater inscriptions of the ancient world, since these cover everything from festivals to architecture. Those in Athens are mostly to be found scattered through Pickard-Cambridge (see General, above). Those of Delos are dealt with by P. Bruneau, *Recherches sur les cultes de Délos* (Paris 1970) 70ff., 312ff., and many theater problems there are discussed by M.-C. Hellmann, *Recherches sur l'architecture de Délos* (Paris 1992) 87ff., 373ff. Many from Aphrodisias are to be found with an excellent commentary in C. Roueché, *Performers and Partisans at Aphrodisias* (London 1992). Some relevant ones from Asia Minor are given in an appendix to D. di Bernardi Ferrero, *Teatri classici in Asia Minore* (Rome 1966–) vol. 4. There are very few works in English like I. Ringwood, *Agonistic Features of Local Greek Festivals Chiefly from Inscriptional Evidence* (Poughkeepsie 1927), and it is now very outdated. But all these studies will be scarcely accessible to those without an ability to read the original language.

IC. Artifacts

Bieber (see General, above) collects a wide variety of artifacts, but does not discuss problems of interpretation, and tends to use the evidence uncritically. A.D. Trendall and T.B.L. Webster, *Illustrations of Greek Drama* (London 1971), is a valuable collection of illustrations mainly of Attic and South Italian vase painting, with excellent short discussions of each piece illustrated. On the whole Trendall and Webster here tend to overestimate the connection of the "tragic" vases with theatrical performances. A.D. Trendall, *Red-Figure Vases of South Italy and Sicily* (London 1989), is a highly accessible and well-illustrated introduction to South Italian vase painting by the great expert. J.R. Green, "On Seeing and Depicting the Theater in Classical Athens," *Greek, Roman, and Byzantine Studies* 32 (1991) 15–50, and O. Taplin, *Comic Angels* (Oxford 1993), are essential reading for anyone concerned with the relation of vase painting to theater: Green concentrates on the Attic material Taplin's emphasis is on the South Italian. S. Pingiatoglou, "Komödiendarstellung auf einer Choenkanne," in H. Froning et. al., *KOTINOS: Festschrift für E. Simon* (Mainz 1992) 292–300, publishes a choral scene from comedy on fragments of an Attic *chous* of ca. 360 B.C. This vase may be a late representative of the *komos* series, and, if so, would indicate that the latter also shows comedy. E. Simon, *Menander in Centuripe* (*Sitzungsberichte der Wissenschaftlichen Gesellschaft an der Johann Wolfgang Goethe-Universität Frankfurt am Main* 25.2, Stuttgart 1989), argues that early 3rd-c. B.C. vases from Centuripe in Sicily already depict scenes from Menander's *Theophoroumene*. Almost no general books have been devoted to the relationship of the dramatic terra-cotta figurines or the dramatic wall paintings and mosaics with the theater. The most important special studies are L. Bernabò-Brea, *Menandro e il teatro greco nelle teracotte liparesi* (Genoa 1981), a superbly illustrated study of the terra-cotta masks and figurines in Lipari, especially important for their securely datable Early Hellenistic New Comic masks, and S. Charitonidis, L. Kahil, and R. Ginouvès, *Les Mosaïques de la Maison du Ménandre à Mytilène* (*Antike Kunst* Beiheft 6, 1970), the publication of the Mytilene mosaics. Of crucial importance for the relationship of Hellenistic art and New Comedy is J.R. Green, "Drunk Again: A Study in the Iconography of the Comic Theater," *American Journal of Archaeology* 89 (1985) 465–483. The Terence manuscript miniatures are published by L.W. Jones and C.R. Morey, *The Miniatures of the Manuscripts of Terence Prior to the Thirteenth Century* (Princeton 1930), in two volumes, one of illustrations and one of commentary. K. Weitzmann, *Illustration in Roll and Codex*[2] (Princeton 1970), is the main protagonist of the theory (which we criticize) that luxury book illustrations existed in antiquity and served as the source of many of the images found on the surviving artifacts.

ID. Theater Buildings

In English, the most complete general introduction to the Theater of Dionysus at Athens is still A.W. Pickard-Cambridge, *The Theater of Dionysus in Athens* (Oxford 1946), and, for the earliest phase, W.B. Dinsmoor, "The Athenian Theater of the Fifth Century," in *Studies Presented to David Moore Robinson*, vol. 1 (St. Louis 1951) 309–14. The most recent general treatment of the Theater of Dionysus is L. Polacco, *Il teatro di Dioniso Eleuterio ad Atene* (Rome 1990). W.W. Wurster, "Die Architektur des griechischen Theaters," *Antike Welt* 24 (1993) 20–42, is a very useful short survey. For the controversy over the circularity or rectilinearity of the early orchestra in the Theater of Dionysus, see E. Gebhard, "The Form of the Orchestra in the Early Greek

Theater," *Hesperia* 43 (1974) 428–40, and E. Pöhlmann, "Die Prohedrie des Dionysostheaters im 5. Jahrhundert und das Bühnenspiel der Klassik," *Museum Helveticum* 38 (1983) 129–46, both in favor of a rectilinear classical orchestra. Arguments against this view appear in N.G.L. Hammond, "More on Conditions of Production to the Death of Aeschylus," *Greek, Roman, and Byzantine Studies* 29 (1988) 5–33, esp. 5–9, which develops a theory about the configuration of the pre-*skene* theater first made in "Conditions of Dramatic Production to the Death of Aeschylus," *Greek, Roman, and Byzantine Studies* 13 (1972) 387–450. The chief point in favor of a rectilinear orchestra is the fact that other early theaters are roughly rectilinear or trapezoidal: a useful quick survey can be found in C. Ashby, "The Case for the Rectangular/Trapezoidal Orchestra," *Theater Research International* 13 (1988) 1–20. For the *theatron* and *prohedria*, see M. Maass, *Die Prohedrie des Dionysostheaters in Athen* (Munich 1972). The controversy stirred up by the discovery of mid-4th c. B.C. pottery in a cleaning operation around the New Temple of Dionysus (and the stoa and wall H-H supposed to be contemporary with it) is accessible in J. Travlos, *Pictorial Dictionary of Ancient Athens* (New York 1971) 537–52. Travlos' downdating of the phases of the Theater of Dionysus has some following, but the pottery finds on which they rest have not been properly published and Travlos' theory cannot sustain the criticisms made by H.-J. Newiger, "Zwei Bemerkungen zur Spielstätte des attischen Dramas in 5. Jahrhundert v. Chr.," *Wiener Studien* 89 (1976) 80–92, and F.E. Winter, "The Stage of New Comedy," *Phoenix* 37 (1983) 38–47. Winter's article and R.F. Townsend, "The Fourth-Century Skene of the Theater of Dionysos at Athens," *Hesperia* 55 (1986) 421-38, are important recent discussions on the appearance of the "Lycurgan" *skene*.

The only complete work on the other theaters generally is still Bieber (see General, above), useful for its plans and illustrations. E. Frézouls has published many studies on the architecture of the ancient theater, perhaps most useful for its illustrations being "Aspects de l'histoire architecturale du théâtre romain," in *Aufstieg und Niedergang* II 12.1 (Berlin 1982) 343–441. Amphitheaters are now the subject of a magisterial study by J.-C. Golvin, *L'amphithéâtre romain: essai sur la théorization de sa forme et ses fonctions* (Paris 1988). Individual theaters have been published in detail by archaeologists; and perhaps just as important, many of the confident reconstructions of earlier scholars have been revised. There are now excellent reconstructions in G.C. Izenour, *Roofed Theaters of Classical Antiquity* (New Haven/London 1992), of examples of the Odeon and other similar types of building; Izenour has a very useful treatment of the Theater of Herodes Atticus in Athens. The so-called theater-temples of Italy and Africa are dealt with authoritatively by J.A. Hanson, *Roman Theater-Temples* (Princeton 1959). C. Courtois, *Le Bâtiment de scène dans les théâtres d'Italie et de Sicilie* (Providence/Louvain le Neuve 1989), collects and illustrates with good plans what evidence remains for the scene buildings of Roman theaters, showing usefully how they developed and adapted throughout the empire. Other recent books that illustrate plans of Roman theaters are K. Mitens, *Teatri greci e teatri ispirati all' architettura greca in Sicilia e nell'Italia meridionale* (*Analecta Romana Instituti Danici* 13, Rome 1988), and A. Neppi Modona, *Gli Edifici teatrali greci e romani* (Florence 1961). J.-C. Moretti in the new journal *Topoi* (1991–) has provided important surveys of the bibliography of theaters in Greece and in the East, which supplement earlier surveys such as that of D. di Bernardi Ferrero, *Teatri classici in Asia Minore,* 4 vols. (Rome 1966–1974), which is invaluable for its plans. But only four theaters have been properly published in the whole of Asia Minor, though we may hope for further important publications from Hierapolis and Aphrodisias. For Gaul there are good plans in the series of essays edited by C. Landes, *Le Théâtre antique et ses spectacles* (Lattes 1992).

II. Origins of Greek Drama

Much of this vast material is treated somewhat confusingly in A. Pickard-Cambridge, *Dithyramb, Tragedy and Comedy,* revised second edition by T.B.L. Webster (Oxford 1962), but it is now out of date. The dramatic vases are to be found in the collections of monuments illustrating ancient drama by T.B.L. Webster, *Monuments Illustrating Tragedy and Satyr Play*[2] (*Bulletin of the Institute of Classical Studies,* supplement no. 20, London 1967), and *Monuments Illustrating Old and Middle Comedy,* second revised edition by J.R. Green (*Bulletin of the Institute of Classical Studies,* supplement no. 39, London 1978). The Attic protocomic (?) choruses with pipers are also conveniently listed, illustrated, and discussed by J.R. Green, "A Representation of the *Birds* of Aristophanes," *J.P. Getty Museum: Greek Vases* 2 (1985) 95–118. The return of Hephaestus has been last studied by G.M. Hedreen, *Silens in Attic Black-figure Vase-painting* (Ann Arbor 1992), and "Lenaean" vases are collected by F. Frontisi-Ducroux, *Le Dieu-masque* (Paris 1991). Komasts have not yet been studied as a group, though the Corinthian vases have been collected by A. Seeberg, *Corinthian Komast Vases* (*Bulletin of the Institute of Classical Studies,* supplement 27, London 1971), and many early Attic examples can be found in H.A.G. Brijder, *Siana Cups 1 and Komast Cups* (*Allard Pierson Series* vol. 4, Amsterdam 1983). Brijder has also studied a most interesting vase in detail in "A Predramatic Performance of a Satyr Chorus by the Heidelberg Painter," in H.A.G. Brijder et al., eds., *Enthousiasmos: Essays ... presented to J.M. Hemelrijk* (Amsterdam 1986) 68–91. The relation of drama to ritual has been often studied in detail; two good examples are R. Seaford, "On the Origins of Satyric Drama," *Maia* 28 (1976) 209–21, and W. Burkert, "Greek Tragedy and Sacrificial Ritual," *Greek, Roman, and Byzantine Studies* 7 (1966) 87–121. Aristotle's discussion of origins has been hotly debated with different results, and one does best to consult the latest translations and commentaries on the passage, e.g., by S. Halliwell, *The Poetics of Aristotle* (London 1987), or R. Janko, *Aristotle: Poetics* (Indianapolis/Cambridge 1987).

IIIAia. The Great Dionysia

For Attic religious festivals in general and including the dramatic festivals, see H.W. Parke, *Festivals of the Athenians* (Ithaca 1977), and E. Simon, *Festivals of Attica* (Madison 1983). On the Dionysia and Lenaea, Pickard-Cambridge (see General, above) is the standard work. For a recent discussion of Peisistratus' unification of Attica through the reorganization of Attic cults, see F.J. Frost, "Peisistratos, the Cults, and the Unification of Attica," *The Ancient World* 21 (1990) 3–9. W.R. Connor, "City Dionysia and Athenian Democracy," *Classica et Mediaevalia* 40 (1989) 7–32, reviews the evidence for the early history of the Great Dionysia and argues that the festival was founded only at the end of the 6th c. B.C. by the Athenian democracy. Ritual aspects of the Dionysia are discussed by S.G. Cole, "Procession and Celebration at the Dionysia," in R. Scodel, ed., *Theater and Society in the Classical World* (Ann Arbor 1993) 25–38. S.D. Goldhill, "The Great Dionysia and Civic Ideology," *Journal of Hellenic Studies* 107 (1987) 58–76, examines the festival from the perspective of its political and ideological function. The most important discussion of the number of comic contestants at the Dionysia is W. Luppe, "Die Zahl der Konkurrenten an den komischen Agonen der Zeit des Peloponnesischen Krieges," *Philologus* 116 (1972) 53–75.

IIIAib. The Lenaea, Rural Dionysia, and Anthesteria

For the other Attic dramatic festivals consult Parke, Simon, and Pickard-Cambridge (listed under The Great Dionysia, above). The organization of the Rural Dionysia is studied by D. Whitehead, *The Demes of Attica* (Princeton 1986) 212–22. Ghiron-Bistagne (see Actors in the Classical Period, below) 86–97, looks at the evidence for dramatic activity at the deme level. N.W. Slater, "The Lenaean Theater," *Zeitschrift für Papyrologie und Epigraphik* 66 (1986) 255–64, argues for and attempts to locate a Lenaean theater, separate from the Theater of Dionysus.

IIIAiia. The Choregic System

The most detailed discussion is in Pickard-Cambridge (see General, above) 75–78, 86–92. J.K. Davies, *Athenian Propertied Families 600–300 B.C.* (Oxford 1971), examines the demographics of the "liturgical class" in his introduction (xvii–xxxi) and Casson (see The Athenian Theater Audience, below) gives a detailed insight into their economic conditions. The attitudes rich Athenians held toward liturgies and the means they used to avoid them are studied by M. Christ, "Liturgy Avoidance and Antidosis in Classical Athens," *Transactions of the American Philological Association* 120 (1990) 147–69. *Antidosis* is also discussed by V. Gabrielson, "The Antidosis Procedure in Classical Athens," *Classica et Mediaevalia* 38 (1987) 7–38. D. MacDowell, *The Law in Classical Athens* (London 1978) 161–64, explains the laws and regulations governing liturgies. Valuable also is MacDowell (see The Choruses, below) 65–69, with further discussion of the rules governing the recruitment and exclusion of *choregoi*. A link between some illustrations of theatrical scenes and choregic dedications is argued by H. Froning, *Dithyrambos und Vasenmalerei: Beiträge zur Archäologie* 2 (Würzburg 1971).

IIIAiib. Judges

Far too much has been taken for granted with respect to the manner in which prizes were handed out at the dramatic festivals, yet nothing could be more crucial to such widely studied aspects of Athenian drama as its competitive context, the role of the audience, and popular reception. Apart from a four-page discussion in Pickard-Cambridge (see General, above) 95–99, English readers have only M. Pope, "Athenian Festival Judges—Seven, Five, or However Many," *Classical Quarterly* 36 (1986)

322–26, who made the suggestion criticized in the introduction to IIIAiib that there were ten judges but only as many votes were counted as assured placement. This is far too simplistic a solution. Pope does not mention III 119 or G. Arrighetti, "Il papiro di Ossirinco n. 1611 e il numero dei giudici negli agoni," *Dioniso* 45 (1971–74) 302–8, who is more critical of the ancient testimony. The problem deserves more attention.

IIIAiic. Freedom of Expression

More or less standard expressions of the festival license theory can be found in K. Reckford, *Aristophanes' Old and New Comedy* (Chapel Hill 1987) 461–82, and S. Halliwell, "Aristophanic Satire," *Yearbook of English Studies* 14 (1984) 6–20. Several studies have appeared recently that apply Bakhtin's theory of carnival to Old Comedy: J. Carrière, *Le Carnaval et la politique* (Paris 1979); W. Rösler, "Michail Bachtin und die Karnevalskultur im antiken Griechenland," *Quaderni Urbinati di Cultura Classica* 23 (1986) 25–44; and somewhat oversubtle and opaque in its presentation, but still of great interest, S. Goldhill, *The Poet's Voice* (Cambridge 1991) 167–222. A.T. Edwards, "Historicizing the Popular Grotesque: Bakhtin's *Rabelais* and Attic Old Comedy," in R. Scodel, ed. *Theater and Society in the Classical World* (Ann Arbor 1993) 89–117, offers a much more discriminating view of both Bakhtin and Old Comedy. J. Henderson, "The Demos and Comic Competition," in J.J. Winkler and F.I. Zeitlin, eds., *Nothing to Do with Dionysos?* (Princeton 1990) 271–313, criticizes the carnivalists and those who regard the effect of political statements in comedy as limited only to humor. Both groups would isolate comedy from its political context by buffering it with concepts of otherworldliness, fictionality, and comic aestheticism; although the carnivalists do argue for an abstract political content in the "deep structure" of comedy, it is at the expense of its manifest political invective. Henderson argues, as we do, that comic satire and abuse are effective contributions to Athenian political discourse and do not differ essentially from their counterparts in forensic and political rhetoric. S. Halliwell, "Ancient Interpretations of *onomasti komodein* in Aristophanes," *Classical Quarterly* 34 (1984) 83–88, shows how the presuppositions and methods of Hellenistic scholars are responsible for manufacturing much of the information about *komodoumenoi* and about censorship that appears in our scholia. Halliwell argues that both the decree of Antimachos and possibly the decree of Syrakosios are inferences from the text. A.H. Sommerstein, "The Decree of Syrakosios," *Classical Quar-*

terly 36 (1986) 101–8, argues for the historicity of this decree and revives a theory that it was a ban on mentioning those involved in the scandals of the mutilation of the herms and/or the profanation of the mysteries. This theory is effectively challenged by S. Halliwell, "Comic Satire and Freedom of Speech in Classical Athens," *Journal of Hellenic Studies* 111 (1991) 48–70. Halliwell's study is a thorough examination of the reports of censorship legislation and of comedy's relation to the general law of slander. Halliwell, like Henderson and like ourselves, sees comic license as ultimately derived from a combination of its political context and its festival occasion, but whereas Henderson stresses the political, as we do, Halliwell stresses the festival context. J.E. Atkinson, "Curbing the Comedians: Cleon Versus Aristophanes and Syracosius' Decree," *Classical Quarterly* 42 (1992) 56–64, argues a variation on Sommerstein's theory, that Syrakosios' decree was to protect those wrongly implicated in the scandals of 416 B.C. Many of Halliwell's criticisms could be applied to Atkinson. The laws of slander and *hybris* are explained by MacDowell, *The Law in Classical Athens* (see The Choregic System, above) 126–32.

IIIB. The Greek World from Hellenistic
to Imperial Times

There is in English no overall survey of festivals in the Greek world, nor of the hundreds of dramatic festivals in it, as is pointed out by P. Herz, "Die musische Agonistik und der Kunstbetrieb der Kaiserzeit," in Jürgen Blänsdorf, ed., *Theater und Gesellschaft im Imperium Romanum* (Tübingen 1990) 175–195 with a useful bibliography. A useful introduction to the detail of only one festival is S. Mitchell, "Festivals, Games, and Civic Life in Roman Asia Minor," *Journal of Roman Studies* 80 (1990) 183–93. An entire book was written about this inscription by M. Wörrle, *Stadt und Fest im kaiserzeitlichen Kleinasien (Vestigia* 39, Munich 1988). Likewise a specific area is treated by A.J.S. Spawforth, "Agonistic Festivals in Roman Greece," in A. Cameron and S. Walker, eds., *The Greek Renaissance in the Roman Empire* (London 1989) 193–97. Roueché (see Inscriptions, above) is a good introduction to the interesting and unique festivals of Aphrodisias and much else. G.M. Sifakis, *Studies in the History of Hellenistic Drama* (London 1968), deals with most of the Hellenistic inscriptions, and remains the basic work on the drama of that period. Also useful is B. Gentili, *Theatrical Performances in the Ancient World* (Amsterdam 1979). C.P. Jones makes much use of inscriptions in his important survey of "Greek Drama in the Roman Empire," in R. Scodel, ed., *Theater and Society in the Ancient World* (Ann Arbor 1993) 39–52.

IIIC. The Roman World

The only survey of the area are chapters in L. Friedlaender's *Sittengeschichte:* there is a translation of the seventh edition by L. Magnus and others, *Roman Life and Manners in the Early Empire* (New York 1965), but, being originally written in 1906, this is out of date. There is interesting general material also in P. Veyne, *Le Pain et le Cirque,* abridged as *Bread and Circuses* (London 1990), as well as D. Balsdon, *Life and Leisure in Ancient Rome* (London 1969). H. Scullard, *Festivals and Ceremonies of the Roman Republic* (London 1981), is useful for details. E. Jory gives a good overview in "Continuity and Change in the Roman Theater," in *Studies in Honour of T.B.L. Webster* (Bristol 1986) 143–52. A survey of recent epigraphical studies is to be found in M. Le Glay, "Épigraphie et théâtres," in Landes (see Theater Buildings, above) 209–21. The Etruscan origins are treated by T.P. Wiseman, "Satyrs in Rome?" *Journal of Roman Studies* 78 (1988) 1–13. But for the most part one must refer to discussion of the individual passages and inscriptions, e.g., M.G. Geer, "The Greek Games at Naples," *Transactions of the American Philological Association* 66 (1935) 208–21, and J.R. Arnold, "Agonistic Festivals in Italy and Sicily," *American Journal of Archaeology* 64 (1960) 245–51. The inscriptions for the Secular Games are treated with bibliography by A.E. Gordon, *Illustrated Introduction to Latin Epigraphy* (Berkeley 1983) 100.

IVAi. Actors in the Classical Period

There is relevant material scattered through Pickard-Cambridge (see General, above) esp. 126–56 and 279–80, but the most valuable general work is P. Ghiron-Bistagne, *Recherches sur les acteurs dans la Grèce antique* (Paris 1976). Ghiron-Bistagne also includes an annotated catalog of actors that supplements the list in J.B. O'Connor, *Chapters in the History of Actors and Acting in Ancient Greece* (Chicago 1908): both are now superseded by I.E. Stephanis, *Dionysiakoi Technitai* (Heraklion 1988), written in Greek. D.F. Sutton, "The Theatrical Families of Athens," *American Journal of Philology* 108 (1987) 9–26, shows that the early acting profession centered on professional families. G.M. Sifakis, "Boy Actors in New Comedy," in G.W. Bowersock, W. Burkert, and

M.C.J. Putnam, eds., *Arktouros: Hellenic Studies Presented to Bernard M.W. Knox,* (Berlin/New York 1979) 199–208, and the same author's "Children in Greek Tragedy," *Bulletin of the Institute of Classical Studies* 26 (1979) 67–80, give some insight into the structure of acting troupes and the training of actors. F. Jouan, "Réflexions sur le rôle du protagoniste tragique," in *Théâtre et spectacles dans l'antiquité: Travaux du Centre de Recherche, Strasbourg 7* (Leiden 1983), focuses on the relationship of the star actor with the audience and the poet.

IVAii. The Artists of Dionysus

The Artists of Dionysus are well treated in Pickard-Cambridge (see General, above) 279–321, which also prints without translation a few of the main inscriptions. For the later period, where we know more about athletes than actors, Roueché (see Inscriptions, above), appendix 3, provides a valuable commentary and translation of some late inscriptions of Aphrodisias concerning the Artists and the athletic guild. There are important remarks on the synods of athletes and theater performers in F. Millar, *The Emperor in the Roman World* (Oxford 1977) 456–63, especially in regard to their relations with the imperial authorities. But, as is normal, the Artists tend to be mentioned in passing by historians, e.g., P. Fraser, *Ptolemaic Alexandria* (Oxford 1972) vol. 1, 201ff., deals with the powerful cult of Dionysus in Egypt, in which both the kings and the Artists were involved, while H. Lavagne, "Rome et les Associations Dionysiaques en Gaule," in *L'Association Dionysiaque dans les sociétés anciennnes* (CEFR 89, 129–48, Rome 1986) deals with an interesting group of inscriptions from Gaul.

IVAiii. Classical and Hellenistic Acting

Pickard-Cambridge (see General, above) 135–231 has valuable chapters on the distribution of parts among the actors in the surviving playtexts, on delivery, on voice and enunciation, gesture, and costume. Several recent works (all in English) attempt to reconstruct the original performance of ancient tragedies. Chief among these is O. Taplin, *The Stagecraft of Aeschylus* (Oxford 1977), the monumental work that inaugurated the trend to "performance criticism" in classical studies. The interest of Taplin's work for reconstructing Aeschylean tragedy goes far beyond the book's focus on entrances and exits. O. Taplin, *Greek Tragedy in Action* (Berkeley/Los Angeles 1978), is a shorter, more accessible, and general treatment of the visual dimension of nine tragedies. More recently R. Rehm, *Greek Tragic Theater* (London/New York 1992), offers a reconstruction of the significant action of six tragedies (four overlap with Taplin). For Sophocles and Euripides, see also D. Seale, *Vision and Stagecraft in Sophocles* (Chicago 1982), and R. Halleran, *Stagecraft in Euripides* (London 1985), and, for Aristophanes, C.W. Dearden, *The Stage of Aristophanes* (London 1976). A great deal is known, from the texts and artifacts, about comic costume, but most studies are highly specialized: in addition to Pickard-Cambridge and Dearden, one should consult L.M. Stone, *Costume in Aristophanic Comedy* (New York 1981). There is no easy introduction to the masks of New Comedy: D. Wiles, *The Masks of Menander* (Cambridge 1991), is very unreliable. One should consult Pickard-Cambridge, Bernabò-Brea (see Artifacts, above), and the introductory sections of T.B.L. Webster, *Monuments Illustrating New Comedy*[2] (*Bulletin of the Institute of Classical Studies,* supplement no. 24, London 1969). A third edition of this work will appear very soon, edited by J.R. Green. The most important general studies of the classical stage and its resources are: P.D. Arnott, *Greek Scenic Conventions in the Fifth Century* B.C. (Oxford 1962); C. Hourmouziades, *Production and Imagination in Euripides* (Athens 1965); and Dearden (above). Among recent special studies of acting resources are R. Rehm, "The Staging of Suppliant Plays," *Greek, Roman, and Byzantine Studies* 29 (1988) 263–307, and J.P. Poe, "The Altar in the Fifth-Century Theater," *Classical Antiquity* 8 (1989) 116–39. In arguing for the importance of the central orchestra as primary acting space, Rehm minimizes the importance of the *skene* and rejects the existence of a low stage, but does so without consideration of the archaeological material. The best case for the low stage is put by E. Billig, "Die Bühne mit austauschbarem Kulissen," *Opuscula Atheniensia* 13 (1980) 35–83, a very important discussion of the appearance of the classical stage building, though one should be very cautious about his tendency to equate material (wood or stone) with the form of the stage (*Kulissenbühne* or *Architekturbühne*) and even more cautious about his reasons for thinking that comedy required a different stage from tragedy. D.J. Mastronarde, "Actors on High: The Skene Roof, the Crane, and the Gods in Attic Drama,"

Classical Antiquity 9 (1990) 247–94, discusses the use of the *mechane* and the form and function of the *skene* roof.

IVAiv. Republican and Imperial Actors and Acting

There is a reasonable survey of some of the points discussed here in R.C. Beacham, *The Roman Theater and Its Audience* (Cambridge, Mass., 1992), who offers a reconstruction of a republican theater stage. A useful list of all Roman actors is given by H. Leppin, *Histrionen* (Bonn 1992). Both these books include valuable bibliographies. A good survey is that of E. Rawson, "Theatrical Life in Republican Rome and Italy," *Papers of the British School at Rome* 53 (1985) 97–113, while B. Levick, "The Senatusconsultum from Larinum," *Journal of Roman Studies* 73 (1983) 99–115, provides a commentary on the complex legal problem of acting. But the only accessible work on Roman acting techniques, which requires an investigation of the many monuments, is the brief and unsatisfactory monograph of K. Neiiendam, *The Art of Acting* (Copenhagen 1992). One would have to consult the literary scholia, e.g., in J. Basore, *The Scholia on Hypokrisis in the Commentary of Donatus* (Diss. Baltimore 1903), to get a better picture. Roman actors' organizations are studied by J. Jory, "Associations of Actors in Rome," *Hermes* 98 (1970) 224–53.

IVBi. The Athenian Audience in the Fifth and Fourth Centuries B.C.

There exist no complete studies of the Greek theater audience: the most important is Pickard-Cambridge (see General, above) 263–78. The capacity of the Theater of Dionysus is studied most recently by L. Gallo, "La Capienza dei teatri e il calcolo della popolazione: il caso di Atene," in *Studi salernitani in memoria di Raffaele Cantarella* (Salerno 1981). For recent arguments against the presence of women in the theater, see N. Wilson, "Observations on the *Lysistrata*," *Greek, Roman, and Byzantine Studies* 23 (1982) 157–63; the case for the presence of women is well put by A.J. Podlecki, "Could Women Attend the Theater in Ancient Athens?" *Ancient World* 21 (1990) 27–43, and, more positively, by J. Henderson, "Women in the Athenian Dramatic Festivals," *Transactions of the American Philological Association* 121 (1991) 133–47. The basic study of the *theorikon* is J.J. Buchanan, *Theorika* (Locust Valley, N.Y. 1962), which must be supplemented by N. Valmin, "Diobelia und Theorikon," *Opuscula Atheniensia* 6 (1963) 171–206. E. Ruschenbusch, "Die Einführung des *Theorikon*," *Zeitschrift für Papyrologie und Epigraphik*

36 (1979) 303–8, presents strong arguments for dating the introduction of the *theorikon* around 350 B.C. The *architekton* is discussed by T.L. Shear, *Kallias of Sphettos and the Revolt of Athens in 286 B.C. (Hesperia* supplement 17, Princeton 1978) 56ff. D. Bain, *Actors and Audience* (Oxford 1977), studies interaction between the actors and audience as revealed by the playtexts and by performance techniques, particularly audience address and asides. The literary reflection of the change in the status of the dominant segment of the Athenian audience is given some attention by L. Casson, "The Athenian Upper Class and New Comedy," *Transactions of the American Philological Association* 106 (1976) 29–59.

IVBii. Roman Audience and Society

As always, the best survey of the evidence is still that of L. Friedlaender (see The Roman World, above) in his chapter on games. For two important and detailed articles bearing on this topic, see E. Rawson, "Discrimina Ordinum: The Lex Iulia Theatralis," *Papers of the British School in Rome 55* (1987) 83–114, and Rawson's article on "Theatrical Life" (see Republican and Imperial Actors and Acting, above), which cover advances in our knowledge of the law and theatrical inscriptions. F. Abbot, "The Theater as a Factor in Roman Politics under the Republic," *Transactions of the American Philological Association* 38 (1907) 49–56, remains a useful collection of information. M. Wistrand, *Entertainment and Violence in Ancient Rome* (Gotheburg 1993), is very idiosyncratic, but has a useful survey of the views of the imperial writers. A number of relevant articles with bibliography can be found in the collection edited by Blänsdorff mentioned under The Greek World, above, and the conference proceedings edited by Landes mentioned under Theater Buildings, above.

IVBiii. Emperors and Theater

The best and very readable analysis of a theater riot driven by claques is C.R. Whittaker, "The Revolt of Papyrius Dionysius," *Historia* 13 (1964) 348–69. Roueché (see Inscriptions, above) gives a fine summary of the use of claques for political ends and as social control in the empire. The introduction of A. Cameron, *Circus Factions* (Oxford 1976), is worth reading for the later developments of the claques in the circus in Byzantium. Beacham (see Republican and Imperial Actors and Acting, above), in chapter 6, deals with the stage of the empire. There is, however, no suitable introduction in English to the general place of the theater in political life, in either Rome or the Greek cities of the East. There is a perceptive essay by J.-M. André, "Die Zuschauerschaft als sozialpolitischer Mikrocosmos zur Zeit des Hochprinzipats," in Blänsdorff's collection (see The Greek World, above), 165–73.

IVC. Music

M.L. West, *Ancient Greek Music* (Oxford 1992), provides an excellent survey of what is known about ancient music and is accessible even to those without musical or classical training. The same author's *Introduction to Greek Metre* (Oxford 1987) is the best short survey of Greek verse rhythm. Pickard-Cambridge (see General, above) discusses forms of delivery (156–67) and provides a brief survey of dramatic music (257–62). Texts and transcriptions of ancient musical scores can be found in E. Pöhlmann, *Denkmäler altgriechischer Musik* (Nuremberg 1970). Of great interest are the reconstructions of ancient music in *Musique de la Grèce antique* by the Atrium Musicae de Madrid under the direction of G. Paniagua, recorded in 1978 under the *Harmonia Mundi* label, and, more recently and fully, in the two-volume (four compact disk) set by P. Tabouris, called *Melos Archaion* under the *Paian* label. Translations of many of the major ancient writers on music can be found in A. Barker, *Greek Musical Writings*, 2 vols. (Cambridge 1984–89). Regarding pipers on Greek vases, one should consult Taplin (see Artifacts, above) 70–78 and 105–10.

IVD. The Chorus

The best general discussion is Pickard-Cambridge (see General, above) 232–57. Statistics for choral participation in Greek tragedy down to the time of Euripides' *Medea* can be found in M. Griffith, *The Authenticity of the Prometheus Bound* (Cambridge 1977) 123. A.M. Dale, "The Chorus in the Action of Greek Tragedy," in *Collected Papers* (Cambridge 1969) 210–20, offers a concise and "classic," if too rigid, statement of the conventions governing the tragic chorus. The most important discussions of the decline of the comic chorus are G.M. Sifakis, *Studies in the History of Hellenistic Drama* (London 1967); T.B.L. Webster, *Studies in Later Greek Comedy*[2] (Manchester 1970) 56–63; R.L. Hunter, "The Comic Chorus in the Fourth Century," *Zeitschrift für Papyrologie und*

Epigraphik 36 (1979) 23–38; and Pöhlmann (see Dissemination of Athenian Drama, above) 29–55; and K.S. Rothwell, "The Continuity of the Chorus in Fourth-century Attic Comedy," in *Greek, Roman, and Byzantine Studies* 33 (1992) 209–25. The basic works for dance are L.B. Lawler, *The Dance of the Ancient Greek Theater* (Iowa City 1964), and G. Prudhommeau, *La Danse grecque antique* (Paris 1965). D.M. MacDowell, "Athenian Laws About Choruses," *Akten der Gesellschaft für griechische und hellenistische Rechtsgeschichte 5, Symposion 1982* (Vienna 1989) 67–77, studies the laws governing the recruitment and the exclusion of choreuts. J.J. Winkler, "The Ephebes' Song: *Tragoidia* and *Polis*," in Winkler and Zeitlin (see Freedom of Expression, above) 20–62, is an interesting and influential recent study, which argues that participation in dramatic choruses was part of basic military training in Athens, a view criticized in the introduction to IVD.

V. Mime and Pantomime

E. Fantham, "Mime: The Missing Link in Roman Literary History," *Classical World* 82 (1989) 153–62, gives a brief survey of early mime, with emphasis on the literary implications. C. Garton, *Personal Aspects of the Roman Theater* (Toronto 1972), has a useful chapter on Sulla and his interest in mime. Beacham (see Republican and Imperial Actors and Acting, above) has a survey of Roman mime and pantomime in chapter 5. Very valuable are articles by E.J. Jory, especially "Publilius Syrus and the Element of Competition in the Theater of the Republic," *Bulletin of the Institute of Classical Studies,* supplement 51 (1988) 73–81; "The Early Pantomime Riots," in A. Moffat, ed., *MAISTOR: Classical, Byzantine, and Renaissance Studies for Robert Browning,* (Canberra 1984) 57–66; "The Literary Evidence for the Beginnings of Imperial Pantomime," *Bulletin of the Institute of Classical Studies* 28 (1981) 147–61. K. Coleman, "Fatal Charades," *Journal of Roman Studies* 80 (1990) 44–73, provides an excellent introduction to the more outrageous spectacles of the Roman entertainment industry, while D. Potter, "Martyrdom as Spectacle," in Scodel (see The Great Dionysia, above), 53–88, provides a later gruesome complement. Important are the lists of Latin and Greek performers provided by Leppin (see Republican and Imperial Actors and Acting, above) and Stephanis (see Actors in the Classical Period, above).

Glossary/Index

Page references are given for the more important discussions and passages.

acclamatio (pl. **acclamationes**): Lat. "shouting at": orchestrated rhythmic shouting by claques, usually of supporters under a leader. Pp. 306, 315–17, 319, 325–27

aditus maximus (pl. **aditus maximi**): Lat. "chief entrance": each of the entrances to the orchestra from the side, usually through a vaulted entranceway. P. 84

agon (pl. **agones**): Gk. "competition," and so "festival": the verb *agonizo* means "compete." The term is also used to refer to a formal debate in tragedy and especially Old Comedy. Pp. 65, 109, 162, 187, 287, 291, 350

agonothetes (pl. **agonothetai**): Gk. "competition administrator": the sponsor of a Greek festival, usually paying for it in part, and responsible for its administration. Pp. 104, 143, 193, 200, 203, 205f., 215, 243f., 246, 277

agora: Gk. "market place," cf. Lat. *forum:* the central open place in Greek cities, where government buildings were located and markets and some festivals were held. Pp. 115, 123, 133, 135, 169f., 184

Alexandria: the Greek capital of Egypt founded by Alexander the Great in the 4th c. B.C., and one of the most important centers of Hellenistic culture. Pp. 5, 18, 20, 249, 319, 325, 370, 379, 388

amphitheater: Gk. "double-theater": a Roman development of the theater for the purpose of spectacles and hunts in the 1st c. B.C. Pp. 307, 318, 320, 373

analemma: (pl. **analemmata**): each of the side support walls of the Greek theater, built out from a slope. P. 84

antidosis: Gk. "exchange": in Athenian law, an exchange of property between a candidate for a liturgy and someone he claims to be better

425

suited to perform the liturgy but who contests this claim. Pp. 126, 140, 144–46

architekton: Gk. "chief builder": the manager of a Greek theater. Pp. 125, 288f., 295, 297, 299

archmime or **archimim-us/-a:** (pl. **archimim-i/-ae**): Gk. "chief mime actor": a professional mime. The term seems to refer both to the head of a troupe and a role. Pp. 218, 279, 372, 374f.

archon (pl. **archontes**): Gk. "ruler": one of nine chief Athenian magistrates, and esp. used of the "eponymous archon," after whom the Athenians named the year. Also used of magistrates in other Greek cities. Pp. 104, 108f., 113, 122, 124, 132, 135–36, 139, 143f., 154, 158, 161f., 180f., 184f., 198f., 205, 223, 230, 289, 300, 352

Atellan-farce or **Atellana:** a native Roman, originally Oscan, genre of farce and parody, notable for its fixed masked characters, and its freeborn actors. Pp. 207f., 211, 215, 281, 307, 324, 326, 369

Attic: "of Attica," the territory administrated by Athens and of which Athens was the capital. Passim

aulaeum: (pl. **aulaea**): the Roman stage curtain, which rose from a slot in the stage proper. Pp. 371, 384

basilica (pl. **basilicae**): each of the large halls at either side of many Roman stage buildings, communicating with stage and *aditus maximus*. P. 85

Byzantium: later Constantinople, now Istanbul. Capital of the Eastern Roman Empire from 330. P. 19

canticum (pl. **cantica**): Lat. "song": the songs of early Roman comedy. P. 331

cavea ima, media, summa: Lat. "lowest, middle, highest theater seating": the horizontal divisions of the Roman theater by means of encircling passageways, *praecinctiones*. Pp. 84–86, 306–17

Charonian steps: an underground passageway from the stage to a place in the orchestra, derived from the name of the mythical ferryman of the dead, Charon. Pp. 82, 258, 397f.

choraules (pl. **choraulai**): Gk. "choral piper": a pipe-playing chorus director. Pp. 204, 369, 385f.

choregia (pl. **choregiai**): Gk. "chorus driving": in Athens, the duty imposed upon a wealthy citizen of financing and organizing the training of a chorus for dithyramb or drama. Pp. 122, 125, 127, 139–57, 230, 265, 287, 351f., 394

choregos (pl. **choregoi**): Gk. "chorus driver": a citizen who performs a *choregia* (q.v.). Pp. 39–41, 44f., 48, 57, 65, 106, 115–17, 122–29, 136, 139–59, 161, 172f., 176f., 180, 197f., 204–6, 223, 236, 290, 332, 351, 358f., 369

chorus: Gk. "choros" implies both group dancing and singing. Pp. 53, 57f., 69f., 81, 89–95, 126, 135, 139, 148–50, 153–56, 195, 197, 201–3, 212, 260, 331–34, 338f., 347–70, 377, 380, 385, 389, 394f.

circus: Lat. "racecourse" = Gk. "hippodrome": esp. the Circus Maximus in Rome. Pp. 207f., 212, 214, 307, 311, 318–20, 324, 328f.

Colosseum: the Medieval name for the "Flavian amphitheater" dedicated in Rome in 80. Pp. 242, 311

cuneus (pl. **cunei**): Lat. "wedge": the wedge-shaped section of seats in the Roman *cavea*. Pp. 84, 86, 311

Delos: the Greek island that was a center of the cult of Apollo. Pp. 44–46, 48, 82, 204f., 272

Delphi: a center of the cult of Apollo on mainland Greece with an important festival called the Pythia. Pp. 44–46, 112, 188, 201f., 239, 243–46, 249–52

deme: one of the districts or townships in Attica outside of Athens. Pp. 116, 121–32, 135, 150, 174, 296f., 360

demos: Gk. "the people," i.e., the sovereign democratic body at Athens and in other Greek states, but esp. "the common people," and often "supporters of the democratic constitution" (as opposed to aristocracy or oligarchy). Pp. 167, 171–72, 178

diazoma: Gk. See *praecinctio*. Pp. 80, 82

didaskalia (pl. **didaskaliai**): Gk. "teaching": normally, a term used to describe a list recording the details of the Athenian dramatic productions, and, in the plural, esp. used of the surviving inscriptions that do so. Pp. 41–43, 123f., 136f., 176, 227–29

didaskalos (pl. **didaskaloi**): Gk. "teacher": director of a dramatic chorus and drama; frequently the poet. Pp. 39–44, 126, 129, 131, 134–37, 178, 197, 201, 337, 352, 360, 394

Dionysia: a festival of Dionysus, Greek god of wine and masks, and esp. the Great (or City) Dionysia at Athens. Pp. 3, 12f., 39–45, 48, 103–32, 138–44, 147–56, 174f., 196–200, 222, 226–29, 236, 240, 287, 291, 300, 302f., 351

dithyramb: a choral dance and song usually in honor of Dionysus. Pp. 40f., 45, 48, 57f., 90f., 95, 99, 101, 106f., 112, 115–17, 120, 125,

131, 140, 143, 147–60, 204, 206, 236, 290, 333, 337–40, 342, 345, 348, 352f.

ekkyklema: Gk. "out-roller": a contraption that was rolled out of the door of the Greek stage, supporting a tableau. Pp. 61, 258, 261f., 270–72, 340, 397

emboliari-us/-a (pl. **emboliari-i/-ae**): a solo performer of an *embolimon,* usually a singing and dancing mime.

embolimon (pl. **embolima**): Gk. "insert": in Greek, originally a generic choral song, then an entr'acte in a Roman performance. Pp. 173, 349f., 354, 371

ephebe: young Athenian men undergoing military training. Pp. 106, 111, 125, 228, 289, 298, 352, 396

episkenion (pl. **episkenia**): the wall of the *skene* (q.v.), which is visible rising above the level of the *logeion* (q.v.). Pp. 81, 83

Etruscan: refers to the Greek-influenced civilization of Etruria north of Rome, which was hostile to the expanding empire of the early Romans. Pp. 207, 210–12, 379, 380

exodiari-us/-a (pl. **exodiari-i/-ae**): performers of *exodia* (q.v.).

exodium (pl. **exodia**): Lat. from Gk. "a closing song": a farce closing out Roman dramatic performances, mostly an Atellan or mime, and sometimes parodying the previous drama. Pp. 211, 307, 322, 371, 394

exodos (pl. **exodoi**): Gk. "exit": the exit and exit song of the chorus in Greek drama. Pp. 161, 332, 347, 350, 357, 394

exostra: Gk. "what is shoved out": apparently a Hellenistic stage device to allow the sudden appearance of gods on high. Pp. 258, 261, 272f., 397

faction: a group of supporters of a dramatic star. The Blues and Greens are imperial circus factions. Pp. 306, 314–16, 318f., 323f., 327f., 382

Fasti: Lat. "official festival calendar": used to describe an important inscription recording productions at Athens. Pp. 12, 20, 22, 24, 39–41, 43, 89, 115, 119f., 129, 226, 228

forum: Lat. the political center of Rome, and the place where gladiatorial and hunting games were given. It was adapted for more complex spectacles in the mid-1st c. B.C. Pp. 307, 380–81, 387

freedman: a former slave who has been freed but usually remains under obligation to the former master. The Roman emperor's freedmen (i.e., "imperial freedmen") often held positions of enormous power. Pp. 275, 279f., 310, 320

frons scaenae: Lat. "stage front": the facade of the Roman stage building above the *pulpitum* (q.v.), ultimately made of stone, three stories high. Pp. 84f., 87

histrio (pl. **histriones**): Lat., allegedly Etruscan for dancer, then actor and pantomime. Pp. 211, 276, 278, 371

hospitalia: Lat. "<rooms> for guests": the name given by Vitruvius to the two doors to the left and right of the central door on the Roman stage. Pp. 273, 396

hypokrites: (pl. **hypokritai**): Gk. "actor": originally "responder," later accompanying actor to a pantomime or tragedian. Pp. 221, 228, 257, 265–67, 369, 386

hyposcaenium: the room(s) below the stage, equipped in the postclassical period with wooden machinery for special effects. Pp. 85, 397

hypothesis (pl. **hypotheseis**): Gk. "plot"; used to describe the short summary introducing a play in the manuscripts; also a longer form of mime with a plot in several acts. Pp. 21, 25f., 376–78

infamis (pl. **infames**): Lat. "of ill repute": a legal term indicating a loss of certain civil rights. Pp. 275–77, 374

iter versurae (pl. **itinera versurae**): Lat. "versura-way": a term used by Vitruvius to describe each side entrance to the Roman stage. Pp. 84

ithyphallic: Gk. "with erect *phallos*" (q.v.). Pp. 65, 70, 96, 98, 104

kerkis (pl. **kerkides**): Gk. for *cuneus* (q.v.). Pp. 80, 82f., 289, 396

kitharode: Gk. "a singer to the lyre": esp. in later times, one who sang tragic arias to a lyre accompaniment. Pp. 191f., 202, 204, 237, 369, 386f.

knights: the equestrian class in Rome, who occupied by right the first fourteen rows of the *cavea* (q.v.). Pp. 275, 277f., 281–83, 306, 309, 311, 316, 319, 325, 387

koilon: Gk. "hollow": as Lat. *cavea*.

komast: Gk. "reveler": but describes particularly the costumed dancers on early Greek vases. Pp. 44, 89–101

kommos (pl. **kommoi**): Gk. "dirge": but used to describe a choral lament or similar scene in a Greek tragedy.

komodoumen-os/-e (pl. **komodoumen-oi/-ai**): real people ridiculed or represented in a Greek comedy. Pp. 165–85, 291

komos (pl. **komoi**): Gk. "reveling": any drunken procession, esp. one accompanied by music and song or dance, also a term used in antiquity to describe a Dionysiac chorus. Pp. 41, 44, 53, 65, 89–101, 106, 112, 161, 339, 350

koryphaios (pl. **koryphaioi**): Gk. "chief": lead singer and dancer of a chorus. Pp. 70, 353, 360, 363f., 394

Lenaea: an Athenian festival of Dionysus in February/March. Pp. 3, 39–43, 120, 122–24, 132–38, 141, 156, 161, 177, 222, 227f., 287, 351

Lenaean vase: two series of 5th-c. B.C. Attic vases showing a mask or masks of Dionysus on a pillar along with female worshipers. There is no certain connection with the Lenaea. Pp. 94, 97, 123

liturgy: Gk. "undertaking of public work": a euphemism for the imposition on wealthy Athenian citizens of certain financial responsibilities such as the *choregia* (q.v.). Pp. 116, 139f., 142, 144–49, 152, 157, 254

logeion (pl. **logeia**): Gk. "talking place": in the Greek theater the stage proper, above the roof of the *proskenion* (q.v.). Pp. 81, 87, 396

ludus (pl. **ludi**): Lat. "game": the plural "games" is equivalent to "festival," and can be private or public, as part of the Roman festival calendar. Pp. 207–10, 213–18, 277, 308

maenianum (pl. **maeniana**): a horizontal section of the Roman theater, equivalent to e.g., *cavea ima* (q.v.). P. 311

mechane (pl. **mechanai**): Gk. "machine": stage machinery, but esp. the crane. Pp. 61, 258, 261, 268–70, 397

metic: a resident foreigner at Athens. Metics had certain obligations but were not empowered to exercise the rights of citizens. Pp. 106, 113, 122, 135, 139, 286, 351

Middle Comedy: Athenian and Athenian influenced comedy ca. 385–330 B.C. Pp. 66, 71f., 166, 172f., 179f., 350, 354

mime: a spoken drama that could involve dancing, singing or music, with fixed characters, and with or without masks, often used as an end piece after Roman dramatic performances. Pp. 87, 187–90, 204, 208f., 239, 241, 272, 275, 277, 281, 319–23, 327, 329, 369–78, 388f.

monody: Gk. "solo song": esp. songs sung by the actors in Greek drama without choral accompaniment. Pp. 333, 347f., 351

munerarius: (pl. **munerarii**): Lat.: the official, usually a wealthy man, charged with, or voluntarily undertaking, the performance of a *munus* (q.v.). P. 213

munus (pl. **munera**): Lat. "official duty": at Rome in particular, private games, usually gladiatorial, given by a private individual as an obligation, e.g., on the death of a father; from the 1st c. B.C., games donated by individuals for the public not as part of the regular festival calendar, and esp. gladiatorial games and spectacles. Pp. 207–10, 213–15, 218–20, 387

New Comedy: the Greek comedy of Menander and his contemporaries, beginning about 320 B.C. Pp. 71–78, 81, 166, 173–74, 188, 222, 256, 258, 284f., 287, 350, 354, 386, 393, 400–402

New Music: the avant-garde Greek music, esp. of the 5th c. B.C., which tended to greater complexity and a liberation of the music from the constraints of verse. Pp. 155, 332–34, 336–48

odeon/odeum (pl. **odea**): Gk./Lat. "singing place": a covered theater, esp. for musical performances. In classical Athens, the Odeon of Pericles built beside the Theater of Dionysus. Pp. 80, 105, 110

Old Comedy: Athenian comedy of the 5th c.–ca. 385 B.C. Pp. 65–68, 71f., 160, 165–85, 188, 222, 256–58, 287, 290, 400

onkos (pl. **onkoi**): Gk. "swelling": the exaggerated high crown of the Hellenistic and Roman tragic mask. Pp. 72, 257, 260, 280, 398f.

orchestra: Gk. "dancing place": the area of the Greek theater in front of the *skene* where the chorus performed. Pp. 64, 66f., 79–88, 133, 158, 214, 306–8, 310, 332, 350, 358, 372, 396–98

padded dancer: a type of costumed comic komast (q.v.), found on Corinthian and Attic vases of the 6th and 5th c. B.C. Pp. 90–93

pantomime: Gk. "all mime": a dancer of mythical themes, who wears a mask but does not speak. Pp. 87, 138, 188, 209, 215, 235, 239, 241, 248, 276, 278–81, 318–20, 323, 325–29, 369–73, 377–85, 388

Papposilenos: Gk. "grandad silen": the aged father of the satyrs in Greek satyrplay.

papyrus (pl. **papyri**): ancient paper and the Egyptian bullrush from which it was made. Pp. 2, 18, 19

parabasis (pl. **parabases**): Gk. "coming forward": a scene of Old Comedy in which the chorus comes forward to address the audience directly. Pp. 12, 162, 173, 178–79, 305, 332, 335f., 350, 353, 361f., 394f.

parasite: Gk. "eating alongside": a term describing a clever accomplice, always a free person, who is a fixed character in Middle and New Comedy. Pp. 71f., 374, 396, 401

paraskenion (pl. **paraskenia**): Gk. "what is beside the skene": the areas to each side of the Lycurgan (at Athens) and Hellenistic stage proper,

cials and guests in the theater, also the front rows of seats where this privilege was exercised. Pp. 65, 80, 82, 132, 288f., 297, 299–301, 396

proskenion/proscaenium (pl. **proskenia/proscaenia**): Gk./Lat. "what is before the scene-building": the building in front of and abutting the *skene*. Its roof is the *logeion* (Greek) or *pulpitum* (Roman theater). Pp. 80–83, 85–87, 261, 313, 371, 387, 396

protagonist: Gk. "first competitor": the chief actor of a troupe. Pp. 223, 228, 230, 267

pulpitum: the Roman stage. P. 85

pyrrhiche: originally a Greek dance of young men in armor, then any massed dance, esp. part of a spectacle. Pp. 147, 153, 192f., 367f., 373, 384, 388

rhapsode: Gk. "song-sticher": a declaimer of epic song. Pp. 192f., 237, 251

satyr: the mythical follower of Dionysus, part horse (or goat) and part man. Pp. 41f., 53f., 69f., 89–101, 188, 192, 194–96, 200, 203, 207, 212, 273, 338, 364, 395

scaena: v. skene.

scaenae frons: v. frons scaenae.

scholion (pl. **scholia**): a note written on the margins of a medieval manuscript. Pp. 21, 22, 24–36, 168, 176f., 184f.

senate: the patricians who formed the highest Roman class and were entitled to seats in the orchestra. Pp. 213f., 216, 253, 276, 282, 306–8, 310f., 316, 319, 323f., 326, 382

Silen/Silenus (pl. **Sileni**): a mythological beast, part horse and part man, often confused with a satyr even in antiquity. The chief Silen is the Silen *tout court,* also called Papposilenos (q.v.). Pp. 89, 98, 395

siparium: (pl. **siparia**): Lat. from Gr.: apparently a curtain (not the *aulaeum*) that blocked the view of the stage, before which mimes could act. Pp. 50f., 272, 371, 384

skene/scaena (pl. **skenai/scaenae**): Gk./Lat.: the stage building; but also used in plural as the painted scenery. Pp. 61, 66, 68, 79–88, 218f., 258, 270–74, 297, 303, 396

skenographia: Gk. "scene painting." Pp. 63, 273

stasimon (pl. **stasima**): Gk. "a standing piece": a choral ode in Greek tragedy after the *parodos* (q.v.) and before the *exodos* (q.v.). Pp. 341f.

stichomythia: Gk. "line-talking": a form of tragic dialogue in which two (or more) speakers exchange usually one line each, but sometimes two or three lines or half lines.

stupidus (pl. **stupidi**): a fixed character in mime with bald head and prominent ears. Pp. 374–76

subsellia: the places in the orchestra of the Roman theater, where the chairs of the Senate were placed. P. 84

synagonistes (pl. **synagonistai**): Gk. "fellow competitor": an actor other than the protagonist (q.v.) of a dramatic troupe, i.e., the deuteragonist or the tritagonist. Pp. 221–23, 225f., 230, 248–50, 253, 267, 304, 386

synchoregia (pl. **synchoregiai**): Gk. "*choregia* along with": a *choregia* (q.v.) shared by two or more people. Pp. 122, 125–29, 142f.

technites (pl. **technitai**): Gk. "artist": member of a guild of the Artists of Dionysus. Pp. 186, 196–202, 205, 214, 232, 237, 239–55, 371

tetralogy: Gk. "four tales": the four parts of an early Greek tragic performance, viz., three tragedies and a satyrplay.

theatron (pl. **theatra**): Gk. "viewing place," and originally only the seating area. Pp. 64, 79–83, 86–88, 286–305, 398

theologeion (pl. **theologeia**): Gk. "god-speaking-place": a part of the roof of the Greek *skene* (q.v.) where gods could appear above the heads of the actors. Pp. 261, 397

theorikon: Gk. "festival (money)": a cash dole at Athens designed to ensure that all citizens could afford to participate in the civic entertainments, esp. buying seats at the Dionysia. Pp. 286–88, 293–96

thymelic: Gk. "of the *thymele*": apparently the altar or pedestal in the middle of the orchestra, where musicians could perform, and so "musical," as opposed to the stage. Pp. 187, 210, 239, 245, 396

thyroma (pl. **thyromata**): Gk. "doorway": apparently the opening in the stage facade (*episkenion*) of the Hellenistic theater, which could also accommodate a *pinax* (q.v.). Pp. 47, 75, 81, 258

tragoidos (pl. **tragoidoi**): Gk. "tragic actor": esp. later the protagonist of a troupe of actors of Greek tragedy, and so the troupe itself. Pp. 45f., 360, 369, 385

tribunal (pl. **tribunalia**): the place above the orchestra entranceways of the Roman theater, from which important officials could view the stage. Pp. 84, 308

valva regia (pl. **valvae regiae**): Lat. "royal door": the central door of the Roman stage. P. 86

vela: Lat. "sails": the canvas coverings of the Roman theater, drawn across to protect the audience from the sun. P. 51

venatio (pl. **venationes**): Lat. "hunting": wild beast hunts that took place in theaters adapted for the purpose. Pp. 50, 209, 214, 387

versura (pl. **versurae**): the structures on each side of the Roman stage, in which was set the side door to the stage. P. 84

Index of Personal Names and Places

Does not include source authors, for which see the Source Index

437

Source Index

Plates

Plate 1A. I 124. Attic column krater in the Mannerist style. Basel BS 415. Courtesy, Antikenmuseum, Basel.

Plate 1B. I 125. Attic bell krater, Kleophon Painter. Copenhagen 13817. Courtesy, Department of Near Eastern and Classical Antiquities, National Museum, Denmark.

Plate 2A. I 126. Attic calyx krater, Dokimasia Painter. Boston 63.1246. Gift of William Francis Warden. Courtesy, Museum of Fine Arts, Boston. Side A.

Plate 2B. I 127. Attic calyx krater, Dokimasia Painter. Boston 63.1246. Gift of William Francis Warden. Courtesy, Museum of Fine Arts, Boston. Side B.

Plate 3A. I 128. Sicilian calyx krater, Dirce Painter. Berlin F 3296. Courtesy, Antikenmuseum, Berlin, Staatliche Museen Preussischer Kulturbesitz. Photo: Jutta Tietz-Glagow.

Plate 3B. I 129. Fragments of Apulian vase, Konnakis group. Würzburg H4696 and H4701. Courtesy, Martin von Wagner-Museum, University of Würzburg. Photo: K. Oehrlein.

Plate 4A. I 130. Sicilian calyx krater, Capodarso Painter. Syracuse, Museo Archeologico Regionale "P. Orsi" 66557. Courtesy, Soprintendenza aí Beni Culturali e Ambientali, Syracuse.

Plate 4B. I 131. Attic chous. Vlastos collection, Athens. Drawing by E.R. Malyon after E. Gilliéron.

Plate 5. I 132. Attic calyx krater. Malibu 82.AE.83. Collection of the J. Paul Getty Museum, Malibu, California.

Plate 6A. I 133. Apulian calyx krater, Tarporley Painter. New York 24.97.104. Metropolitan Museum of Art, Fletcher Fund, 1924. (24.97.104)

Plate 6B. I 134. Apulian bell krater, McDaniel Painter. Boston Museum of Fine Arts 69.951. Gift of Otis Norcross. Courtesy, Museum of Fine Arts, Boston.

Plate 7A. I 135. Apulian bell krater, Schiller Painter. Würzburg H5697. Courtesy, Martin von Wagner-Museum, University of Würzburg.

Plate 7B. I 136. Attic pelike, Phiale Painter. Boston Museum of Fine Arts 98.883–11. Gift of H.L. Pierce. Courtesy, Museum of Fine Arts, Boston.

Plate 8. I 137. Attic volute krater, Pronomos Painter. Naples, Museo Nazionale 3240. Drawing by E.R. Malyon.

Plate 9. I 138. Attic figurines. New York 13.225.13, 14, 16, 18, 19, 21–23, 25–28. Courtesy, Metropolitan Museum of Art, Rogers Fund, 1913.

Plate 10A. I 1139. Figurine from Myrina. Athens NM 5027 (Misthos 544). Courtesy, Hellenic Ministry of Culture.

Plate 10B. I 1140. Figurine from Myrina. Athens NM 5060 (Misthos 543). Photo DAI Athens, NM 194.

Plate 10C. I 1141. Figurine from Myrina. Berlin 7969. Courtesy, Staatliche Museen, Preussischer Kulturbesitz.

Plate 10D. I 1142. Ivory statuette. Musée du Petit Palais, DUT 192. Courtesy, Ville de Paris, Musée du Petit Palais.

Plate 11A. I 143. Mosaic. Naples, Museo Nazionale 9985. Alinari neg. no. 12057.

Plate 11B. I 144. Mosaic. Naples, Museo Nazionale 9987. Alinari neg. no. 12195.

Plate 12A. I 145. Mosaic, Mytilene. After S. Charitonidis, L. Kahil and R. Ginouvès, *Les Mosaiques de la maison du Ménandre à Mytilène* (= *Antike Kunst,* Beiheft 6, 1970). Pl. 6.1.

Plate 12B. I 146. Mosaic, Mytilene. After S. Charitonidis, L. Kahil and R. Ginouvès, *Les Mosaiques de la maison du Ménandre à Mytilène* (= *Antike Kunst,* Beiheft 6, 1970). Pl. 5.1.

Plate 13. I 147. Miniature illustration of Terence, *Phormio* 2.3. Vaticanus Latinus 3868.

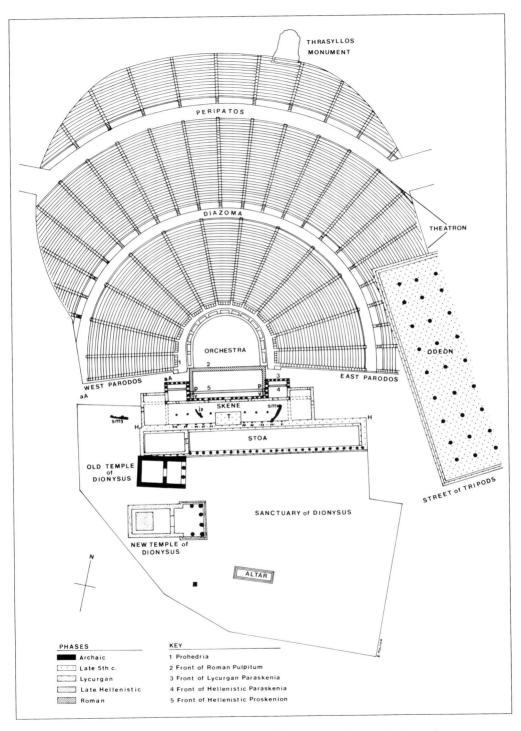

Plate 14. I 148. Plan of the Theater of Dionysus at Athens. Drawing by
E.R. Malyon.

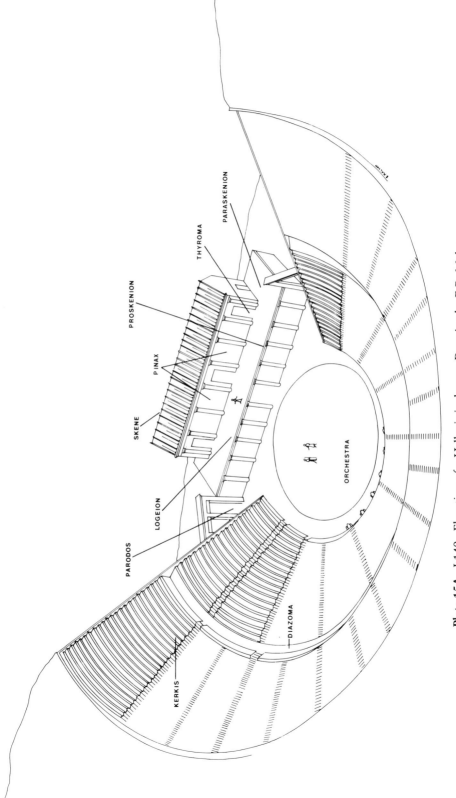

Plate 15A. I 149. Elevation of a Hellenistic theater. Drawing by E.R. Malyon.

Plate 15B. I 150. Model of the theater at Epidaurus by K. Hinrikus. Courtesy, Royal Ontario Museum, Toronto.

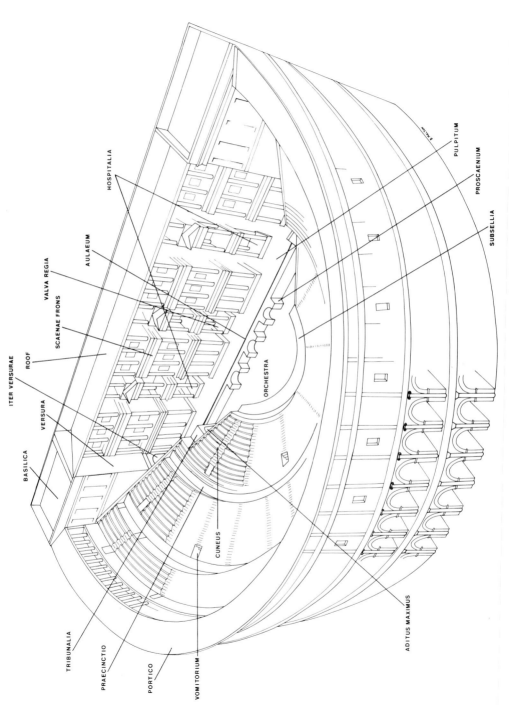

HOSPITALIA

AULAEUM

VALVA REGIA

SCAENAE FRONS

ROOF

ITER VERSURAE

VERSURA

BASILICA

TRIBUNALIA

PRAECINCTIO

PORTICO

VOMITORIUM

CUNEUS

ORCHESTRA

ADITUS MAXIMUS

PULPITUM

PROSCAENIUM

SUBSELLIA

Plate 16A. I 151. Elevation of a Roman theater. Drawing by E.R. Malyon.

Plate 16B. I 152. Theater of Bosra.

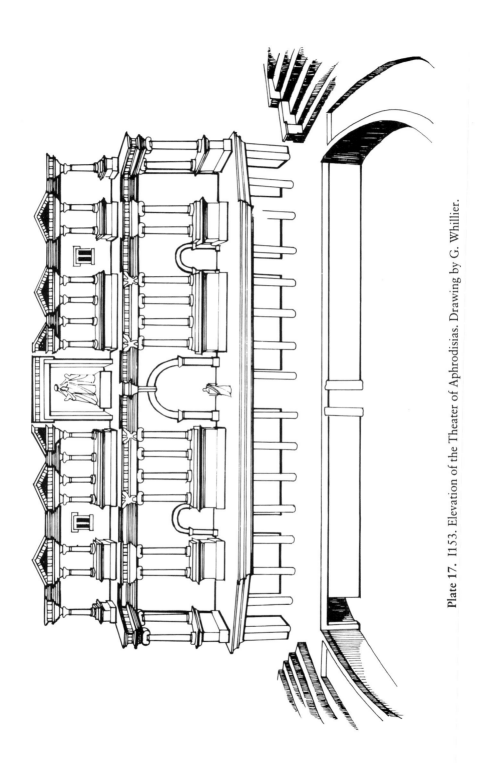

Plate 17. I153. Elevation of the Theater of Aphrodisias. Drawing by G. Whillier.

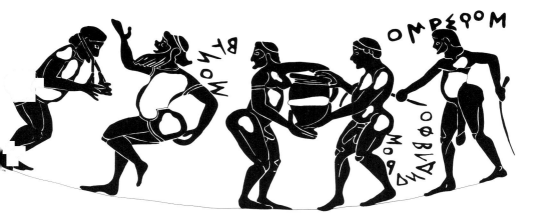

Plate 18A. II 2. Corinthian krater. Louvre E 632, upper band. Drawing by E.R. Malyon.

Plate 18B. II 2. Corinthian krater. Louvre E 632, lower band. Drawing by E.R. Malyon.

Plate 18C. II 3. Corinthian amphoriskos. Athens NM 1092 (664). Drawing by E.R. Malyon.

Plate 19A. II 4A. Attic cup. Florence 3897. Courtesy, Soprintendenza Archeologica di Firenze.

Plate 19B. II 4B.

Plate 20A. II 6. Attic cup. Boston Museum of Fine Arts 20.18. Gift of the heirs of Henry Adams. Courtesy, Museum of Fine Arts, Boston.

Plate 20B. II 7. Attic stamnos, Dinos Painter. Naples MN 2419. Alinari Art, New York. (Anderson 25941).

Plate 21A. IV 279A. Transcription of the music from Euripides, *Orestes* 338–44 (first *stasimon*). After M.L. West, *Ancient Greek Music* (Oxford 1992) 284.

(I grieve, I grieve—your mother's blood that drives you wild. Great prosperity among mortals is not lasting: upsetting it like the sail of a swift sloop some higher power swamps it in the rough doom-waves of fearful toils, as of the sea.)

Plate 21B. IV 279B. Transcription of the music from Euripides, *Iphigenia in Aulis* 784–92. After M.L. West, *Ancient Greek Music* (Oxford 1992) 286.

(I pray neither I nor children of my stock may ever have those prospects that the Lydian women rich in gold and the Phrygians' wives will think on as they ply their looms: 'Which man will pull my fine hair to tears and ravish me amid the ruin of my fatherland?')